MW01028161

Edited by Michael Sragow

Agee: Let Us Now Praise Famous Men,
A Death in the Family, Shorter Fiction

Agee: Film Writing and Selected Journalism

Produced and Abandoned: The National Society of Film Critics
Write on the Best Films You've Never Seen

Victor Fleming

Victor Fleming

An American Movie Master

MICHAEL SRAGOW

Pantheon Books *New York*

 Published in the United States by Pantheon Books, a division of Random House, Inc., New York, and in Canada by Random House of Canada Limited, Toronto.

Pantheon Books and colophon are registered trademarks of Random House, Inc.

Library of Congress Cataloging-in-Publication Data

Sragow, Michael.
Victor Fleming : An American Movie Master / Michael Sragow.
p. cm.
Includes bibliographical references, filmography and index.
ISBN: 978-0-375-40748-2 (alk. paper) 1. Fleming, Victor, 1889–1949.
2. Motion picture producers and directors—United States—Biography.
I. Title. PN1998.3.F62S63 2008
791.4302'32092—dc22 2008015255

www.pantheonbooks.com

Book design by Soonyoung Kwon

Printed in the United States of America

FIRST EDITION

2 4 6 8 9 7 5 3 1

To my mother, Kaye Sragow, who taught me how to read;
to my wife, Glenda Hobbs, who taught me how to write;
and to my friend Pauline Kael, who taught me, by example,
to trust my most personal reactions to the movies.

Contents

Victor Fleming

INTRODUCTION

The Real Rhett Butler

"A composite between an internal combustion engine hitting on all twelve and a bear cub"—that's how a screenwriter once described the movie director Victor Fleming. An MGM in-house interviewer discerned that he had "the Lincoln type of melancholia—a brooding which enables those who possess it to feel more, understand more." Known for his Svengali-like power and occasional brute force with actors and other collaborators, Fleming was also a generous, down-to-earth family man, even in a sometimes-unfathomable marriage. He was a stand-up guy to male and female friends alike—including ex-lovers. He was a man's man who loved going on safari but could also enjoy dressing as Jack to a female screenwriter's Jill for a Marion Davies costume party. After he married Lucile Rosson and fathered two daughters, he reserved most of his social life for the Sunday-morning motorcycle gang known as the Moraga Spit and Polish Club. His ambition in the early days of automobiles to become a racetrack champ in the audacious, button-popping Barney Oldfield mold grew into a legend that he'd really been a professional race-car driver. (Well, he had, but just for one race.) He was one of Hollywood's premier amateur aviators. Studio bosses trusted him to deliver the goods; many stars and writers loved him.

Victor and Lu Fleming's younger daughter, Sally, encouraged me to write this book after she read an appreciation of her father that I'd written for *The New York Times* on the occasion of *The Wizard of Oz*'s sixtieth anniversary in 1999. She asked what led me to take on Fleming as a subject. For decades I'd known and loved the half-dozen great movies he'd directed before salvaging *The Wizard of Oz* for MGM and *Gone With the Wind* for the producer David O. Selznick in 1939—movies like *The Virginian* (1929) and *Red Dust* (1932) and *Bombshell*

(1933). But as I told Sally, I'd only recently seen the first film he made after that historic year—*Dr. Jekyll and Mr. Hyde* (1941)—and I'd been astonished by its candid sexuality and by how much better it was than its reputation. Sally, who sprinkles frank convictions with spontaneous wit, laughed and said, "*Dr. Jekyll and Mr. Hyde*—that's the film that's most like Daddy." It didn't take long to find out that Fleming was a man of more than two parts.

In 1939, the MGM publicist Teet Carle, trying to sell Fleming as a subject for feature stories, noted how remarkable it was, even in what we now consider the golden age of Hollywood, for a director to be "a man like Fleming who has really lived through experiences." Moviemakers like Fleming, who came of age in the silent era, forged their characters beyond camera range. Andrew Solt, the co-writer of Fleming's disastrous final picture, *Joan of Arc* (1948), told his nephew Andrew Solt, the documentary maker (*Imagine*), "Victor Fleming's story is the perfect Hollywood story, from A to Z; it represents the picture business of his time better than anyone else's." What the elder Solt meant, of course, was that Fleming's story wasn't merely about the picture business—it was about what men like Fleming brought into the picture business.

Fleming was born on February 23, 1889, in the orange groves of Southern California, and became an auto mechanic, taxi driver, and chauffeur at a time when cars were luxury items and their operators elite specialists. During World War I, he served as an instructor and creator of military training films as well as a Signal Corps cameraman, and after it, Woodrow Wilson's personal cameraman on his triumphant tour of European capitals before the beginning of the Versailles peace conference. Fleming became a friend to explorers, naturalists, race-car drivers, aviators, inventors, and hunters. His life and work are the stuff not just of Hollywood lore but also of American history. It may seem puzzling that he hasn't inspired a full-length biography until now. But he left no paper trail of letters or diaries, and he died on January 6, 1949, before directors had become national celebrities and objects of idolatry.

Long before sound came into the movies, Fleming had mastered his trade, directing Douglas Fairbanks Sr. in two ace contemporary comedies, *When the Clouds Roll By* (1919) and *The Mollycoddle* (1920). Fleming was part of the team that perfected Fairbanks's persona as the cheerful American man of action, deriving mental and physical health from blood, sweat, and laughs in the open air. The director and the international phenomenon were friends from Fleming's early days as a cameraman and Fairbanks's as a star. They became merry pranksters on a global scale, whether hanging by their fingers from hurtling railroad cars or turning a round-the-world tour into one of the first full-scale mockumentaries (*Around the World in Eighty Minutes*). Fleming forever credited Fairbanks with establishing action as the essence of motion pictures. Fairbanks also set his pal an example of the art of self-creation. The son of a New York attorney who abandoned Douglas's family in Denver when the boy was five, Fairbanks turned himself into a model of dash and vim. Fleming was born in a tent; his father died in an orange orchard when he was four. But he metamorphosed from a Southern California country boy into a Hollywood powerhouse known for mysterious poetic talent, a courtly yet emotionally and sexually charged way with women, and a macho sagacity that spurred the respect and fellowship of men.

Many of Fleming's silent pictures boast a prickly, evergreen freshness that emanates from their spirit of discovery. He designed his Fairbanks films as if they were pop-up toys, playing with special effects, animation, and the audience's knowledge of Fairbanks as a movie star. (Later, he brought some of that modernism into *Bombshell* and parts of *The Wizard of Oz.*) He became a household name in Hollywood. When the author of *What Makes Sammy Run?* and screenwriter of *On the Waterfront*, Budd Schulberg, and his boyhood pal Maurice Rapf played at being studio executives like their fathers (B. P. Schulberg and Harry Rapf), Maurice would name King Vidor his prize director, and Budd would counter with Vic Fleming.

That other underrated director, Henry Hathaway (*The Lives of a Bengal Lancer*), who trained with Fleming, once declared, without reservation, "Clark Gable on the screen is Fleming . . . He dressed like him, talked like him, stood like him, his attitude was the same toward women. He was funny." But Hathaway hit closer to the truth when he said, "Every man that ever worked for him patterned himself after him. Clark Gable, Spencer Tracy, all of them. He had a strong personality, not to the point of imposing himself on anyone, but just forceful and masculine."

Among the stars of the major studios' heyday, Gable was the charismatic cock of the walk; Gary Cooper, the natural aristocrat; Tracy, the grudgingly articulate Everyman. Fleming shaped each man's legacy. Seven years before *Gone With the Wind*, Gable broke through as the hero of Fleming's *Red Dust* (1932); its screenwriter, John Lee Mahin, Fleming's close friend and collaborator, evoked the director in the character's brusque authority, technical savvy, rough-edged humor, and lodestone sexuality. Gable was a projection of the Fleming who, on meeting the Olympic swimmer Eleanor Saville in 1932 at the Ambassador Hotel, genially snapped, "Nice legs, sister!" (And that's *all* he said.)

A few years before Fleming partnered with Gable, he turned Gary Cooper into the paradigm of a chivalrous cowboy in *The Virginian.* Cooper became known as "the strong, silent type" less because he was silent (the Virginian is a joker and a genial if haphazard conversationalist) than because his banked intuition made every syllable count, gave richness to each casual gesture and weight to every decisive one. Cooper was the Vic who knew how few words it took to express emotion. When the producer of *The Virginian*, Louis "Bud" Lighton, wired Fleming that Lighton's mother had died, he wired back, simply,

Dear Bud

Vic

A few years *after* Fleming partnered with Gable, he forged a bond with Spencer Tracy that won Tracy the best actor Academy Award for *Captains Courageous* (1937). "He is probably the only guy in the world who really understands me," Fleming said. "We're alike: bursting with emotions we cannot express; depressed all the time because we feel we could have done our work better." In *Captains Courageous* and other films, like *Test Pilot* (1938, co-starring Gable), Fleming and Tracy succeeded in creating characters who conveyed, physically and facially, more knotted-up notions and feelings than they could put across in words. "Fleming was quite inarticulate in explaining something to an actor, but he had such a way of getting around his inarticulateness that the actor would get it just like *that*," said the Paramount propman William Kaplan, snapping his fingers.

With Gable, Cooper, and Tracy, Fleming mined some of the same territory as Hemingway and his creative progeny. The stars he helped create have never stopped hovering over the heads of Hollywood actors, who still try to emulate their careers, or of American men in general, who still try to live up to their examples. The director's combination of gritty nobility and erotic frankness and his ability to mix action and rumination helped mint a new composite image for the American male. Fleming's big-screen alter egos melded nineteenth-century beliefs in individual strength *and* family with twentieth-century appetites for sex, speed, and inner and outer exploration. His heroes were unpretentious, direct, and honest, though not sloppily self-revealing.

To Olivia de Havilland, "Vic was attractive because he was intelligent, talented, handsomely built, and virile in a non-aggressive way. He was also sensitive. A potent combination."

"Every dame he ever worked with fell on her ass for him," said Hathaway, naming "Norma Shearer. Clara Bow. Ingrid Bergman." (He could have added Bessie Love and Lupe Velez.) Fleming helped turn Shearer and Bow into stars, and became the first director to bring out Bergman's full sexuality, in *Dr. Jekyll and Mr. Hyde*. From the start, he was as much a woman's director as a man's director. Fleming and Bow's collaboration in *Mantrap* (1926) has won belated recognition as groundbreaking comedy. Bow's embodiment of guilt-free sexual energy exploded stereotypes of the vamp and the girl next door and made clear to everyone that she had "It." (She didn't actually make the movie *It* until a year later.)

Much of Fleming's attractiveness came from his vigor. He kept revitalizing himself away from movies with an anti-Hollywood home life and round-the-world travel and hunting. With his six-foot-two-inch frame and broken-nose profile and eyes that could narrow to slits and intensify humor or emotion, he looked as if he could handle himself on and off the movie set. Actors felt energized by the sight of this tall, powerfully built figure reflexively brushing back his mane and training a sharpshooter's vision on their performances and on all the workings of the set. Craftsmen felt secure serving a director who could correct errors on the run, from lax ad-libs to skewed camera angles or faulty props. The cinematographer Harold Rosson, who collaborated with everyone from René Clair to John Huston, said, "Victor Fleming knew as much about the making of pictures as any man I've ever known—all departments." And Fleming kept growing and extending his versatility for decades. To Hathaway, who worked with Fleming mostly during the silent era, "Fleming was the realist." If a story was set in a certain place, "he wanted to go where it said it was made." When talkies took over, Fleming was able to move indoors when necessary. He re-created Indochina in a studio for *Red Dust* and reveled in artifice on the most beloved flight of fancy of them all: *The Wizard of Oz.* This director knew how much visual detail an audience needed to make illusions feel real, and how much had to be contained in one shot. In that sense he was the Lucas or Spielberg of his day.

He was also the Sydney Pollack of his day. Male and female stars alike, Judy Garland as well as Gable, de Havilland and Bow as well as Cooper and Tracy, delivered, simultaneously, their boldest and most characteristic performances in Fleming's movies. Unlike the stage-trained directors who invaded Hollywood in the sound era, Fleming had no set vocabulary to communicate with his actors. He relied on every ounce of his own being, expressing in face, tone, and body language the desired pitch of a performance and the impact he wanted for a comic or dramatic situation. To the sophisticated producer David Lewis, who watched Fleming film *The Virginian*, "he had an inner power that made him almost hypnotic."

Fleming had the emotional advantage of being a Californian and an outdoorsman in an industry dominated by transplanted urban Easterners. In his book *The Industry* (1981), the producer Saul David characterized directors of Fleming's stripe as "The Old-Time Wild Men":

> They are intensely physical men who make physical movies in a physical world. Strength is their religion, endurance their pride, and alcohol their undoing. They are clannish and contemptuous of everything most of the world thinks is moviemaking. They are boorish and overbearing, tend to vote "wrong" and use socially unacceptable epithets in public. They are an unutterable pain to the Hollywood New Yorkers and a boon to caricaturists—but no one has yet figured out how to make big outdoor movies as well as they do without them.

What gave Fleming special sway in Hollywood was that he was an Old-Time Wild Man who could also be elegant, intelligent, and at ease indoors. (And he knew how to handle his alcohol.) Going through a roster of gifted directors who'd bridged silent films and talkies, the cult silent star Louise Brooks listed "Eddie Sutherland, the gay sophisticate; Clarence Brown, the serious repressed; Billy Wellman, the ordinary vulgar. Fleming combined all of them with a much finer intellect."

Fleming didn't actively cultivate the Old-Time Wild Man image—he never enlisted a publicist to increase his visibility. Then again, he didn't have to. When colorful fables clung to him like barnacles—even Mahin said "he was part Indian, and proud of it"—Fleming did nothing to scrape them off. Not only were his movies successful and acclaimed, but with female stars as different as Shearer and Bow falling hard for him, and male stars copying him, his personal reputation was stratospheric.

"He was always the biggest star on his sets," said the MGM publicist Emily Torchia. "You could tell that by the attitude of the people who were there around him—he was very well appreciated," says the former MGM child star John Sheffield ("Boy" in the Johnny Weissmuller *Tarzan* movies). In her book on MGM, *This Was Hollywood* (1960), Beth Day observed, "Tall, silver-haired director Victor Fleming was privately considered by many feminine employees 'the handsomest man on the lot' " and drew as much attention at the commissary as the man everyone knew as the King—Gable. Fairbanks had been billed as the King of Hollywood, too. But throughout his career, Fleming didn't just serve Hollywood royals: he put them on their thrones. When he guided fresh young talents, he saw them whole and inside out, tapping qualities that turned them into new American archetypes.

When talkies ruled and production boomed and the Hollywood studios became dream factories, fellows like Fleming and his favorite writers (Jules Furthman, Mahin) developed the special seen and spoken language of "golden age" sound movies. This audiovisual dialect of expressive actors punching across snappy or suggestive talk in the molded light of a square frame was intensely stylized. It was also unabashedly emotional and sometimes cunningly erotic, even after the enforcement of the Production Code made explicit lovemaking verboten. Vintage Hollywood styles often felt more real than the slangy, jittery realism of today because the characters were substantial enough to cast long shadows and special effects didn't swamp their crises and predicaments.

If he'd died before directing *The Wizard of Oz* and most of *Gone With the Wind* (in the same year) instead of a decade afterward, Victor Fleming would remain an outsized figure in American culture. *The Virginian* was a Western milestone as influential as John Ford's *Stagecoach*. *Red Dust* was a classic sexual melodrama, fierce and funny—the peak of Hollywood's few-holds-barred approach to sex before the enforcement of the Production Code. *Bombshell* predates Howard Hawks's *Twentieth*

Century (1934) as *the* seminal showbiz screwball comedy. *Captains Courageous* proved that movies *without* sex appeal could be smash hits and that something non-mawkish could be fashioned from tales of surrogate fathers and sons. And *Test Pilot*, an incisive look at what happens to flying partners when one gets married, brought the first wave of sound-film buddy pictures to a resounding culmination. Fleming's daring matched his taste, tact, and craft. He frequently demonstrated that free adaptations of beloved novels could both honor their sources and become their own enduring works of art and entertainment.

When Hathaway, Tracy, Gable, and others called Fleming the real Rhett Butler, they were referring not only to manner but also to mind. Rhett and Fleming shared the cynic-idealist's ability to rise to a challenge realistically and, with competence and wiliness, achieve a tough nobility. From Fleming's day to our own, American directors who navigate the whirlpools of movie-industry politics often generate denser moral and emotional environments in their films than the wanly virtuous or frivolous worlds too often found in independent fare. Fleming's artistry lay in the way he molded other men's material. What's extraordinary about his work is how often he fully realized or even transcended that material, not how often it defeated him. What's extraordinary about his life is that he filled it with as much passion and adventure as he did his movies.

I

Born in a Tent

Victor Fleming got his biggest professional break when he began working the camera for Douglas Fairbanks Sr., the actor and producer who set the early-twentieth-century standard for all-American exuberance and athleticism. Fleming often photographed Doug in robust Westerns—frontier sagas such as *The Man from Painted Post* (1917) or contemporary cowboy tales like *Wild and Woolly* (1917). Before Fleming entered the service in World War I, he may even have shot pieces of Fairbanks's *Modern Musketeer* (1918), which featured a fictional Kansas cyclone twenty-one years before *The Wizard of Oz.*

The humor and heroism of these Fairbanks mini-epics must have been piquant for Fleming. His family had enacted a *real* hardscrabble pioneer story, complete with a rampaging twister. When they migrated from Summersville, Missouri, to San Dimas, one of the sparser, dustier outposts of Southern California's Citrus Belt, they became part of America's national saga of farm-raised men and women staking out their piece of the emerging middle class. As Carey McWilliams wrote in *Southern California Country* (1946), the Citrus Belt featured settlements that were "neither town nor country, rural nor urban." San Dimas was a scrubby bucolic province in America's first burgeoning suburbia.

Fleming's parents, William Richard Lonzo and Eva (née Hartman) Fleming, set out for California on February 20, 1888, the day after a tornado ripped through their county, demolishing at least three houses. Their destination: Pasadena. Their itinerary: one train across the Ozarks, from Cabool to Kansas City, then another to California on the Atchison, Topeka, and Santa Fe—the line celebrated by Judy Garland in *The Harvey Girls* (directed by George Sidney, who apprenticed under Fleming, in 1946). Eva's Methodist minister had officiated at their wedding in Houston, the county seat of Texas County, Missouri, just a week and a half before.

Lon and Eva were one of the first Summersville couples to go west to seek their fortune during the famed mid-1880s California land boom. The Santa Fe laid its final tracks in California's Cajon Pass (between the San Gabriel and the San Bernardino mountains) in 1887, catalyzing a price war that fanned get-rich-quick dreams throughout the Midwest. The competing railroads, the Santa Fe and the Union Pacific, slashed the cost of tickets and exploited the nineteenth-century equivalent of saturation advertising—"publicity, settlement agents (with branch offices in Omaha, New York, New Orleans, London, and Hamburg), lecturers, exhibits, and inspired news stories"—to promote Southern California's seductive climate and soaring economy in agriculture and real estate. For a transportation expense of not much more than $25 per person, the Flemings could migrate to a state with fields hyped to be so fecund that "half an acre in lemons is sufficient for the support of a family."

Eva's older brother Mal had been living in Southern California for several years, driving a stagecoach filled with passengers and mail. The Flemings had a better handle than many Midwesterners on California realities. Edward Hartman, Eva Fleming's grandnephew, says, "Jobs were so scarce in those days, Lon must have known someone who knew that someone was hiring."

Thirty-two and already afflicted with a heart condition when he and Eva made their way to California, Lon had left Missouri once before, possibly to mine for silver in the Idaho Territory. His parents were farmers who had moved to Summersville from Bledsoe County, Tennessee. Established in 1807 on former Cherokee nation land, Bledsoe County was also in the path of the 1838–39 "Trail of Tears," the forced evacuation of the Cherokee to Oklahoma Territory. Those two facts, along with some Bledsoe families' claims of Cherokee blood, are the sole basis for the Hollywood-bred myth of Fleming's Native American ancestry. (Victor once described the Flemings' ancestry as English, but their origin is obscure.) Lon's father, John Fleming, likely joined a Confederate unit from Missouri during the Civil War: his name appears on a list of taxpaying Texas County veterans, with a *C* beside it. He died not long after the war ended, and a year later Lon's mother, Neoma, remarried to another farmer, Alfred Farrow. Lon lit out for the territories as early as 1870, when he was fourteen, around the time that his mother gave birth to the first of her two Farrow boys, and probably didn't return to Missouri until the latter half of the 1880s. By then, two married younger sisters had died (another younger sister and a brother, twins, had died in infancy), and his youngest sister had wed and started drifting out of family records.

Residents of Summersville knew the man who would become Victor's father, this thin fellow with a handlebar mustache, by his initials, WRL. Only the modest, unaffected Eva, who had moved to town with her family three years before, called him Lon. He won her with his good looks and manners, his air of having seen the far horizon, and a touch of fatherly authority. "To Miss Eva Hartman. Bee Wair of temtation [*sic*] and remember that contentment of mind makes one happy. Your friend, WRL Fleming." That's what he wrote in her autograph book on February 8, the day before their marriage. Yvonne Blocksom, her granddaughter and Victor's niece, said Eva's prize story from her trip west took place at a Harvey House restaurant along the way. "She was such a farm girl and she thought he was such a gentleman. And on the first meal of the trip, they had finger bowls. And she was completely nonplussed and didn't know what to do and asked him, 'What's this for?' And he showed her, and he said, 'Eva, keep your voice lower, please.' She was so embarrassed."

Niceties like finger bowls weren't part of Eva's upbringing. Lizzie Evaleen Hartman (Eva was short for Evelyn, the name she later adopted for herself) was born nineteen years earlier in the village of Buckhorn near Bloomsburg, Pennsylvania, in the east-central part of the state; Fleming's own speech patterns echoed his mother's Pennsylvania Dutch inflections. The Hartmans' earliest recorded ancestor was John Hartman, who lived outside Philadelphia and fought for General George Washington at the Battle of Germantown in October 1777. They came from German stock: Lewis Shortley Hartman, Eva's father, changed his first name from Ludwig around the time he became a private in the Seventy-ninth Pennsylvania Infantry during the Civil War. He joined the Army in February 1864, served in the Battle of Atlanta under General William Tecumseh Sherman on July 22, and got his discharge in October. When he returned to his Buckhorn farm, the scene resembled the postwar vignettes in his grandson Victor's *Gone With the Wind.* Two young sons saw his muddied figure approach their house and ran inside to warn their mother of the ragged stranger bearing down on them.

Lewis and Clarissa Hartman's children—those who survived beyond early childhood—knit closely together. Three died in infancy, and one at age five, but the remaining six, as well as Lewis, all ended up in Southern California. The family's first attempt to begin anew, in Summersville in 1885, had also come from a railroad pitch, for land around Missouri train-stop towns like Cabool. (The Kansas City, Fort Scott & Gulf Railroad had just completed its line through Texas County.) The way the story came down to Yvonne Blocksom: "The family's farm in Pennsylvania wasn't doing well or something, so Grandpa Hartman decided they should go to one of those real estate things, you know, come down and we have wonderful land and it's for sale for nothing and what not, so they went down to Missouri, and Nanny said it was just plain hardpan rock stuff, and it was a terrible place." The most money the Hartmans made came from selling oak for barrel staves.

California may not have looked any better than Missouri to Lon and Eva when they debarked in Pasadena, after four days on trains. The land *was* cheap. It was also brown and arid, not the green pastures of the promotions. Hucksters hoping to sell real estate still greeted newcomers with pig roasts and brass bands, but the predicted rise in settlement hadn't panned out, so banks had begun to limit credit, and properties were selling at panic-driven prices. Settlers often laid claim to the little available water with the fait accompli of a diverted sluice.

For seven decades, the main source for Fleming's life story has been *Action Is the Word*, a studio-edited autobiography from 1939. Although embellished by the MGM publicity chief, Howard Strickling, the finished document boasts a color and energy missing from Strickling's earlier attempts to tell Fleming's life story. *Action* retains its share of banalities and inaccuracies, but many pages of it crackle with the brass-tacks vitality you find in Fleming's few surviving notes, memos, and letters. Near the start of *Action*, Fleming states that his father "put in the first water supply system at Pasadena." Lon Fleming did not engineer or supervise the system—no Pasadena records mention a Lon or WRL Fleming—but his first California employment *was* digging for water and installing lines in and around Pasadena, ready work for brand-new Californians who couldn't leap right into citrus ranching. Lon and Eva went to live in a tent community for water-industry laborers near La Cañada, just northwest of Pasadena (bordering the present-day Rose Bowl). "They were living there as an employee of whomever he worked for," says Edward Hartman. "Contract workers lived in tent areas they had put up. He was probably hired for four, five, six months at a time, and they provided tent housing, things like that."

Eva gave birth to Victor Lonzo Fleming on February 23, 1889. Victor's handwritten family notes state that Dr. Nat Dalrymple delivered him at the Banbury Ranch near present-day La Cañada Flintridge—the same doctor would deliver his sister Arletta on February 9, 1891—and that his birth was registered at Pasadena. (His father got the name from a favorite younger cousin, Victoria Sullivan, who was living in Idaho. Victor would name his own older daughter Victoria.)

Despite the reverse migration of disillusioned wealth seekers after the land boom waned, Lon and Eva stayed on and persevered as citrus ranchers. They moved to a northern Pasadena neighborhood in 1890. In mid-1892, perhaps to lessen the financial burden on Lon during a ruinous drought, Eva took three-year-old Victor and her one-year-old daughter to Missouri to see their relatives, including her sister Arletta, her daughter's namesake. But she returned in September and brought along her brother Ed. He had toiled side by side with Lon in La Cañada in 1889 before going back to Missouri and now aimed to set down his own roots in the Pasadena area.

In the fall of 1892, the Flemings moved to the hamlet of San Dimas, about thirty miles east of Los Angeles. Once part of the Rancho San Jose as the village of Mud Springs, it never attracted many settlers even under a more enticing name. Still, says Edward Hartman, for the Flemings and for Ed, managing citrus ranches in San Dimas "represented a fresh start out of construction work and pipeline work." They hoped to earn enough from this form of sharecropping to purchase their own spreads. Victor's notes say that after leaving the Banbury Ranch, his parents went to the twenty-acre Saulsbury Ranch in San Dimas. (Banbury and Saulsbury were names of absentee owners.) In 1893, Ed began managing the nearby Caldwell Ranch. "A family named Caldwell from back East owned it," says Edward Hartman. "They paid my grandfather for planting it. They paid him for the trees, and paid him for the fertilizer. He'd have twelve wagons, six going into the stockyards in Los Angeles and six coming out all the time, to haul the fertilizer out to all these places . . . Lon was doing the labor work [on the Saulsbury Ranch]. He was out taking care of the trees."

Lon and Eva had approximately two thousand trees to shield from gophers and to defend from frost with oil-burning smudge pots. The labor was intense and exhausting. "What they did, they watched the irrigation furrows all the time. They watched [for] gophers, and you had to make sure that [all the trees] had the stakes up. Those trees, I would guess, were not over four or five feet tall at the time, and so they needed tending all the time to make sure the stakes weren't broken and that the furrows were okay for irrigation and the gophers were not eating everything up and destroying everything," says Hartman. It could take as long as seven years to raise a profitable crop, and in the days before refrigerated trains, spoilage was a constant hazard. Irrigation water had to be bought, then conveyed through concrete pipes. Mal Hartman, by then a railroad engineer and married in Salida, Colorado, sent Lon and Eva money to see them through.

On May 31, 1893, Lon left home after breakfast and didn't come back for lunch. Eva—more than seven months pregnant with their third child—went looking for him. She found him in the orange orchard, dead of a heart attack. According to Edward Hartman years later, the story passed down to the family about Lon's death "was very graphic, and very definite. Lon was stricken in the orchard, and Eva went out and found him out there, and [he was already dead] and she had his head in her lap, and grandfather went out, and she said, 'Don't go away.' And so he waited [with her] that evening, and the next day he went out and said, 'Okay, Eva. It's time to go.' "

Lon was actually buried on June 1, the day after Eva first cradled his dead body. But the intensity of the tale and the way it prolongs her time in the orchard with Lon suggest the depth of the widow's shock and grief. "Sister Eva takes it hard, as you may believe," Ed wrote Mal on the day of Lon's death. "He has been as well as usual all the time and able to work, but you know death by heart affliction is very sudden." The family laid Lon to rest in Pomona according to Hartman custom, with a short graveside service.

When Eva had her second daughter, on July 8, she named her Willie Ruth. Only the immediate family ever knew Ruth as "Willie," but by naming this daughter Willie Ruth and her son Victor Lonzo, Eva had passed her beloved Lon's initials, WRL, down to another generation. "She loved the man dearly," Edward Hartman remembers. "You could just tell all the way through her. She was a one-man person." After Eva's mother died in Missouri in 1894, she expressed her gratitude to her sister Arletta for saving a lock of their mother's hair. "I never thought to have a bit of poor Lon's. It was such a shock to me I did not have very much thought about me. I have often been sorry since. Lon had such nice curls on his head. *Oh dear*, *oh dear*; isn't it hard to part with our dear ones."

Decades later, Victor would write, "There is little room in my life for sentiment and soft words." He overemphasized his toughness; with close family and some friends and lovers he could overflow with "sentiment and soft words." But he did assume a life-goes-on posture toward death that may have stemmed from experiencing his father's abrupt demise and burial. In *Action Is the Word*, Fleming tersely writes, "When I was about four years old my father died. My uncle, Edwin [*sic*] Hartman, a San Dimas citrus rancher, took me into the household and there I went to school."

It was a period of change and sacrifice for the Fleming and Hartman families. On April 9, 1893, Ed Hartman had married Mary Jordan, a petite redhead he'd met while doing farmwork in Missouri, and she instantly became "Aunt Mamie" to the Flemings. Eva moved with Victor, Arletta, and Ruth into Ed and Mamie's place before the newlywed couple had much chance to make their own home. Clyde, Mamie's first child, arrived in February 1894. Meanwhile, Eva began commuting on a train to be a nurse's aide at Queen of Angels Hospital in Los Angeles. "It was either that job or a packinghouse in San Dimas," says Edward Hartman. "Los Angeles was a place where she could easily find employment. She wasn't going to work as a domestic." With Eva and Ed out earning a living, Mamie had the Fleming brood to manage as well as her own son. Hartman tradition has it that Ed simply told Mamie, "You take care of 'em." (Ed's brusque treatment of Mamie might have influenced Victor's later marital relations.) For a time, Mamie breast-fed both Ruth and Clyde. With the birth of her daughter Edna, Mamie found herself in charge of five children, with Victor the oldest at age six. No wonder her hair went gray before she turned thirty-seven.

Despite the burden, Mamie was a warm, nurturing force, "probably the best loved of all the Hartmans in those years," says Christy Kelso, a great-granddaughter and the family historian. "[The Hartman household] became the center of family gatherings every Sunday . . . Victor showed the same devotion to her as everyone else. He came to visit one Christmas in the 1930s bringing a baby lamb. But it never became dinner. She turned it into a pet, named it Christmas, and it had the run of the house. During his Christmas visit in 1940, he gave her a check for $10,000, something he would never have been able to do while his uncle Ed was alive." Ed was tightfisted with Mamie. "She was very short, and since she spent so much time in the kitchen cooking for the orchard workers, she repeatedly asked Ed to lower the window there so she could have some air while she cooked. But he would never do it. The day after his funeral in 1938, she had workers at the house lowering that window."

Ed gave his family a firm anchor—and Victor a primary role model—with his perseverance, energy, and resourcefulness. In addition to managing citrus groves and hauling fertilizer, Ed began a side business raising bees necessary for the maintenance of the orchards. Ferociously individual, he sold his lemons and oranges independent of growers' associations and in good time prospered as a rancher and then as a buyer and seller of ranch properties and a moneylender to fellow ranchers. He would set up his finance operation under a large tree in his yard in San Dimas every Saturday, with a leather bag of gold coins and a pistol in a shoulder holster. His humor reflected his conservatism and self-reliance, traits he shared with many rural Southern Californians. ("A pious and conservative lot" is how McWilliams described the older residents of the citrus towns.) A favorite saying of Ed's later years was that "Henry Ford ruined the country" with the forty-hour week. Victor followed Ed's example. Even in an industry where men toiled twelve or more hours every day except Sunday, Fleming the film director would be known as a hard worker.

After Lon died, Eva's brother Mal canceled the couple's debt to him, but she had lost whatever nest egg she and Lon had accumulated. Sidney Roger Deacon offered her and her children security. Sid owned a nearby citrus ranch and well with his younger brother, Ira, and a third brother living in Chicago. Eva was twenty-nine and Deacon thirty-seven when they got married in 1897, in Pomona. "I think [the marriage] was Nanny's doing. She set her sights on him, because he was not an aggressive-type person, and Nanny was," says Edward Hartman. "It was a very small community. Everybody knew each other." Deacon, a carpenter who had grown up in Waukegan, Illinois, was easing out of ranching at the time of his wedding to Eva; his stated occupation was "water developer." He and his brother sold water to the Covina Irrigating Company, as well as peddling fruit trees on the side. Their well was so productive that shortly before the birth of their daughter, Sid and Eva were able to sell it to the Covina company for $10,000.

A lean fellow with a clipped mustache and eyeglasses, and big ears protruding from his head, Sid Deacon took Anglo-Saxon reserve from his English immigrant parents and added his own gravity. Before marrying Eva, he had built a new house in San Dimas.

Early poverty, like an Indian genealogy, became part of Victor Fleming's legend, but his main childhood home was a spacious three-bedroom bungalow nestling comfortably against a hill on five acres. The kitchen boasted a dumbwaiter to the cellar; the backyard outhouse had three seats, a sure mark of respectability for a growing household. Sid the carpenter milled sliding oak doors to separate the dining room and parlor. He erected a barn and tapped an artesian spring in the back, and planted orange trees in front. And Uncle Ed and Aunt Mamie eventually lived roughly a half mile away. "The whole family worked as a cohesive unit, and saw to it that the kids were taken care of," says Edward Hartman. In adulthood, Fleming remembered working on Uncle Ed's ranch when he was ten, learning how to blast tree stumps with dynamite. In a bit of Hollywood hyperbole, he claimed one stick went off in a delayed reaction and hospitalized him for three months.

Life in San Dimas wasn't easy. Apart from a Chinese peddler from Azusa who sold vegetables, Eva had to do her shopping in Pomona, and took her children to a Methodist church in Lordsburg. But practicing rural survival rites like shooting gophers, coyotes, and rattlesnakes gave young Victor an ease and skill with firearms that garnered him a reputation as a crack shot whether aiming for big game on safari in Asia and Africa or shooting pests in Bel-Air. And as the Deacons and Flemings relaxed in their backyard, they got a glimmer of the heaven on earth promised years before in the railroad ads.

The screenwriter and director Robert Towne, another Southern California native, once eulogized the unspoiled atmosphere he knew as a child. Brought back decades by "an old postcard" or the air on Catalina Island, he remembered "the warm dry itch across your skin . . . the mountains and sky and the pastels of lavender, salmon, and blue . . . [the] messy green shade [of pepper trees] overhead, tiny dry leaves and red-green bee-bees crunching on the cracked sidewalk . . . a whiff of dry weed, cactus, and wet paint on an open porch." Eva would summer in San Dimas, without Sid, after he moved the family to Los Angeles. Her relatives began going to the shore and setting up tents to escape blistering heat, but she preferred San Dimas to Redondo Beach.

Eva gave birth to Sid's daughter, Carolyn Evaleen (named after his mother), in August 1899. By then, Eva's youngest brother, Loid, had arrived in San Dimas—living for a spell with her and Sid, in 1897. Ed and Mamie had given Missouri one last try but, scared off by another Midwestern twister, had returned for good. The Hartman patriarch, Lewis, moved to San Dimas in 1901 and, at age eighty-five, had become the town's oldest man by the year he died (1914).

Longevity and a close family life were Hartman traits; another was musical talent, going back to the Hartman family band, which played at the Bloomsburg Fair in the nineteenth century. Blocksom recalled that both Carolyn and Arletta "played the piano and they sang and painted." (Ruth, Blocksom's mother, "was the businesswoman in the family.") Blocksom also said that Carolyn was "totally different from the other two girls. She was a Deacon. She had the advantages, and got to go to a private school. Arletta and my mother went to public school." Edward Hartman says that Eva remained especially close to her first three children. "In talking with her and the way she talked about Vic, Arletta, and Ruth, they were separate from [half sister] Carolyn in [her] feelings. There was still that bond between the Flemings and her, and naturally for Victor because he was the firstborn . . . There was a special bond there."

In Hollywood, Victor would be known, in Leonora Hornblow's words, for "great strength, great vitality—but it wasn't just energy. You knew there was somebody there." Hornblow, the wife of the producer Arthur Hornblow Jr., said, "When he talked to you, he looked at you and, believe me, in Hollywood that was rare." Victor's early years in San Dimas provided him with an inexhaustible well of emotional substance. "You can't understand the closeness of this family. A lot of love, and a lot of respect," says Edward Hartman. "Nanny could motivate anyone to do anything," said Blocksom of Eva. "She was not the huggy kind, particularly, but she was there, and you knew it, and you wanted to do what she wanted you to do . . . You knew she loved you, and she took good care of everybody. Even with Uncle Vic, I never saw what you'd call fondness shown, physically. It just radiated, but not physically."

Sid Deacon gave Victor much of value, too—the mechanical expertise that would feed his enthusiasm for cars and planes, then land him a job in movies and earn him a reputation for exacting film craftsmanship. "[Sid] had him work with him drilling water wells, which he didn't like," says Edward Hartman. "The wells had internal combustion engines fueled by natural gas. They had a flywheel and a big belt, maybe twenty feet long. Pa Deacon probably taught him a lot of mechanical things that carried through. He had an above-average mechanical ability and knew how things worked. His philosophy was, you thought out what you were going to do first. Think about it, make good plans, and do it the best you possibly could." Around the turn of the century, Deacon began investing in desert property and also dreamed of becoming a water baron. But a Deacon family venture into a water company (along with an Azusa orchardist) went bust. Deacon and his brothers sold their ranch in the spring of 1904; Ira and Sid (with his family) moved back to Los Angeles. Sid couldn't resist the job opportunities and potential for wealth in the growing city. But Ed bought the house Sid had built for Eva, and it remained a gathering place for the clan until Mamie died in 1942.

"The only thing I ever heard about my grandfather and oil was that he had been very, very lucky," says Deacon's grandson, Rodger Swearingen (Carolyn Deacon's son). Between 1900 and 1921, when asked to list his occupation for a city directory or a Census, Deacon would switch between "water developer" or "water locator" and "oil explorer" or "oil promoter." What he did was practice the ancient art of witching (or dowsing). He used a forked twig to uncover subterranean water (he then also drilled wells) and placed a cylinder filled with crude oil between forks of copper tubing to locate new oil (which was supposed to cause the cylinder to rotate). Although this may conjure images of the humbug Wizard of Oz, many wildcatters and small operators put their faith in dowsing rather than the relatively new science of geology. Witchers and prospectors like Deacon taught themselves rudiments of earth science, learning to spot oil from natural gas bubbling through water or iridescence slicking across mud or salt domes pushing to the surface of the ground. Using observation and intuition, witchers would discover the gushing Spindletop well in Texas in 1901. "I used to go prospecting with him in the Mojave Desert," says Edward Hartman. "He knew that quartz formations were one of the signs of gold possibly in the vicinity. And he'd tell me, 'Dig here, the ground will be soft.' And sure enough, it was."

When Deacon moved to Los Angeles, oil had already been drilled there a dozen years before. He bought options on oil wells in Texas and Oklahoma with part of the money he got from selling his water well, and he kept dowsing and prospecting, too, advertising his services in the classifieds of the Los Angeles newspapers. "To teach you how to locate water, oil and minerals," read one; "S. R. Deacon, locater of gold, silver, oil or water," read another. He still practiced carpentry as he moved his family to three different houses in four years—the first two rented, the last one bought (perhaps a sign of improving fortunes, though he didn't strike it rich for another decade and a half). Despite the novelty of indoor plumbing for kids raised in San Dimas, the peripatetic life couldn't have been easy on the Fleming children and their half sister. "As soon as [Arletta and Ruth] graduated [high school], they went to work," Blocksom said. "They went to work for Bullock's, the big department store downtown at the time. You had to make your own living; I think they moved out as soon as they could. They couldn't wait to get out of the house."

At times, Victor would play the household prankster. "This is what my mother remembered," says Swearingen. "They all had to share the same bathroom. And one day, Vic announced that he was sick and tired of seeing women's hair in the basin whenever he came in to shave. The next day—it was either Arletta or Ruth—when they finished their cup of coffee, they found a big wad of hair in the bottom of their cup."

In *Action*, Fleming recalls, "I quit school in the seventh grade . . . I was 14 years old." He said the same to an MGM reporter for the in-house magazine *The Lion's Roar* in January 1944, adding that on a salary of $135 a month he set aside enough money in a year ($312) to buy the *Encyclopaedia Britannica*. He also set aside enough time to read all thirty volumes—not as the magazine writer and editor A. J. Jacobs recently did, as a stunt for a book deal, but out of his drive for self-improvement. He was the perfect example of an autodidact. Fleming told his daughters and his niece that he dropped out in the *eighth* grade, but he was consistent about feeling his lack of education and the need to compensate for it. Blocksom remembered that "he told me when I was struggling with school, he went through the dictionary, bit by bit by bit, and the encyclopedia. So he was quite learned, I would say, but he did it himself." The *Lion's Roar* reporter wrote, "He is still trying to catch up on his education. An unresolved fact drives him crazy."

Until 1905, says his Army record, Victor did take classes at Los Angeles's Polytechnic High School, including "intensive study of scientific and engineering subjects." The Hartmans' artistic bent hadn't yet affected Victor, who was by and large an adolescent gearhead. Eva put together a scrapbook for anything he did as a schoolboy between 1901 and 1904 that could be classified as artwork. Inside she pasted a machine-printed fortune that read, "She will have a dutiful and handsome son." On the following pages she affixed typical schoolroom assignments such as an agricultural map with regions labeled and shaded according to farm products, a map of the westward expansion of the United States, drawings of a trunk and of a barn and farmhouse, and a map of the landscape of *The Lady of the Lake.* Her son puckishly signed the last one "Victory Fleming."

Victory for Fleming—independence and success—would come in ways his mother never anticipated when she and Lon worked the citrus groves. To her undoubted delight, it *would* have a lot to do with art.

2

Cars, Cameras, Action!

Victor Fleming is an American boy, born a Yankee and bred of staid, Yankee parents. He set out on a personally conducted tour to conquer the world some years ago, and he has succeeded in some respects. His mother wanted Victor to become President of the United States. Victor, in turn, didn't, and still fails to like the idea.

—PARAMOUNT STUDIO RELEASE, 1928

Early American adventure films and comedies had an infectious, antic movement. Even the machines—cars and motorcycles, trains and planes—behaved with improvisational abandon. Heroes and heroines soared to improbable heights by seizing on opportunities with confidence and prowess. Yet these flights of fancy weren't all make-believe. They had emotional roots in the experiences of filmmakers who made up their lives as they went along. Fleming's early years, like those of other directors such as Allan Dwan and Marshall "Mickey" Neilan and producer-stars like Fairbanks, were breathless amalgams of industry, gamesmanship, and hustle.

In 1928, a Paramount publicist described Victor Fleming as a Yankee tinkerer who showed his mechanical aptitude from infancy, when he'd quiet down only if he could hear his mother pedaling a Singer sewing machine. "His teachers say that as a schoolboy, Fleming was 'a holy terror,' " the studio release goes on. "But it was that terror that they called on when the school bell broke down. He had a mechanical mind." Beneath the hype lay elements of truth. Fleming's fascination for machines and especially cars—not pictorial composition—led him to photography and movies. "Because automobiles were rare and pictures of them accordingly interesting, it was a natural step for me to experiment with an old box camera," he said in *Action Is the Word.*

Autos did come first. He had wanted to become a race-car driver like Barney Oldfield ever since Oldfield took Los Angeles by storm in 1903, setting a 65.6 mile-per-hour one-mile dirt-track speed "record" in a Winton Bullet. (Oldfield, ever the showman, always set crowd-pleasing "records" at his appearances.)

Although Fleming's most famous racing scenes would be aerial (*Test Pilot*) or aquatic (*Captains Courageous*), his youthful history with auto racing added to the allure he would later radiate in Hollywood. His record wasn't as extensive as it would become in studio handouts. He probably did cross paths, though, with three California race-car pros he mentioned in later years. Charles Soules and Joe Nikrent were part of renowned racing families. Ted "Terrible Teddy" Tetzlaff appeared in a Mabel Normand one-reel comedy in 1913 and fathered the cinematographer Ted Tetzlaff. Beginning in 1907, Fleming put in hours at Agricultural Park (future site of the Los Angeles Memorial Coliseum), which started hosting contests in 1903 for local amateurs as well as exhibition matchups for visiting professionals such as Oldfield. It was quite a spectacle for a young man with a hankering for speed. In 1903, there were no more than a few hundred cars in all of Southern California. Fleming said he worked on two of Oldfield's racers: the Peerless Green Dragon and the Blitzen Benz. If he did work on the Green Dragon, it was in 1904 or 1905, and on the Blitzen Benz, 1910. Oldfield would travel only with his manager and publicist and would hire local mechanics to help him tune, prime, and patch his cars. Fleming doubtless responded to Oldfield's nervy masculine showmanship.

As the Paramount story said, Fleming "refused to become a preacher, teacher or a civil engineer, as his parents suggested." Victor itched to get both his hands on gears, wheels, and engines—he was, for most tasks, ambidextrous—so he went to work in 1905 as a machinist with W. W. Whitesell & Co., a large downtown dealer of Columbia and Rambler bicycles and one of California's first auto agencies. It sold the Eldredge, a two-seat, 8-horsepower runabout with a top speed of twenty miles per hour. In *Action*, Fleming told of delivering a car to a Santa Monica physician. (He described it as an Oldsmobile, but most likely it was an Eldredge.) The scenario was fit for a Harold Lloyd or Buster Keaton comedy. Exploiting his storyteller's license, Fleming stated his age as fourteen and described the mission as his initial foray into traffic.

For starters, he had to use a stick, not a wheel, to steer the car, "and the sensation of riding was not unlike that aboard a mobile Gatling gun." On "the old winding dirt roads," covering less than twenty-five miles "took one day over the National Boulevard through Culver City, which was merely an outpost then, long before it became the home of Metro-Goldwyn-Mayer studio." Near disaster struck on the fringes of Los Angeles when

> the key that held the timing gear fell off. I walked to the shop where the smithy gave me a squarehead horseshoe nail and a hearty laugh. The nail worked in place of the key. Beyond Culver City, at what is now Clover Field airport [and today is Santa Monica Airport], the gas line broke. I chewed a piece of dead tree limb to make a plug, then got a strip of rubber tubing at a farmhouse and completed the repairs. The car was delivered that night and I slept in a cheap hotel room, to return by train in the morning.

Nothing dulled Fleming's appetites for cars and speed and automotive tinkering, not even picking up a live electrical line that "put a crease in his [right] hand," says Rodger Swearingen, Carolyn's son. (Fleming's Army documents record a scar on his right palm.) He acquired all the skills of a mechanic *and* a "demonstrator" who knew how to turn an operating lesson for a wealthy customer into a classy experience. Someone like Fleming, a Mr. Fix-It who could drive and teach, would be a smart hire for any client who could afford him. He could wheel a car out from a dealership and instruct the owner in its use—and often the owner would ask if he needed another job.

In mid-1908, when Earle C. Anthony, an automotive entrepreneur and future broadcasting pioneer, assembled a small fleet of four-passenger Thomas Flyers for a Los Angeles taxi service, Fleming became one of the city's first motorized-cab drivers. Simultaneously, Anthony was promoting Chalmers autos in speed and endurance competitions, and Fleming nursed hopes he could get behind the wheel of a race car. His experiences as a cabbie honed his reflexes and fed his craving for practical joking and action.

A decade and a half later, he told the cinematographer James Wong Howe what a hair-raising challenge it was to skitter through Los Angeles in a cab. There were so few cars that the city hadn't yet felt the need for traffic cops or signal lights, and hacks had to navigate at their peril among horse-drawn carriages and electric trolleys. The Flyers had the edge on speed and maneuverability over horse-drawn hansom cabs. But the motormen operating the beloved red cars of the Pacific Electric Railway ruled the streets—and they would compete to run over Anthony's taxis. Fleming confessed to Howe that cabdrivers found a way to get back at them. "We'd wait until it rained, rained really hard, and when the streetcar would stop on the corner, we'd take our cabs and run over that front part, cowcatcher, they called it." The motormen would soak in the rain as they tried to bend the cowcatchers off the pavement.

When Fleming couldn't parlay his cab job into a racing slot, he took a position as a mechanic and later a demonstrator at the Los Angeles Motor Car Company, a Locomobile dealership whose burly, flashy owner, Brian J. Leavitt, helped promote the cream of Southern California's automotive talent by sponsoring individual contestants as well as entire races. Fleming also could have worked on racing crews in Corona from 1913 to 1916, and in Playa del Rey (at the Los Angeles Motordome) circa 1910–13. But Santa Monica was the sole place that cropped up in all his race-car stories, and he made his strongest connection to professional racing there between 1909 and 1911. The Motor Car Dealers Association of Los Angeles put on the Santa Monica races as promotional events, with a roster composed, in most years, entirely of West Coast drivers.

With the Locomobile job came another big change. Vic began a brief, childless marriage to Clara West Strouse on April 7, 1909, at the parsonage of Trinity Methodist Episcopal Church, South, in Los Angeles. He was twenty, still legally a minor, so when he applied for the license, he put his age as twenty-two. Having turned sixteen in July, Clara was roughly eight months past California's age of consent for women. Her father had died in 1903 (in Fostoria, Ohio, where he owned and managed a plumbing business), and she was living in California with her mother and her mother's second husband (a salesman). It may not have been the happiest of households—Clara's older sister chose not to move with them to the West Coast—and after the wedding Clara moved in with Victor and his family. Eva always spoke well of Clara. Yvonne Blocksom recalled seeing her picture: "All I remember of the photo is that she was quite beautiful." The couple then rented furnished rooms with a private bath at the Munn Hotel near

Victor's new workplace. Only one thing is known about this marriage: her beauty and his charisma couldn't hold it together for long.

In September, C. N. Cotton of Deming, New Mexico, bought Leavitt's Locomobile agency with part of the fortune he'd acquired as one of the first national marketers of Navajo rugs. (He also exploited cheap Navajo labor by supplying gangs of workers to the Santa Fe Railroad and paying them in scrip usable only at his Gallup store.) Cotton installed his son, Charles, as the agency's manager, and Charles became a mentor and friend to Fleming for decades. (Clara, sadly, would barely be a memory.) Although Locomobile withdrew from racing and focused on stunts designed to prove the car's comfort and durability, such as having drivers take high-society women on long-distance land cruises, Charles Cotton didn't completely retreat from the high-speed arena. He built the grandstand for the Santa Monica races in 1911 and arranged for Fleming to enter his one documented professional race, which took place on October 14.

Fleming, who drove a Locomobile, received no advance publicity, unlike most drivers in his nine-car field. But the newspapers did list "Vic Fleming" the day of the event. He was part of the "baby" group, composed of stripped-down stock models with engines up to 230 cubic inches, able to reach speeds in the fifties. (The bigger cars could hit the nineties.) More than fifty thousand spectators lined up at 8:30 a.m. for the running of the "medium" race (cars with engines 231 to 300 cubic inches) and the "heavy" race (cars with engines 301 to 450 cubic inches). The "baby" cars raced at 10:45 a.m. Then came the major contest, the "free-for-all," at 1:30 p.m., including drivers from both the medium and the heavy classes. Starting in front of the grandstand on Ocean Avenue, the roughly triangular eight-mile road course ran south to a sharp ninety-degree turn onto Nevada Avenue (later named Wilshire Boulevard). This was nicknamed "Dead Man's Curve" as a warning for racers to slow down—luckily, no one yet had died there. Then the course made a straightaway to the Soldiers' Home on San Vicente Boulevard, followed by a final S turn along San Vicente. Although his car didn't break down, Fleming didn't finish the hundred-mile race; he was flagged after completing 10 of the 12.5 laps and being lapped twice by the leaders (the average speed was fifty-three miles per hour). Fleming's modest showing in his one pro race helped convince him to drive only as an amateur and serve pros as a ride-along "mechanician."

The Cottons soon left the car business and entered real estate and then the oil market, developing holdings in the Signal Hill oil fields and establishing the Jurgins Oil Company. (Signal Hill was immortalized by Upton Sinclair in his novel *Oil!*) Locomobile's departure from racing and Cotton's decampment from the agency left Fleming at loose ends. His professional racing dreams had hit the skids, and his marriage to Clara was already falling apart. Young and inexperienced, she wasn't emotionally suited to be the spouse of a man who aimed to be on the move—and was now floundering.

Fleming forged more lasting bonds with other future directors logging time around autos in Los Angeles, such as Marshall "Mickey" Neilan, soon to become the favorite moviemaker of the first female superstar, Mary Pickford. Neilan was born in San Bernardino in 1891 and, like Fleming, had a pronounced mechanical facility and a father who died when he was young. He left school even earlier than Fleming, at age eleven, and made his way onto the stage of the Belasco Stock Company in Los Angeles. He also performed as a juvenile for a San Francisco company that included Lawrence Griffith, who would earn acclaim under the name of David Wark or D. W. Griffith. As Neilan grew up, he alternated acting and car jobs, becoming a bit player moonlighting as a chauffeur and sometimes the other way around. In 1909, Neilan was living with his mother in Los Angeles, but in 1910, he moved to the home of the theatrical impresario Isaac M. Peyton as his full-time chauffeur. Possibly with Griffith's help, Neilan had started acting at the Kalem studio in Santa Monica by 1911. Fleming and Neilan would have crossed paths in the Los Angeles auto world when Neilan was driving for Griffith.

Fleming's protégé Henry Hathaway said Victor used to say that when he drove for Cotton, the five-year-older man grilled him about his ambitions, discovered that he wanted to "get into the motion picture industry," then drove him over to the Griffith studios himself. "That's where you get a job in pictures. Go in and get yourself a job," Cotton told Fleming. "Talk to the manager. Talk to the head man. Walk in and say you know about cameras." According to Hathaway's retelling of the story, Fleming went in, came out, and said, "I got a job." It's an anecdote with some emotional truth to it. But Hathaway got the elements of the story confused. Fleming's introduction to movies didn't occur in Los Angeles. It happened up the coast in Santa Barbara and became a treasured tale of American film's infancy.

Fleming's benefactors were a host of talents at the American Film

Manufacturing Company, including Neilan's new boss, Allan Dwan, a seminal figure in American movies. (Dwan would go on to direct Fairbanks in 1922's *Robin Hood* and John Wayne in 1949's *Sands of Iwo Jima*.) Dwan had become the top filmmaker for the company, known as the Flying A because of its winged trademark. A former electrical engineer with a degree from Notre Dame, he got to observe movie production in Chicago when experimenting with mercury vapor arcs for lighting. He had talked his way into becoming a scenario writer when the Flying A sent him on a reconnaissance mission to find out what was happening to a unit that was roaming through the Southwest and California, filming one-reelers with real cowboys, on the run. They had moved from New Mexico and Arizona to San Juan Capistrano, where Dwan met up with them. Flying A filmmakers were wise to present a moving target. Agents of the group known as the Motion Picture Patents Company, or simply "the Trust," strove to protect the Edison Company's patents on motion picture technology by any means necessary, ambushes and sabotage included. Spies of the Trust dogged the trail of independents like the Flying A, who ignored licensing fees. And other independents were competitive to the point of vandalism.

Catching up with the cast and crew, Dwan discovered that their alcoholic director had abandoned them, so he took on the directing job himself. He then continued casting about for unusual locations, filming one-reelers wherever he found picture-worthy settings. Eventually he settled in La Mesa, a dozen miles north of San Diego. (Hathaway's mother, a musical comedy actress stranded in San Diego, began performing for Dwan, who used Hathaway as a juvenile bit player.) For a year in La Mesa, Dwan put out films at the rate of two a week. Neilan was his scout and actor as well as the driver of Dwan's elaborate car, a Mitchell Six. When Dwan went looking for new locations and headquarters, Neilan suggested Santa Barbara, a sleepy coastal town that was a three-hour train trip from Los Angeles. It impressed Dwan with a variety of potential shooting sites: picturesque cliffs and spacious beaches; hills and mountains glinting with streams and dramatically cut by gullies; nearby Santa Cruz Island, with its primitive beauty; and aristocratic Mediterranean mansions, with their airy luxury. On July 6, 1912, the Flying A moved into a makeshift studio on an abandoned ostrich farm and began churning out one- and two-reelers.

The year before, Fleming had become the chauffeur for a prominent Santa Barbaran, a wealthy retired merchant and banking heir named Clinton B. Hale. "A chauffeur in those days was quite somebody—like a pilot is today," John Lee Mahin once explained. For Fleming it was a steady job in a pretty spot when he was going through hard times. Clara didn't join him in Santa Barbara; on grounds of desertion, he filed for divorce. By the time he had the papers served at the Venice Apartments in L.A. in 1912, Clara had gone back to Ohio. (She protested the desertion charge, but the divorce became final in 1915. Eva told her grandchildren that Clara succumbed to the 1918 flu pandemic; Fleming's daughters remember hearing that she died of sunstroke.)

Tooling up Hale's several luxury cars while living in a boardinghouse, Fleming was one of fifteen thousand Santa Barbara residents in the second decade of the century. It was a relaxed, pleasant town, and he even had family close at hand—his sister Arletta worked there as a clerk at a millinery shop. His new flame was the stage actress Charlotte Burton, a beauty from old Santa Barbara stock and, at twenty-one, herself a veteran of a failed marriage, with a six-year-old daughter also named Charlotte. Burton grew up in San Francisco. She had been acting in theatrical stock companies when the movie business lit up Santa Barbara. Her divorce—and the Flying A—brought her down the coast. In November 1912, the studio signed Burton to star in pictures and lauded her in its announcement for her "superb figure" as well as her "cleverness." Her relationship with Fleming lasted several years. He began hanging around the Flying A and its footloose crews, watching pictures being made. He hired Albert Witzel, the photographer of choice for early movie stars and a forerunner of the glamour-master George Hurrell, to take a portrait of him for his new gal. Compare it with photos taken a year or two before, and the change is startling. The slablike lines of the chauffeur's face suddenly seem hewn from red marble, and the right eyebrow is cocked as if he's about to fire a fatal gaze on an adoring lover.

Dwan, thanks to Neilan, entered Fleming's life at that time, too. "We developed some sort of engine trouble in that car we bought," Dwan told Peter Bogdanovich, "and all the mechanics in Santa Barbara didn't seem to be able to fix it." Neilan said he knew a chauffeur for a wealthy family: "If I can find him, he knows more about engines than any guy I ever met." So he and Dwan drove around looking for this fellow and at the estate where he was working did find a tall young man shooting a .22 with a Maxim silencer at a target in the garage.

> Mickey said, "There he is now," and we drove up behind him. Without even looking at us, he said, "One of your tappet valves is stuck." Anyway, while he was fixing the car, I looked around the garage and saw over in the corner a bunch of photographic equipment—still cameras. So I said to him, "Are you interested in photography?" He says, "You bet I am—I like it very much." And he showed me some very pretty things he was doing. So when he got through with the car, I said, "How'd you like to go into the moving-picture business and be a photographer?" He said, "Well, that sounds pretty good, but I've got to eat—do you pay for it?" I said yes, so he joined us.

In reality it wasn't so immediate. Fleming told Paramount in 1928, "I wanted to start in at the bottom. A person can't begin at the top in any business. If he does, he'll undoubtedly lose his balance and slip off someday." So, probably following Cotton's advice, he begged the company's president, Samuel Hutchinson, for a job, *any* job, offering to work for nothing. Hutchinson complied and soon sent Fleming a note praising his efforts and awarding him a salary that applied even to his first "free" days at the Flying A. (Fleming framed the note.) Fleming often said, "My introduction to the business was an order to repair an old Williamson camera that had been chewing up good film in the manner of a buzzsaw with cordwood. I discovered that the brass plate was fouling the film and replaced it with a new aperture plate of steel." But his first regular job at the Flying A was simply to drive cast and crew out on location. Fleming wrote in *Action* that the Flying A cameraman Roy Overbaugh was "instrumental in placing me in the [developing] laboratory, from which I graduated to become an assistant cameraman." (Vic and Charlotte and Roy and his girlfriend would go on double dates.) Overbaugh, Hutchinson, Neilan, and Dwan all deserve credit for helping to launch Fleming's career.

Fleming next struck up a friendship with Wallace Reid, a budding cowboy star who had "transferred his affections from bucking horses to racing automobiles. We had the love of speed and the interest in engines as a common bond and I can still remember some of the rides we took in those early vintage automobiles. Wally was a good mechanic. He was also reckless, a quality that was equaled only by the generous nature which made him one of the most lovable characters in the field." Reid would be a top name at Paramount/Famous Players–Lasky from 1915 until his untimely death in 1923. (Introduced to morphine as a painkiller, he became addicted to the drug and died in a sanatorium.) There's no proof, but if Fleming did occasionally do some "doubling for a star as an auto driver or an aviator," as his publicity suggests, the star was likely to have been Reid. In the actor's 1919 movie *The Roaring Road*, he plays an auto salesman who goes against the wishes of his car-dealership boss and races on the Santa Monica road course. For Fleming, it would have been a case of entertainment imitating life.

Yet another nascent Hollywood luminary was hanging around racing cars back then. Howard Hawks, the Pasadena rich kid who became Fleming's pal, traced their relationship to a dirt-track race Hawks said they competed in when he was about eighteen and Fleming, now going back and forth between Los Angeles and Santa Barbara, was about twenty-five. "[When] I used to drive a race car," Hawks told the film critic Richard Schickel,

> in one race there was a fellow coming up on the outside and I put him to the fence. We weren't very polite about driving in those days. I won the race. After the race was over, I saw the fellow coming and I thought, Oh Lord, here we go. I'm going to have a fight. Instead he came up and he said, "That was pretty good. But," he said, "you better not try it again because next time I'm going to run right into you" . . . We used to be on the point of a fight many times, but we never quite got into it. We always had to laugh before it started.

Hawks's biographer, Todd McCarthy, has written, "True, false, or merely exaggerated, the story sets the tone for an enduring friendship that had a strongly competitive edge but that the men never allowed to become endangered by personal or professional jealousy, despite repeated opportunities over the years." The story was probably false: an early example of Hawks's retrospective one-upmanship. Hawks entered Cornell University in the fall of 1914. Fleming stayed enrolled in the hard-knocks school of early filmmaking.

In those days, knowing how to drive a car was as crucial to the makers of outdoor adventures as knowing how to ride a horse. Fleming wrote for a 1944 *Lion's Roar* article that in 1914 "we used to load director and principals in one car, cameraman and crew in another, and go looking for scenery that would look well as background. Sometimes we changed stories to suit the scenery!" As he put it in *Action*, cowboy actors brought "their own props from the bunkhouses and corrals," and autos were so rare "that few actors knew how to drive and not many cared to attempt it. As a result, those of us who could drive were invariably used to double for the stars in those early thrill scenes when automobiles were in the picture." Cowboys left the studio an hour early so they could ride to location on horseback. "The natives were never quite sure whether it was a hanging party or a movie outfit that rode down upon them before the sun was high in the heavens. We frequently used them for atmosphere."

It was a good thing that Fleming had grown up with California landscapes, for he saw less of them when he became a cinematographer than when he was a driver—as a cameraman he had to carry equipment in his lap en route, and it blocked his view. Dwan and his Flying A compatriots put a premium on speed, utility, and movement. They were, Fleming wrote in *Action*, making *motion* "pictures and we moved nearly everything but mountains. We employed house painters and carpenters who could achieve their art with brush, hammer and nails, because regular stage technicians were familiar only with canvas scenery and structures of but one dimension. We even took on 'powder monkeys' from the mines to work as actors, because in the movies we used real fire, and when the script called for an explosion we didn't do it with bass drums, but dynamite."

Without ego inflation, Fleming painted a self-portrait of a gutsy youth making his way into a brave new aesthetic world sans stuffiness or rules:

> There was no science of artificial lighting. It was the California sunlight, of course, that originally brought the motion picture industry to the West. In addition, we had the advantage of a variety of scenery which no stage artist could hope to duplicate. On one side there was the Pacific, on the other the snow-peaks of the Sierra and in between the rolling range. When the script called for a train scene we set up near a railroad right-of-way and if there happened to be water in the story, we located on a stream, or down beside the sea. Work began at 7 o'clock in the morning and we knocked off about 4 in the afternoon, usually with our picture in the can.

According to *Action*, even during Fleming's days with the Flying A, its crews fell prey to marauders. When he was assisting Neilan on camera during a location shoot in La Mesa, "bullets began to sing around the camera from a mesquite thicket. It was evident that the sniper wanted to wreck the camera rather than the operator, but that didn't prevent me from flattening on the ground, and I wasn't alone." The culprit, Neilan decided, was somebody who "wants to put us out of business"—and not necessarily an agent of Edison's patents group. "There was war among the independents in those days and on some occasions it filtered on down through the ranks."

Nevertheless, the company put out two pictures a week so efficiently that many casts and crews ended up with four free days out of every seven. That left plenty of time for Fleming and Burton to savor Santa Barbara's balmy hills and beaches or take that three-hour train ride to Los Angeles.

Despite, or perhaps because of, some scrappy filmmaking conditions, the pioneer cinematographer Overbaugh spoke of his Flying A years as a lark. Before the California outpost got a lab of its own, the film was edited on the camera negative, then sent to Chicago for printing. During one period of economic squeeze, the moviemakers could use only four-hundred-foot rolls of film instead of thousand-foot rolls (one thousand feet—roughly ten minutes' worth of film—was the standard length of a one-reeler). When the action outlasted a four-hundred-foot roll, the actors would "play statue" until the cameraman could reload and let the director finish the scene. "There were quite a few incidents," Overbaugh summarized, with amusing understatement. When a planned collision of two cars—one filled with dummies—went awry, the impact caused mannequins to "skyrocket" into State Street, where onlookers fainted dead away.

Dwan, the top man on the lot, said the corporate officers in Chicago were hands-off and congratulatory. "They didn't make any comment except 'Fine, keep them coming.' " Of course, Dwan made it easy for the company to be appreciative. He was a thrifty, all-business filmmaker. "We never shot over two thousand feet. I was very sparing with film—all of us were. Very often, if I had gone out and hired twenty extra horses and men for a chase, I'd make two or three extra chases since I was paying these men for a certain period of time, and so I accumulated a library . . . That was economical and saved us from doing it over and over." Dwan even married within the company, to the leading lady Pauline Bush, in 1915.

"In the 'middle ages' of silent pictures," Fleming once wrote, "a director concentrated on telling his story through action and pantomime. It wasn't particularly important what an actor was thinking while walking—or running—through the scenes. By makeup and broad 'mugging' plus explanatory titles, you established your player's type and let it go at that." But as he said in *Action*, "There was some fine acting in those old flickers on occasion and always there was the gamble of hardship and danger against fame and fortune."

One of the few Flying A players to make a lasting impact was J. (Jack) Warren Kerrigan—"a tremendous figure in those days. He was a wonderful individual, big, handsome, had a Roman-type nose," said Harold Lloyd, who watched him from afar when Lloyd was an extra and Kerrigan was a star at Universal. "He was certainly the star of that lot," said Lloyd. Fleming recalled, "He was known as the Gibson Man, because he seemed to be the masculine type which served as model for the drawings by Charles Dana Gibson, who was then America's foremost illustrator . . . When he came to us at American Films, Kerrigan still considered pictures as a temporary medium, good enough to join between theater engagements. He became the idol of the screen." Jack Kerrigan was also gay. "Quite a lady himself" is how Allan Dwan described him many decades later.

There was some raw kidding between the silver-screen idol and the ultra-heterosexual cowboy extras and crew, but there was also enough hard-nosed tolerance in the corps for all to get on with their jobs. In an enclave like the Flying A in Santa Barbara, everyone knew he or she was part of the same celluloid circus. Kerrigan was powerful enough to promote his twin brother into the position of business manager at the Flying A. And when Kerrigan, the studio's top gun in front of the camera, had a showdown with Dwan, the top gun behind it, the outcome was clear. Hutchinson, like many a latter-day studio chief, fired Dwan. Dwan ended up in L.A. at Universal. (Before long, so did Wallace Reid—and Kerrigan.)

Just as Fleming's connections with Dwan, Neilan, and Overbaugh brought him into Santa Barbara moviemaking, they'd soon propel him back to Los Angeles. Under Dwan's aegis, Neilan became a director at Universal and parlayed that experience and another acting stint (this time at Biograph) into powerful jobs at the Kalem studio in Santa Monica—first as a producer-director and head of his own unit and then as production chief. Neilan hired Overbaugh to head his camera department with Fleming as his assistant. Although the locale had changed, the business hadn't. Wherever he went, Fleming still found himself most often shooting "horse operas," again at the rate of one or two a week. These dramatic shorts, mainstays of theatrical bills that also included brief comedies and newsreels, remained in demand even after most theaters started scheduling features of increasing length, from forty and fifty minutes up.

Not yet the intricate complexes they'd become over the next two decades, the Los Angeles studios were patches of bungalow offices and bare-bones stages with wooden platforms for flats and muslin or canvas reflectors, deflectors, and diffusers. A single business often ran several studios simultaneously—Kalem already had one studio in Glendale and one in Santa Monica, and in 1914 Neilan established a new site for Kalem in Hollywood at the former Essanay Studios.

In these rough-and-tumble days, Fleming got the broken nose that added to his hard-bitten handsomeness. His daughters believe their father smashed his proboscis in a racing crack-up, but the premier silent-film historian Kevin Brownlow heard that the real culprit was Art Acord. Also a veteran of the Flying A (he replaced Kerrigan when the star went to Universal), Acord was the most rambunctious of the cowboy actors who would rodeo or ride the Wild West circuit in the spring, then ranch in the fall and find picture work in the winter. "World Champion Bulldogger" in 1912, he won renown for his off-camera fistfights with Hoot Gibson. "With both alcohol and fury in his veins, Acord was as spectacular a sight in the barroom as he was on a horse," writes Brownlow. The fight with Fleming may have erupted when Acord starred in a 1913 two-reeler called *The Claim Jumper*, whose cast featured a future actor-director friend and MGM colleague of Fleming's, Jack Conway. Brownlow writes that Acord "broke Fleming's nose, when Fleming cast doubt upon his cowboy origins." But could Acord's authenticity ever have been in doubt? More likely, Fleming ridiculed the improbable chirp that emerged from the mouth of the square-jawed Acord, who was destined to speak only four lines in a sound film (a 1930 Gibson, *Trailin' Trouble*) before committing suicide in Chihuahua, Mexico.

"When something went wrong we could not sing out for a new camera," wrote Fleming. "We poked our head down in the works and made repairs, while Neilan and the crew stood by without any too much patience." It was at Kalem's Hollywood studio that Fleming first branched out into comedy by shooting entries in the slapstick Ham and Bud series starring an endomorphic Mutt and Jeff team—the six-foot Lloyd Hamilton and the four-foot-eleven-inch Bud Duncan—and, sometimes, Neilan himself. "The legend of the great silent-film director who dissipates his own success in a welter of fast parties and bootleg liquor has at least some basis in reality: the crippled career of Marshall Neilan." That's how the film historian Richard Koszarski summarized Mickey Neilan. The biographer Jack Spears nailed him as "the Hollywood version of the Scott Fitzgerald image in a fabulous period of bad booze and good times. 'I can stand anything but to be bored,' he once said." Hailed as "the youngest Big director in the motion picture industry" in 1918, "Mickey was a genius who didn't grow up until it was too late," said that dazzling comedienne, Colleen Moore. Fleming had the luck to know him on the rise. Neilan would soon start making a string of Mary Pickford movies of enduring charm, including *Rebecca of Sunnybrook Farm*, *The Little Princess*, *Stella Maris*, *Amarilly of Clothes-Line Alley*, *M'liss*, and *Daddy-Long-Legs*, as well as *Tess of the D'Urbervilles* with his second wife, Blanche Sweet.

As the studios consolidated and their bosses became true moguls, Neilan refused to blunt his criticism, even if its ethnic slant marked him as an anti-Semite—just as Fleming's gibes at David O. Selznick would brand him as one decades later. Said Lina Basquette, who acted for Neilan in *Penrod* (1922), "You must remember that lots of people were anti-Semitic in those days. They just didn't say so the way Mickey Neilan did." Budd Schulberg, who liked him "a lot," says Neilan shared some Gentile directors' "built-in resentments of the Jewish bosses," who were "not the greatest people; not the greatest *Jews*. It was something these directors expressed more amongst themselves, when they were bitching about things." Neilan made Louis B. Mayer uneasy with his irreverence and sauciness from the moment the fledgling producer met the already-renowned director on the set of Mayer's first Hollywood movie, *In Old Kentucky*. In 1924, Mayer's company and the Metro and Goldwyn Studios merged into Metro-Goldwyn-Mayer, and Mayer celebrated with lengthy staff-wide pep talks. Neilan walked out of one proclaiming, "Oh, shit! I've got a picture to make!"

Still, Neilan's ability to wring the best out of his actors impressed his bosses—and Fleming. "Irishmen like Mickey or Jack Conway or Tay Garnett had a great deal of ham in them," Basquette recalled. "With them talking you through a scene, and with the music playing in the background, why, they could get a performance out of a turnip." Neilan would act out the movie's parts himself for his actors, then lie back during shooting to see if the performers were merging his conceptions with their own broad or subtle talents. Ironically, his last work in movies would be as an actor for a very different kind of director, Elia Kazan, in *A Face in the Crowd* (1957). He brought his old silent-comedy chops to the role of a stuffed-shirt senator who needs media coaching from Andy Griffith's megalomaniac TV personality, Lonesome Rhodes. Griffith recalled, "We were shooting a scene in a duck blind, I believe it was, and he started sinking, his feet started sinking, in the marsh, you know. And he did it like a silent movie. He was waving his arms around saying, 'I'm sinking,' but all with his arms. We all got amused at that." (Kazan cut that scene but retained a reference to how ridiculous the senator looked shooting ducks.)

To Neilan, the signal traits of screen actors were "beauty, personality, charm, temperament, style, and the ability to wear clothes"; the guiding emotional intelligence would belong to the director. Fleming hadn't been a stage actor, and he did his job differently from Neilan. Like Neilan, he saw the need for a director to convey the essence of a scene and then calmly observe where the performers would go before he built on it. But for Fleming, the process wasn't a matter of pre-acting the parts or chewing them over in the manner of an art-theater director. He used his immense presence and vitality, his psychological cunning, and his powers of physical suggestion to throw the meaning of the drama into the souls of his actors as unerringly as a crack ventriloquist throws his or her voice into the mouths of sidekicks. Then he let the action take on a life of its own.

Consider the testimony of Gene Reynolds, a child actor who became a notable television director. He collaborated closely with Fleming when the filmmaker was retaking some shots for the credited director, Richard Thorpe, on *The Crowd Roars* (1938). In his one big moment, Reynold's character learns that his mother has died. Dissatisfied with Reynolds's performance, Fleming talked him through the scene. Sixty-five years later Reynolds remembered, "The emotion in his voice made me get it. *His* emotion overtook me, so I did it and he got it in one or two takes. You could communicate as an actor with Fleming because he was not afraid of seeming vulnerable. Fleming got you to sense *his* belief in the scene. I could see it touching him, so it touched me."

In 1915, Dwan catapulted Fleming into the first ranks of filmdom—and a literal Hollywood Babylon—when he brought him into the Triangle Film Corporation. D. W. Griffith, one of the three producers that Triangle was named for (the others were Mack Sennett and

Thomas Ince), was in California shooting his mad masterpiece *Intolerance.* Brownlow has noted that an entire post-Griffith generation of Hollywood action directors cut their teeth by helping the Master on this project, and Fleming was one of them. *Intolerance* put him at the center of the most elaborate live-action scene in movie history: Griffith's unbridled imagining of Persia's ruler, Cyrus, storming Belshazzar's Babylon. In his *Adventures with D. W. Griffith*, the cameraman Karl Brown says that Griffith "used dozens of assistants, each in charge of this unit or that." He dressed them all in antique battle regalia and planted them among the extras on Babylon's celestial walkways or parapets, or among the troops marching to assault it. They had their own battalions: "Another hundred to von Stroheim, another to Woody Van Dyke, more to George Hill, Vic Fleming, and so on." They'd move their men based on the signals they got from Griffith's first lieutenant, Monte Blue, either from the report of his revolver or from the waving of a red, green, or yellow flag.

Fleming would go on to film the most famous crane shot in movie history for *Gone With the Wind:* the camera moving back and up to take in the wounded and dying soldiers of the Confederacy. Here he had a firsthand look at its most illustrious precedent: Griffith moving up and in on Babylon as its citizens crowd the streets for the Feast of Belshazzar. Using two elevator-mounted cameras on a moving platform, Griffith was able to hold in focus each member of his cast of thousands. In the red-tinted siege scenes, the flames of Babylon burned as vibrantly as those of Civil War Atlanta would on the Selznick lot more than twenty years later.

Fleming had never been east before Dwan brought him along to shoot at the Triangle studios in New York City. "New York was the mecca to which nearly everyone in the business hoped to go, sooner or later," Fleming wrote in 1939; "now," he mused, "the New York people head for Hollywood." For the young man with the broken nose and daredevil attitude, who had used his native intelligence and ingenuity to hammer and drive his way into a career in a fledgling industry, this was a leap into "fast company." His breakthrough would come with an actor-producer whom Griffith didn't understand: Douglas Fairbanks. Fleming's first filmmaker-star relationship was different from the ones he would have with a slew of child actors like Reynolds or even with Cooper, Gable, and Tracy. When you shot or directed Douglas Fairbanks, the goal was to bottle electricity.

3
The Importance of Shooting Doug

Fairbanks proved to be a crucial influence on Fleming, personally as well as professionally. Fans knew him as "Doug." He was the epitome of the self-created individual—F. Scott Fitzgerald's Gatsby on a jungle gym. He almost never spoke of his roots. With a swarthy complexion emphasized by a constant deep tan and gray-blue eyes sparkling under his receding brown hair, "he often enjoyed telling some people he had American Indian blood, others Italian or Spanish, or whatever amused him at the moment," wrote Douglas junior to Richard Schickel. (His son said that Douglas's brother Robert was even darker.)

Fairbanks's real story might have tarnished the world-beating super-straight image he coined long before his screen debut. His father was a Jewish attorney, Hezekiah Charles Ulman, who helped Ella Marsh settle the estate of her late first husband, John Fairbanks, and win a divorce from her second husband, a hard-drinking Georgian. Then Ulman married Ella and moved her to Denver from New York in search of a lucky mining strike. Already the mother of two sons (John Fairbanks and Norris Wilcox), Ella gave birth there to Robert (in 1882) and Douglas (in 1883). Frustrated at her new circumstances and Ulman's frequent absences, she eventually threw the man out and took the last name of her first husband for herself and for her younger sons, too. When Douglas turned fifteen, the English actor Frederick Warde stopped in Denver with his troupe, and the plucky teenager, with his mother's help, talked his way into becoming head of the spear-carriers with the company back in New York.

After two seasons touring with Warde, Fairbanks hung out at Harvard, discovered gymnastics, spent time in Europe, and spun his wheels in odd white-collar jobs. He started acting again at age eighteen and by twenty-two had become a marquee player on Broadway. He married above his actor's station, to a tycoon's daughter, Beth Sully. In exchange for her hand he became a soap salesman for one of her father's companies, but he was soon back onstage, establishing his new persona as a teeth-flashing battler for good—a happy acrobat and laughing champion. He seemed to spring from nowhere and everywhere. He made mysterious public references to experiences at Harvard and abroad, but no reporter could pry much specificity or truth out of him or the two Fairbanks brothers, John and Robert, who became his business partners.

Fleming, who grew to love fine tailoring and workmanship, must have learned something about "class" from Fairbanks—and something about mystique, too. Knowing that people presumed *he* was half-Indian, Fleming did nothing to dissuade them and in fact may have egged them on. But, more important, Fleming knew that he'd helped Fairbanks invent and sustain a screen personality that tapped into the essence of movie magic. Shortly before Fairbanks's death in Fleming's year of triumph, 1939, the director made the star's credo the title of his studio autobiography. "Douglas Fairbanks believed in the theory of action in pictures, a belief I continue to share with him now. In this business *action is the word.* By action alone can we show characterization on the screen."

Of course, Fairbanks didn't immediately realize his trademark character on the screen. After shooting a test at Famous Players in Long Island in 1914, he signed on to make movies with D. W. Griffith's company at Triangle–Fine Arts. Griffith wrote in *Variety* that Fairbanks "has definitely abandoned his old (stage) associations for that time at least." Douglas Fairbanks Jr. wrote to Schickel, "He went out West as a way of killing time during a summer lull in New York and also because so many of his colleagues and friends were doing the same thing. It was largely an experiment on his part that not only promised to pay well [$2,000 a week!], but would also incidentally satisfy his curiosity about the Far West." Griffith had agreed to be his director, then basically reneged on the deal. They weren't a good fit. To Griffith, the grandest gestures in movies belonged to the filmmaker. Although Fairbanks Sr. always respected Griffith (and vice versa), only a few years after he joined Griffith at Triangle, Fairbanks told Hollywood columnist Louella Parsons, "The director is much overestimated. It is the actor and the scenario writer who should get credit for the success of a production."

Fairbanks came to Griffith as a matinee idol wielding a sizable contract. On Broadway he had crafted a persona as a virile blithe spirit puncturing the banality of office routines and uptight social politesse. He'd established a preference for scoring laughs and gasps with physicality. He had his own way of turning a set into a circus ring for comic-dramatic calisthenics and making his jumps over buffets or banisters seem thrilling and spontaneous. A walk upstairs on his hands, a pull-up on the rim of a balcony, a leap over a wall—these were his stock-in-trade. The opposite of a baggy-pants comic, Fairbanks was an impeccably turned-out comedian, and his targets were both boorishness and foppishness. He had a perfect combination of gifts and personality for the popular art of the movies. Only his future actor-partners in the creation of United Artists—Charlie Chaplin and Mary Pickford (who became Fairbanks's second wife)—would rival him in audience affections. Ultimately, his pop-culture influence would dwarf theirs: he inspired not only musical stars like Gene Kelly, comedy stars like Cary Grant, and action stars like Errol Flynn, Tyrone Power, Burt Lancaster, and Jackie Chan but also the creators of Superman and Batman.

The history of comic-book superheroes starts with Fairbanks's Zorro. And as far as traditional *adult* fantasies go, the greatest of all male romantic leads, Cary Grant, modeled himself on Fairbanks. Grant wrote touchingly about being on the same boat as Doug and Mary Pickford when Grant made his first voyage from London to New York in 1920: "Once even I found myself being photographed with Mr. Fairbanks during a game of shuffleboard. As I stood beside him, I tried, with shy, inadequate words to tell him of my adulation. He was a splendidly trained acrobat, affable and warmed by success and well-being. A gentleman in the true sense of the word . . . It suddenly dawns on me as this is being written that I've doggedly striven to keep tanned ever since, only because of a desire to emulate his healthful appearance." The longtime *New Yorker* critic Pauline Kael noted how much Grant and Fairbanks had in common—from "shattered, messy childhoods, and fathers who drifted away and turned to drink" to their mix of part-Jewish backgrounds with Christian upbringings. "And, though they represented different eras, they were loved by the public in similar ways—for their strapping health and high spirits, for being *on* and giving out whenever they were in front of an audience, for grinning with pleasure at their own good luck. Grant's later marriage to Barbara Hutton—Babs, the golden girl, 'the richest girl in the world'—had a fairy-tale resemblance to the Fairbanks-Pickford nuptials."

In 1915, that adulation was out of reach for Fairbanks. With the director Dwan, the cinematographer Fleming, a young screenwriter named Anita Loos, and an actor just turning director, John Emerson, attached to Griffith, the key influences were almost in place to ratchet Fairbanks up a notch. But they were still darting all over the map. Dwan and Fleming were going back and forth between Hollywood and New York. Fairbanks had moved to Hollywood, hoping to be supervised by Griffith, only to find a director who had his hands full with *Intolerance.* Loos, a self-schooled wunderkind from San Diego who'd been selling scripts by mail to Griffith since 1912, showed up in Hollywood newly divorced from a brief marriage. Pleased, Griffith put her to work—writing the titles to *Intolerance.*

Harry Aitken was the executive who had hired Fairbanks for Griffith's company, along with a few dozen other Broadway stars for the Triangle units, including Sir Herbert Beerbohm Tree. Under the guidance of Aitken and a Griffith production man, Frank Woods, Fairbanks emerged as the smashing success of Triangle's blanket sign-ups of Broadway talent. *The Lamb,* a comic adventure suitable to Fairbanks's satiric daredevilry, was Aitken and Woods's idea. (The director was Christy Cabanne; Griffith concocted the story and received a supervisory credit.) It was the first in a succession of Fairbanks sagas about dandies who find their inner he-men in the West—though, given his characters' youthful high spirits, they should be called he-boys. The New York premiere of *The Lamb* drew such political and cultural bigwigs as Mr. and Mrs. William Randolph Hearst, Rupert Hughes, Ignacy Jan Paderewski, and the director of the Metropolitan Opera, Otto Kahn. In *Action,* Fleming recalled attending it: "We were all at high tension because Triangle was about to introduce an unheard of innovation to motion picture audiences. On September 23, 1915, *The Lamb* opened at the Knickerbocker Theater at $2 a seat. It seemed to me that all the celebrities in New York were there that night, although they appeared to be as curious as I was." Part of their curiosity came from Triangle's innovation of *triple*-billing productions from their three individual units: "not only *The Lamb,* but full side dishes of *The Iron Strain* [from Ince], with Dustin Farnum and Enid Markey, plus *My Valet* [from Sennett], with Raymond Hitchcock." *The Lamb* was the hit of the evening. And Fleming felt he'd seen the future of the movies.

Fleming deemed Shakespeare inferior to Fairbanks as cinematic material—"As beautiful as Hamlet's soliloquy is in literature, it couldn't be adequately filmed." When he used Shakespeare as a point of comparison, he was licking an old wound. After *Intolerance,* Triangle's most prestigious item was the Emerson-Loos production of *Macbeth* starring Tree. Loos always stated that *Macbeth* was her first collaboration with Emerson, and she invariably said that her credit embarrassed her: "*Macbeth*, directed by John Emerson and written by William Shakespeare and Anita Loos." Her script sheared the drama to the bloody essentials of the corrupted lord and his corrupting lady, and honed down the verse to compact inter-titles. But Tree insisted on delivering the play complete. So Emerson employed two cameras—a dummy that stayed trained on the star while he orated, and a real one that caught only the action that Loos extracted from the full text. The weightier challenges for the moviemakers included a night victory celebration for Macbeth's army shot with banks of lights. Tree himself found "this nocturnal scene deeply impressive." On at least one occasion, though, the "curse of the Scottish tragedy" that has doomed many a theatrical production threatened this screen version, too. Emerson followed Elizabethan tradition to the extent of casting the three witches with padded men; then, in an ambitious stroke of special effects, he had their fingers wired so that when they intoned, "Double, double, toil and trouble," a lightning bolt would blast from each of their hands. On shooting day, one bolt set a witch aflame. According to Loos's biographer, Gary Carey, the burning witch howled, "My tits! My tits are on fire!"

The film did a nosedive at the box office. The very name of Shakespeare, wrote a *New York Times* reporter, "bears the taint of highbrowism, and because one has been inveigled into the theater at some time to sit through a badly staged and acted performance of one or more of the cycle of dramas, the mere mention of a movie 'Macbeth' conjures up memories of tedious hours." Whether Fleming shot *Macbeth* (the film and most of the credits are lost), he knew its sorry history, and the lesson he gleaned couldn't have been clearer: "Motion pictures should meet the requirement of that qualifying adjective"—they should always be *motion* pictures.

In a trumped-up quotation that is often used and never footnoted, Fairbanks declared, "D.W. didn't like my athletic tendencies. Or my spontaneous habit of jumping a fence or scaling a church at unexpected moments which were not in the script. Griffith told me to go to Keystone comedies." The source is an identical third-person passage from a 1929 *Photoplay* history of Hollywood: "Griffith was not pleased with the new star's athletic tendencies. Fairbanks seemed to have a notion that in a motion picture one had to keep eternally in motion and he frequently jumped the fence or climbed a church at unexpected moments not prescribed in the script. Griffith advised him to go into Keystone comedies." All of this may derive from Fairbanks's disastrous attempt to make a Keystone-style farce in 1916's *Mystery of the Leaping Fish*. In reality, Griffith never tried to fob off Fairbanks on Mack Sennett. A month before the opening of *The Lamb*, Griffith said that his new star "has already proven himself of such great worth in pictures that we have engaged him for an exclusive three years' contract." *After* the opening of *The Lamb*, it's possible—as Allan Dwan thought—that Griffith, a ladies' man himself, grew to envy Fairbanks's masculine charisma. That's why Dwan figured Griffith assigned his great new star to Dwan's unit. At any rate, that master of Victorian melodrama, Griffith, was not the man to nurture a twentieth-century eternal adolescent like Fairbanks.

Better suited to harnessing his roiling energy were rugged craftsmen like Dwan and Fleming, who'd joked and improvised their way with eclectic casts through countless unforgiving locations and didn't let Broadway stardom stymie or intimidate them. Their challenge was formidable: modulating Fairbanks's constant motion, loosening his emphatic poses, and keeping the expressions he developed for live theater—always smiling, and always with the high beams—from scaring away the up-close movie audience. Fairbanks Jr. somewhat snobbishly noted:

> The fact of the matter is that none of my father's directors had really very much autonomy in any department. They were in effect directors of good but not necessarily great reputations who were expected to be intelligent, responsible and knowledgeable aides, "super-assistants," day-to-day, hour-by-hour coordinators and executives on the set, but who were also clearly required to follow my father's instructions. In short, while he encouraged the honest expression of views and welcomed their reactions, he always reserved the right to overrule them.

Fairbanks, however, did permit collaboration in ways his friend Charlie Chaplin didn't. Dwan considered Fairbanks one of his favorite actors; he guided Doug through swift early melodramas as well as his epic *Robin Hood*. But Dwan said, "You had to keep working with him, he'd lose the character." Fairbanks would strike a pose with one arm signaling at stars and the other pointed to the ground, and Dwan would ask him, "What the hell was that? What's in your other hand?" Dwan acknowledged that Fairbanks "did a lot of creating, a lot of the stories, the movements, the gags," but also insisted, "We all did. Vic Fleming was our cameraman and he used to come up with ideas, too. Sometimes we'd invent them at the spur of the moment."

Fairbanks could be temperamental. Dwan called him that "very actorish, petulant, shrewd, creative man." Even his son admitted, "If something went wrong, he was quick off the trigger. When a dog bit me, he damn near killed it (pause)—matter of fact, I'm not sure he didn't." So the members of his entourage both kept him on an even keel, cushioning his down moods and jealousies, and provided invaluable sounding boards. "Douglas Fairbanks was a man who never read *anything*," said Margaret Case Harriman, daughter of the Algonquin Hotel owner and Fairbanks friend, Frank Case. Fairbanks's practice "was to glance at [scripts] rapidly and then hand them over to someone more fond of reading than he." As Dwan noted, his performing demanded constant attention, because otherwise he'd revert to stances he learned from public-school declamation exercises.

Fairbanks Jr. declared that his father carefully separated his work and home lives, but he also stated that Douglas senior's closest friends included the screenwriter and script editor Tom J. Geraghty and Kenneth Davenport, an ex-actor who wrote the script for *The Nut*, served as Fairbanks's secretary, and reportedly ghostwrote some of Fairbanks's inspirational writings, such as *Laugh and Live*. Fairbanks's best movies were the happy results of on-the-spot creative teamwork. It's no diminution of Doug's talent to say that he had to rely on others to come into his own. They included creative friends like Geraghty and Davenport, Dwan and Fleming, and, of course, Beth Sully Fairbanks. Angel-faced Bessie Love, his frequent co-star and for a time Fleming's own girlfriend, took notice of Beth's influence. Love first worked with Doug and Beth on Dwan's *Good Bad Man* (from Fairbanks's own scenario), about a cowboy Robin Hood who gives stolen money to illegitimate children because he mistakenly believes he *was* one: "It was no secret that she was not exactly wearing the pants, but [was] the manager. She was a little bit stern, a little bit the manageress. But never mind, she was a good one."

Dwan and Fleming shot the pictorially ravishing *The Half-Breed*, written by Loos from a Bret Harte story, "In the Carquinez Woods," in the big-tree country of Calaveras and Tuolumne counties. Doug portrayed a mixed-blood frontiersman as one of Nature's noblemen. Beth, determined that her husband not be seen as "a dirty savage," nudged the director toward opening the film with Fairbanks emerging from a river bath in an Indian thong. Big-star beefcake was born.

John Emerson and Anita Loos barreled into Fairbanks's destiny when Emerson rifled through a pile of scenarios gathering mites in Griffith's studio and tumbled on some sassy work by Loos, full of cutting-edge parody and horseplay. Emerson was "basically an actor and ninety percent bluff," in Dwan's estimation. "Anita had the ideas. He milked her." The show-off wit of the titles was a turnoff to Griffith, but Emerson realized they could be the perfect complement to a live-wire presence like Fairbanks's. This star's brand-name vigor and continuous smile italicized his acting anyway, and the robust tenor of his performing punctured stuffed shirts and deflated pretension. Enlisting Fleming behind the camera, the team had a photographer nimble enough to follow this actor-acrobat wherever he might roll—and daring enough to inspire some amazing stunts of his own. Within a few months, this new team would pool their skills and turn Fairbanks into the glorious embodiment of a burgeoning, cantankerous America. *His Picture in the Papers* (1916), the first Emerson-Loos-Fairbanks film, about the meat-eating heir to a publicity-hungry health food tycoon, hit the mark. It established its leading man as a wholesome rapscallion who could be summarized in a Loos title from Fairbanks's 1916 vehicle *The Americano* as "an all-around chap, just a real American." Fleming worked on a fistful of these movies as well as several more that Fairbanks did with Dwan, and made his directing debut after World War I with two of Fairbanks's smartest, fizziest comedies, *When the Clouds Roll By* (1919) and *The Mollycoddle* (1920).

Knockabout crewmates like Vic were a crucial part of Doug's creative equation. And of course, Fairbanks was the perfect figure for Fleming to hook up with at this point of his life. As a star and pop philosopher, he was, like Teddy Roosevelt, committed to combining the most vigorous aspects of America's regional cultures, rubbing shoulders with cowboys and the theatrical crowd at the Algonquin. "Fairbanks and I both preferred laughter and fun at any cost," Fleming remembered. "He was the sort who would play leapfrog over the stuffed furniture in a Broadway hotel lobby and I was likely to join him, although it was never possible for me to jump so high, or to shinny up a polished marble pillar with equal agility."

Fairbanks turned his own physique into the epitome of modernization. His body was one of the machine age's prime examples of a well-tuned device that with proper maintenance responds to its owner's every whim. The escapist comedy adventures that Fairbanks made with Dwan, Emerson, and others connected with contemporary audiences because they contained within their fantasy a comprehension of real life. In February 1917, Fairbanks broke off with Griffith and formed his own Douglas Fairbanks Pictures Corporation at Adolph Zukor's Artcraft Pictures. A prestigious special distribution arm of Paramount, Artcraft operated like the "boutique" companies of today—except its mainstays were two superstars, Fairbanks and the Pickford Film Corporation's Mary Pickford.

In 1939, the trailblazing American film historian Lewis Jacobs wrote that Fairbanks's action comedies "called for a degree of intellectual appreciation and their huge success at this time signified how perspicacious both audiences and film makers were becoming." If one wants to understand the blockbuster appeal Fairbanks had between 1916 and 1922, the best place to start is Alistair Cooke's astute, penetrating 1940 essay "The Making of a Screen Character." (Perhaps the middlebrow taint Cooke acquired as host of *Masterpiece Theatre* has kept it out of anthologies.) Drawing on his memories of watching Fairbanks movies "as a small and absorbed child," Cooke declares that Fairbanks

> was the abnormal norm of the man in the street, and his audience never mistook him for a Don Juan, a character actor, or a comedian or acrobat simply. He was a muscular itinerant preacher sailing gaily into the social novelties and the occupational neuroses of a new era dizzy with growing pains. He could do this without any doubt of his popularity because Fairbanks had the feel of the popular pulse—he knew to a degree the median limits of romance, prejudice, social conservatism; he knew them instinctively because they were his own.

Emerson and Loos gave Fairbanks the right framework for the wonderment of normality made lively and writ large, handing him outlandish roles that he could fill out to perfection. He popularized the expression "Gee whiz!" His heroes were walking, vaulting, somersaulting flights of fancy, but with frontier-Yankee traction to them. By the time they finished an hour's worth of exploits, they managed to clear the air of hypocrisy and cant and publicize the power of positive thinking—no, positive *action*—without losing their self-satiric smile.

Fairbanks's effortless straddling of these qualities has to do partly with the wit of Emerson and Loos and Dwan and partly with the bravado of Fleming and other men like him in Fairbanks's company. These strapping fellows placed little value on their own hides and would risk them for a laugh or a dare. Fairbanks must have responded to Fleming's magnetism. "Uncle Vic had the kind of charisma that arrived in the room ahead of him and lingered for a while after he left," says Edward Hartman. "He seemed to radiate something." In one of his first assignments at Triangle, Fleming shot a Dorothy Gish vehicle called *Betty of Greystone* under Dwan's direction. The cast included Norman Selby, who'd been known in the boxing ring as Charles "Kid" McCoy and was famous for his "corkscrew punch," which felled opponents with an abrupt, devastating snap. Dwan remembered that Kid McCoy/Selby taught Fleming how to throw that punch (at Vic's request) and that Fleming later knocked a "whole damn crew cold with it." The crew Fleming knocked cold may have been the company Dwan assembled for Fairbanks's *The Good Bad Man.* "Doug wasn't that fond of fighting," Dwan said. "Matter of fact, he always walked away from trouble; but he was always eager to see new things, find new thrills. The three of us had a lot of fun."

Bessie Love, Doug's co-star on that picture, remembered a bet Fleming and Fairbanks made to avert the boredom of a long ride on the Santa Fe Express. They wanted "to see which of them could go from their compartment and drawing room to the dining car, without touching the floor . . . they 'walked' through the coaches, hanging on to anything overhead and clinging to the seats, which faced each other." Dwan, recalling a similar stunt or the same incident in a different way, suggested that the men had been "walking" along the outside of the train, clutching lips and sills and staring in at the passengers through their windows. There *is* a photograph of Fleming and Fairbanks clinging to a Santa Fe caboose, with Fleming holding on to a chimney cable and Fairbanks, his legs flying over the side, hanging from Fleming with his right arm around his chest. The columnist Dan Thomas reported ten years later that they'd shout "Boo!" at unsuspecting passengers while the train barreled along at sixty miles per hour. "Vic Fleming [was] taller—could do it," Dwan noted, but the stunt had the same punch line for both of them when they found themselves locked out of the train, praying it would stop. Railroad stunts—or variations on this one stunt—pepper both men's stories, including a gag involving "a suitcase of valuable bonds . . . false mustaches and locked compartment doors" that Fleming told about on the set of *The Wizard of Oz.* If Fairbanks was the workout addict in the company, Fleming was the catalytic risk taker.

In a story that became part of Hollywood oral history (Lewis Milestone handed it down to the musician and wit Oscar Levant, and Milestone also relayed it to the actor Norman Lloyd), Fleming once asked Fairbanks to leap from a twelve-foot height. When the actor balked, saying it was "too dangerous," Fleming said, "I'll show you," and made the jump. So Fairbanks went ahead and did it—then immediately called for an ambulance because he had broken an ankle. As the vehicle was taking Fairbanks to an infirmary, Fleming turned to an assistant and said, "You better get another ambulance. I broke my ankle, too." (In the Milestone-Levant version, it's both ankles; in a version told by John Lee Mahin's son Graham Lee, the jump is from a burning hayloft.)

Fairbanks's greatest trick is that in his action movies, as in Fred Astaire musicals, none of the perspiration shows. Credit goes partly to Fleming's prestidigitation. In *The Good Bad Man*, Dwan and Fairbanks wanted to shoot the Western hero with the archetypal name of "Passin' Through" jumping his horse over an impossibly wide ravine. Fleming's ingenuity saved the day: He photographed Fairbanks's approach *and* jump over flat land, with the paper blotting out the bottom half of the frame. Then Fleming rewound the film. He positioned his camera and composed the picture so the width of the ravine would seem to equal the distance of the jump—and exposed the film again, this time with the paper over the *top* half of the frame. Double exposing the film with this makeshift matte convinced audiences that Passin' Through had nailed a formidable leap, no sweat. Similarly, in *The Half-Breed*, Fairbanks bends a sapling to the ground and then uses it for a vault. Dwan remembered attaching a steel rod to the sapling so it would function as a catapult, but Fairbanks's sometime stunt double, Richard Talmadge, said the bit was done simply by reversing the film—an explanation that fits the slight inconsistencies of Fairbanks's supposed forward motion, and becomes patently obvious when the scene is run backward.

Fairbanks broke with Griffith in 1917 because the Great Man hadn't paid any attention to the upstart after *The Lamb* and had, according to Doug, established "the names of actresses by connecting them with mine, in violation of my contract." He made Emerson and Dwan the production heads, Loos the chief scenario writer, and Fleming supervising cameraman of the Douglas Fairbanks Pictures Corporation. Their first production was another Emerson-Loos-Fleming comedy, *In Again–Out Again* (1917). By now, Fleming was living at the new downtown Hotel Stowell, a favored hangout of the young film crowd. He was such an integral part of the team that when the production needed a set built in a hurry, Fairbanks took his recommendation and hired a college-boy pal of his named Howard Hawks, who was studying mechanical engineering at Cornell. Hawks never gave Fleming credit for starting him in the film business, but it was the Fairbanks picture that led to more work for Hawks at Artcraft's parent company, Paramount.

By the third Fairbanks Corporation production, Fleming was mounting a reputation outside his circle of collaborators. "The Fairbanks photographer is hardly more than a boy and his exceptional work has often caused wide comment," read Fleming's first piece of personal publicity, upon the release of *Down to Earth* in 1917. Highlighting the film's "extraordinary, unusual night photography," a promotional item planted in papers on opening day described how, "with the aid of flare lights and a special photographic device, Cameraman Victor Fleming filmed a scene of the popular actor relaxing on the ground looking up at the stars." Fleming's utter disdain for visual orthodoxy, whether as a cameraman or as a director, makes his body of films rich and surprising simply for their mise-en-scène.

From collaborating with Fairbanks, Fleming learned how to time and frame a portrait of a star so that audiences would have their fill of his or her personality. He also learned how to plot out a course of action so that a leap or a tumble, a smile or a tear achieves absolute persuasiveness. A lot of Fairbanks films are tales of gradual maturation that seem like quick-change character studies because the star is always in motion. It takes most of five reels for a Western lawman to remove his Eastern-outsider disguise and reveal his authentic self to his true love in *The Man from Painted Post;* or for an office worker in a button business to put his fantasies of European aristocracy in perspective in *Reaching for the Moon.* But the photographer Fleming had the film sense to put the camera in the right places to make these extended skits appear emotionally mercurial. Fleming shoots relatively unadorned acrobatic moves like Fairbanks swinging himself onto the side of his father's chair in *His Picture in the Papers* or vaulting onto a horse in his Westerns the way Astaire insisted directors shoot his dance moves. Fleming presents Fairbanks full-body, in compositions that emphasize athletics *and* character traits like impatience and ebullience.

It took MTV only a few years to convince filmmakers hungry to evoke sensation that they should "destroy geography" and create queasiness in the audience by *not* letting them know the starting point or the direction of the next fist, bullet, laser, or spear. Moviemakers like Dwan and Fleming spent their careers *creating* geography. Whether Fairbanks was pretending that a spit of beach was a desert isle in *Down to Earth* or foiling assassination attempts in the imaginary kingdom of Vulgaria in *Reaching for the Moon*, viewers could feel as if they were *inside* a fantasy—even, in these cases, inside fantasies within the fantasy. The delight comes not from shock but from settling into the contours of a fun house big enough to fit an Everyamerican's universe, circa 1917. Fairbanks's transformation sagas still play like perfect catch-alls for topical parodies, glorified or debunked pop stereotypes, and romances sealed in midair.

If Fairbanks's action heroes inspired the creation of Superman and Batman, his movies helped catalyze comic-book graphic artistry with their breakneck mixture of visual ambition and vulgar excitement. Like vintage comics, a madcap mini-masterpiece like *The Matrimaniac*—with photography credited to Fleming, though no credits survive on-screen—keeps producing frissons that tremble like surreal found art. This story of an elopement gone wrong contains riotous tableaux: a mule doing an impromptu hind-legs dance with Fairbanks and a parson; Fairbanks balancing on phone lines like a high-wire walker or a modern-art mobile. (The movie climaxes with a marriage ceremony performed over the phone. The day I re-watched it, in September 2004, the news carried a story of a U.S. soldier in Iraq wedding a girl back home the same way.)

Dwan shared Fleming's curiosity, range, and sensitivity, and the cinematographer had plenty to learn from Fairbanks's other directors. Joseph Henabery, who worked for Fairbanks as an assistant director before taking the helm of *The Man from Painted Post*, was a shrewd exploiter of locations. He took a camera unit to the Yosemite Valley to shoot a brief mountain-climbing scene in the early part of *Down to Earth*. But a later shot of Fairbanks in full Great White Hunter regalia, commanding loin-clothed dark-skinned natives, might have been filmed anywhere from Long Island to Santa Monica. With little more than blinding light and tropical flora, it conjures a torrid spot on the equator. Most of *Down to Earth* hinges on Fairbanks's ability to convince some upper-crust hypochondriacs that they're on a desert island, not a spit of beach. It's as if Fairbanks were proclaiming that all the world's his studio. Fleming's camerawork here is remarkable for its ingenuity and clarity *and* for the way his images abet humor and satire. When Doug directs a ship's hand to guard the land beyond the beach from the patients, he newly dubs the seaman "a wild man from Weehawken." This sunbaked fellow, getting the message, adopts a caveman's pose near the top of a sandy hill in a composition that's as startling as it is funny.

When Loos and Emerson stumbled at answering Doug's demand to concoct a Western shot in the real West, Henabery and Fairbanks came up with a story of a range detective posing as a greenhorn rounding up rustlers for *The Man from Painted Post*. It's the sort of square Western that the hero of *Wild and Woolly* would devour; it's as if Fairbanks made his revisionist Western comedy, then decided to do the straight version. But it's a well-paced shoot-'em-up, and a feel of fresh air courses through it. "Nice and cool up here," Fleming wrote his mother from the Hotel Connor in Laramie, Wyoming, "and it's rained a couple of times. We are going to camp out on the ranch where we work." Fleming's use of the Wyoming hills gives *The Man from Painted Post* a hint of grandeur.

It was evidently as a result of the prestige and popularity of his work with Fairbanks that Fleming got his key job in the Signal Corps during World War I, which led to his assignment as chief cameraman for President Wilson's European tour. These experiences would burnish his reputation as an American original—a self-taught virtuoso—and turn him into an even more dynamic character: a rough-hewn man of the world.

4

In Manhattan for the Great War

When the United States entered the Great War in April 1917, every healthy male between the ages of twenty-one and thirty-one anticipated induction by autumn and then service in the field. The twenty-eight-year-old Fleming didn't appreciate the bump it would put in his career path; in what looks like an attempt to lower his chances of going in the first wave of draftees, he changed his birth year to 1888 on his draft card. But once he was called up, he didn't flinch from the challenge. He wrote his mother in August that John Fairbanks arranged to have Fleming's draft exam take place in Laramie, Wyoming, where he was shooting *The Man from Painted Post.* "Hope I pass it" was his comment. And he did.

After he squeezed in one more Fairbanks picture, *Reaching for the Moon,* the Army inducted him "with what appeared to be the rest of Hollywood" on October 18. He arrived at Camp Lewis, outside Tacoma, Washington, on October 23. In a letter to his mother that night—"I have made up my bed and am going to hit it very soon"—his only complaint is about the crowding in the car on the way. "All the boys say it is great up here," he adds, and "one can't expect too much because things are so new up here they have not had time to get things running smooth."

His "first job in the army was to peel potatoes with a kitchen police detail at Camp Lewis," Fleming wrote in *Action.* He was initially a private in the Ninety-first Division of the American Expeditionary Force, known as the Wild West Division because the bulk of its draftees came from California, Idaho, Montana, Nevada, Oregon, Utah, Washington, and Wyoming. The Army dammed this flood of men into the division's 166th Depot Brigade before assigning them to units. According to Fleming, he "had enlisted in the Officers' Training Corps"; unfortunately, "before the commission came through, my number went up in the draft." Had Fleming remained in the Ninety-first Division and the 316th Field Signal Battalion, he might have seen battle in France as a combat photographer.

A few days after his arrival at Camp Lewis, Major Charles Wyman, the division signal officer for the battalion, summoned Fleming to his office. Wyman had received a telegram concerning Fleming's enlistment, either from the War Department, as Fleming remembered it, or from the office of the chief signal officer. The way Fleming recounted the interview, Wyman told him, "We have about thirty-five hundred applications from the infantry for service in the Signal Corps. They all want to get into the photographic division. They all say they're A-1 cameramen, or laboratory experts. What we want you to do, Fleming, is to get ten good men out of the bunch."

Fleming wrote that he "knew there weren't that many cameramen and laboratory specialists in the country, but I kept my lips buttoned." Wyman's nephew Richard V. Wyman remarks that "Charley was not one to make up figures, and he might have said there were 'a lot' or 'many' from which to pick ten." Wyman, perhaps unwittingly, had orchestrated an ideal match of job and soldier. After Fleming chose those men, he was transferred to Fort Sill, Oklahoma, and became a soldier in the 251st Aero Squadron and the Aviation Section of the Signal Corps, in part devoted to making "pictures from the air that would help the artillery locate its target." (Eventually, the Army handed aerial photography from the Signal Corps to the newly formed Army Air Service. The Army Air Corps had temporarily disbanded in 1911.)

Although the Signal Corps was founded in 1861 to take charge of all field communications, it had not kept up with technology and had trained its officers and soldiers mostly in semaphore flags and telegraphy. Still photographs had no place in the Signal Corps of the Civil War, and prior to World War I the Army used motion picture photography only for isolated events, like the Wright brothers' flight in 1907 at Fort Myer, Virginia. But on July 21, 1917, it designated the Signal Corps "the bureau which will obtain the necessary photographs to form a comprehensive pictorial history" of the war. Fleming would become a member of the fledgling Photographic Section.

Once he put on the uniform, Fleming hoped to be in the thick of the action. He later said that what *he* really wanted to become in the war was a machine gunner or an aviator, but the Army rejected his efforts to enter the field of battle. Even officers far removed from Hollywood recognized Fleming's importance as the chief cameraman for Fairbanks, the most inspiring producer-star of his day and a phenomenal wartime fund-raiser and morale booster. And Fleming "found compensation in the knowledge that motion pictures had served a great many purposes in the war, apart from their ordinary utility as entertainment." He would use his unique experience to serve his country first as a maker of training films, next as an instructor, and ultimately as a cameraman for military intelligence.

The Army intended to use Fort Sill as the base for its school of land photography, probably because it had already become a center for instruction in multiple fields, including gunnery and aviation. It was an apt spot for a private from the Wild West Division. Fort Sill dated to frontier days and had been the prison holding the Apache chief Geronimo before his death in 1909. Starting in September 1917, its School of Fire trained field artillery officers in the thousands, peaking at two hundred a week. Fort Sill also turned out one hundred air service observers a week. The ranks were a lot thinner for the Photographic Section. In August 1917, it numbered only twenty-five men, with cinematographers especially scarce; it could field only four motion picture cameramen as late as March 1918. Fleming answered to a couple of scholarly captains, Olin O. Ellis and Enoch Garey, and under their command did breakthrough work, creating some of the first military training films. "These films were used to demonstrate . . . the whole machinery of the guns," he recalled. They "gave recruits about everything there is in gunnery except the feel of hot metal and the smell of powder." Sadly, a series of arson fires in the 1920s incinerated those films. But the experience grounded Fleming and his colleagues in wartime reality. "It was my first consideration of the camera as a weapon of warfare and it was highly impressive."

Fleming nonetheless viewed Fort Sill as just a step along his way. In a telegram to his mother sent on Christmas Eve, he says, "Everything is fine" but he expects "to get somewhere soon." He didn't have long to wait. Late in 1917, the Signal Corps hierarchy realized that equipment for the Photographic Section would be easier to acquire in New York. In January 1918, Fleming was making gunnery films at the School of Fire at the rate of one or two every couple of days. He and twelve others from the 251st Aero Squadron got their orders to transfer from Fort Sill to the new photography school at Columbia University.

Standing out in the group was the wiry, six-foot-five twenty-five-year-old Ernest B. Schoedsack, the co-creator of the epic documentaries *Grass* (1925) and *Chang* (1927) and then the epochal fantasy *King Kong* (1933). Within a month, Fleming had finished the last of his fifteen training films and was Manhattan-bound.

In his February 9 letter of recommendation for Fleming, Captain Ellis suggested that Fleming and two others receive commissions "should their work at Columbia prove satisfactory." The letter testifies to Fleming's ability to impress people in a matter of weeks; it also points up the stature of his civilian connections. "Private Fleming was Douglas Fairbanks's cameraman. In fact, we have found him to be more than a cameraman. He understands the motion picture game from the ground up, and he has ingenuity, conception and imagination, which made him a most valuable man in our work."

The U.S. School of Military Cinematography established at Columbia taught six-week courses in motion picture and still photography. Although more than seven hundred men would attend its classes and enjoy the many off-base diversions of Manhattan, the Army treated the school as a military secret. It hid in plain sight at 116th Street and Broadway, and went public only after the war ended.

Fleming arrived on February 9. He wasn't the sole Fairbanks cameraman on campus. Three days earlier, Harris Thorpe had arrived; he'd worked on *Wild and Woolly* under Fleming's supervision. An East Coast cameraman named Harold "Hal" Sintzenich had helped develop the Columbia curriculum. Sintzenich was a seasoned veteran of New York and New Jersey studios, but in his diary he responded to Fleming's arrival with youthful alacrity: "Vic Fleming, cameraman for Douglas Fairbanks, has been put in charge of the movie men, temporarily. An awfully good fellow." Sintzenich and Fleming spent the next day "examining for men who are to go to France." Ray June, who would later shoot Fleming's *Treasure Island* and *Test Pilot,* also taught there at some time, but the "chief" or "senior" instructor of motion picture photography was Second Lieutenant Carl L. Gregory. Like Dwan and the other film pioneers, Gregory had earned a college degree in another field—chemistry, from Ohio State University. Then he worked briefly as a cinematographer for the Edison Company in 1909 and became a jack-of-all-trades (including writing and directing) for the Thanhouser Film Corporation of New Rochelle, New York. Tending the egos of movie-industry vets became a sizable task for Gregory, their supervisor. Schoedsack, for example, who would scale Gotham's heights with *King Kong*, brushed off his Columbia experience with the words "I taught them how to put a camera on a tripod." But Gregory's faculty offered students a high-level practical education in lenses, composition, and lab work as well as "news value, historical record and war caption writing." It culminated in "lectures on work under actual field conditions in the trenches and at schools of fire located in nearby training camps."

Wesley Ruggles was one student who took advantage of everything he could. A former Keystone Kop, Ruggles went on to direct the first Academy Award–winning Western, 1931's *Cimarron*. And there was an activated reservist named Louis (formerly Lev) Milstein, a cutting-room assistant, posted after Columbia to the propaganda division of the Army War College in Washington, D.C. He hoisted equipment for a cameraman documenting Medical Corps operations, made health films about the benefits of good posture and dental hygiene, and edited combat footage. After the war he adopted the name Lewis Milestone and directed the most celebrated of all World War I movies, *All Quiet on the Western Front* (1930). Another Signal Corps enlistee, a former worker at the World Film Corporation, got his first taste of trade-paper coverage when he was in the Army. *Moving Picture World* noted, "Joe Sternberg has been stationed at Columbia University, where he will be engaged in important work connected with the preparation of a film which will be used as an aid in training recruits." Later, a Hollywood producer persuaded him to change *his* name, and Jonas Sternberg became Josef von Sternberg, the director who made Marlene Dietrich an international star in a string of poetic melodramas.

Young women from Barnard happened by now and then, but the U.S. School of Military Cinematography was a wholesome enclave at the edge of a New York scene heady with its own exploding cultural vitality. This was a time when Broadway was considered a barbaric camp at the barricades of proper etiquette and study. A contemporary music professor at Columbia, Daniel Gregory Mason, complained that "Jewish tastes and standards, with their Oriental extravagance, their sensual brilliance and intellectual facility and superficiality," had corrupted Broadway. But Broadway hadn't yet infiltrated Mason's—and Carl Gregory's—campus. Sintzenich's diary entries of his time at Columbia read like a training camp fit for Fairbanks. Calisthenics and military drill followed reveille; then it was time for practice with twin semaphore flags and the single-flag signaling system known as wigwag. The cinematographers scrimmaged on Columbia's football field between afternoon classes and lectures on cameras and lighting, fitness and health. For a bit of spice, female instructors taught French. To conserve time, Central Park, rather than nearby Army schools of fire, hosted semaphore classes as well as field trips that were meant to echo battlefield conditions.

Even the boys' nights out were salubrious. On March 13, Sintzenich recorded, "In the evening went down to the Strand with Wruggles [Wesley Ruggles] and Fleming to see Mary Pickford." The film was *Amarilly of Clothes-Line Alley.* It must have been a kick for Fleming to watch his pal Fairbanks's paramour, Pickford, as directed by his even older buddy Marshall Neilan. The next week Hal and Vic plunked down their money to see "Terrible Teddy" Tetzlaff's onetime co-star Mabel Normand at the height of her comic-dramatic prowess in *The Floor Below.*

On March 28, Sintzenich sketched a vignette of Manhattan hospitality that transports a reader to a more formal, gracious time. "Arrangements were made for the company to go to the theatre tonight and a supper after, of which about 100 took advantage . . . We went down in formation." The image of a hundred men in uniform marching seventy blocks to see a hit Broadway musical, Sigmund Romberg's *Maytime*, seems something out of *Yankee Doodle Dandy.* But it happened, and Fleming was part of it. (The following month the Columbia soldiers regrouped to see Al Jolson in *Sinbad.*)

Fleming got his lieutenant's commission and an assignment that sent him briefly to Washington, D.C., on May 13. His mother, vacationing in Long Beach, California, mailed him a postcard that elicited a revealing response. "How do you like eating everywhere and anywhere?" he wrote his mother on May 22.

> I have been doing it for so long now that it's hard to imagine any other way—and it looks as though I shall be eating that way for some time. *But* some day I am going to have a house in California—wife and all that goes with it. That will be much better. I am going back to Columbia University tomorrow. Have finished my work here. It's fearful hot in Washington. Would hate to have to stay here all summer . . . It's much better to be an officer than a private. You are somebody and have

> liberties—live like a regular human being. Never felt better and had less in my life.

Of course, almost any man, even one who signed his name as an "affectionate son," would be circumspect about love and marriage when writing to his mother. But bringing up having a house and wife in California without mentioning Clara, whom he'd divorced for desertion just three years earlier, suggests that Fleming was capable of ruthless movement in his emotional life. His ex-lovers would always speak well of him, but not his wives. Clara Strouse is a silent part of Fleming family history. By 1918, she presumably had died; her memory seems to have expired before her. Fleming's second marriage, fifteen years hence, would be rife with oddly mixed emotions.

One friend he made at Columbia, Carl Akeley, would affect him as much as Fairbanks. "Akeley's talents were spread across so many fields that he deserves the rank of Renaissance Man," wrote Kevin Brownlow. In 1886, practicing a unique version of taxidermy that became state-of-the-art, Akeley stuffed P. T. Barnum's elephant Jumbo. He became devoted to Africa and its animals and befriended another lover of the Dark Continent, Theodore Roosevelt. He survived a bull-elephant trampling and killed a leopard with his own two hands. He was a sculptor, naturalist, wildlife photographer, conservationist, and creator of the compressed-air cement gun. He invented the gyroscopic Akeley camera, capable of fluid movement in any direction and at any tempo.

While his cameras were being used for aerial reconnaissance and he was attached to the Corps of Engineers, Akeley improved searchlights and remote-control devices for light projectors and placed his evolving photographic designs at the disposal of the Signal Corps. In early May, Fleming and others accompanied Akeley and Signal Corps equipment inspectors to perform tests on Akeley's new "pancake" camera, lightweight and popular with newsreel photographers, and the next month Fleming started teaching an advanced class in its use.

As Fleming put it in *Action*, around the same time "some letters reached me from California advising that someone had been conducting a strangely thorough investigation into my record. A few days later, I received orders to report to General [Marlborough] Churchill, commanding [the Military Intelligence Division] in Washington." The Army was appropriating the new lieutenant so he could perform classified and experimental duties. A group called the American Protective League conducted the investigation of Fleming's "loyalty, integrity and character" in June. Established by the Department of Justice in 1917 and lasting until 1919, the APL was manned by as many as 250,000 civilian secret agents. They were supposed to report suspicious activity, conduct interrogations, and make arrests. But when there wasn't enough to keep them occupied, they turned in draft dodgers and maintained surveillance on industrial plants with defense contracts. They also raided German-language newspapers.

Called upon for testimonials to his patriotism and character, Fleming showed himself to be a savvy young man on the rise, naming half a dozen people on the basis of their clout and celebrity more than their knowledge of his character. Under the category noted on the form as "known by," he listed his friend and sometime employer Charles Cotton; the Los Angeles city official Glen MacWilliams Sr., father of the Fairbanks cameraman Glen MacWilliams Jr.; and, of course, Fairbanks. Under "recommended by" (meaning they wrote letters and/or were interviewed directly on Fleming's behalf), Fairbanks topped the list. The others never again show up in Fleming's story, but they included Jules Brulatour, who inspired the opera-impresario segment of *Citizen Kane*, and Donald J. Bell, who co-founded Bell & Howell. Brulatour distributed raw film stock for Eastman Kodak, a key position in the photo industry; he was also an occasional producer and later the agent for the actress Hope Hampton, his second wife. Brulatour gave Fleming a letter of recommendation. In a follow-up interview he said, "Fleming is very intelligent, bright, and I think he would be a very valuable man as a moving picture photographer for the government." He added he knew Fleming "three years in a business way only," and "whether he would make a good officer or not for the Army, I am somewhat doubtful . . . Regarding his patriotism, I do not know him well enough to speak, as I have not been in touch with him lately."

Bell, who said he had known Fleming a little over two years, had no qualms, calling the lieutenant "very, very patriotic . . . absolutely an American straight through." He even backed up Fleming's contention in *Action* that he had "been very anxious to get into the aviation service." But just how well he knew Fleming is debatable. The APL delegate writes, "Mr. Fleming's people are from Oklahoma, he thinks. Mr. Fleming's father [Sid Deacon] is interested in oil properties out there."

Fairbanks, then on the West Coast (Fleming had supplied an East

Coast address), appears to be the sole source for a Los Angeles report that lauds Fleming's mechanical facility but says he "expressed considerable dislike over the prospect of being drafted, stating that he hated to be taken from his work just at a time when he was making good. When [Fleming was] recently interviewed, however, by Douglas Fairbanks in New York after having entered the service, he stated that he was supremely happy and well satisfied with his lot. That he wouldn't get out of it for anything in the world." The investigator's signature at the bottom of the report belongs to Cecil B. DeMille, the head of Hollywood's APL chapter. The shadow of DeMille and the American Protective League would loom throughout Fleming's life, to the formation of the anticommunist Motion Picture Alliance for the Preservation of American Ideals in the 1940s.

One of Fleming's first confidential assignments was shooting high-speed movies of exploding ordnance at the Aberdeen Proving Ground in Maryland. He noted in *Action* that "it was delicate business and we soon learned that a charge of TNT can be as unruly at the starting point as it is on landing." If you believe an earlier account of his life, he learned all about dynamite in San Dimas.

Fleming underwent the security check so he could chronicle comings and goings at the port of Hoboken, New Jersey, where three million doughboys eventually shipped out to Europe. He ended up spending much of his war time in Hoboken. It was an important post. In 1914, seventeen German ships had been stopped and kept at the port under harbor neutrality acts, and the government had maintained rigid control of it ever since, seizing the piers outright when America entered the war. Naming Hoboken a port of embarkation, the United States put part of the city under martial law and shuttered all saloons within a half mile.

For a young cinematographer with a knack for kinetic imagery and an appetite for power, filming the troops assembling at Camp Merritt, New Jersey, boarding a ferry at Alpine Landing, and then debarking at Hoboken must have been a pleasure as well as a duty. (Fleming's footage is preserved at the National Archives.) A real-life cast of thousands provided him with a charge that may have rivaled assisting Griffith with the Babylonian hordes of *Intolerance*. Fleming's main responsibility was to keep the action clear while providing evidence of military scope and efficiency, but his compositions demonstrate the understated snap that classical moviemakers achieved simply by putting the camera in the right place. The formations of the men are as memorable when they're huddled en masse on the ground, waiting for the next move, as they are when they're marching. In images from an epoch before people reflexively adapted their conduct for movie cameras, there's an endearing poise in the shots of Red Cross women pouring drinks for the servicemen and handing them rations. The embarkation center footage contains purely documentary shots of officers scanning paperwork, but there are also frames that rival those in Vidor's *The Crowd:* rows of female secretaries stooped over their desks and a wall-length filing cabinet stretching from the floor to some high windows. Fleming conveys the tension and drudgery in tasks like loading the Belgian relief ship *Remier* with supplies, and the controlled tumult of troop ferries docking at Hoboken.

The high point of his Hoboken footage, though, comes when the liner *Leviathan* participates in an abandon-ship drill. During this full-dress rehearsal for catastrophe, Fleming's ability to keep lines of action in deep focus in one setup after another brings out the drama beneath the matter-of-factness. After the lifeboats are lowered, life rafts slowly slither down the sides of the ships, like rubbery mollusks. In the transfer of men from rafts to boats, one or two fall overboard and splash around in life preservers, and with the exercise nearly complete, the rafts bob around empty, filled with water. In *Action,* Fleming recalled "one occasion when a thousand men were struggling in the water and all life boats were overside." It looks more like a few hundred men, and very few of them are struggling. Whatever the count, this cameraman achieves indelible documentary impact.

On August 25, Ellis once again demonstrated his trust in Fleming. He wrote from the War Department's Office of the Chief of Staff in Washington, asking "Dear Fleming" to make an official report about a lieutenant who had been "insubordinate" at Fort Sill. Perhaps to his chagrin (he did hate the heat), Fleming was sent back to Washington himself in Indian summer and stayed on through most of the fall, working for the Army War College's propaganda division from September to November. Although no specifics are known, he processed film from France and edited it into civilian propaganda films for the Committee on Public Information. On September 30, he was promoted to first lieutenant and given "one of the precious blanket passes. Which meant that I might go anywhere at any time, without question. It was a rare honor, but it was also the instrument which kept me in service long after the war ended."

What he called "a confidential mission" took Fleming to New York, where he was when the armistice was declared on November 11. He hankered to get back to Fairbanks and filmmaking and civilian fun and, on November 16, wrote a letter to his immediate superior, Captain Charles F. Betz, stating that he'd been left in limbo. Betz, a career officer, counseled patience with a letter addressed to Fleming at the Friars Club:

> Suggest you "hold fast" for the time being. Nothing definite can be stated now, but it is believed that within the next two weeks instructions will be issued from the War Department in which case we will know exactly how to act. There have been quite a few who have jumped to the conclusion on the spur of the moment of getting out, and which caused rather harsh comment. You have done such excellent work that a few weeks delay would not cause any great hindrance to you. Suggest that you "go slow" for the time being. If anything comes up will keep you posted.

The same day that Betz gave his advice, November 18, President Woodrow Wilson announced that he would personally head the American delegation to the Paris Peace Conference in December. "My orders," Fleming wrote decades later, "were to accompany him." With a recollection of mingled irritation and excitement, he went on: "So it was that when the war was over, I was still in it as far as military discipline and rigid obedience were concerned. But in compensation, the voyage to Europe and the adventures there as a member of Wilson's party, provided some of the most interesting incidents in my life."

5

Filming the Conquering Hero: With Wilson in Europe

"No one in America, or in Europe either, knows my mind and I am not willing to trust them to attempt to interpret it," President Wilson said in October 1917. So a year later he determined that only he should head a delegation to sell European allies on his Fourteen Points—planks of a treaty for a just and lasting peace that would also serve as the Covenant of the League of Nations, his United Nations prototype.

In his final task for the Signal Corps, Fleming photographed the ecstatic citizens of the victor nations who swarmed Wilson in Europe. They broke the boundaries of the movie frame with a show of approval that visibly buoyed the president. "Whether Europeans were cheering Wilson's Fourteen Points, celebrating the end of the war, thanking Americans for military help, or simply responding to a unique and exciting event was not clear," Wilson's biographer Kendrick A. Clements writes in *Woodrow Wilson: World Statesman* (1987). "Being human, Wilson enjoyed the adulation." Fleming caught the essence of the spectacle and provided critical data for Americans debating whether Wilson let the cacophony cloud his judgment. In Clements's positive account, Wilson "did not fool himself that securing the peace he wanted would be easy."

A few years before, in 1915, this president had hosted the first White House screening of a movie: Griffith's *Birth of a Nation.* His reported reaction—"It is like writing history with Lightning. And my only regret is that it is all so terribly true"—became part of essential movie lore, though nobody has ever nailed down the source of the quotation. For this trip, he was lucky to take along a cameraman able to capture international diplomacy at flash point.

"I don't know what you will think of this news," Fleming wrote to his mother on November 27. "But I won't get home for Christmas. I have to go to France with President Wilson on the peace trip. We will be gone about six weeks from the time we leave—go to England, France, Italy and maybe Germany. I tried to get out of going but they won't let me. Anyway, it will be a great trip, and worth much to a young chap for the knowledge he will gain, of course." The assignment's prestige had started to sink in: "It is really quite an honor when you stop to think of it."

Fleming wasn't kidding, though, about seeking "to get out of going." He'd been on the brink of a professional breakthrough just before the war, and may have seen his Hollywood career slipping away. But once Fleming came on board, he found himself caught up in history in the making. On November 27, the White House announced that the president and his delegation would travel on the *George Washington*, a German passenger liner the U.S. government had impounded and turned into a troop carrier during the war. The ship boasted a crew of 525 and had enough room for twenty-seven hundred passengers. On this voyage it would contain a few hundred diplomats, scholars, and soldiers, including Fleming and four other Signal Corpsmen.

As the novelist John Dos Passos neatly put it fourteen years later in *1919*, the second volume in his trilogy *U.S.A.* (1937), "On December 4th, 1918, Woodrow Wilson, the first president to leave the territory of the United States during his presidency, sailed for France on board the *George Washington*, the most powerful man in the world." Amid the blare of military musicians and a happy, noisy throng, the ship left Hoboken's Pier 4 at flood tide, 10:15 a.m. In footage that can be seen at the National Archives, Fleming's camera glances upward at the presidential flag and then stays focused on the cheering crowds as the ship glides out. Wilson's well-wishers race along at eye level; the ship goes a short distance before a viewer realizes that they're running along the rooftop of a pier building. (This "found" tracking shot has the inexorable pull of Francis Ford Coppola's harbor and rooftop scenes of roughly the same period in *The Godfather: Part II*.) Patriots spill out of windows and doorways; an ebullient mob waves handkerchiefs below.

Flag wavers line the piers, biplanes cut the air in blocky loops and zigzags, and a Navy dirigible circles watchfully, with eerie evenness, until the *George Washington* sails past Long Island. Wilson received a send-off more tumultuous than for any previous American leader. An escort of five destroyers fired off a twenty-one-gun salute. "We replied, and the din was terrific," noted the Columbia history professor James T. Shotwell, the president's adviser on economic and political history.

It was a bang-up start to Fleming's first ocean voyage. He'd made his initial trip to the East Coast just four years before, but here he was, listening to popular anthems like George M. Cohan's "Over There" as he drank in the intoxicating imagery of the ship's steam underlining the New York skyline. On board and in Western Europe, *he* was wielding the camera that would catch the tour for the record, and for posterity. (Fleming's chronicling of the Wilson trip was always meant to be archived: it was the first time film would be considered as important as presidential papers.) Shipping out was a dizzying continuation of his wartime experience, with its blend of service and growth as well as a smattering of showbiz.

Wilson's company and the ship's crew soon assembled for a portrait. Fleming focused on the delegates, then tilted his camera up to depict the crew forming a diamond shape as they hung from every corner of each deck. Even more magnetic for Wilson's delegates than the movies shown nightly was the camera recording them during the day. On December 9, Shotwell wrote, "I nearly forgot to say that the Military Intelligence took our pictures this morning, not merely as a group but individually, and then took film of us for a movie!" The same day Charles Seymour, a Yale history professor who was chief of the delegation's Austro-Hungarian Division, was writing to his family:

> We have at our table the Signal Corps officer who is responsible for all the pictures to go into the war records and who is to make all the pictures of the Conference. He took still pictures of the Inquiry group all together, then individual pictures of each of us; then moving pictures of groups of three of us at a time, talking and smoking . . . All these movies go into the war records and copies are sent back to the Committee on Public Information. So keep a watch for movies of the President's party.

Edith Benham, First Lady Edith Wilson's social secretary, wrote of being filmed by Fleming on December 11, two days before the landing in Brest, in northwest France: "So up we went and made fools of ourselves talking animatedly for the movie man and posing for the cameras."

Fleming was the one who thought *he'd* made a fool of himself. President Wilson's chief bodyguard, Edmund W. Starling, was walking on a small promenade deck during the second day at sea when he noticed Fleming—"an enterprising young photographer"—cranking his camera as Starling approached him. Fleming "had turned and fled" before Starling could introduce himself. Fleming spread the word that shipboard footage of the president would be projected before the next scheduled movie. As Starling recalled, "A man in a dark overcoat and gray felt hat could be seen walking slowly around the deck. Finally he turned and walked toward the camera. There was a gasp of astonishment, then a roar of laughter as the features of his face developed into the countenance not of the President, but of myself. The President and Mrs. Wilson turned and waved at me, laughing. The young photographer was embarrassed."

But not demoralized. Fleming leaped at the chance to film an abandon-ship drill, with the president and the delegates looking on in life jackets. Two days after the drill, a severe storm made the headlines back home, as Fleming rolled his camera on dark skies, roiling seas, spume-drenched bulkheads—and then shards of sun piercing the newly calm Atlantic.

Wilson turned Fleming into a catch-as-catch-can portrait artist, stealing close-ups of the president doing paperwork in his stateroom. Outside, whether Fleming depicts Wilson chatting up correspondents, ambling on the deck, or staring thoughtfully at the Atlantic, Edith is at the president's side, usually with his aide and physician, Admiral Cary Grayson. One reason for Wilson's spare presence on the journey out was the onset of a cold. Because of the momentousness of his mission and the euphoria surrounding him, Wilson may have felt unusually vulnerable. On December 12, after the evening movie, the crew serenaded Wilson, and all the officers and guests joined in. "At the end, just before the lights went up, a group of fifty bluejackets who had gathered unseen in a corner of the dining room, sang 'God be with you till we meet again,' " noted Raymond Blaine Fosdick in his diary. (Fosdick would eventually become an undersecretary general of the League of Nations.) "The president was visibly affected. His head was bowed and I could see the tears on his cheeks." In a testament to Fleming's work, a *New York Times* dispatch stated, "Nothing has pleased [Wilson] more than the moving picture taken of him with the assembled crew on the forward deck, in which the president shook hands with everyone, from the grimy fireroom gangs to the men of the upper decks."

Eighteen American destroyers accompanied the *George Washington* as it pulled into Brest, the principal city of Brittany, on December 13.

"The town was a veritable mud-hole," Grayson noted in his diary. "Yet today when the *George Washington* steamed into the harbor, the sun was shining brightly, and the sea was as tranquil as the proverbial mill-pond." In Fleming's scenes, the ships spread blithely across the water, dreadnoughts at their ease. A sailor on the *George Washington* uses semaphore to signal them and the greeting party; the crew hoists the tricolor to flap alongside the Stars and Stripes. In *Action*, Fleming writes that when French and American officials reached the ship,

> Gen. John J. Pershing, commanding the AEF, was the first man to stride aboard the ship. I was endeavoring to be the first ashore, because I wanted to shoot that moving scene on celluloid. The general became lost in the winding companionway below decks. I rounded a turn at considerable speed and collided with him head-on. Now a lieutenant who bumps unceremoniously into his commander-in-chief had better pull himself together promptly and explain. I lost no time. Pershing readjusted his cap to its customary rakish angle and eyed me as I stood at attention. A faint smile came to his lips. "Lieutenant," he said crisply, "will you direct me to the president? This damned alley is confusing."

"If we do not heed the mandate of mankind," Wilson said in his initial speech in France, "we shall make ourselves the most conspicuous and deserved failure in the history of the world." The images Fleming set on film were often stately, monumental—retinues proceeding down piers decorated with Allied flags and full-dress parades moving along roadways. But those phenomenal crowds are always pushing in. The task of documenting the action required alertness and flexibility. After a greeting from Brest's mayor, and shouts of "*Vive l'America*" from his audience (throughout the country, the French held "*Vive Wilson*" signs or draped them across streets), Wilson's motorcar convoy whisked him to the railroad that would bring him to Paris on December 14. French President Raymond Poincaré and Premier Georges Clemenceau met him at the railway under Fleming's eye. Then the cameraman leapfrogged the delegation to find the best possible vantage point on the Champs-Élysées. He managed to catch both the front lines of spectators and the masses maneuvering for position, as well as the parade's motor convoys speeding ahead and a group of women on the sidelines holding the banner for the American Red Cross.

Here, Fleming was not alone. The Signal Corps wisely enlisted five or more other cameramen—including an aerial cinematographer—to cover the presidential route and, in Fosdick's words, the "riot of color and fun" surrounding it.

President and Mrs. Wilson and most of the official party stayed four miles from the train station, at the Hôtel Murat, the three-hundred-year-old mansion in the heart of Paris. The Hôtel de Crillon on the Place de la Concorde put up the rest of the delegation, including Fleming. "An American," Fosdick noted, "can have anything he wants in Paris today—he owns the city. The girls even try to kiss him on the streets."

Another American in Paris for the peace conference was a twenty-four-year-old theatrical producer, Walter Wanger. His future credits as a movie producer or production executive would range from *Stagecoach* (1939) to *Invasion of the Body Snatchers* (1956) and include two epic fiascos—Joseph L. Mankiewicz's *Cleopatra* (1963) and Fleming's *Joan of Arc* (1948). Fleming and Wanger met at the end of 1918. Wanger had spent part of the war working for the Committee on Public Information in Rome, learning the rudiments of film editing by re-titling and often rearranging Signal Corps newsreels for Italian audiences. Now he was an aide to Shotwell, who described him as "a very jolly boy." Wanger "assured" Shotwell "we were going to have major-generals do our laundering, and all things on a similar scale!" Wanger flirted with the Foreign Service, but years later would say that after seeing the effects of films on public opinion, "I decided this was going to be my niche." Wanger once referred to Fleming as "my cameraman at the Peace Conference." Fleming, though, was not Wanger's man: he was Wilson's. On December 18, he was placed at the president's disposal "until he otherwise directs."

Fleming became Wilson's personal cameraman. In his footage are dozens of iconic images of Wilson in his top hat and one-of-a-kind winter coat—a calf-length fur piece made of kangaroo pelts, a gift from an Australian admirer. Fleming also was in the perfect place to photograph "the international actors of the theater of war." He told an anecdote about Wilson reviewing the troops. At one point, Pershing blocked Fleming's angle on the president and was so engrossed in conversation that he didn't hear the cameraman's request to move two feet to the right. Noticing a cloud about to cover the sun, Fleming roared, "Get out of the way!" Pershing smiled and moved three feet to the right.

Fleming's stories fit the photographic evidence. At the reviewing stand at Humes, "Black Jack" Pershing betrays an attractive, unbuttoned sense of humor, laughing with the president, nudging him to look in the cameraman's direction, then snapping a salute just for Fleming.

The day after Christmas the Wilsons crossed the English Channel. King George V, Queen Mary and Princess Mary, Premier David Lloyd George, and various other politicians greeted the president at Charing Cross Station. Two million people filled the sidewalks. Fleming shot the more regally paced British reception, with its fancy horse-drawn carriages, liveried drivers and riders, and row on row of cavalry, to provide a president's-eye view of the parade, sometimes from within the route itself, the horses nobly clomping right in front of him. Nothing deterred the British crowds, whether in London or outside the Lowther Street Congregational Church, where Wilson's grandfather had preached in Carlisle, Scotland.

Pope Benedict XV, who had helped inspire Wilson's Fourteen Points—and who would canonize Joan of Arc in 1920—welcomed the president on January 4. There would not be another presidential visit to the Vatican until 1959, when President Eisenhower met Pope John XXIII. Fleming may have been the first person to shoot motion picture film at the Vatican; unfortunately, whatever he filmed has been lost. When Wilson spoke on the balcony of the palace at Milan on January 6, *The New York Times* reported, "a tremendous demonstration took place . . . stretching as far as the eye could reach." Fleming's footage pictures a happy horde whose number seems to approach infinity. As Wilson, benign victor and peacemaker, orates next to a U.S. flag, Fleming pans from right to left and then from left to right. He takes in all of a crowd so dense, euphoric, and turbulent that it makes the classical architecture appear to float and bob on a squall-tossed sea.

Fairbanks had taught Fleming well about creating celluloid legends. In a peak of mythmaking, Fleming filmed Wilson standing alone in the prow of the launch that took him from Italy to the *George Washington.* Wilson, having shed the kangaroo pelts for a proper black overcoat, basks in the affection of the crowds onshore and beams back at them. He places his arms jauntily akimbo when he doesn't use his right hand to tip and wave his top hat. For fleeting seconds, a viewer feels, as Wilson must have, that he *was* the American destined to unite Europe and prevent future wars and make the world safe for democracy. Then the smile fades; impatience, or maybe doubt, creeps into the picture; he turns and asks for a time-out or direction. But it's a sensational example of one of the first staged photo ops.

After six days of preliminaries with the Great Powers—Great Britain, France, Italy, the United States, and Japan—the first plenary session of the Paris Peace Conference began in the Salle de la Paix of the French Ministry of Foreign Affairs on the Quai d'Orsay. Fleming's task, though, was filming dignitaries in their limousines and carriages arriving and departing; he couldn't bring his camera into the Salle de la Paix. He trained his lens appreciatively on the rare picturesque sight—the elegant costumes of some Asian delegations, or the dramatic mane of Poland's President Ignacy Paderewski. But he must have felt stranded on the outside of these historic proceedings. He was ready to go home.

Wilson shipped back to the United States on February 14, returning to Europe at the end of the month. The two thousand soldiers and sailors on board the *George Washington* must have made Fleming feel as if he were on a mammoth, floating version of a Fairbanks set. Fleming shot them blowing off steam in athletic ways. There was a rope-climbing race, a slap match on a pipe eight feet higher than the deck (the loser was the one who fell off), and a mock boxing match funnier than Fairbanks's in *His Picture in the Papers* and just as full of parody bravado. En route, Wilson's private secretary, Joe Tumulty, suggested that the president disembark in Boston, not Hoboken, as a poke in the eye of his political opponent, the Republican senator Henry Cabot Lodge. Ill prepared for the change, the skipper nearly stowed the ship between two large rocks until a passenger came to the rescue: an assistant secretary of the Navy, Franklin D. Roosevelt, who recognized the spot, near Marblehead, Massachusetts, and adjusted the course to Boston.

On February 5, Griffith, Pickford, Chaplin, Fairbanks, and William S. Hart had announced the creation of United Artists, which promised to "protect the great motion picture public from threatening combinations and trusts that would force upon them mediocre productions and machine-made entertainment." (Hart withdrew after three weeks.) Keen to join Fairbanks, Fleming, scheduled to return with Wilson on his second trip to Europe to ratify the treaty, looked for a way out of the military and back into his moviemaking life. Since he was still assigned only to Wilson, he was stationed at the White House. He wrote, "I took a chance and typed my formal discharge on a sheet of White House stationery. Admiral Grayson came down the stairs on some hurried mission and I met him. 'Will you sign this, Admiral?' I handed him the paper. He held it on the polished banister and scrawled his signature with my fountain pen. An officer of the Army had written his own discharge and an officer of the Navy signed it."

Fleming didn't stretch the truth too far. He did handwrite the first draft of his discharge, in standard military language on White House letterhead. But Grayson signed the typed version neatly, betraying neither rush nor the curve of a banister. Fleming received his official discharge on March 7 and headed for New York for a few days before returning to California.

For all his eagerness to wiggle out of the job, being Wilson's cameraman had put Fleming at the top of the heap. As an observer, Fleming had sensed the story, and as a craftsman he had known how to get it. Without the evidence caught in Fleming's camera, future generations wouldn't be able to judge the potency of these epochal demonstrations for themselves.

6

The Importance of Directing Doug

Douglas Fairbanks Sr. was committed to exploring all the possibilities of movies. Charlie Chaplin remembered ruminating with him over life's meaning or lack of it one night at the summit of a large water tank. " 'Look!' said Douglas, fervently, making an arc gesture taking in all the heavens. 'The moon! And those myriads of stars! Surely there must be a reason for all this beauty? It must be fulfilling some destiny!' " In the thrill of his epiphany, Fairbanks focused on Chaplin and asked, "Why are you given this wonderful talent, this wonderful medium of motion pictures that reaches millions of people throughout the world?"

"Why is it given to Louis B. Mayer and the Warner brothers?" Chaplin answered.

Fairbanks responded with laughter and a history-making idea. With Pickford and Griffith, Chaplin and Hart, Fairbanks founded United Artists, a movie production, financing, and distribution company that had everything except a back lot. It allowed its partners to operate like independent producers.

After he left the Signal Corps, Fleming shot the first United Artists release, *His Majesty the American*, for Fairbanks and the director Joseph Henabery. This 1919 action romp about a virtuous, mysterious New York adrenaline addict who finds fresh adventures in an Old World country called Alaine, the home of his long-lost mother, fires up a proven Fairbanks formula with throwaway bravura. In one of the New York scenes, Henabery and Fleming use a cutaway set of six rooms in a racketeer's building to open up a hive of criminal activity as if it were an ant farm. (Jerry Lewis would use a similar set for *The Ladies Man* four decades later, just as Jean-Luc Godard and Jean-Pierre Gorin would in 1972 for *Tout va bien.*) The Fairbanks humor never flags. When he takes a detour to Mexico, he lights his cigarette on the sunbaked earth.

And the action in Alaine has a sweep and a cast of many hundreds (if not thousands) that dwarf the relatively modest dimensions of Fairbanks's previous European frolic, *Reaching for the Moon.*

Fleming moved briefly into his mother's spacious new home, and as Fairbanks's marriage fell apart and his romance with Mary Pickford thrived, Fleming grew close to Mary's younger brother, Jack, who had a yen for fast cars and chorus girls. (Jack died in 1933, at age thirty-six, of general dissipation from substance abuse and venereal disease; Vic was an honorary pallbearer.)

Theodore Reed, another of Fleming's close postwar friends, had worked his way up in Fairbanks's creative ranks during Fleming's Signal Corps service—and no wonder. He had the same breadth of experience that made Dwan and Fleming and the Signal Corps brethren such good company. Born in Cincinnati and reared in Detroit, Reed had a background that combined athletics, science, and storytelling. As a teen he'd been a semipro baseball player; he later earned a master's degree in chemistry at the University of Michigan; he became an actor in a theater troupe that toured throughout the Midwest; and he did time as an efficiency expert. When Reed met Fairbanks in 1918, during a Detroit stop for a Midwest Liberty Loan tour with Marie Dressler and Chaplin, he was a reporter and publicist with the *Detroit Free Press,* married, and the father of three children. Striking an immediate rapport with Doug, Reed took a leave to join Fairbanks and company on the road; because he looked a lot like Chaplin, he could stand in for him on the tour when exhaustion waylaid the comic genius. (Reed renewed his partnership with Chaplin as the sound supervisor on 1931's *City Lights.*)

After the bond-selling tour, Reed returned to the newspaper, but Fairbanks dangled a Hollywood job in front of him. The prospect of fending off a frigid, flu-bugged Detroit winter with rationed coal helped make Reed's decision easy. What's more, his wife Helen's parents had moved from Wisconsin to Pasadena; when they heard of his prospective new employment, they bought Ted and Helen a house west of downtown Los Angeles. Reed began his decade-long stint with Fairbanks by editing scripts, writing titles, and helping Fairbanks cook up scenarios. A selection of his words for the silent Western *Arizona:* "Arizona: Where the burning rays / Of the noonday sun / Assay two men— / And find—but one." (In 1930, Columbia approached Fleming to remake *Arizona* as a talkie.)

Fleming rejoined the Fairbanks production unit in March 1919. Reed, by now Fairbanks's production manager, hit it off with Vic as quickly as he had with Doug. Reed's fourth child, Robert, became Fleming's godson. Robert says Fleming visited their house well into the 1920s, and he appears to have been a likable, rowdy god-dad. "On one of Fleming's visits to our house," Robert recalls, "we were playing a game of blind man's bluff, and each of us was armed with a club made of rolled-up newspaper. We crawled around the living room floor, swinging our weapons wildly and hitting one another from time to time. I recall returning from the game after taking a hard blow and complaining to my mother, 'Vic's a rough guy,' pronouncing it 'wuff.' "

Like his creative partnerships and friendships, Fleming's family was prospering. Late in 1918, Sid Deacon finally struck it rich in oil when some wells he had helped locate in Texas began to produce (given the timing, it was likely in Burkburnett, the scene of MGM's 1940 film *Boom Town*). His initial payday was a stunning $100,000. With part of that money, he bought a large Swiss-chalet-style house, with a big front yard lined with palm trees, at 1618 Crenshaw Boulevard. He also invested in the Signal Hill oil fields. But wealth and a more upscale neighborhood didn't change Eva Deacon. "She still was a farm woman, let's put it that way," Fleming's niece Yvonne Blocksom said. "She was the only one with a chicken house. The chickens were fenced in on two sides of a three-car garage. When the old hens stopped laying, we'd have chicken for dinner. She'd chop the head off herself. She had a vegetable garden and grape arbor, too." In Blocksom's phrase, Eva "did not *live* wealth. She did everything herself—her own laundry, cooking, her own housekeeping, stuff like that."

The only way for Fleming to keep going up in *his* career was to become a director. He made his directorial debut with *When the Clouds Roll By* (1919)—a comic masterpiece that expands its fan base every year at museum and festival showings. His ascendancy was a natural outgrowth of Fairbanks's reliance on his collaborators and Emerson's dependence on his cameramen and assistants for staging scenes. Ted Reed is sometimes credited as Vic's co-director on *When the Clouds Roll By*, but with a bit of pre–Orson Welles panache, the art titles not only name the creators but also picture them—including Fleming alone as the director, sporting a jaunty cap and waving the camera out of his face with a jeer and some rolled-up script pages. Reed functioned as an assistant to Fleming on this boundary-busting movie, which attested to

Fairbanks's widening aesthetic reach. "An extravaganza of the most fantastic sort," read the review in the *Los Angeles Times*. "Whether it will prove a strikingly popular film there is no denying the fact as far as the trappings of the story are concerned the conventional Fairbanks situations have been neatly covered up."

Actually, *When the Clouds Roll By* does more than cover up the "conventional Fairbanks situations." It subverts them. Fairbanks plays the kind of character he helped reform in *Down to Earth*. He's the willing victim of a depraved psychiatrist-neurologist. This persuasive quack uses Fairbanks, a lowly employee in his uncle's New York investment firm, to establish how easily psychological tricks can destroy a man. Knowing that Fairbanks harbors self-destructive superstitions, the mad doctor mercilessly augments them by prescribing awful diets and sabotaging every aspect of the young fellow's existence, including his apartment's plumbing. When Fairbanks bumps into an equally superstitious beauty from Oklahoma, played delightfully by Kathleen Clifford, love has a chance to conquer all, but Clifford's boyfriend from back home comes east to bilk her dad in an oil-grab scheme, with help from Fairbanks's uncle. Clifford does choose Fairbanks over her old beau. The doctor, though, connives to bring the Oklahoman and the uncle to the couple's wedding party—and Fairbanks is accused of fraud. Roused beyond the power of superstition, he chases after Clifford when she leaves New York on a ferry and a train. His first reward comes when insane-asylum orderlies unmask the doctor as an escaped inmate. But it takes Fairbanks's bravery during a sudden catastrophe—a flash flood that swamps the train and an entire town—for him to expose the Oklahoman as a creep and assert his own worth when he rescues Clifford.

The movie boasts two scintillating fantasy scenes. At the start, the quack's accomplice serves Fairbanks a late supper of onions, lobster, Welsh rarebit, and mince pie. Fleming dresses up actors as these foods—they could be the progenitors of the Fruit of the Loom clowns—and depicts them knocking around boisterously inside Fairbanks's stomach. In his ensuing marathon nightmare, Fleming springs one surprise after another. A hydrocephalic stranger reaches for Fairbanks in his bed. When Fairbanks slaps him down, he falls and bounces back like a tin figurine in a pinball game. White shadowy hands cover the room. Fairbanks escapes them by catapulting out of bed and through a wall, landing in a ladies' club—shades of the GIs imagining themselves at a garden club in John Frankenheimer's *Manchurian Candidate.* (Appearing before proper middle-class women must be a show-biz primal fear.)

Escaping through a hanging sea painting, Fairbanks quickly lands in and clambers out of a pool, only to find his four-course dinner chasing after him. In slow motion he makes his frantic getaway, hurdling a few fences before pulling off a somersault and a flying mount onto a waiting horse. Breaching yet another wall, he goes through one more time-space warp into a house that's cut away like the crime hive in *His Majesty the American,* permitting viewers to see the action inside as on a theatrical set. Fairbanks strolls up walls and across the ceiling and does a handstand upside down. The return of the attacking foods leads to a hundred-yard dash over rooftops. The sequence arrives at its breathless end as Fairbanks plunges into a chimney and winds up in a metal canister, subjected to merciless drumming. As he wakes up, we realize that one of the doctor's goons has been stomping around outside Doug's window, impersonating a janitor, and hurling two garbage cans and a bucket.

Technically and imaginatively, the sequence is a tour de force. In 1919, "slow motion" was not a common term, let alone a typical device. (Fleming's experience with high-speed photography in the Signal Corps had obviously given him ideas for its application to comedy.) The wall-and-ceiling walk caused such a sensation that *Literary Digest* exposed the mechanics behind it—basically, "a room open at one side and revolving on an axis like a squirrel cage" and a camera positioned to revolve alongside as Fairbanks kept his balance on the ceiling, walls, and floor. (A pair of Stanleys would embellish the same trick for future generations: Donen in 1951's *Royal Wedding,* and Kubrick in 1968's *2001: A Space Odyssey.*) With crazed bursts of pop poetry, this sequence announces and then brings home the movie's point. When his mind gets tossed off balance, Doug's exuberant physicality becomes subordinate to his warped thoughts and feelings.

Seeing Fairbanks display his athletic abilities through a Lewis Carroll looking glass magnifies their *emotional* power even as it makes them disconcerting. If any film punctures the criticism that Fairbanks exists in his own closed system, it's this one by Fleming. Throwing the usual Fairbanks universe topsy-turvy allows Doug to make deeper connections with the audience and the other characters. Few Fairbanks courtship scenes are as beautifully balanced as the ones here, in which

Clifford matches her leading man's every nervous tic and gesture with her own fluttery, oddball grace.

Early on, the deranged scientist tells Fairbanks to stop smiling, because that expression "is the mark of the idiotic." The put-down plays on Fairbanks's advertised image as "America's Greatest Exponent of the Smile" and presages the moment when Fairbanks's "Sense of Humor" actually saves him in this movie. During the chaotic breakdown of Fairbanks and Clifford's wedding party, Fleming stages another strange interlude, this time without putting the protagonist to sleep. Unable to pursue his true love, reduced to hiding in the closet when cops block every exit at the doctor's behest, Fairbanks freezes. As he does, the camera penetrates his brain, where costumed representatives of Worry and Discord seize the throne of the fair lady Reason while an impotent jester lies at her feet. Only when the asylum orderlies unmask the doctor as a loon does the jester inside Fairbanks's brain—the embodiment of the hero's Sense of Humor—restore Reason to her throne. Humor does it with an ancient, still-good joke: "Have you ever heard the one about the old maid in the sleeping car?" The climactic deluge that tests Fairbanks's strength—it's a lot mightier than the digital flood in *Evan Almighty*—makes the world seem new enough for him and Clifford to start afresh. It's as if God's brain had to clear, too.

When the Clouds Roll By established several hallmarks of a Victor Fleming production. It was technically innovative in its stagecraft and use of artificial lights. "We had even passed an era old-timers remember as something preceding Noah's flood—the day of the overhead mercury lights which gave everyone a ghastly green appearance," Fleming reminisced, years later. "But because we didn't yet understand all we needed to know about light, our actors wore blue, pink or yellowish shirts. This was to cut down the halation." Along with cunning sets, the movie boasted brawny location work. Vic shot some of it at Seal Beach, California, and, for the flood, built a reservoir and a town at the foothills of the Cascade Mountains. He mixed the full-scale action with miniatures. He aimed to escape stage blocking and photographed Fairbanks from unconventional angles away from "stage center," hoping, he said, "to give the action a more 'real' quality."

He also demonstrated his willingness to do anything to get what he needed from performers. A publicity item noted that Clifford "couldn't make her tear ducts work" when she was supposed to weep over her character's apparent breakup with Fairbanks, "so Director Fleming, when he had her rehearsing on the set, deliberately berated her. Finally the temperamental little girl became so worked-up and nervous that she burst forth in great heart-rending sobs, and then the fiendish director yelled, 'Shoot, camera,' and laughed finally at her because he had secured just what he desired." According to the publicity, it was hard for Fleming to make Clifford believe that "he was only getting her to play a crying part" until they screened the scene together "and they realized the harsh methods had obtained excellent results." Clifford's nephew, the stage actor Micky O'Donoughue, says he doubts she would have needed the berating. Hardly a "little girl" at age thirty-two, and experienced in British theater and on Broadway, she came from "a wild and unusual family of incredible talents."

Clifford and Fleming began a four-year romance with her moving into his new place on Gardner Street. A zesty brunette with large, expressive eyes, Clifford was a former chorus girl turned vaudevillian. In 1921, a besotted critic called her "intensely unselfconscious about everything that she does. I've seen her breeze into a musical comedy with an opera glass in one hand and a pretzel in the other. She ate the pretzel as unhesitatingly as she looked over the members of the chorus with the opera glass and passed opinions upon them."

Born Kathleen O'Donoughue in Ireland and raised as part of a traveling theatrical troupe in England, Clifford had performed in America since 1902 and, at just five feet one inch and 101 pounds, created a male-impersonation act called "The Smartest Chap in Town," wearing formal male duds, including top hat and monocle, or a newsboy's outfit with cap, performing songs she'd written herself. (Such acts, long popular in vaudeville, were rooted in nineteenth-century British music halls and made famous by the often-imitated Vesta Tilley.) She was cute enough for Irene Castle to suspect, in 1913, that she might steal the heart of Vernon Castle before their dancing team had even begun.

Clifford had the same blithe, roguish quality as Fairbanks. She went from (in her nephew's words) "running out of money in Ireland and having to urinate in a bottle so her mother could sell it as medicine" to performing in musical comedies with Al Jolson in New York, and later hitting the vaudeville circuits with her "Smartest Chap" turn; she broke into motion pictures in a 1917 Paramount serial. Her mother hawked patent medicines as "Madame Clifford"; that's where Kathleen got her new last name. She also created a new history for herself. Her publicity stated she'd been born in Charlottesville, Virginia, because, according to her nephew, "someone had told her that the courthouse in Charlottesville had burned down during the Civil War, so she gave that as her birthplace because she didn't think there was any way it could be traced!"

In New York to direct Constance Talmadge in *Woman's Place*, Fleming writes Clifford in 1921: "Right now I want you to understand that I am not having a 'great time' or 'lots of fun' or enjoying myself greatly, as you seem to think. I'm not at all happy—having a thoroughly miserable time and wish I were with you, 'where I belong.' Now just what do you think of that." The following year he addresses her as "Dear Pie" from the Algonquin Hotel. "Just another day away from you, that is about all it amounts to," he writes, saying he's going to the world-championship light-heavyweight bout between Benny Leonard and Lew Tendler the next night, and he's "seen no shows and the pictures are rotten."

In another love letter that fall, Fleming writes, "Darling, my love, I have been coming home for several evenings expecting a letter from you and no luck. Always met by Old John Disappointment at the desk. Do you think that is a nice way to treat a perfectly good husband who loves you, do you?" He tells Clifford of a rained-out day on location (for *Dark Secrets*) forty miles out from New York City on Long Island, with no interiors ready to take up the slack. He reports, "Tom [Geraghty] and everyone liked my last picture," *Red Hot Romance*, and hopes his new one (*Anna Ascends*) will be better, "but I don't see how it can knock the world dead," and asks her if she's seen James Cruze's *Old Homestead*, which he hears is "a great picture." He signs the note, "Worlds of love, Victor," with a P.S.: "And please do write. Love thee."

What's most revealing about this letter is its easy, affectionate tone with a worldly beauty who was actually two years older than he (despite the press calling her a "temperamental little girl"). Fleming's conquests would be legion, but they always spoke of him as a man who took good care of them.

If he and Clifford *had* been romantically involved throughout the filming of *When the Clouds Roll By*, Fleming might still have yelled at her or nudged her to make a point if there had been any lull or hesitation in the filming. Even if a performer can *eventually* deliver on a part's requirements, Fleming learned early that a director needs results on demand. He was acclaimed for what he wrought. A *New York Times* reviewer, after stating that *When the Clouds Roll By* and the next Fairbanks-Fleming production, *The Mollycoddle* (1920), have "extraordinary scenes," declared, "That as Victor Fleming directed both 'When the Clouds Roll By' and its successor he is entitled to [take credit for] much of the cinematic works."

The Mollycoddle is as refreshing and pleasurable, though neither as far-out nor as iconoclastic, as *When the Clouds Roll By*. (The title is nineteenth-century slang for a milksop or a mama's boy.) It offers a more intense and stylized version of a *Wild and Woolly* adventure. Here Fairbanks isn't even a Western *fan* when the action picks him up: he's what the *Times* review and his leading lady call "a foreign American"—a Europeanized dandy at play in Monte Carlo. Cultivated beyond his native wit and instincts, Doug's mollycoddle character has lost the frontier-taming vitality of his Arizona forefathers. But a trio of "American college boys" named Patrick O'Flannigan, Ole Olsen, and Samuel Levinski—a melting pot on six legs—discover that despite his cane, monocle, and cigarette holder, Fairbanks is an American, not an Englishman. They resolve to crack his overrefined veneer and see if there's a true Yank below. They shanghai him onto the boat of the rich Dutchman (Wallace Beery) who's been hosting them on an Old-Europe-to-Wild-West vacation tour, not realizing that Beery has been smuggling diamonds from a mine in Hopi Indian country for cutting and finishing on the Continent and that Beery suspects Doug of spying on him for the Secret Service.

Only one of the Fab Three's lady companions, played by Ruth Renick, comes right out and says of Doug, "He has the makings of a man." (She turns out to be the real secret agent.) But all approve as he toughens up with duties in the stokehold, and the guys give him a new tweed outfit: "Suit by O'Flannigan—Cap by Olsen—Shoes by Levinski." By the time the mollycoddle leaves the ship, Renick has revealed her identity (and Beery's) and enlisted Doug in her crusade. Once he finds his way to Arizona, and sheds his sensible tweeds for cowboy duds, the stirring fragrance of western zephyrs wafting off the Apache Mountains and successive bouts of do-or-die action change this mollycoddle into a real man—and, once again, his father's son.

What makes the movie so appealing is the way it touches on the common desire of ordinary men and women to shuck all traces of comfort and etiquette and to sharpen reflexes and senses in the great outdoors. Doug's attempt to join an Indian dance may trigger alarms on P.C. meters, but even the orthodox should see that his I'll-try-anything attitude is disarmingly democratic. Doug the revitalized frontiersman displays a good-humored noblesse oblige both to the Hopi and to the college boys, far removed from the cutthroat ethos promulgated in twenty-first-century wilderness adventures. The famous Fairbanks smile suggests not inherited arrogance or smarminess but a gleeful acknowledgment of his own luck.

In Fairbanks's movies, if not always in his self-help books, his humor makes his most relentless proselytizing for healthy activity and good cheer palatable. It did in his off-set shenanigans, too. During the making of *The Mollycoddle*, Fleming and Fairbanks knocked off early one day to jaunt over to Chaplin's studio with three of their crew members. Spontaneously, they marched through Chaplin's offices silently and deadpan, then started running at a dogtrot, still in single file. Chaplin was working on *The Kid*, but they jogged straight through his set, not saying a word—and Chaplin, getting the stunt, joined right in, flapping along at the end of the line in the Little Tramp's big shoes. With Fairbanks leading the way, they toured the entire lot, without breaking formation or uttering a peep. When they got to Chaplin's studio swimming pool, they dived in and swam the length of it, with Chaplin bringing up the rear in his Little Tramp costume and makeup. As Fleming told the tale to a reporter a few years later, he and Fairbanks and their men got out of the pool, "started running again and drove off in perfect silence, dripping wet, and went home."

The Mollycoddle emerged as a marvelous follow-up to *When the Clouds Roll By*, with the same casual authority at mixing comedy, fantasy, and adventure. The history of the hero's forebears begins with a tableau lifted from the painter Frederic Remington: Doug's grandfather and a sidekick fending off Indians from a water hole. (Fairbanks pads himself out and ages his face to play the role of the mollycoddle's ancestor; he also plays a Wild West sheriff forebear.) When Doug explains to Renick that he's heard New York is wild, Fleming cuts with the directorial equivalent of a deadpan to Western gunslingers raising hell on Wall Street. He uses simple line and figure animation to illustrate Beery's smuggling operation. The sequence serves as a visual palate cleanser, and also echoes later in the mind.

When Fleming shoots some of the desert action, he uses long shots that reduce Doug's figure to an animated speck among the buttes and ledges. And when Doug shows Renick his notes on the Dutchman's operation, the drawings that he's made within a flip book have a comic-strip-and-caption quality. The movie is always visually alive; there's a brief use of subjective camera when the picture rotates with the hero's stomach as he feels queasy in the stokehold, watching his fellow stoker shoveling coal. The killer climax is a landslide that the *New York Times* reviewer declared

> outdoes anything of the kind in the memory of the writer. Half a mountain, it seems, moves down the steep slope, through an Indian village and over half a dozen people protected by a thin ledge . . . [Fairbanks] even challenges the landslide to beat him at its own game and demonstrates that he and Wallace Beery, the villain of his story, can roll and tumble, and fall and slide, down a steep mountain with quite as much concentration on getting to the bottom as any rock that was ever started anywhere by the single-purposed force of gravity. The two men start fighting in a tree at the top of a mountain and are still at it after they have dived over a waterfall, several precipices, many feet of rough ground and two or three brick walls below. Camera tricks? Some of it, but none that can be noticed and more that must have been performed exactly as it is seen.

The greatest milestone of *When the Clouds Roll By* and *The Mollycoddle* is artistic: they mark American moviemakers' early grasp of the ineffable. They convey what Graham Greene articulated when he wrote, "Only the cinema is able in its most fantastic moments to give a sense of absurd unreasoning happiness, a kind of poignant release: you can't catch it in prose."

7

Scaling Paramount Pictures

If Fleming had remained with Fairbanks for many more years, his career might have stumbled like Ted Reed's. Reed stayed a Fairbanks colleague for a decade. He became a full-fledged director with *The Nut* (1921), the last of Fairbanks's modern comic adventures—in part, a Chaplinesque satire of mechanical obsessions. But the success of *The Mark of Zorro* (1920) persuaded Fairbanks, after *The Nut*, to concentrate on heroic period spectacles that consumed months in production. Fairbanks turned to Fred Niblo (*The Three Musketeers*, 1921) and Dwan (*Robin Hood*, 1922) to direct these epics; Reed later served the company as a production manager on *Don Q, Son of Zorro* (1925) and *The Black Pirate* (1926). One of Reed's lasting contributions never made it into the film history books: as the first director on *I Wanted Wings*, in 1941, he designed Veronica Lake's peekaboo hairdo; Mitchell Leisen got the directing credit.

Fleming, though, maintained his partnership with Anita Loos and John Emerson, making three of their snappy, ultracontemporary scripts in rapid succession. By then, Emerson had given up directing. When he and Loos broke with Fairbanks, Emerson gave a series of physical ailments as his public excuse. Some were genuine.

After Emerson and Loos married and took a European tour, they adapted Rachel Barton Butler's *Mamma's Affair* as a vehicle for that deft comedienne and Loos friend, Constance "Dutch" Talmadge. They surrounded Dutch with veterans of the hit 1920 Broadway stage production. Effie Shannon repeated her crowd-pleasing performance as the mother whose psychosomatic (or hypochondriac) attacks keep her at the center of attention every time the spotlight—or her daughter—threatens to stray from her. Emerson and Loos cast Kenneth Harlan as the doctor who, at the movie's comic pinnacle, takes one look at the family and realizes that it's the daughter who needs to be cured of mom-induced neurasthenia.

"To direct," Loos wrote in 1978, "John chose a newcomer, Victor Fleming." (Fleming actually worked for the producer Joseph Schenck, who was married to Constance's sister Norma at the time and later co-founded 20th Century, which eventually merged with Fox. Schenck also sent the director to another Broadway play, *The Broken Wing*, to scout it as a possible Talmadge vehicle.) Fleming's industry and unexpected enthusiasms snared Loos's interest. "I respected Vic's enterprise," she wrote, "and was intrigued by the interest he took in things outside the movies. I recall one night when Vic was bringing me home from a party and we stopped to watch a fleet of fireflies skimming about Beverly Hills. 'Those small insects have mastered a problem that's never been solved by science,' Vic informed me. 'They can produce *light* without *heat*!' "

Fleming focused his attention on Talmadge. *Mamma's Affair* would be no more than stagy piffle with a dynamite opening if not for Fleming's loving treatment of his lead actress. Loos and Emerson kick off their comedy-drama with a burlesque prologue set in the Garden of Eden. Proud of this addition, the team devoted much of an article they wrote on the script to "Eve forcing Adam to let her eat the apple by throwing a fit of hysteria," the point being "that 'nerves' have always been woman's greatest weapon to secure what she wants." The movie's introduction exemplifies wiseacre humor circa 1921 *and* Fleming's gift of putting over outrageous material without fuss. Eve is a babe in a foliage-decorated body stocking, Adam is a scrawny, thatch-haired, Keatonesque caveman, and the snake is a low-tech hand puppet with the infectious effrontery of Burr Tillstrom's Ollie (or maybe Robert Smigel's Triumph, the Insult Comic Dog). When the snake urges Eve to eat the forbidden fruit, Adam says, "Nix on that. We ain't supposed to eat the apple," and warns him to stay away from his family. So the reptile advises Eve to escalate her complaints about Adam denying her any pleasure. "I never see anything but this old garden," says Eve. The bit is funny and offhand in its daring. It's as if the flight from paradise were the source story for all domestic hilarity from Aristophanes to boulevard farce to sitcoms.

Then the stage material begins. Shannon plays Mrs. Orrin, a rich, not-so-merry widow who has tied her sweet, beautiful daughter, Eve (Talmadge), to her own solipsistic mood swings. Fleming knows where the laughs are and where the audience's affections are, too. Eve, on the verge of going out for the first time without her mother (with some girlfriends, to the theater), decides she has to kiss her mom goodbye. Talmadge is so tragicomically vulnerable and Shannon so farcically dominating that you feel an "uh-oh" rise in your throat without the benefit of a setup. Eve cancels the theater trip and cuts short her first evening party to be home with her ailing parent. Ma Orrin and her best friend and enabler, Mrs. Marchant (Katherine Kaelred), plot to marry Eve off to Marchant's son, Henry (George Le Guere), a bespectacled mama's boy who resembles the epicene young Joe E. Brown, and set the date to coincide with Mrs. Orrin's birthday. But when Dr. Harmon (Harlan) observes the melodramatically tremulous matriarch and the furtively coughing and shaking Eve, he decides the young woman must be saved—and can be saved only if he separates her from her mother. Mrs. Orrin is reluctant to lose her "prop in all life's sorrows," but Eve reaches what the titles call "the breaking point" with a nervous outbreak of loathing and self-loathing that ends with her fainting.

Fleming handles Talmadge as knowingly as the doctor does Eve, but far more exquisitely. In this film she has a wholesome, quizzical voluptuousness, with a full, slightly down-turned mouth and eyes that flash out of deep triangular sockets. When she wakes up in the good doctor's care, she exhales a delicious air of freedom. Fleming tenderly shoots her pulling a wrap around a slip or negligee, one tiny strap still showing on her shoulder. Talmadge is a fresh, spontaneous actor. When Eve mimes a fit to disturb her mother's plans for her, Talmadge cues the audience into Eve's fakery without wrecking the illusion—she goes as far as she can with the gag, right up to writhing on the floor like a dog chasing its tail.

A smattering of wit keeps the mix of mirth and heartbreak lively. Eve delights in a rugged piece of pulp fiction called *Pirate's Revenge;* then her mother grabs it and substitutes gushy ladies' novels in which "marriage is the sacred road where two souls meet." Fleming gives satisfying weight to the doctor's setting things straight. "Mother love is beautiful," he says, "but you've never known it. Your mother is a hysterical, selfish vampire."

At age thirty-two, when he filmed *Mamma's Affair*, Fleming was a "mature" figure in the giddy world of early Hollywood; Constance, for instance, was ten years younger. And Harlan's doctor typifies an image found in several Fleming silent movies: a worldly and virile yet temperate man.

You lose patience with the doctor character when he clings to spurious notions of male pride. He spurns Eve's advances twice: first because others might think he's after her money; second because of her superficial dishonesty when she throws that artificial fit. Eve ultimately convinces the doctor that she had to provoke him before he would acknowledge his own authentic feelings. "I can't let you go because I love you," he says, finally. "That's what I've been trying to get at," she responds. By the end he's happy with his "bald-faced, brazen, scheming little darling." As Fleming made future films his own, his notions of love and honor grew more complex and often involved a man and a woman divvying up traditional male and female roles. But *Mamma's Affair*, though stagy and dated, still has a smidgen of audacity. Its revolt against a cloying nuclear family is timeless and true to the period; so is its cry for healthy sexual love.

The movie was obliquely true to Fleming's own experiences. He did know genuine mother love with Eva, who resisted the spoils and spoiling of wealth even after Sid Deacon made his fortune, and Fleming was as frank with her as any mother could require of a son. In an undated letter from the Algonquin Hotel around this time, Victor wrote his mother, "I just finished cutting the picture we made out there" and in about three weeks "will begin a new one with Constance." Given that Fleming never drew family members into the film business, the reference to Constance connotes a certain intimacy. Fleming followed *Mamma's Affair* with one more Emerson-Loos-Talmadge movie, *Woman's Place*, this time starring Dutch as a flapper who loses a mayoral race but becomes a political force behind the scenes. Harlan co-starred as her on-and-off-and-on fiancé, an established political boss. No print has survived.

Fleming's relationship with Clifford ended in early 1923 when she was linked to the scandalous divorce of the operatic diva turned actress Geraldine Farrar and the screen heartthrob Lou Tellegen. Clifford had been one of Tellegen's lesser flings—she spent a wild few days in a San Francisco hotel with him in 1918—but Fleming had little tolerance for cheating. (He didn't leave Clifford empty-handed. He had advised her to invest in Signal Hill oil wells; by the time they split, one of the wells had begun to produce. Clifford opened a chain of flower shops with the proceeds. Fleming didn't kick her out of his Gardner Street house. Instead, *he* moved out, to a small place in the Hollywood Hills.)

The last of Fleming's Emerson-Loos productions, *Red Hot Romance* (1922), about an heir to an insurance fortune, harked back to Fairbanks's globe-spanning satirical adventures. According to the terms of his father's will, the hero gains his millions only if he successfully sells insurance for a year. His best bet is to peddle it in a land where there *is* no insurance—specifically, the tropical country of Bunkonia. There he runs into two giant problems. Rapacious international forces have been engineering a coup d'état in Bunkonia—and his fiancée's father has become unwittingly enmeshed in it as the American consul. The hero parodies imperial capitalism and Fleming's old boss Woodrow Wilson when he proclaims, "This country must be made safe for democracy and insurance!"

The surviving print of this movie is a shambles, combining bits and pieces of the setup with most of the last two reels; when I viewed it at the Library of Congress, it was sandwiched around an entirely different movie, Lois Weber's *Midnight Romance* (previously thought lost). The script *does* survive; to judge from it and the available footage, Fleming's movie is an amiable, slaphappy curiosity, with another of the director's clever animated interludes (this time a lampoon of urban crowding) and one bizarre twist. At the climax, an all-black U.S. Marine unit saves the day, whipping wicked white authority figures and their mobs into order.

Is the imagery racist or antiracist? Are audiences meant to savor the supposed irony of blacks laying down the law to unruly whites? The sequence leaves contemporary viewers amused and perplexed, especially since the most prominent black character, the insurance salesman and heir's right-hand man, is played by a broad blackface comic, Tom Wilson. The movie does provide happy echoes of knockabout Fairbanks vehicles like *Reaching for the Moon* and *His Majesty the American*, but it may have taught Fleming a lesson in the uses of star power: Basil Sydney, as the hero, is no Fairbanks. There's no sparkle to his smile. And there's not enough spring to his step. When Fleming uses a Fairbanks trick from *The Half-Breed* in *Red Hot Romance*, filming Sydney dropping off a wall, then printing it as if he's scaling it, Sydney doesn't move with enough authority to make the charade convincing.

In the midst of completing *Red Hot Romance*, Fleming began a seven-year stint with Paramount/Famous Players–Lasky. His studio debut, *The Lane That Had No Turning* (1922), was released almost simultaneously with his final Emerson-Loos comedy. For Paramount, though, he'd made a melodramatic farrago set in French Canada and based on a Sir Gilbert Parker novel. It centered on a budding opera star (Agnes Ayres), but was filled with soap-operatic twists involving her increasingly unhinged hunchback husband (Theodore Kosloff) and a hidden will. The film won praise in *The New York Times* for "two scenes where double exposure is used with dramatic effect."

During this honeymoon period at Paramount, Fleming helped Howard Hawks land his first sizable studio job as one of four production editors in the scenario department. Hawks gave sole credit for his hire to an even bigger name, Irving Thalberg, the not-yet-thirty "boy genius" of Universal then en route to mythic stature with Louis B. Mayer at MGM. Hawks would say that Paramount's Jesse L. Lasky declared, "Thalberg says you know more about stories than anybody else he knows, so I'd like to have you."

But who would have been the more likely Hawks supporter—Thalberg or Fleming, his best pal? In his reminiscences, Hawks became addicted to retrospective one-upmanship; he downplayed Fleming's talents and contributions. Still, they *were* best friends. Probably speaking about the time in Fleming's life after he split from Clifford, Hawks said that Vic once dropped by his house for a visit and ended up staying for five years. That turns out to be another Hawksian exaggeration, but Howard and his brother Kenneth lived in a couple of houses in the early 1920s that became havens for high-powered bachelors like Fleming and the actor turned director Jack Conway. John Gilbert also participated in the single-guy high jinks. Eddie Sutherland, a vaudeville-comedy veteran who later directed giddy hits like *International House* (1933), became part of the Hawks group, too, calling it "a dandy little household." Sutherland may have embellished the facts when he said one house had a rain machine, "so if you were sitting there with your fiancée or something and you didn't want [her] to go home, you'd turn on the rain, and when you decided she should go, you turned it off." But Sutherland was being real when he remembered Fleming at that time as "a tough guy, a great big strong fellow," who also had a keen sense of what would work for him on-screen. Fleming bailed out on *Behind the Front*, a service comedy presenting "the first nonsense side" of World War I, and recommended that Sutherland take it over.

Gilbert and Conway probably brought Thalberg into the fold. They and a writer named Jack Colton had already formed a Thalberg friendship group nicknamed "the Three Jacks." Thalberg's longtime story editor Samuel Marx described Colton as "a world-weary homosexual who could be persuaded over drinks to discuss revealing intimacies of love between males," while Conway and Gilbert "relentlessly stalked the beauties of Hollywood, of which there was a plentiful supply." The Three Jacks introduced the seemingly ethereal Thalberg to "the pleasures to be derived from sex." Later, Hawks and company pitched in, too. Thalberg's two great loves were both linked, in varying degrees, to Fleming: Constance Talmadge and Norma Shearer, who fell for Vic on the set of *Empty Hands* (1924).

The screenwriter John Lee Mahin, who got to know Fleming a few years later, thought the Hawks brothers gave him swank and refinement. "Howard had class, you see. Vic had innate class, but he wasn't born to the purple like Howard was. He didn't have the advantage of his young life, the rearing." Yet Fleming's years with Fairbanks, Emerson, and Loos had already spruced him up smartly. He may have found it socially and sexually useful to foster the illusion that he had a roughneck background and rose from abject poverty. Bessie Love knew him professionally from her days as a Fairbanks co-star and romantically by the time she appeared in *A Son of His Father* (1925). When Kevin Brownlow interviewed her in 1971, she said, "I loved Vic," and recalled, "I once asked him where he came from, where he went to school. There was a long pause. 'Oxnard,' he said. I took no notice. It was only later I discovered that he had come from a very poor background." Love remembered that he used to pronounce "-ing" as if it were "-een"—as in "eateen and drinkeen" and "singeen." (She said Marshall Neilan did that, too.) Fleming once told Howard Hawks's formidable and socially prominent mother that she taught him how to use a knife and fork; Love thought Mrs. Hawks took that statement literally.

In 1929, Love married another Hawks brother, William, who for many years acted as Fleming's agent. Other women went back and forth between Fleming and the Hawkses throughout the 1920s. Howard was briefly engaged to Pauline Starke, who had starred in Fleming's *Devil's Cargo* and *Adventure*, both supervised by Hawks. In 1926, Howard met his first wife, Athole Shearer, because Fleming had been wooing her sister, Norma; and in 1928, Kenneth Hawks married Mary Astor, the female lead of Fleming's *Rough Riders*.

Ferocious yet friendly competition, with a patina of class, formed the basis of all this Hawks-Fleming bonding. Hawks's tale of them meeting during an auto race hit on its essence. The unapologetic masculine ardor flaring out of their best buddy pictures (say, *Ceiling Zero* for Hawks and *Test Pilot* for Fleming) reflects their offscreen connection. Hawks once recounted to Joseph McBride that he and Fleming "just started" calling each other Dan: "He'd say, 'Dan, what are you gonna do?' And I'd say, 'Dan, I don't know.' And we'd go out and get into some kind of trouble." (Fleming's daughters tell similar stories about Hawks and their father calling each other Ed.) These two talented fellows swam through the same hormonal Hollywood atmosphere. They extended the chemistry of adolescent chums well into adulthood. Even given occasional jealousy on Hawks's part, their friendship was one of the purest things about them. After Fleming's death, Hawks's propensity to contend he had the upper hand as a person and a pro may give a sour cast to almost all the anecdotes Hawks would tell about his best friend. But scrape away Hawks's self-promotion and you can still feel the shared zing of two world-beaters rivaling each other zestfully at every macho pastime.

"I think I got about an hour and three-quarters flying, and they made me an instructor," Hawks said of teaching flying down in Texas during World War I. "There were two or three thousand cadets down there," he said, "and about seven or eight planes. They didn't even have enough planes to train people." He must have been a decent teacher, because the Army Air Corps kept him at it. And in 1921 he probably encouraged Fleming to become an aviator, joining other movie-land pilots such as Cecil B. DeMille and Wallace Beery. Fleming took instruction at Rogers Field in Los Angeles and Clover Field in Santa Monica. One of his instructors was Gilbert Budwig, an early test pilot.

Hawks told Peter Bogdanovich that he and Fleming "built a couple of airplanes. One of them was very fast, but it was also very heavy. We used to call it the 'Cast-Iron Wonder.' We knew if we could get up, we could go faster than anything around, but it broke its landing gear every time it landed!" Inevitably, Hawks characterized Fleming as a pilot easily spooked compared with himself, a paragon of coolness:

> We built an airplane for racing, he flew it in the first race, won the race, and landed it and the landing gear broke. And I said, "Next time you better let me fly it." And I flew it and won the race and the landing gear broke when we landed. We flew it in four races and won four races and every time broke the landing gear. Then we gave up on that airplane. He was funny. He came in one day and wanted a drink. "Well," he said, "I'm through flying." I said, "Why?" "Well," he said, "you know that new airplane? I landed it—perfectly good landing—right out in the middle of a landing strip," he said. "I pulled the lever

> and let the wheels down. What I meant to do was put the flaps up." "Oh," I said, "Vic, anybody does that." He said, "That isn't what I'm talking about. I'm so sore about doing that to a new airplane, I went in and had a cup of coffee and they passed me the sugar and I unwrapped the sugar, threw the sugar away, put the paper in my coffee cup." He said, "I have no business flying any more." But he did.

Indeed, Fleming kept improving his standing in the flying world. After soloing for more than three hundred hours in a secondhand Curtiss JN-4, or "Jenny"—a popular instruction vehicle favored by barnstorming pilots—Fleming mastered another slow-moving war-surplus trainer, the Standard J-1, then a Catron & Fisk CF-15, often used for racing and aerobatics.

Flying must have given Fleming more satisfaction than his first few Paramount movies. (Most of his Paramount films have been lost.) After *The Lane That Had No Turning*, he shifted gears with *Anna Ascends* (also 1922). It was the film version of Harry Chapman Ford's stage melodrama about an immigrant waitress in New York City's Little Syria district who triumphs over dire obstacles, including a brush with murder, to become a productive, happy American. (In the play she nearly kills a rapist; in the film, a diamond smuggler.) Although *The New York Times* summarized *Anna Ascends* as "a collection of puppets in a mechanical plot," the movie is notable for two reasons. It features an Arab-American as the protagonist (although she was played on Broadway and in Fleming's film by the Irish-American Alice Brady), and it marked the debut of sixteen-year-old Betty Bronson, who credited Fleming with helping her land her most famous part: the title role in Herbert Brenon's *Peter Pan.*

Dark Secrets (1923) starred Dorothy Dalton as an "untamable" society gal, crippled in a riding accident and courted by an Egyptian mystic who offers to cure her in exchange for marriage. (A virtuous Egyptian servant kills the quack and restores the heroine to her true love.) In stills, Dalton has the bold, dark beauty of Anjelica Huston; *Photoplay* noted that because she was nearing the end of a long-term contract, she was making $5,000 a week, "far more than such favorites as Pola Negri or Gloria Swanson." But the movie's main interest was its reliance on the notions of the chic French hypnotherapist Emile Coué (author of *Self Mastery Through Conscious Autosuggestion*). His signature line, "Every day, in every way, I'm getting better and better," became one of the jumping-off points for the satire of Nathanael West in his 1934 novella *A Cool Million.* Along with *The Lane That Had No Turning*'s Theodore Kosloff, Dalton also starred in Fleming's next lost picture, *The Law of the Lawless* (also 1923). This tale of Tartar and Gypsy rivalries on the shores of the Black Sea derived from a story by Konrad Bercovici. *Photoplay* said, "It never seems real anywhere," but Fleming won approval from *Variety:* "In direction the picture is well handled."

Amid all this heavy industry and fine carousing, Fleming managed to romance Virginia Valli, an actress at Universal. "You could always tell who his current girlfriend was by whoever's picture was on the piano," said his niece Yvonne Blocksom, who recalled seeing Valli's photo there. Fleming never guided Valli through a film.

He did direct the frequent Western heroine Lois Wilson in back-to-back Zane Grey adaptations, *To the Last Man* and *The Call of the Canyon* (both 1923). Wilson's niece Sheila Shay (the daughter of the director George Fitzmaurice) says of Wilson and Fleming, "I'm sure she liked him as a director and probably as a person," and, "They seemed to enjoy one another's company." Fleming shot both films in Arizona—*To the Last Man* in Tonto Basin (where he had shot *The Mollycoddle*), and *The Call of the Canyon* in Sedona—and he and Wilson, an expert rider, would go searching together on horseback for picturesque locations. One day, Fleming insisted on roaming into a dead volcano to see, he said, "a pine tree growing right in the middle." Wilson said, "We rode our horses down into that dead crater, and we had a very hard time getting back. I got a little panicky, but we made it. Victor said he found out that the last thing in the world to do is ride down into a dead crater, because it's all ash."

The man Wilson fell for wasn't Fleming but her co-star, Richard Dix. *To the Last Man* was one of Dix's first Paramount movies as a contract leading man, replacing Fleming's old pal, the late Wallace Reid. Dix wasn't the daredevil that Reid was. Vic "gave me a half-broke horse off the range," Dix recalled. "He was a photographic horse, black and white spots . . . I had to run the animal around in a circle and there was a ditch a foot deep. About the fourth time around the horse stuck a foot in a bush and I went with him. I had more than 8,000 thorns in me. I got up and laughed it off, because I wanted to impress the director."

It was probably harder to laugh off the knowledge that Fleming was indirectly responsible for Dix's breakup with Wilson. On *To the Last Man,* Wilson said, "Vic Fleming wanted to go to the Grand Canyon for some scenic locations. We were camped on the floor and had to ride these small but wiry little mountain ponies up a steep path carved out of the side of the canyon wall. There was scarcely enough room for one horse; one slip, and horse and rider would plunge over the side." Dix didn't want her to make the ride, but Wilson enjoyed it. "I don't think I could love a woman who wasn't afraid of a thing like that ride," Dix said. She replied, "You can't love me, because I wasn't afraid." The romance fell apart before they made their next picture, *The Call of the Canyon*.

It's particularly cruel that these two Zane Grey Westerns have been lost, along with Fleming's later epic *The Rough Riders*. (The only surviving copies are said to be at Gosfilmofond of Moscow, but repeated inquiries there haven't turned them up.) They were the movies Fleming was most likely referring to when he spoke of silent directors winging their productions from novels instead of just shooting scripts. (A location still from *To the Last Man*, reprinted in 1944, shows him directing the actors book in hand.) These movies are also tantalizing predecessors to Fleming's *Virginian*.

Zane Grey had followed Owen Wister's lead as a novelist of the West who depicted frontier heroes evolving in chivalric directions under the influence of Eastern women. *To the Last Man* took off from a real-life feud between cattlemen and sheep ranchers, but *The Call of the Canyon* was an out-and-out "flapper Western" about a World War I vet (Dix) who goes West to regain his health and summons his Jazz Age sweetheart (Wilson). *Motion Picture News* called it "a picture 'that kills two birds with one stone.' It has society life in the effete East, jazz (marathon) dances of the '400' and striking feminine fashions for the folks who like these ingredients in their film fare and it has red blooded western scenes, thrilling physical combats, wonderful shots of the Arizona canyon country, a terrific prairie storm."

Ranchers living outside Flagstaff might have taken it as a portent of the apocalypse when they saw thunderbolts spring up from the ground one September night. These sheets of lightning were actually fifty arc lights on a train rattling through Arizona for the sequence depicting jim-dandies from the East partying their way to the West. But the "terrific prairie storm" the press loved so much was a masterpiece of carpe-diem moviemaking, not special effects. Right after Zane Grey and Jesse Lasky visited the company's main Oak Creek Canyon location, real lightning, rain, and hail inundated northeast Arizona, wreaking havoc on the unpaved road between Oak Creek Canyon and Flagstaff. For several days, cast and crew lived with the threat that the flood might fill the canyon. The cook emptied his pantry, and the men emptied their pockets in nonstop poker games, and the women huddled together for warmth and sleep. The cinematographer James Wong Howe shot several hundred striking feet of film. Then the company made it out to Flagstaff.

Howe shot both of Fleming's Zane Grey films (the first with the help of Bert Baldridge), and Hathaway took care of props and assisted Fleming. Hathaway said Fleming once used a tin cup as a reflector to get the right amount of eye light on a Wilson close-up, and Howe went even further. When Fleming said he wanted "a silhouette picture of Dix under the tree" and then decided he needed a close-up, too, Howe ordered Vic and the grips to hold a bank of tin coffee cups so they could reflect "the light off them onto Dix. And they shook a little so it looked just like the shadows of tree leaves coming on the guy's face. Just like Burnett Guffey, when he shot *Bonnie and Clyde* and he picked up a Coke bottle to shoot through." On one of the Zane Grey pictures, Howe remembered Fleming showing off his marksmanship:

> We were riding along the trail, about 1,500 feet up, and suddenly he rode in front and he waved his hands. He said, "Stop, everybody, get off. There's a rattlesnake up here in front." We got off and went down there, and there was a rattlesnake. He got a stick and he got ahold of the rattlesnake's neck and picked it up and looked at it and finally he threw it down. He always carried a little .22 pocket pistol, and a hatchet. He used to chop his way through the woods to get cameras set up, you see. So he said, "Now, fellows, I want to show you what a good shot I am. Without looking at this snake, I'm going to turn around and I'm going to shoot this snake right through the head." So we stood there, "Go ahead, go ahead." So he pulled this gun out, pointed it, and he pulled the trigger and he hit the snake right through the head. My assistant, name was Archie Stout, he was there. He said, "You're such a good shot, let me see you shoot this cigarette out of my hand." [Vic] said, "Hold it up." He stood about eight feet away. And he aimed and he shot, and you know what? He shot him right through the finger!

Decades later, Howe explained to Norman Lloyd that Fleming knew the snake would fasten on the gun glittering in the sun and fix on the position of the barrel, giving Fleming a clean shot.

Also on the *Canyon* set was the future producer of *The Wizard of Oz*, Mervyn LeRoy. He had a small acting part in the picture; Wilson said he was "just a very attractive bright boy who would do anything the director asked him to do to help the picture along."

Fleming was beginning to feel his clout in and out of the picture business. On November 9, 1923, an Orange County judge slapped him with a $25 fine for driving his Duesenberg over thirty-five miles an hour in a Seal Beach speed trap. Earlier that year the California legislature moved to abolish speed traps, but some communities like Seal Beach had ignored the ban. So Fleming appealed. He lost in superior court, but his lawyers, from the Automobile Club of Southern California, won a reversal in the Second District Court of Appeal—"a judicial knockout"—and a stunning vindication when the California Supreme Court overturned the law and dismissed Fleming's case.

Fleming made no public statements on the matter himself, but when he *was* quoted, about moviemaking, he was beginning to sound august. Suddenly Fairbanks's seat-of-the-pants creative sidekick was advocating film schools. "The finished photoplay of today," he said at the time of *The Call of the Canyon*, "is as different from the two-reeler of ten years ago as Egyptian hieroglyphics are from modern paintings." Whereas a decade earlier a budding director could pick up what he had to know from hanging around a studio, "it is questionable whether he can learn through ordinary channels now how to make a superproduction of 1924." Audiences "demand art, subtlety and realism in photoplays. Pictures can only be made with these qualities by specialized training."

The two Zane Grey pictures were box-office successes; Paramount would film more than half a dozen Grey titles in the 1920s and remake them in the 1930s. And studio executives realized that in Fleming they had a major creative commodity. Paramount would proudly declare his next picture, *Code of the Sea* (1924), "A Victor Fleming Production," right on the opening title card.

8

Courage and Clara Bow

Bravery under stress was a natural theme for "outdoor" directors, and as a man and a professional Fleming had a bone-deep feeling for it. He'd wandered into a profession that enabled him to turn one of his ruling appetites—voracity for action—into a creed. Physical bravery was integral to his sportsmanship. It also fed his yen for knockabout jokes and urge to complete any task swiftly. Artistic and existential bravery were significant for him, too, but here the quality became more complicated. Fleming had dared big by leaping into a quicksilver creative and social life. He'd had help from Dwan and Fairbanks, Emerson and Loos, but he was a self-made man in a self-made industry and a freewheeling town.

The zest of early moviemaking came from its participants' unself-consciousness—they thrived on happy accidents and turned whatever made them work into rules of play. The gifted recognized principles that clicked for them and stayed on the lookout for new ones. Fleming never lost his sense of directing as a job, but it was a job he practiced with the intensity of an artist. At times he did movies that he'd dreamed about; at other times he took on assignments. So he was a creative force *and* a hireling, alternately and often simultaneously. His personality usually came through, and it had a homegrown sophistication: heartfelt and crusty, yet sometimes brashly satirical.

His personal life had the same brand of complexity. Though he became a sought-after figure socially, he kept one foot in Hollywood and one foot out. He was a ladies' man and, from all accounts, an honorable one. His leading women fell in love with him on location, but they also spoke well of him back in Hollywood. Given his mix of pride, curiosity, and practicality, it's not surprising that the overriding characteristic of Fleming's work is its variety, especially in the hell-raising

1920s. That's also when he carved a romantic chessboard out of Hollywood.

His aura of ruggedness and stoic courage caused his peers to speak of him in Hemingwayesque terms, but Fleming's two silent seafaring adventures focused on the redemption of cowards. *Code of the Sea* (1924) derives from a story by Byron Morgan, who wrote racing scripts for Wallace Reid (including *The Roaring Road*, Fleming's one possible foray into stunt driving). It registers as a dress rehearsal for Fleming's prestigious adaptation (several films later) of Joseph Conrad's summa of gracelessness under pressure, *Lord Jim* (1925).

In *Code of the Sea*, Rod La Rocque, who had the dark good looks of Robert Downey Jr., plays the hero, Bruce McDow, with some of Downey's volatility (though little of his skill). Bruce carries a family curse: he's the son of a craven lightship skipper who steered away from his post during a storm and was responsible for a passenger ship's fatal crash. Jacqueline Logan, sweet-faced and sensible, plays Jenny Hayden, Bruce's true love and the daughter of the man who captained the ship that piled up on the Barrier Reef. In the opening scene, Bruce loses his first berth—he succumbs to vertigo at the prospect of climbing a mast. One old salt says with a sneer that book learning has taught Bruce not merely to look before he leaps but never to leap at all. Jenny gets him a job on his father's old lightship. There he must overcome the presumption that he inherited his dad's yellow stripe.

The movie may be a potboiler, but it's involving and audacious—a premium example of Fleming's feisty virtuosity. He'll do anything to put over this pulpy story. He twirls the camera from Bruce's dizzied point of view so that the masts of a ship seem to dance. He presents Bruce's inner demons as outer ghouls—gap-toothed, scrofulous heads that encircle the hero and paralyze him, even when Jenny's dress catches fire. Fleming doesn't let the primal story get too far away from the elements. When Bruce decides to prove to himself that he isn't a coward, he places his hand over a burning kerosene lamp (a gesture that anticipates Peter O'Toole's T. E. Lawrence). These flourishes make the movie teeter on the brink of macho camp, with the masochism and rabidity common to Mel Gibson and Sylvester Stallone. They also give it a brute vivacity, which the picture needs, because the human characters are so humorless. Bruce's ragged mongrel terrier provides the one effective comic counterpoint. The hero's debonair rival for Jenny's hand, Ewart Radcliff (Maurice B. Flynn), the heir to a passenger-ship fleet, has an aggressive bull terrier that is always putting Bruce's mutt on the run. When Bruce finds his sea footing, the mongrel soaks up his master's new forcefulness. (From this point on, Fleming is a maestro of doggy theatrics. His canine prowess would peak with the extraordinary scene of Frank Morgan's Pirate, in 1942's *Tortilla Flat*, re-creating a church service for a half-dozen dogs.)

Filming began in San Francisco in February 1924, and some scenes set on Bruce's first schooner and on the lightship were shot at sea, eighteen miles out from the Golden Gate. Fleming might have shot most of the seafaring scenes near San Francisco and the complicated climax at San Pedro, where Logan bruised her right arm and side during filming when a mooring rope broke and part of it struck her. Erratic but thrilling, the final storm sequence mixes miniatures of storm-tossed ships with location shots of real ships and depictions of men and women in peril presumably done on wet sets or in studio tanks. Fleming would become known for his fearlessness at blending different types of footage, and sometimes, as in *Captains Courageous*, he did it so deftly and with such an acute understanding of the audience's attention that the stitch work is barely visible.

The seams do show in *Code of the Sea*, yet Fleming displays his killer instinct for finding the red-hot center of a turbulent sea tale, even one that gets mighty spongy. Bruce McDow is in charge of his lightship, Captain Hayden is trying to skipper his ship home, and Jenny is on the Radcliff family yacht (to keep her far away from Bruce) during the climactic gale. Bruce must choose between holding the lightship's position to ensure that Captain Hayden's ship avoids the Barrier Reef and steering the lightship toward the yacht where Jenny fears for her life. Captain Hayden hopes that Bruce will leave his post and save Jenny. Instead, Bruce does something riskier: he tells the lightship sailors to stay put and makes for the yacht in a launch, by himself.

When a horse-drawn lifesaving crew gallops to the rescue, its members shoot a line out to Bruce, who ties it to his waist, leaves his wave-tossed skiff, and swims out to save Jenny. With Bruce steeling himself on the yacht's deck, the lifesavers establish a winch to haul the passengers in a makeshift shuttle. Of course, Bruce insists on being the last man on board; the boat breaks up with him still on it; and everyone expects him to die. The documentary details of the operation, and the sight of waves hitting the passengers as they lurch to shore, are frightening, and Fleming pushes the heartbreak as far as he can without enraging the audience or deflating its hopes. As the dawn breaks, Bruce's mother stands on the rocks and searches the horizon like one of J. M. Synge's mournful matriarchs in *Riders to the Sea*. Bruce's trusty mongrel finds him washed up on shore, alive. Jenny and Bruce embrace. And Bruce's newly emboldened mutt gives chase to the bull terrier.

Code of the Sea didn't impress the critics, but it gave Fleming his best chance to flex his muscles since *The Mollycoddle*, and in Hollywood it increased his growing directorial star power. The director "was mistaken for the leading man on location," stated a newspaper item for the next Fleming production, *Empty Hands*. "A lady visitor at Yosemite Lodge where the company put up while on location, made audible remarks anent his handsome and commanding appearance! Jack Holt was well camouflaged behind a week's growth of whiskers at the time and enjoyed the joke on his director as much as the rest of the company, including Norma Shearer." Shearer probably enjoyed it more. She, too, fell in love with her director.

Shearer had wanted to act since she was a teenager. She owed her success partially to the connections and influence of her uncle (who had married an actress) and the tenacity and drive of her mother, Edith, who moved Norma and her sister, Athole, from Montreal to New York City. D. W. Griffith told Norma that she'd never make it after he used her as an extra in *Way Down East*, and Florenz Ziegfeld rejected her for his Follies. Shearer persisted anyway, until her made-in-New-York movies and serials earned her and her mother a trip to Hollywood with a contract waiting for Norma at the Mayer studio. She gamboled through a half-dozen pictures without creating a stir until she starred in *Broadway After Dark* for the director Monta Bell (who'd assisted Chaplin on *A Woman of Paris*) and followed it with *Empty Hands* (1924), made on a loan-out to Paramount. Four years from her woes as a bit player, she was on the brink of major stardom—and adult independence.

Fleming called *Empty Hands* "an 'Adam and Eve' story." *Variety* called it yet another variation on J. M. Barrie's *Admirable Crichton* scheme—"desert island stuff, with a man and a woman." Except this time the "desert island" is the Canadian wilderness, where the father of the heroine, a worn-out flapper, has dragged her away from a debauched life. Holt plays her dad's chief engineer, who saves her from a rocky death when she's swept down some rapids in a canoe. They end up in virgin territory: the sylvan mountains of Lake Arrowhead, in the

San Bernardino National Forest. "After a few days on location in this romantic setting," Shearer wrote in her unpublished autobiography, "I developed a big crush on the sweet man who was the director of this picture."

Norma thought of Fleming as a substitute for Andrew Shearer, her father. Andrew was "a gay blade" and a "sport." He'd "sown plenty of wild oats," built two homes for his wife and daughters, and designed the modern hockey stick before his lumber and construction company went belly-up and he ceased to be a presence in his family's life. Shearer wrote of Fleming:

> Because he was fifteen or twenty years older than me [eleven, in fact] I found him very endearing. His few silver hairs and kind gentle ways attracted me enormously. I supposed psychiatrists would have said my love for my father, whom I was missing so much, expressed itself in my romantic yearning for this mature man—this undoubtedly was the basis for my tender affection which must have overwhelmed me one moonlit night as we sat in a hammock on the terrace of the hotel overlooking the beautiful lake. I found myself saying, for no reason at all, "Mr. Fleming, would you kiss me?" And to my surprise he did and I loved it.

Mother Edie disapproved of what that "sweet gentle kiss led to," which Norma characterizes as "a most beautiful friendship." The actress said, "I had a lovely time courting this mature man—the first I had known." She said she loved "his amazing hands" and the way he called her "dear darling." And Victor even knew how to throw Edie off balance. "Sports cars were his passion, and he drove a beautiful dark grey Duesenberg too fast—except when Edie was in the back seat—because she would scream 'Victor!' and hit him on the back and he would pretend she had knocked him off the seat onto the floor."

Yet even if she looked askance at Norma and Vic's fling, Edie must have been euphoric over their cinematic liaison. Howard Hawks said, "When Lasky saw the finished picture, which Victor Fleming made, I thought he'd break both legs getting out of the projection room to sign her." Norma's performance propelled Thalberg, newly ensconced as Louis Mayer's production chief at MGM, to cast her in a prestigious film, *He Who Gets Slapped* (released later in 1924). Fleming, too, won praise, for directing the stock story in (as the *Los Angeles Times* put it) "a breezy, refreshed style." Fleming himself marveled at its ease of production: In 1944, he pictured "a group of people on a river bank in Yosemite National Park in 1924. In the group are Norma Shearer and Jack Holt, our principals; a cameraman, a couple of automobile drivers, a bit player or two, and myself . . . Less than ten people in the production unit to make that picture! Contrast that with the huge resources Metro-Goldwyn-Mayer and other major companies put behind a production today! More than ten persons will be engaged in the research alone if it is a big production."

Despite his later reputation as a "man's director," Fleming launched or cannily revamped a host of female stars from the 1920s on. As Shearer rode the crest of her *Empty Hands* success, she was happy to be seen in Fleming's company. The Los Angeles reporter Grace Kingsley, running into her one afternoon in October, praised the star's elegant taste and noted that her companion, Fleming, "seemed quite devoted." But the affair between Shearer and Fleming didn't affect the director's eye for the potential of his next leading lady, Pauline Starke. In *The Devil's Cargo* and *Adventure* (both 1925—and both lost), he turned Starke from a long-suffering starlet into a happy hell-raiser. And she thrived under his guidance. *Photoplay* once asked her to name the moment when movie producers found out that she had sex appeal. She credited *The Devil's Cargo:* "For the first time in my life I had a role that meant something, and I loved it." She plays a gambler's daughter and casino chanteuse during the Sacramento gold rush of 1849 who falls for a crusading newspaper editor and ends up uniting with him against vigilantes and a drunken steamboat stoker (Wallace Beery). Starke carried the picture with the critics and the public—from then on, she'd win comparisons to the robust, erotic Gloria Swanson. Fleming rebuilt Old Sacramento on the Sacramento River and filled it with a couple hundred cast and crew, slaking his growing thirst for the epic. The erstwhile mechanic in Fleming listed among his requests to Paramount's props chief "a stern-wheel river steamboat of the type used in 1850" and "a Washington hand press."

In Fleming's 1925 *Adventure* (based on a Jack London novel of the same name), Starke played a maverick globe-trotter who enters into partnership with a plantation owner on the Solomon Islands and defends him against usurers who covet the hero's land and stir up the locals. (Wallace Beery again pops up as one of the bad guys.) Hawaii's

Olympic swimmer Duke Kahanamoku made his first appearance for Fleming in this movie and said he "nearly drowned" after swimming four hundred yards with Starke to a ship and then, on the return swim, getting tangled in seaweed. Critics took *Adventure* for what it was—as *The New York Times* put it, "a compact serial." Its most influential scene was "a table duel." Two men place a loaded revolver, a lit cigarette, and a match on a table in the middle of a room; only when the burning end of the cigarette starts to ignite the match can the men jump for the gun. Fleming mastered ritualized machismo—and directors would emulate him for decades.

Fleming also began talking like a studio employee, telling a Paramount flack that a typical 1925 picture was a "staple article," yet "a staple article of superlative quality." He might have been thinking of his third 1925 movie, *A Son of His Father*, another lost Western, which *Variety* dubbed "one more of Harold Bell Wright's handsome hero and dirty villain stories." Wright's best-selling celebrations of frontier virtues included *The Shepherd of the Hills*, frequently filmed (most famously by Fleming's former assistant Henry Hathaway, with John Wayne in 1941) and still performed today as an outdoor play in Branson, Missouri. Paramount hoped that *A Son of His Father* would start a series of Wright adaptations, and chose Fleming to launch it based on his success with Zane Grey. Fleming's female lead, Bessie Love, remembered in her memoir that after the production, when she "asked him, frankly, why he had agreed to make such a bad film," Fleming "asked me, frankly, if I knew how much money the film had made." Of course, Love had met Fleming on the set of *The Good Bad Man* nine years before. It was on *A Son of His Father* that she "got to know him pretty well; he was as big as a bull moose and one of my beaux." Yet Love thought "he could be cruel." Fleming's crew warned him not to fire a gun near an electrician who suffered from shell shock, but the director went ahead and did it anyway. "I asked him why he'd been so cruel—of course, he didn't think he was. I suppose he felt the man had been through a war, he could take it."

Not even Fleming's nonstop run of romances, from Valli to Shearer to Love, kept him from his family. His sister Ruth got divorced and returned to their mother's house late in 1924. Fleming was an attentive uncle to Ruth's daughter Yvonne. "He was at Nanny's one day and he grabbed my chin and turned my head up and said 'Open your mouth.' And he hollered to Nanny, who was out in the kitchen,

'Mother, come here!' So he said, 'Yvonne has to have her teeth straightened. I will take care of it, I will call you and tell you who the dentist is, and you will see that she gets to the dentist.' So that's how I got my teeth straightened." Yvonne thought of him as "a precisionist." She'd iron his handkerchiefs for him, "and if those corners weren't exactly done, they had to be redone."

Fleming spent every Christmas dinner at his mother's house, with Arletta's son Newell sitting on one side of him and Yvonne on the other. Yvonne remembered that "he would come with his pockets full of $20 gold pieces, and everyone got a $20 gold piece for Christmas." When Ruth bought a new house of her own, Vic gave her the down payment. In 1925, he also urged his favorite sister, unsuccessfully, not to marry Dick Kobe, nine years her junior, saying, "He's going to find another woman, and it will never last." But it did, more than fifty years, until her death. Fleming's largesse was the only sign of his Hollywood success. He never brought over his girlfriends, and Yvonne said, "He never talked about himself. He was very, very private."

When *A Son of His Father* opened, Fleming was already nearing completion on his next picture, one that would land him an upgrade of his contract at Paramount and increase his prestige. "I have just witnessed the first two reels of *Lord Jim*, which Mr. Fleming is now producing," Jesse Lasky told *Moving Picture World* in August 1925, "and I am certain that it is greater than anything he has ever before directed. I very deeply admire both the man and his work, and it is our aim to keep him with Paramount for many years to come."

No major writer, James Joyce included, has been more difficult to adapt than Joseph Conrad. What makes his fiction great is also what makes it hard to film—in Graham Greene's words, "its strange removal of action to the second hand, its shades of thought." (Probably the best Conrad adaptations are Hitchcock's 1936 *Sabotage*, loosely based on *The Secret Agent*, and the 1952 *Outcast of the Islands*, directed by Greene's friend and collaborator Carol Reed.) When Greene wrote that the object of filmmaking "should be the translation of thought back into images" and that "America has made the mistake of translating it into action," he might have been thinking of Fleming's *Lord Jim*. Fleming and his screenwriter, John Russell, aim at concision and dispatch as they present Jim's momentary moral blackout during a crisis at sea and his tragic attempt to work out his own salvation by restoring order and morale to a jungle village.

Watching the picture is direct and visceral, nothing like the knotty experience of reading the book. Yet Fleming imparts a remarkable amount of Conradian flavor into the look and feel of the movie. His Lord Jim wants to be a man of heroic action, but when he gets his chance to prove himself—and save the Mohammedan pilgrims on the *Patna*, or at least go down with the ship—he listens to the voices of the corrupt skipper and crew, not to his conscience or to the passengers crying for help. Then he becomes a penitent, self-destructive saint: a character of mixed gallantry, which would become a Fleming specialty.

Fleming's spruce film, like Richard Brooks's bloated 1965 version (shot by David Lean's photographer, Frederick Young), demonstrates how difficult it is to turn a figure with a crippled self-image into the anchor of a sprawling adventure. In Brooks's spectacle, Peter O'Toole comes off as a neurasthenic even though the actor is at his most athletic—indeed, 1982's *My Favorite Year* used O'Toole's swashbuckling fantasies from *Lord Jim* to illustrate the prime of his Errol Flynn–like character. In Fleming's, Percy Marmont seems, at first, impossibly fey—a sad reflection of early Hollywood's Anglophilia. (Even *The New York Times* noted that he lives up to the part "in all except bulk.") But Fleming, shooting on the back lot and in the Los Angeles harbor, creates a strong tissue of atmosphere and incident. He gradually extracts from Marmont's elusive presence the sardonic humor and strength he needs to bind it together. Fleming's own naïve *and* worldly background connected him to what Greene isolated as the Conradian formula—the virtues of "courage, loyalty, labour" set against "the nihilistic background of purposeless suffering." And Fleming responded decisively to the screenwriter Russell's skill at sifting Conrad's themes and action to dramatic essentials. (Russell next adapted that classic action novel about deception and valor, *Beau Geste*, with stunning success.) The outcome is a lucid, moving film about catastrophe.

Paramount boasted of employing an 881-man crew and more than 500 extras at one time in *Lord Jim;* Fleming keeps everything in balance. From the beginning, he uses compositions that hold the characters in clear focus while the dockside shops and piers vanish in a line that stretches into the horizon. It takes Fleming no more than a few title cards and vignettes to establish Jim as an upright English sailor who sees a top berth on any ship, even one as shabby as the *Patna*, as a stepping-stone to a skipper's position. Speedily and indelibly, the director etches the casual racism of every other white man on the *Patna* and the equivocal position of the human cargo, Muslim pilgrims en route to the Red Sea. When the steamer hits a rock or a derelict ship in a murky night and threatens to go down, Jim's—and our—understanding of the situation comes in an instant. There's no way the scurrilous Cap'n Brown (Noah Beery) and his crew are going to risk their necks for eight hundred Muslims.

Fleming already knew the emotional dynamics of melodrama inside out. Where he excels in *Lord Jim* is in the *poetry* of disaster: the rustling movement of the sleeping pilgrims when the collision in the dark disturbs their sleep; the fog and mist clouding Jim's judgment literally as Brown and his men urge him to jump into their lifeboat; close-ups that home in on Jim's confusion just as he's about to take that leap.

These touches display the knack for synesthesia that the best silent directors would bring into the talkies. With crack staging and timing, Fleming turns the *Patna* crew's dumbfounding realization that their ship made it to port into a black-comic knockout: the Port Office master pulls open the shade on his window and there's the *Patna*, docked at the pier behind him.

Inevitably, in any Conrad adaptation, some dialogue devolves into abstraction, such as when the sympathetic trader Stein says to a sailor at the Court of Inquiry that it's futile "trying to judge a man's soul by his actions." But the filmmakers deploy their metaphysics much more sparingly here than Brooks did in his version, counterpointing it with earthiness and humor. After his judges cancel his seagoing certification on the grounds of desertion from duty, Jim leaves the court exactly as an onlooker is telling a mangy canine, "Get out, you cur." Of course, Jim thinks he's the one being called a foul dog.

Lord Jim marked Fleming's coming of age as a creator of thinking-man's spectacles, not only because of his mastery of intimacy within scope, but also because of his ability to meld a diverse cast into a winning hand. Jim agrees to reform Stein's outpost in the village of Patusan, which Stein's drunken, unscrupulous agent Cornelius (Raymond Hatton) has been running into the swamp. Duke Kahanamoku plays Tamb' Itam, the villager who becomes Jim's stalwart right-hand man out of love for him. (In real life he was a hero, too, winning three gold and two silver Olympic swimming medals for the United States.) Shirley Mason as Jewel, the daughter of Cornelius's abused and long-dead native wife, conveys the underlying innocence and ardor that *would* attract a starry-eyed soul like Jim.

The film combines the *Patna*'s skipper with Conrad's dangerous aristocratic raider, Gentleman Brown. When Cap'n Brown, a couple of *Patna* veterans, and the deposed Cornelius raid the village, Jim foils them but decides to give them safe passage rather than an eye-for-an-eye brand of native justice. He vows to forfeit his own life to the village leader Doramin (Nick De Ruiz) if Brown and his men slaughter any more Patusanese.

The director shows his mettle when he stages Jim's resulting self-sacrifice. The corpse of Doramin's son, Dain Waris (George Magrill), lies in state when Jim takes his fateful walk, idly running his hand across the vine-laden rail of a bridge, blithely demonstrating that he has no gun and has accepted his fate. Doramin shoots—and Jim totters back across the bridge and into the arms of Jewel. As promised in the opening quotation from Conrad's final pages, Jim ends up "inscrutable at heart, forgotten, unforgiven, and excessively romantic."

Between *Empty Hands* and *Lord Jim*, a number of characteristic Fleming projects went unrealized, including a Zane Grey Western, *The Border Legion*, and *Outcasts of Poker Flat*, based on the celebrated Bret Harte story that had last been filmed in 1919. The most intriguing was a remake of the 1918 Sessue Hayakawa hit, *The Honor of His House*—a love triangle with a Japanese-American girl at its apex and a Japanese and an American at its corners. Fleming's later political foes would accuse him of anti-Semitism, but the necessity for cross-racial understanding crops up often as a theme in his work.

Fleming might have considered the circus movie *The Mountebank* (released as *The Side Show of Life*) beyond his range then, like the World War I service comedy *Behind the Front*. And he probably thought the oil-well melodrama *Tongues of Flame* beneath him; it went to his old pal Joseph Henabery. Though Vic's detractors have branded him a roughneck, his studio bosses thought him qualified to follow *Lord Jim* with a high-society melodrama, *The Blind Goddess*. Fleming had to orchestrate a plot that combined courtroom theatrics with the mother-daughter suds of *Stella Dallas*. The cast boasted Esther Ralston, star of *The American Venus*, as the daughter of a New York political boss (Ernest Torrence); Louise Dresser as the mother she never knew; and square-chinned Jack Holt (Chester Gould's visual model for Dick Tracy) as the girl's fighting district-attorney fiancé. Holt resigns his post to defend Dresser from the charge of killing Ralston's father. The author of the original novel, Arthur Cheney Train, was a Harvard-educated lawyer turned storyteller long before Scott Turow; Train's most popular creation, Ephraim Tutt, was once as famous as Charlie Chan. But the scribblers who would have a lasting effect on Fleming's career were the screenwriters on *The Blind Goddess*, the husband-and-wife team of Louis Lighton and Hope Loring. They and Fleming won praise from critics for "a pace that keeps the audience keyed up all the way." Lighton would eventually collaborate with Fleming as a producer on three classics—*The Virginian*, *Captains Courageous*, and *Test Pilot*.

Hoping that a jolt of barnstorming energy would rev up a potentially stuffy big-star contraption, Fleming directed Ralston, on location, to jump into a big Hispano-Suiza roadster (borrowed from Jack Pickford) and race alongside a real Santa Fe passenger train carrying her fictional father. The car was known internationally for its get-up-and-go. (Luis Buñuel hailed Buster Keaton's *College* for being "as vital as a Hispano-Suiza.") The problem was that Ralston couldn't drive. Ralston recalled that Fleming "yelped, 'Oh, God. I hear the train coming now. Somebody put it in gear for her. I hope you can at least steer. Just follow behind the camera car and stay in the road!' " She did, at eighty miles an hour in her recollection, until she had to wave at Torrence, who, as her father, was standing on the train's rear platform. "I took my hands off the wheel and waved, and almost plowed into the camera car ahead of me. I grabbed the wheel and swerved to miss it, almost overturning the Hispano in the ditch. From then on, Mr. Fleming decided to use a double for my future driving scenes."

Ralston "couldn't squeeze a tear" in the courtroom for the character's dead father until Dresser came over and murmured, "Esther, dear, my beloved mother is in the Hollywood Hospital, dying of cancer. They just phoned me and said if I could get right over there, I'd be able to see her once more before she dies. I can't leave until we do this scene." Ralston began sobbing, and Fleming ordered, "Get her close-up . . . quick." Fleming sometimes cooked up soap operas to get what he needed from his actors, but this was no desperate ploy: Dresser did rush to the hospital once the scene was done, and her mother died an hour after she got there.

Ralston, a compact, well-behaved blonde, was Hollywood's idea of a smart young leading lady. Clara Bow, Fleming's next star (and next lover), was anything but. When Joseph Moncure March described a redheaded flapper in his notorious 1928 verse novel, *The Wild Party*, he must have modeled her on the flame-haired Bow, who was dubbed the It Girl two years earlier.

> A rogue—
> But her manner was gay and delicious.
> She could make a Baptist preacher choke
> With laughter over a dirty joke.

From 1925 to 1933, the entire moviegoing world knew this ravishing live wire as the epitome of the jazz baby: "naughty of eye" and "expressive-lipped"; "cute, lecherous; lovable, treacherous."

Well, maybe not "treacherous"—except in the minds of scandalmongers and pop moralists. Bow was a generous and plucky gal, on and off the screen. Her multifaceted beauty was dreamy, spellbinding, and spine-tingling. She wasn't merely a movie star but a battered Hollywood heroine. On ambition and street wit alone, she pulled herself out of Brooklyn tenements, escaping from a sexually abusive father and a murderously unbalanced mother who once tried to slit the teenage Clara's throat when she was sleeping—catalyzing, among other repercussions, a lifelong case of insomnia. Clara's father put her mother in an insane asylum, where she died while her daughter was appearing in a picture.

Becoming a performer in a disreputable fledgling art form, Clara managed to use her disadvantages and her psychic wounds to invent her own acting grammar and vocabulary built on uninhibited energy and movement. Her swift, intuitive mastery of a new erotic syntax made her a revolutionary star. She was all the more alluring—and, to some onlookers, "dangerous"—because her sexuality informed her overall life force. Neither a vamp nor a Goody Two-Shoes, she provided the figure of the girl next door with a healthy sex drive.

Her best-known picture was Clarence Badger's 1927 adaptation of Elinor Glyn's *It*, but her juiciest vehicle was the movie that led up to it: Fleming's *Mantrap*. Its Sinclair Lewis source novel has been forgotten, but Lewis was coming off an unprecedented string of critical and popular successes (*Main Street*, *Babbitt*, *Arrowsmith*) when *Mantrap* came out in 1926, and the movie was a plum assignment for Fleming. The director was ready for it. He saw that it was a new kind of sex comedy, celebrating a spunky, unstable erotic heroine (Bow) while poking fun at both her honest, backwoods-trader husband (Ernest Torrence) and the elegant urbanite (Percy Marmont) who almost steals her away. Professional critics took Lewis at his word when he called it "a straight, out-and-out romance of an unspoiled country . . . the most captivating love and adventure story I have ever conceived or told." But young James Agee, writing to his friend and mentor Father Flye during his summer vacation from Exeter, hit the right note when he called it "always amusing" and "a sort of relaxation for Lewis" from "working on the biggest thing yet," which turned out to be *Elmer Gantry.* Of course, *Mantrap* still had elements of social commentary: it popularized the concept of the "social climber."

Whether on a Paramount set or on location at Little Bear Lake in the San Bernardino Mountains, Fleming sustains a summery tone from start to finish. Vincent Lawrence, fresh from Broadway, consulted on the script and instructed Hathaway and Fleming on the importance of structuring scenes rather than concocting clever titles. Lawrence had a benign influence; he'd later work on *Test Pilot* and Fleming's unfortunate 1946 *Adventure* (no relation to the silent Jack London piece). On its own terms *and* as an interpretation of the novel, the movie is a small comic masterpiece, though Lewis ended up hating it. (He told an audience at a movie theater where he was spotted that he was glad he'd read the book first, because he wouldn't have been able to recognize it from the movie.) It's consistently sprightly, as befits the theme that erotic attraction bubbles constantly beneath the surface of social life, even in the Canadian frontier town of Mantrap Landing.

Most romantic comedies, especially ones revolving around triangles, build to a clear amorous resolution. *Mantrap*'s characters don't know or can't accept what they want, especially the sophisticated Ralph Prescott (Marmont), a New York City divorce lawyer, and the flirty Minneapolis manicurist turned rural wife, Alverna (Bow). At the end, they all drift back to where they started, sadder and wiser and a little bit funnier, too. The movie begins with comical vignettes contrasting the sexual hunger of Mantrap Landing's general-store operator Joe Easter (Torrence) with the sexual disgust of Prescott, a bored Manhattan attorney. Annoyed rather than flattered when a well-put-together blonde plays footsies with him under his desk, Prescott escapes into a hallway. There he runs into a business neighbor, Woodbury (Eugene Pallette), who beckons him into *his* office—past a display of papier-mâché legs and sashaying models (he runs a hosiery company)—and suggests that a vacation in the north woods will be therapy for Prescott.

James Wong Howe, returning as Fleming's cinematographer, said it was the director's idea to start with Prescott's client crying in his office: "He had me open up on her little hand-mirror showing the lips being made up and I would dolly back." When she puts the mirror down, we get our first view of Marmont's lawyer, looking stern and stressed. Speaking in 1970, Howe remembered the gal as Bow, though it's the skillful Patty DuPont as Prescott's blond client (Fleming would use her in his next Bow picture, too). In a pungent counterpoint, we first see Joe in a marvelous tableau, modeling hats for local squaws; Torrence is priceless when he presents his wares to his audience with an obsequious deadpan. He's been out of circulation far too long, and when he discovers that dames in the 1920s display more than their ankles, he decides he needs a trip to Minneapolis. Fleming told Howe, "You go ahead and shoot the montage of Ernest Torrence coming to town from the woods by yourself," and Howe thought, "That's wonderful." In Minneapolis, Joe meets Alverna, a manicure girl who finds this endearing lug a welcome change of pace from slick city beaux. Even before Bow's entrance, the movie's zest and innovation outstrip even Fleming's Fairbanks pictures: the camera glides among the characters with a skin-prickling emotional alertness. When Bow does arrive, she provides a power surge that never leaves the picture. From the moment Alverna waggles her way out of a taxi, Fleming lets Bow take charge of the film as if she were stuffing a hotel key down her blouse.

Alverna parades down the row of barber chairs until her attention snags Joe Easter like a magnet does a filing. She likes this "big boy from way back"—she really likes him. And the camera loves her. Arthur Jacobson, Bow's sometime lover, who served as a second cameraman or assistant director on several of her films, said, "She was what we called a freewheeling actress . . . The cameramen they put on her pictures got used to her. They knew how to light and how to follow her with the camera, because once she started to play a scene you never knew where she was going to be. No director wanted to hold her down. They let her go!"

In the wild, the city slickers are unmanned. Fleming was a whiz at the anti-buddy movie before he perfected the buddy movie in films like *The Virginian* and *Test Pilot*, as he proves with his swift limning of

Prescott and Woodbury's disastrous woodland partnership. Prescott's earnest awkwardness clashes so keenly with Woodbury's know-it-all assurance that when Easter arrives on their campsite Prescott reacts to him like a godsend. Prescott is glad to go back with Easter to Mantrap, although as soon as he gets there he knows in his gut that a real mantrap awaits him: Easter's new wife—Alverna. Bow shows her native acting genius in Alverna's interaction with Prescott: she instinctively reads how he reacts to her all-out physicality (even before she makes a move on him), then puts him at ease.

It was Fleming who put Bow at ease. The twenty-year-old star thought him "older a great deal than I am, and very strong." In 1928, she told Adela Rogers St. Johns:

> I liked him at once, though I didn't feel in the least romantic about him. But soon we became great friends and he had a tremendous and very fine influence on my life. He grew fond of me at once. And he began, with his strong intellect and understanding of life, to guide me in little ways. He showed me that life must be lived, not just for the moment, but for the years. He showed me what a future I might have as an actress, because I had made a place for myself that people seemed to want. He was very patient, and he taught me a great deal.

The "great friends" became lovers. He advised her to be careful in her friendships—and predicted that in a year she would be a great star.

Happily, *Mantrap* has the ambience of a frolic, not a tutorial. It was a watershed moment for Bow, for Fleming, and for Howe. It's the rare comedy—like *Midnight*, or Fleming's later *Bombshell*, or *The Lady Eve*, or *Some Like It Hot*—where the scintillating craftsmanship carries its own sense of humor. However fast or slow his affair with Bow, something on this movie energized Fleming and electrified his co-workers. *Mantrap* makes observational humor cinematic. It's unpredictable as well as funny, particularly when, at an excruciating pace, Howe's camera slowly pans around the Easters' welcome party for Prescott while a grim reverend and neighbors from the nearby Hudson Bay Company outlet paralyze rambunctious trappers with a heavy dose of holy attitude.

The look of the film may suffer at times from primitivism—the "day for night" techniques used for a night burglary now seem woefully inadequate—but the sophisticated feeling behind the camera-work hasn't dated and fits the heroine's frisson.

"She was bad in the book, but—darn it!—of course, they couldn't make her that way in the picture. So I played her as a flirt," Bow told a reporter, underlining her meaning with, the reporter wrote, "a sidelong glance." Alverna channels all her vitality into flirtation; she stands for life amid a mob of pious zombies. Fleming and Bow leave little doubt that neither Easter nor Prescott will ever manage her: that's what catalyzes the comedy. Fleming wisely pushes the material toward an evenhanded satire. Both the slick attorney and the wholesome bumpkin are Silly Putty in this lady's hand, yet each of these guys could use some kneading. You root to see them fall before her. Prescott does try to leave Mantrap before he gives in to temptation and betrays his friend. Alverna lies in wait at a bend of the river to intercept his canoe; Howe's lens takes in her hobo sack of goods and then her calves before it moves up to her gorgeous, irresistibly expectant face. Prescott can't resist. Who could? Yet there's nothing fatale about this femme. Ultimately, she revives Prescott's appetites and makes Easter see that she's worth the trouble.

There's tenderness to this movie's sexiness—maybe that's why it was a favorite with both its stars. On a packet of production stills, Bow wrote to her sons, "From *Mantrap*—the best silent picture I ever made." In 1991, a *Toronto Star* reader responded to a request for "magic movie moments" with an experience he'd had seeing *Mantrap* at a "nostalgia cinema" in England:

> Just before the lights went down, the ushers parked a frail, shriveled old man in a wheelchair beside my aisle seat. As the voluptuous "It" girl romped with her handsome leading man on the screen, this shrunken man beside me was overcome with emotion. His sobbing, groaning, and whimpering were so distracting that I wound up watching him as much as the movie. Then, when the lights came up, the theatre manager bounded up on stage and announced: "Ladies and gentlemen, I would like to introduce to you the man whom you just saw making love to Clara Bow on screen."

It was, of course, Percy Marmont.

In a tragedy or soap opera, Alverna's itchiness would doom her to eternal disappointment—even Lewis's book leaves her hurting. But here, as later in *Red Dust*, Fleming has a healing comic vision. She's better off with Easter than with a tonier and more forbiddingly "honorable" man like Prescott; Easter just has to hold on to her when she slips a little. It's a trick Fleming couldn't master with Bow in real life. But *Mantrap* was the start of an affair to remember.

9

A Lost Epic: *The Rough Riders*

Fleming and Bow may have set the screen and the box office ablaze (at a cost of $216,584, *Mantrap* netted $415,600 in rentals), but exactly when their affair turned serious isn't clear. In their few weeks between pictures back in Los Angeles, they followed separate tracks. Bow was still an outsider. Though Fleming was living not far from Bow's Hollywood Boulevard home and then in the Hollywood Hills, he was becoming a member of "the Club"—literally. In 1925, the Hollywood Sixty Club, a group that tried (and failed) to build a "clubhouse" for moviemakers, proudly announced Fleming as one of its founders, along with Chaplin, Howard Hawks, John Ford, and other luminaries. But Hollywood never took to Bow. "Most people in Hollywood were burying their pasts," says David Stenn, author of *Clara Bow: Runnin' Wild* (1988):

> She was exhuming hers. They were doing everything behind closed doors, and she was talking to the press. Esther Ralston told me a story on herself that I thought revealed a lot about Clara and Hollywood. She and Clara were shooting *Children of Divorce* and the day they wrapped, Esther was having a big party. Esther was very proper—blonde, petite, pretty—and she lived in a big mansion. And everyone in Hollywood was invited: that is, all the right people. So Esther was getting dressed in the dressing room and Clara walked by and lingered in the doorway and said, "You're having a party, ain't cha, Esther?" And Esther said, as if it had just hit her, "Oh Clara, would you like to come?" And Clara Bow stood in the doorway and said, "Oh, no, I know you don't want to invite me." This is the biggest star in Hollywood—and she's a pariah to the point

> where no one even pretended to accept her. And Esther *liked* her. I mean, there are plenty of people around who don't like the big female stars today, but they sure put on a great act.

"Clara did strange things," even the besotted Arthur Jacobson had to admit. "Someone told her she shouldn't leave her two dogs in the backyard. She brought the dogs into the spare bedroom, and had someone cover the floor of the room with dirt. When she sold the house, she had to replace the floor." (Fleming would later use his knowledge of Bow's helter-skelter home life to enrich *Bombshell.*)

When the Mayfair Club, a more successful and elitist version of the Hollywood Sixty Club, held its first formal dinner dance at the Biltmore Hotel, the lady on Fleming's arm was Norma Shearer. The Hollywood Sixty Club would serve dinner to anyone who could cough up $15; the Mayfair Club was much snootier. Mary Astor described it as "a social experiment" to see whether Hollywood mainstays could find a space without gawkers or press to "be themselves": to eat and dance and (especially during Prohibition) drink. "But as for movie people being themselves," Astor wrote, "it was absurd. The men wore top hat, white tie and tails. Everybody got a good look at everybody else, and who was with who, and who got drunk, and who looked terrible, and the columns duly reported the long lists of important names the following day; and if your name wasn't there you called the paper and raised hell." The galas sometimes doubled as charity benefits, and the organization was exclusive—a nonmember couldn't come as a guest to two galas in a row. A local madam did manage to puncture the group's airs: she sent fifteen employees to infiltrate a dance, all dressed in red. At the club's glittering first night in August 1926, Fleming had his last known date with Shearer; his pal Hawks had his first date with Shearer's sister, Athole, his future wife; and Astor went with Hawks's brother Kenneth, her future husband.

Patsy Ruth Miller, the performer turned writer who had played Esmeralda to Lon Chaney's Quasimodo in *The Hunchback of Notre Dame* (1923), was in a good position to understand the Hawks-Fleming allure; she married John Lee Mahin, who in the 1930s became Fleming's favorite screenwriter. She knew how men like Hawks and Fleming denigrated the flaccid side of make-believe and treasured their risky real-world pursuits. In Miller's *That Flannigan Girl*, a 1939 roman à clef that mingles perceptions of the Hawks clan and Vic, she portrays a pair of brothers from Pasadena's upper crust—"tall, loose-jointed men, big-featured and soft-voiced." The figure resembling Howard Hawks possesses "a smile that had very little mirth." The brother more like Fleming has "a fullness, a softness that his brother never had," also a protective way with women and perhaps with other men—he boasts of rescuing an assistant director from suicide. (Vic said he did, too.) Accused of being "just a hidebound Pasadena boy," the Fleming figure says Hollywood puts out "entertainment for morons" and declares, "Acting's a hell of a way for a man to earn a living . . . You get punch drunk from hitting yourself in the face with a powder puff." The character's exuberance for flying charms her—until he dies in a plane crash.

Fleming himself kept flying throughout the 1920s. Near the end of the decade, a *Washington Post* movie columnist spotted him enjoying an aerial bout of tag in a checkered biplane over Santa Monica. But William "Wild Bill" Wellman, a filmmaker of Fleming's robust temperament and roving pedigree, got the call to make *Wings* (1927), Hollywood's landmark flying epic, even though it was written by Vic's recent collaborators Loring and Lighton. In World War I, Wellman flew in the Lafayette Flying Corps of the French Foreign Legion. Douglas Fairbanks had met Wellman at a high-school hockey match in Boston. When Doug read a newspaper account of the young man's wartime exploits, the star cabled the aviator with the words "When it's all over, you'll always have a job." Wellman possessed chiseled, camera-ready looks, and Fairbanks tried to make him an actor. But Wellman felt ridiculous in wigs and makeup and wanted a post on the other side of the camera. It took him only four years to work his way up from messenger boy and assistant propman and assistant director to director. Once he did, his ascent to the top ranks was even swifter. B. P. Schulberg, first as an independent producer and then as Paramount's production chief, championed Wellman—and Wild Bill landed the prize of *Wings.*

Fleming was another of Schulberg's favorites. But it was Schulberg's boss, Jesse Lasky, who handed Fleming an equally ambitious assignment: *The Rough Riders* (1927), a salute to Teddy Roosevelt and his command of the First U.S. Volunteer Cavalry during the 1898 Spanish-American War. Fleming had already made his reputation as what Astor called "a good 'big production' man." *The Rough Riders* was enormous. Fleming would shoot most of it in San Antonio, Texas, partly on the same International Exposition parade grounds where

Roosevelt trained his troops. Wellman would shoot *Wings* in San Antonio, too, and at the same time, because the location contained both air and land Army bases. Wellman got complete cooperation from the War Department: fliers from across the country flocked to San Antonio. And Fleming had the use of up to twelve hundred soldiers from the Army's First Cavalry Division. "The town was lousy with movie people," Wellman wrote—and even lousier with military people. And, as Wellman continued, "if you think that contributes to a state of tranquility, you don't know your motion picture ABCs."

Wings endures as a milestone of aerial moviemaking and a war film of enduring vitality. *The Rough Riders* would be a casualty of big-studio neglect, surviving only in bits and pieces, and in legend. But for Fleming, it was a grand cinematic exploit. And for Lasky, *The Rough Riders* was a personal crusade. He had once told his son Jesse junior that he'd been a bugler for the First Cavalry. He now would spare no cost in setting the record straight. (Budgeted at $500,000, the film came in at $1.2 million.) He hired Hermann Hagedorn, secretary of the Theodore Roosevelt Association, to concoct a historically accurate screen story and serve as research guru. Even after Lasky and Fleming added the contributions of John Goodrich (who delivered a romantic triangle) and Keene Thompson and Robert N. Lee (only Thompson worked with Fleming on location), they arrived at an account that—apparently—was faithful to Roosevelt's 1899 memoir of the same name. "Apparently," because the only evidence that survives comprises a record of the editing continuity at the Motion Picture Academy library, a few minutes of spectacular footage cut trailer-style (housed at the Library of Congress), and, at the Museum of Modern Art in New York, editing-room dupes and trims from the cast-of-thousands scenes.

The loss of *The Rough Riders* is serious, because what does survive has the size and charm of popular legend and the detail of history. In the brief Library of Congress reel, there's percussive power to the action shots. And the romantic leads—Mary Astor as the regimental belle Dolly, Charles Farrell as the Harvard man and New York millionaire Stewart Van Brunt (known as Van), and Charles Emmett Mack as Dolly's Texas hometown sweetheart, Bert Henley—all look charged up. Astor has a swooning grace and an intriguing shadow in her eyes; Farrell and Mack have the grit, sensitivity, and gruff humor that already characterized Vic's leading men as well as his brand of storytelling. The MoMA footage of men swarming in and out of long boats, or marching on parade grounds, or embarking and debarking or boarding mules onto military ships suggests an exultant urge to express, on a mammoth scale, the discipline and sporadic chaos of Army life. Teddy Roosevelt wrote that the Rough Riders were an eclectic crew of "born adventurers," and Mary Astor wrote that Fleming did "get the feel of the period, the zeal for a cause, the heat and dust of Texas."

What *hasn't* been lost are the fables attached to this film's making. Wellman recalled the simultaneous shooting of *The Rough Riders* and *Wings* in San Antonio as "the Armageddon of a magnificent sexual donnybrook." Lasky, still in love with the Roosevelt movie's subject decades later, said that it was "a smashing hit as the big road-show special of its year." Astor simply dubbed it "the high spot of 'having fun making movies.' "

The fun started with the search for a Theodore Roosevelt. According to Lasky, "We notified all our exchanges of our need" and found a look-alike in the Midwest. The road-show program stated that Hagedorn put up a $500 reward for the person who found the man who most resembled TR. A Los Angeles apartment-house manager read the announcement in a pamphlet at the Million Dollar Theatre and then "came face to face on the sidewalk" with Frank Hopper, a former Montana businessman and sometime stage actor "employed as a representative of a book concern." He was Roosevelt's spitting image, and when he lost twenty-five pounds (Hagedorn promised $5 for every pound lost whether or not he got the part), Hopper won the role. But after Lasky put him in Fleming's hands, the director said, "Hopper won't do." Lasky tried to persuade him otherwise, but Fleming held his ground. "Only in looks [is he a dead ringer for Roosevelt]," Fleming said. "In every other way he's the direct opposite. Roosevelt was aggressive, dynamic, stormy. This guy hangs his head. He trembles when you speak to him. He's so timid he's afraid to ask what time it is. If you've got a picture where he'd be working behind a ribbon counter, he'd be perfect—but leading the Rough Riders up San Juan Hill? . . . The audience would roll in the aisles."

None other than the movie producers' morality czar, Will Hays, provided the solution. Hays, formerly President Harding's postmaster general, drew on his cabinet experience and said to Lasky, "Suppose you introduce [Hopper] to me with the greatest deference and respect, and I act as if I'm meeting the president himself." So when Hopper entered Lasky's office, the mogul and the czar snapped to attention. Lasky turned to Hays and asked, "General, may I present you to Theodore Roosevelt?" And Hays responded, "Sir, I am happy and proud to make your acquaintance. The resemblance is remarkable. I see you have the same character, the same undaunted courage—and your eyes reflect a passionate love for your country." Addressing Hopper only as Roosevelt and always in tones of homage, Lasky buttressed the actor's self-worth until "there was just the suggestion of a swagger in his gait. I grabbed the phone before he could get back to the set and told Fleming to give orders to everyone up and down the line to treat the fellow as if he were dealing with royalty, and to feign absolute sincerity in order to build up his ego." It worked. By the time filming began, Hopper was raring to impersonate TR in all his bluster, demanding to get his boys food "if I have to burn up all the red tape between here and Washington."

Production trains for *The Rough Riders* pulled in to San Antonio on August 18 carrying cavalry units and turn-of-the-century wooden-wheeled supply wagons still in daily use in Army operations on the border with Mexico. Fleming and company arrived the next day on a special Southern Pacific car. "The heat bore down as only Texas heat in August can," wrote Astor, "but we had no time to think of our discomfort in the noise and turmoil of our reception. The crowd at the station shouted; a military band blasted its welcome above the noise of the crowd; Mayor [John W.] Tobin gained sufficient quiet to make a welcoming speech and present me with roses and gratifying compliments."

With a sizable budget resting on his back and a company of 150, not counting all the military extras, Fleming plotted out every minute of the schedule to avoid getting bogged down far from Hollywood. The first three days of shooting went off like gangbusters and "almost finished off" Astor and some of her colleagues. But Fleming and his cinematographer—again, James Wong Howe—were depending on full sunlight. On most days the clouds went in and out. After that marvelous three-day start, the weather turned so rainy and steamy that it shut down production for ten days. Ennui never afflicted Astor, who enjoyed the attentions of the cavalry and fliers. "We were lionized, partied, dated almost to death. On the days when we could work, we hurried back in the late afternoon, hot and sweaty, for a swim at the country club or at Brackenridge Park, followed by a dinner and dance at the Gunter Roof or Kelly Field."

When Fleming could pick up the pace, it was intense. Determined to send shock waves through even the most sprawling images, he pushed Howe into devising what Howe recalled was "a crude version of the crab dolly." Howe and Paramount's special-effects-department camera expert Frank Madigan put together "a device like a cart on aeroplane wheels and a two-armed thing with a counterbalance and a camera on each arm. You could lift them up or drop them down as you pulled the cart along to follow the action."

Fleming gave them action worth following. In *The Rough Riders*, Theodore Roosevelt wrote, "Half the horses of the regiment bucked, or possessed some other of the amiable weaknesses incident to horse life on the great ranches; but we had an abundance of men who were utterly unmoved by any antic a horse might commit." Fleming corralled four hundred broncos and hired experienced rodeo riders to mix in with the actors. Howe shot tests of them. "Well, I never saw so many fellows tossed in the air," he said. "These fellows, they weren't really good riders. They just thought they wanted to get in the movies, you see. I think there were forty or fifty of them taken to the first aid camp. It was dusty. The horses, the minute they started bucking, they kicked up so much dust, and all I could see was people, fellows going up through that dust in the air."

The assistant director, Henry Hathaway, knew Fleming from the seat-of-the-pants Zane Grey pictures and the frolicsome *Mantrap*, but on *The Rough Riders*, Fleming brought his protégé to tears, pushing him to stress point during the staging of the Rough Riders' departure from San Antonio to Tampa, Florida. Veering away from TR's account of an organizational breakdown, Fleming planned it as an exultant parade to the Aranas Pass train station, complete with three hundred cheering local extras. It was Hathaway's job to settle the logistics.

> Fleming was sitting on his ass and I set up this whole damn parade and had to do most of it at nighttime to get ready. In the morning he wanted to see if the start of the parade would come into view. At that time I'd gotten the whole thing ready so that he wouldn't have to wait too long. I ran all the way from where the parade was up to the camera and I was out of breath. I said, "It's all ready, Vic." He looked at me and said, "Oooooooh, I worked so hard." Oh, I was so mad. He was a cruel man. He's the kind of guy who picked the wings off flies.

Fleming was always a hard-driving joker, especially to men he liked and trusted like Howe and Hathaway. On *The Rough Riders*, he struck up a jovial friendship with the associate director Earl J. Haley and made him a thousand-dollar "quit smoking" bet. When Haley fell off that wagon in 1930, he wrote Vic a $1,000 check—and to his astonishment, the director cashed it. (Uncle Ed would certainly have approved. Haley's son Stan says the incident became a cherished family story.)

On the day the company shot the departure of the Rough Riders, Hathaway probably did sense something off balance. The top-billed star of *Wings* (albeit for a relatively small part) was Clara Bow, and she chugged into town at 4:00 a.m. the previous morning. Eluding the welcoming committee, she went straight to her hotel, and when she did step out, on September 15, it was to witness Fleming shooting his parade—and to declare her engagement to "Vickie" (her latest pet name for him).

The timing was not choice. Bow had recently announced that she was engaged to the smoldering actor Gilbert Roland. Indeed, Roland told a reporter that this engagement to Fleming was just a ploy to win *him* back. Roland produced a wish-you-were-here telegram signed "Lots of love" from his "Clarita," and said he'd wired her back that their affair was "all off" because he wouldn't share her "with several other suitors."

It all made for amorous chaos and fresh material for reporters who rarely tired of field updates from Bow's romantic battlefronts. Bow had already gone through with a joke application for marriage to a Yale amateur poet named Robert Savage, who thought it was no joke—and slashed his wrists to demonstrate his seriousness. And of course, Fleming had in recent weeks been seen cheek to cheek with Norma Shearer. The Society of Cinemaland column in the *Los Angeles Times* noted, "We were quite sure that there was some sort of love affair between Fleming and a popular young star who is not Miss Bow—but now the little Clara is quite sure that the Victor has gone to her heart. And what are Gilbert Rowland [*sic*] and Robert Savage saying about this?"

Years later, Bow told a movie magazine that she knew she'd been "impetuous and thoughtless." She *had* been having an affair with Roland—"I did not consider myself engaged to him but our relations were of a very friendly nature." But when she got to San Antonio, her "friendship" with Fleming "was renewed. We talked engagement sincerely but here again I thoughtlessly did something which placed both

Victor Fleming and Gilbert Roland in embarrassing positions"—that is, announce the engagement in order to be " 'a good sport' and give a publicity man trying to gin up some ink 'a break.' " When it came to speaking with the press off the cuff, the girl couldn't help it; she was always lively and unpredictable (and inconsistent). She visited one San Antonio newspaper and told reporters that Fleming had proposed in a letter and that they'd been engaged for ten days before they announced it.

No wonder Hollywood viewed her as a sexual flibbertigibbet. If anyone is responsible for propelling that view into the twenty-first century, it's Wellman. A director of great force who got a winsome performance from Bow in *Wings*, Wellman was also an agreeable if unreliable storyteller, with the uncanny knack of embedding a grain of honesty in not-so-cultured pearls of wisdom. "A motion picture company lives hard and plays hard, and they better or they will go nuts," he wrote in his memoir, stating a truth that all Hollywood's great wild men have adhered to, from Fleming and Wellman to John Huston and Robert Altman. Like Bow herself, but with a yarn spinner's hyperbole, Wellman gleefully mixed up Bow's image with reality:

> To begin with all the young actors in *The Rough Riders* and *Wings* fell in love with Clara Bow, and if you had known her, you could understand why. This presented a problem to both Vic Fleming and me, but a far greater problem to Miss Bow. She took care of it—how I will never know . . . She kept [Buddy] Rogers, [Richard] Arlen, [Gary] Cooper, [Charles Emmett] Mack, a couple of pursuit pilots, and a panting writer all in line. They were handled like chessmen, never running into one another, never suspecting that there was any other man in the whole world that meant a thing to this gorgeous little sexpot—and all this expert maneuvering in a hotel where most of the flame was burning.

Contrary to popular perceptions, Arlen and Rogers didn't vie for Bow's affections during the making of *Wings* or even in the movie. Onscreen they competed for the second female lead, Jobyna Ralston (though their characters actually had the hottest friendship with each other); offscreen Arlen and *Ralston* fell in love and got married after the movie wrapped. Despite her billing, Bow as scripted was the weakest corner of a romantic quadrangle: she plays the girl next door who can't get Rogers's attention until the final scene. Still, her arsenal of wholesome flirtations keeps her character alive and gives the action on the ground a lift whenever *Wings* doesn't soar into the clouds.

Fleming was probably more pivotal than Bow herself to the romantic goings-on in San Antonio. Rogers later said he got "a little flirtation" going with Bow one night, but "was too scared to do anything about it" because "Vic Fleming was a *tough* guy, rough and tough. I was scared to death of him." Meanwhile, Fleming was playing the fairy-tale godfather for his *Rough Riders* leading lady, Mary Astor. On the rebound from John Barrymore, the first great love of her life, Astor had become engaged to the production manager Irving Asher—and Astor's mother, who accompanied the actress to Texas, conspired with the director to keep Astor away from Los Angeles and Asher as long as possible. Her part could have been done in a week; Fleming spread it out for months, from August into October, the whole run of the production. As Astor and Asher grew distant, John Monk Saunders, the dashing Rhodes scholar who wrote the original story of *Wings*, decided to give Astor the rush. When she signaled she was giving in, "Vic smiled a knowing smile; Mother kept out of the way (she was, she assured me, happily entertained by a cavalry captain); rumors were carelessly but pointedly dropped that back in Hollywood [Irving] was seeing a good deal of a former girlfriend; and I didn't care whether we got home by Christmas."

Bow knew *Wings* would be another breakthrough: her first part in a bona fide super-production. Apart from trying to be a right gal for a publicist friend, is it so hard to comprehend why she'd make her announcement during that heady time? After all, when she spoke about Fleming, she described him as the man who gave good counsel when she had what future generations would call "an identity crisis" over becoming a star. "You couldn't deceive him with any false glitter," she said. "He steered me straight a lot of times when I was going 'haywire.' " She said when they got engaged in 1926, "I began to read again, and to enjoy music, and to grow calmer about many things."

It's testimony to Fleming's fortitude that he had a calming effect on Bow during what she called their engagement, because at that time he was experiencing the kind of pressure that would make lesser directors crumple. On September 21, Paramount's West Coast production manager, Sam Jaffe, came to San Antonio to take the pulse of the studio's runaway productions. Both *The Rough Riders* and *Wings* suffered from the weather. If Fleming wanted absolute sun, Wellman wanted sunlight with a few clouds to contrast with the speeding planes; gray skies did neither of them any good. After Jaffe left, Fleming doubled his efforts to pick up the pace wherever he could. (Bow returned to California on September 25.) Astor wrote that they "worked like slaves to make up the lost time," doing "twenty scenes in one day." One bout of running down a road in the Texas heat, wearing corsets and heavy Gay Nineties clothing, made her collapse and knock off for three days.

The urgency to bring off the special-effects-laden action scenes grew particularly intense. Hathaway was preparing shots of an American observation balloon when the same Frank Madigan who helped Howe create the crab dolly arrived with Fourth of July pyrotechnics—small devices that could whirl around in the air before detonating like bullets, setting off smoke clouds and giving audiences the impression that they were "exploding in the balloon." Hathaway instructed his crew: "Set your things so there's no way of hitting the balloon," which was carrying a stuntman. He caught a break when the first explosive device grazed the balloon, rebounded, and went off. "The next one goes, hits the balloon, blows it up. Thank God there was only one man ['the second man chickened out'] because he climbed out and slid down the cable. Boy, was he raw—his hands, his legs that he wound around the cable."

As usual, Fleming's practical-joke side escalated with risky circumstances. He asked Howe, "Jimmy, you want to take a ride in [the balloon]?" Howe said, "Sure," so Fleming said, "Take your camera up there and get a shot." Howe recalled, "He put the camera in this basket and he let this thing up there, and we got some shots . . . Then I said, 'Victor, take us down.' I must have been up about 150 feet or so . . . and Fleming I would see down there swinging this rope. You know what he was trying to do? He was trying to get it loose up there . . . He's crazy. Vicious."

Fleming's production returned to California on October 21 and moved to Santa Cruz for twenty-one days of shooting, re creating the Cuban invasion and several major battles. The push to get the movie done was staggering and so was the size of the production: in addition to the 150-strong company, the 1,200 extras included 250 African-Americans as members of the all-black Tenth Cavalry. Hathaway organized a string of explosives to go off while the Yanks were making a river crossing. Before shooting he ordered his special-effects guy to put one charge down at the last minute, right before Charles Emmett Mack hit a particular spot, for prime dramatic effect. But when Fleming called "Action!" and Mack made his mark and Hathaway was supposed to punch a nail on a strike board to set off the explosion, he couldn't remember "which damn nail" to strike. Fleming stopped the camera to dry off and regroup everyone who was wet. But Hathaway's freeze delay saved a life—not Mack's, but the special-effects technician's. He hadn't been able to lay the charge in time. "He was so scared and he thought he was going to get the hell blown out of him." Hathaway was thinking, "If I'd have hit that nail, he'd have been pieces."

Fleming used miniatures for the sinking of the *Maine* (Paramount production records show Wilmington, California, as the location for shots of the searchlights and the gun deck) and reassembled the cast and crew for unspecified reshoots between December 28 and January 8, 1927. The *Variety* critic alluded to "considerable trouble with the film before it was ready to be shown," and the negative buzz might have tainted the trade paper's review. Most critics applauded, including Mordaunt Hall of *The New York Times*, who reported the audience's delight at the comic interplay of Noah Beery, as Sheriff Hell's Bells of Roaring Forks, New Mexico, and George Bancroft, as Happy Joe, who breaks jail to join his troop. There was a subplot of cowardice; Bert bolts from the battle lines but achieves salvation when he ignites the charge up San Juan Hill. Still, the movie pivots more on buddy-film reversals: Hell's Bells and Happy Joe, Farrell's Van and Mack's Bert, take turns bonding under pressure. Hall singled out Farrell's ability "to express his emotions with a sense of humor" as well as his and Mack's "sincerity" in the scene of Van singing military songs as he hauls the mortally wounded Bert to the hospital tent. "You can't call a man a coward—if he dies trying!" reads the title card. Mack died in a car accident on March 17, two days after the film's New York premiere. Fleming served as one of the pallbearers.

It's doubtful that Bow met Gary Cooper when he did his small, attention-getting part as a fatalistic flier in *Wings* (they *may* have collided on the two-day train ride from L.A. to San Antonio). But Bow did co-star with Cooper, and fall for him, on their next film, Frank Lloyd's *Children of Divorce* (1927)—catalyzing a temporary break with Fleming. ("It's all right to be directed by a man you don't know very well, but having the man you are engaged to direct you just doesn't work out," Bow said. "When a man likes you real well, you know, you can get away with anything.") After Frank Strayer's negligible *Rough House Rosie*, *Hula* came around a few months later, with Fleming attached to it. By then he was ready to forgive her and direct her; Bow and Cooper were no longer an item. (Cooper thought that what broke them up was Bow's inability to shake her feelings for Fleming.)

Ever the pro, Fleming would turn Cooper into the It Boy by setting him up to be a sexual icon in 1929's *Wolf Song* (co-starring Lupe Velez, also a lover to Fleming and Cooper at different times). And he'd perfect Cooper's screen image when he directed him in *The Virginian* later that same year. But for now, he had another kind of superstar on his hands: Emil Jannings.

10

From *The Way of All Flesh* to *Abie's Irish Rose*

When Paramount seduced the German star Emil Jannings in 1926 with $400,000 a year—and the rare guarantee that his films would be shot in sequential order, "according to plot instead of according to the set-builders' convenience"—B. P. Schulberg (Budd's father) assigned Fleming to Jannings's first American production, *The Way of All Flesh* (1927). Schulberg reckoned that one outsized personality demanded another. Jannings was an international acting potentate with transcontinental charisma. He saw himself as a cinematic demigod: maybe that's why he maintained that he was born in Brooklyn to Americans of German descent, when actually he was born in the aptly named Rorschach, Switzerland, to an American-born father and German mother. A carnival strongman who rose to become "Kaiser of Berlin's theatrical world" and then, after Ernst Lubitsch cast him as Louis XV in *Passion* (1919), Kaiser of Berlin's film world, too, he relished his position and enacted it with noblesse oblige. He made a point, when he first reached Hollywood, of shaking hands with everyone on Paramount's staff. (He had no love for America: he stayed for less than three years and, after returning to Germany in 1929, destroyed his reputation with support for the Nazis.)

The *New Yorker*'s Elsie McCormick summed up Jannings as "a large, beaming, childlike personage who looks out upon the world with the expression of a good-natured cherub. This cheerful ingenuousness somehow makes those around him feel that he should be pampered like a youngster and protected from adult annoyances. Even his impressive size does not prevent the women with whom he is associated from developing a maternal attitude."

He was not going to get any mothering from Fleming, who babied only his girlfriends. And during *The Way of All Flesh*, even that well of warmth was running low. Bow started filming *Children of Divorce* with Cooper on November 26; within a week reporters took her comments that she and Fleming "have had a slight disagreement and the wedding is postponed." She told Adela Rogers St. Johns a year later that she "needed romance" and her and Fleming's "feeling for each other became more and more that of close friendship and less and less that of lovers." Several years later she added, "I couldn't live up to his subtlety." Cooper's attraction was more direct: Bow famously bragged to Hedda Hopper, "He's hung like a horse and can go all night!"

Fleming never made a public statement about any of his affairs; by then he knew how changeable Bow could be (they would get back together before the break of summer). On the rebound, he went out with a Bow manqué, a bobbed redhead named Alice White, who in 1930 was named by Cecil Beaton as one of the most beautiful women in the movies, along with Lillian Gish, Dolores Del Rio, Norma Shearer, and Greta Garbo. Her background was almost as juicy as Bow's. Born Alva White (possibly out of wedlock) in Paterson, New Jersey, raised by her Italian immigrant grandparents, she ended up with them in Los Angeles, and found her way into movies as a script girl for von Sternberg and for Chaplin. Dubbed "Peter Rabbit" for being "so stubby and fat and pink-looking," she caught fire in front of a cameraman who was snapping some test shots for a new lens, and Chaplin made her a stand-in. She then performed her own extreme makeover, shedding forty pounds, losing her spectacles, and straightening her hair. Beginning as an extra (notably in 1924's *Thief of Bagdad*), she was still an extra when Fleming first dated her, but she was angling to be an actress. She also was determined to be as frank as Bow about her escapades. Her first kiss with Fleming, she wrote in a published diary, was "a nice little-boy kiss. No thrills." But "a girl can't help liking Victor. He's so awfully nice and sort of babies her."

Fleming reveled in his burgeoning status. In March 1926, when Kathleen Clifford married the banker Mirimir Illitch, he sold the Gardner Street house and moved to his bachelor house on Cove Way in Beverly Hills, not far from his friends Arthur and Lu Rosson, around the corner from Buster Keaton, and down the road from both Chaplin and Fairbanks. The ad he composed bursts with pride:

HERE'S A BARGAIN
AM MOVING TO BEVERLY HILLS

> Will sell my beautiful English stucco bungalow at extremely low price. Six lovely rooms and a separate small bungalow for maid. 1632 Gardner, just south of Hollywood Blvd. See it today. Owner, GR 7220

Early in 1927, Fleming also bought a spread north of Encinitas to provide an escape from Hollywood and to host friends like Fairbanks and lovers like Bow and White. He paid $250,000 for the eleven-hundred-acre Meadowlark Ranch (he purchased even more land later) and announced plans (unfulfilled) to expand the residence into a Spanish-style hacienda. It remained "a very modest house," his niece Yvonne Blocksom said, with two bedrooms, a living room, a dining room, and a screened-in porch. "No pretense. Uncle Vic was not one for pretension." He did clear a landing strip, plant grain to feed the livestock, and fill the land with horses, cattle, and Poland China pigs—a special show breed. "Part of the ranch was on the other side of the road. An old stone house, a waterfall. And the horses were all loose-running, so if we wanted to ride, we had to go out there and lasso them." Edward Hartman, at age seven, was tucked into bed there one night when a voice startled him: "Move over, kid, I'm getting in." It was Douglas Fairbanks. (And a far more innocent time, echoing the days of bed sharing in frontier inns.)

Fleming enjoyed playing the paterfamilias; it was good research for his new movie. Although *The Way of All Flesh* borrowed the title of Samuel Butler's severe novel about patriarchal tyranny, it was a tearjerker for daddies. The script originally carried the title *The Man Who Forgot God*, from an unrealized project by Bruce Barton, the advertising-meets-religion guru of the Roaring Twenties, who interpreted Jesus as the ultimate promoter, entrepreneur, and organization man. Barton had written an update of the David and Bathsheba story—a fable that would find its way into parts of Fleming's *Red Dust*. But Jules Furthman's screenplay for *The Way of All Flesh* is about a chief cashier (Jannings) with a half-dozen kids and a doting wife (played by none other than Belle Bennett, the self-sacrificing mother in 1925's tearjerker for mommies, *Stella Dallas*). He falls from grace and contentment when the bank director asks him to transport bonds to a distant city. In the original script he went from

Weimar to Berlin, but the shooting script Americanized the action to Milwaukee and Chicago. On the train, he meets a bottle-blond floozy (Phyllis Haver), who gets him to commit drunken adultery in the Windy City; then she swipes the bonds and splits. In a glitch of fate that preserves the antihero's honor, a railroad runs over a thug who has picked Jannings's pockets and scavenged his identification papers. But Jannings cannot tell the truth, recover his identity, *and* keep his good name. He becomes one of the anonymous urban poor and, in a climactic twist, chooses to preserve his reputation (and his family's) and accept a prison term for his own murder.

The Way of All Flesh was an ideal conveyance for Jannings's adroit masochism. (Unfortunately, even this famous film has been lost.) At the time of its premiere, Jannings praised "Mr. Fleming and Mr. Schulberg" for filming it in sequence and for completing shooting "in six weeks—in Germany they would have taken six months." A master of makeup, Jannings also appreciated the care Fleming and his assistant—Hathaway again—took in preparing the look, up to a custom hairpiece that extended his hairline when the character was young. Its removal, of course, then made him look old. (George Westmore, Hollywood's pioneer of creative makeup, and/or one of his sons, conceived the look.)

In his posthumously published (1951) memoir, Jannings wrote that he and Fleming

> discussed every scene as a matter of principle. He usually asked: "How do you want to do this, Emil?" I told him what I thought, he listened attentively and responded: "If that's what you feel—good! Do it!" But then he watched like a hellhound. His often repeated, whispered "Too much!" liberated me more and more, all in a sense of friendship, and I realized to my astonishment that a very different Jannings came out of the shell—a simpler, less burdened, more matter-of-fact person. I believe that it was Fleming's great fortune that he had never been an actor. With his natural artistry he personified what every actor wishes for—the ideal audience!

It took time to reach that accord. Fleming was accustomed to megaphoning his directions to actors who followed them immediately. The German star, said Fleming for public consumption, insisted on dissecting every change and discussing "the situation so thoroughly that Jannings became in fact the character of the story, feeling the same emotions, venting the perfect reactions. It did not take me long to realize that Jannings can never give a true Jannings performance when he feels that he is acting. And that is why I say that an actor who acts is never a good actor."

Jannings requested that Fleming go on to direct *The Last Command.* (That didn't happen because of scheduling conflicts with *Abie's Irish Rose.*) Still, Hathaway, who thought Jannings was a problem drinker, witnessed titanic clashes between them. The day they shot the cashier antihero waking up with a hangover, Jannings took "about three or four slugs of whiskey," said Hathaway; then Jannings fell asleep. Fleming "went over and turned out that light and quietly left . . . Jannings woke up on a dark stage about two hours later." Hathaway claimed Jannings threw a fit, summoned Schulberg to his dressing room, and called Vic a "son of a bitch." Fleming responded, "I don't want to work with any autocratic German son of a bitch who's drunk. You can take me off the picture, I don't care."

Jannings's next director, Josef von Sternberg, who became the director of *The Last Command* and then was invited to Germany for *The Blue Angel*, told a slightly different version, with an acid moral. According to von Sternberg, Jannings loved practical jokes, except when they were played on him—any reference to those "would bathe him in gloom." Fleming simply asked him to perform his sleeping scene with "more conviction," and Jannings, "needing no such spur," fell into such profound slumber that Fleming, unable to rouse him, moved his crew to another set and continued filming. "Jannings awoke eight hours later no longer the object of intense interest, alone and abandoned on a pitch-black stage. Except on that occasion, he was never alone, behaving as if the Earth were worthless unless it revolved around him."

After the Sturm und Drang, the movie was a critical and popular success and, along with *The Last Command*, won Emil Jannings the first Academy Award for best actor (in a ceremony that didn't take place until 1929). Fleming's use of a moving camera as a mood reader and probe won comparisons to F. W. Murnau's and E. A. Dupont's collaborations with Jannings on, respectively, *The Last Laugh* (1924) and *Variety* (1925). Even a Paramount publicity item singled out the way the camera follows Jannings "around one room, down a long hallway and into a second room, recording every action on the way." Berlin critics contemptuous of the movie's pathos-laden finale still praised Jannings and Fleming—one even called it the star's "greatest success."

There was a strong dissenter: Luis Buñuel. He had no use for Jannings: "For him, suffering is a prism cut into a hundred facets. That's why he's capable of acting in a close-up from 150 feet, and if one were to ask even more of him, he'd manage to show us how an entire film could be made of nothing but his face." Buñuel treated Fleming as a skilled opponent: there's a poetic rightness to the premier avant-garde director of his time attacking the man who would go on to make two of the most popular movies of all time. "Devoid of authentic emotion, Victor Fleming's film is, ultimately, a counterfeit. Although technically excellent, this film shares with many others the distinction of appealing more to our tear glands than to our sensibilities. One could hear the tears falling on the theater floor. Everyone was exposed deep down as a crybaby at the showing of *The Way of All Flesh.*" Edmund Wilson disdainfully referred to the movie's "ballast of American hokum." But Yvonne Blocksom, who saw it at age twelve, fondly recalled not only the film but also its sniffling audience.

Few Hollywood directors worried about their international reputations. What was significant, even at relatively lighthearted Paramount, was their standing within their own company and industry. Fleming was now near the top. Frank Tuttle and Clarence Badger (*It*) held tidier paychecks, but neither had bettered Fleming's critical and box-office record.

Out of the studio, Fleming was sustaining *some* kind of relationship with Alice White—and with Bow, too, who, after a few months, was cooling on Cooper. "Gary was big and strong, but Victor was older and understood me," Bow said. "You know I have always been terribly lonesome. I have no brothers, no sisters, no mother. I need someone to soothe and quiet me. Victor was like that. I mothered Gary, but Victor mothered me."

In case Victor needed some mothering, there was the soft shoulder of Hedda Hopper, not yet a fearsome gossip columnist but a forty-two-year-old actress and divorcée when Fleming squired her to Hollywood events like the premiere of *Seventh Heaven.* When Hopper did become a columnist, in 1938, she championed Fleming in ultra-personal terms, raving about "that great shaggy head of his, with his fine, sensitive features and hands like a surgeon," or "blue eyes, iron grey hair, and bronzed face . . . almost as dashing as Rhett Butler."

Motion Picture magazine completed its 1928–29 series on the "love-lives" of Hollywood women by proclaiming Fleming one of the two "Beau Brummells of Hollywood" (the other was the leading man Ben Lyon) and noting, "Many of the men have commented on their honorable mentions [in the series]. But not Victor Fleming. A real sheik doesn't talk, we take it, unless he is love-making."

How did he keep his balance if he wasn't sounding off? His older daughter, Victoria, said, decades later, "Daddy used to bring his girlfriends around to Mother for her approval." When Victoria said "Mother," she meant *her* mother, Lu, then the wife of the director Arthur Rosson. But years before Vic and Lu changed their relationship from friend and confidante to husband and wife, there was another love bout—and another movie—with Bow.

Hula (1927) is the sort of cheerfully flimsy picture that critics and serious fans disparage, with some cause, for being unworthy of its stars and creators. Reteaming Fleming and Bow, Paramount wanted to recapture the magic of *Mantrap*. In little more than a year, the director and the star, as well as being an on-and-off item in the fan magazines, had acquired enough luster to put a shine on any property—including one about the farmer's daughter. In this case it's a Hawaiian plantation owner's daughter named Hula (Bow) emerging into ripeness when a handsome British engineer, Haldane (Clive Brook), arrives on the scene.

In his unpublished notes on Fleming, Kevin Brownlow rightly puts this movie in the category of silent-star vehicles of the mid-1920s that are comparable to star-oriented network-TV series. But seen fresh, the movie has a flighty charm. Fleming didn't stint on craftsmanship. "We worked down on the Lucky Baldwin place," Hathaway remembered, "now the Los Angeles County Arboretum in Arcadia. Beautiful location. That big old wooden house there and the lake around it, palm trees. We used the Queen Anne cottage [it also appeared in the TV series *Fantasy Island*] for one of those plantation-type wooden houses."

Fleming taught Hathaway that "it's better to have one tree in a cross or back light than a forest in flat light." *Hula* is lush and lively, like *Mantrap*, but with less satiric edge and more florid romance. A *tropical* wilderness movie, *Hula* embraces the Bow image minted in *Mantrap* and cemented in *It* and takes a giant step into the primal. The heroine doesn't grow out of the urban erotic renewal of jazz babies and flappers, though she would appeal to them. Her untamable sexiness represents how any normal red-blooded girl would feel in Hawaii, a state of nature if not yet a state. Hula's dad (Albert Gran) hangs out with boringly dissolute Westerners. One of the harshest laughs of the movie comes when Fleming pans around this gluttonous, inebriated crowd the way he did around the teetotalers in *Mantrap*.

Hula's guiding light proves to be a half-Hawaiian, half-Caucasian cowboy (Agostino Borgato). In its own not-so-naïve way, the movie ridicules the negative concept of "going native." By the end, the uptight Brit gets the message that native is better. Forget the machinations of the rotter who lusts for Hula, the female rotter who lusts for Haldane, and the ultimate villainess, Haldane's wife (Patty DuPont). What's memorable about the film are precisely the scenes that made it disreputable: Hula's opening skinny-dip, where she flicks at a flower with her toes only to have a bee sting her on her thigh (yes, silent-film lip-readers, the legend is true: you can distinctly see her mouth form the words "Oh, fuck!"); her rump-first meet-cute with Haldane in his room, where she's gone to fetch her scruffy dog from under Haldane's bed; her grass-skirt hula (more of a soft-shoe dance than authentic Hawaiian hip wriggling), which she does at a wingding of a luau, instinctively knowing it will drive her loathsome admirer wild and jolt her proper-gentleman hero into action. They all build to the moment when she visits Haldane in the shack he's set up next to his dam site and puts her toothbrush next to his. Never has the urge to "shack up" been so economically expressed.

Fleming's affection for his star—and her sensitivity to it—keep the film light and limber. It's a cinematic love letter written in the eyes and torso of the respondent. The whole thing would collapse if there were anything coy about it, but Fleming doesn't exploit his lover; he leads her toward an irresistible performance. Her boldness is unconstrained. She rides her horse into her dining room; she admits she set off dynamite to bag her man. Her movements have a speedy grace, whether she's showing off her bee-stung thigh or fingering the cleft in Haldane's chin. Brook later said, "For all the acting I did, they might as well have poured me out of a bottle." But Brook is a perfect foil for Bow—if this bit of British sterling melts before her, *no one* has a chance when she puts her mind to it. According to Budd Schulberg, B. P. Schulberg had a fallback plan to ballyhoo White as a "blonde Clara Bow" if *Hula* flopped. But *Hula* was boffo. And White ended up being remembered, in Lew Ayres's phrase, as "a poor man's Clara Bow."

William Kaplan, a Paramount propman, said Bow was just a conquest for Fleming on *Mantrap*, but by the time they made *Hula*, "Vic was fascinated with her. It was a *very* serious thing." (Kaplan thought Fleming was juggling White and Bow during *Mantrap*.) Was Vic looking for Lu Rosson's approval when he dined with the Rossons on June 12, possibly with Bow? In mid-July he helped Bow seal her new Paramount contract: he had her take out the morals clause, as he later did with his own contract at MGM. And on July 24 he took her to a college-themed night at the Montmartre Café, where they joined the "special dance contest" late in the evening and were "noted as graceful dancers on the floor." Shortly afterward, without Bow, he accompanied the director Herbert Brenon on a trip to London, where Brenon was doing exteriors for *Sorrell and Son*. Fleming had no role in the shoot—the cameraman was James Wong Howe—so he might have gone for personal reasons, to test Bow's maturity and loyalty. In his development notes on *Bombshell* five years later, Fleming said of the director-hero's relationship with a Bow-like star named Lola, "He went out of town on location for two weeks, and that ended things between Lola and him. She couldn't stay true to him twenty-four hours."

Upon his return, Fleming and Bow were sighted at the local premiere of the Edward Everett Horton stage vehicle *Going Crooked*, on August 29. But that was it. Fleming wasn't "social" or maybe "showy" enough for Bow, according to her friend and future stepmother, Tui Lorraine. And Bow was too much of a sexual gadabout for Fleming. A few years later, Bow mused that he was "too much older" and "gosh, he was too subtle."

In those *Bombshell* notes, Fleming describes his alter ego, Brogan, as "a big, handsome he-man, who has made most of Lola's successful pictures. He falls for every new girl he works with. His ego is equal to that of a star." When Lola was untrue to him, "he didn't care because he had Alice Young." Alice Young was to Alice White as Lola was to Clara. Fleming didn't cast White in any of his pictures—even Mervyn LeRoy, not the most exacting director, said "she was never much of an actress" and couldn't remember where to move without "an off-camera semaphore system." But Fleming helped her secure the female second lead in Paramount's adaptation of Anita Loos's smash novel *Gentlemen Prefer Blondes* (1928). He and White looked "perfectly devoted," according to the *Los Angeles Times*, at the film's premiere, but White dismissed engagement talk. "And when Alice 'pooh's' you, you certainly stayed poohed," the reporter noted. Lu Rosson held a luncheon party for White at the Montmartre Café in mid-November, but there was still no engagement announcement, and by Christmas the relationship was over. It's hard to tell who poohed whom. White was no more than a dalliance for Fleming, and Fleming a comfort or amusement for her.

When Howard Hawks directed *The Cradle Snatchers* in 1927, he inserted a shot of a business card for "The Club 400" with the name "Victor Flemen [*sic*]" scrawled on it. Fleming was becoming such a hot property for Paramount that this humorous personal reference was more like an industry shout-out. After the back-to-back critical-commercial success of *The Way of All Flesh* and financial sensation of *Hula*, Paramount turned to Fleming with hopes of committing box-office larceny: transferring the mammoth stage take of the 1924 Broadway smash, *Abie's Irish Rose*, to the movie box office. In the twenty-first century, that title may not set off reverberations the way it did in the twentieth, but for decades any proper Jewish boy bringing home a fetching Gentile girl was apt to hear his parents call her Abie's Irish Rose.

The dubious credit for that moniker goes to the playwright Anne Nichols's ghetto-garish hunk of mawkish, stereotypical humor, in which every Jew is materialistic and every Irishman is raring for a fight. Of course, there's a treacly sweetness behind the concept. The differences between the widower-fathers of Abie Levy and Rosemary Murphy dissolve in the sight of their children's happiness and twin grandchildren's beauty. The material would be more persuasive if it didn't make you feel that the human ingredients of the melting pot were atavism, greed, suspicion, and stupidity. But the play struck a thunderous pipe-organ chord on Broadway and across the country. Paramount's Lasky wrote, "Practically every major studio in Hollywood was bidding for *Abie's Irish Rose.* In order to grab the plum for ourselves I finally offered the highest price we had ever put out for a play or book—$500,000 against 50 per cent of the profits." To seal the deal, he succumbed to all of Nichols's demands, including approval over "cast, screen play, wardrobe, advertising."

Only partial prints of the movie exist, but even in abbreviated form it's slow going—the equivalent of the over-elaborate stage-to-screen transcriptions produced in the wake of *The Sound of Music* (1965). Ernst Lubitsch, who had recommended that Warner Bros. buy *The Jazz*

Singer, went to Paramount when Lasky won the bidding war for *Abie's Irish Rose* and was reported to be favored to direct it. It would have been an insane choice—the Lubitsch touch was sophisticated, not gemütlich. But as ever in Hollywood, an expensive, supposedly "presold" product backed at the highest levels of a studio exerted its own magnetism.

The film provided a welcome career jolt for Nancy Carroll. After appearing as Roxie Hart in a Los Angeles production of *Chicago* and being screen-tested all over town, she needed this kind of launch to become one of the true comic sirens of her era in films like the 1930 classic *Laughter.* Handpicked by Nichols after she stomped off the lot, fed up by high-handed treatment, Carroll said she had "one great trouble in that picture: it was difficult for me to cry." Luckily for her—and amusingly for social-cultural historians who major in bias and prejudice—J. Farrell MacDonald, who played her father, "stood just off the set, and talked in a low voice about being heartbroken because his little girl was going to marry a Jewish boy. He looked so exactly like my father would have looked if I had married one that I burst into volumes of tears. I cried so hard that I stained my baby face, and the shot had to be retaken."

Charles "Buddy" Rogers, the co-star of *Wings* and later the third husband of Mary Pickford, took the role of Abie, epitomizing the Hollywood tradition of "write Jewish, cast Gentile," even in an ethnic comedy. ("Do it this way . . . Do it *my* way," Fleming would bark at him.) It makes sense that Carroll and Rogers look relaxed only in France during World War I, when Rosemary sings at a YMCA hut and Abie, impromptu, plays the piano for her. Back in the States, the avalanche of bad comic dialogue proves that you *can* stop the music. *Variety*'s pan of *Abie's Irish Rose* as "two hours and ten minutes of title gags" was one of the most astute critiques the trade paper has run in its long history. It also "outed" its pseudonymous reviewer, "*Rush,*" with the tagline explanation, "(*Rush,* Al Greason, is of the Protestant faith)."

Of course, Protestants have a pivotal symbolic role to play in *Abie's Irish Rose*, too; as soon as Rosemary arrives from California and meets Abie in New York, he turns to a Methodist minister in New Jersey to marry them. It's as if a tolerant Waspishness were the social-cultural ideal toward which all ethnic subcultures must tend. Fleming can't separate the movie's heartiness from its bogusness: there's something inescapably fraudulent about the ease with which Jewish and Catholic chaplains meet on the battlefield and conclude that Jew, Christian, and Muslim all cry out at journey's end for the same God. (The chaplains, of course, turn out to be Levy's rabbi and Murphy's priest.) When cultural benchmarks appear dated, it's tempting to view them as relics from innocent times, but even as a stage piece *Abie's Irish Rose* was widely reviled, and *Variety* was right on top of its shortcomings as a movie:

> The laborious sentimental play upon bigotry, continued reference to the brotherhood of Jew, Celt and the rest of mankind—including the Mohammedan—is wearisome, and seems for the most part to have been pushed in. Under the Constitution, and specifically in the subway rush hours, these things go without saying. There is something also not so very tactful about the elaborate technical exactitude of the Jewish and Roman customs, even to the point of assuring the audience in a program note that a real rabbi and a real priest acted as expert advisors in these details. If these things are right they will speak for themselves to such auditors as are concerned in their correctness.

The Danish-born character actor Jean Hersholt, who plays Solomon Levy, achieves a weary authenticity. (Hersholt became better known for his altruism; Buddy Rogers, his Abie, won the Jean Hersholt Humanitarian Award in 1986.)

Working again with his *Way of All Flesh* screenwriter, Furthman, Fleming did what he could to energize the movie under Nichols's constraints. Apart from a few transitions—such as fading from battling schoolboys to marching troops—and some shots of the Yanks in France that have a *Big Parade*–like heft, Fleming's efforts proved feeble. He may have been weakened by his first reported attack of kidney stones; propman Joseph C. Youngerman said, "I had to hold a glass of water in front of him every half hour." When the movie opened, it was, *Rush* later reported, "an utter flop" as a two-dollar-a-ticket reserved-seat special. It left Lasky stunned: "I can't understand why it didn't do phenomenal business, since the picture was every bit as bad as the play!"—a nice quip, except that a bad play plastered on the screen makes for an even worse movie. By then, shrewder films patterned on the play, like the 1926 George Jessel vehicle, *Private Izzy Murphy*, might have tapped the ethnic-comedy market dry.

Also, another stage epic of Jewish assimilation, *The Jazz Singer*, had opened on October 6, 1927, revolutionizing the medium and revving up audiences with a new ingredient: sound. Eight weeks after its April 19, 1928, premiere, Paramount pulled *Abie's Irish Rose* out of circulation, added sound to a handful of sequences (including Carroll tap-dancing and singing "Rosemary" and "Little Irish Rose"), and shaved fifty minutes off its original 129-minute running time. Recalling the events four decades later, the cinematographer Hal Rosson confused *Abie's Irish Rose* with *The Jazz Singer* when he told Leonard Maltin, "One of the things that we had was a death scene, and the Jewish boy's father was a cantor (I hope I'm not mixing this up) and he sang the Kol Nidre. And when that hymn came from the loudspeaker in the projection room, it was a fantastic moment." Actually, what Rosson shot was Hersholt chanting the mourner's prayer, or Kaddish, for his shiksa-marrying son. Al Jolson sang Kol Nidre for his dying cantor-father in *The Jazz Singer*—which really *was* the Kaddish for silent movies.

By the time *Abie's Irish Rose* made its debut, Paramount had lent Fleming to Samuel Goldwyn for *The Awakening* (1928). Goldwyn designed this tale as the first solo vehicle for Hungary's blond beauty Vilma Banky, who'd previously enjoyed success co-starring with Ronald Colman. She starred as Marie, a pure Alsatian peasant girl who rouses the anger of her countrymen when she falls in love with a German lieutenant (Walter Byron) before the outbreak of World War I. Influenced by the Lillian Gish–Colman hit *The White Sister* (later remade by Fleming with Helen Hayes and Clark Gable), another story with an injured soldier-hero and a heroine who enters a religious order, the movie premiered with a synchronized score, including an Irving Berlin theme song, "Marie." (The song survives not in its original waltz tempo but in the lively Jimmy Dorsey version from the 1930s; the movie has been lost.)

Never content to exploit one star when he could also be nurturing another, Goldwyn brought his French discovery Lili Damita to *The Awakening*'s set. "When I first come [to Hollywood]," Damita told *Motion Picture*, "Mr. Goldwyn think I am lonesome so he bring over to dinner, Victor Fleming . . . Mr. Goldwyn think maybe eef I like someone here I can forget and not want to go back right away to Paris. We have our pictures taken together on the set—we eat dinners. He ees a good man to keep a woman from being lonesome." (Errol Flynn would marry her in 1935.)

Fleming's main sexual playmate at this time was the twenty-year-old Lupe Velez, who'd co-starred with Fairbanks in *The Gaucho* and was making *Lady of the Pavements* for Griffith. "And Victor Fleming!" she told *Motion Picture*. "I like him because he is a devil with womens . . . But I am more than a devil than he is. That is why I never fall in love with him." Of all Fleming's dalliances, Velez may have been the least serious. Velez said of herself generally, "I have flirt with the whole film colony. Why not? I am not serious. What harm is a little flirting? No I do not kiss many mens. But when I kiss them, they stay kissed!"

Fleming was often seen with the author of *The Awakening*'s original story, Frances Marion, the former Hearst reporter who had become a favorite writer for stars like Mary Pickford and Norma Talmadge. Marion's third husband, the cowboy actor Fred Thomson, had died on Christmas Day 1928 (of tetanus after a kidney stone operation). Fleming, a friend for a decade, joined other pals like Hedda Hopper and Marie Dressler in bolstering the spirits of Marion and her two sons. He took her to the wedding of the actors Ruth Roland and Ben Bard in March, and later dressed up as Jack to her Jill for a Marion Davies costume party at Davies's Santa Monica estate.

Frances Marion and her fourth husband, the director George Hill, whom she married in 1930, figured in a story about Fleming and Louis B. Mayer that she made famous in her 1972 memoir, *Off with Their Heads*. The MGM film editors Blanche Sewell and Margaret Booth asked the directors and Marion to meet with a "tall, shy youth" in "a shabby suit" in a studio projection room. It was Walt Disney, who'd come to sell Mayer on the idea of distributing his cartoons. As soon as Fleming saw Disney's Mickey Mouse short, he exclaimed, "It's terrific!" and continued, with his long arms thrashing, "Man, you've got it! Damndest best cartoon I've ever seen! Let's have the other one." It was a Silly Symphony with "a garden in spring . . . a west wind blowing . . . the leaves on the trees stirring . . . then the flowers began dancing together like an exquisite ballet." Hill and Fleming "praised it, though not with the enthusiasm they had lavished on Mickey Mouse."

When Marion managed to drag Mayer into the screening room, the prancing flora disturbed Mayer—and Mickey Mouse turned Mayer's stomach. "Goddamn it! Stop that film! Stop it at once! Are you crazy! Is this your idea of a practical joke? I've a mind to fire all of you!" Fleming snapped, "Keep your shirt on, L.B. What the hell's the matter with you? Got elephant blood, you're scared of a mouse?" Mayer defended himself, saying, "It ain't myself I'm thinking about, it's the poor frightened women in the audience . . . All over this country pregnant women go into our theaters to see our pictures and to rest themselves before their dear little ones are born . . . Every woman is scared of a mouse, admit it. A little tiny mouse, admit it. And here you think they're going to laugh at a mouse on the screen that's ten feet high, admit it. And I'm nobody's fool and not taken in by your poor judgment." He slammed the door on Mickey, Disney, and their new director-fans.

A great story, but is it true? For one thing, Mayer later launched a cartoon series about a cat and mouse, Tom and Jerry. It was Nicholas Schenck in New York, the head of MGM's parent company, Loew's, who nixed a Disney deal with Metro for the Mickey Mouse cartoons. And the way Marion told it, the disastrous meeting with Mayer took place in 1928—a year before Disney went to work on the Silly Symphony shorts. On the other hand, Disney did try to broker a deal with MGM again in 1930, when Fleming was on the move from Paramount and might have been looking for a deal from Mayer himself. Mickey was fresh on Fleming's mind when he filmed his next picture (and last with Douglas Fairbanks), *Around the World in Eighty Minutes*—and included a cameo appearance by Disney's plucky rodent.

Fleming noted of the Fleming-like director in *Bombshell* and the screen personalities he'd created, "If it were not for him they would not be where they are." Fleming knew what made a star—whether it was a tiny animated mouse or a tall drink of water like Gary Cooper.

11

Creating Gary Cooper

On July 14, 1928, Paramount announced that Fleming would direct Paramount's "first all-sound picture" from the hit show *Burlesque*, with Nancy Carroll signed for the role Barbara Stanwyck created on Broadway as the long-suffering mate of a drunken dancer. Fleming left the picture because the studio delayed production, reluctant to cast the stage lead, Hal Skelly. Two months later, Fleming heard Paramount *was* shooting its first all-sound picture, but it wasn't *Burlesque*. The studio had mandated Roy Pomeroy, its despotic special-effects boss, to move Paramount into talkies, and the first film designated to get the Pomeroy treatment was a William Powell vehicle called *Interference*. (The director Lothar Mendes had already done the silent version.)

Fleming told Henry Hathaway, "Come on. Let's go and see what the hell this is, making a sound picture." When a cop at the soundstage door barred their entrance, under orders not to let *anyone* in (it was "guarded like the Bank of England," quipped Hathaway), Fleming marched straight to B. P. Schulberg and asked, "Are you only going to have one director for sound? What the hell is this, Ben? We're all going to have to know about it. This son of a bitch [Pomeroy], he can't direct all the pictures. We've gotta make more, we're all going to have to get into it; it's here to stay. So let's find out about it." (John Cromwell made *Burlesque* in 1929—with Carroll and Skelly—under the title *The Dance of Life*.)

Fleming's next Paramount film at least had singing interludes, but even without them *Wolf Song* (1929) would have been a smash. For the first time since he worked with the Fairbanks team, Fleming molded a fresh male performer for maximum star impact, doing for Gary Cooper what he did for Shearer in *Empty Hands* and Bow in *Mantrap* and Pauline Starke in *The Devil's Cargo*. In *Wolf Song*, Fleming's eye detonates Cooper's sensuality while giving him a nude bathing scene like the one he gave Bow in *Hula.* It helped turn Cooper into the It Boy.

Cooper had blamed Fleming for his breakup with Bow. Asked why he didn't marry her, Cooper said, "Too late," then muttered that she had "a fellow [Fleming] she's flipped for." Lupe Velez, Cooper's co-star, had been the lover of both Fleming and the crooner Russ Columbo, who also appeared in the movie. Of Fleming, she had said, "He's on everybody's love-list!" Cooper was on everybody's love list, too—and Velez fell for her leading man. Cooper admired Fleming as a director. "Coop loved him," said Joel McCrea, a friend of Cooper's and a wily cowboy and comedy star himself. "I know he adored Victor," said Cooper's wife, Rocky. The ever-professional Fleming, without hesitation, turned Coop into a sex object.

Fleming understood Cooper without being much like him. Victorian gentility was a big part of Cooper's background. The son of British transplants to Montana—a lawyer from Birmingham who became a judge, a mother from Kent who yearned for the old country—Cooper had hoped to be an editorial cartoonist, but newspapers didn't accept his work. He stumbled into movies as a stunt rider. In person, he shared Fleming's immediate sensory impact. Like Fleming, he was a womanizer and *not* an exploiter.

Playing a cowboy, he stole *The Winning of Barbara Worth* from its stars, Vilma Banky and Ronald Colman. He did a couple of quickie Westerns, including one for Fleming's pal Arthur Rosson, before Wellman gave him an attention-getting bit in *Wings* as a fatalistic cadet who nibbles a chocolate bar and announces, "Got to go and do a flock of figure eights before chow." He tells the heroes (Richard Arlen and Buddy Rogers), "Luck or no luck, when your time comes you're going to get it," then saunters out of their tent—and crashes. This cameo alone made him a romantic hero. Imposingly lanky, with a long, thin face and features whose impassivity intensified any inkling of thought or emotion, Cooper didn't need a female co-star for women in the audience to go crazy for him. He had a torrid liaison with the camera.

He did, however, need a decent script and an ounce of inspiration. After a half-dozen or so forgettable vehicles, *Wolf Song* gave him both. Under Fleming's direction, Cooper displayed elemental ardor. Soon, he began to base his acting career on stoic power, on holding in more than giving out. Fleming helped him perfect that style, too, in their subsequent film, *The Virginian* (1929). But before an actor can make understatement eloquent, he must learn the power of direct statement. That's what Cooper did as Sam Lash in *Wolf Song*, "the tall silent boy from Kentucky," who heads out for St. Louis instead of marrying a girl back home and raising a family on his father's land. Sam thinks he's not "the marryin' kind." It's 1840 when we meet him picking his way down from the Rockies with two other trappers, Rube Thatcher (Constantine Romanoff) and Gullion (Louis Wolheim). In a flashback, we learn that they met at a St. Louis bar when Thatcher and Gullion got into an eye-gouging, bottle-breaking fight over a girl, and Sam made away with her—which impressed rather than antagonized them. By now they've traveled together for three years. When the two grizzled older guys talk about the pretty gals in Taos as they head into that town, they wonder whether Sam will get in trouble with a woman just like he did in Albuquerque.

Fleming introduces Taos with a turbulent vignette—elders of the Spanish elite interrupting a cockfight when they nab a peasant boy and girl rolling in the hay. Lola Salazar (Velez), the local don's daughter, bites her knuckles in excitement as she looks on from her window. The other trappers decide to "likker up" before they attend the town ball. Instead, Sam goes bathing in a river. The sun glints off the water, and the camera frames him low on his waist to show that he's not wearing anything. His pals warn him that one of these days a girl will get him and drag him down. At the ball, Sam proclaims, "*I want a gal to dance with me.*" Lola, smoldering, volunteers.

Edith Head was almost a decade away from becoming Paramount's chief costume designer. In her posthumously published autobiography, she recalled that Fleming "wanted Lupe to be so sexy that most of the time her bosom would be hanging out. I went to Mr. Fleming and said, 'Don't you think that's a little inconsistent? Women did not uncover their bosoms in those days.' He told me, 'Edith, if no woman had ever shown her bosom in those days, you wouldn't be here.' " And Fleming didn't stop there: his camera comes up so close to Velez's Lola that we see her heart heaving in her chest. (Off-screen, Fleming didn't take Velez so seriously. Tom Mix, the cowboy star who was Velez's current lover, phoned her nightly—perhaps guessing she was changing from "his Mexican spitfire to Coop's little lamb." Velez demanded quiet whenever Mix called her, but Vic would cry out, "Kees Tony for me, Tom!"—referring to Mix's horse. One observer noted, "Lupe never complained.")

Sam wins Lola against her father's wishes, but the film's real contest is waged between their love and the call of the wild. The Western writer Harvey Fergusson's novel drew on frontier New Mexico and the author's own troubled marriage; John Farrow's script follows the book, dramatizing the explosive consequences of a mountain man settling down and exchanging male partners for a wife. The key creative ingredient, though, was Fleming's mastery of ambivalence. Sam leaves Lola to hunt and trap again, but he feels her against him when he tries to sleep on the trail. Fleming deploys slow dissolves and superimpositions to conjure her ghostly presence next to Sam's body.

The guy can't take it; he heads back to his wife, only to be wounded in an Indian ambush. His painful trek to Taos takes on the feeling of a sexual mortification. Whatever Lola wants, Lola gets, but at significant cost. Fleming and his cast are adult enough to mix ecstasy with anguish, and romantic victory with personal defeat; Sam is not the same man at the end, and if he's more open and vulnerable, he's also scarred and weakened. Reviewers damned the picture as an attempt to broaden the base of a routine Western with florid amour. But Fleming's movie is *about* the clash between a trapper's wandering ways and his love life. *Wolf Song* anticipates Peter Fonda's marvelous *The Hired Hand* by forty-two years as it captures confounding erotic fluctuations.

The print of *Wolf Song* at the Library of Congress contains the nude bathing scene, not the musical score and sound effects or the sequences of Columbo, Velez, and Cooper singing—which made Cooper perhaps the first singing cowboy, and definitely the first singing mountain man. But *Wolf Song* was never an all-out sound movie. Fleming had not yet broken into talkies, and he was growing impatient. His blowup at Pomeroy and Schulberg helped persuade the studio to open up the new technology to all directors and crews, and that decision paid off with Fleming's next collaboration with Cooper (and with Hathaway)—a milestone in movie history.

Cecil B. DeMille filmed Owen Wister's 1902 novel, *The Virginian*, in 1914; Tom Forman directed it in 1923, and even Douglas Fairbanks considered it as a starring vehicle, but finally dropped it, apologizing to Wister: "I didn't seem to myself to physically fit it. For more than a year I looked for an actor who filled your ideal and finally gave it up in despair. Suppose I admire the character too much to find anyone to satisfy me." Fleming's version wouldn't even be the first large-scale sound Western: *In Old Arizona* beat it to the screen in January 1929. But in the spring of 1929, Fleming and his producer, Louis Lighton (co-writer of *Wings*), jumped off from the 1902 stage adaptation that Wister wrote with Kirk La Shelle and managed to breathe spontaneity, humor, and unpretentious complexity back into the story. Lighton and Hope Loring had written *The Blind Goddess* for Fleming, but Lighton's service as the producer of *The Virginian* sealed their partnership and friendship.

They spoke the same plain language and shared tastes for similar experiences. Before his eyesight deteriorated, Bud Lighton, a college athlete, trained to be an Army flier. After World War I ended (he never saw action), he wrote for newspapers and did fiction on the side. His aviation stories caught Hollywood's attention. Lighton and Loring collaborated on lucrative screenplays (including Bow's career-defining *It*), but in her lively, bitter memoir, *The Shocking Miss Pilgrim: A Writer in Early Hollywood* (1999), Frederica Sagor Maas, who'd worked on several Bow vehicles, including *The Plastic Age* (1925) and *Hula*, heartily disparaged them. She called Lighton's British-born wife Loring "a manipulator and fast talker" who, in Maas's view, knew that the "tall, handsome" Lighton "looked like a producer," then "got him elevated to play the role." Even if Maas's argument were true, Loring's shrewdness alone couldn't account for Lighton's success as a producer.

The Virginian showed the Lighton-Fleming team's ability to revivify classic stories. Once again, a ranch foreman called only the Virginian must juggle his love for a New England schoolmarm named Molly (Mary Brian), his antagonism with a cattle rustler, Trampas (Walter Huston), and his tangled friendship with his all-too-affable friend Steve (Richard Arlen). The moviemakers rose to the challenge of introducing the Virginian's frontier code to the burgeoning youth culture of the late 1920s. "The film is about the struggle of youth at the threshold of adulthood," writes Richard Hutson, a professor at the University of California, Berkeley, "for the young adults have, in effect, been left to themselves to work out their lives without much interference from a more adult world." Children and babies are a constant presence in this film's Medicine Bow, Wyoming; boys play rustler and enforcer instead of cowboys and Indians. But the main action traces what it means to "play the baby" as a man—and what it means to act, however cruelly, as a grown-up in this frontier culture.

The Virginian never wears its meanings on its denim sleeves. Like *Captains Courageous*, that other Lighton-Fleming adaptation of a beloved novel, *The Virginian* is a piece of "traditional" filmmaking that contains more substance than most of its "revisionist" successors. From the moment the Virginian and his crew appear on-screen, singing as they herd five hundred head of cattle, Fleming makes the audience feel part of a vital, changeable way of life. In a feat that the Coen brothers would duplicate seventy-eight years later in *No Country for Old Men*, there is no background music in the movie. The sound camera takes in Cooper's assured, easy manner on a horse ("Gary Cooper on a horse—that's a scene," said the Western director Anthony Mann) and lets us hear the animals low and the cowboys cluck and croon. In this universe, the competence of the workingman reigns supreme; proficiency and loyalty will be primary virtues.

James Drury, the star of TV's *Virginian* (1962–71), hit on one element of this character's appeal when he said that playing the part "was the most wonderful gift for an actor." *Not* having a past allowed an actor to suggest, trailing behind him, "quotes of glory that you really didn't deserve . . . It gave an aura of mystery to the character that was irreplaceable." In Fleming's movie, it's a *sunny* aura of mystery. As he did in his lost *The Rough Riders*, Fleming harks back to the Teddy Roosevelt–Douglas Fairbanks brand of hero, the cheerful self-created man of action. Fairbanks had realized that he was physically too compact and temperamentally too jumpy to play the soft-spoken, laid-back fellow who embodies Roosevelt's injunction to tread softly and carry a big stick. Under Fleming's guidance, though, Cooper was perfect. And Arlen was ideal as the Virginian's lovable, malleable buddy Steve. Cooper's Virginian falls into a slouch. Arlen's Steve keeps pulling himself into a stretch, as if to rouse himself—the way a man does waking up in bed, only Arlen does it fully clothed and standing up. The two pals share a signature hello-and-goodbye whistle that registers like a quail call. When they first exchange it in the movie, they haven't seen each other for about four years.

Walter Huston's Trampas, a black-clad horse thief with a mustache made for twirling, soon tries to horn in on a three-way flirtation among Steve, the Virginian, and a senorita at a saloon. The Virginian suggests that Trampas back away. Trampas responds, dead seriously, "When I want to know anything from you I'll tell you, you long-legged son of a . . ." The Virginian sallies back, with lethal humor, "If you want to call me that . . . smile!"

Trampas isn't ready for a showdown, but the herding, the birdcall, and the dare reverberate through the film (and through film history). A train whistle signals the near arrival of Molly the schoolteacher, but first cows must be cleared from the tracks. Steve helps her off her car and into town, but when the railroad steam spooks a little girl's cow into a trot, Molly panics; and before Steve can tell her there's nothing to fear from the mild animal, the Virginian lifts Molly out of the street and onto his horse. He exploits his own picturesque heroism, but Molly sees through his deception in a minute. She also knows that he's sounded a mating call.

The Virginian represents the aggressive drive of the West and Molly the force of Eastern civilization. The Virginian has a childish side. He cajoles Steve into helping him mix up the babies waiting to be christened at the community's meet and greet for Molly, then pins the misdeed on Steve. But he does it to get closer to Molly; we hear her chime in to his laughter, off camera, as she begins to succumb to his silliness. Howard Estabrook's screenplay (from an adaptation credited to Grover Jones and Keene Thompson) opens up the stage play with dialogue by Edward Paramore and a snatch or two by Joseph L. Mankiewicz, writing his first lines to be spoken on-screen after a few years writing titles. Mankiewicz, who thought Fleming "a very, *very* attractive man," told his son Tom, "It's amazing: you ask people as a trivia question 'Who directed *Gone With the Wind*?' and nobody knows; you give them a second clue—it's the same guy who directed *The Wizard of Oz*— and they say Mervyn LeRoy. Victor Fleming was either a wonderful director or the luckiest son of a bitch in the world." And Fleming was at an early summit of luck *and* talent in *The Virginian.*

In the scene Mankiewicz took credit for, Molly compels the Virginian to discuss *Romeo and Juliet.* Comically and admirably he says he feels that Romeo should have stridden through the front door and settled things with Juliet's father, man-to-man. That's how the Virginian operates. As a ranch foreman, he has become a man of authority, unlike his friend Steve, who simply wants to keep rambling unattached through life, even if it requires thieving off other men's stock. (Trampas is like Steve's evil twin: he shows up at Molly's party "in the cool of the evenin', when the food and women and liquor is ready.")

Fleming proves as deft with sounds as with images. In a prime piece of foreshadowing, the Virginian catches his friend putting a brand on a ranch's stray calf, and Steve rides off singing, "Bury me not on a lone prairie." (Even "a lone prairie" instead of "*the* lone prairie" feels right and rough and real.) Steve will be buried, but not alone, for he joins Trampas in a large-scale rustling job and the Virginian tracks the gang down. What follows is one of the most wrenching cowboy lynchings ever filmed, because the victims *are* guilty and according to the hero's code deserve this punishment. Steve and two other rustlers *will* face the rope; the only question is whether the Virginian's gang will catch up with Trampas and a couple of other culprits in time to string them all up simultaneously. An unobtrusive pan slowly isolates the Virginian from the lynching party and those about to be hanged. Deliberately ignoring his old friend, Steve gives away his goods and hands his gun to Eugene Pallette's Honey to deliver to the Virginian, first tucking a note inside the holster: "I couldn't have spoke to you without playing the baby." Two whistling quails startle Steve and the Virginian into looking at each other. Then Steve does his quail whistle—and the rope snaps.

It was Steve who made the clean break, by joining up with Trampas. Molly doesn't see things that way until the town matriarch compels her to compare the Virginian's posse with her own pioneer forebears, and Molly realizes that what *should* concern her is how killing Steve affected the Virginian. But the coil of vengeance doesn't stop. While escaping the posse and hiding high on a cliff, Trampas had already nearly murdered Molly's man by shooting him in the back. The day that our hero and Molly ride into Medicine Bow to get married, Trampas declares, "This town isn't big enough for the both of us," and says he'll kill the Virginian if he doesn't leave by sundown. As the critic Robert Warshow wrote,

> What is needed now to set accounts straight is . . . the death of the villain Trampas, the leader of the cattle thieves, who had escaped the posse and abandoned the Virginian's friend to his fate. Again the woman intervenes: why must there be *more* killing? If the hero really loved her, he would leave town, refusing Trampas' challenge. But the Virginian does once more what he "has to do," and in avenging his friend's death wipes out the stain on his own honor.

Warshow goes on to say that no stain can be "truly wiped out" and that the movie "is still a tragedy" because the hero confronts "the ultimate limit of his moral ideas." But the Virginian fills out that limit with grace and honors his code without apology or explanation. In a gesture full of significance, he kills Trampas with Steve's gun. In the movie's final image, the hero and Molly clasp each other as she says, simply, "I love you."

"I was extremely impressed with Fleming as a director," wrote David Lewis. This producer whose credits would range from *Dark Victory* (1939) to *Raintree County* (1957) wrote in his book, *The Creative Producer*, "He was far and away the best I had any contact with. I later visited his set a couple of times. He seemed inarticulate, but knew exactly what he wanted and how to get it. He was a powerful, handsome, overwhelming man. He had a great rapport with Gary Cooper and Richard Arlen. He later was known as a man's director, but he did very well with the women in the cast, too. He was the first really fine, creative director I saw at work." Fleming knew how to help the invaluable Eugene Pallette—with his growly voice and doughy yet doughty presence—look at home in the rugged landscape and get the homey wit out of his declaration to buy a quart of liquor "and get off in a corner and kind of slowly strangle it to death." Mary Brian, spirited and charming underneath too-heavy makeup, said Fleming "was serious when he needed to be, but he had a funny sense of humor. I think the good directors at that time knew that our hours were so long and tedious, that they must give us time to play a little bit."

Walter Huston faced as much pressure as his younger co-stars. The Broadway icon had starred in only one stilted sound feature (*Gentlemen of the Press*) and a handful of shorts when he landed in the Sonora locations of *The Virginian.* "The air was chilly when I was introduced to Gary Cooper and Dick Arlen," he recalled. "They thought I was another bohunk who had come out to show the hicks how it was done." Fleming asked Huston if he could ride a horse. "Now I was in a pretty pickle. I had never ridden even a mule in my life. If I said I couldn't they would laugh at me, and if I said I could and fell off they would laugh much harder." So to "a sprinkling of slightly derisive laughter" he said he hadn't ridden since he was a kid.

"Well," Fleming said, "you've got some riding to do in this picture. Maybe you'd better get your hand in." Huston had an hour to learn his lines for his first scene and to master riding a horse:

> After three or four tries, I managed to get into the saddle, but my perch there was precarious to say the least. Fortunately the

> horse was a gentle beast . . . Striking a nonchalant pose, I said, "Get up, Joe," and walked him across the field, headed for an oak tree. I dismounted there, tied the reins to the tree and sat down to study my lines. I was reading when I heard an eerie sound I had never heard before. It emanated from a rattlesnake. I leapt away, snatched up a rock and bashed the head in.

In his first scene as Trampas, Huston and his horse had to climb to the crest of a hill to give some orders to his gang:

> As they scampered off, I was to break into song, roll a cigarette, and make an exit by riding off downhill. I managed to get to the top of the hill all right, but in my anxiety to give my movement haste, I made the mistake of spurring my mount. He was standing on a rocky ledge and, in rearing, slipped on the hard surface and fell. I stepped off him in time and did not get hurt. During the making of the scene I was not the slightest bit nervous, but after Fleming yelled "Cut!" I realized what I had been through and had difficulty concealing my nervousness. Seeing the rushes, I was surprised to see that during the entire scene I had continued to smoke a cigarette . . . I was Trampas just as sure as if I had been born of his fictional mother. I acted as he would under the circumstances. It is a strange truth—an actor will do things that his own character would never do.

His efficient dismount of the falling horse "gained me admittance to the esoteric circle of stunt men."

Lighton and Fleming "had an almost wordless communication; they were decidedly on the same wavelength," wrote Lewis. Arlen once said that Lighton almost fired Cooper because he was somnolent and disengaged. If so, Lighton never referred to it. In a Yuletide letter to his family back in Arkansas, he labeled a spate of films he'd done in his new position, including *The Virginian*, as "some fairly good pictures, in spite of the newness of it all. The satisfaction of that is a fair recompense for the amount of work. They're not nearly good enough—but they're at least stepping-stones . . . That's enough to ask, I expect—that the work comes out all right."

Another time Arlen said that Velez distracted Cooper when she showed up on location for a few days, especially since she had been one of Fleming's lovers, too. But these anecdotes sound like carryovers of the Virginian and Steve's joshing from the film, or Arlen, Cooper, and Buddy Rogers's carryings-on in the months right after *Wings*, when this trio was so close others dubbed them the Three Musketeers. Cooper's performance has a brilliantly calculated stutter to it. Some of the pauses were even written into the script, and his stalwart sort of stammer meshes beautifully with Arlen's effusiveness, just as it clangs eloquently against the verbal steel of Huston's Trampas.

"The most underrated actor I've ever worked with was Gary Cooper," Henry Hathaway said. He remembered Cooper forgetting his words only once on *The Virginian.* The actor then looked up from under his hat "to see if Fleming was mad at him, and both the look and the hesitancy in his speech came from that one scene." Estabrook agreed that this cautiousness became part of his interpretation of the role: "Cooper was so hesitant, so diffident about his approach to the characterization that it became marked on the screen. He was so perfect, he didn't even realize what he was doing, but he had infinite courage and the ability to carry himself through." Estabrook thought it was ideal that "in this case, his acting was tinged with alarm and apprehension."

Cooper gave pride of place to *The Virginian,* calling it "a sort of exclamation point in my career," in an eight-part as-told-to series that ran in the *Saturday Evening Post* in February and March 1956. "Well, It Was This Way: Gary Cooper Tells His Story" had a summing-up feeling to it, as if Cooper knew the many ailments and operations he'd had were catching up to him. (He'd die five years later, of cancer.) He self-mockingly blamed *The Virginian* for pinning him with his ultra-laconic "yup" and "nope" image. But he also reported it as his moviemaking great adventure:

> It was the first major talkie ever filmed outdoors and well do I remember our awe at the size of our production setup. Before sound came in we only had to wind up the camera and we were in business. Now, moving to our location near Sonora in the High Sierras, we were accompanied by a caravan of trucks, cranes, tractors and enough mobile generators to light up a small town. We had telephone linemen, road builders and track layers. We had radio engineers, sound directors, dialogue directors, voice coaches and sound-effects men. And off to one

side, feeling obsolete, we had some old-fashioned actors and an old-fashioned movie director . . .

The camera was now enclosed within a four-wheeled, soundproofed structure built like a brick smokehouse, so its whirring gears wouldn't disturb the microphone. The microphone itself, a fearsome bucket full of charcoal granules, was suspended from a small crane mounted on a dolly, the whole assembly looking like a steam shovel.

To see the camera and microphone in action, imagine a small ridge down which plank tracks have been laid. Over the ridge I come, driving ahead of me a herd of bawling cows, crowding them as close to the microphone as I can get. As I pass the brick smokehouse and the steam shovel, their drivers start down the track, keeping pace with me. The cows, seeing these weird contraptions, grow a mite nervous and pick up speed. Pretty soon we are really high-tailing it, the smokehouse and the steam shovel careering along beside us. This, of course, only encourages the cows. The smokehouse and the steam shovel, already out of control, need no encouragement. By the time they sail off the end of the track in a cloud of dust, I've got a junior-grade stampede on my hands. The equipment stops, relatively intact, but some of my cows never come back.

Aside from difficulties with our "portable" equipment, we had a battle of another kind. Fleming clung to the old-fashioned notion that he was making a picture with voices. The sound director . . . supported by his army of electronic engineers, was convinced he was making a radio program with faces. There was little fraternizing, and nothing much in the way of a co-operative exchange of ideas. What is more, on their impressive sound stages in Hollywood, surrounded by all their abracadabra and awe-inspiring gear, the sound moguls had been getting by with it. Up here on his own stamping ground, Fleming grew less and less impressed. Trouble brewed.

There came finally the scene in which I caught my old friend Steve, played by Dick Arlen, with a rustled herd of cows. We were to play it in semi-closeup, squatting on the ground, with the camera shooting across Dick's shoulder into my face. My opening line was, "Ah'm sorry, Steve, that ah had to come up with you at a time like this."

We took our places. The steam-shovel operator lowered the boom and nearly scalped both of us with the bucket of charcoal. There was one more formality, because it was no longer enough to hold up a slate in front of the camera on which would be chalked, "*The Virginian,* Take 147." The sound track had to be cued in, too. For this purpose they had invented the slapstick. The boy would hold the slate up in front of the camera, cueing it in, and then he would bring the slapstick down on top of the slate. Clack!

I watched the take boy nervously. He held the slate in front of my nose, brought the stick down with a violent slap, and wham, he blew my lines right out of my head. After three attempts, I thought I was all right, but that was only my opinion. If I got my lines across to the satisfaction of the sound director, Fleming complained that I looked like a schoolboy making his first public recital. If I pleased Fleming, the sound director . . . would claim I came through the microphone like something abandoned by a soap opera. With this heckling I began to disintegrate fast. Finally I couldn't even remember my line, let alone act it out. Fleming and the sound director weren't speaking to each other when that day's work went into the ashcan . . .

That night in our tent, Arlen came up with an idea. "Since I'm turned partly away from the camera in this scene," he said, "I'll write down your line on my chaps. When you look past me toward the camera, your line will be staring you right in the face where you can't forget it."

The next morning, I took a look at the bold print on the inside of Arlen's chaps, and away I went. Fleming applauded. The sound director looked sour.

"He stammered. The line wasn't smooth," he said.

"But didn't you catch the expression on his face?" asked Fleming. "He has discovered his best friend to be a cow thief. Wouldn't you stammer, too?"

"I don't care about the expression on his face. I was listening to the sound track, and it didn't have enough punch . . . All right, fellows, back where you were. We'll take this one over."

"Who's directing this picture?" asked Fleming after a slow recovery. "You or me?"

> "This is sound, and sound—"
>
> Right then and there Fleming made a firm and violent stand, and, after that, movie directors began regaining their authority. They've never suffered serious competition since.

In February 1961, just three months before Cooper's death at age sixty, Hedda Hopper asked him if his favorite Western was *High Noon.* "No," he answered, "I think it's *The Virginian.*" He recalled Vic's old nemesis Pomeroy: "He'd set up a spook joint, no visitors allowed. The sound department wanted to direct; there was quite a hassle when Vic Fleming put his foot down and said, 'You know sound, I don't, but I'm the director and I'm directing.' It was a good decision."

Four years later, Coop's and Vic's old lover Clara Bow, afflicted with schizophrenia and a recluse for three decades, was watching a broadcast of *The Virginian* in the modest Culver City home she shared with a live-in nurse. Ninety-six minutes after Mary Brian told Cooper, "I love you," Bow quietly died. She, too, was just sixty years old.

12

A Woman's Film and a Man's Adventure at Fox

In 1927, six months after the spectacular success of *Mantrap*, Paramount raised Fleming from $1,750 a week to $2,000. But in the immediate wake of the sound revolution, the studio had neglected Fleming and other seasoned pros. His long-term contract expired before he shot *Wolf Song* and *The Virginian.* One Paramount producer who recognized Fleming's worth was David O. Selznick. After those back-to-back hits, the director let Selznick know that Fox had offered him $3,250 weekly and that he wanted to concentrate on "epics, not melodramas." Selznick badly wanted to reteam Fleming with Cooper, Lighton, Paramore, and Keene Thompson to follow up their stellar work on *The Virginian.* Despite Selznick's efforts, Paramount didn't make a counteroffer, and Fleming did make a deal with Fox.

When Cooper talked about Fleming being "old-fashioned" on *The Virginian*, he was being complimentary and, in his clipped way, ironic. Fighting to keep the movie alive visually as well as aurally, Fleming was ahead of his time. In a memo pillorying B. P. Schulberg's Paramount regime, Selznick wrote that Schulberg mistakenly considered Fleming "old-fashioned" and "impossible for talking pictures." (Selznick listed among Schulberg's sins turning down Hawks "as an absurd incompetent" and Wellman as an "incompetent, a has-been and a maniac." Schulberg also fired Jules Furthman and mistreated other Selznick and Fleming friends and collaborators, past and future, including Lewis Milestone, George Cukor, Janet Gaynor, and Constance Bennett.) Selznick soon left Paramount to become West Coast production chief of RKO.

Fleming's long run at Paramount and lucrative two-picture agreement at Fox enabled him to indulge his passions and also to be exceptionally generous to his family. In August 1929, he flew Howard Hawks and the Rossons to the Cleveland Air Races in his new Travel Air, a high-end luxury model with a closed cabin. (They became part of a search for a downed plane on the return trip.) In 1930, he gave his nephew Newell Morris his Cord roadster, though the lad was only fourteen. Then he startled and delighted his niece Yvonne with a Ford roadster. "I was fifteen years old in 1931," she said, "and he thought it was high time that I had a car . . . He just rang the doorbell one day and there he was: 'I got your car here. Come on, let's go.' Of course, I'd never driven. At fifteen, you're not supposed to be driving. He hastily taught me, and I was so glad. He was a wonderful driver."

Thumbing his nose at Schulberg, Fleming brought Furthman and Bennett along with him and made a property as gabby as they come for his first Fox picture, *Common Clay* (1930). This proved to be a commercial trendsetter, creating a new pattern for (as *Variety* put it) "the tragedy of the sweet, trusting young thing who goes wrong." With *Common Clay*, Fleming tuned up another breakthrough vehicle for a female performer, this time Bennett, daughter of Richard Bennett and eldest sister of Joan. Constance had achieved an early vogue in silent pictures, but she took three years off in the mid-1920s to marry a playboy, Philip Morgan Plant, and frolic in Paris and Biarritz. When the Plants' union fell apart, Hollywood beckoned: aside from a marriage into wealth, acting was the only way Constance knew to make money. She was a natural performer, but not yet a star. *Common Clay* would make her one.

In this update of a 1915 play first filmed in 1919, Bennett portrays the heroine, Ellen Neal, as a bright, lowborn gal who gets in over her head with the smart set. In one of Furthman's contemporary twists, she starts the movie as a speakeasy hostess—and persuades the judge (and the audience) after a raid that she really was only a hostess. He convinces her that if she stays at that job, she won't be a hostess very long. So she goes into service at the mansion of the fabulously wealthy Fullertons. There, even the butler paws her over. Hugh Fullerton (played by Lew Ayres), the heir to the family fortune, offers what she thinks is love and protection. But Ellen is a summer fling for Hugh (partly because he doesn't realize the depth of his feelings).

When she becomes pregnant and he doesn't answer her letters, she hires a lawyer. They file suit for improper relations with a minor against Hugh *and* his friend Coakley (Matty Kemp), who's bragged of knowing Ellen intimately from the speakeasy. (He didn't.) Revelations flare up in the courtroom scenes: Ellen's "mother," Mrs. Neal (Beryl Mercer), turns out to be the best friend of her real, dead mother, who threw herself into the Hudson River rather than impede the career of Ellen's VIP father. The rich fellows' attorney, Judge Filson (Hale Hamilton), realizes that he's Ellen's long-lost dad. Ellen decides that the proudest thing to do would be to drop the case and bring up baby alone. Suddenly Filson and the Fullertons want to make things right. But Ellen won't be won over until Hugh, repentant and besotted, swears that she is all he wants from life. Fleming's picture has the sharp trajectory of a feminist crusade. *Variety* was on the money when *Rush* wrote that the "original play had the 'ruined' girl rather abject about it all. Now she has been made an utterly defiant heroine."

Fox put *Common Clay* on its slate before the Motion Picture Producers and Distributors of America adopted the morality-policing Production Code in 1930 and four years before the code developed teeth. In January 1930, Fleming told the code's Colonel Jason S. Joy that he was willing to develop two awful alternate story lines. One would have hinged on the young couple's comedy-stunt marriage in a New York nightclub, the other on a Tijuana marriage that Hugh's father refuses to recognize because there is no official record of it. Happily, Fleming pursued neither.

The code administration tried to make filmmakers dilute their work at the script stage by specifying material that state and city censorship boards would cut from the finished movie, but the theatrical pedigree of *Common Clay* must have protected it. Despite voluminous suggested emendations and a smattering of changes in the dialogue, Fleming followed Furthman's script almost to the letter. The most revolutionary act in the making of *Common Clay* was filming it in sequence, a practice as unusual then as it is now. It had worked for Fleming in *The Way of All Flesh*, and it worked for him in *Common Clay*. The movie gets talkier and more static as it goes along, but the forward motion of the speakeasy raid at the beginning propels a viewer into the cozy seductions and stagy courtroom histrionics. With Fleming, as with Wellman, the director's urge to get on with things often made his material bristle. *Common Clay* half-bristles, half-creaks, and Bennett pulls you through.

Throughout Fleming's career, and even throughout individual productions, he zeroed in on some actors and left others alone; mostly, he knew what he was doing. Sixty years later, Lew Ayres said he felt Fleming wouldn't have cast him as Hugh if he'd had his choice of leading men. "He had been handed me and it was my first assignment after

All Quiet on the Western Front, and for some reason, he was a very different type than I . . . Very macho, I guess you'd say. Very positive." Ayres was unable to characterize Fleming's directing beyond "some of his ideas were good." Yet the completed picture proves that Fleming knew exactly where to draw the line between Hugh's upper-crust charm and ingratiation. Like many directors of his generation, he used manipulation to tame his ensembles. Hugh *needs* to be borderline effete for the melodrama to work and for Ellen to emerge victorious; it was good for Ayres to feel half the man that Vic was.

The director had to recognize that the critical performance was going to be Bennett's. And she was on target. She plays a paradigm of tarnished virtue without ever becoming a nagging pain. She uses her blond sparkle and her mischievous, longing eyes to create a woman who doesn't know her own sexual strength. When she gives in to amorous weakness, her husky voice becomes a bruised whisper. The courtroom scenes hand showstopping numbers to Mercer as her "mother" and Tully Marshall as her grandstanding lawyer, but it's Bennett who holds the show together and mints the newly refined image of a reformed, unflappable flapper.

Selznick cited this movie to cap his indictment of Schulberg for misusing Fleming: Schulberg had doubted the director who turned *Common Clay* into one of the most successful talkies to date. "Constance Bennett had that audience at Loew's State Theater so much with her in *Common Clay* yesterday that if she had walked into the theater she probably would have been mobbed," wrote Louella Parsons. "I have never seen more tears shed in one afternoon over a heroine's plight." (Parsons, by now an established Hollywood character, reveled in superlatives.)

Fleming's next Fox film, *Renegades* (also 1930), is a French Foreign Legion adventure starring Warner Baxter as the head of four ne'er-do-wells who are considered morally unreliable even among the other legionnaires in North Africa. Myrna Loy plays the Mata Hari–like spy who sends Baxter, a former French army officer, into disgrace, and Bela Lugosi, in his juiciest pre-*Dracula* role, plays the Arab leader whom Baxter and then Loy think they can turn into a continent-dominating dictator. Peopled with nihilistic, greedy, and unstable antiheroes, *Renegades* flirts with being prophetic and terrific, but doesn't make good on its promise.

Dated colonial-adventure attitudes and conventions limit and taint it. Baxter takes Loy to the Arabs' camp to punish her, only to see her become the chieftain's mistress—which marks her, in Baxter's *and* the movie's terms, as the lowest sort of fallen woman. The antiheroic legionnaires' redemption comes when they give in to their conventional guilty consciences: faced with their former barracks mates, they reflexively renew their loyalty to the West and turn their guns on their Arab collaborators. Reviewers drubbed the picture. They were probably responding not to the vigorous, clear action but to the confusions at the movie's core.

Nevertheless, *Renegades* has an arid visual grandeur—Fleming scouted the Mojave Desert locations in his own plane—and patches of scruffy vitality and humor. One shot of the four men crawling into a fort with their butts in the air boasts the same tense visual humor as the Cowardly Lion, Tin Man, Scarecrow, and Toto sneaking into the witch's castle in *The Wizard of Oz.* The square-cut, angry Baxter and the slinky, teasing Loy sustain a crackling tension. Their dual erotic death foreshadows Jennifer Jones and Gregory Peck's in Selznick and King Vidor's *Duel in the Sun.* Loy called *Renegades* "a happy film": Baxter had skill and charm, and Fleming was "a man's man and master of his craft." Before *Renegades,* Loy had been cast as "Burmese, Chinese, a South Seas islander, a couple of Mexicans, and . . . a Creole." Even though she was playing a vamp again, *Renegades* pushed her into the mainstream.

Some of the fun took place off camera. Loy remembered:

> I was supposed to operate a machine gun. One day on the set a man was explaining the apparatus to me, so simple it seemed a child could work it, and he told me to look through the sights and move the gun, to get the feel of it, I supposed. Victor Fleming, the director, happened to be standing near and almost directly in front of me. I sighted the gun and in moving it must have pressed the wrong thing, for it started shooting. There were blanks in it, of course, but the way both Mr. Fleming and I jumped one would have thought it really loaded with bullets. He jokingly intimated that there were probably several actors who would like to have been in my position with a loaded machine gun.

Lugosi imbues the warlord with a self-regarding ripeness that deflates Baxter's vengeful fury and Loy's canny, manipulative sexuality. The screenplay (by Furthman) hands Lugosi a refrain—"What do you think?"—that becomes funnier with every repetition. It's always used after the Arab muses on some outrageous atrocity, such as "I'm going to crucify every dog of a Christian if taken alive, or maybe I just burn them in slow fire. What do you think?" The script required Lugosi's chieftain to read the riot act to his native troops for losing ground, and the director wanted it done in a language not readily understandable to Americans. Lugosi's torrent of exotic verbiage echoed through the desert and delighted Fleming—until, at a preview in New York, a large segment of the audience started howling with laughter. It was the star's Hungarian-born fan base. When Fleming collared the theater operator for an explanation, the manager, who was also Hungarian, explained that Lugosi had been spouting in Magyar. A loose translation would run, "The hell with you sons-of-bitches. You are the lowest shits I've ever had anything to do with. You're a lousy bunch of beggars. You are lower than the asshole of a drunken frog on a rainy day." Fleming dubbed the imprecations into Arabic.

The year at Fox helped Fleming consolidate his mastery of the latest sound technology. If he saw his family infrequently, he was still a bountiful figure in their lives. After his niece Yvonne spent two years at UCLA, he paid for her to finish up at UC-Berkeley, then—thinking back to his Signal Corps days—he suggested, "Why don't you go to Columbia? I think that you'd learn more there." She didn't want to go to a big city far away, and she did want to be part of Berkeley's vaunted history department. "It was to be one year, but I had such a good time and was doing so well, I approached him again, and said I'd like to go back." He said, "I was just going to buy a twin-engine plane, but I'll buy a single-engine plane so you can go back to Berkeley." She demurred; he insisted. "Well, I'll do it," he said, "and you just consider it my sacrifice." Yvonne remembered, "That's the way he talked. He was very generous, and very fond of Mother. I know she was his favorite." In 1933, his cousin Clyde Hartman lost his painting business and became the Hartman family handyman, among his other odd jobs. Fleming reacted the way the rest of the family did, hiring Clyde for repair and construction work at his ranch.

Clyde's son Edward, born in 1924, got privileged glimpses into Fleming's life at Meadowlark Ranch. "I would either wash the walls, sand, or do prep work. Vic would do ranch work or meet with Mr. Frost, the caretaker. Mrs. Frost would do the cooking for us. We had a lot of canned tamales. I think Vic bought them by the carload." Fleming hadn't lost his appetite for speed and his scorn for traffic cops. In his Pierce-Arrow, he'd drive to Encinitas down the Pacific Coast Highway—as Edward recalls, "A three-lane highway then, with a center lane for passing. When he'd hit it, he would barrel down the middle lane at something like sixty miles per hour before he turned onto a rural road that led to the ranch. Any time I was with him, the police never stopped him, but several times I remember he laughed because the police car was so far behind the officer didn't see he had turned off. At times, it was scary. We never had much in the way of conversation, but he seemed to like the company."

He was tight about money outside family circles. Blocksom once went "riding with him in his car down Wilshire Boulevard, and there was a new building, an auto dealership that was going up on the left side of the road, this beautiful building, this gorgeous auto dealership, and I said, 'Gee, that's good-looking,' something like that, and he said, 'I own that,' and I said, 'Oh, how wonderful,' and he looked at me and said, 'I want to tell you something right now. Don't ever make a million dollars. Because you'll never know who your friends are.' " (When Fleming said "I own that," he meant he leased the lot; from Dodges to Nashes to Buicks, it was always a site for auto dealers, and is now Beverly Hills Porsche/Audi.)

No longer was he popping up in all the fan magazines as the favored beau of this or that starlet, but Bow had made him a focus for suspicions of romantic scandal. In 1932, for example, the *Los Angeles Examiner* investigated his supposed secret marriage in Mexicali to a nightclub dancer named Joan Blair. Blair's mother said it was "all a joke, started by someone trying to kid the girl." The newspaper checked it out nonetheless before shelving the item.

Bow would later say of Vic, "Of all the men I've known, there was a *man*." In 1929, though, she got engaged to the singer Harry Richman, who'd had a hit singing Irving Berlin's "Puttin' On the Ritz," which eventually contained an encomium for another Bow lover, Gary Cooper ("Dressed up like a million-dollar trouper / Trying hard to look like Gary Cooper / Super duper"). The actress-turned-writer Patsy Ruth Miller, in her unpublished memoir, said, "I only met Clara Bow once, but that time was memorable. It was at the wedding reception, when I got married to Tay Garnett." Garnett was about to direct the singer in a picture, and Miller "was curious to meet Harry Richman, whom I had seen in New York; he had a certain crude charm, twirling his top hat, prancing across the stage, and bellowing out the latest jazz." It would have been impolite not to invite Bow, Richman's betrothed. At the event, held in the backyard of her Beverly Hills home, Miller thought everyone could find a chair without place cards. The problem was that Bow plunked herself down in the bride's seat of honor. Thinking quickly, Miller asked the studio trio she and Garnett had hired to stop playing Strauss waltzes. "They set to with gusto playing, if I remember correctly, Charleston, Charleston, da, da, de, da . . . It worked. Miss Bow began swaying in her seat, then, unable to resist the lure of the music, she rose and grabbed Harry Richman, and started doing the Charleston. Quick as a flash, I was in the chair at the head of my table."

Miller, who became close friends with Fleming when she married her *next* husband, John Lee Mahin, said Vic "had what might be called an old-fashioned sense of chivalry, of courtesy toward women. He had sort of a protective attitude toward women which some modern girls might object to, but which I found very appealing. I never heard Victor say anything disparaging about a woman, even about Clara Bow . . . If asked about her [he] only said, 'She's a nice kid. A bit flighty, perhaps. But a sweet kid.' "

Bow sometimes blamed Cooper for her breakup with Fleming, just as Cooper blamed Fleming for his breakup with Bow. Another cowboy star, Rex Bell, would eventually stabilize her love life, but not even Bell could get her to settle down at this time. He was romancing the It Girl in California while newspapers were exploding with headlines about Bow's 1930 trip to Dallas to see another long-term lover, a married Dallas urologist, Dr. William Earl Pearson. When the scandal was cresting in July, Fleming spotted Bell in the Fox commissary. "Hey, Rex!" he reportedly whooped. "How's our girl?"

Meanwhile, Fleming was spending more time with Arthur and Lu Rosson. Especially Lu. The middle child of a German saloon keeper who had two other daughters and kept taverns first in Brooklyn, then on Manhattan's Upper West Side, she was born Louise Irana Niedermeyer (on March 22, 1895), later changing her first name to Lucile. When her dad died at age thirty-five of a burst appendix (in 1906), the family's fortunes plunged. "They were *very* poor," Sally Fleming says she was told. "And my grandmother insisted that they live on the top floor of a tenement on Ninety-third Street, near the Jacob Ruppert Brewery. She would send those three girls, in complete misery and embarrassment, to collect horse droppings to use for growing vegetables in a garden she kept on the roof." Lu's mother, Emily Niedermeyer, was a talented cook (a gift she passed down to Lu). She took in boarders and served them "fantastic dishes." She made the three girls' clothes and raised them "in a strict Germanic fashion. You know, if they touched the silverware before dinner, they were sent away from the table. They didn't have a lot of money, but they maintained their dignity."

The clock tower of Ehret's Hell Gate Brewery, topped with crossed beer barrels, loomed over the neighborhood. Lu's family lived at 181 East Ninety-third Street; also struggling next door, in a three-room apartment at 179, were the Alsatian tailor Sam "Frenchie" Marx and his ambitious wife, Minnie, who nursed showbiz aspirations for their five sons, Leonard, Adolph, Julius, Milton, and Herbert. Thanks in part to their mother's drive, the sons, renamed Chico, Harpo, Groucho, Gummo, and Zeppo after their move to Chicago in 1910, would succeed in vaudeville, Broadway shows, movies, radio, and television. Harpo described the block as "a small Jewish neighborhood squeezed in between the Irish to the north and the Germans to the south in Yorkville." The side of it the Marxes (and the Niedermeyers) lived on was indeed, Harpo wrote, "the tenement side," cruelly facing a string of "one-family brownstone townhouses." (The block now borders the Carnegie Hill neighborhood made famous in numerous Woody Allen movies.)

"I'd like to be able to say that my mother knew the Marx Brothers growing up," says Sally. "But she never spoke about them, and I don't think she did. Her mother, from the stories I heard, was very reclusive." Just to the south of them, Yorkville-bred Bert Lahr (born Irving Lahrheim, the son of a Prussian upholsterer) was reading penny dreadfuls and dreaming of the theater. Just to the north, that future Irish-American icon, James Cagney, was teaching himself how to hoof and also how to speak Yiddish. But Lu's mother kept to herself (she didn't know Plattdeutsch, the German dialect spoken by the Marxes *en famille*, or Yiddish, which increased her isolation). And her family had no propensity for showbiz. Lu's older sister, Georgiana, went to work for the phone company at age seventeen. Lu left school in the seventh grade and by age fifteen had a job in an advertising agency as an office assistant.

Arthur Rosson, nine years older than Lu, was a movie-struck stock-exchange clerk. Within two years he was *in* movies at the Vitagraph studio in Brooklyn, working as a stuntman and sometime actor. Arthur and Lu got married on June 2, 1912, when Lu was three months pregnant. "Lu's theory was, if you want to get married, get pregnant," said Blocksom. In December, Lu gave birth to their daughter in Hoboken, New Jersey, and named her Helene, after Arthur's mother. Then they started for California. By the time Fleming got to be their neighbor, in 1926, Arthur had won a reputation as a versatile director, able to shift from melodramas to frothy comedies; his brothers had solidly established themselves, too, Richard as an actor turned director and Hal as a stuntman turned cinematographer. Hal would shoot many movies for Vic, including *Abie's Irish Rose;* Richard would get a co-director credit on Hawks's *Scarface* and also contributed to Fleming's *Joan of Arc;* Arthur got a co-director credit on Hawks's *Red River.*

Lu couldn't have guessed that she was marrying into a moviemaking dynasty. The patriarch, Arthur Rosson Sr., was a British jockey turned coachman who married a Frenchwoman (Helene's maiden name was Rochefort). He had worked for the banking titan J. Pierpont Morgan, and he curbed any family rowdiness with the threat of his riding crop. Maybe it was the zest and esprit of the family that made Arthur and his two brothers and three sisters quit jobs as clerks or office boys or stenographers and work in or around movies, first at Vitagraph in Brooklyn and then in California. Gladys, Art's middle sister, was the only one who became an executive. The rest started out as stuntmen and/or actors; the men became directors, the other Rosson siblings, Ethel and Helene, homemakers after brief stints as silent-film actresses. But Gladys signed up as DeMille's secretary in 1914, rose to the position of secretary-treasurer of his production company, and stayed with him until she died in 1953. She was also DeMille's beloved "head mistress" of a three-woman platoon filled out by the screenwriter Jeanie MacPherson and the actress Julia Faye.

Fleming had known Arthur and Lu since before World War I. Fleming's early moviemaking pals Allan Dwan and Wallace Reid directed and wrote a 1913 film that gave Arthur his first acting job in California and also featured Marshall Neilan in a bit part. Rosson started out as a Western director and retained a gritty reputation for knowing how to handle everything from canyon rock slides to cantankerous horses. Around the time Fleming moved to Beverly Hills, Rosson gave him a pistol that was supposed to have belonged to Pancho Villa. All the Rosson men were known as hale, inventive filmmakers.

If there was one big difference between Fleming and the Rossons, it was how they turned filmmaking into a family affair. Fleming rarely tried to involve any family members in the movie business. The closest he came, in the late 1930s, was getting Yvonne Blocksom a research job at MGM, where her Berkeley history degree came in handy. (Her specialty was "old English and European stuff.") Even so, she said, "I was on many of the sets, but I never tried to get on any of Uncle Vic's sets when he was working. I felt it would be an imposition. I tried to keep out of his personal life, and I was grateful for his making the contact at the studio so I could get my job there." It was merely an innocent, affectionate stunt when Arthur and Lu's seven-and-a-half-month-old daughter, Helene, became the "star" of a 1913 Allan Dwan half reeler, *Our Little Fairy*. Dwan's camera followed her as she woke from a nap, took her bath, breakfasted, shredded flowers in the garden, got into a jam jar and a mud puddle, and imitated the grown nude's pose in *September Morn*. It's doubtful Fleming would have approved of the intrusion.

Lu, however, was a Rosson only by marriage. She was not a theatrical type—she was not even movie-star pretty. She was a good housekeeper and hostess and, in a way, sexy. "She was famous for her tennis legs," says her daughter Victoria. Both daughters say the first bond between Vic and Lu was culinary. "He used to go to their house because my mother was a fabulous cook," says Sally. Fleming and the Rossons sailed and dined and danced in the same social circles. Mary Astor wrote that she drove to Santa Barbara after work, one day in 1927, "to spend Saturday evening and Sunday with Vic Fleming and Art and Lou [*sic*] Rosson and Howard Hawks and Athole Shearer, and went out in Howard's Chris-Craft." Fleming's friendship with Lu grew more intimate over time, but it didn't heat up for a couple of years.

Meanwhile, Fleming reestablished his friendship with Douglas Fairbanks, who was then at a crossroads of his own. He'd made an exciting, moving swan song to swashbuckling—and to silent moviemaking—in his *Three Musketeers* sequel, *The Iron Mask* (1929). After that, his first two sound pictures—a production of *The Taming of the Shrew* co-starring Pickford (also 1929) and a big-business musical comedy, *Reaching for the Moon* (1931), with all but one of Irving Berlin's songs cut out—misfired and let down Fairbanks and what was left of his public. The making of *Shrew* had magnified his temperamental differences with Pickford—his carefree manner and practical jokes enraged rather than reassured her. He was getting antsy at his and Mary's mansion, Pickfair, and he needed a recharge or an escape.

Fleming, more of a globe-trotter by now, may have been the one to propose a round-the-world jaunt. And it was Fleming who probably devised an itinerary that included big-game hunting. The two men bought an elephant gun and tested it at Meadowlark Ranch. Even braced against a eucalyptus log, Fairbanks, the smaller man, couldn't handle the gun's recoil. It lifted him off the ground and sent the log flying several feet in back of them, to Fairbanks's chagrin and Fleming's covert amusement. (Edward Hartman, who witnessed this with Rodger Swearingen, merrily adds, "Rodger and I ran behind the barn after that, because in those days that's what little kids did when you heard a grown-up cursing!")

Doug and Fleming then invited the cameraman Henry Sharp and Chuck Lewis, Doug's right-hand man, to join them in turning their trip into a deliberately minor movie, *Around the World in Eighty Minutes.* It was good timing for Fleming. Negotiations for a new directing slot at Columbia had run aground, along with a proposed remake of Fairbanks's silent Western *Arizona.* The notoriously unreliable Howard Hawks said Fleming got $100,000 for signing with Columbia's studio chief, Harry Cohn, because he told Cohn he could bring in stars. Fleming then recommended that Cohn hire Hawks—and as usual in a Hawks story, no good Fleming deed goes unpunished. In Hawks's version of reality, Cohn tells him, "I want you to make pictures for me. You make good ones, and you can get the stars. And I think the director's the important thing." Hawks replies, "OK, Fleming stuck you, but I'm just going to ask you for just what I got on the last picture because I like the way you think."

Did Hawks turn Cohn against Fleming with that statement? Probably not—Hawks might have made up the whole thing, except for Fleming recommending him. When Columbia announced Fleming for *Arizona*, it was slated to start in three weeks with Jack Holt in the lead; maybe Cohn needed a director like Fleming, known for swiftness and proficiency, but Fleming lost interest.

With *Arizona* on the rocks, *Around the World in Eighty Minutes* was a good excuse for Vic to travel and to see if he could make an early sound film with the same seat-of-the-pants ease as an early silent. It would be a proto-mockumentary, with Fairbanks and Fleming playing themselves. Fairbanks's roughly $118,000 budget didn't earmark any payment to Fleming as director or himself as producer-star. Of course, the existence of any budget at all showed that it was never intended simply to be a home movie. Fairbanks's sidekick Chuck Lewis said that Fleming tried to map out a scenario and Fairbanks always found reasons to balk at his efforts. Fairbanks knew that circling the globe in modern conveyances wouldn't yield the adventures that greeted the heroes of Jules Verne's *Around the World in Eighty Days.* He soon learned that his own presence engendered most of the trip's excitement. A policeman who chased them down after a riot in a Chinese opium den was simply a fan of Doug's hoping to snag an autograph. The king of Siam assigned Vic and Doug a courtesan each; Vic advised Doug that the best way to save face was to accept the gift. "Just give her your autograph," he added, as Doug turned in.

None of this made it into the movie. But it probably helped push Fleming and the commentary writer, Robert E. Sherwood, into a frolicsome series of riffs on Fairbanks's own stardom and his action-oriented filmmaking. (Sherwood was an Algonquin wit and film critic as well as a movie writer since 1926 and a playwright since 1927's *Road to Rome.* He was also a longtime supporter of Fairbanks.) It's fitting that Fairbanks walks into the film by stepping out of a title-credit picture of himself. *Around the World in Eighty Minutes* deconstructs itself as it goes along, mixing star-in-the-street stuff with bald sleight of hand. Fairbanks introduces his audience to his small crew and to the real movie magic of lightweight sound and photo equipment, but he also gleefully exploits the magical fakery of the movies. He asks for a pointer, and a golf club enters his hand. He aims the club at a spot on a slide-projected map (a map heavily oriented toward Asia) and winds up on a ship, where he demonstrates how to keep fit in close quarters.

Movie stuff and real life intersect everywhere in this film. The costar of Vic's *Lord Jim* and *Adventure*, the Olympic athlete Duke Kahanamoku, greets them in Hawaii and takes them surfing. The actors Sessue Hayakawa and Sojin (the Mongol prince from Fairbanks's *Thief of Bagdad*) meet them in Japan. Sherwood's script becomes a running parody of the era's travel and real-adventure films. "Every travelogue has got to mention these things. Here they are: the contrast between the old and new Japan: rickshaws—elevated trains." And that's what we see. Unfortunately, there's nothing inherently parodic about most of the footage, either in style or in content. (The reason the pasted-on commentary clicks in a goof like Woody Allen's 1966 *What's*

Up, Tiger Lily? is that it brings out the essential silliness of the material.) Fairbanks and Fleming set themselves up on-screen as dueling pals, with Fleming as "the menace," goading golf-crazy Doug to get to the job at hand—making a movie. But the movie's tone flutters from earnest to comic to ingratiating. Bessie Love recalled, "When Doug went abroad he got red carpet treatment. Vic would go look at the country. He was very upset by India. They would just prop up corpses in the street by the walls—for identification."

Fleming's most relaxed moment comes when he corners Doug in a sunken Japanese bath. Robed from calf to shoulder, Fleming cuts almost as saturnine a figure as Richard Nixon walking in dress shoes on a beach. But there's a twinkle underneath his long-suffering pose. Doug prods him to peek at the early-morning mores and manners of their hostesses. Fleming wittily labels it "window shopping." Next we see a dapper Fleming advancing to a young woman's doorway in the manner of "a second-story man." He has an endearing, formal self-consciousness—there's a touch of self-burlesque to his voyeurism, possibly from being uncomfortable in front of the camera. Fleming doesn't photograph as the dynamo he was in real life, but he and Doug share an understated, manly rapport: the star's joviality seems less strident when he shares the frame with his old pal Fleming.

The movie captures a time when an American star could say "the world is essentially funny"—not *life*, but *the world*—and Americans, at least, could laugh along with him. The movie is innocent about the world, but savvy about the increasingly central role of movies (and the legerdemain of moviemaking). The picture gets more antic as it nears the finish line. In the most thrilling sequence, in India, Doug and Vic mount elephants and join a leopard hunt. Doug kills one, and Vic wounds another that must be tracked down and destroyed in a nearby village. So far, so real. But when Fairbanks goes on the attack against a tiger who has dragged human prey from another village into the jungle, the sequence becomes a parody of Hollywood films that try to intercut stars on a soundstage with wild animals shot by second units on location. The fur flies behind bushes as it does when the Cowardly Lion beats up on the Winkies in *The Wizard of Oz.* The payoff comes when the action fades to Doug grappling half-asleep with a tiger-skin rug. He tells Vic, "I had the most terrible nightmare—I dreamt I was in *Trader Horn*!"

While Fairbanks and company visit Siam, they watch a performance of a classical Siamese dance troupe; Fairbanks says that the rhythm beneath the exotic moves and music is the same as the fox-trot, then tries to demonstrate that notion by twirling a Siamese gal around a ballroom. Out of nowhere, he announces, "Now, here's Hollywood's most famous star dancing to Siamese music. C'mon, Mickey!" The film turns into a cartoon, and Mickey Mouse prances out from a doorway on the right side of the screen. Against a temple backdrop, the mouse pulls off a mix of traditional Oriental choreography and American folk dancing. His hands try to pull off elegant courtly gestures, but his feet can't help tapping or clogging. He slants his eyes for a second or two, in a mixture of frustration and homage—no slur intended, all in good fun—then does a series of keep-on-truckin' clogs that would make R. Crumb proud.

It's a genuine novelty: the rarest Mickey Mouse cartoon. How it ended up in *Around the World in Eighty Minutes* remains anybody's guess. United Artists (of course) released the movie, and UA had agreed to distribute Disney's cartoons after the animator had fulfilled his still-running contract with Columbia. But no Disney cartoon received an official UA release until the summer of 1932; *Around the World* opened in December 1931. And Disney kept no record of any contract or correspondence between him and Fairbanks. Disney must have known that Fairbanks and Fleming were big fans of his. By then Doug had told the press that only Mickey Mouse fully exploited the capacity of the sound film: "These cartoons get their tremendous appeal from the perfect rhythm, in comedy tempo, of the little characters and of the accompanying sound. It is not merely synchronization; it is more than that; it is a rhythmic, swinging, lilting thing, with what musicians call the proper accent-structure." So Disney might have simply done Doug a favor and cooked up that Mickey cameo for a renowned, vocal supporter.

Around the World in Eighty Minutes was just a lark for Fleming—as a movie, its prankishness is its saving grace. More important, it once again solidified his friendship with Fairbanks. The star was the one who reached out to *him.* Not only was Fairbanks at loose ends professionally, but stress lines were showing in his marriage. In the movie, Doug starts to make time with a pretty Japanese girl, and Vic warns, "I'll tell Mary on you, young fella," an in-joke twice over, because Fleming was six years younger. When the Asian voyage ended, Fairbanks sailed for New York with Lewis, but Fleming, this time with some color film, headed to Africa for a Kenyan safari. In *Action*, he recalled that he once "let a wounded rhino get within twenty feet before I fired. Her own momentum carried her forward and she went down at my feet. She was actually protecting her calf and her courage was magnificent. I hated to pull the trigger."

According to Anthony Quinn, when Fleming returned, he had a fling with Katherine DeMille, Cecil B.'s adopted daughter. It went unreported until Quinn wrote his as-told-to autobiography, *One Man Tango*, in 1995. Quinn had met Katherine at Paramount in 1936 and married her the following year; when he discovered that at age twenty-six she was not a virgin, he wouldn't be satisfied with her as his bride until she made a clean sweep of a confession. In a fit of macho hysteria, Quinn feverishly thought:

> Shit, she had been with Clark Gable? How could I compete with someone like Gable? Or the director Victor Fleming, another of my predecessors? In my lunatic paranoia, I imagined Gable and Fleming on the set of *Gone With the Wind*, comparing notes on Katherine, and laughing at me. Oh, how I hated that movie! I would not see it for more than forty years, until I had beaten back the ghosts, but even then it was a torture . . . When she told me Fleming had taken her to a ski lodge in Aspen, and asked that she lie around naked with him when they were not on the slopes, I wanted to kill the bastard.

Lu Fleming's great-granddaughter Kate Harper, a relation to the DeMilles through her mother's marriage, knew Katherine well in her later years and thought her "a gracious and dignified woman" who "deserved far better than Quinn's Mexican machismo." Quinn is the sole source for the fling with Katherine, but Fleming *was* operating at high energy in every way throughout the early 1930s. He hatched a new travel plan and travelogue with Fairbanks when the friends reunited at the Hotel Del Mar in San Diego. The round-the-world trip had inspired Fleming to propose a bolder, less jokey documentary, centering on a pontoon plane tour of South America, down the Amazon. As if talking about our era's reality-TV craze, Fairbanks touted "*natural adventure*" and boosted the notion that "*the new fiction is fact.*" But the trip and the movie never happened—it was probably too risky for Fairbanks—and its demise cooled the friendship. Edward Hartman says his father grumbled that Fairbanks lacked Fleming's relish for hard labor: when the friends went to work on Fleming's boat in Newport, "Vic got down on the deck and we sanded and sanded, but Fairbanks would disappear someplace."

Shortly after he returned, Fleming took what would be the most momentous step in his career by signing his first contract with MGM. At the same time, he slaked his thirst for adventure by buying the aircraft that had been chosen for the Amazon adventure. The black and orange Lockheed Sirius, a muscular low-wing monoplane, was the same model that Charles and Anne Morrow Lindbergh had used to map international plane routes. Lockheed had built this particular plane for the Baltimorean Charles Hutchinson—he hoped to break a New York–to–Paris speed record, but instead crashed the plane on its first flight (he pleaded lack of ease with its controls). Fleming poured money into retooling it for shorter distances. With a forty-two-foot wingspan, it was bigger and more difficult to operate than Fleming's previous aircraft. He flew it with Douglas Shearer (MGM's sound chief and Norma's brother) as his co-pilot, but the plane was beset with mechanical problems, including a cracked oil tank that forced a landing in Reno. Within two years, he sold it back to Lockheed. His experience with this monoplane would plant the seeds for one of his critical and commercial triumphs, *Test Pilot*, at his new studio.

13

Guiding Gable in *Red Dust*

On October 2, 1931, Fleming received the most important document of his professional life. MGM delivered a letter of agreement for him to direct "one photoplay" within a seventeen-week period for a salary of $40,000. (Several days later, *Variety* announced that MGM had showered him with fifteen scripts.) For most of the 1930s, similar notes would fly back and forth between Vic's lawyers and the studio, because he resisted any long-term contract.

Fleming would soon become *the* MGM director. In 1971, for an oral history project at Columbia University, the producer Pandro S. Berman, who joined MGM in 1940, was asked whether the reputations of MGM's big directors should really have gone to the producers. "I would say except in the case of one man," Berman said. Who was that? asked Charles Higham. Vincente Minnelli? Not to this producer's eyes. "Victor Fleming was such a powerful man and so strong that he wouldn't do anything until it was his way," said Berman.

Fleming would thrive equally under his old pal Thalberg and his new admirer Louis B. Mayer. But Fleming's first MGM picture, *The Wet Parade* (1932), was an intolerable Thalberger—a barely viewable film made out of an unreadable book. Upton Sinclair, who had earned his reputation as a muckraker by exposing tainted meat-processing plants in *The Jungle*, had personal reasons for writing this exhausting fictional screed against John Barleycorn: alcoholism took his father's life.

Sinclair had no illusions about his Prohibition propaganda. He admitted, "When I finish my very bad Prohibition novel, I hope to write a very good one about Russia." Not only did anti-Prohibition voices like H. L. Mencken mock the novel; so did his sometimes sycophantic friend Fulton Oursler (*The Greatest Story Ever Told*), who advised, "For God's sake, throw it in the fire."

Nonetheless, Thalberg paid $20,000 for the rights and paid Fleming twice that much to direct it. Fleming gave the project his all, even when kidney stones once again began to plague him. They incapacitated him on and off throughout the 1930s, with severe pain that could make him short-tempered. The only long-term solution then was surgery, which he eventually had. But during *The Wet Parade*, he managed to keep functioning despite the attacks. The script clerk Morris Abrams said the director "came to work on a [tiltboard] with armrests like actresses used and was carried from set to set. He wouldn't quit work." *The Wet Parade*'s ingenue, Dorothy Jordan, remembered him as a "very sensitive, very dedicated man . . . basically, he was a big person. He never did petty things or little things."

Mary Craig Sinclair wrote that in a meeting with her and her husband, Upton, Thalberg "explained that he could not make a Prohibition picture, but gave his word that he would hold the balance fair and give both sides. He did this, and with excellent results." The Sinclairs—but few others—were satisfied. In a tale of two families ruined by alcohol, Robert Young and Jordan play the juvenile leads, and Jimmy Durante plays Young's partner when the hero becomes a Prohibition agent. Durante's crack for a *Photoplay* columnist, "They're grooming me for drama, so they can save John Barrymore's salary," is sprightlier than any line in the script. Myrna Loy played a small part, and all this Fleming fan had to say about the production was that the Cyrano-like Durante kept staring at her pert nose off camera and exclaiming, "Moyna, where'd you get that schnozzola?" Walter Huston does give a memorable performance as a dangerous blowhard, a Democratic ward politician (Young's father); the only indelible scene is his brutal murder of his wife (Clara Blandick, later Auntie Em in *The Wizard of Oz*). The screenwriter, John Lee Mahin, said that the film tanked "because it didn't take a stand." Well, that's one reason.

From this unpromising beginning grew a director-studio alliance and a writing-directing partnership that extended to most of Fleming's top sound films, including *Red Dust*, *Bombshell*, and *Captains Courageous*. Mahin, the son of a leading advertising executive (John Lee Mahin Sr.), was born in Winnetka, Illinois, in 1902, and moved with his family to New York when he was sixteen. He attended Harvard, reviewing movies for the Boston *American*, but dropped out after two and a half years to work as a full-time newspaperman in New York.

"I think it's the best thing in the world," he said, "because you've got to write something every day . . . Getting your stuff edited, you learn terseness. You realize how important editing is." Mahin entered show business as an actor—"a thin, reedy juvenile," he said. He had a bit part in Eugene O'Neill's *Great God Brown* and appeared with Robert Montgomery and Hume Derr, soon to be Mahin's first wife (of five), as a song-and-dance team in *Bad Habits of 1926*. When Montgomery's solo success broke up the act, Mahin and Derr married and moved upstate to restore a country house in Rockland County; Mahin commuted to New York to write copy at an ad agency while doing magazine fiction on the side. He regularly met Ben Hecht, who lived in Nyack, on the West Forty-second Street Ferry, and one day in 1928 Hecht announced that he and his playwriting partner, Charles MacArthur (then nicknamed "Nutsy"), the hottest writers on Broadway after the success of *The Front Page*, were going to Hollywood to write a film for Sam Goldwyn (*The Unholy Garden*). Hecht asked Mahin if he'd like to come along: "work with us, give us something to sneer at." Mahin went as Hecht's "secretary." As Mahin's eldest son, Graham, remembers the story, the three writers went on the 20th Century Limited, his mother left from La Guardia Field on a DC-3, and Graham and his governess traveled on the Cunard Line via the Panama Canal. When Mahin assisted Hecht on *Scarface* two years later, it made the young man's name. *The Wet Parade* was one of the first films he wrote for MGM. F. Scott Fitzgerald would come to regard Mahin as "one of the half dozen best picture writers in the business" (the only other screenwriter Fitzgerald singled out by name was Robert Riskin).

Mahin was urbane. Fleming was elemental. Mahin could be a two-fisted drinker—he carried the spirit of the Jazz Age all the way through the Depression and World War II—but he couldn't handle his booze. Vic could handle his *and* Mahin's. Graham Mahin said, "My dad was a drunk. I mean, he was a Hollywood drunk, like most of the people were. Like Duke [John Wayne] was a drunk, like Ward Bond was a drunk, like all those guys, but, you know, it was fashionable to drink a lot . . . My father had this thing when he was drinking; he would just open the car door wherever he was and pee. It could be in the middle of an intersection. But Victor would say, 'Now, John, we can't do that.' And Dad would get back inside." Mahin himself said he and Fleming knew each other "the way women do when close . . . If I was in trouble, Vic and I would see each other that night."

Over the years, Mahin stood up consistently for Fleming's character and talent, but to his son Graham, Mahin never downplayed the dark corners of his friend's life. "Everywhere you went, really strange shit happened with Victor," he once said. John recalled the two of them visiting a saloon and brothel in Mexico when Fleming noticed a new man behind the bar. Victor asked, "What happened to the other bartender that was here?" The new guy answered, "He was fooling around with a pistol and shot himself." Fleming replied, "You're kidding—how'd he do that?" The fellow picked up a pistol from behind the counter to demonstrate—and shot himself. As Mahin's story went, he and Fleming sped out of there.

Whenever Mahin was in a fix, Fleming could get him out of it. Mahin once nearly lost an eye in a car accident, when the rearview mirror broke in his face while he shielded his wife. Fleming wouldn't let the local doctors take the eye out—"just put it together with cotton," he growled—and got a specialist to fly down from Canada. ("It was always funny," Graham recalled. "I mean, it worked, but when he got very tired or anything, it would wander off and go into his head.")

Professionally, the pair's reliance was mutual. "Victor would talk about something, about dialogue," remembers Graham, "and my father would say to him, 'Verbs, Victor, verbs. You and the cameraman give the adjectives, just verbs is what we want.' " Howard Hawks, who took credit for introducing Mahin to Fleming, said, "He had a lot of talent, but he worked well only when he was with me or Victor Fleming or somebody like that—he had to be told what to write, and then what he wrote was really good." Hawks's condescension may have come from Mahin's willingness to call Hawks an awful liar whenever he took credit for Fleming and Mahin's work. Fitzgerald, again, wrote admiringly, "A Bob Sherwood picture, for instance, or a Johnny Mahin script, could be shot by an assistant director or a script girl." Mahin saw himself as a yarn spinner, not a technician. He told novelist-screenwriters like Scott Fitzgerald and James M. Cain, "I never wrote 'close shot,' 'long shot,' 'medium shot' or anything . . . It's all horseshit. You write your story; you're a storyteller; write the dialogue where it should take place and if you have a good director he'll start with a closeup and pull back, or whatever."

Mahin's preference for a script full of verbs would help Fleming fulfill his appetite for on-screen action. Fred E. Lewis, a wealthy real-estate investor, world traveler, hunter, and amateur zoologist, would help Fleming satisfy his yen for real-life adventure. "Restlessness, I suppose, is an emotion which one shouldn't try to explain," Fleming said in *Action.* "You have it or you don't, and it has varying effects on different people."

In 1930, Fleming and Charles Cotton, along with Lewis, bought a strip of bayfront property in a Southern California coastal town, Balboa, and built luxurious vacation homes. Lewis, unlike Fairbanks, was the real thing when it came to sailing, and he was much more than another Carl Akeley. It is likely that he was Fleming's own Disko Troop, a living prototype for the seasoned skipper in *Captains Courageous.* Nine years older than the director and born into Gilded Age wealth in New York, Lewis was a charismatic naturalist in the era in which zoos still relied on wealthy patrons not only to build their facilities but also, at times, to supply the animals themselves. Collecting baby mammals typically meant killing one or more of their parents, meaning that Lewis also had the skills of a big-game hunter.

Right after *The Wet Parade*, Fleming leaped at the chance to join him for an animal-collection voyage on his diesel-powered yacht, the *Stranger*, which Lewis had custom-fitted to transport live animals. Lewis had planned a five-month sail to collect walrus, reindeer, and perhaps some bears in Alaska. As they headed into Alaskan waters, Fleming, off the starboard bow, "made out a ship through the glasses and her name was the *Nanuk*. Aboard her was W. S. Van Dyke, my fellow director . . . He was, with his crew and technicians, freezingly engaged in filming the picture *Eskimo.*"

The expedition ended up hauling away a three-hundred-pound baby walrus, three black bear cubs, three reindeer, and two Kodiak bear cubs for the San Diego Zoo. The Kodiak cubs were captured after Fleming shot their mother, who weighed nearly a ton. Fleming had the bear pelt made into a rug and put it in his bedroom during his second marriage. "I used to enjoy rolling around in it," says his daughter Victoria.

Fleming, needing to return to Hollywood, cut his adventure short after that, flying home from Juneau. He quickly committed to direct *The White Sister*, a remake of the high-toned Italy-set soap opera that had been a silent hit with Ronald Colman and Lillian Gish. But MGM had a drifting production called *Red Dust* that needed an immediate course adjustment. Wilson Collison's 1927 play pivoted (in far different ways from the finished movie) on a sexual triangle—the brusque, competent manager of a rubber plantation in Cochin China (present-day Vietnam), a prostitute from Saigon, and the classy wife of the manager's new specialist in surveying. The setting was exotic; the material, turgid. Early plans to have Fred Niblo direct Garbo in the picture (with several different projected co-stars) went nowhere. Perhaps because of the French colonial backdrop, the producer, Hunt Stromberg, next put Jacques Feyder in charge; the Belgium-born director had made an acclaimed French silent version of Zola's *Thérèse Raquin* in addition to Garbo's last silent film, *The Kiss.* Now Jean Harlow was to play the streetwalker, with one of the silent screen's great lovers, John Gilbert, as the hero. In the talkie era, without stage experience or sound technicians who knew how to mike his light and charming voice, Gilbert had grown unsteady. Teaming him with Harlow was supposed to buck him up.

Mahin wrote the script, by the skin of his teeth. "We were starting the picture with about ten pages of script and were going to spitball it as we went along." (That sounds like Hollywood hyperbole, but the Production Code correspondence backs his story. Viewed against the uninhibited finished movie, it also illustrates how toothless the code could be, when handled properly, before 1934. Mahin's *Scarface* didn't fare as well: censorship fights kept the film from opening until a month after *Red Dust* did in the autumn of 1932.)

The turning point for *Red Dust* came when Mahin saw an up-and-comer playing a lady-killer chauffeur in William Wellman's *Night Nurse* and told Stromberg, "There's this guy, my God, he's got the eyes of a woman and the build of a bull. He is really going to be something." Stromberg looked at Mahin as if he thought the writer "was queer or something," but finally said, "By God, you're right." Clark Gable made thirteen movies in the single year before *Red Dust* and was well-known on the Warner Bros. and MGM lots (if not to Mahin or Stromberg!) for his smoking physical presence. He hadn't carried a film by himself, but he'd already partnered a handful of the era's sirens, including Garbo (*Susan Lenox, Her Fall and Rise*), Barbara Stanwyck (*Night Nurse*), Norma Shearer (*A Free Soul*), and, most often, Joan Crawford (*Dance, Fools, Dance*; *Laughing Sinners*; *Possessed*).

It was natural to link him up with Harlow, the sound film's update of Clara Bow. Harlow was born Harlean Harlow Carpenter in Kansas City, and Gable in Ohio. Each had youthful experiences of Hollywood—Harlow as a precocious eighth grader at the Hollywood School for Girls, Gable as a West Coast theater actor who made Hollywood his base at the age of twenty-two. Harlow's mother was so devoted to her daughter's stardom that she'd ice Jean's breasts before each shot to perk them up. Gable had a series of lovers and wives who helped teach him art and "class" and even, in the case of Pauline Frederick, temporarily fixed his lousy teeth. Indeed, in 1931, his first wife, Josephine Dillon, the Portland acting coach who felt she'd given him discipline, confidence, and naturalness as an actor, threatened to sell her story of how she made Gable who he was unless Louis B. Mayer paid her to keep quiet. She wound up with $200 a month—out of Gable's salary! In a thank-you note to Mayer, she offered her teaching skills to MGM and said, "I wish I could do something about John Gilbert's voice for you. I know it can be done." It's poignant to think of Gable's ex-wife wanting to aid Gilbert just when Gable was taking his place. (In 1932, Gable stopped the payments.)

Gable and Harlow may have been homegrown, but they were also wised-up. They projected a democratic and down-to-earth sexuality and smarts that made them ideal fantasy figures for Depression audiences. By the time Stromberg brought them together for *Red Dust*, they were crack camera actors. Yet they didn't know their own strengths; they were still insecure.

With Gable in, Feyder was out. Mahin described Feyder as "a sweet, delicate Frenchman who didn't know too much." The screenwriter called him "an old-timer"; actually, Feyder had some glory years ahead of him. In 1935 he made *Carnival in Flanders* in France, in 1937, *Knight Without Armor* in Britain. But Stromberg needed a robust presence on the set and initially hired Rowland Brown, an attention-getting, volatile director who had recently made *Quick Millions* (1931) and *Hell's Highway* (1932). The *Los Angeles Times* noted that Brown was "famous for his departures from the set"; in the case of *Red Dust* he departed before shooting began. Gable hadn't yet worked with Fleming, but the star had done a 1931 film called *The Easiest Way* for Vic's old friend Jack Conway.

The director-star rapport must have been immediate. Fleming shared more with Gable than with Cooper. Gable had grown up on an Ohio farm. He'd worked part-time as a garage mechanic and labored as a rigger and tool dresser and cleanup man at Oklahoma oil wells and refineries. Like Fleming's stepfather (but with less success), his father had dreamed of founding his own oil empire. Fleming and Gable knew how much toil went into failed dreams but hadn't let that knowledge blunt their ambitions or dull their appetites.

According to studio conference notes, Fleming came onto the production realizing that *Red Dust* hadn't found its "driving dramatic force." With Howard Hawks as an unofficial adviser, he tore apart the original piece. A play that in the studio précis reads like a big mess became one of Hollywood's lasting comic-romantic melodramas about sex, love, honesty, and duty. "Just thinking out loud, suppose we change the order of the entire story," Fleming said. "Open up as Hawks felt with a stunning dramatization of a rubber plantation in the throes of Hell. Let's forget about the play and its feeble motivations and see what characters we can evolve whose own emotions will give us the situations. We open on the plantation as the red dust is furiously blowing. The rebellious and faithless coolies are deserting at all turns and we characterize Dennis [the hero] as almost giving up the fight."

Americanizing the characters and also vitalizing them, Fleming and Mahin arrived at a startling blend of high and low romance and comedy. They gave the men and women caught in this hellish part of Cochin China more facets and harder edges—any angels here are fallen, any devils have real sting. That push toward complexity pays off in adult entertainment value. Dennis Carson (Gable), born into the rubber trade, has tired of living with one sloppy, drunken co-worker, Guidon (Donald Crisp), a cheerful, simple Chinese cook, Hoy (Willie Fung), and one friend he trusts, observant, mellow Mac (Tully Marshall).

Dennis's exhaustion opens him up emotionally instead of burning him out. Guidon returns from a trip to Saigon with a prostitute named Vantine (Harlow). Dennis tells Mac that he's sick of whores being the only women available to him, but Vantine is frank and funny and has standards: she won't tumble for a foul drunk like Guidon. She wins Dennis over, gets him into bed. It's her rotten luck that the next boat brings in gung-ho but green-at-the-gills Gary Willis (Gene Raymond) and his upper-crust-lovely, Philadelphia-born wife, Barbara (Mary Astor).

From the moment Dennis and Barbara lock eyes in a mirror, they're goners. Vantine knows it because Dennis turns brusque and rude to her, feeling that her presence lowers and vulgarizes him. In fact, Barbara refers to Dennis and his crew as "civilized barbarians," a locution that suits the film's brute elegance. Barbara, Dennis, and Vantine dance out a roughhouse gavotte, with Gary and Guidon breaking in at crucial points. Gable has his cocksure stride and Astor a magnetized grace. And Harlow has, as the critic Gerald Weales puts it, a walk that's "a marvel. It contains little of the teasing seductiveness that Hollywood sex goddesses are supposed to display. Her sexuality is direct and matter-of-fact; she moves like an athlete."

In this masterpiece of erotic choreography, Dennis dazzles Barbara with masculine aplomb. First, he cures her boyish husband of jungle fever. Then, when Gary does his first full day's work, Dennis shows Barbara the plantation. The ensuing documentary about creating rubber ends when Dennis splashes rubber milk with acetic acid to make it stiffen. A monsoon comes up suddenly and drenches both of them. Dennis picks Barbara up in his arms and doesn't let her go until he's kissed her, long and hard, back in her room.

What makes Gable so sexy in *Red Dust* is that he isn't the John Gilbert great-lover type: he's fresh in every sense. When he comes up with seductive patter or a bold and winning gesture, he's not overly practiced. Making things up as he goes along, he surprises even himself. He *is* in love with Barbara. That's what drives Vantine batty, not merely because she loves him as much as Barbara does, but because she knows what Dennis denies—he loves Vantine in a way, too. The movie is as lusty, funny, and sad as it should be. It wrings humor and pathos from the unfairness and ruthlessness of love, and hopefulness from the varieties of love.

The play wasn't even *about* adultery—the equivalent of the Gary Willis character dies before any hanky-panky. The movie is about respecting another man's marriage. It isn't prescriptive. If Gary weren't a good fellow, and if he didn't hero-worship Dennis; if the idea of wooing Barbara weren't tied up in Dennis's head with the thought of leaving Cochin China; if Vantine weren't around to call a cheat a cheat, and to supply a more suitable alternative—who knows?

"They would go through the script," said Graham Mahin, "and they'd break it into cards, or pieces of cardboard, or whatever. And they'd look at it and say, well, does it fit into the story? [And if my father said no], Victor would say, 'Don't throw it away, I like the scene. We'll put it somewhere—we'll put that bit in somewhere else.' " *Red Dust* kept changing during shooting, growing bolder and keener and cruder. The scripted finale, for example, had been protracted and talky. In the finished version, Fleming has Barbara catch Dennis and Vantine in a sexy tussle, so that Barbara thinks Dennis is a heel before he says anything. (Donald Ogden Stewart supplied the amusing coda.)

Fleming's direction is more than assured: it's electrically instinctive. William Kaplan said it simply: "He had a knack of [knowing] what a man would do under certain conditions." And women, too. The exactness of the extra seconds Gable looks at Astor is matched by the moments when she registers her troubled response and then covers it up. In the script, after they kiss, Barbara says, "You should never have done that." In the movie, she says, "*We* should never have done that."

Fleming savors the intensity of their passion as well as the heartiness of Harlow's high jinks; Vantine sometimes plays the joker, but she's too consistent and candid with Dennis and Barbara to make a fool of herself. The male relationships are equally detailed. Dennis starts the movie by saving Gary's life and ends it by saving his marriage, with Vantine's quick-witted help. Reluctantly, he responds to the canine devotion that Gary extends to him as his boss and wilderness mentor. Fleming left Gene Raymond to his own devices when it came to playing Gary, but the director probably saw that the actor's neediness was working for the character. Gary proves disarmingly semi-aware in his touching eagerness to please both his wife and Dennis; he may know when "Babs," as he keeps calling her, gets upset, but he never suspects the reason. He intuits that Dennis understands his love for her, but not exactly why. Gary's character is entirely different from his counterpart in the play. The younger-brotherliness he extends to Dennis may reflect Mahin's growing friendship with Fleming. At one point, Gary tells Dennis his and Babs's old dream of living thirty-five miles up the Hudson from New York—just what Mahin once did with his first wife, Derr.

Filming on sets from MGM's *Tarzan*, Fleming achieved a texture far denser than what John Ford got shooting on location in his light, enjoyable 1953 African remake, *Mogambo*. (Also starring Gable, with Grace Kelly and Ava Gardner, *Mogambo* is an airier movie all around.) Astor remembered the constant dampness from the rain machines and Fleming "being tough about our complaints: 'So what! Everybody sweats in the tropics—that's the way it is!' " The propman Johnny Miller testified to Fleming's insistence on evoking the right atmosphere when he spoke of the director ordering him to assemble a flotilla of moths to interrupt a rubber-company meal and "fix one of 'em so it would light on Gable's lip." Even though Miller discovered it was a tough season for gathering moths, and they're impossible to train anyway ("I know, because I tried it"), he "did figure out a scheme which had about one chance in a million to work . . . I took one of the moths and put a little glue on it. I shut my eyes and threw that moth at Gable and it landed smack-dab on his lip, just like Fleming ordered."

"I see the most gorgeous shot of Barbara," Fleming said in his conference notes. "When holding her in his arms he suddenly lifts her up to him and kisses her passionately. I see a close up shooting down on her face to catch the madness that is sweeping over her. Her eyes are open wide—she trembles—she is more alive now than she's ever been in all her life." Fleming thought if the scene were "emotionally and psychologically sound," they would "hit upon a terrific situation in the story." He adds, "If Gable were really the 'great lover' type (which he isn't)—in other words if it were Freddie March or Valentino or Jack Gilbert (in silent days)—we would write it out and play it for a fierce sex scene."

In a June 1969 *Reader's Digest* story, "What It Was Like to Kiss Clark Gable," Astor provided the most intimate account of Fleming commanding a set (she later revised it and formalized it slightly in her book *A Life on Film*). "Now I don't claim to have total recall," she wrote—but she really did, starting with the early scene where she arrives by riverboat at the rubber plantation.

> Clark, the handsome superintendent, escorts me with great politeness along the dock to the house, away from the camera. Vic stops the first take and says, in front of everybody, "Mary, *please*! Go to your dressing room and take off that damned girdle. We need the bounce!"
>
> We had completed several days on the plantation set—and many shots of Clark carrying me through the mud, gasping from the force of a "monsoon."
>
> We had just finished the continuation on the stage inside where he carries me up the veranda steps into my bedroom, soaking wet, breathless.
>
> Fleming said, "OK, let's move in on a tight two."

The scene in the script reads, "Dennis suddenly kisses her. Barbara at first recoils, but cannot take her lips from his. She raises her hand as if to strike him, but it stays suspended. As he kisses her, he slowly lets her down to her feet, his mouth still on hers. Then he takes his lips from hers, and smiles."

Now Clark was a husky guy and a good sport, but it was not practical for him to be a hero and hold me up for the hour or so the shot would take to line up and shoot. So first of all, a stool had to be found which was the correct height to support most of my weight. Out of sight, of course; they were cutting about elbow high.

A prop man and a carpenter shoved a stool under my bottom as Clark hoisted me up, his right arm supporting me under my knees, his left under my shoulders.

From behind the camera: "Too high! Too high! Her head's gotta be lower than his." The carpenter started in with a saw on one of the legs.

"Wait a minute! Check it in the finder, first. Let's see where you're going to be, kids."

"Clark, just before you kiss her, swing her an inch or two, so we get your full face."

We tried it.

Vic said, "Too much, too much—back just a little." Peering through the camera lens.

Clark said, "It's uncomfortable. I'll never hit it right."

"Yes, you will. Just clear the key light on her neck, see it?"

"Why don't you move the camera?" asked Clark.

"I don't want to move the camera. It's a natural move, Clark."

"OK, OK."

. . .

[During a break, while the stand-ins took the set] I had my usual bad-tempered argument with the makeup man about too much makeup. He pursued me, carrying a powder puff like an extension of his arm.

Soothingly he said, "The freckles are coming through on your forehead, Mary. Let me just touch it up with a *leetle* bit of pancake."

"OK, but no lipstick, Harry—you know what Mr. Fleming said. All that rain. I'd never have any makeup left."

"Looks so naked."

"That's what he wants."

. . .

[For the rehearsal] I hoisted myself onto the stool. As Clark took his position he cracked, "Hey, you've lost weight!"

The head gaffer, kneeling under the camera, asked Clark, "This gonna be too hot?" Indicating an eyelight.

"Gee-sus it is hot," Clark replied. "It'll make me squint, Gus."

"No it won't. We really need it."

"Then it's not too hot. Whadja ask for?"

The gaffer grinned and said, "Got anything in the fifth on Saturday?"

"Yeah, I gotta honey."

"Lemme in on it, huh?"

"Sure, later."

Finally Vic came in from behind the camera so that he could talk to us quietly. And we started to think about the scene. What happened previously, relationships, emotional levels, etc.

"Let's just move through it once," Vic says. "The look needn't be very long, Clark. Mary, keep it simple. Real. Just *be* there."

He turned and disappeared behind the lights.

"Let's make one, okay?" He calls. "Don't need a rehearsal. Just mean it. Think. Feel." To the camera crew: "Can we go?"

Hal Rosson didn't like that. "No rehearsal? Well, let me check their position when they kiss. We could move in, you know."

Vic said, "I don't *want* to move in, goddam it. I don't want to move the camera. Let the *people* do it, not the camera."

Rosson interrupted to say, "Give us a look, people."

Clark leaned his head close to me and our lips were barely touching. Loudly, he asked, "How's this?" I jumped a little and he said, "Sorry, baby."

"No good. We're just getting the top of your head."

We maneuvered fractional changes, our noses getting in the way.

"Hold it, hold it! That's fine, if you raise her just a little—too much, too much. Right there, that's beautiful, perfect."

Clark whispered to me, "That's where we were in the first place."

The assistant director checked his watch. It was getting close to lunch time. "OK, can we go? Let's wet 'em down!"

Clark said, "Here we go, baby," as we unwound and he helped me down from the stool.

We went over and stood just off the set in a shallow bathtub arrangement made of tarpaper and two by fours, and the man in the raincoat turned the hoses on us. After the heat of the lights, the water felt icy and we gasped and yelled as it hit us.

The assistant said, "Let's go, let's go! Let's get 'em while they're wet!" The makeup man popped in to wipe a drop from the end of my nose. "Git outta there, Harry!"

Now it was quiet. Now we were ready to go. To do what they paid us all that money for. To use our acquired ability to concentrate, to focus all our thoughts and emotions on the scene.

This is what they'll see up there on the screen in the theaters, although that isn't what you think of at the time. The best way I can describe what happens is with the phrase, "as though"; we think and act "as though." As though at that moment we were in the grip of an emotion bringing us violently together in the first taste of lips . . .

Somebody's laughing. Out there behind the lights.

It was pin-drop silence. Then somebody chuckled from behind the camera. Clark's head jerked up, shocked, mad. Then the whole crew started laughing into loud guffaws.

Vic said, "Cut it! Cut it!" then came in to us. "It's a very hot scene, kids, but not *that* hot! You're steaming!"

And we were, literally. The hot lights had vaporized the water on our clothes and skin, and it was rising in waves.

After the laughter and kidding and the joke was over, the problem remained. Everybody made a suggestion to solve it.

Then there was the question of lunch time. After lunch we were scheduled to move to another set—a "dry" scene. During lunch time I was to have my hair set and a new makeup. If we waited until after lunch to get this sequence shot, the production would be held up for at least an hour for the hairset and makeup renewal. And time was valuable.

The problem was solved. The water had to be heated. Since the source for the hoses couldn't be heated, we simply stayed in position with the lights on until we stopped steaming. To prevent our drying out, [the propman Harry Edwards] kept us wet by pouring teakettles of warm water over our heads and shoulders.

To the assistant director [Hugh Boswell], who must keep things on schedule, it's all very hurry-up, very urgent. But the situation has given the rest of us the sillies. Somebody says, "Clark, wanna deck of cards? You and Mary could play a hand of gin rummy while you're waiting!"

And all the time the assistant director is chanting, "Can we go? Can we go, fellas?"

There's a muscle in my shoulder that's beginning to complain. "Can I stand up a minute?" I ask.

"No, Mary," Vic says. "We're all set. Don't move out of it. Wet 'em down a little more." The warm water dribbles on our hair. Clark says, "What, no soap?"

"Okay, roll 'em!"

And the scene was shot . . . And it was a print. "Lunch everybody. One hour! Crew back in a half hour."

The weird part of it all is that it never occurred to anyone, including Clark and me, that all this might have had a bad effect on the mood, or on our ability to play a love scene convincingly. But that's the way it was. The way it always is. The way it is today, on any movie set.

Under Fleming's guidance, Gable and Astor did manage to conjure a suitable romantic cataclysm for Dennis and Barbara—and after it, for a while, Vantine hovers around the edges. Harlow, though, earns her star billing as Vantine deftly deflates the lovers' high-flown image of themselves. She's a marvelous clown, slapping around naked in the plantation's big water barrel. Carried away with good humor and exuberance, the nude Harlow shot up on her feet in the rain barrel and proclaimed, "Something for the boys in the lab!" Knowing that the footage would get around, Fleming jerked the film right out of the camera. It was one of those times when the assistant director Willard Sheldon saw two facets of Fleming at once: "Very hard-nosed, yet he had this sensitive side which always surprised me." He helped Harlow imbue Vantine with an understated poignancy, especially when Dennis offhandedly treats her like a whore. The wardrobe man Ted Tetrick said, "I felt he pulled things out of people based on what he wanted. Never above, never below."

When her partners praised Harlow's timing, they weren't merely talking about her ability to put over Mahin's crackling innuendos and euphemisms, such as Vantine scraping the bottom of a parrot's cage and asking, "What have you been eating, cement?" Harlow's Vantine is magnetic when Dennis puts her down and she struggles to show him that she could be the right gal for him—without airs and ambitions, she can buck him up as he does his duty. Dennis has built his authority by displaying strength and loyalty in an unforgiving land; he comes to realize that he can be honorable with the whore, not with the pedigreed married woman. And that comprehension hurts. The jolly ending carries a tinge of pathos. Dennis looks happy with Vantine; still, when he fleetingly recalls Barbara, he looks wounded.

If the stars were "playing themselves," Harlow would have been the wounded one. Midway through filming, on Labor Day 1932, her husband committed suicide, when she was in their house and would find his body. Just two months before, Harlow had married Paul Bern, a literate MGM executive and Thalberg's dearest friend. On paper, he seemed a good prospect to provide a stable family life. Bern, though, was deeply troubled and impotent. As Harlow's biographer David Stenn uncovered in his analysis of this tragic scandal, the MGM damage-control machine, normally so reliable at protecting the studio's human assets, delayed the arrival of police and raised suspicions of a cover-up. It would take weeks to deflate the suspicion that Harlow drove her husband to suicide. Production resumed two days later, as Fleming shot around Harlow and staged scenes with Gable, Astor, and Raymond. It was possible that Harlow would be replaced and her scenes reshot. Mayer offered her role to Tallulah Bankhead, who called his doing so "one of the shabbiest acts of all time." But during the week, emerging details of Bern's life before Harlow, such as his previous, common-law marriage to a woman who was obsessed with him, began to swing public feeling Harlow's way. On Monday, September 12, Harlow returned to the set.

MGM's efficient publicists got a story out to the papers that Harlow had telephoned Irving Thalberg on September 11. "This staying around home is driving me crazy," she said. "I've got to get busy—to forget." Her stepfather, Marino Bello, and a nurse, Adah Wilson, accompanied her. The sound mixer Bill Edmondson said, "The day she came back, she was really subdued, and for the Baby to be subdued was *something*." Astor reported that Fleming asked, "How are we going to get a sexy performance with *that* look in her eyes?" Yet she deflected any show of sympathy and was, as Edmondson put it, "a trouper."

According to Mahin, it was Harlow's sad luck that the next day required retakes of the rain-barrel scene. One of her feisty, laugh-getting lines was "Don't you know? I'm La Flamme, the gal that drives men mad!" Mahin said she asked, "I don't have to say that, do I?" His response: "I'm sure you don't." In Mahin's account, Fleming shot that bit, but didn't use it. Another report says that Stromberg and Fleming had begun auditioning alternative actresses; when Harlow made her reentrance, Gable was rehearsing a test scene with one of them. Harlow tapped the woman on the shoulder and said, "I'm sorry, honey, but the part's taken." In this version, Harlow's first comeback line was Vantine's sardonic statement upon seeing Dennis return from Gary's drainage project: "Well, if it ain't old massa Fred, back after all these years."

When he wasn't dealing with turmoil and temperament on the set, Vic was wooing Lu Rosson—though his daughter Victoria says Lu was the one with courtship on her mind. It was unusual—perhaps unprecedented—for Fleming to bed a married woman, especially the wife of a friend. Yet Arthur Rosson and Lu had been living apart for half a year, since he moved out of their Rexford Drive home in Beverly Hills and into his own place. And something about the adrenaline-pumping whoosh and excitement of Vic's life in these months connected with Lu's inchoate yearning for a change.

"I think she was just an unhappy woman," says Victoria. "She was unhappy in her first marriage, and I don't think she ever had plans to move forward, at any time." But Vic and Lu shared similar struggling childhoods, including limited schooling and the early loss of a father. Both had an instinct for jokes that defused situations or exploded them. Fired up from his expedition with Lewis, in the middle of bringing to life a movie with a volcanic id and a complicated view of adultery,

Fleming may have allowed the intensity he always poured into his work to spill over, with Lu's abetting, into their friendship.

Vic was collaborating with Arthur's brother Hal when he started his affair with Lu. It's surprising partly because, in the words of Cecil B. DeMille, "there was never a family of more vividly distinct individuals, neither was there ever a family of more close-knit unity and loyalty." (He said he always thought of them as "The Rossons.") Arthur and Lu's marriage may have started to fall apart in the late 1920s. In 1927, Paramount had initially assigned him to *Underworld*, the Ben Hecht–written gangster movie. But Hawks, who was at Paramount then, said, "He went up to San Francisco, as I remember, to go to the prison there, but unfortunately got tight, so they had to fire him." The director Josef von Sternberg took over (with Hathaway as his assistant director) and turned the film into a smash. By 1929, Rosson was directing Hoot Gibson cowboy talkies at Universal. Shooting Westerns took Art away from home, often to Arizona.

Around this time, Lu acquired her first nickname—from the song "True Blue Lou," a hit from the show *Burlesque*, the one Vic was slated to direct before it was made as *The Dance of Life*. The song is about "a dame in love with a guy" who sticks by him even though she gets nothing back: "Who fought to save him, smiled and forgave him? True Blue Lou." Lu later insisted that relatives, including grandchildren and great-grandchildren, call her Truie.

Lu knew the man she set her cap for—Fleming didn't hide or tone down anything for her, including his hard-guy joking and mockery. In the late 1920s, a tiny, densely furred monkey called a pygmy marmoset became a frequent pet and fashion accessory for Hollywood women. Alice White took hers on the town in a satin purse. Lu often carried hers in her coat. Vic and Lu "were out somewhere, having lunch," his daughter Victoria recalls. "And the marmoset peed on Daddy. So to show his disgust, he caught a fly, mashed it on the table with a knife, put it in his mouth, and made a big show out of eating it. He stuck his tongue out at Mother, and there was a single leg of the fly on it." Victoria also remembers a story Lu told of Vic shooting down a hummingbird at Meadowlark Ranch, where they had occasional assignations. "He must have used a pellet gun, I don't know for sure." Then he dressed it "for Thanksgiving, the feathers off and everything . . . in a position with the 'drumsticks' sticking up." Since Lu loved hummingbirds, "she was probably horrified. She was a bird lover . . . He did have a sadistic sense of humor."

Thinking of the Gable persona Fleming helped create in *Red Dust*, Pauline Kael asked, "What man doesn't—at some level—want to feel supremely confident and earthy and irresistible? . . . And for women, if the roof leaks, or the car stalls, or you don't know how to get the super to keep his paws off you, you may long for a Clark Gable to take charge." That combination of competence and sexual certainty, and the air of challenge that went with it, were part of what drew Lu to Vic. (He also may have had what Kael called the "little bit of male fascism" that makes certain actors "dangerous and hence attractive.") On August 15, Rosson started shooting a low-budget Tom Mix cowboy picture, but Universal swiftly replaced him because of "illness." If he *was* having problems holding his liquor and it was beginning to diminish him as a professional and as a man, Fleming would have presented a seductive contrast. Of course, how he viewed his affair with Lu is even more of a mystery than how he regarded his on-and-off-and-on entanglement with Bow. Perhaps, given Fleming's simultaneous attraction and revulsion to show business, Lu offered a perfect blend of her own: she knew the demands of film production, but had no showbiz ambitions except to marry a respected moviemaker—more specifically, a powerhouse like Vic.

He rewarded her devotion with a public regard that could be downright courtly. "I remember one lovely story about Victor," Ben Hecht said in 1957.

> He was a great ladies' man, and terribly handsome, very strong, very gentle, talented, successful, rich. He used to sit at the directors' table at Metro, and there used to be topics come up for discussion, and they usually had to do with dames and bragging. One time the topic came up as to how many women one had loved, and the boys began. I remember Joe Mankiewicz led off with quite a high number, and his brother, and a couple of directors. Everybody had from ten to thirty. When it came to Vic to answer, he said, "One." He dumbfounded the table, and they said, "Who was she?" He said, "I'm married to her." This was the first time gentlemen's words had been heard at this table.

Sans the Philadelphia patina of class that Barbara has in *Red Dust*, what Lu represented to Vic might have been what Barbara represented to Dennis: someone out of "the life."

Before Lu, Vic might have thought there was no room in a real director's day for a conventional family. Vera Gebbert, the daughter of Fleming's frequent cameraman at Paramount, Charles Edgar Schoenbaum, recalled her dad telling her that Vic "took great pains, worked around the clock, Saturdays, sometimes Sundays. My father got up at 4:00 a.m. every day, wouldn't get home until eight or nine; he'd have lunch with Vic. Victor was never tired, never complained—I never heard a bad word about him."

Yet while working those hours at Paramount, Vic found himself spending more and more time with Arthur and Lu Rosson, and his friendship with Lu became sexual. During or right after the completion of *Red Dust*, Rosson discovered the affair. "Rosson caught them," says Sally, "and he told them if they were going to be screwing, they ought to be married." (Arthur Rosson Jr. heard it differently: "My dad was going to shoot Fleming" but was talked out of it.) But if Arthur "caught them," it was at the home he had already abandoned. And Lu may have *wanted* to get caught, to push her marriage to its sorry resolution.

A couple of weeks before the *Red Dust* premiere, Lu established a six-week residency in Reno, where the divorce went through on November 23 on grounds of cruelty. Rosson never countered with a charge of adultery, and there was no alimony.

Eventually, Rosson pulled his life and career back together, establishing a long-term relationship with DeMille as an ace second-unit director. In 1940, he married Odetta Bray, a singer and dancer from Hawaii, and had two more children, a son and a daughter. Up to his death in 1960, he racked up formidable achievements like the Indian attack in DeMille's *Plainsman* (1937) and the cattle stampede in Hawks's *Red River* (1948), earning a rare "co-director" credit on the latter, just as his brother Richard had on *Scarface*. And he would lead the Hebrew slaves out of Egypt in DeMille's *Ten Commandments* (1956).

Red Dust was an instant crowd-pleaser. "I went to see it at the Pantages," says Gebbert, "and even at a preview you could tell it was going to be a hit." Abel Green, the Samuel Johnson of *Variety* slang (and soon to be the trade paper's editor), called *Red Dust* "sure-fire b.o." and declared, "it means a lot for Gable, who's been tossed around on the Metro lot quite a bit." He also noted, "John Mahin, the adapter, has some nifty language punctuating the proceedings. It's censor-proof yet punchy, with lots of extra stuff read into it both by the histrionic interpretation and, best of all, the audience's own mental reactions. That makes it 100%." As he reached the decade's midsection and his own vital midlife, Fleming was 100 percent, too.

14

Pioneering the Screwball Comedy: Jean Harlow in *Bombshell*

While Lu Rosson was signing property agreements before her divorce from Arthur Rosson, Fleming was giving interviews about his new version of *The White Sister*, long slated for Helen Hayes and now featuring Gable. Fleming said that when it came to remakes, what mattered was "the original idea": in this case, turning an aristocratic virgin, an Italian soldier, and God into a romantic triangle.

Fleming and the producer Hunt Stromberg assigned Donald Ogden Stewart to update F. Marion Crawford's novel, setting it during World War I rather than the 1880s. A Yale-educated satirical novelist who contributed dialogue to *Laughter* (1930), Stewart later wrote that Stromberg, Fleming, and Sam Zimbalist, Stromberg's assistant, "were a daily delight to work with, and a revelation to me of the Hollywood psyche." According to Stewart, Stromberg recognized only the "reality" of whatever he'd already seen in pictures; at the same time, he would measure the effectiveness of a scene by whether, in Stromberg's words, "a dumb Scranton coal miner" could understand it.

Stewart strove to satisfy his own "rather high standards of truth," and Fleming knew how to get that truth across to the cast. "When Vic got a scene going, really going heavily," said Morris Abrams, once again Vic's script clerk, "he'd sit there and tears would roll down his face. Or he'd mouth the words along with the actors. He was a hell of a man, high-strung and intense, but he handled himself well. How he got performances out of actors, I don't know. I only know that if the scene was very heavy, the set would get quiet, the lights would go down, and he would go off in a corner with the actor and talk very quietly. And the actor would come back and do it."

Stewart was "very pleased and deeply satisfied" at the playwright Philip Barry's praise for the first two-thirds of the film. (Later, Stewart would write the script for the film version of Barry's *Philadelphia Story*.)

The screenwriter's enthusiasm faded when Hayes wouldn't play one of his scenes. Stromberg called in Hayes's husband and Ben Hecht's partner, Charles MacArthur, to rewrite it and then make over the script's last third. "That was the moment when the fun went out of Hollywood" for Stewart. Even if he stayed to the end, it's hard to see what he could have done to transcend high-flown Victorian melodrama.

At least Fleming brings the same conviction to the best and worst parts of the film. For a while, Hayes's fluttery artificiality *works*, expressing the newly released giddiness of a sheltered noblewoman. Gable is part man of the street, part Nature's nobleman: he's light on his feet even in army boots, an ideal object of schoolgirl reverie. No chemistry cements Gable and Hayes; no biology simmers beneath the surface. But Fleming puts some zing into the opening sequences: they have the melancholy-tinged euphoria that became one of his specialties. Gable's car rams into the one Hayes and her dreary fiancé (Alan Edwards) and forbidding father (Lewis Stone) are riding in as a carnival explodes around them. "In the carnival scenes and the convent scenes," Fleming said, "there were many temptations to stop, to spend a great deal of time catching this bit of landscape, that group of picturesque characters, a lovely corner here and there . . . Beauty we must have in pictures, but it must be beauty in action."

Beauty in action is exactly what he gets on the winding small-town boulevard filled with giant bobbing heads and costumed stilt walkers. In its luster and its whimsy, it's almost a prelude to the Emerald City, and Fleming, proud of his handiwork, put his own face on one of the bobbing heads. Gable pursues Hayes, once under the front end of a two-man costume horse, with the screenwriter, Stewart, under the rear end, revealed in a quick, funny cameo. Hayes's high-pitched refinement lends some pathos to Gable's tender wooing of her. She's discovering the delight of childish things as well as adult passion.

Then comes a cavalcade of catastrophes. Her father races to stop her from meeting Gable in the barracks as she speeds to meet her lover where he really is (at the officers' club, in town)—and the family cars nearly crash head-on. Her father dies when his car runs off the road. The will reveals a debt-ridden estate. Gable goes to war. In the only thrilling sequence, the Germans shoot him down over enemy territory; the Italians report him dead. So Hayes becomes a nun—and even after she learns he's alive, she refuses to renounce her vows. Fleming wanted to close the film with Gable simply walking away, but Catholic clergy pressured MGM to make sure, as in previous versions, the White Sister's would-be suitor really dies at the end.

Lillian Gish wrote that Hayes, disappointed in the rushes, called Gish to ask how she, Ronald Colman, and *their* director, Henry King, "had achieved certain effects." Gish asked Hayes what the on-set atmosphere was like; Hayes replied, "Oh, you know, the usual stories and jokes." "Then you're not going to get it," Gish told her. "You cannot set up a camera and take a picture of faith."

Gish was a great actress, but King's version of *The White Sister* is sanctimonious. André de Toth said that Fleming "was Henry King with balls," and that holds true even with this impossibly masochistic and high-minded material. Fleming thought the scene in which Hayes tells Gable that she won't renounce her vows one of the best he'd ever filmed. He knew that's when Hayes had to pay off—as René Jordan put it, "The Gable blow-torch style could by then melt an iceberg, but not Helen Hayes in a nun's habit." *Variety* applauded: "Pre-eminently a woman's picture and one of the strongest of recent entries in that direction."

A week after *The White Sister* premiered, Louella Parsons noted that Lu Rosson took in some recent prizefights with Fleming and Howard Hawks, and reported, "The Lou [*sic*] Rosson–Victor Fleming romance continues to interest Hollywood." But Fleming's next project would make him look back with laughter at a previous love. "A dramatic character sketch of Lola, a Clara Bow type—in fact, one is tempted to think that it is Miss Bow who is being dramatized." So began the October 25, 1932, MGM reader's report for the play *Bombshell* by Caroline Francke and Mack Crane—a serious examination of a Hollywood star losing her bearings.

Mahin explained:

> That came in, again, as a very purple movie, a treatment about this poor girl who worked all her life and in the end committed suicide. Nobody understood her, and she had all these people on her, her father and her brother. It was a tragic thing. I said, "Let's turn this into a comedy. It's funny. You must have known people, Vic, in the early days . . ." He said, "I know one right now, Clara Bow. She was my girl. You'd come into the room—there's a beautiful Oriental rug with coffee stains and dog shit all over the floor, and her father'd come in drunk."

No behind-the-scenes Hollywood film has been sharper than *Bombshell.* It revels in the ironies of the industry and popular press building a star image around the merest fragment of a diva's life. *Bombshell* is unique because it's such a *happy* satire. Fleming, unlike the studio reader, could see Bow's whirlwind personality as the basis for a comedy. By casting Harlow as Lola Burns and getting her loosest screen performance—her humor is as jiggly as her braless, corset-free look—Fleming ensured that the audience would always cheer on Lola, even after she makes lousy decisions. We see what she doesn't: her problem isn't her distance from "real" life at the studio but the rapacity of all-too-real parasites at home. Topping the list are her sporting-man "Pops" (Frank Morgan, Fleming's future Wizard of Oz, in an amusing sketch of a lesser humbug); her current gigolo lover, the Marquis di Binelli di Pisa, a.k.a. Hugo (Ivan Lebedeff, nonpareil at unctuousness); and her conscienceless sponging brother Junior. (Ted Healy demonstrates a lethal knowing deadpan in this role; in vaudeville he'd groomed the Three Stooges as *his* stooges.)

Fleming sees Lola as a creature made for and by the movies. For her, staying away from movies is suicide. Indeed, the innate movie-ness of Lola makes Space Hanlon (Lee Tracy) her only suitable life partner: he's the studio's director of publicity.

"He has a crush on Lola," Fleming said in his script notes. "It has taken a strange form, this love of his. If he openly declares it, he will be just another sucker falling for her. If he yields to her suggestion that they cut out fighting and get together, he will be letting her make a sucker out of him. He wants to and he does dominate her. He is jealous of her men, treats her cruelly, then does something nice to make up for it. Every day they row with each other, but always come back for more."

Rather than Space, the man's man in the picture is Vic's alter ego, Brogan (Pat O'Brien), who directs Lola in the real Harlow's role in *Red Dust*—one of the many ways this movie turns in-jokes inside out. Brogan, like Fleming, is the master of his set and, on his nights off, a romancer who won't push his advantage. But even he is susceptible to Space's pinpoint flattery. When Brogan lambastes the Marquis for distracting Lola, Hanlon calms him: "Is this the old smooth-tongued, easygoing Brogan? The one genius in Hollywood that hasn't got any temperament? The guy that used to keep his stage as quiet as a church and put as much work through in a day as those other piano movers put through in a week?" (Later, trying to puncture the director's allure, Hanlon splutters that Brogan is "a bluebeard.")

By filming this spot-on characterization of his own pre–*Gone With the Wind* reputation, Fleming was proving that he was more than the studio's top piano mover. As George Sidney said, he was a *big* man, with the ability to see where the power lay in Hollywood and the capacity to savor the fun embedded in its tinselly cynicism. In notes penned throughout April 1933, *Bombshell*'s producer, *Red Dust*'s Stromberg (billed as the *associate* producer, under "A Victor Fleming Production"), envisioned the movie as an entertainment exposé comparable to *The Front Page*, which he pegged as "the first play that presented the cyclonic inside of a newspaper office." Lola would be "a composite of any and all stars who have reached for the moon and arrived there," uninhibited and willing to show off her wares as lustily as Harlow did in *Red Dust*.

Stromberg wanted the movie's milieu to reflect his vision of "Hollywood as a crazy house, a burning Rome," and "a very miserable place . . . because the heart of Hollywood is miserable." He saw Space Hanlon as Howard Hughes, "a tall, lanky, good-looking guy." He emphasized that the movie must be "*real*," not "a satire or a burlesque, nor . . . [a] wallow in the mud." Based on Stromberg's notes, Jules Furthman took the first shot at the script.

Fleming, with *The White Sister* behind him, had embarked on another zoological trip with Fred Lewis, this time bagging snakes in Cedros, Cape San Lucas, and the Guayanas, including a boa constrictor that he adopted as a pet and dubbed Effie. (It became known for occasionally wrapping itself around the legs of unsuspecting dinner guests.) When Fleming got around to compiling his own notes on *Bombshell*, after his return on July 3, he made only one passing reference to Furthman's pages: describing Lola's sadness over lost possibilities, he says, parenthetically, "Play the episode as Furthman has written." It would be their last collaboration.

Fleming knew *Bombshell* had to be slaphappy. By the time he put it through Mahin's typewriter, it had become equal parts satire, burlesque, and wallow in the mud. Yet it remained real. And Space Hanlon became a forward-tilting fast talker with his eyes always popped toward the main chance. He, not Jim Brogan, proves to be Lola's odd true love and the movie's conquering antihero—the über-director of the studio universe. Fleming and Mahin achieve Stromberg's end by their own brash comic means. Their creation *is* to the world of the soundstage and the publicity office what *The Front Page* is to newspapers: a booby-trapped bouquet. With refreshing modernity, it blends raw back-lot atmosphere and location work (in Tucson and at various Los Angeles hotels, including the Ambassador, the Huntington, and the Beverly Hills) with privileged views of the actual MGM assembly line. Fleming grasps the diverse elements of the Dream Factory and spins them like plates on sticks in a vaudeville twirling act.

The citizens of the fictional Monarch Studios in *Bombshell* live in a world of make-believe even outside the studio gates. From the start, when a butler named Winters (Leonard Carey) calmly presents her with sauerkraut juice instead of orange juice for her breakfast, no one levels with Lola. Nearly everyone around her is either a chiseler or a glad-hander, because everyone depends on *her* for employment or needs to keep peace between her and the front-office suits. She *can* count on her blowsy maid, Loretta (the ultra-relaxed Louise Beavers), who wears an evening wrap for a negligee: she explains to Lola, "The negligee you give me got all tore night befo' last." "Your day off is sure brutal on your lingerie," Lola replies, in a line the Production Code couldn't squelch—and Loretta responds with a knowing smirk.

What does *Lola* want? Oh, love and respect all right. How she aims to get them changes from scene to scene. As Space tells Monarch's boss, Gillette, "She's great copy because she doesn't know what she wants and wants something different every day, and that's a story—!" At the start she's convinced that her supposedly aristocratic lover, the Marquis, is her salvation. Brogan calls the boyfriend "a no-good immigrant." Space quips, "Some guy with an Ellis Island accent happens to have a dress suit with a hair-ribbon across his chest, (and) you dames get a pedigree and start reaching for the tiara!" He later tells Lola, with broad irony, that the Marquis is "a cultured, charming gentleman. We need men like him in this country. We're still pioneers and backwoodsmen."

There's an air of self-satire to the period xenophobia. When Space refers to the press pack as "You Comanches," it's more guttural wit than racism. That also goes for the sequence in which Space arranges for immigration officers to snatch the Marquis from Lola's arms at the Cocoanut Grove—and for reporters to be present when he's zipped off to jail. "Modern journalism's speeded up like everything else, sugar," Space explains, when a newsie sells Lola a paper, minutes later, with a story about the Marquis already in it. Space is half-right and prophetic. But Lola sees through him—and through the Marquis, too. She joins the Brogan-Hanlon camp and calls the Marquis a "big patent-leather peanut vendor."

What's spiritually attractive about Lola is her generosity. If she has any real affection for a man, she cannot hold a grudge. Shortly after she demands that Gillette discharge Space, he comes to her literally hat in hand and tells her he's been planning a new image for her as a proper lady. She gets so far into this different "part" that she takes to heart a sob-sister interviewer, Mrs. Titcomb (Grace Hayle), who asks her, "In the grueling midst of your career—doesn't there ever come a longing for the right of *all* womanhood?" In another passage the Production Code protested to no avail, Mrs. Titcomb muses, "The call of motherhood is so strong in some women. And fatherhood in men, too. I sometimes think that's what killed Mr. Titcomb."

Space orchestrates a showdown at her house between the Marquis and Lola, with Brogan joining in, to amuse the press and to shock two ladies from the home committee of the orphanage who are interviewing Lola about adoption. As a bonus, Pops, Junior, and Junior's latest louche girlfriend (Isabel Jewell) also make the scene. The usually acute James Harvey, in his *Romantic Comedy in Hollywood*, lodges the caveat that "there is something finally unpleasant in the film's making *such* a joke out of the idea of Harlow having a baby." He sees it as the "cruelest" example of the movie winning laughs at its star's expense and credits Harlow for the "enthusiasm, skill and intelligence" that transcend the meanness of the material.

The movie's identification of Harlow with Lola, though, is slippery and playful. True, it shows Lola with the boxer Primo Carnera in the opening montage; Harlow had been slated to appear for MGM in *The Prizefighter and the Lady*, in which Carnera did a bit. Of course, Lola also runs through Harlow's scenes from *Red Dust*. But the gist of the comedy is that the real Lola differs humorously from the movie Lola—just as the real Harlow differed, tragicomically, from MGM's bombshell. And the thrust of the film's *satire* is that Lola is, in many ways, like her audience. She may know all the ugly machinations of the Dream Factory. But she gets her thoughts of proper behavior from the nicer movies being made all around her—and from the same popular press that either paints her as an irrepressible party girl or sends Mrs. Titcomb to question, then counsel her on womanhood.

Fleming and Mahin peppered the first hour with gags that would resonate with starry-eyed fans and influential Hollywoodians. Some of the jokes do double duty. The mooching father, brother, and secretary (Una Merkel) who make free with Lola's booze and money obviously derive from Bow's father, cousin, and hairdresser-turned-personal manager, Daisy DeVoe. But Lola's casually piratical clan also echoes the gaudy materialism and greed of Harlow's mother, Jean, and her second husband, Bello. "I felt sorry for the Baby," said Abrams. "All she did was work while her family took her money, just like the girl in the movie. She would come in at 6:00 a.m. each morning for makeup and hair and wardrobe and rehearsal, then shoot 'til dinner or later—and in they'd stroll in the middle of the day, dressed to the nines and riding high. They were parasites."

When Space asks Lola to go to the Cocoanut Grove "for Collegiate Night," Fleming must have been thinking of his last date with Bow at the Montmartre Café. Lola's Marquis, Hugo, reflects the propensity of 1920s and 1930s sirens (Mae Murray, Gloria Swanson, Constance Bennett) to wed titled Europeans, sometimes of questionable stock. "He's got royal blood in his veins," says Lola. "I don't care if he's got a royal flush in his kidneys, tell him to scram!" replies Brogan, with a cheerful brutality that Fleming might have underplayed had he not already been having constant attacks of kidney stones. And Fleming's script notes state that "the Nut," the bowler-hatted madman who keeps popping up like a movable jack-in-the-box and declaring himself Lola's husband, was based on an actual loony who did the same to Bebe Daniels.

When Lola finally wearies of the rat race—or of being around the rats who run it—she hightails it to Desert Springs (think Palm Springs), hoping to decompress in a plush resort. Space tracks her there. But the publicist's irritating presence helps make her vulnerable to a vision of class from a bygone era: "Gifford Middleton of Boston." Sporting a polo player's figure and with a rich woodwind timbre to his voice, Gifford—the high point of Franchot Tone's screen career—saves her from the Nut (who has followed her onto one of the resort's bridle paths) and smothers her in blandishments. She's doomed when he murmurs, "Your hair is like a field of silver daisies." With a flourish worthy of Prince Charles, he adds, "I'd like to run barefoot through your hair." (At least Tone knew how good these scripted lines were. In later years he took credit for ad-libbing them.) Abetted by C. Aubrey

Smith and Mary Forbes as his parents, he acts a bassoon-toned romantic buffoon to upper-crust perfection.

From the days of *When the Clouds Roll By* and *The Mollycoddle*, Fleming knew the ingredients of a satisfying comic wrap-up, and *Bombshell* has a doozy. The Middletons keep Gifford from marrying Lola, partly because of her vulgar movie-star popularity and partly because, after they meet Pops and Junior, they're wary of her bloodlines. Lola returns happily to Hollywood. She and Space shed their emotional armor and declare their love. But she soon discovers that the Middletons were actors hired by Space to humiliate her and propel her back to the studios. And no sooner does Space assuage her fury with a kiss than she learns that the Nut is really an actor hired by him, too. The movie ends as it begins, in merry chaos. It's a masterpiece of comic engineering.

If Fleming were not otherwise engaged with Lu Rosson, he and Harlow might have made a match. Fleming's friend Hawks had a one-night stand with her, then abandoned her. But Hawks was a sucker for a different, boyish athletic type (Mahin told Scott Eyman that Hawks was "disconcerted by the moisture she secreted during sex"), and for him Harlow was nothing more than a conquest. Vic didn't have a type. He was what Czech novelist Milan Kundera called an epic Don Juan, appreciating the objective variety of the feminine. But Fleming's relationship with Harlow was friendly and protective, not amorous. Charles Cotton's son remembers Vic squiring her for a beach day to Balboa without a hint of hanky-panky—to this boy, the glamour girl was down-to-earth and approachable, especially for a star nearing the acme of her popularity and critical approval.

MGM, though, was doing a lot of worrying about Harlow. She was having an affair with Max Baer, the heavyweight contender known as much for his easy charm as for his deadly punches. (Ron Howard demonized him in his boxing film, *Cinderella Man*.) Louella Parsons had alluded to the affair in her column and had asked Baer's wife about it. Dorothy Baer started talking divorce. MGM's publicity department doubted that, so soon after the suicide of her second husband, Paul Bern, Harlow's reputation could withstand another scandal. The pressure was on to make Harlow respectable. To her biographer David Stenn, what followed had all the earmarks of a studio-arranged marriage. On the set of *Bombshell* she proposed to her cinematographer,

Hal Rosson. He'd already photographed three Harlow hits, including *Red-Headed Woman* and *Red Dust*, and he'd established a jovial, trusting relationship with his star. No one had ever made her look better. But there was not even flirtation until Harlow made him a marital offer he couldn't refuse. Arizona, unlike California, didn't require a six-day waiting period. Justice of the Peace Earl A. Freeman married them in Yuma. In an interview with the *Los Angeles Times* on September 24, six days later, Harlow said, "Hal's exquisite quality of friendship, his vast capacity for loyalty," and "his divine sense of humor" made him the one for her. Her interviewer also noted that Harlow and Hal "insist the influence of the desert stars while on location with 'Bombshell' " swayed them toward their sudden elopement—just the sort of romantic hooey that *Bombshell* makes hash of. (Rosson's nephew Robert Terry visited his uncle after the wedding, and Harlow kissed the boy good night. "Her whole family, they weren't much," he recalls. "They were just interested in her for the money she could make them.")

The Rosson-Harlow nuptials were only the first in *Bombshell*'s talent base. Vic and Lu were next.

The circumstances were murky, but this much is known: Sometime between Vic's return from the Lewis trip and his completion of *Bombshell*'s first cut, Lu told him she was pregnant. And on September 26, 1933, the day before the film's first preview, he drove her 240 miles to Yuma, where Freeman married them, too. True to Fleming's long-standing story that he announced his retirement after every movie, he gave his occupation on the license application as "Retired—from motion pictures." They exchanged no wedding bands, and there was no honeymoon. According to Lu, Vic ordered Freeman, "Let's leave the 'love' out of the ceremony." Fleming drove back to California and deposited Lu at her old home. The marriage would stay secret for the next three months.

Some time and in some way after that, Lu told him she was not pregnant. The details of her mistake, deception, or self-deception only entered family lore in her sad tirades after Fleming's death in 1949, when, Sally observes, "Mother would get six Schlitzes under her belt and start to tell horrible stories." It's possible that in panic, Lu had impulsively sprung the oldest marital trap in the world. She knew of examples close to home and *in* her home: Lu's daughter Helene was two months pregnant when she married Jaime del Valle (later a famed radio director). And Mildred Harris had coerced Fleming's friend and neighbor Charlie Chaplin into marriage under the pressure of a pregnancy that turned out to be false, too.

Fleming's reaction was to tell Lu she could not share his Cove Way house until she was really pregnant. For nearly a year, she continued to use her old house as her social base and legal address until she did become pregnant the following May.

But Sally observes of those circumstances, "Let's be honest about one thing. They were adults. They had been friends up to that point for several years. And that long friendship is what kept them together."

Fleming gave no outward sign that he felt panicked or rushed into marriage. He rarely let his private complications get in the way of his job duties or amateur enthusiasms, and he didn't then. He immersed himself in *Bombshell* when he returned from the Lewis trip, and on September 23, he even kept an appointment to join Charles Cotton in the California state skeet-shooting championship in Santa Monica. On October 6, he boarded the *President Hoover* in San Francisco, bound for Hawaii and another animal-collection voyage with Lewis. Married or not, he was going to take his usual post-film getaway, plans he had made weeks earlier. Taking Lu to Hawaii, where they would be greeted by ship news reporters, would have ended the secrecy.

Fleming ensconced himself at the Royal Hawaiian Hotel in Honolulu for a couple of weeks until Lewis sailed in from San Pedro, and then spent the next two months sailing around the Hawaiian islands with the millionaire oilman N. Paul Whittier and his wife, the silent actress Olive Hasbrouck. They collected specimens for San Francisco's Steinhart Aquarium—yellow tang, butterfly fish, and moray eels—and were not scheduled to return until December. But another kidney stone attack forced Fleming to cut the trip short and sail back with Whittier on the luxury liner *Lurline*.

With the notable exception of his "engagement" to Bow, Fleming had kept his personal life largely out of public view—maybe that's why the real-life Space Hanlon, MGM's Howard Strickling, thought he was "the shyest, most bashful guy." Fleming separated parts of his existence from his extended family, too. His niece Yvonne said she and her family didn't even meet Lu until well after the marriage. "We could never figure out why in the world he married her."

A court case would force him into going public about the marriage—although not about its unusual living arrangement. In December, the MGM cameraman Paul Lockwood filed a $150,000 lawsuit accusing Fleming of "alienating the affections" of his wife, Marjorie DeHaven, a pert, big-eyed brunette and sometime dancer. She was the daughter of the stage stars Carter DeHaven and Flora Parker, and the older sister of Gloria DeHaven.

Such lawsuits were common in Los Angeles in the depths of the Depression—practically a weekly occurrence—until California finally outlawed them. Lockwood contended that the director "debauched and carnally knew" his twenty-one-year-old wife, dangled the prospect of a film career, and had an unnamed friend lure her to San Francisco and then abandon her on October 4, two days before Fleming sailed for Hawaii.

Fleming and his lawyer, Howard Henshey, knew the suit was coming, so Henshey made what, for Fleming, was a rare phone call to publicize his marriage. On December 18, 1933, the same day Lockwood filed suit, Walter Winchell's column reported in its typical slang that Vic and Lu "were secretly welded in Yuma months ago." Newspapers jumped on both the lawsuit and the wedding announcement, and the story made national news, sometimes with a photo of Mrs. Lockwood in a demure pose. Henshey filed a point-by-point denial to the accusations.

Nothing came of it. The case was never heard. When Lockwood attempted to divorce his wife the following year, a different tale emerged. He charged that his wife had become "infatuated" with Fleming—not that they'd had sexual relations or that an unnamed man assisted the scheme—and that he found a note from her saying she was about to go to Honolulu with "her true love." That's when Lockwood drove to San Francisco with her father and found her there in a sanatorium. (If she had taken the same train as Fleming to San Francisco, it was not disclosed.)

Mrs. Lockwood never appeared in court for the divorce trial. Because she refused to undergo a court-ordered psychiatric examination, Judge Georgia Bullock, under the state law of the time, could not grant the divorce. (A divorce went through on other grounds in 1936.)

For every possible scenario, there's a question, but no information to answer it: Did Fleming seduce a fragile woman in some erotic yet misogynistic panic of his own? Was studio pressure brought on Lockwood to alter his story, or was there a secret cash settlement? Did Fleming impulsively set up a sexual encounter, then change his mind? Was it all a legalized extortion attempt? Or did Mrs. Lockwood become so infatuated with Fleming that she followed him—and did this truth force Lockwood to revise his accusations?

The matter faded away, and Fleming reerected his wall of privacy. But Victoria used to hear jokingly from her half sister, Helene, that occasionally her father would find a woman hiding in his car in the studio parking lot. It was a recurring echo of the Lockwood case.

Meanwhile, *Bombshell* was turning into Fleming's most contemporary, of-the-moment film since *Mantrap*—and its pace reflected the racing current of the director's life. Louis B. Mayer's cutting chief, Margaret Booth, said, "I worked alone [in the editing room] and then Fleming came in. He was a *wonderful* man"—and a daring director, in his prime. "Nobody had ever cut anything that fast; I cut it very snappy, which was unusual then. Everybody at the studio said, 'Oh, it isn't going to be any good.' And of course it was terrific." At least that's how it played at its Hollywood premiere. "*Bombshell* was a SENSATION, a WOW, a SUCCESS, and what an evening," wrote Harlow's mother to Jean's agent, Arthur Landau, even though Louis B. Mayer snubbed her daughter by stopping and saying only, "God, [Lee] Tracy has great lines." In a night letter to Nicholas Schenck, Mayer urged him to hold the film back from release in order to build a proper campaign: "Don't believe we should spend money on picture that has no possibilities but BOMBSHELL has not only star value but is truly great entertainment."

In 1989, Booth confessed that at the film's sneak previews, MGM thought it "a dud." She said, "People then didn't appreciate it like we do now. It's more of a hit today." After it opened, the manager of the Fox Granada Theater in Kansas City, Kansas, complained to Mayer, "Box office returns on *Bombshell* and *Lady Killer* indicate pictures on Hollywood are not wanted. Suggest you change title *Going Hollywood* to *Going Gay* or similar title." For a knowing, urbane farce, *Bombshell* still did well—at $761,000, its gross more than doubled its $344,000 cost. And it had a far-reaching influence: the director Stanley Donen, his co-director and star, Gene Kelly, and his screenwriters, Betty Comden and Adolph Green, screened *Bombshell* before they created *Singin' in the Rain.* In its own time, *Bombshell* solidified Fleming's reputation as one of the few directors who could do anything in sound that he did in the silents, from adventure to erotic melodrama to sophisticated farce.

15

Treasure Island

While Fleming was making his next picture, the quintessential pirate adventure, *Treasure Island*, Hollywood was going through an abrupt and concentrated climate change. The rising Hays Office censor Joseph Breen had done everything he could to heat up the animus between the Catholic Church and Hollywood's Jewish moguls. In a letter to Father Wilfrid Parsons (the editor of *America*), he called the studios' Jewish leadership "probably, the scum of the earth." When Breen became the head of the newly formed Production Code Administration office, he set out to give the code teeth. He succeeded. The innuendo-laden adult humor audiences had enjoyed in movies like *Red Dust* and *Bombshell* would now have to be camouflaged or abandoned.

Before the studios began to feel Breen's bite, Fleming had already started preparing his adaptation of Robert Louis Stevenson's beloved 1883 adventure about the plucky lad Jim Hawkins, the murderous one-legged rascal Long John Silver, and their search for buried treasure on a tropic isle in the eighteenth century. Luckily for Fleming, it was family fare, but with a violent, sometimes terrifying edge that would grow ever rarer in studio pictures after the growth spurt of the Production Code. *Treasure Island* had been filmed at least twice in the silent era, but not even Maurice Tourneur's 1920 version, with Lon Chaney in two roles (including the blind pirate Pew), achieved the pop-cultural penetration of, say, Fairbanks's *Three Musketeers* or *Robin Hood.* With this hale and hearty blockbuster, Fleming would succeed where the gifted Tourneur had failed.

In the spring of 1934, Fleming and his producing partner, Stromberg (who would get a full producer's credit on-screen for *Treasure Island*—an uncommon occurrence for a Fleming picture), knew they had the opportunity to craft a fresh image of a children's classic.

According to Jackie Cooper, who played Jim Hawkins, Fleming and Stromberg lobbied in vain to film in the South Seas instead of on Catalina Island (off the Southern California coast); to purchase a true oceangoing frigate; and to shoot in color, as Fairbanks did with his 1926 two-strip Technicolor hit, *The Black Pirate*. (Fairbanks's technical supervisor on all matters piratical, Dwight Franklin, advised Fleming on buccaneering, too.) Mayer turned these requests down; Fleming threatened to walk.

"If Fleming didn't do it, then Mr. Mayer was not happy with any other director," Cooper recalled. So, while not giving in to Fleming's demands, Mayer placed every in-house resource of an MGM superproduction at his disposal. Studio publicity trumpeted "more than two years of preparatory work in the studio research department." The production accumulated antiques, including "thirty-five genuine flintlock rifles," and manufactured stunning facsimiles, such as "ten large cannon with a range of a mile each." Crewmen paved mock-ups of eighteenth-century roads and walkways with several tons of cobblestones. In Oakland, California, MGM dressed the estuary wharf of the Alaska Packers Association to look like the Bristol docks. A private collector supplied Catalina with tropical birds. A second unit was sent to Hawaii (Maui, mostly) for additional boat shots and rowing shots.

For the *Hispaniola*, the three-masted, square-rigged sailing ship of Stevenson's tale, MGM salvaged the hulk of the whaler *Nanuk*, which had survived the production of *Eskimo* (the film Fleming had encountered on vacation in Alaska), and erected period decks and masts on top of it. "If you dove in the water and swam down a few feet, you could see the other hull right underneath it," Cooper said. "But it stayed afloat, this thing, and it sailed. Actually, underneath there were the motors moving it." (Cooper insisted that the *Nanuk* was a yacht and that Joseph Schenck had lent it to Mayer.) Cooper ended up having to wear a wig, because he'd cut off his boyish bob when it looked as if the picture would fall through.

The most critical construction was the script. Leonard Praskins and the future leader of the Hollywood Ten, John Howard Lawson, each took a swing at it. To avoid what Stromberg called "the leisurely start of the story," these scripts began with Captain Flint burying his loot at Treasure Island. The novel's colorful, mysterious brigands—even Billy Bones, whose tumultuous residence at the Hawkins family's Admiral Benbow Inn sets Stevenson's tale in motion, and the menacing blind man Pew, who hands Billy the black spot that seals his doom—entered the tale as bold buccaneers rather than spooky enigmas. Early drafts depicted Long John Silver losing his leg and gaining a wooden stump in a mutiny. No wonder Stromberg recalled, "We began to feel we were leaving too little to the imagination. When Billy Bones arrived at the Inn, there was, for those who would see the picture, nothing mysterious about his character. He was mysterious to Jim Hawkins, perhaps, but *not* to the audience."

Fleming eventually cut this material and made the Admiral Benbow Inn, once again, the story's point of origin. To speed things up further, he eliminated the character of Hawkins's father (after all, he begins wasting away just three pages into the narrative) and turned young Jim Hawkins into the man of the house and the sole protector of a pretty mother (Dorothy Peterson). With Fleming's new favorite, Mahin, in charge of the script (he would receive sole credit), the moviemakers built suspense while balancing coziness and risk, picturesque action and grotesquerie. In the finished film, Jim is a lad we first see baking a cake for his mother's birthday. Shortly afterward, he begins to serve as a trusted aide to the dissolute, apoplectic Billy Bones (Lionel Barrymore), who uses the Benbow Inn as a hideout. Without resorting to narration, Fleming and Mahin walk us right inside Jim Hawkins's head. The movie's Jim seems a few years younger than the book's, but he has a large thirst for thrills. And with the age difference, his gullibility becomes more understandable, his perils more pronounced.

Mahin and Fleming perceived *Treasure Island* as an elemental melodrama whose complexities derive from divided allegiances among the characters, not from psychological torture underneath their skin. "Character to the boy is a sealed book," wrote Stevenson in an essay defending the emotional authenticity of his work; "for him a pirate is a beard, a pair of wide trousers, and a liberal complement of pistols . . . The characters are portrayed only so far as they realise the sense of danger and provoke the sympathy of fear." The moviemakers bravely embellish Stevenson's caricatures. Watch this movie at an impressionable age and it's your *Treasure Island* for life. Watch the movie in adulthood and you have to adjust to its high-on-the-hog acting and broad-stroke storytelling. But adjust you will. The *New Republic*'s Otis Ferguson, the best American film critic of the day, called it "a picture so good in some ways that any but the most determined can see what fresh possibilities in the way of beauty and free movement lie in this new art of the screen." Mahin and Fleming hit on a hyperbolic tone that's scary, comical, and disrespectful of propriety—that's what Ferguson meant when he wrote that they caught "the frank swagger of the story."

Barrymore's scowling, growling Billy petrifies the inn's clientele with tales of seafaring men less "genteel" than himself who would slice and dice Spanish dons, ravish their women, and drain their feminine blue blood into punch. (The content is Stevenson, the words pure Mahin.) You know you're in good hands when Dr. Livesey (Otto Kruger) enters the picture and, in a ringing line from Stevenson, vows to Billy that if he doesn't stop brandishing his cutlass, he'll "hang at the next assizes." Kruger makes Dr. Livesey's righteousness function as an invisible shield. And "Lionel Barrymore was just marvelous as Billy Bones," Mahin remembered years later. "He had that shiny black beard; N. C. Wyeth had drawn color pictures of those characters, and his face was like that, just shiny from the weather."

Fleming swiftly sketches Black Dog (Charles McNaughton) and Pew (William V. Mong) and the other scoundrels who go after Bones's sea chest as part of a rogues' gallery that stretches to infinity, or hell. In a breathtaking and brutal variation on Pew's death scene from the book (one of the good guys' horses tramples him), Dr. Livesey crushes the sightless brigand *twice*. His carriage horses knock Pew down; then both sets of carriage wheels create ruts in his body. (On location, Fleming used an Oakland riding-academy manager as the coachman, after forcing the fellow to shave off his grandiose mustache.) At its fringes, this *Treasure Island* is a Halloween cartoon. The score, with its insidious theme song—"Fifteen men on the dead man's chest / Yo-ho-ho and a bottle of rum!"—employs a pastiche chantey and occasional bouts of minstrelsy to form a not-so-silly symphony. There's something Disney-like about the way Fleming coordinates the score with images of desperate men straight out of Wyeth illustrations—pockmarked, wart-laden pirates in billowing capes tramping up lonely seaside lanes under lowering skies. (Fleming was thinking of Wyeth when he promised a columnist an "exact picturization of the book.") When Jim croons the dead-man's-chest song as Billy Bones walks the hills outside the inn, dirty dealings float through the air. Fleming's *Treasure Island* belongs to the realm of good bad dreams.

After Jim saves the treasure map from Black Dog's crew and delivers it to Squire Trelawney (Nigel Bruce) with Dr. Livesey, the Squire hastens to outfit a ship for his treasure hunt. In Stevenson, the Squire falls "in talk with" Long John Silver on the Bristol dock and hires him as sea cook. Mahin sharpens the action. The introduction of the sea cook and Jim at Silver's Spy-Glass Inn had been, in previous scripts, too "long," noted Mahin, "and not at all pictorial. Instead, in the final scenario, we have Jim, a boy in transports of delight, rushing here and there on the ship during his first moments aboard. Boy-like, he kneels down to sight a cannon, and through the porthole he sees a man with one leg!"

In this exhilarating presentation of the movie's extraordinary good-bad guy, Fleming's camera swings with Hawkins's point of view until it fixes on Silver (Wallace Beery), who soon accepts the job of sea cook and takes the Squire up on his offer to replace a vanished crew. (Beery signals the audience that Silver is behind the seamen's disappearance.) When Long John approaches the Spy-Glass Inn with Jim, he buys a whistle for his young friend—then uses it to alert his mates. With comical rapidity, they cease brawling and assume mellow, amiable postures as Dandy Dawson (Charles Bennett) sings and strums his mandolin. It's the kind of stunt-like transformation found in Roaring Twenties movies set in speakeasies. And it's typical of the filmmakers' drive to keep the story dynamic as well as fable-like. Dandy Dawson, a Mahin-Fleming invention, is a true "dandy" who loves fine lace and sings Robert Herrick's "Gather Ye Rosebuds While Ye May" but keeps a dagger hidden in his tricornered hat. "I like pretty things," he tells Jim ominously, after Long John introduces them, and notes that with their similar shoe size, they're like "two sister craft." Jim never gets close to this predatory figure again.

Long John and Jim, though, become fast friends, because Silver treats the boy as a peer. In his script notes Fleming remarks, "What would help make the kid and the audience like him, even though he does slit throats, is the way he explains to the kid the necessity of one pirate having to kill another, etc.—it's just a matter of business, that's all." In a way, it reflects the child star's relationship with his director. When giving interviews at the time, Cooper said, "One thing I hate is to be treated like a baby. Mr. Fleming didn't try any of that stuff on me. He's my pal." (Fleming, for his part, called Cooper "a great kid," able to discuss everything from "screen stories" to "the Chinese situation.")

Because Mahin and Fleming respect Stevenson's structure, their version plays faster than the half-hour-briefer (ninety-minute) Disney

CHRISTY KELSO COLLECTION

On her own: Eva Fleming with Victor, Arletta, and newborn Ruth, September 1893, Pomona, California.

CHRISTY KELSO COLLECTION

CHRISTY KELSO COLLECTION

(left) Starting out in California: Victor Fleming's parents, Lon and Eva, in Pasadena, 1891. *(right)* Eva and her second husband, Sid Deacon, early 1920s.

CHRISTY KELSO COLLECTION

KEVIN BROWNLOW COLLECTION

(top) Fleming in Santa Barbara, 1912. *(bottom)* Fleming is in the passenger seat of this camera car (year unknown), but his first goal in life was to become an automobile racer.

KEVIN BROWNLOW COLLECTION

First lieutenant Victor Fleming of the Signal Corps mans a Bell & Howell camera while acting as Woodrow Wilson's personal cameraman with the Presidential Peace Party, 1918.

TOPICAL PRESS AGENCY/HULTON ARCHIVE/GETTY IMAGES

Fleming filmed iconic images of President Woodrow Wilson in his top hat and kangaroo-pelt coat, touring the European capitals in triumph before the Versailles peace conference. Here Wilson is flanked by French prime minister Georges Clemenceau and British prime minister David Lloyd George.

Fleming and the "It Girl," Clara Bow, at the start of their affair, making *Mantrap* (1926).

ARCHIVE PHOTOS/HULTON ARCHIVE/GETTY IMAGES

Fleming and another lover, Bessie Love, on location for *A Son of His Father* (1925).

HULTON ARCHIVE/GETTY IMAGES

Four Conquests

© BETTMANN/CORBIS

(above) Samuel Goldwyn's new discovery, Lili Damita, visits Fleming on the set of his Goldwyn-produced picture, *The Awakening* (1928). *(below)* Fleming with Ingrid Bergman at the New York City premiere of *Joan of Arc* (1948). Their affair was over, and he would be dead two months later.

SALLY FLEMING COLLECTION

Family portrait: Fleming, Vicky, Lu, and newborn Sally, 1937.

SALLY FLEMING COLLECTION

Fleming bought this 81-foot yacht from Frank Morgan to sail up and down the Pacific coast and kept Morgan's name for it, *The Dolphin*.

SALLY FLEMING COLLECTION

The polio scare of 1946 prompted Fleming to purchase Knapp Island, near Vancouver, British Columbia, and to use this spacious house as a family retreat.

Douglas Fairbanks and Fleming were masters of pranksmanship. Here Fairbanks hangs off the roof of a caboose by hanging on to Fleming's chest.

ARCHIVES OF THE NATIONAL FILM SOCIETY BY PERMISSION OF JOHN C. TIBBETTS

Fleming cleans the camera lens as John Emerson directs Arline Pretty and Fairbanks on *In Again, Out Again* (1917).

Fleming did his only on-screen acting when he directed Fairbanks and costarred with him in *Around the World in Eighty Minutes with Douglas Fairbanks* (1931). This photo was carefully posed to create the illusion that Fairbanks and Fleming were roughly the same height.

KEVIN BROWNLOW COLLECTION

(above) Fleming trains his eye on (*from left*) Ernest Torrence, Percy Marmont, and Clara Bow in *Mantrap* (1926), on a set in the Famous Players-Lasky Studios. James Wong Howe is at the camera. *(below)* Fleming (at the camera), John Emerson (with megaphone), and Douglas Fairbanks (on horse) shooting the comic western *Wild and Woolly* (1917).

KEVIN BROWNLOW COLLECTION

On location in San Antonio for the lost epic *The Rough Riders* (1927). George Bancroft holds a cigarette in one hand and his army hat in the other; James Wong Howe sports a white cap; Henry Hathaway, his head popping out of the crowd at his director's feet, awaits orders from Fleming, who holds the megaphone; and next to Fleming sits a visitor, Clara Bow. This photo was taken on September 15, 1926, when she announced she and Fleming were "engaged."

PHOTOFEST

Fleming directs Clark Gable and Vivien Leigh as they stroll down Peachtree Street in the studio-built Atlanta of *Gone With the Wind* (1939).

PHOTOFEST

Producer David O. Selznick and Fleming confer over the troubled script.

GREG GIESE COLLECTION

Selznick, Leigh, Fleming, Carole Lombard, and Gable celebrate at the wrap party.

WILLARD CARROLL COLLECTION

Judy Garland, Fleming, Myrna Loy, and Frank Morgan at Fleming's going-away party on *The Wizard of Oz* (1939).

COURTESY OF CAROLE SAMPECK FROM THE LOMBARD ARCHIVE/JEAN GARCEAU COLLECTION

Sunday fun. Three members of the Moraga Spit and Polish Club: Gable, Ward Bond, and Fleming. Bel-Air, 1946.

HULTON ARCHIVE/GETTY IMAGES

Composer Jerome Kern visits Jean Harlow and Fleming on the set of Fleming's first musical, *Reckless* (1935).

PHOTO BY PATSY RUTH MILLER, KEVIN BROWNLOW COLLECTION

Fleming vacationing on the Rogue River in Oregon just before he went to work on *The Wizard of Oz*.

KEVIN BROWNLOW COLLECTION

The strain of filming *Joan of Arc* shows in this 1947 portrait.

adaptation from 1950. Fleming's team holds true to Stevenson's charged tableaux technique—they recognize that the relative impact of each episode is a matter not of length or adrenaline but of intensity of feeling. ("There was a fine sequence of the ship getting under weigh," Otis Ferguson wrote, "one of the most lovely I have seen.") And they pick up on the mildest suggestions of suspense and wit. Just when you think there couldn't be a more righteous gentleman than Dr. Livesey, along comes Captain Alexander Smollett (Lewis Stone), who orders the sailors' blades "tipped" (or blunted) when he fears they know they're on a treasure hunt. (It's another Mahin-Fleming invention.) Smollett borders on the prescient during the sea voyage. But he flits with foolishness after Silver's mutiny. Smollett, Livesey, and Trelawney, along with a few good men, abandon ship and defend themselves in an empty island stockade. The stalwart captain flies the British flag and won't pull it down even though it presents the pirates with a target. He's determined to create a spot of England—a true-to-the-book incident that plays today like a piece of satire.

Stone is Stevenson's Smollett to the unpliable upper lip. The film's most audacious re-creation, though, may be Charles "Chic" Sale's Ben Gunn, a crazy-eyed man in beard and tatters who's been marooned on the island for three years and tells Jim that he can save his friends from Silver's scurvy bunch. Sale moves with a painful, ecstatic angularity: it's as if he's astounded that his limbs are still attached to him. Mahin seizes on a subtle conversational tic in Stevenson's book to compose a manner of speech for this castaway that's riotously and emotionally true. Ben has been alone in the wilderness for so long that he transforms dialogue into monologue, and vice versa; "says you" and "says I" and "says he" punctuate every turn of his thought. Cooper gets the last laugh when Jim, in a bout of disgust that his friends take this loon quite seriously, mutters, "Says he, says them, says I, says nobody."

Because of Cooper's baby-faced youth, Fleming could cut down on Jim's awkwardness and indecision without losing the boy's alternately awestruck and despairing perspective. "At twelve going on thirteen," Cooper said in his as-told-to autobiography, *Please Don't Shoot My Dog* (1981), "it was the hardest work of my life, and some of the most unpleasant." A lot of the unpleasantness came from co-starring with Wallace Beery, a prima donna who reacted to Cooper shooting some relatively harmless flash powder on his foot as if he'd been mortally wounded. Although Mahin thought "all the pirates were good," he "didn't think Beery was too good. He was so funny when he got the script. He said, 'I don't want to play this thing.' Then somebody told him it was a great classic and then Beery was saying, 'Oh, you can't touch a word of this picture. This is a classic.' " Part of Beery's bluster came from physical agony. "Beery was in terrible pain most of the time, with that leg strapped up in back of him," said Cooper. "He just hated it. He'd pick scenes as often as possible sitting down, or sitting on the ground where they could dig a hole and stick his leg into it."

For Cooper, his director provided most of the "bright spots." He urged the young star to play old. "Fleming would tell me not to whine, to try to act more mature. It was the first time anyone had made me think about what I was doing, really to consider my character and how to make him come alive." He later told Burt Prelutsky for *Emmy* magazine that Vidor and Fleming were his best directors, explaining, "When I was a kid, directors were always offering me bicycles whenever they wanted me to play a difficult scene. Instead of trying to communicate with me, they always tried bribes. By the time I was nine, I had eight or nine bikes in the garage. Fleming would speak to me like an adult. He would talk to me about the scene. I felt he respected me. As a result, I would break my neck to please him."

Cooper proved wise beyond his years when it came to handling the rude, unpredictable Beery. Mahin said that in "the last shot of the last day of the picture," Jim had to cry at Long John's departure, and Fleming demanded, "Come on Jackie, you've got to get to work. Let's stop fooling and finish the darned thing." Cooper said, "Okay, Uncle Wally, be mean to me." Beery let loose with "You little son of a bitch, I've had it with this leg . . . I've got pains, varicose veins." Before long, Jackie, "crying like a trouper," turned to his director and said, "All right, Vic, roll 'em!"

Cooper saw that Fleming was in touch with his own inner twelve-year-old. When the cast arrived by seaplane at a secluded spot in Catalina Island, "a sort of a large rowboat came out to the seaplane to pick us up." Cooper's teacher stepped out on the edge of the boat before he and Fleming were off the seaplane—and "of course the boat went out from under her and she went in the water. With the water filling up her clothes and herself filling up her clothes, she looked like a balloon in the water, spouting great streams of salt water, and pilots and people were jumping in trying to save her—she couldn't swim, the poor thing. My mother was screaming. They got her out, but she was large and heavy to get out. All Vic Fleming kept yelling was 'Jackie, throw your schoolbooks in the water, throw your schoolbooks in the water!' He and I were hysterical while this poor woman half drowned," Cooper recalled, chuckling.

The actor needed to put his trust in Fleming, especially in physically uncertain scenes such as Jim's race up the riggings of the *Hispaniola* with the pirate Israel Hands (Douglas Dumbrille) in pursuit. "Jackie's perch sixty feet above the deck was precarious," said Fleming. "The roll of the boat made it hard to maintain the balance of the cameras built on parallels over the edge of the boat. It was necessary to cover the mike boom to avoid the whistling of the wind."

For Fleming, "the most difficult scene mechanically" was Smollett's flight under fire from the *Hispaniola.* "The cannon being fired from the ship and the men in the small boat firing muskets back required several days to photograph. It was necessary repeatedly to remine the ocean, dry off the guns and the players, and reshoot the scene, although it consumes less than two minutes on the screen." On the set for one of those days, Philip K. Scheuer of the *Los Angeles Times* observed, "A small charge of dynamite had to be planted each time in a fathom or two of water, its location marked by a cork. On signal there would be a puff of white smoke from the ship, a count of three, and then the charge would be set off. When there wasn't a mix-up in signals, the skiff would either be too near or too far from the charge. As we departed, Victor Fleming, the director, was slowly going crazy. He didn't even say good-by. Just 'Cut!' "

Editing was the ultimate rewrite on *Treasure Island.* Mahin had written and Fleming had filmed the book's melodrama-charged sequence of Jim's witnessing the buccaneers handing Silver "the black spot," just as Pew had handed it to Billy Bones. "But at this point," Fleming said, "the preview audience grew restless; they shifted in their seats; they rattled programs; they coughed, all signs of diminished attention. It was obvious that their sympathy was with Jim, the Squire, Livesey." So Fleming "confined the issue to Long John's defense of Jim. This simple change, absolutely, at the next preview, eliminated the break in audience attention we had noticed here."

Final cut on the movie, of course, belonged to Mayer. According to Cooper, Mayer was crestfallen for two reasons. First, Cooper, his biggest child star, the uncrowned prince of male weepies since *The Champ* (1931, also co-starring Beery), hadn't a single good bawling scene in the whole picture. And the climax of Long John slipping away under the eye of Ben Gunn didn't provide a suitable theatrical crescendo for the friendship between the pirate and Jim Hawkins. So LB "had a new ending written—Jim Hawkins frees Long John Silver just before the end of the film, but first, he cries because his piratical friend will be gone forever." This capper has caused Stevenson scholars to charge the film with sentimentality ever since.

Still, the relationship between the boy and the buccaneer generally cleaves to the novel. From the time he lies hidden in an apple barrel and eavesdrops on Long John laying plans for mutiny, Jim sees through the pirate's feigned innocence. Yet even after he witnesses Long John commit cold-blooded murder, he retains a reluctant admiration for the man's leadership, cleverness, and persistence, just as Long John appreciates the boy's true grit even after Jim brags of setting the *Hispaniola* adrift and bollixing the pirates' plans. Cooper and Beery are at their best when Long John and Jim are enjoying each other's mettle. The characters' mutual admiration needs no underlining. Small wonder that Cooper was to write, "We were all unhappy at the summons to return to work." Beery hated the idea of Cooper getting a climactic showcase, so he flubbed lines and stalled and stretched a day of retakes into a week. As for the director, Cooper said, "Fleming nearly had a stroke; to him, the idea of mucking about with a Stevenson ending was damn near sacrilegious."

Mayer, however, did know his audience, and he didn't stint on promotion. *Treasure Island* initially grossed $565,000 over its enormous $825,000 budget, then was revived both in the United States and overseas. It was during a London revival that Graham Greene, then a film critic (and a great one), compared it favorably to the nautical adventure *Midshipman Easy*, by Carol Reed, his future friend and collaborator on *The Fallen Idol*, *The Third Man*, and *Our Man in Havana*. Wrote Greene: "The story of *Treasure Island* has a deeper, more poetic value" because "the buried treasure, the desert island, the horrifying murder of the faithful sailor, the persons of Long John and blind Pew, all these have symbolic value. *Treasure Island* contains, as *Midshipman Easy* does not, a sense of good and evil. Even a child can recognize the greater dignity and depth of this Scottish Presbyterian's *Mansoul* written in terms of an adventure-story for a boys' magazine."

Treasure Island solidified Fleming's reputation as a "big picture" man and a reliable moneymaker. Ever since 1929, he had wanted to do "epics, not melodramas," but this at least was an epic melodrama.

He was firming up his marriage, too. Lu was devoted, even witty. Vidor would say, "Fleming was very sort of tough with his wife, always," but Victoria thought she was happy playing a supporting role and was "completely subordinate and quiet. He was a big director and she was his very little wren of a wife." As far as his niece Blocksom could see, "She spent her days playing cards and gambling. She was a great gambler, so [now] she had money to gamble with. But Uncle Vic wanted children." Lu visited Vic on Catalina, the site of a great casino, while he was filming there in May—Sally says her mother joked years later, "It was a dark and stormy night"—and gave birth to their first child, Victoria Sue, on January 28, 1935.

16

Introducing Henry Fonda, Farewell to Jean Harlow

A fan of Fleming's since Vic's Paramount days, David O. Selznick was in the middle of his brief but spectacular producing stint at MGM, designed, said his father-in-law, Louis B. Mayer, to take pressure off the ailing Irving Thalberg, who suffered from a bad heart. Under various working titles, including *Salute*, *There Goes Romance*, and *A Woman Called Cheap*, Selznick, using the pseudonym Oliver Jeffries, cooked up the original story for Fleming's first musical, *Reckless* (1935), with the director himself. Ten writers, including Joseph Mankiewicz, Philip Barry, S. N. Behrman, and Val Lewton, had some involvement with the script; P. J. Wolfson got credit for the final screenplay.

Selznick and company loosely based the film on the mysterious demise of Smith Reynolds, the R. J. Reynolds tobacco heir who died of a gunshot wound to the head. His widow, torch singer Libby Holman, contended that it was suicide; the state of North Carolina nonetheless accused Holman and Reynolds's best friend, Ab Walker, of murder. Holman was an easy target, being Jewish, bisexual, and culturally and politically adventurous, but the family successfully petitioned the state to drop the case because the evidence was not decisive. (Holman's biographer Jon Bradshaw argues that Reynolds's death resulted from Ab and Libby trying to wrest Smith's gun from his hand.) Parallels to Holman run a zigzag path through *Reckless*.

The movie's heroine, Mona Leslie (Jean Harlow)—also a Broadway musical star, but not Jewish, bisexual, educated, or culturally and politically adventurous—makes the mistake of eloping with a flamboyant, confused swell named Bob Harrison (Franchot Tone). His one accomplishment in life is founding the SAML: the Society for the Admiration of Mona Leslie. Bob's belated recognition that he still loves the highborn woman (Rosalind Russell) whom he jilted to marry Mona leads to his suicide. The media and the district attorney accuse Mona of murder, and Bob's snooty father (Henry Stephenson) threatens to bring their fight over the custody of his grandson to trial. Her support through all her troubles is the fellow who really loves her: Ned Riley (William Powell), a sports promoter who catapulted Mona from the sideshow circuit to headlining shows on the Great White Way. (Two weeks before the premiere of *Reckless*, MGM publicity chief Howard Strickling wrote Howard Dietz, his New York counterpart and a friend of Holman's, assuring him there was "nothing ever done here to connect Holman case with RECKLESS and will be doubly careful in the future.")

After the arduous *Treasure Island*, *Reckless* must have seemed like a cakewalk for Fleming, who had wanted to do a musical ever since *Burlesque* fell off his schedule in 1929. Fleming became acquainted with Broadway's brand of personality-infused musical theater in his Columbia/Army days, when he and his company saw Al Jolson, in *Sinbad*, step to the footlights and announce that he had been hunting down barbed wire to weave a sweater for the kaiser. Selznick obviously intended *Reckless* to be "Metro Goldwyn Mayer's mammoth musical melodrama" of 1935 (to quote the poster copy). He aimed to star Joan Crawford as Mona and surround her with a clutch of top players: not just Powell as Ned and Tone as Bob Harrison but also, as Mona's granny, May Robson, who had recently been Frank Capra's Apple Annie in *Lady for a Day* (1933). "So this picture looms as of the multiple stellar variety," noted one press release. But along the way, Harlow fell for Powell. MGM, hoping to capitalize on the eruption of this romance into the newspapers, pulled Crawford out and put Harlow in—though the story now seemed (to Harlow and others) a vulgar echo of her marriage to Paul Bern.

Powell urged Harlow to stay in the picture because walking out would enrage the studio into suspending her and further cloud her image. Selznick later wrote, "I thought she could do well by it and was for the substitution, even though I certainly never would have planned a musical for Jean Harlow," who was no singer or dancer. Virginia Verrill dubbed her vocals. The choreography interlaced long shots of Harlow's dancing double (Betty Halsey) with the star herself, swaying her shoulders, swinging her arms, and executing a cartwheel and some skips and bounces.

But *Reckless* doesn't fail because of Harlow's inadequacies; it fails because it plays like a sober and archaic Broadway version of the inside-showbiz melodramas that Fleming had already satirized to cinders with *Bombshell.* In *Reckless,* instead of a sponging family, there's the square, straight-shooting grandma (Robson). Instead of *Bombshell's* dozens of Hollywood hustlers, there are Ned Riley's redoubtable lieutenants. They're Runyonesque and funny-tough yet also *righteous* New Yorkers, played by *Bombshell's* uncouth brother, Ted Healy (Smiley), and Nat Pendleton (Blossom), who had appeared with Powell in *The Thin Man.* Space Hanlon in *Bombshell* was as wily, witty, and manipulative as he was amorously abashed. In *Reckless,* the otherwise similar Ned Riley is more wounded and smitten. And Tone, as Harrison, is a rakish version of Gifford Middleton without the comical corkscrew of his *Bombshell* character.

Indeed, nearly everything Fleming played for laughs in *Bombshell* he played for melodrama or poignancy here, and his heart wasn't in it. Nor did he have the instinct for backstage byplay that he had for soundstage hustle and flow. *Bombshell,* though broadly satirical, boasts a veracious edge. *Reckless* is stagy, even for a film about the stage.

Fleming was at his best in the modest moments of *Reckless.* Mona and Bob play out their madcap courtship on a merry-go-round and in a fun house. Ned is charming when he backs a lemonade stand for little Eddie (Mickey Rooney), whose street-corner rival has begun selling peanuts. It's the movie's glitz that dulls. The title number is a surreal mini-epic that follows Mona from a high-society cruise to a wild dance in a cantina with a flamboyant bandit who exits, Fairbanks-like, on a swinging rope after she's shot dead. There's no exuberance or lift beneath its nuttiness. The most amusing aspect of the other big number, "Everything's Been Done Before," is the way the choreographers position the chorines. In glittering sheaths with big bows across their breasts, they regularly block out the star in order to maintain the illusion that it's Harlow and not her double executing the high kicks.

The rest of the movie sets out to prove, without any farcical or histrionic fizz, that there's nothing worse than a mistaken marriage for everyone surrounding the bride and groom. Ned gets as depressed as Bob. Mona's public turns fickle, even though a coroner's inquiry clears her and Ned. After she gives birth to Bob's son and seeks full custody of the child, she relinquishes any claims on the Harrison family fortune. In a twist out of *Common Clay,* that gesture wins over her snobby father-in-law, but she still must face down a jeering audience during her Broadway comeback. She wins *them* over with a heartfelt plea for understanding. As a result, despite the potentially snappy ambience, this film is even more stupefying than *The White Sister.*

"Mr. Fleming was a real gentleman," said Rosina Lawrence, one of the chorus girls. Maybe Fleming's focus was on keeping an even keel while striving to get the picture done at all. There were minor delays due to Ted Healy's tonsillitis and the wrestler Hans Steinke walking off the set when the director ordered the 310-pound Man Mountain Dean to sit on him. (Another wrestler, Ernie Haynes, replaced Steinke; in the bit that's in the film, Dean executes a fierce throw-down and then simply pins Haynes.)

Midway through, the hair specialist Marcel Machu answered an SOS to save Harlow's overbleached locks from "falling out all over the place." (Selznick installed Machu in a bungalow at the studio.) Fleming, Machu said, "almost killed himself when he found out the picture might not be finished."

At least Powell displays his specialty of being simultaneously seductive and satirical. He mutters, "All in good time, my pretty," before springing Mona from a woman's detention center. He's boyishly debonair when bantering with Rooney about his lemonade stand doing better than Ned's sports-promotion business. And Fleming shows his knack for making female performers sparkle by getting a gracious performance out of the often-grating Russell as Bob's jilted Jo. And because Fleming made Russell relax, she helped *him* put an unusually tense Harlow at ease in Jo's scenes with Mona.

The still photographer Ted Allan noted on *Bombshell* that when Harlow "was working with Franchot Tone she felt she could compete with his stage training by flaunting her body." That's not apparent in *Bombshell*, but it is in *Reckless*, where Tone plays all-out pathos, and for keeps. Nonetheless, "Harlow was fun, and nice," said Robert Light, who played Jo's brother. "I remember she was doing pirouettes in front of a mirror to see how she looked . . . Someone said, 'Hey, Jean, you don't have anything on underneath.' And she said, 'Yeah, I know.' That was her!" Fleming's partnership with Harlow ended with *Reckless.* In two years, she was dead of acute nephritis.

Although *Reckless* disappointed Harlow's and Powell's fans, MGM proposed a three-year contract for Fleming's services at a $3,000-a-week salary. He never signed it. As the legal department put it, "Pursuant to an understanding . . . with Mr. Mannix"—Eddie Mannix,

Mayer's troubleshooter—Fleming continued working picture to picture. (June Caldwell, a former secretary to Mannix, recalled that Fleming, unlike other directors, never stopped by the office; instead, Mannix visited Fleming on the set.) When Fleming went to Fox for *The Farmer Takes a Wife*, it was a freelance assignment, not a loan-out from MGM. Set in 1853, this leisurely, elaborate, and romantic Americana unfolds on the Erie Canal, before the railroad stole much of its importance as an avenue for westward expansion.

With this movie, Fleming once again introduced a future star—Henry Fonda—while connecting or reconnecting with several talents who drifted in and out of his career. The play, taken from the novel *Rome Haul*, by Walter D. Edmonds (best known today for *Drums Along the Mohawk*), was written by Frank B. Elser and Marc Connelly (who would contribute mightily to *Captains Courageous*), though Edwin Burke, not Connelly, wrote the screenplay. Margaret Hamilton, later the Wicked Witch of the West in *The Wizard of Oz*, here plays a friend of the heroine's. And shortly before Fonda starred in the play, which made him a Broadway marquee name, Fleming's fellow veteran of President Wilson's European tour Walter Wanger, still a producer at Paramount, put the actor under contract. Wanger had nothing else to do with *The Farmer Takes a Wife*, but he would become Fleming's final producer on *Joan of Arc*.

Jane Withers, the one surviving cast member of *The Farmer Takes a Wife*, proud seventy-five years later of being "the first person in B films to reach the Top 20 at the box office for two years running," invests a comical little character named Della with her trademark exuberance. Exuding the ticklish affability of a precocious girl next door, she becomes a foil for Slim Summerville's busybody and odd-job man, Fortune Friendly, as he explains that the Erie Canal has been the main conduit for goods and immigrants flowing from the Eastern to the Western states. Withers loved doing *Farmer* partly because she "loved Henry Fonda. It was Henry's first picture, and I was there his first day. He was shaking all over; he was a nervous wreck, and my heart went out to him."

In later years, Fonda repeated, in different ways, "I was very fortunate in my director." To the writer-director Curtis Hanson, he simply said, "I was in love with him before we started the picture." Of course, Fonda was also fortunate in his role. Dan Harrow, the farmer of the title, works a canal boat so he can save money to buy a farm—and faces the jeers of canal workers who parade their contempt for farmers. He and his cook, Molly Larkins (Janet Gaynor), fall in love. Molly adores everything about the canal, including its menfolk's propensity for brawling. Dan has no allegiance to the Erie, and is also the first man she's ever met who shies away from a fight. When Dan finally takes his fist to Molly's former boatman, Jotham Klore (Charles Bickford), it's because he thinks he must restore her honor. And even after he beats Klore into the water, he refuses to assume Klore's position as the canal's reigning tough guy.

Dan possesses the unassuming rural rectitude—and the humor and checked strength—that Fonda would immortalize when he played the title role in John Ford's *Young Mr. Lincoln* four years later. Indeed, Fleming's film made that greater picture possible. Fonda's resemblance to Lincoln inspired Winfield Sheehan, the Fox production chief and executive on *The Farmer Takes a Wife*, to commission a script then called *Young Lincoln.*

Fleming had already proven his ability to help an actor locate his charm for the camera with Cooper and Gable. Fonda developed a capacity for understatement similar to Cooper's and was an even more comfortable fit than Coop for Fleming's ideas. It had taken several years in New York—years spent sharing an apartment with James Stewart, Joshua Logan, and Myron McCormick, and wearing out shoe leather seeking work—before Fonda, at twenty-eight, landed his breakthrough role in *The Farmer Takes a Wife.* A month after he stopped playing Dan Harrow onstage, Fonda began re-creating the character on a movie set. Decades later, he said he thought the only difference would be working

> outdoors and there's real dirt here and there's water in the canal and there are real horses pulling the canal boat and there's a real fire in the blacksmith's forge—it's not fake, it's real. And if it's real that helps me, because in the theater you have to *make* reality out of papier-maché, so to speak. So that's the first thing. And we're into this scene I had with Janet Gaynor that first day and I said a line the way I had in the play. Victor stopped and I could see him sort of wondering what to say and he finally came over and sort of put his arm around my shoulder—we were friends by then—and turned me and said, "Hank, you're mugging a little."

"Mugging" was a calculated dig—Fleming knew that for a serious New York actor like Fonda, mugging was "a dirty word." Fleming, Fonda said, "was aware I'd done this play, of course, and he was smart enough to realize that I was probably doing it the same way. So he said, 'You don't have to act like in the theater,' and pointed to the camera. 'That big eye; that lens—that's your audience, and it's just as close as it is to you right there—even closer if it's a closeup lens. So you don't have to do anything that you wouldn't do as you would in reality.' " Fonda "was in shock for a little while thinking, 'My God! Mugging!' So I just pulled it right back. It wasn't too difficult. I was lucky in a director who knew how to explain it to me." And when Fonda needed to show fire, Fleming knew how to ignite it. The director goaded him into "putting some realism" into his fight with Bickford. Fonda ended up breaking a bone in his hand. Happily, it was the last scene on the production schedule.

Gaynor had been a box-office mainstay at Fox as well as the studio's artistic anchor ever since she appeared in F. W. Murnau's 1927 masterpiece, *Sunrise,* capturing the spark in the childlike emotions of a country wife whose husband is drawn to "the Woman from the City." Although stereotyped as a paragon of domestic virtue, she often showed surprising range, as in Frank Borzage's 1929 *Lucky Star,* where she starts out emphasizing a tough, needy farm girl's slyness and selfishness before letting her gamine charm emerge softly and coltishly. (Gaynor won the first best actress Academy Award for her roles in *Sunrise* and two other Borzage films, *Seventh Heaven* and *Street Angel.*) She didn't hold a grudge against Fleming for *Bombshell,* in which Alice Cole, described as a "Janet Gaynor type," was depicted as Harlow's wholesome opposite.

"You know, he was a very big and rugged man, and an absolutely charming man," she said in 1958.

> He knew exactly what he wanted. It was all worked out in his mind. But when he presented it to you, it was very simplified. He was almost inarticulate sometimes. It seemed difficult for him to explain all the things he wanted you to do in a scene, but yet you knew he knew, and before he okayed a scene, you knew what he wanted, and you did it. He didn't create under the camera, because you see this was a talking picture. All of that went out with silence. Of course, he was creative in the rehearsals.

Fleming mussed her image up a little. Seen today, the relationship between a canal man and a cook like Gaynor's Molly Larkins raises questions that only the book answers. Edmonds's novel *Rome Haul* decorously states that Dan and Molly have a sexual relationship from her first night on their boat. Edmonds, in effect, cuts from Molly's "skirt lifting above her knees" and her telling Dan, "You've forgot to blow out the lamp," to Dan waking up "with lazy contentment" the next day, when "his hand could still feel the warmth in the blankets beside him." That transition might have passed muster in Hollywood's pre-code days. Broadway allowed Dan and Molly (in Brooks Atkinson's words) to "set up unlawful housekeeping in the best tradition of canal sociology." By 1935, Fleming and the screenwriter, Burke, had to keep everything perfectly chaste.

Yet the charged bitterness Gaynor brings to Molly's complaints about Jotham Klore, her aggressiveness at pushing the virtues of the canal, and her general erotic awareness give Molly's pursuit of Dan a pleasing hum. These two may not act on primal impulse, but their feelings are naked enough when they give each other the eye. And there's something hazily romantic about even a minimalist love story set on a boat or a barge, on a river or a canal, as the great French filmmaker Jean Vigo sensed when he made *L'Atalante* with Jean Dasté and Dita Parlo the year before. The two movies share a similar emotional trajectory: a young couple in love battle their divergent impulses as they make their first joint boat trip, accompanied by an older, eccentric third hand (Summerville in *Farmer,* Michel Simon in *L'Atalante*) who reunites them after they drift apart. Fleming is no Vigo when it comes to psychological lyricism, but Dan's slow-burning American courtship of Molly conveys steady warmth.

In *Young Mr. Lincoln,* in 1939, John Ford *wanted* to include an encounter between Fonda's Lincoln and a very young John Wilkes Booth, but the studio objected. Fleming got away with something similar in *The Farmer Takes a Wife.* Molly and Jotham Klore, en route to Rochester from Rome, swap pleasantries with the touring actor Junius Brutus Booth and his son John Wilkes. Boor that he is, Jotham tells Junius that his Richard III was difficult to understand but fine, and declaims, "My horse, my horse, my kingdom for a horse!" And Fortune Friendly wonders if Junius might have an ailing tooth he could remove with his newly acquired dental tools. Then young John leaps onto Klore's canal boat and scans a paper filled with political news from Illinois, where a former congressman has declared that no Western states coming into the Union should permit slavery. When Friendly says they'll be hearing a lot about this man—Abraham Lincoln—John Wilkes says that he expects to be just as famous someday.

William Tuttle, part of the makeup crew on this film and later on *The Wizard of Oz*, remembered Fleming as "a very strong person" who didn't tolerate "too much clowning around" but had a crackerjack sense of movie comedy, especially with Summerville and Andy Devine as an affably whiny canal character. When Devine was supposed to get a city gal drunk so Summerville's Friendly could pull her tooth out without pain, "Vic was very tickled by it; he broke up and had the two of them do it a couple of times—it cracked up everybody. He was great at pantomime," Tuttle noted. "He didn't have to have words for the humor."

Apart from such high points as the Wilkes incident and the tooth extraction, Fleming's Americana in *The Farmer Takes a Wife* is more forced than Ford's was in those amiable down-home frolics *Judge Priest* and *Steamboat Round the Bend* and than Ford's would be in his Lincoln masterpiece (Fox films all). Fleming places too much weight on musical and pugilistic outbursts. The atmosphere courts the soporific when the canal men aren't brawling or breaking into song.

The music has the double burden of brewing a spirit of community and commenting on changing times. Fleming tries to convey a huge historical shift in the transition from a male chorus singing, "I had a mule / Her name was Sal / Fifteen years on the Erie Canal," to a similar chorus chanting, "I'll be working on the railroad / All the livelong day." One of Fleming's specialties (one can see its influence on David Lean) was juxtaposing the intimate and the epic, but in *The Farmer Takes a Wife* there's an unclosed gap between his engagement with his core ensemble and his broad, crude work with the supporting players and extras.

Reviews were mixed. "The narrative starts slowly and never responds to pulmonary first aid," wrote *Variety*. But *The New York Times*, in addition to applauding what it thought "an affectionately amusing photoplay," singled out Fonda: "He plays with an immensely winning simplicity which will quickly make him one of our most attractive screen actors."

Part of the problem with *The Farmer Takes a Wife* is the studio ambience. Sheehan, the producer, feared a lingering winter (although production began in early April), so he wouldn't take the company to the actual Erie Canal. He first scouted locations in Sacramento, then decided to build the canal on the Fox lot. (Fleming later did some location shots in Sonora.) A storm washed out the canal set and sank the barges; Fleming was briefly hospitalized with another kidney stone attack. By the third week of shooting, *The New York Times* suggested the production "seems subject to a jinx." But Fleming, according to Withers, maintained an even attitude. She was most excited to join the picture because "at that time, Fleming only did A movies and I only did B movies." She came to "like him very much. He was very quiet, very gentle; I couldn't stand the ones who'd yell and scream and holler. Mr. H. Bruce Humberstone [who in 1937 directed Withers in *Checkers*] used to yell, and I had to tell him, 'If you keep your voice down and let people know exactly what you want, you get more.' He thanked me!"

One thing Withers liked was that "mugging" happened to be the only dirty word Fleming ever used on the set. "On most of my sets I'd start a swearing box where someone would put in 25 cents for every nasty word. I can't think of how much I made that way for different organizations. But Mr. Fleming, a very handsome man, just couldn't have been nicer. He was not gruff and not rough, and allowed no tacky language—and even though I was underage, I had been on some sets where people would really let go! Everybody was well mannered, everything went very smoothly, and I had such a good time."

17

Bagging Game on Safari, Losing *The Good Earth*

While *Scribner's* magazine serialized Ernest Hemingway's nonfiction novel about a safari, *Green Hills of Africa,* from May through August in 1935, Fleming was experiencing the real thing in the same terrain.

Hemingway peppered his narrative with literary discussion, including his most famous proclamation: "All modern American literature comes from one book by Mark Twain called *Huckleberry Finn.*" But Fleming, who went on the safari as his vacation after *The Farmer Takes a Wife*, wasn't discussing Twain, Gertrude Stein, or Stephen Crane with his fellow adventurer, Charles Cotton. Going by Cotton's safari diary, their cultural excitement came from whatever they could pull in on a portable radio: a cowboy program from Pittsburgh or the NBC show with the pianist-bandleader Eddy Duchin, which they got at four in the morning.

Fleming's hunting trek through what was then called British East Africa (now Kenya) helped gain him Hemingway's respect when Howard Hawks tried to team them up in 1941 to film the writer's safari-inspired short story "The Short Happy Life of Francis Macomber." (The always underrated Zoltan Korda did film it, superbly.) The director later urged Clark Gable to come with him on another safari in 1939—until their prolonged involvement with *Gone With the Wind* scotched their plans.

Fleming and Cotton left Nairobi for the wilderness on July 4 and, once they hit their stride, stalked game with guns and cameras every day until late August. They dined on fowl and fresh meat, and occasionally conversed with British officials and Anglo-American travelers. In Cotton's journal, big-game hunting comes off as a test of endurance as much as sporting skills; they "ran into locust so thick they made a dark cloud in all directions."

Fleming's mechanical skills came in handy for Cotton; when a pump casting broke on one of their vehicles, Vic simply repaired it with some wire. Help went both ways. Fleming woke up one morning running a fever of 103. Cotton found him still in bed, "wringing wet," as the fever broke at the end of the day, and put him into dry clothes and bedding.

They journeyed through hard brush, with high thorns pricking the horizon, until, on July 12, they found themselves on "a very beautiful spot right on the bank of the Tana . . . Real African mahogany and other tropical vegetation a very pleasant contrast from what we have been going through for the past weeks." Cotton shot and killed a bull elephant. Fleming wounded an elephant without being able to finish him, but killed his share of East African antelope, gazelles, rhinos, warthogs, and crocodiles.

In Africa, as in Hollywood, Fleming remained a confounding combination of sturdiness and ailments. "Vic developed something wrong with his eyes," Cotton records, "and we had to put cocaine in them and give him sleeping powders. Stayed up until 10 with him then he went to sleep." Soon he was back on his feet.

Although Fleming never vanquished his most dearly sought prey—a bull elephant—on August 1 he killed a rhinoceros near the Kinno River, right before the animal would have slammed into Cotton. "She charged right at Vic and me," Cotton writes. "It was Vic's turn to shoot so we all waited until she was just 8 yds from me thinking all the time that she was bluffing, but just as she got there I saw that she did not intend to stop and told Vic to shoot. In one half second I would have shot to save myself."

Her offspring ran into the bush. Everyone felt "terrible," Cotton continues, "but if they had not shot her I am sure I would have been hurt." It was the second mother rhino Fleming killed in his travels.

On August 21, he and Cotton crossed paths with a British hunter and another Californian on safari, which is how they learned of the death of the humorist and actor Will Rogers six days earlier. A *Hollywood Reporter* review of *The Farmer Takes a Wife* suggested that Fleming had originally designed Slim Summerville's Fortune Friendly for Rogers; it would have fit his sly folksiness and built on his role as a Mississippi patent-medicine peddler in Ford's *Steamboat Round the Bend.* Fleming never got to work with the cowboy humorist (who really *was* part Cherokee), even though they had a mutual friend in Fred Lewis, whose Diamond Bar Ranch near Whittier was next to a ranch Rogers had there.

Fleming and Cotton wound up their travels at the Dutch Trading Company about 110 miles from Nairobi, "where [Theodore] Roosevelt did a lot of hunting." They made it into Nairobi the following afternoon, "had a fine hot bath and an excellent dinner and went to bed early, ending our safari." A year later, Cotton shipped four cases of trophies to the Broadway department store in Los Angeles for use in a window display.

Of course, long before "runaway" filmmaking, Hollywood directors like George Hill would travel four continents on assignment. Six years younger than Fleming, Hill was also a cameraman from the silent days (they might have worked together on the Loos-Emerson *Macbeth*). He'd recently emerged as a major MGM director because of Marie Dressler's Oscar-winning hit, *Min and Bill* (1930), and other acclaimed and profitable talkies such as the prison drama *The Big House* (1930) and the gangster film *The Secret Six* (1931), all written by his wife, Fleming's friend Frances Marion.

Despite their volatile marriage and prolonged estrangement and divorce (Hill was a depressive and a secret alcoholic), Thalberg teamed Hill and Marion on a choice assignment in 1933: Pearl Buck's Pulitzer Prize–winning 1931 novel, *The Good Earth*, about Chinese farmers enduring poverty, famine, and the corruption of wealth. (The director Tod Browning, of *Dracula* fame, had been announced but withdrew for unknown reasons.) In December 1933, MGM launched an ambitious trip through China, where Hill filled "250 cases of film" with background action and atmosphere.

Under the direction of General Ting-Hsui Tu of China's Central Military Academy, expeditions went out on buying missions. They'd arrive at a rural estate and purchase "everything movable on the farm. The plows and implements, the cooking utensils in the kitchen, the used clothing in the house, furniture, bamboo doors and windows, matting partitions—the water wheels for irrigation." They also had hundreds of items made, including baskets. Hill left after several months, but Tu continued his work.

Back in Los Angeles, Hill swerved his car from children crossing a street and smashed into a telephone pole. The resulting pains and treatments, along with his chronic drinking and depression, the tension of being around his ex-wife, and disagreements with Thalberg over *The Good Earth*, eventually leveled Hill. Alone in his Venice beach home, he shot himself, fatally, in the head. Thalberg assigned the film to Fleming.

Regardless of his all-American profile, Fleming and *The Good Earth* might have been a better match. As a filmmaker and an adventurer, he had an appetite for the epic and the exotic—and along with Cotton, he'd recently endured "locust so thick they made a dark cloud," a key ingredient of *The Good Earth*. The novel summoned his agrarian memories. "It is a story that might be laid in any of our farming states, or in any country of the world," he said. Thalberg assigned the screenwriter Talbot Jennings to the script, and when Jennings arrived to take his orders from Thalberg's associate Albert Lewin, he found Fleming and Lewin swimming through a sea of previous drafts. Much as he'd later do with *Gone With the Wind*, Fleming said, "Throw 'em all out. We'll start all over again and work from the book." Publicly, Fleming stated, "The only major change we are making in the adaptation is that of reducing the dialogue from smooth, Biblical-like utterances to the simple, direct speeches of simple, illiterate people. The dialogue of the novel does not make good motion picture dialogue, though it reads very well. The characters are sensitive people of great depth and feeling, who, like many fine but illiterate characters in real life, cannot adequately express themselves."

His safari break reenergized him. He named his cabin cruiser *The Missy Poo* after his daughter, Victoria, nicknamed Missy. On the Saturday of Thanksgiving weekend, he flew in his Waco from Los Angeles to Ensenada in a James Cagney–sponsored air race publicizing a casino in the Mexican coastal resort. (His "competitors" included Wallace Beery and Howard Hawks.) A wire service article in December hailed him as not only one of Hollywood's best-dressed men but also "the most nonchalant" on that list. And now he was at the helm of MGM's current super-production.

Thalberg decided to make *The Good Earth* at MGM and on California locations, with a mixed cast headed by Paul Muni as the male lead. He had promised to fill the cast with English-speaking Chinese players; every day Lewin tested Chinese actors as well as American and European actors in Chinese makeup. Today, some of Lewin's reports read as straight-faced comedy, such as "Leonid Kinskey: Russian accent still noticeable; doubtful if he can ever overcome it entirely. Nevertheless, worth serious consideration as Ching." (The role went to Ching

Wah Lee.) Or, of the dazzling Anna May Wong: "not as beautiful as she might be." (Wong's potential role, Lotus, the dancer who becomes the hero's No. 2 wife, went to the charm-deprived Tilly Losch.) On the same day Thalberg announced Fleming as the director, October 30, 1935, he officially pegged Muni to play Wang Lung and Luise Rainer to play O-Lan, Wang Lung's No. 1 wife.

Fleming selected a five-hundred-acre stretch of California hills and valleys for his main location. He terraced the hills for two miles on each side of the canyons and had them hand-sown with grain, then organized the valley floor in patches of Chinese vegetables. Poultry, pigs, water buffalo, dogs, and donkeys acclimated themselves to the MGM-nurtured farms of Wang Lung and his friend and his uncle. The company tapped an aqueduct, erected a huge pump, and employed modern irrigation techniques to make ready for a harvest in eight months; during filming, the company also used Chinese waterwheels and windmills.

Shortly before Christmas, Fleming scheduled surgery for kidney stones, expecting to be back on his feet in time to start filming in January. He would have weathered it easily, except for a blood clot that formed in one leg. Doctors confined him to bed, and his niece Yvonne remembered that when she visited him at his house, "he was like a caged tiger"—one who, sadly, couldn't keep his biggest picture yet from slipping through his claws.

After so much costly preparation, Thalberg had to make a move. Speedy, worldly W. S. Van Dyke, Fleming's best possible replacement, begged off so he could finish *San Francisco.* As the official MGM production history put it, "Here was a great picture, under way so far as locations, casting, and all operative details were concerned . . . and no director." In late 1935, Thalberg approached Sidney Franklin, and on January 21, 1936, he took over, deeming the physical layout Fleming had prepared "altogether excellent." But he considered the script Fleming had prepared "too Occidental" and ordered a new script written with more "Oriental flavor." Franklin ended up directing with (in Pauline Kael's words) "his usual lack of imagination, individuality, style. He was the MGM heavyweight champ"—and a thorn in Fleming's side a few years later, on *The Yearling.*

18

Spencer Tracy and *Captains Courageous*

No matter how odd the circumstances of Lu's pregnancy, the delight Fleming took in parenting surpassed the disappointments of forfeiting *The Good Earth* and *They Gave Him a Gun*, an antiwar adventure set to star Spencer Tracy. (Mayer had lured Tracy from Fox with a promise of leading roles.) Victoria turned one as Fleming was recuperating. A few weeks later, she piled some twigs in her tiny fists and gave them to him. He wrote, "Missy gathered up these beautiful things to her daddy one March morning—her first gifts to him," then lined a jewelry box with cotton batting and preserved these gifts. By the end of March 1936, he had recovered sufficiently from his surgery and embolism to travel to Dayton, Ohio, to look at new airplanes, and from there sent his daughter a telegram in baby talk.

That colleagues noted a transformation in Fleming is evident in an item found in Louis Lighton's papers. Among the notebooks and scraps of paper containing scribbles of story and film ideas, Lighton wrote, "Vic's parenthood." Under the guidance of Lighton and Fleming, and with that thought in the background, the movie version of *Captains Courageous*, Rudyard Kipling's virtually plotless 1897 novel about a spoiled young man's redemption through labor on a New England cod fleet, became a moving paradigm of fathering.

In his final year at Paramount, Lighton made two standout productions with Fleming's directing and acting protégés: *The Lives of a Bengal Lancer* and *Peter Ibbetson*, both directed by Henry Hathaway and starring Gary Cooper. When Lighton moved to MGM in 1936, it was natural for Thalberg to pair him and Fleming. They shared a professional past and a forthright aesthetic.

Budd Schulberg said Lighton, like Fleming, "was very un-Hollywood, not mixed up in the social scene, seemed to stay apart from that." Elia Kazan, in *A Life* (1988), wrote that the producer consciously made films dealing "with individual standards, never politics; with courage and decency, privileges and responsibility . . . Lighton's work goal was to capture a single, strongly felt human emotion, one he believed in himself." Lighton respected all the old "tough" directors, including John Ford and Hathaway, but "his particular favorite" was Fleming.

Kazan observed of Lighton, "perhaps because he had no children, his best films dealt with children," including *Captains Courageous.* In 1931, Thalberg approached Kipling to purchase screen rights to the poems "Gunga Din" and "On the Road to Mandalay" as well as *Captains Courageous* and *Kim.* Three years later, Thalberg optioned the novels for $25,000 each. He assigned Lighton to both as soon as the producer arrived at MGM in 1935.

MGM's pre-Lighton treatments for *Captains Courageous* didn't win Kipling over. An attempt to inject the story with sex prompted the author to inform the studio that "a happily married lady codfish lays about a million eggs at one confinement." Kipling died in January 1936 and Thalberg in September. By then Lighton had taken charge of the production, and he quickly dispensed with vulgar notions.

At the end of April, with Fleming back on his feet, MGM announced that he would direct the picture and Freddie Bartholomew would star in it. (Lighton wanted to make *Kim* with Fleming and Bartholomew, too.) Franchot Tone was reported to have nailed down the adult lead a year before, but Tracy was luckier casting. It would be the first of five Fleming-Tracy collaborations. The actor was closer to the director in temperament, though not in background, than Cooper, Fonda, or even Gable. Both Fleming and his new star radiated complicated moods and feelings beneath a tough-smart surface.

According to Lighton (via Kazan), Fleming would say, "A good actor is one who, when he's asked what he does for a living, will drop his head, kick a little shit, and speaking with a bit of shame, mumble, 'I'm an actor.' " He might have been thinking of Tracy. Tracy was born in 1900 in Milwaukee, and his hard-drinking Irish-American father owned a trucking company; his mother's ancestors had founded Brown University. He settled into acting at Ripon College and went on to the American Academy of Dramatic Arts in New York. It took Tracy eight years to become a breakout stage star with the prison drama *The Last Mile*, in 1930. Although John Ford snatched him up for a prison comedy called *Up the River,* it would take more than half the decade for Tracy to have the same impact on-screen. When he did, he became, as *Time* declared, "cinema's no. 1 actor's actor." But he was a conflicted man—a boozer and a married Catholic whose lasting romantic connection would be to a woman not his wife, Katharine Hepburn. "Spencer always thought acting was a rather silly way for a grown man to make a living," Hepburn wrote.

He arrived at MGM at the end of 1935 after an unsatisfying five years at Fox, where he'd kept busy in character roles—eighteen films, including loan-outs, between 1932 and 1934—and where stardom had eluded him. By the time he entered MGM, he and his wife, Louise Treadwell, had weathered his intimate friendship or affair with Loretta Young and an embarrassment of drunk-and-disorderly charges stemming from binge drinking. To explain his carousing, studio publicists forwarded the story that Tracy felt God had punished him for his vices by making his son, John, born in 1924, deaf.

Hepburn's biographer William J. Mann in *Kate* (2006) traces the roots of Tracy's drinking further down in his psyche, painting the actor as bisexual or gay, in torment over the gaps between his secret erotic identity and his supermasculine Hollywood image. Mann effectively deflates the romanticism that usually surrounds Tracy and Hepburn—an image cultivated by Hepburn from nearly the week after Tracy's death in 1967—but his evidence for the star's homosexuality is built entirely on stories that passed through George Cukor's circle. Mann's single source is party bartender Scotty Bowers. After two tours with the Marines in World War II, he worked at a Richfield gas station that he ran as a male bordello "arranging introductions between returning servicemen and older gentlemen." Bowers said he had sex with Tracy repeatedly in the guest bungalow on Cukor's estate, where Tracy lived for the last few years of his life.

Mann summoned a number of testimonials to Bowers's veracity and Cukor's implicit trust in him, but no direct statement from Cukor himself. And even the director grew wary of the rumors rampant in his crowd. One of his regulars, a supporting actor named Anderson Lawler, was a key component of a tale often used to portray *Gable* as a bashful bisexual. Cukor called Lawler "a great and bitchy gossip," but also "an idiot—full of half-assed sophistication."

Tracy's alcohol-fueled escapades stayed out of the press after he joined MGM. The studio's publicity chief, Howard Strickling, a suave, efficient "fixer" with connections to pliable police officers and reporters, confessed that he ordered the studio's security chief, Whitey Hendry, to have an ambulance ready to rescue Tracy from the scene of any trouble in a bar. But the studio also invested Tracy's moviemaking collaborators with much of the responsibility for keeping him away from booze. While co-producing *Mannequin* (1937), Joseph Mankiewicz ensconced the star in his own home.

The poetic Irish lush was a cliché long before the 1930s, but offscreen Tracy seemed determined to put flesh on it. "I would get drunk and disappear in the middle of a film, get into fights, become a complete bum," he admitted to Stewart Granger. "At the beginning, the studio heads and my friends would rally round and cover up for me, but eventually the only one left who seemed to care at all was Victor Fleming."

He was likely speaking of the bender he went on after Thalberg's death on September 14, 1936, the day *Captains Courageous* had been scheduled to begin principal photography. Tracy was not close to the production chief, but like many others at the studio, he was uncertain about his future when Thalberg died of a heart attack at age thirty-seven. MGM rescheduled the picture to start after Thalberg's funeral three days later, but Tracy's drinking held it up for another five days.

Granger wrote up Tracy's version of the episode nearly twenty years after Tracy's death, and it may not be reliable in its details, which are flattering to Tracy, with Fleming putting him up at his Cove Way home. Tracy said Fleming fetched him from a Los Angeles drunk tank, "squared the press, the police and the studio," had his Filipino servant clean him up, and had his own doctor examine him:

> I was lying there feeling like death when Vic came in with a case of Scotch. He put it down beside my bed and went to the door. Turning back, he said, "Spence, I've just talked to the doctor. He tells me one more bash like that and you'll be dead. I want you to do me a favor. Drink that whole case of Scotch. It's the last time you'll see me, Spence, I'm through," and he went out and left me alone. I was dying for a drink but I knew it wouldn't be just one. I knew that I'd lost my last friend and there would be nobody left to give a damn about me. Either I took Vic's advice and drank the whole case or I shouldn't take another drink, ever. I decided to give it up.

That's not quite how it happened, though, says Edward Hartman. He remembers the emergency phone call that came in one mid-September evening. Fleming told Hartman's mother, Gladys, "We're missing Spencer. Can you help us find him?" He also had enlisted his sister Ruth, and she, Gladys, and Clyde Hartman went in different directions. "They had some list of these places where he went, where he was known to go." Some details after that, including who found Tracy, are in dispute, but in the Hartman version Gladys got him bundled into a cab and put him in Good Samaritan Hospital. There he kept "screaming, yelling, pawing the walls"—and doctors threatened to place him in restraints unless Gladys stayed with him overnight. (She did, but Edward says she "was pretty disgusted with him.")

Fleming's next step: shrewdly stashing Tracy away in San Dimas, a dry town far from prying eyes and studio gossip, at Ed and Mamie Hartman's house. Fleming's aunt and uncle "wanted to make sure they got some food in him," says Edward.

The additional delay kept Fleming's tensions close to the skin. It didn't require much of a remark from Jules Furthman—probably a crack about Tracy—to set off the director during lunch in the MGM commissary. George Sidney, who began at MGM that year in the shorts department, was a month shy of his twentieth birthday when he saw the outburst. "Vic sat at one end of the table with [Furthman] in the commissary and got into an argument; Vic pulled him out of the chair and dragged him out of the commissary and started hitting him; then they made up and sat down and had lunch."

Despite his self-doubts, Tracy had been developing a performing style that suited the Lighton-Fleming mode: "to capture a single, strongly felt human emotion" in a vigorous, unostentatious way. "Spencer does it, that's all. Feels it. Talks. Listens. He means what he says when he says it, and if you think that's easy, try it," said Humphrey Bogart. Tracy told Phillip Trent, who played his son in *The Power and the Glory* (1933), "Always remember, the camera's picking up what you're thinking."

Tracy liked to discuss acting with reporters far less than he did with other actors. But in 1962, making Stanley Kramer's *It's a Mad, Mad, Mad, Mad World*, he tossed out a couple of nuggets about his approach: "That business of not being typecast, that just bores me. I've always played the same character. Larry Olivier says the way to act is, learn your lines and get on with it. I'm Spencer Tracy with some deference to the character. When a person says he's an actor—he's a personality. The whole idea is to show your personality. There are people who are much better technically, but who cares? Nobody cares."

"Fox had him playing villains," Mayer said, "and he probably would never have been anything more than a good character actor if I hadn't seen something about his face—something more important than his acting ability. We signed him, found just the right stories for him [before 1940, all of Tracy's MGM scripts were chosen for him] and he became Spencer Tracy the star, not Spencer Tracy the actor." In 1936, Tracy had enjoyed critical success under Fritz Lang's direction as the target of a lynch mob in *Fury;* he'd also been in a blockbuster, but only as the second male lead under Gable in the period romantic melodrama *San Francisco.* In *Captains Courageous,* he would be the center of what *Variety* aptly labeled "a big money picture of the sea," comparable to MGM's *Mutiny on the Bounty.* He became the focus of Fleming's effort to contain Kipling's anecdotes in a well-knit narrative about shifting friendships on a Gloucester schooner, the *We're Here*—culminating in a race between that vessel and its longtime rival, the *Jennie Cushman.*

The script elevates a minor character, Manuel, a warmly rugged Portuguese fisherman, into the protagonist. It also adds some Christian spirituality to the redemption of the spoiled rich boy Harvey Cheyne. (The adapters tailored the part to Bartholomew, four years younger than Kipling's callow youth; about the only Kipling dialogue in the film is the remarks by sailors calling Harvey a "Jonah," a harbinger of bad luck.) One thing Mayer must have seen in Tracy's face—the soulful magnetism of his eyes—anchors Manuel's guidance of Cheyne into young adulthood. Tracy had scored with audiences and critics as a priest in *San Francisco,* and he'd go on to win a second Oscar for playing Father Flanagan in the lachrymose *Boys Town* (1938). The moviemakers reconceived Manuel to exploit Tracy's capacity for muscular Christianity—make that muscular Catholicism. (He played Flanagan again in *Men of Boys Town* and a priest evacuating children from a hospital in *The Devil at 4 O'Clock.*)

Marc Connelly and Dale Van Every, as well as John Lee Mahin, got screen credit for the script. Mahin did the final draft and shepherded it through filming. Two-fisted Catholicism came naturally to this non-Catholic screenwriter; twenty years later he wrote John Huston's island-set World War II fable, *Heaven Knows, Mr. Allison,* with

Deborah Kerr as a nun who helps a Marine played by Robert Mitchum find the faith to fight the Japanese who occupy the island. (The nun and the Marine agree they "both belong to pretty tough outfits.")

But Mayer was the one who made Christian symbolism with a Catholic overlay part of MGM's house style. He wrapped a clerical collar around Tracy before Warner Bros. did it with Pat O'Brien for *Angels with Dirty Faces* (1938) or Paramount did it with Bing Crosby for *Going My Way* (1944). He was indulging his appetite for (in his grandson Daniel Selznick's words) the "pomp and respectability" of the Roman Catholic Church. He also inoculated his studio against the Catholic morality police. In January 1934, before the Production Code clamped down, Archbishop John J. Cantwell of Los Angeles had summoned Mayer, Sheehan from Fox, and J. J. Murdock from RKO to discuss morality in pictures and hint at a possible nationwide Catholic boycott. In March, Joseph Breen, about to become the Production Code chief, wrote to the archbishop of Cincinnati, John T. McNicholas (soon to help found the National Legion of Decency), "Most of the men and women who write the film stories are pagans. Of course, these write film stories that are based upon pagan philosophy and the result is that we are slowly making our audiences *pagans.* How could it be otherwise?"

Still, it's doubtful that any of Fleming's creative team saw the Catholic reworking of *Captains Courageous* as either a compromise or a sop to studio critics. Christian salvation entered his films again and again, often in his stiffest pictures, such as *The White Sister, Adventure*, and his strangled *Joan of Arc*, but also in livelier entertainment like *Tortilla Flat.* (Even in *Gone With the Wind*, Scarlett O'Hara fears hell.) And Garson Kanin, a prime builder of the posthumous Tracy myth, wrote that the star told him he'd felt drawn to the priesthood while a boy attending a Jesuit prep school, Marquette Academy: "The priests are all such superior men—heroes. You want to be like them—we all did."

Lighton and Fleming had become powers at Paramount during an era when studio executives considered producers, and directors who could function as producers, the crucial arbiters of a script. They worked that way at MGM, too. Studio legal files connect fourteen writers to *Captains Courageous.* But even an early "temporary incomplete" script reflects Lighton and Fleming's decision to make Manuel emerge as the principal figure in Harvey's transformation.

Kipling's novel offers a fictional commentary on the United States depicted in Theodore Roosevelt's book of speeches and essays on civic philosophy, *The Strenuous Life* (1900). The novelist-critic John Seelye, who writes with command and affection about both novel and film, says that Kipling's Harvey embodies what Roosevelt saw as "America's faults: [he is] spoiled, lazy, corrupted by his father's prosperity and his mother's indulgence." Seelye goes on to argue that when the movie depicts Harvey with the cod fleet, Fleming (unlike Kipling) "concentrates on an aspect of American culture that puts a heavy emphasis on immersion in a primitivistic environment as a means of attaining wisdom. Harvey is redeemed not by hard work but by love, a Christian burden lacking the Protestant ethical dimension. It is more in the spirit of Eleanor than Theodore Roosevelt."

Actually, Fleming puts equal stress on love and hard work. But love *is* newly crucial to the narrative. And as Mahin followed Fleming's orders to deepen Manuel, providing a narrative trajectory even Kipling knew was lacking in the book, the screenwriter did emphasize Manuel's Catholicism. The cook, Doc (Sam McDaniel), clarifies the connection between Manuel and Emmanuel, the Christ, by enunciating every syllable of Man-u-el. As Seelye notes, not only does the script characterize him as "a pious Catholic," but Manuel's dory has the number 3—"suggesting the Trinity." In his first scene, as he rescues Harvey, Manuel wears a large glistening crucifix that reappears only twice: when he's lecturing Harvey about honesty and, later, just before he dies, when the *We're Here*'s mainmast snaps and its cables rip him apart.

But *pace* Seelye, is *Captains Courageous* an allegory of any kind? Its Christianity, after all, is on the surface. The movie starts at the tail end of Easter vacation. And when Harvey waxes sympathetic about Manuel's father "drowning out on the ocean, all alone at night," Manuel delivers a homily based on Luke 5:1–11 but ending on a note of his own: "The Savior, he see my father all tired and wet down in the water. So he light the harbor buoy and he say, 'Come on up, old Manuel. I so happy you come up here to help us fish.' "

The text is spiritual, but the subtext depicts a great chain of fatherhood connecting God's son, the Savior, with Manuel senior, Manuel junior, and Harvey. Jesus wants good fishermen like Manuel and Manuel senior to fish in heaven. "Oh, I think the Savior, he the best fisherman," says Manuel. "But my father, he come next!" Mahin, the sole author of this interlude, punctuates this Sermon on the Dory with Manuel hooking a huge cod and Harvey landing his first fish, an enormous halibut. (Bartholomew called these rubber props "electric fish": battery-powered windshield-wiper motors made the fake cod and halibut flop, just as they would make the wings of the flying monkeys flap in *The Wizard of Oz.*)

Harvey and Manuel employ the hand lines favored by Manuel's father, not the trawls used by other fishermen—and this activity helps Tracy bring the speech a lifelike spontaneity. (The *New Republic* critic Otis Ferguson took aim at the inflated rhetoric of the sermon, this "backbreaker about heaven," as he called it; then he observed, with relief, that Tracy "finally comes through all such obstacles like a bull through a picket fence.") After Manuel's death, Harvey confirms his manhood by using his earnings to buy twin candlesticks for Manuel's father, as his friend wanted, and his own candlestick for Manuel. During the memorial service for Gloucester men lost at sea (when we finally learn Manuel's last name, Fidello), Harvey tosses a wreath into the port's waters to honor him. His father does, too, and as the current links the wreaths, the young and the older Cheynes unite with the two Fidellos. (In one of the glaring differences between the works, in the novel Harvey calls the service "a sort of song-and-dance act, whacked up for the summer boarders.")

Manuel's Catholicism doesn't exclude the community values and superstitions of the crew of the *We're Here*, or the dynamism they share with Harvey's father; Fleming, like Kipling, was a Teddy Roosevelt kind of guy. The entire first act is as much about Harvey's yearning to become part of a group as it is about his father neglecting him. In the movie, Harvey's mother is dead, and his father unconsciously gives up the responsibility of raising his son to the staff of the Green Hill School in Connecticut. Logic might ascribe the prep school scenes to the blue blood Mahin, but in fact most were Connelly's. This Broadway playwright and sometime collaborator of George S. Kaufman had already won a Pulitzer Prize for *The Green Pastures*, a stage retelling of the Bible in African-American dialect (or, as it was called at the time, "Negro patois"), and had written the script for and co-directed the 1936 screen version.

Of all the pictures he contributed to, Connelly considered *Captains Courageous* "the only one with which I was truly happy." New to MGM, he misread the Lighton-Fleming relationship to the studio, seeing the director as "left pretty much alone" and concluding that was because he was "a pariah" or in "general disfavor, owing to his contempt for the jackal practices he frequently encountered in the studio world." Connelly didn't realize that this solitude was a hard-won prize. But he did get the big artistic picture: "Instead of the usual concoction of half a dozen channels, siftings, sievings to a final result, three men set down and tried to produce a pretty good picture—and I think we did, as a matter of fact."

The picture is a study of what later generations would call "tough love." The first act demonstrates why it's necessary. In Connelly's beautifully wrought opening scenes, Harvey hosts three schoolmates at his father's estate (the exterior of Selznick International's headquarters) in order to manipulate one of them, Charles (Bill Burrud), into making him a member of "the Buffalos." Acting like a mini-Machiavelli, he thinks his only way of joining the club is to bribe Charles with a first edition of *Treasure Island*, then threaten him with Mr. Cheyne closing down the car dealership of Charles's dad. With his precocious self-possession and natty hat and suit (you can't see that he's wearing short pants), Bartholomew has the silky wickedness of Michael Corleone. At school, Harvey's teacher, Mr. Tyler (Donald Briggs), calms Charles and tries to talk sense to Harvey. As punishment, Harvey is put "in Coventry"—a state in which, for forty-eight hours, he receives the silent treatment from classmates before, during, and after classes, and must not speak to anyone himself.

When Harvey persists in talking to his colleagues at the school's newspaper office (after all, his father paid for the equipment), a weedy lad named Wellman decides that socking him in the jaw won't break Coventry's rules. (The references to William Wellman and *Treasure Island* show Fleming's rare ability to keep his sense of humor even at grandiose MGM. At the time, Wellman was working on two Selznick pictures, *Nothing Sacred* and *A Star Is Born*.)

This is not, as today's viewers might infer, a Depression-era condemnation of upper-class morals. The Green Hill headmaster, Dr. Finley (Walter Kingsford), tells Harvey's father that his goal in suspending the boy for the remainder of the year is to turn out "another splendid citizen" like Mr. Cheyne (Melvyn Douglas). What's remarkable about Bartholomew's performance is his skill at getting across the disconnect between Harvey's duplicity and his untapped emotional and intellectual potential. He makes you feel that Mr. Tyler is not coddling or sentimentalizing Harvey when he says that the boy is deeply unhappy and formidably talented. You know Mr. Tyler is getting all this not simply from Harvey's academic performance but from his racing mind's surfeit of energy.

Mahin said he told Fleming, "Geez, this is a beautiful kid, Vic. It seems to me you're not getting the closeups of this kid." And Fleming replied, "Wait till we need 'em. Wait till they have some effect . . . When he starts crying and breaking, that's when we'll go in to see him." But Fleming does give us a tight close-up of Bartholomew near the beginning, coolly reading his effect on Charles, his mark.

Mahin may have felt protective of Bartholomew's part because he'd poured a little of his own son into it. Graham Mahin remembered his father and Fleming taking him on their "script vacation" to a Wisconsin fishing lodge in the summer of 1936, when he was nine. They didn't try to shelter him from rugged behavior any more than the crew of the *We're Here* does Harvey. First they set him up with a guide to learn big-cast fishing while they went drinking. ("They were both pretty into drinking then," says Mahin.) The lodge contained a slot machine that Fleming quickly figured out was fixed, and he confronted the manager, who apologetically took the machine apart, removed the slug that kept anyone from hitting the jackpot, and returned Fleming's quarter. The director's next pull of the lever brought an avalanche of coins, and he stuffed them all in his pockets. That day they went fishing for muskellunge ("muskies"), and Graham caught a twelve-pounder, which quickly became one of Fleming's practical jokes. "He had it cooked for me and brought it around and everyone knew—it was the local gag—everyone knew that I wasn't going to be able to eat it."

In *Captains Courageous*, the headmaster imagines that Harvey will be "rusticating" at home with his dad. But Mr. Cheyne, still insensitive to his son's needs, takes Harvey on a transatlantic crossing, not realizing that the ocean liner merely gives him another grand setting in which to act like a young lord. Betting a couple of boys already sick of him that he can down a counter full of ice-cream sodas, he soon stumbles on deck and falls into the water far below. The overhead shot of Harvey tumbling into the ocean, his head scraping the top of the motion picture frame, and the connecting shot that pans up from Harvey's bobbing head, across a span of dark and roiling sea to Manuel's dory, are magnificently eerie. As the fog enshrouds the boy, he crashes out of "our" world—the moviegoer's world—into an entirely different culture and also into a past decade or century; Fleming's Kiplingesque fishing fleet is made up completely of tall-masted schooners. There are no steam-powered trawlers, or two-way radios, to be seen. Fleming's creation of a marine world of American fable may be why many lovers of Kipling carry the memory of the film being totally true to the novel. The inventive and supremely accomplished British director Michael Powell applauded how "faithfully" Fleming caught Kipling and wrote, "The film of a book, particularly of a great book, very seldom equals it, but in this case I think it did." (He even suggested that Canada rename the historic ship known as *Bluenose II* the *Captains Courageous.*)

When Manuel plucks Harvey from the water, then blows his conch-shell horn to signal the *We're Here*, there's magic in the dense, moist air. Fleming downplays the otherworldliness of the captain, Disko Troop (Lionel Barrymore), but he doesn't eliminate it. Disko's son, Dan (Mickey Rooney), says Troop "thinks like a cod." Could there be a more pithy statement of the uncanny? Harvey's shipboard nemesis Long Jack (John Carradine) soon calls the boy a "Jonah." And maybe Harvey *is* a maritime jinx. Disko's reckless race against the rival *Jennie Cushman* to be the first ship back to Gloucester with a full load of cod causes the mainmast to snap, sending Manuel into the drink. Even before that, Harvey persists in upsetting the ship's chemistry for a good deal of the running time.

Mahin viewed Manuel as "half Portuguese and half black," and Seelye puts Manuel, with his deep-tan makeup, in an American literary tradition "in which white children are assisted toward wisdom by people of color who then die or are simply removed from the scene." Hence, he is "a fisher of men" (to Seelye) *and* "the latter-day saintly Uncle Tom," even, perhaps, a relative of Huckleberry Finn's friend Jim. (The au courant term is "magic Negro," with examples such as Will Smith in *The Legend of Bagger Vance* and Don Cheadle in *The Family Man.*) But what Manuel feels for Harvey is paternal fondness, and what Harvey feels for Manuel is filial love mingled with hero worship. When Manuel tells Harvey that he'll use some of his earnings to buy a purple suit and canvas-topped shoes, and then step out with a series of ladies, he halts his musings on the opposite sex to ease Harvey's fears of girls intruding on a boy's world.

If Fleming throws the focus of Harvey's coming of age on Manuel's unaffected surrogate fatherhood, he also accents the fisherman's immediate goal: getting Harvey to mesh with the crew. The vignettes of men competing for the biggest catch give way to images of them forking fish and pitching them into the ship and down the hold, and chopping and hooking bait with assembly-line steadiness and momentum. You see and hear how their sea songs keep their spirits up and set a satisfying rhythm when they're swinging knives. "They had tons of fish packed in ice, and every so often they'd have to throw it away and get a new batch in," Bartholomew recalled. The frozen codfish came from Boston, and some live halibut were shipped in special tanks from Alaska. (Rooney said he couldn't resist sneaking a fish or two into Bartholomew's bunk during location shooting on Catalina Island.)

Fleming's achievement of complexity within simplicity on such an oversized production seems astounding, but he and Lighton fought for it every step of the way. Lighton procured a real Gloucester schooner, the *Oretha F. Spinney*, to serve as the *We're Here*. Late in 1935, a second-unit crew logged fifteen thousand miles on it from Massachusetts through the Panama Canal to California, shooting "atmosphere" along the way. But after it arrived, the crew found that either the new construction on deck or the Pacific swells made it roll to one side. For the rival schooner *Jennie Cushman*, Lighton acquired John Barrymore's former yacht, the *Mariner*.

Fleming aimed to shoot much of the movie off Catalina Island, where he'd made *Treasure Island*. But *Captains Courageous* had far lengthier and more intricate nautical sequences, and marine and weather conditions that autumn made outdoor filming nearly impossible. Although in later years Rooney and Carradine insisted they were at sea for weeks, a contemporary profile of Tracy states the principal cast "set sail" for a mere three days. (Tracy got some extra nautical experience when Fleming took him to Balboa for coaching from Fred Lewis, whose *Stranger* was then the official training vessel for California Sea Scouts.)

The first day of filming on the Catalina waters started with a 5:00 a.m. wake-up call. By 6:30, an equipment barge had set out for the *We're Here* so Hal Rosson could supervise the construction of a camera platform on the side of the ship while the principal actors studied their lines on deck. A Gloucester fisherman taught the supporting cast how to chop and hook bait, while the voice coach Arthur Rosenstein instructed a second team in sea chanteys. Shooting began at 1:00 p.m., after lunch, but the fog needed for the scene lifted at the wrong time, a wind came up, and at 4:30 Fleming was forced to wrap for the day, having put only a take or two in the can.

This director had a track record of adapting his methods and equipment to difficult locations. On *Captains Courageous* he utilized a unique rig to capture the shots of the schooner race: the "iron egg" to steady the camera ("a kind of pod strapped to the mast, stabilized by a gyroscope," Rooney would recall) and a self-wiping windshield to keep the lens clean. But ingenuity couldn't compete with unpredictable seas and winds, so Fleming moved most of the film to MGM's Stage 12. "You'll never know what he went through," Tracy said. "Six months, mostly on a process stage, with only three sections of boat to work with—the stinking smell of fish—and Freddie Bartholomew limited to four hours of work a day—and Fleming himself sick as a dog half the time." (Jack Conway took over for two weeks in late January 1937 while Fleming recovered from a second operation for kidney stones, this one without complications.)

At the studio, the filmmakers had to plan precisely and artfully to create a 3-D mosaic. Even the pivotal shot of Manuel standing in his dory as he sees Harvey floundering in the fog is second-unit work with Tracy's double. But Fleming's cutting of the rescue is so intuitive that the disparate visual components are indistinguishable. Ralph Winters, a top film editor for five decades, said, "Usually, when you shoot process, your camera stays pretty well anchored. Fleming would move anchor even when he was working with a process plate, and if the process image became grainy, so what? It worked all right dramatically."

James Havens, the "marine director," was in charge of the background footage as well as key images of the race between the *We're Here* and the *Jennie Cushman.* Havens shot off the coasts of Eureka, Monterey, the Pacific Northwest, and Catalina before sailing to Mazatlán, Mexico, to finish the tragic end of the race. When the *Jennie Cushman* tries to cut in front of the *We're Here* and neither Troop nor Captain Cushman (Oscar O'Shea) gives an inch, their audacity and foolhardiness give you the shivers. And the potent studio-filmed climax of Manuel's death merges with the second-unit footage without dropping a stitch.

The film's real-life tragedy involved a sailor, not a star. MGM paid $30,000 to the widow of a Norwegian sailor who was swept over the side of the *Mariner* during a storm off the Mexican coast. The second unit had gone looking for bad weather for a storm scene that never made it into the finished picture. "*Courageous* is all done until we can get a few shots at sea—whenever God sends a nice storm," Lighton had written his family. "And we have boats scattered all over the ocean looking for that."

James Wong Howe, who had worked with Rosson before working with Fleming in the early 1920s, said directors like Fleming "will not move the camera unless it's absolutely necessary to follow the actor. They play most of their shots with a stationary camera, allowing the actor to play within the frame. They'll cut with the camera. They'll establish the shot and let the action dictate where the cuts should be." *Captains Courageous* proves how subtly mobile and expressive Fleming's camera could be. The result is a wedding of emotion and rhythm resembling Kipling's best poetry rather than his prose.

Fleming and Rosson reckoned correctly that to make the movie all of a piece, the camera on the land sequences needed to be as fluid as the constantly rocking camera at sea. They track Mr. Cheyne as he departs his mansion, the sure swing of the camera movement echoing the crisp authority of his orders to his servants. The camera soon ambles through the hallways of Green Hill with Mr. Tyler as he tries to settle Charles, the target of Harvey's attempted bribery, and talks sense to Harvey. Throughout, there's a pleasing unity to motion and emotion, even when the scenes are still. Doc's gentle waking of Harvey on the *We're Here* has a sly, woozy wit, culminating with the cook concluding to the little braggart, "You sho' is a tonic to yourself." Everything that unfolds in Gloucester is magical, including the casting of the normally villainous Jack LaRue as a priest. He brings a non-creepy intensity to his consolation of the boy.

Fleming grew close to Bartholomew and gave him rides on his motorcycle. As director, he stays focused on Harvey's actions and reactions, whether the boy is downing the chocolate sodas that make him sick or responding with shock to Disko's slapping him ("You hit me!"). The actor rises to each moment in one of the great, unaffected child performances. The way Fleming and his team frame Harvey's story and Bartholomew embodies it, you never consider it the tale of a brat getting his comeuppance—it's about a boy finding out what makes him *him*.

By age twelve, Bartholomew had already appeared in such celebrated literary adaptations as George Cukor's *David Copperfield*, Clarence Brown's *Anna Karenina*, and John Cromwell's *Little Lord Fauntleroy*. Born in Dublin, raised in London and onstage there since age three, he wasn't destined to mingle well with Fleming's raucous crew. Keith Carradine recalls his father telling him that when Fleming asked Barrymore to cuff Harvey and send him sprawling into a pile of fish, "he really did it, because the kid was being such a pain in the ass."

Mahin put a more positive spin on it. "Freddie always came in, in the morning, very hale and well and dewy-eyed. And poor old Barrymore, he had this open-sore ulcer on his leg. Mickey Rooney would come in hung over, and they'd be like, 'Oh, gee, here he comes.' So when [Barrymore] had to hit him in the scene, onto this big pile of fish, he says to Vic, 'You really want me to hit him, huh?' Vic says, 'Yeah, make it good, because I'm only going to do one take.' It really stunned him." Height differences were another issue. Rooney, at sixteen, had already reached his full height of five feet three inches, but Bartholomew was hitting an adolescent growth spurt, so Rooney wore lifts to stay taller. "And so they had one woman whose only job on the set was which shoes should Mickey or Fred wear that day to keep them at the proper height," says Bartholomew's widow, Elizabeth. Still, Rooney considered Bartholomew "a great actor." Gene Reynolds, who played one of the Green Hill boys, liked Bartholomew immensely and chalked up any friction between him and the rest of the cast to his British manners. Tracy said, "You never have to fake any scenes with Freddie." When Tracy had to pull him over the side of Manuel's dory, it "tore the skin right off his ribs. He didn't bleat, not a bleat."

Bartholomew faced enormous pressures. The aunt who had brought him up accompanied him to the set and was soon to embroil him in two court fights. In 1937, his parents, in vain, tried to wrest him from her guardianship, and she strove, unsuccessfully, to get MGM to cancel his contract. But none of that impinged on the Harvey he created for *Captains Courageous.* Bartholomew was sturdier than he looked. He described the filming as "one long outing" and said he and the principal cast "grew very close" and "cried like a bunch of babies as we said our goodbyes."

"Vic had a very special manner [with Tracy]," said Edward Hartman, who visited the studio set and affirms Tracy's recollection of the fishy stench. "He seemed to be very quiet with him, not coaching, but just talking with him in a very gentle manner." The unusual rigors of Tracy's role went beyond the curls and Portuguese accent, and even beyond the physical challenges of working on a wet, rocking set and standing hip deep in water for hours. It was Tracy's first shot at solo stardom in an MGM epic, and Fleming was sensitive to his root insecurities. The special care paid off in the performance. A welter of emotion emanates from Tracy's core. His accent does waver; it seems equal parts French, Swedish, Yiddish, and Irish. And the curls ironed into his hair for two hours every day sometimes droop because of all the working and waiting he did in and on the water. No matter. Tracy creates a sailor who carries the wisdom of the home and the world within him without making a big deal about it.

Tracy called his performance "hammy"—but it isn't. He imbues what could have been a figure of unmediated goodness with explosiveness and edge. According to Kazan, Lighton would say, "When a man gets angry in life, he'll walk away. If he's sad, he'll conceal it. Emotion is and should be private. Actors are proud of their emotions; they show them off. When they do, I don't believe the scene." Tracy paraded his doubts about the role to the press, but his sheepishness about playing Manuel strengthened his acting. He told the film magazine writer Gladys Hall, "I didn't want to play Manuel, you know. Fought against it like a steer, thought the characterization would be phony. Didn't know how the pieces would fit together."

He studied dialect performances by Edward G. Robinson and Paul Muni, and found a Portuguese sailor from San Diego "who *was* Manuel. The expression in his eyes, the way he walked, the way he sat, the way he used his hands, his knowledge of boats. Then he began to talk and—he spoke better English than I do!"

Fleming didn't lavish the same attention on all his players. Billy Gilbert, who was Mr. Pettibone in *His Girl Friday*, had an atypically subdued bit part as the soda jerk on the passenger liner who mixes Harvey's near-fatal ice-cream sodas. He and Fleming probably disagreed on whether Gilbert should perform any of his trademark tics and sputters. "He got the dark side of Mr. Fleming," says his sister-in-law, Fay McKenzie.

> Now Billy really was a beloved character. They would bring him into a block comedy scene. Many times, they just needed something funny, and Billy was very inventive and could write stuff, and could give them what they needed.
>
> Evidently, Fleming was awful to him. He really humiliated him. And he wasn't used to that kind of treatment. All I know is that he was furious at how he had been treated. And this is the story. They broke for lunch, and he's sitting in the commissary, and he's looking at the table where Fleming is seated, and he had a glass of water and was thinking he'd like to throw it at him. But then, suddenly, a glass of water flew at Fleming, and

Billy looked down, quick, in his hand to see if he'd actually done it. And it scared him.

Fleming recorded the singing of Tracy and the rest of the cast right there on the set, even though Douglas Shearer had devised sophisticated methods of prerecording and lip-synching long in use at MGM for musicals and "straight" movies alike. A musician played for Tracy out of camera sight while the actor worked a dummy hurdy-gurdy. Fleming used a wax playback track to cover medium and long shots of Manuel singing and playing. But for most of the musical scenes, the director simply shot multiple takes with two cameras to get all angles. Fleming had progressed from *The Farmer Takes a Wife*, in which the thundering male choruses were fit for concert halls. Here he weaves the two main tunes—Manuel's ballad "Little Fish" and the jolly work song "Tishimingo" (with its chorus of "Oh, what a terrible man!")—in and out of the action. They lend the film an unusual springiness for a production of its size. Harvey reaches his peak of euphoria when he's able to contribute his own gibe against Captain Cushman:

Oh, he might have been a grocer
But a first-class seaman, no sir!
Oh, what a terrible man!
Oh, what a terrible man!

Gus Kahn got screen credit for the lyrics and Franz Waxman for the music, but additional contributions came from Lighton and the irrepressible Mahin, who once jokingly said to Jerome Kern, "I write songs."

"Little Fish" comes into play as we feel the profundity of Harvey's maturation under Manuel's influence. Their relationship reaches crisis point when Harvey fouls up one of Long Jack's trawl lines so Manuel can win a bet that he catches more fish with his hand lines. Manuel forfeits the contest to Long Jack when Harvey brags about his sabotage, and ignores the boy until he confesses to Long Jack. Harvey also apologizes to Long Jack for inadvertently filling the wiry seaman's arms with fishing hooks. But the boy's penitence rouses Long Jack to anger instead of mollifying him, and when he threatens to beat Harvey's ears off, Manuel responds with white heat: "Don't get me mad, Long Jack. I get all crazy and sick inside." Indeed, an unsettling glare irradiates his face; then he goes belowdecks and comforts the mortified Harvey. "We all got be ashamed once," Manuel says, "so we don't do things again we be ashamed of." He sings a new version of "Little Fish," joining the chorus, "Yeah ho, leettle feesh / Don't cry, don't cry," with new words: "You'll be a *balea* by and by"—"That mean beeg feesh, whale," he explains. Fleming regarded this scene, with its close-ups of Bartholomew fighting back tears, as one of his own top three. What's moving is not its sadness but the sight of a boy growing into himself. Tracy partners Bartholomew beautifully throughout this sequence. Early in the film, when Manuel first explains to Harvey why he sings, he says he just finds the songs in his mouth—feelings hit him like trade winds and keep coming out. But before he croons "Little Fish" after his face-off with Long Jack, he explains to Harvey, "I gotta sing every time I get mad." His singing is a way of turning negative energy positive—and making positive energy lyrical.

For Harvey's odyssey to be over and for him to connect with his real father, Manuel must be sacrificed. Lighton and Fleming kept working on Manuel's death almost to the end, striving for a balance between pathos and cruelty. What requires a willing suspension of disbelief is also what makes the scene extraordinary: Manuel knows he's cut in two as soon as he hits the water. The snapping of the mainmast was present in the script early, but only in Fleming's final notes do we find the inspired stroke of Manuel screaming out his horrifying condition to Doc in Portuguese, so Doc can tell Disko to cut him loose. "He's stove in," Doc tells Disko. "All the bottom half of him's gone. But he don't want the kid to know."

The element of self-sacrifice does more than ennoble the seaman. It heightens the emotions shared by *all* the characters and particularizes the action beyond a tragic stroke of fate. Manuel insists on determining the manner of his demise, and that becomes his final gift to Harvey. He demonstrates not just grace under pressure but grace in extremis. (Tracy remembered shooting his final scene "in iced water for three days running" in shots that took hours. But he was safely encased in a steel cage camouflaged by rigging; he sank down a mere three feet while water chutes and airplane motors created waves and pneumatic rockers swayed sections of the *We're Here*.)

Otis Ferguson, a Navy veteran, hailed *Captains Courageous* as "a corking yarn" and praised its "uncanny genius for the shipshape, that inimitable seaman's order in a cramped confusion of halyards, rope ends, buckets, pin and tackle, hatches and capstans and standing gear." The French agreed. "One must be insensitive to resist the profound emotion of this film," pronounced *Paris-Soir.* "Fleming has made this film with incomparable technical perfection." Even the *Times* of London observed that the Americans "have shown here a remarkable capacity for absorbing their author's mind," and "in fact, in some passages it almost seems to out-Kipling Kipling." James Shelley Hamilton of the National Board of Review imagined Kipling's ghost noting all the changes from the book and then admitting "they had made a good show of it."

Before those kudos, Fleming found himself fighting the studio. In early February 1937, he threatened to "leave the lot" if MGM didn't present the film as "Victor Fleming's production of *Captains Courageous.*" Although still working without a long-term contract, he said the MGM executive Benny Thau had promised him that credit. Eddie Mannix backed up Fleming, but in March he again risked Mayer's ire. The studio chief was trying to avoid paying Thalberg's estate—that is, Fleming's former lover Norma Shearer—what Thalberg would have been owed if alive. This time, Fleming went over Mayer's head to Nicholas Schenck, the president of Loew's in New York, and told him the studio had united behind Shearer and that shortchanging her would cost the company its Tiffany image. Schenck concurred.

Fleming shot final retakes on March 18, 1937, after which Tracy went into the hospital for a thyroid operation. "It looks all right, as nearly as you can tell before a preview," Lighton wrote his family. "Bartholomew is very good, and Spencer Tracy is excellent. Hope it's all right. It's been a lot of work." In the end, he was satisfied.

It's amazing how much *Captains Courageous* and its director meant to its cast. After Fleming finished with Bartholomew, he growled, for comic effect, "Now we can get this kid off the set!" and mimed a kick. Bartholomew, playing along, leaped off and hit an iron railing, breaking a front tooth. Fleming thought he must have really kicked him or forced him to jump, but Bartholomew, his widow says, knew he hadn't. The tooth was capped. Years later Bartholomew joked, "To my dying day, I'll be able to brush my teeth and think of Victor Fleming."

Rooney raved about Fleming: "He was a fabulous character . . . and so competent that you just knew he could have stepped in and filled any job on the production crew because Fleming was, above all else, a real technician who understood film and filmmaking." Although Rooney's character suffered most from the expansion of Manuel, Fleming handed him and Barrymore an unforgettable moment. On the *We're Here*, Disko and Dan are all business, but in the final sequence, back home in Gloucester, Dan leans on Disko's knee and the skipper lovingly pats the boy's head—they are a father and son once again.

19

Test Pilot

During all the tumult, illness, and complications of *Captains Courageous,* Vic and Lu conceived a second child. "The stork will stalk the Victor Flemings in February," the *Los Angeles Times* announced on December 23, 1936, and their new daughter *was* born on February 16. But settling on a name took months. "They're still trying names on the Victor Fleming baby. And after seven weeks they can't find one that fits," ran one column in April. Victoria's sister was called "Little Bit" before Sara Elizabeth was settled on. But that quickly became Sally.

Nearly twenty years after Fleming promised his mother that "some day I am going to have a house in California—wife and all that goes with it," he finally did. That spring, he put $60,000 into buying property and building a ten-room house in Bel-Air, a still-expanding district of West Los Angeles. Designed by Kirtland Cutter, who also did the Balboa beach house, the new home sat on eleven acres of rough chaparral in Moraga Canyon. It was substantial and comfortable—the strong, silent type, built almost like a fort, with walls made with two-by-six studs, not two-by-fours, and bars on the daughters' bedroom windows as a shield against kidnappers. In addition to a basement workshop and darkroom, Fleming installed a massive safe built to withstand the house's destruction by a wildfire. The family had moved in by the time he started *Test Pilot* in December.

The daughters say the products of the workroom were usually quite delicate. "He liked to have things to do," says Victoria. "He made a big bamboo bank to hang on the wall. He made a round box that opened up, and a penguin out of a walrus tusk." Sally says there was also a carved pelican with "a tiny fish in its beak" and her father presented them with "a mailbox with our address, 1050 Moraga Drive, engraved on it. A tiny silver mailbox. On the end of this teeny chain was this piece of silver."

"It was a lovely house," said their neighbor, the film editor Watson Webb. "Very warm and cozy and very attractive, sort of a combination of Early American and a California ranch house. And totally unpretentious, not like something you'd find in [contemporary] Bel-Air for somebody who was big and successful."

Of course, there was nothing unfashionable about it. The special-effects whiz Jack Cosgrove (who would work on *Gone With the Wind* and *Joan of Arc*), the MGM composer and arranger Adolph Deutsch, and the singer Allan Jones (who'd appeared in *Reckless*) were already neighbors, and the Gary Coopers lived nearby. Lu had selected the spot. A pair of hundred-foot pepper trees attracted her, and Fleming had the house built around them. "One was close to the swimming pool, and another shaded the porch," said Victoria. Vic and Lu had separate bedrooms, hers in wallpaper and chintz, his in knotty pine; his enormous bed included a carved headboard, and the Kodiak bear rug dominated the room.

He lured a butler away from Deutsch: tall, dour, half-Indian, half-African-American Osceola Slocum, who also doubled as a chauffeur for Lu and the girls. Slocum's wife, Robbie, was the live-in maid. The daughters eventually also had a live-in governess; early on, their father quickly discharged a nurse after she slapped one of them and he discovered the handprint.

Friends took notice of Fleming's settling into traditional masculine maturity. Hawks's biographer, Todd McCarthy, surmises that Vic's fidelity to Lu prompted Hawks to *continue* womanizing, as if Vic had left the field to him; now Hawks could at last beat him at something. Fleming's circle embraced Lu. With small groups such as Webb and the Lightons, Vic and Lu made a lovable couple. He was affectionate and attentive toward his wife, and, Webb said, "Lu was very warm, very nice, very easygoing, not attractive by standards of Hollywood glamour, but attractive as one who made a contribution to a group of people."

Joan Marsh Morrill had a small role in *The Wet Parade* and is best remembered today as the poster girl who comes to life in *All Quiet on the Western Front.* She thought Lu was "a lot of fun, a great personality, and great around the house; I remember a copper bowl always filled with yellow nasturtiums." Whatever Lu's elusive charm, she was making Vic a family man. Nearly everyone knew of his womanizing past. Patsy Ruth Miller, now married to Mahin, thought Lu "very pleasant" but "not the sort of easygoing woman who would have accepted" philandering.

Captains Courageous had been one of MGM's biggest grossers of 1937 as well as an Academy Award nominee for best picture, editing, and script, and Tracy won his first Oscar for best actor. Had it not split MGM's vote with the prestige-laden *The Good Earth*, it might have garnered nominations for Bartholomew and Fleming (Sidney Franklin was nominated for directing *The Good Earth*). On paper, *Test Pilot* didn't promise similar critical and financial success. The generic title had kicked around the studio since 1933; pulp fiction writers such as L. Ron Hubbard had published stories with the same name. Gable was always attached to MGM's version; in 1933, he and Harlow, along with Wallace Beery and Jimmy Durante, were slated for one incarnation of it, and MGM arranged with the War Department to film at Wright Field in Dayton, Ohio, before changing plans.

Nine writers ultimately had a hand in what became Fleming's version, including, of course, Mahin. The official credits went to Frank "Spig" Wead for the original story and Vincent Lawrence and Waldemar Young for the script. (Lawrence was the playwright who taught Fleming, on *Mantrap*, that words in movies live or die on their dramatic context.) Wead was an authentic Annapolis-meets-Hollywood personality: in 1957, John Ford even made a John Wayne film about him, *The Wings of Eagles*. Wead had graduated from the U.S. Naval Academy and flown in World War I before breaking his back falling down a flight of stairs in 1927; then he became a playwright and screenwriter. Hawks had turned Wead's 1935 play *Ceiling Zero* into an entertaining picture in the Fleming vein—indeed, Fleming, Wellman, and Tay Garnett had been on the wish list of the producer, Hal Wallis, before Hawks got the job.

Test Pilot turned out even better than *Ceiling Zero*—and, as on *Captains Courageous*, Fleming and the producer Louis Lighton were the two who pulled it together. The final product is full of characters and performances from MGM's stock company, including Lionel Barrymore as the crusty, benevolent owner of Drake Aviation and Marjorie Main as a savvy landlady. Yet it's a vibrant, personal picture.

Getting it made took persuasion. "Vic Fleming was the most exacting man on a job I ever knew," the MGM production manager Eddie Mannix said. "Nobody wanted to play [*Test Pilot*]. Fleming brought it to me. I said, 'Vic, I don't understand it.' He said, 'I don't know what's wrong with it.' Nobody understood it. I said, 'Come up and read me a sequence.' I said the thing is underwritten. He said, 'But we'll show you.' I said, 'I'm sold.' He had that confidence."

Myrna Loy and Clark Gable didn't understand the story, either. According to Hedda Hopper, Loy's initial reaction was: "It's incredible, it's unbelievable, the dialogue is stilted and insincere, the theme is absurd." Gable testified that when he read the script, "I wanted out because I didn't understand what the story was getting at. But the director . . . explained the character and I was happy with the part and still am." Loy would eventually call the picture "a personal favorite of mine."

On the page, only Fleming could sense the potent tension between the Kansas farm girl Ann Barton (Loy) and the mechanic Gunner (Spencer Tracy) as they vie for the focus of the flying ace Jim Lane (Clark Gable). And on the page, only Fleming could see how powerful it would become to portray the true rival to Ann *and* Gunner as the wild blue yonder: "the lady in a blue dress," an aviator's ultimate seductress.

Fleming's own flying time had begun to decrease sharply as his schedule became busier at MGM. He flew only seventeen solo hours in 1937, and by the end of 1938, his pilot license had lapsed because he hadn't put in the minimum number of hours in the air required to keep it active. "I just didn't have the heart to lie about it," he said. "You have to fill out a form that says among other things you have flown fifteen hours during the past twelve months, and I couldn't say I had without lying." But an ambitious youngster, Sid Luft (he'd become Judy Garland's third husband in 1952), remembered him as a regular presence at the Santa Monica Airport, where Fleming kept his Waco. "I was a kid then, building up my flying time and trying to get my commercial [license]. We'd just occasionally have some dialogue in the hangar." Luft admired the Waco: "A nice airplane; it could cruise close to two hundred miles per hour. I had a Monocoupe I bought for $1,500. We used to bullshit about his plane and mine, and he seemed to know what he was doing."

Fleming's comprehension of the risks run by test pilots ran deep. The Lockheed Sirius that had bedeviled him in 1932 ended up in the hands of the Australian aviation pioneer Sir Charles Kingsford Smith, that nation's Charles Lindbergh. "Smithy" had made the first transpacific flight from Oakland, California, to Australia, and set a record for flying solo between Australia and England—nine days and twenty-two hours. He had also briefly done stunt flying in silent pictures.

Kingsford Smith, who named the Lockheed the *Lady Southern Cross* and had it painted a bright blue, set another record with the plane in 1934, flying from Hawaii to Oakland in less than fifteen hours. Then he hopped down to Los Angeles, where the movie studios as well as local officials feted him. His last stop was with Fleming at MGM. If he expected pleasant conversation about the future of aviation, what he faced were blunt complaints from the aircraft's former owner. "I never did have any luck in that plane," Fleming told him in front of reporters. "It was always getting mysterious things the matter with it . . . Why, one time I flew in to Reno and had to come back by train. I developed a leaking tank. That's why I sold it." Kingsford Smith and his navigator "exchanged glances and smiled"—they had endured the same problem over the Pacific. Swamped in debt, Kingsford Smith wanted to sell the plane, possibly even to sell it back to Fleming. But he couldn't find a buyer. He was competing in the 1935 England-to-Australia air race and operating on a thirty-six-hour sleep deficit when, on November 8, 1935, he crashed the plane into the Bay of Bengal.

Test Pilot placed similar life-or-death aeronautics into a Fleming-Lighton specialty—a buddy picture with the emotional intensity of an irresistible doomed romance. Gable's Jim Lane, the test pilot for top-of-the-line Drake Aviation, uses dames and the bottle to siphon off tension after he breaks speed and altitude records. Spencer Tracy's Gunner is as reliable and punctilious as Jim is seat-of-the-pants and breezy. Loy's Ann Barton, a college-educated beauty, wins Jim's heart and complicates both men's lives.

MGM promoted the film—the only time Gable, Tracy, and Loy appeared together—as "The Captains Courageous of the Air." Loy thought it a prime example "of what big-studio moviemaking could be: the writing, the directing, the photography, the technical expertise, the casting of that impeccable stock company."

It also received a considerable publicity boost from a newly syndicated columnist, Ed Sullivan, who sought to raise his profile outside of his home city, New York, by sponsoring a "King and Queen of Hollywood" contest. Ballots ran in papers that carried his column, and though it's facile to surmise that a studio fix was in, Gable and Loy, who won, *were* at the peak of their popularity during the filming of *Test Pilot*. The "Queen" title didn't stick to Loy, but "King" did to Gable for the rest of his life.

In early December, Sullivan presented the actors with tin crowns for a newsreel, and in his account Fleming ended up directing the segment. Sullivan, whose wooden manner in front of a camera would become legendary with his long-running TV variety show, kept scrambling his consonants and saying Loy and Gable were the choice of "twenty million ficture pans." Fleming halted filming and announced, "Stop being nervous, Sully, and let me hear you do it right this time." A more revealing interchange took place when Sullivan had to cede the mike to Gable. "You might pretend to understand English even as Gable speaks it," Fleming lectured. "Listen to him. He's saying words and there must be a reaction from you." Later he told Sullivan, "Don't worry about it. Some of the alleged stars of this business are just as bad in scenes where they have to stand and listen. They're all right if they can talk, but listening is the severest strain."

The opening scene in Burbank has a beautiful bustle to it. Jim Lane is running late to break a cross-country record with the Drake Bullet. Gunner, fed up with waiting at the airport, goes to Jim's hotel room, where one girl (Virginia Grey) waits for Jim as he arrives with another (Priscilla Lawson) on his arm. It's not yet panic time—as the reactions of Gunner and Drake tell us, it's Jim's standard procedure. Fleming retained his veracious edge, improvising around the script. Martin Spellman, who played one of the kids crowding the Drake Bullet near the runway and yelling for Lane to break a record, recalls Fleming telling Gable, "This scene needs a line from one of the kids in the crowd." So Spellman got to ask Lane for his autograph. In the finished film, the crowd noise crushes that line, but it was smart for Fleming to treat Lane as a blue-sky star.

The Drake Bullet breaks an oil pump (somewhat like Fleming's Lockheed), forcing Jim to land in a Kansas field in front of the droll, admiring eyes of Ann Barton. "You're a funny-looking gazebo," she tells him. She also sees him as a modern-day prince who rode into her field on a plane rather than on a white horse. Ann knows that for all Jim's dash, he's not chivalrous. He still represents the larger world, a new life, the unknown.

The following sequence captures the giddiness of an impossible impromptu courtship. Ann and Jim generate the helium high lovers can get just before Cupid aims and stings. Jim is a romantic figure, but he's determined to make light of romance. They spend a day rooting for the home team at a baseball game in Wichita, then pop into a movie. As the lovers on-screen pitch woo, Ann mock-melts against Jim. (Fleming shot the flowery film within a film himself. The woman on-screen, Mary Howard, went on to play Ann Rutledge in *Abe Lincoln in*

Illinois.) Before long, Ann is whooping it up in a borrowed twin-cockpit plane as Jim performs loop-the-loops.

Loy, typically a lithe charmer and occasionally sublime, rarely seemed as free, easy, and original in her banter as she is in these scenes. (It rivals her *Thin Man* badinage with William Powell.) The odd turns of phrase like "funny-looking gazebo" click because of the way Ann savors them. She glides like a corn-fed goddess who knows that even for a world-beater like Lane, she doesn't have to push the allure. And Gable isn't the confident seducer of *Red Dust.* Jim turns up the emotional heat, all right, but also lets himself be hooked.

The scowl of Tracy's Gunner can't bring them earthbound when he arrives with a new oil pump. Jim has neglected preparations for the next day's flight, and Ann's presence is a further irritant. While Jim and Ann sweet-talk in the front seat of her car, Fleming frames Gunner brooding in the back. It's a perfect composition for a romantic triangle—and the entire film can be read that way, since Gunner's life focuses on Jim. After Jim takes off, Gunner tells Ann that she'll realize his departure is a good thing in the end, but flying over the baseball field, Jim gets an ache that grounds him again. He returns to the farm, warns Ann she'll be sorry, then sweeps her up in the air. They marry (offscreen) in Indianapolis.

These long yet chipper opening scenes stir up roiling complications. Ann loves Jim's untutored instinct. When anything takes him by surprise, he turns his head and glares—"like a big bear," she says, or "like a cross between an Indian and a gazelle." (She likes those "ga" words.) But she's stumbled into an improvised life that's as scary as it is exhilarating. Once Jim returns to New York, he refuses an assignment, and Drake fires him. So Ann, Jim, and Gunner begin looking for shared digs. The chemistry among the three is sensational. The movie is always fresh because Jim and Gunner constantly befuddle each other.

Fleming meshes the human and mechanical stories as cunningly as David Lean does in *Breaking the Sound Barrier* and Philip Kaufman does in *The Right Stuff.* Indeed, when Levon Helm's Ridley hands Sam Shepard's Chuck Yeager a piece of gum before each flight in *The Right Stuff,* he's echoing Gunner and Jim's good-luck ritual of pasting a wad of gum on each test plane's fuselage. And when Ridley starts Kaufman's movie with his talk of that demon that lives in the sky, he's carrying on the tradition of Jim Lane, who talks of that "girl in the blue dress" who teases and taunts him and tries so hard to slap him down that he slaps her back. Ann says she wants a blue dress; she even says she wants to be slapped. Loy pulls off a portrait of love that includes everything, including a streak of masochism.

Gable is part id, part kid. Tracy is like a high-school idealist, struggling to keep his best friend the star athlete in fighting trim. Gunner is sympathetic to Ann when he sees that she loves Jim as deeply as he does. Yet what moves her isn't what Gunner says—being a test pilot is "death every time you make a move"—but the break in his voice and the tears streaming down his face when he says it. Ann articulates what she sees as her three choices: She can try to get Jim to drink sarsaparilla with her instead of booze with the boys, knowing it won't dull his shrieking nerves. Or she can try to ground him altogether, which would make him hate her and make her hate herself. Or they can go on as is, pretending they're both happy and at peace, until at last he falls to earth. After that declaration, Gunner and Ann take turns melting down.

Tracy is at once urgent and at ease. He delivers a great silent performance as a man whose powers of feeling and understanding dwarf his limited eloquence. That gap accounts for some priceless big-mug comedy. When Ann playfully insists that Jim buy her a nightgown without her help, Gunner becomes Jim's model. Marginally less clueless about women than Jim, he suggests that they can't go wrong with pink.

The deep and genuine affection between the men, and role-reversal scenes like this one, have caused insightful critics like John DiLeo to ask, "Spencer Tracy as a gay man in love with his straight best friend?"—and answer in the affirmative. If you watch this movie with that question in mind, it can be simultaneously gripping and campy, like the scene of Montgomery Clift and John Ireland hefting each other's pistols in Hawks's *Red River*. There *is* a homosexual element to the bond between Gunner and Jim, and neither Tracy nor Gable is afraid to bring it out. But there's less of a physical spark between them than there is between Clift and Ireland. On the airfield, they're a team, and off it Gunner has absorbed himself into the most tough-minded kind of hero worship—the kind that recognizes his hero would be nothing without him.

In his script notes, Fleming suggested that Gunner act "very motherly" toward Jim, but in the playing the two conjure an intense adolescent relationship with the undefined, generalized yearning that accompanies it. Gunner also clicks with Ann as a kindred spirit; they're like an older brother and kid sister. He loses himself in Ann's analysis of the futility of domestic life with a test pilot—it hits him hard as he watches them cavort at an amusement park, where Jim admonishes Gunner, "Why don't you be gay for once and give yourself a shock." But he doesn't merely wallow in self-pity. He's judging the potential wreck of all three lives if Jim plays his string out to the end. (Indeed, one reviewer in 1938 thought Gunner's big dark secret was that he carried a torch for Ann.)

Gunner is fatally injured in Jim's final test flight of a B-17 bomber. As he's dying, he says the one blessing of going first is that he won't have to tell Ann that *Jim* has died. Of course, Jim is uppermost in his mind: he has been the most important person in Gunner's life. With heartbreaking simplicity, Gunner says Jim didn't know how good Gunner was: "You just loved me." And when Jim begs him to hang on "for my sake," Gunner answers, "That's all I'd come back for, if I could."

It may be Tracy's finest moment on-screen—and under Fleming's direction, Gable matches him. For Mahin, Gable was the "amazing" one. Jim never says, "I love you or something," back to Gunner, the way Mahin recalled, but Gable has the power to get across grief and a fear of what life will be like without his best friend. He wasn't afraid to shed tears over a male friend, though he would balk at crying over Scarlett's miscarriage in *Gone With the Wind.* (Shot for several days on the MGM back lot, the scene, with a studio-built shell of a B-17 set ablaze, attracted such attention that gawkers in private planes often disrupted filming.)

Terrific working partners though not off-set pals, Gable and Tracy, Loy wrote, "had a lively exchange, which actually seldom went on with many people during filming." Maybe Tracy also sensed how well he would come off in the film. He approached it with his usual intensity. "I remember him working out this business of nut cracking," to be performed during one of Gable's big scenes, "which he worked out very carefully all night long," Joseph Mankiewicz said. "Christ, he used up five pounds of nuts, and then he pretended on the set it had just occurred to him. It was perfectly timed so he would never crack a nut on Clark's line, but you would always have to cut to him."

Brinksmanship aside, Tracy and Gable had the kind of rapport that, used properly, sharpened both. The MGM publicist Howard Strickling thought, "Tracy would give his right arm to be Gable: loved, worshipped, respected," while Gable "would give his right arm to be recognized as an actor's actor, like Tracy." Gable told Mahin he always wanted to be able to nail a scene on the first take: "Start fooling around and [Spence will] kill me."

Generally, good-natured goading ruled. Fleming surmised to the *Hollywood Reporter* that he might end the film "with a long shot of Gable's ears flapping in the wind." Gable referred to them all by nicknames: of course, he was King and Loy was Queenie, but Tracy was the Iron Duke, and Fleming the Monk. (The MGM publicity whiz Frank Whitbeck came up with Tracy's moniker as if to extend the studio's royal family.) On Gable's birthday in February, Carole Lombard sent her man two tickets to a sightseeing blimp that circled Los Angeles, and the special entertainment was the studio's up-and-coming juvenile musical star Judy Garland, who sang satirical lyrics about Gable's recent dud *Parnell.* (She had sung "Dear Mr. Gable: You Made Me Love You" on the radio a year before; in three weeks she would be signed to play Dorothy in *The Wizard of Oz.*)

Loy thought it all "got a little out of hand" one day at March Field in Riverside, when officers tried to persuade both male stars and Fleming to fly to Catalina Island in one of the B-17s. Tracy resisted, despite the other men's merciless taunts, and confided to Loy, "The first thing they'll do, they'll head for a bar. You know I can't do that." Loy, not knowing Fleming's history with Tracy's drinking, accepted that explanation. She thought Tracy took his revenge when he failed to show up the next day, making everyone think he'd gone on a bender. Then, "a few minutes before noon, Spence strolled nonchalantly onto the set, bid everyone a jaunty good morning, and went to work." Loy helped dissipate the tensions by scolding the actor and Fleming.

Hawks's *Ceiling Zero* had been a hit a couple of years earlier, but it didn't approach the critical and popular sensation of *Test Pilot.* That may have sharpened Hawks's competitive edge when he was preparing *Only Angels Have Wings* in the wake of *Test Pilot*'s success. Hawks borrowed the most original scene from Fleming's blockbuster, bent it to his own ends, and later implied he came up with it in the first place.

The two movies share similar subjects but diverge in mood and theme. *Only Angels Have Wings* is unswervingly romantic in its presentation of mail pilots flying perilous routes through the Andes; the uncertainty of their lives adds to the intensity of their camaraderie. *Test Pilot* expresses the elation of men pushing their reflexes to meet the power and speed of new technology—and the tragic futility of their attempts to adjust the rest of their lives to their professional quest. Unlike Hawks's film, *Test Pilot* views the daredevil life as a prolonged adolescence. Just as Fleming had done, Jim must let go of his roistering ways to raise a family and tend to the rising generation.

The films, though, match up precisely in their pivotal dramatic sequences. In *Test Pilot,* Jim's plane catches on fire in the National Air Races in Cleveland, but another flier, Greg Benson—Jim's replacement for Drake—crashes his plane and is killed. Of course, all the competitors later celebrate at a bar. As they sing "If I Had the Wings of an Angel," a businessman proposes two champagne toasts. The first, to Jim, is wildly popular, but the second, to the late Benson, gets the businessman pushed from the saloon. The men say they've never heard of Benson; Jim says he must have crashed because he wasn't good enough for "the girl in the blue dress" and she slapped him down.

In *Only Angels Have Wings,* the aviators react exactly the same way when Jean Arthur's chorus girl expresses shock that the station chief, Cary Grant, would eat the steak that another pilot ordered before he was killed in a crash. They say they never heard of the man; Grant has already said he crashed because he wasn't good enough for the job.

Both these anti-wakes depict fliers asserting their right to honor their own dead in a way that enables them to get on with the business of cheating death. But in attitude the two films couldn't be more dissimilar. In *Test Pilot,* Jim then tumbles into a four-day multi-city bender; it's the start of the narrative runway that leads to his retiring from flying and taking up a new career as a pilot instructor. (In one of Fleming's favorite moments, he gives half his prize money—$5,000—to Benson's widow, played by Gloria Holden. She's now a widow with three children, just as Fleming's mother had been after his father's death.) In *Only Angels,* the scene instead begins the heroine's education. She must learn that a pilot needs a gal who can bear the pressure and "stick."

Hawks may have tried to outdo Fleming with the same scene as part of their friendly rivalry. It would not be the last time he took a dramatic idea from a peer and made it say what *he* wanted it to say: the entire plot of *Rio Bravo* (1959) emerged from his disdain for Fred Zinnemann's *High Noon* (1952). But Hawks went further with *Test Pilot,* saying he wrote the original story and some lines for the movie when he was at MGM, even though he'd left the studio in 1934. He also insisted that everything in *Only Angels Have Wings*, no matter how outlandish, was "absolutely true." If so, that resonant death scene may have been part of a truth that he and his friend Fleming had perceived together.

In *Test Pilot*, Fleming used Benson's crash, staged at the Van Nuys Airport, to indulge in an operatic stroke. When an ambulance picks up Benson's body and drives away, he shows the bent, awkward body of his widow running across a field to catch it. The visual eloquence compensates for the dramatic non sequitur. (Everyone knows the widow and the children are there; wouldn't someone stop the ambulance until the driver knew her wishes?) Before Holden's scene with Gable, Fleming kept her in tears for fifteen minutes. He may have misjudged her casting and performance—then best known as Mrs. Zola in *The Life of Emile Zola*, now best known for the title role of *Dracula's Daughter*, she's a little bit undead herself—but the anecdote conveys his commitment to the performance and the material.

What startles contemporary audiences about the sequence at the National Air Races is the spectacle of pilots speeding in aerial circles, like Nascar stars. Some will find in it a transporting quality that Nascar races don't have: spectators crane their necks to the sky instead of locking into a blur on asphalt. Planes in formation suddenly make darting moves like willful dragonflies. The money and prestige of a big MGM production enabled Fleming to send three camera crews to pick up footage from the Thompson Trophy race and to film a simulated race the next day with some of the same pilots. To make the footage in Van Nuys meld with the Cleveland footage, he elevated the camera platforms and had the cinematographer Ray June shoot down on the action to eliminate the mountains in the background.

Every aspect of *Test Pilot* allowed Fleming to test his virtuosity. On a micro level, he had Douglas Shearer record Gable with a lapel mike to capture dialogue above the rumble of the aircraft. On a macro level, for the film's climax, he had at his disposal the entire heavy bombardment fleet of the Army Air Corps. That's because General Henry H. "Hap" Arnold, then deputy chief of the Air Corps, saw the film as an ideal public relations ploy for the Boeing B-17 Stratofortress.

It was the public's first glimpse of the four-engine bomber that would go on to distinguished service in both theaters of World War II. To emphasize its size, Fleming showed two mechanics struggling to polish the bottom of one wing. While *Test Pilot* was being made, the Air

Corps had just thirteen of the aircraft; they were still considered experimental, and Congress had not fully funded production. The Air Corps flew twelve of them to California and put nine in the air at a time for Fleming's second unit at March Field. The innovative aviator and technical director Paul Mantz co-engineered the impact of the flying scenes. Not since Wellman's *Wings* and Howard Hughes's *Hell's Angels* had a filmmaker shot such a fleet with so many cameras and from so many angles and positions on the planes.

In a scenario unimaginable today, General Arnold enthusiastically took part in the movie's publicity, appearing on the Maxwell House *Good News* program—MGM's radio house organ—to salute test pilots as "the unsung heroes of this flying game." Arnold told the radio audience that the Flying Fortresses "are the culmination of the work of these masters of the air," and the ones in the film were the same that had recently completed an eleven-thousand-mile round-trip from Miami to Buenos Aires.

Fleming did not accurately portray the details of testing military planes. He smudged the facts on purpose: these planes' specifications were military secrets (as mentioned in the prologue). For instance, the Air Corps never tested the diving capabilities of pursuit aircraft, as Lane does, and the B-17 is said in the film to have a five-thousand-mile range, when its actual range was less than two thousand miles.

Fleming committed other inaccuracies strictly for dramatic effect. In the climactic Flying Fortress crash, the sandbags doubling in the test for bombs are not only piled too high; they're also put in a position to crash the bulkhead and knock out Tracy. Then Gable heaves sandbags over the side at a point when, as one real-life test pilot observed, the "plane, spinning like a top, should have shot him into space by centrifugal force alone in ten seconds."

Test Pilot nonetheless popped the eyes of the public and reviewers alike, from the trades ("One of the outstanding successes of the year," the *Hollywood Reporter* wrote) to the major dailies ("A bang-up aviation drama," said *The New York Times*). Even National Socialist reviewers in Germany praised the film's technique and dramatic force as well as Gable's valor, although "many critics were shocked that it represented a man in such a serious position as a test pilot as drunken and irresponsible."

It was the second Fleming picture in a row to win multiple Oscar nominations—for picture, editing, and original story but again not for direction. Tracy won his second straight Academy Award not for Gunner but for his Father Flanagan in *Boys Town.* Maybe the sacrificial element of *Test Pilot* seemed too close to Manuel in *Captains Courageous.*

Even Tracy's young daughter, Susie, asked Fleming at the premiere, "Don't you like my papa? That's the second time you've killed him." Actually, with *Test Pilot,* he fashioned a lasting tribute to friendship. Saul Bellow told fellow author James Salter that after he saw the film, he turned to his wife and asked, "Why don't we have friends like that?"

20

Salvaging *The Great Waltz*

In April 1938, the *Hollywood Reporter* mentioned that Fleming "almost cracked up in his own cabin plane, a few days after *Test Pilot* trade raves." Nothing else seemingly went wrong for Fleming in the spring of 1938. *Test Pilot* and Warner Bros.' *Adventures of Robin Hood* were the only new hits packing theaters; throughout the first half of the year, exhibitors desperate to fill seats rebooked old favorites like *Dracula, The Count of Monte Cristo, King Kong*, and Fleming's own *Treasure Island.* MGM was still pressuring him to sign a contract, but he continued working on a handshake deal with Mannix.

His beloved Victoria, "Missy," was three and Sally one. He was pouring more energy and effort into his Bel-Air home, including now a sizable pumpkin patch, which he was using to set up his land for an eventual orchard. Around this time he wrote:

> I am the only farmer in Bel-Air, which is supposed to be a rather exclusive residential colony in Hollywood. My neighbors are famous stars and executives. Carey Wilson, the writer and a studio colleague, is one. Gene Raymond and Jeanette MacDonald, Carole Lombard, Clark Gable and W. C. Fields are others. So far none of them has entered a protest against my own two acres under cultivation. Under the peculiar law of the state, I get special water rates as a farmer. It costs the rest of them more to sprinkle their lawns than I pay for irrigating my farm. And furthermore, if they want homemade pumpkin pie, they come to me for the pumpkins. Mine are the best in this section of the country.

The one farmer in Bel-Air presented a formidable, stylish presence on the MGM lot. As he approached his fifties and his hair began to gray, Fleming began dressing almost uniformly in shades of gray as well; perhaps his only outward sign of eccentricity, it made him look like a jaunty Southern California banker. Gable sometimes adopted the style for himself, but for Fleming it was virtually a daily look, one he kept for the rest of his life. "Flem was very conservative," says the tailor Eddie Schmidt Jr. "He was not a wild man." Schmidt's father made Vic look natty, and his butler, Slocum, kept his wardrobe in perfect order. His niece Yvonne marveled, "[Slocum] would tidy them up and put them at the far right end of the closet. And then the next day he would get in the left-hand side of the closet, and those would be all ready to go. It was beautifully done and he looked like a model at all times. He was absolutely a perfectionist about quality. And he said to me, this was when I was quite young, 'Don't ever buy two of anything. Buy one good thing!' Which I thought was a very good idea." The actor Norman Lloyd remembers seeing Fleming at a distance and thinking, "Now that's the way to look in this town!"

Fleming dressed like the old-school swells Astaire and Cooper, wearing "a lot of Shetland jackets with two-button flaps and side vents," gray trousers, "and understated ties," Schmidt recalls. He wasn't the man for "plaids or a bright white stripe on dark blue stripes."

One legend had it that "he demanded the choicest dressing room and, on location, the biggest trailer." Actually, he got them simply for being MGM's most prominent director, just as, because of his popularity with the stock company, "an extra quota of stars . . . appeared in tribute to him" at the premieres of his movies, though another legend had it that he never attended his own premieres.

Even at his zenith, he may have felt some insecurity about rising from San Dimas into Hollywood aristocracy. One man who thought he saw a taste of this was the freelance director Edward Ludwig. He worked at MGM on *The Last Gangster* with John Lee Mahin around the same time Fleming and Mahin did *Captains Courageous*, and he later directed John Wayne in the anticommunist movie *Big Jim McLain* (1952). Ludwig had a secretary he brought from studio to studio, and he told his nephew Julian that "she would suddenly be close to tears or in tears when he came to check up on things at his office at MGM. She said this director who used to drive for her family kept ignoring her whenever she tried to say hello to him at the commissary. She'd go by his spot at the director's table and he'd not even recognize her." That director was Fleming. When Edward Ludwig heard the story, he explained to the distressed girl that Fleming was "quite a good director and probably had his mind on his next shot." But the last time it happened, "Fleming walked right by her when she was standing in line to pay for her lunch. She just wanted to try to say hello to a guy she once knew, and all the other secretaries thought she was making a pitch for a big director."

That insult set off Ludwig. His nephew recalled, "He went to Fleming's set and told him something like, 'I've got a part in my picture that calls for a big lummox of a driver, someone who knows about cars—you'd look like you'd be perfect for the part!' I think they would have really gone at each other if the other people on the set hadn't separated them."

Ludwig may have been right the first time, when he told his secretary that Fleming had his mind on his next shot. Assuming that she was part of that wealthy Santa Barbaran Clinton Hale's extended family, she may have wrongly presumed that Fleming retained a familiarity with, or respect for, her name. And that anecdote offers a minority report on Vic in this bustling period.

The MGM publicist Norman Geiger said he was just "a real solid guy who didn't take any crap from anybody" and didn't let studio politics affect him: "He knew where he was going and how he was going to get there." Lawrence Bachmann, a junior writer at Metro in the late 1930s, remembered Fleming as "almost a legend at that time." Joseph Newman, who started as an MGM office boy and went on to direct the sci-fi cult favorite *This Island Earth* (1955), considered Fleming to be "a man respected by everybody." To Newman, he was not a mingler like George Hill, Woody Van Dyke, or Robert Z. "Pop" Leonard, but also not a snob: "Just a little bit aloof." Newman said everyone knew he was "also successful [directing] women."

And, of course, children. In July 1938, he assumed command from Richard Thorpe for two days of retakes on *The Crowd Roars* before pitching in for Jack Conway on another pairing of Gable and Loy, *Too Hot to Handle.* Gene Reynolds, a child actor and future TV director, writer, and producer (notably for *M*A*S*H*), who'd had an unbilled role as one of the schoolboys in *Captains Courageous,* acted for Fleming in *The Crowd Roars.* Reynolds played the Robert Taylor character as a young boy ("in those days, the opening reel often showed the stars' characters as children so you'd see the characters being formed"). Frank Morgan played Reynolds's father; the scene took place in a bar where Morgan was getting drunk. Morgan receives a telegram, then sticks it in his pocket; it falls out, and the boy picks it up and reads it. That's how Reynolds's character learns that his mother has died.

"We shot it once or twice, but Victor wasn't satisfied with what I was doing," Reynolds recalls. Fleming approached the boy and instructed him: "You pick up this letter and you read it—this note of your mother dying." And then he said, simply, "You cry." For Reynolds, the secret of Fleming's communication was his own "sensitivity, sensibility, and vulnerability." And Fleming agreed. He isolated "sensitivity—that quickness of inner response on which the director depends in getting across the characterization" as the quality that a filmmaker must not only share with his stars but also "know how to use." Even as a gun for hire or a Mr. Fix-It, he was an actor's director: "Stars and players are the instruments through which [a director] breathes life into a story."

Fleming's largest back-lot salvage job to date arrived one month later. "Vienna seen through American eyes," ran one of MGM's ad lines for *The Great Waltz*—though as its star, Fernand Gravet, pointed out, "there wasn't a single American on the film except for Victor Fleming, and he wasn't originally slated for it." Made in 1938, the year of the story in *The Sound of Music*, and set in the 1840s, it, too, had songs with lyrics by Oscar Hammerstein II, and it, too, conjured a musical fantasy of an Austria brimming with gemütlichkeit. Completed before Hitler annexed Austria but released eight months afterward, it fictionalized and conflated the careers of Johann Strauss Jr. and his father.

It hails Johann junior, or "Schani," as the Waltz King whose music revolutionizes Viennese social life against the background of a student-led revolt against the omnipotent chancellor Metternich and his befuddled absolute monarch, the emperor Ferdinand. Strauss senior never appears on-screen and is notable in the narrative only for trying to get his son to be a bank clerk; when Franz Josef, Ferdinand's nephew, is installed as emperor, the protesters greet it as a victory, though they can't know then that he'll be a benevolent ruler. In small print under the credits, the moviemakers confess that except for Strauss II and Franz Josef I, "the events and characters depicted in this photoplay are fictitious." To squash in-house haggling over the written prologue to the movie, one MGM functionary advised, "Strauss having died about 39 years ago and his second wife having recently died, there is no one living who would be connected."

In bold kitsch strokes, the movie depicts a musical youth culture buoying up bourgeois Vienna, a city where Strauss can gather an orchestra from the ranks of his future father-in-law's bakers. Luise Rainer, fresh from her back-to-back Oscars for *The Great Ziegfeld* and *The Good Earth*, plays the selfless and adoring Poldi, who marries Strauss. Miliza Korjus, a coloratura soprano, plays the cosmopolitan opera star Carla Donner, who almost woos Schani away from Poldi—although Joseph Breen warned against "any suggestion that there is an adulterous relationship between Carla and Schani." MGM had bought the title, which previously graced an operetta in Vienna and London and a Broadway spectacular, and commissioned a whole new script (story by Gottfried Reinhardt; screenplay by Samuel Hoffenstein and Walter Reisch) and score (the composer Dimitri Tiomkin adapting Strauss for Hammerstein).

If Fleming had initiated the project, it might be possible to read in it some presentiment of the conflict he would face between fidelity to his hausfrau, Lu, and rapture for Ingrid Bergman, who in a few years would be enthralled by him and his talent. But MGM brought Fleming onto this film simply to fix it (the studio gave a little work on it to Josef von Sternberg, too). The sole credited director is the Gallic master craftsman Julien Duvivier, who had become one of France's "Big Five" with such masterpieces of poetic realism as *Poil de carotte*, *Pépé le Moko*, and *Un carnet de bal*. Duvivier, like Jacques Feyder (the deposed director of *Red Dust*) and René Clair and Jean Renoir, learned that Hollywood production methods demanded as much political savvy and generalship as sensibility. (The fifth man of the Big Five, Marcel Carné, never attempted the leap.) Duvivier "made magnificent pictures in Paris, where he had charge of everything," said William Wyler the following year. "But in Hollywood he couldn't make a picture. Why? He wasn't given a chance to express himself. Someone else was always overruling him. Believe me, those producers who take authority away from the directors are seriously hurting the business."

The producer-culprit was the Thalberg associate Bernard Hyman. All Hyman's initial choices made sense—the Berlin-born story writer Reinhardt was the son of the fabled theater director Max Reinhardt, who had most recently co-directed the sometimes magical film of *A Midsummer Night's Dream*. Gottfried Reinhardt would become an MGM producer (John Huston's *Red Badge of Courage*) and eventually direct himself (*Town Without Pity*). But Hyman's goal once he hired men like Reinhardt was simply to spread out a deluxe cultural smorgasbord. The composer-arranger Tiomkin obtained four Stradivarius violins at $10,000 each, and MGM spent lavishly for rights to dozens of waltzes.

Reinhardt persuaded Thalberg to hire Korjus, a film novice celebrated in European operatic circles for her *altissimo*, after playing a record of her singing Strauss's "Voices of Spring" over the phone from Europe. And Hyman became a believer after Reinhardt played him a recording of Korjus singing the "Queen of the Night" aria from Mozart's *Magic Flute.* "Transported" by Korjus's high notes, Hyman declared he would put that aria in the picture, and when Reinhardt noted that the picture was about Strauss, not Mozart, Hyman retorted, "Who the hell is going to stop me?" (The original script invokes the aria with a wink, when a starstruck Strauss says he heard Donner sing it at the Imperial Opera; in the film, he refers to seeing *Norma.*)

While the Estonian-born Korjus learned English and shed weight, Duvivier assembled her cast mates and pitched in on Woody Van Dyke's *Marie Antoinette.* Thalberg and Hyman considered Nelson Eddy for Strauss, but when shooting began, all the leads were European. Rainer was Vienna-born—she had worked with *Max* Reinhardt—and Fernand Gravet was Belgian-born and became a film star in France, though Mervyn LeRoy put him under personal contract and he spoke English without an accent. Duvivier shot from May to the end of June. "I got exactly what I wanted," he told his fellow Parisians. "They gave me two million dollars to make my movie." MGM designed a splashy trick magazine spread inculcating the idea that they were making *The Great Ziegfeld* in waltz time. "Korjus—pronounced 'Gorgeous' " was Hollywood's way of introducing its new musical star to the heartland; Korjus later used that line for a self-produced LP.

The studio finalized writers' credits on July 5—and almost immediately sent Duvivier back to France and laid plans to remake his movie. Executives found his *Great Waltz* too dark—often literally, with many atmospheric night scenes—and Korjus's part too brittle. "New policy at MGM," wrote Ed Sullivan. "If a director doesn't measure up to the front office standard he is relieved immediately. Victor Fleming was rushed in on 'Too Hot to Handle.' Then Fleming was rushed in on 'The Great Waltz.' " Fleming began reshoots on August 5 and put Mahin on the movie's payroll three days later. Fleming wanted Mahin on anyway, but hiring him instead of the original writers to create or revamp scenes consolidated his position and froze out Hyman's team. By now, he had become both a master director and one who knew how to throw his weight around.

Even if the front office complained that the dailies were murky or odd, the studio later lobbied for the cinematographer Joseph Ruttenberg to win an Oscar for the movie—and he might be the one most responsible for the film's visual unity. (Fleming would hire him a few years later for *Dr. Jekyll and Mr. Hyde.*) MGM's problem with Duvivier was more basic than unconventional photography. In the record left by his shooting script, Duvivier's hints of sophistication don't fit a scenario that, in exuberant cartoon form, depicts the rise, midlife crisis, and apotheosis of an artist. The story starts with Strauss losing his bank job for writing waltzes on company time. He pulls together an orchestra—the conceit is that every room or workplace in Vienna contains at least one musician—and then makes his debut at Dommayer's Casino.

In reality, Strauss did make his debut there, but it was a rousing historical event: the upstart son challenging the cultural primacy of his disapproving father. In the movie, apart from Poldi and her parents, hardly anyone shows up except Carla Donner and her escort, who insist the music continue despite the owner's intention to close for the night. When she departs to attend a party at her lover's palace (leaving word that Strauss should go there, too), Dommayer huffs off and opens up the windows on the way out, figuring that whoever wants to listen might as well listen for free. The breeze carries Strauss's glorious music into crowded sidewalks and cafés—it's the waltz called "An Artist's Life"—and everyone within earshot surges into the casino. It's the prototype of the music-sweeping-the-nation sequences in movies about jitterbugs or rock and rollers. Strauss arrives at Donner's party flush with success, ready to play along when she decides to risk aesthetic scandal and sing one of his waltzes.

Duvivier then convoluted matters considerably. In the script he shot, Carla kisses Strauss in the palace's "quiet room" before the performance; her noble lover, Count Hohenfried, arrives before that kiss can go anywhere. Then, *during* the performance, she angers Strauss with the way she takes the song-waltz over musically, making it her own with the brilliance of her "embroidered cadenzas" and "coloratura obbligato" and daringly prolonged trill. Strauss leaves spluttering about the honesty of his music and the good Viennese who dance to it. When the movie audience has just gotten a chance to glory in Strauss's music and sample upper-crust sexual confusion, could the composer's disagreement with the singer ever have been made clear and persuasive?

In the Fleming-Mahin version, Carla's performance, relatively straightforward, occurs *before* the flirtation in the quiet room—and it seduces everyone, including Strauss. (Korjus's singing is the only glory in the movie.) And Fleming and Mahin don't merely place the scene in the quiet room afterward: this time Donner caps it by kissing her protector, Count Hohenfried, who adorns her with a dazzling necklace. That's when Strauss comprehends that among celebrities and noblemen, love can be mysterious and enraging. Upon leaving Donner with Hohenfried, Strauss sees Poldi waiting in the street; she's sensed that he (and their love) might be in danger. After a policeman mistakes them for man and wife, Fleming cuts to their wedding party, a corny yet exhilarating Fleming-Mahin invention in which Schani wins a bride and a good business partner (Hugh Herbert) simultaneously.

Luise Rainer says, "They shot all the scenes over because they wanted to have more of Miliza Korjus." Yet it was not about adding more scenes for Korjus but making the ones already there more vivid and accessible. (Fleming's instincts worked: Korjus won a best supporting actress nomination, and Tom Held, who did *Test Pilot*, was again nominated for best editor.) Rainer goes on, "I always jokingly said to my friends that after Duvivier had done the film, it was a film of Mrs. Strauss not Mr. Strauss. Then he was replaced with Fleming, who made a film of Mr. Strauss"—a legend similar to that of Fleming taking over *Gone With the Wind* and putting the focus on Gable's Rhett Butler rather than the women.

Rainer, in truth, retains her big scenes in Fleming's overhaul, though the director did some snipping: for example, Poldi doesn't tell Carla in the diva's dressing room that she intended to kill her. (She does carry a gun, and the full bit even made the trailer.) Rainer found Fleming "a very good man to work with." Unfortunately, she was "rather miserable because the whole thing was supposed to be practically over when he started." Did she think Fleming dashing? "He probably was dashing, but it escaped me. But then, I was very occupied." Part of what occupied her: she was in the middle of her draining three-year marriage to the playwright and screenwriter Clifford Odets. The columnist Jimmie Fidler observed that during a scene with Gravet, "her eyes suddenly filmed over with tears, her voice trembled and she seemed on the verge of breaking down. A tall woman dashed on the set, threw her arm around Luise, and led her away, talking German like mad. The talker was Miliza Korjus and before long she had Luise back at work."

Korjus had battled with Duvivier. In fact, Korjus's daughter, Melissa Wells, a former U.S. ambassador to Estonia, remembers her mother berating the director in Russian and German and declaring, "I don't care, I'm going back to Germany!" She threatened to walk off the movie as long as Duvivier was directing. But when MGM put Fleming on it, he called her "Angel" (he would call Ingrid Bergman that, too), and she nursed hopes that he would direct her in a film about the nineteenth-century soprano Adelina Patti, with Toscanini conducting. When the columnist Sheilah Graham observed Korjus taking direction from the producer Reinhardt in German, Fleming was likely using Reinhardt to help him communicate with someone who had just learned English.

Alfred Hitchcock had made a Strauss movie, *Waltzes from Vienna*, in Britain in 1934; he later referred to it as "the lowest ebb" of his career. But *The Great Waltz* was a smash and set a trend for fictional composer biopics that ransacked entire oeuvres, rearranged works musically and chronologically, and pretended that an artist's life—a make-believe account of his life, at that—was a direct inspiration for those works. *A Song to Remember* (Chopin), *Song of Scheherazade* (Rimsky-Korsakov), *Song of Norway* (Grieg), and *Song Without End* (Liszt) followed.

Duvivier, not Fleming, deserves the credit—and the blame—for many of the form's stock scenes, which here have a spurious freshness. In one *Fantasia*-like sequence, the chattering of birds, the irregular clopping of a carriage horse, the piping of nearby shepherds, and the sounding of a post horn combine to give Strauss and Carla the inspiration for "Tales of the Vienna Woods."

Near the end, Duvivier does pull off a remarkable *coup de cinéma*. When Poldi enters the Imperial Opera House for the debut of Strauss's first opera, the director ratchets the camera back, not in a smooth tracking shot, but in a cannonade of individual images. This swift series of "shock cuts" takes in the grandeur of the theater and leaves her a tiny figure in the distance. Paradoxically, by making us experience Poldi's feelings of smallness, it creates an operatic flourish exactly when the action needs it most.

Fleming remade one large-scale scene: student revolutionaries demonstrating to a Strauss march, led by a line of little drummer boys. Their sunlit assault on Count Hohenfried's house takes the place of Duvivier's more violent and foreboding nocturnal sequence, in which clutches of rebels at various barricades cheered the sight and sound of the singing marchers and upended a patriotic statue. In both versions, Strauss shrewdly rescues Donner from the mob by proclaiming her a friend to the rebels, but he can't save her from the soldiers who pile the protesters into tumbrels.

Again, it's hard to figure how the Duvivier version would have clicked tonally when the sequence always ended with Schani and Donner in one tumbrel and two of Schani's musicians, Dudelman (Leonid Kinskey) and Kienzl (Curt Bois), in another, communicating through a game of charades. The two jokers stage a Three Stooges–like fight in order to distract their guards and let Strauss and Donner escape. This was all more in Fleming's vein, anyway; he always had a healthy affinity for low comedy, from his silent days with Fairbanks to his repeated use of the Three Stooges' mentor, Ted Healy. In *The Great Waltz*, when he isn't deploying Kinskey's Dudelman and Bois's Kienzl as a baggy-pants short-tall comedy team—a sort of Muttski and Jeffski—he exploits Hugh Herbert, as Strauss's bartering music publisher, Julius Hofbauer, for excitable or dyspeptic burlesque effects. Herbert looks as if he'd spontaneously combust if he didn't let out the "Woo-*hoo*!" that had been his vocal signature since his vaudeville days.

Mahin rewrote Hoffenstein and Reisch's script both to tighten its focus on an artist divided between first love and mature love and to give the dialogue the pith it would have in the libretto to a musical comedy. "I thought of you ever since that night," says Schani. "And you walked away, proud and angry," says Carla—dispensing with a half page of verbiage in the previous script. Yet the interchange still falls into cliché.

The Great Waltz gave Fleming a chance to display his film smarts, not his artistry. He and Mahin knew how to maintain a robust emotional through line up to an audacious resolution, with Carla simply announcing to Poldi after her performance in Strauss's opera that he and the singer love each other and that he's going with her to Budapest.

Too bad the filmmakers can't overcome the anticlimax built into the pseudo-inspirational material. In the best Duvivier-shot scene, Count Hohenfried calls on Poldi at the Strauss residence and urges her to fight for her man. As the count, Lionel Atwill movingly blends ardor with mortification, and Rainer shows gracious strength as she tells him he has her "greatest respect." But when the grandeur of the opera world defeats her, she gives up. It was right for Fleming and Mahin to delete Poldi's saying to Carla, "I came to kill you," and to make Carla so bold in her claims on Strauss. You do get caught up in the momentum of mad love. Yet then the lovers turn impossibly high-minded, and Carla reads Johann's mind as they banter in the carriage ride to the boat. She states that Poldi would always be a presence in their lives, coming between them. She sings "One Day When We Were Young," assured that Strauss wrote it for her and that she'll always have a piece of his art and heart. Not long after her boat floats up the Danube, the melancholy Strauss gets his wind back. In a pallid replay of the Vienna Woods ride, the sights and sounds of the river rouse Strauss to create "The Blue Danube."

Gravet said that Josef von Sternberg, not Fleming, was brought in to direct everything from here to the end, and the dancer Dorothy Barrett backs him up. The movie cascades into a montage of Strauss's melodies winning the hearts of waltzers across the Continent and beyond as his sheet music pours off the presses; Barrett was the dancer from Spain, in a dress that Jeanette MacDonald originally wore as a Spanish spy in *The Firefly*. Von Sternberg "did all the montage shots . . . all the little intricate shots and trick shots," Barrett says. (You can also spot Barrett in *The Wizard of Oz*, as the pretty brunette who opens the door to the Emerald City's Wash & Brush-Up Co. at the close of "The Merry Old Land of Oz.")

To gild a rather wilted lily, Carla gets to reprise "One Day When We Were Young" at the scene of Poldi's climactic triumph. After Poldi has shepherded her Schani through the shoals of temptation and temperament for half a century, Franz Josef himself leads all Vienna in celebrating its Waltz King. From the imperial balcony we see Carla in the clouds, warbling soulfully away. Although Fleming's revisions proved critical in making the movie *play*, the press exaggerated their extent, and the picture remained a piece of musical marzipan.

Joseph Stalin, however, found it incomparably tasty. After he saw it in 1939, he canceled awarding a series of medals struck for Soviet filmmakers. "When they learn to work like the Americans," he said, "then they'll get their medals." Partly because World War II curtailed the importing of current foreign films and the return of old ones, Soviet projectors wore out their prints of *The Great Waltz*. The pianist

Dmitry Paperno wrote that it provided "a dazzling contrast to our strictly regulated lives, not to mention the terrible things that were going on in the background, and that the grown-ups tried to keep us from."

When word of *The Great Waltz*'s popularity in the Soviet Union spread after World War II, Korjus, who became a regular host to Soviet émigrés, told her daughter, "I am Stalin's favorite actress"—and Melissa responded, "Please don't tell anybody else about this!" The Bolshoi ballerina Maya Plisetskaya saw it so often that she knew the subtitles by heart. She met Korjus in Los Angeles in 1966 and wrote, "She never did fully believe me when I told her that she had been an inaccessible goddess for an entire nation, a beautiful extraterrestrial, a ray of happiness in the hardest years of the slave state." Korjus's son, Richard Foelsch, says émigrés told his mother a story that originated in Stalin's screening room at the Kremlin (the scene of Andrei Konchalovsky's 1991 film, *The Inner Circle*): whenever the dictator saw her singing "One Day When We Were Young" at the finale, "he would rise from his seat, place his head against the wall, and weep like a baby."

21

Putting Oz into *The Wizard of Oz*

The spate of work Fleming did in the late 1930s drained his resilience and on occasion nearly cost him his sanity. But it also sparked his talents and elevated his stature as both an artist and a Hollywood professional. Sometimes directors, like actors, take on aspects of their greatest creations. Francis Ford Coppola was never more of a film-industry godfather than he was after *The Godfather.* Fleming would never be more of a wizard than he was after *The Wizard of Oz.*

Oz would have been a complex, iffy production under any circumstances—and Fleming shouldered it with little preparation, after one director was fired and another came on simply to readjust the costumes and makeup. Yet Fleming, drawing on his experience in all genres, including comic fantasy, displayed a clear vision and command of the project from the outset. As he told Metro-Goldwyn-Mayer's intra-corporate newspaper, the *MGM Studio News:*

> You may wonder how we make an audience believe there is such a thing as a tin man, a straw man and a cowardly lion which talks. A little psychology was all that was necessary.
>
> First we established the characters. Dorothy, played by Judy Garland, is a Kansas farm girl who wanted to find some place where no one gets into trouble. She runs away from home, meets a medicine man, Frank Morgan, who seems all-wise. Then she is caught in a cyclone. In a subconscious world, she goes to that dream world, Oz . . .
>
> On her farm are three hired men. Ray Bolger is always pretending he has brains, Jack Haley meddles with inventions and talks about having a heart, and Bert Lahr is even afraid of baby pigs, but chatters about courage. So, in Oz, Bolger is trans-

formed into a Scarecrow looking for brains, Haley into a Tin Woodman who wants a heart, and Lahr into a Cowardly Lion who hopes to find courage.

Back home, a neighbor woman was trying to have Judy's dog, Toto, killed for biting her. She is as wicked as a witch, Judy thinks. In Oz, she is a witch. Then that great faker, Morgan, becomes the all-wise Wizard. You take that basis of reality, make things "dream fantastic," add music throughout and adults accept the story and love it as much as children.

Louise Brooks, the cinematic sex symbol of the late 1920s who renewed her fame decades later as a Hollywood memoirist, asked Kevin Brownlow in 1969, "Isn't Victor Fleming an inspired director of the beauty of childhood?"

In *The Wizard of Oz,* he not only captured the beauty of childhood but also defined it for the millions who have experienced it in theaters and in the highly publicized TV showings that began in 1956. It evokes the sometimes-terrifying exhilaration of discovering the world beyond the doorstep—and the anxiety-tinged urge to hang on to "home" before time and circumstance alter it.

The usual stories of Fleming's reluctance to direct the picture because it would be too big a stretch do not survive cursory scrutiny. He brought off *Treasure Island* and *Captains Courageous* with fierceness and delicacy, and both were highly successful at the box office. Paramount had wanted him to direct the studio's first talkie and first musical, *Burlesque*, and he did direct one backstage musical, *Reckless*, and a portion of *The Great Waltz.* And, of course, he had peppered *When the Clouds Roll By* with *Oz*-like whimsy.

What made Fleming resist *Oz* was what would make him hesitate to leave the picture for Selznick's *Gone With the Wind* three months later: he would have to assume command of a formidably complicated and expensive production that had already started shooting. Based on L. Frank Baum's novel first published in 1900, *The Wizard of Oz* was a live-action phantasmagoria that could easily flounder in the execution, like Paramount's all-star 1933 rendition of Lewis Carroll's *Alice in Wonderland*—prominent in Fleming's mind since Bud Lighton produced that botch.

Fleming had squeezed in an Oregon fishing trip with John Lee Mahin following *The Great Waltz* before starting preproduction on

The Yearling. Based on Marjorie Kinnan Rawlings's beloved Pulitzer Prize–winning novel, it boasted equally difficult, if more down-to-earth, requirements for a planned location shoot in the Florida back-country. Spencer Tracy was cast as the father, Penny Baxter, and Gene Reynolds as the son Jody, a character both dreamy and substantial. That's when Fleming got the call for *Oz.*

Although his daughter Victoria says she was told her father viewed *Oz* as just another job, it was one with ineluctable attractions. And Fleming had a compelling private motivation to take on this potential mind fogger. He had always been a dedicated family man, giving advice and financial aid to a real-life Dorothy Gale—his niece Yvonne. Now he was a father of two.

Fatherhood is what Mahin thought attracted Fleming to the picture. "Here Vic . . . suddenly had two little girls. And all his joy was in them. I think he did it for them, for Missy and Sally. I was with him on the set and I could see his whole love for them poured into the picture." Fleming told both Mahin and the producer Mervyn LeRoy (as LeRoy remembered it) that he wanted his daughters to see "a picture that searched for beauty and decency and sweetness and love in the world." Making *Captains Courageous* and *Treasure Island* had been good training. In both, "beauty and decency" rise from the rude awakenings of childhood and adolescence. In *Oz,* Fleming finds "sweetness and love," jagged truth and unpredictable joy, "where the wild things are." He doesn't stint on Baum's loony inventions, and he hits on what makes them transcendent.

At the end of his *Oz* time, Fleming pasted credit sheets from the picture and photos of seven cast members inside two 1903 editions of the book and had the actors inscribe them to the girls. In Sally's, one message reads:

Dear Little Baby Sister,

I hope this book will make you as happy as making the picture has made me.

Love and kisses from Judy Garland
"Dorothy"

The impulse for MGM to make *The Wizard of Oz* predated Walt Disney's entrance into Technicolor animated features with *Snow White and the Seven Dwarfs* (1937). But *Snow White*'s success revived operetta traditions (such as background choruses) that had been going out of style and gave instant Hollywood heat to musical fantasies. Disney's mixture of innovative animation with an integrated score and story, and even specific numbers such as "Some Day My Prince Will Come," exerted a tremendous influence. But in *The Wizard of Oz*, the lyricist E. Y. "Yip" Harburg and the composer Harold Arlen revive operetta *and* slap it silly.

Louis B. Mayer was eager to launch this pleasurable assault on family audiences in the wake of Disney's smash. But Nicholas Schenck applied pressure on Mayer to provide star power for a lavish enterprise that ended up costing $2.777 million. So Mayer at least made a show of trying to borrow Shirley Temple from Fox for Dorothy, probably aware that Fox would refuse. When Fox did the expected, there was no new move to acquire Temple even after the production was delayed and Fleming replaced the first director.

Mervyn LeRoy, Hollywood's "boy wonder" before Orson Welles claimed that title, was a versatile director of hits ranging from the gritty *Little Caesar* and *I Am a Fugitive from a Chain Gang* to the opulent *Anthony Adverse*. He pushed for *Oz* to be his first super-production after Mayer wooed him from Warner Bros. in 1937 (he started at MGM in early 1938). He had long been a fan of the Oz books, starting with the first one, originally published as *The Wonderful Wizard of Oz*. "I'd wanted to make the picture since I was a kid," he told a journalist in 1973.

The announcement that he wasn't directing it confirmed to industry journalists that Mayer wanted LeRoy to help fill the gaps left by Thalberg's death the year before, and by the departure of Selznick from MGM to form his own company in 1935. LeRoy first named Norman Taurog to direct because of the understanding of a child's mentality he displayed in *Skippy* (for which he won an Oscar) and *Boys Town* (which earned him a nomination). MGM even briefly attached Taurog to *The Yearling* when Fleming went on to *Oz*.

The studio, though, reassigned Taurog to *Adventures of Huckleberry Finn*. And LeRoy hired Richard Thorpe—a decision that dumbfounded Arthur Freed, the songwriter making his first foray into producing as an uncredited associate producer on *Oz*. (Freed had been pushing Mayer to make *Oz* as a musical for Garland even before LeRoy came to the studio.) Thorpe had done yeoman work on *Tarzan Escapes* (1936), as he would years later on *Ivanhoe* (1952), but those are vastly different fantasies. Thorpe's footage was flat. "Not his fault," LeRoy said. "He just didn't have the feeling of *The Wizard of Oz.*" So LeRoy canned him, scrapped all his scenes, and went after George Cukor. (Thorpe was the one who ended up making *Huckleberry Finn.*)

On October 26, MGM announced that Thorpe was fighting the flu and that Cukor, "whose work is often rich in imaginative qualities," would probably become the director. "But he wasn't happy in what he was doing," said LeRoy, and Cukor had been committed for years to *Gone With the Wind*, which was finally revving up on the Selznick lot. He stayed on *Oz* briefly and adjusted the look of several characters, including Margaret Hamilton's Witch, Bolger's Scarecrow, and, most drastically, Garland's Dorothy, making everything from her skin tone to her hair color less glamourized and more natural.

Thorpe and the MGM makeup guru Jack Dawn had supplied Garland with a blond wig. Cukor turned to the hair specialist Sydney Guilaroff. "Parting her hair in the middle," wrote Guilaroff, "I pulled it back from her face and shaped it into soft curls hanging down her back. It was a pretty but youthful style." But if Guilaroff and Cukor made Garland look like Dorothy, Fleming made her *act* like Dorothy.

Freed said he eventually focused on Fleming because "that man was a poet. Probably one of the great unsung men of this business . . . I knew he was the right man, from having coffee in the morning and feeling out his mind and the kind of things that he liked." LeRoy agreed and would later say he was "instrumental" in hiring Fleming. "I wish I was as good as he was," LeRoy told George Stevens Jr. "He was a kid at heart."

Some accounts have LeRoy and Mayer calling on Fleming at the director's Balboa beach house. Others have LeRoy taking Fleming to Mayer's home in Santa Monica—which, given Fleming's intransigence, would have been like the Mahatma going to the mountain. On November 1, the news went forth that Fleming was hired. "We got along like a couple of kids," LeRoy told the critic and filmmaker John Gallagher.

It was hardly Fleming's biggest payday; he had been paid $63,333.34 for *Treasure Island* and (in his last year at Paramount) $72,000 for *The Virginian.* For his compressed, intense three-and-a-half-month stint on *Oz*, the studio paid Fleming what had become his usual rate—$3,000 a week—and the director followed his normal process. Fleming's first move was to sign up Mahin for rewrites. They immediately struck a pricklier and more dramatic tone for the movie. Under Thorpe, *Oz* was to open with a limp, coquettish mid-American pastoral featuring a smiling Dorothy gamboling on a pony and chattering to a scarecrow, as if she were blasé over villainous Miss Gulch's threat to Toto. Mahin replaced it with Dorothy scrambling home to tell Uncle Henry (Charley Grapewin) and Auntie Em (Clara Blandick) that because Toto went after Miss Gulch's cat, Miss Gulch "hit Toto right over the back with a rake"—and Toto bit her. (This tale foreshadows Toto's ill-timed capering in the climax: he leaps from the Wizard's balloon and chases an Emerald City feline, causing Dorothy to scramble out after *him* and miss the flight back to Kansas.)

Mahin and Fleming provided Uncle Henry and Auntie Em with a reason for ignoring Dorothy—they're busy trying to fix a faltering five-hundred-chick incubator—and also added a farmhand named Zeke for Bert Lahr to play. With two other hands already in place, Ray Bolger's Hunk and Jack Haley's Hickory, each of Dorothy's Oz friends now had a counterpart in Kansas.

Thorpe, according to LeRoy, had developed such an affection for Toto (the cairn terrier's real name was Terry) that he threw the whole movie to the animal. Fleming decided to treat the dog more casually and shrewdly. Toto is a catalyst of disaster, and his scruffy flashes of spontaneity ground the action. He never stops being a dog, not a fake sidekick. When he enters into the choreography, whether in "Follow the Yellow Brick Road" or in the Tin Man's first woozy steps after derusting, the effect is euphoric and funny.

Fleming also demanded changes of focus and design in both Oz and Kansas. (King Vidor shot the Kansas scenes after Fleming and Mahin reconceived them.) Thorpe's Yellow Brick Road was made of ovals. Fleming remade them to resemble proper rectangular (albeit brightly hued) paving bricks, and also had the Yellow Brick Road curbed, turning it into something more like a Yellow Brick Street, such as those in the Los Angeles of his youth. (Before the automobile age, cities generally used paving bricks—often yellowish beige—instead of concrete and asphalt surfacing.) The curbing may have been a way of keeping the yellow color from bleeding into the rest of the scenery, or, in Fleming's realistic logic, paving bricks meant a street, and a street had to have a curb.

Without Fleming there would have been no Yellow Brick Road song, either. Three weeks before the scheduled wrap of the Munchkin scenes on December 30, Fleming decided there should be more musical punch to Dorothy's farewell to Munchkinland. He commanded Harburg and Arlen to send Dorothy off to the Emerald City with a bang—and with their usual panache, they delivered "Follow the Yellow Brick Road." (Freed may have suggested they make the song "a directive," but it was Fleming who saw the need for it and gave the order.) Aljean Harmetz, author of the groundbreaking and essential *The Making of "The Wizard of Oz"* (1977), writes, "The primer provided by Harburg's lyrics must have been something of a relief to Victor Fleming . . . a man with a rough-hewn masculine effect and little musical delicacy." Evidently, these lyrics were "a relief" because Fleming, who had the musical delicacy to request them, saw how effective they could be in the hands of an alert director.

Fleming knew something about how a struggling farm should feel; he told an assistant director to toss away Auntie Em's costume-department apron and buy a cheaper one at Woolworth. And throughout the film, he revamped decor so he could position the actors more dramatically, both simplifying it and spooking it up. He made the Wicked Witch's giant crystal central to her throne room, then turned her throne around so that a stone buzzard adorning it dominated the scene.

Harburg and the South African–born screenwriter Noel Langley, who received final script credit along with Florence Ryerson and Edgar Allan Woolf (once a vaudeville sketch writer for Morgan), locked in many concepts before Fleming took charge. But the director let in the requisite fresh air. Just as he used sound unself-consciously and freely in *The Virginian*, he made the gigantic Technicolor camera pirouette in *The Wizard of Oz*—his first color film—though then it was a novelty on the scale of the Emerald City's buffing machine.

The film overflows with visual and staging coups. Several Munchkins hide in gardens and flower beds, then seem to sprout from them. The five Sleepy Heads awaken from broken-eggshell beds in what looks like a bird's nest with an ominous saltshaker next to them. In the wake of the Wicked Witch, Munchkinland officials and citizens seek shelter from her fire and brimstone in a whirl, as if, like Dorothy, they were caught in a cyclone. And the Emerald City offers a tough kid's view of divine decadence—its citizens are like pampered, overgrown children devoted to novelty and pleasure. The one big "Merry Old Land of Oz" number is ripe and jolly enough to do the metropolis justice. (Even in the surviving stills, a deleted march of triumph through the city after Dorothy melts the Wicked Witch of the West looks uninspired and cluttered.)

The decision to contrast the pewter and white Sepiatone in the Kansas scenes with the Technicolor in Oz came before any script. LeRoy took credit for the idea. (A sweet, silly *Wizard of Oz* cartoon had the same idea in 1933, but the short went unreleased because of legal problems with Technicolor.) Still, the psychological slant Fleming espoused to the *MGM Studio News* sounds like him and not a publicist, and turns the transition from sepia to color into a gimmick of genius. In the 1946 *A Matter of Life and Death*, which strongly resembles Fleming's 1943 *A Guy Named Joe*, the director Michael Powell depicts earth in Technicolor and heaven in black and white. (In 1942, Powell paid MGM $200 for use of an *Oz* song line, "Because of the wonderful things he does," in *The Life and Death of Colonel Blimp*, released the next year; in his memoirs, he praises Fleming as first among directors who made Mayer and Selznick look good.)

An awkward 1925 *Wizard of Oz* film also had farmhands doubling as a teenage Dorothy's friends, but the cyclone simply whisked these fellow Kansans away to Oz with her—and once there they donned disguises as the Tin Man, Scarecrow, and Cowardly Lion to hide from Oz's evil ruler. (Oliver Hardy, as the Tin Man, was wasted.) That version had a dream framework, too, but the whole movie was a mess, aimed mostly at showcasing the slapstick talents of the star-director-writer, Larry Semon, as the Scarecrow.

The screenwriter Langley said *his* jumping-off point was a nightmare in the magical 1917 Mary Pickford comedy-drama *The Poor Little Rich Girl*, directed by Maurice Tourneur. In that film, the heroine's drug-induced bad dream puts various family service providers in fantasy guises that reveal their true natures. And there are other parallels to *Oz*, such as the way the child takes cliché metaphors literally, so that a two-faced woman actually bears two faces in Pickford's dream, just as the Emerald City's Horse of a Different Color changes into six different colors.

The Wizard of Oz has only one child in it, and she's played by an adolescent. The sixteen-year-old Garland is bound and corseted to appear all of twelve—well, maybe fourteen. Yet Garland, like Pickford in the earlier film, is wonderful at creating a poetic intensification of childhood. On its own rousing musical-comedy terms, *Oz* connects directly to a child's underlying fears and desires, and to an adult's childlike ones. In 101 minutes, it packs as much unruly humor and adventure, and indefinable sensuality, as a full year (or several) of childhood. It reassures kids about their own burgeoning feelings and reminds adults of youth's odd blends of melancholy and elation.

Fleming removed any taint of kiddie-matinee pandering. This is the opposite of fantasies that try to hook preteen audiences with heroes and heroines just like them. It's a plus that Garland's pressed-down bosom doesn't adequately disguise her age. Her teen fervor helps make Dorothy seem as ripe for risky exploits as J. M. Barrie's Wendy in *Peter Pan.* And for today's young viewers, it gives her unexplained orphan status poignancy akin to Harry Potter's. Dorothy's unhappiness on her guardians' farm conveys desperation akin to Harry's, too. Oz is Dorothy's Hogwarts School, even though her aunt and uncle, unlike Harry's, love her. In Baum's original book, Dorothy carries a mark on her forehead—the circle of a good witch's kiss. Harry carries a lightning-bolt-shaped scar on his forehead from his duel with Voldemort.

Baum purists object to the Kansas bookend material in the film, saying that it undercuts the imaginative integrity of Oz as a real if bizarre realm and dilutes Baum's resolve to move fairy tales beyond the gloomy, spook-laden moral fables of Europe into pure entertainment and invention. That analysis denies the actual experience of the movie: the audience registers Dorothy's exploits with an immediacy and depth that don't fade when Fleming reveals the dream nature of Oz. And the whole movie testifies to Hollywood ingenuity and high spirits at their peak.

Harburg, likewise, protested the film's emphasis on Kansas as Dorothy's true heartland—and *his* objection makes some sense. "Over the Rainbow" yearns for the antithesis of a bleak Midwestern landscape. Harburg and Arlen were intent, with their score, on parodying or at least toying with European music-theater notions of rural innocence and corrupted court sophistication.

But the Dorothy of Baum's book does say, "No matter how dreary and gray our homes are, we people of flesh and blood would rather live [in Kansas] than any other country, be it ever so beautiful. There is no place like home." The movie's power depends on an enveloping nostalgia whose source can't be pinned down. After Dorothy proclaims the Scarecrow and Tin Man "the best friends anyone ever had," she says, "I feel as if I've known you all the time—but I couldn't have, could I?"

The shiver she summons in even the most jaded viewer has something to do with the way her dream oscillates between fantasy and reality. It also comes from the movie's eerie, comical grasp about how we create our own destinies wherever we go, often replicating what we think we've left behind. For us, and for Dorothy, Oz becomes the second home that makes us appreciate our first home all the more. Margaret Hamilton said that "home" as expressed in the film is "the place where we belong, where we are welcome, where there is love and understanding and acceptance waiting for us when we come. Home, where we can shed our cares and share our troubles and feel safe and protected." The mesh of prayer and desire in "Over the Rainbow" expresses simultaneously Dorothy's urge to escape and her need to get back to where she once belonged.

That song, along with the others, demanded a vocalist with chops. Although Temple had a perky way with a tune and Jane Withers could pack a musical-comedy wallop, neither could compete with Garland as a singer. Indeed, Freed's musical mainstay, Roger Edens, declared Temple's vocal limitations "insurmountable." From the outset, Freed, a vaudeville-bred lyricist, thought of Garland. So did LeRoy. Freed wrote that Garland would be perfect for "an Orphan in Kansas who sings jazz"—a description that also makes clear how much irreverence and invention he expected from the score.

Freed contemplated hiring Jerome Kern and the lyricists Ira Gershwin and Dorothy Fields, but Kern was too weak from a recent heart attack. MGM also considered the teams of Mack Gordon and Harry Revel and then Al Dubin and Nacio Herb Brown; Freed made a critical hire when he signed Arlen and Harburg instead. Based partly on a musical structure set out by Edens, they aimed to salute three things: the potency of illusions, the liberation that comes with the power to see through them, and the force that positive illusions can retain even after a sound debunking. Their score lays down a satisfying through line. It's riotous and upsetting when Toto pulls back a curtain and reveals the awe-inspiring Wizard to be a fraud. But when the Wizard, in a variation on Baum's climax, gives the Scarecrow a diploma and a doctorate in Thinkology, the Tin Man a heart-shaped watch and a testimonial, and the Cowardly Lion "the Triple Cross Medal" and membership in the Legion of Courage, they embrace those symbols and feel transformed. Yes, the Wizard is a humbug, but in the end his rhetoric and prizes are authentic. He knows how to make Dorothy's pals recognize their own virtues. Although Dorothy contains all their qualities, and the Wizard's wisdom, too, she doesn't require certification; all she needs is a pair of ruby slippers. She lucks into them when she inadvertently kills the Wicked Witch of the East; she earns them when she saves the Scarecrow from the Wicked Witch of the West.

The score makes the characters farcically or ruefully self-conscious about feeling that they're acting out roles. Dorothy's first number in the Land of Oz is giddy and self-satirizing. Carried on waves of adoration, she helps the Munchkins inflate her accidental killing of the Wicked Witch of the East. Similarly, in the middle segment of the "If I Only Had a Brain/Heart/Nerve" song cycle, the Tin Man, pining for a genuine ticker, muses, in the bridge, "Picture me . . . a balcony . . . above a voice sings low," and a female voice sings out, "Wherefore are thou, Romeo?" The use of Adriana Caselotti as the voice of "Juliet" embellished the joke for contemporary audiences. She had previously been the lead voice of *Snow White and the Seven Dwarfs*.

Fleming and his creative accomplices stumbled onto the realization that youngsters experience life with greater-than-adult intensity. Harold Meyerson and Ernie Harburg (the lyricist's son), in their biography of Harburg, *Who Put the Rainbow in "The Wizard of Oz"?* (1993), note that Arlen conceived "Over the Rainbow" as a blend of mature and childish feeling: "It is a song for Nelson Eddy as well as for little Dorothy. The octave leap with which Arlen begins the front phrase, and the other graceful leaps of the first sixteen bars situate this song of yearning in emotional overdrive from the start. The challenge facing Harold and Yip was to balance the power of that emotion against the poignancy and delicacy of its childish context." Thirty years later, his close friend Irving Berlin, working on a Friars Club tribute to Barbra Streisand, sent parody lyrics of "Over the Rainbow" to Arlen, who may have written some of his own—Berlin included a note, "This is better—at least my lawyer thinks so." Berlin's version, never performed, contains the line "If Miss B will sing my song—who needs people?" By then, this song may have been too resonant and revered to parody in public.

Balancing the score's potent longings with Dorothy's youthful quest for identity was a challenge facing Fleming and Mahin, too. But they attack (and conquer) it head-on. The first question Dorothy hears in Oz is, "Are you a good witch or a bad witch?" She replies, "Why, I'm not a witch at all. I'm Dorothy Gale of Kansas." She finds herself as she seeks her way home. The movie is about multiple quests—the Tin Man to see himself as a feeling creature, the Scarecrow as a thinking one, the Cowardly Lion as the brave King of the Forest. Even the Wizard hopes to see himself as "a very good man" if "a very bad wizard."

The consequences of the diverse comedy and drama is a film of unusually elastic allure, earning the allegiance of artists as different as John Waters and Salman Rushdie. This long-lived milestone of family entertainment has an enormous gay following—and not just because the Wicked Witch calls Dorothy "my little pretty" or because the Cowardly Lion embodies an archetypal "sissy," a tender fellow in a half-fey, half-butch package. (Frank S. Nugent of *The New York Times* knowingly and admiringly referred to his "artistically curled mane.")

Dorothy's wondering statement, "Toto, I've a feeling we're not in Kansas anymore," has become one motto of San Francisco's Castro district. That's because Oz is a place where all the characters become what they want to be, including Dorothy. The paradox is that she wants to be a loving, appreciative niece to Auntie Em. *The Wizard of Oz* is the movies' most enduring transformation fantasy because it speaks at once to wanderlust and to the nesting instinct, to a yen for license and make-believe and to a hankering for roots. It's become the center of sing-along screenings for families as well as camp cultists and a homing signal for American service members abroad.

"I viewed the replacement of Richard Thorpe by Victor Fleming with great trepidation," noted Wallace Worsley, a script supervisor who aptly book-ended his career with Fleming on *Oz* by acting as Steven Spielberg's production manager on *E.T.* "Fleming had a reputation for being irascible, quick-tempered, and, some said, sadistic. By the time he took over the picture he must have mellowed considerably, for I saw very little of those characteristics."

From his first day, November 4, to his last the following February 17, Fleming maintained good-humored control. If he "saw a workman sawing or nailing a board in a way he thought was inept, he would go to the man, take the tool, and do it himself. None resented this, and all found it amusing," Worsley wrote. After working with Thorpe, he felt Fleming's attitude "was the difference between night and day." The makeup man William Tuttle ("So many people were involved, I couldn't take credit for the creative part") found the director "very gentlemanly. He didn't put up with foolishness; he was not the most patient person. If you knew what you were doing, he respected you . . . but he would never say, 'That's good enough.' "

Worsley thought the crew "seemed to be in our own world on this picture, far removed from the real one. Five soundstages were reserved to us at all times, with sets being built, shot or struck. The crew was large and our hours comparatively short." Starting at 8:00 a.m., they "were nearly always through between 5:00 and 6:00 p.m." He remembered the production as a hotbed for gambling on horses, with Bolger a prime player. There was plenty of time for it. Filming often halted so Garland could be tutored for a total of three hours out of an eight-hour workday, as required by state law. (MGM kept her busy after hours with offstage preparation and rehearsals.) In addition, because of the intense carbon-arc lamps required to light three-strip Technicolor, Fleming had to stop shooting every hour or two for an hour, to open up the soundstage and ventilate the set—air-conditioning wasn't sufficient.

Frank Leonetti, a lighting technician in Munchkinland, still marvels at the crew's ingenuity at swinging around the already-cumbersome camera in its unwieldy sound shielding, called a blimp. "It used to take six to eight men to put the cameras into the sound blimps and then put them on a dolly or a crane," he says. Leonetti was part of a small army of lamp operators. "The lamps were a lot larger than the ones you have today," he said in 2004, "and not as efficient. For a carbon-arc lamp, you had to put the two [carbon elements] together, trim and feed them, and they had to be changed every half hour. Today we use high-intensity arcs that don't require igniting. One man can produce the light that ten men did in 1939; back then, you needed one man for every two arcs, and I couldn't tell you how many we had." Hal Rosson, once again Fleming's cinematographer, said the production used enough arcs "to light 550 five-room homes."

When Fleming replaced Thorpe, Haley replaced Buddy Ebsen as the Tin Man after an early version of the makeup put Ebsen in the hospital with an allergic reaction. (Makeup artists had sprayed Ebsen with aluminum dust that got into his lungs; for Haley, they substituted aluminum paste. Haley was still laid up with an infection for a week, because the paste got into his eyes.)

In the rush to get a new Tin Man on the set, someone forgot that the character had rusted solid during a rainstorm and been immobilized in the forest for a year. "I worked in a shiny suit of tin with a sparkling tin nose, a bright tin strap around my chin, a glistening tin pot on my head and a coat of brilliant tin paint on my face. I glittered no end—for three days," Haley said. The mistake brought three days of reshoots—$20,000 a day was the well-publicized cost—so Haley would look as if he'd been corroding in the woods.

After settling the makeup and costume matters, Fleming "sort of threw" Haley (the actor wrote) by asking him, "Well, how do you see the part?" According to Haley, "I then told Vic how I had a storytelling voice I used whenever I opened the Oz volumes. It was a soft and sort of wonder-filled voice. Of course, this voice had developed over time, reading the books to my kids, trying to lull them to sleep. But I thought this same soothing quality should typify our dialogue delivery when we were characters in Oz and that we should deliver our lines in a very straight voice when we were real people back in Kansas." Fleming then called a meeting with Garland, Bolger, and Lahr. "We would all be storytellers in the Land of Oz, each with our own unique story to tell, and each to their own idea of the child listener." The singsong of Haley's delivery contrasts beautifully with Lahr's guttural buffoonery and Bolger's airiness. "I tried to get a sound in my voice," said Bolger, "that was complete wonderment, because I was new, so newly made."

All four actors came out of vaudeville, Garland in a singing act with her sisters. For the men, Lahr adopted a popular brand name of the time and turned it into the trio's battle cry: "Smith's Premium Ham!" In a TV interview with Jack Paar in the early 1960s, Garland said the three of them tried to elbow her off the Yellow Brick Road as they skipped along until Fleming, on the camera boom, called out, "Hold it! You three dirty hams let that little girl in there!" He simply could have tired of the "Smith's Premium Ham!" crack.

Lahr told his son John, for John's biography of his dad, *Notes on a Cowardly Lion* (1969), "Vic Fleming had never experienced guys like us. Some legitimate directors can't imagine anybody thinking about anything else, and when he yells 'Shoot' just going in and playing. We'd kid around up to the last minute and go on. You could see he got mad and red in the face." He also could get physical; Edward Hartman noticed Fleming once grabbing Lahr by the arm to make a point.

But Fleming had been working with "guys like us"—including Kathleen Clifford—and blending their acting with outlandish stunts and backdrops throughout his career. The director of Douglas Fairbanks understood outsized theatrical performance as well as any of his stars. Lahr was onto Fleming, though; he knew the director wanted to make sure the movie maintained "a certain mood." Fleming kept the film's emotions true and tangy while acknowledging to the audience that these were top vaudevillians acting out bizarre fantasy characters. With this authentic, flexible base, he could easily insert flashes of black comedy (they're not in the book)—such as the Winged Monkeys scattering the Scarecrow's straw and the Tin Man commenting, "Well, that's you all over."

Fleming's handling of Lahr and Bolger is exemplary, especially in relation to their young leading lady. Lahr uses a repertoire of growls along with a variety of rumbles that sound like nasal events preceding giant sneezes. His tearful expressions break through the makeup, and his gestures alternate crude braggadocio and daintiness; at times, he could be knitting sweaters with his paws. He riotously exposes a feminine neediness beneath low-comic bluster. And when it comes to Dorothy, this "sissy" lion also is a kidding sister. His showstopping "If I Were King of the Forest" is a game of dress-up, with Dorothy acting (per the script directions) "as flower girl and train bearer."

During filming, Bolger complained to Billie Burke, the movie's Good Witch "I'm a professional dancer. That's what I do. I'm a dancer. So of course I don't dance." But his long-legged lopes and stops and drops, and the perilous extended swings of his floppy arms, make for dances of uncanny spontaneity. He's panicky around fire (after all, he's made of straw), but his general affability balances Dorothy's urgency. Her final line to the Scarecrow—"I think I'll miss you most of all"—was the relic of a shorn subplot about her love for the farmhand Hunk. But it's the perfect capper for Fleming's melding of Dorothy's intensity and the Scarecrow's humming affection. Never had the director's keen eye and ear for male and male-and-female bonding born more unlikely or affecting results.

Fleming once had to call "Cut" because the Wizard's throne, surrounded by surging torches, caught on fire. Frank Morgan quipped, "Ah—the hot seat!" As Harlow's grandiloquent hustling father in *Bombshell*, Morgan had cooked up a perfect piece of ham bone, but when he tried out burlesque routines as the Wizard, Fleming clamped down. Years later, at his Virginia Beach home, Noel Langley would regale visitors with his recollection of Fleming shouting, "Is everyone ready?" and Morgan invariably yelling back, "No!"

Fleming wanted the actors to pierce the fourth wall without breaking it. It's something he had done as early as those silent Fairbanks comedies, with their humorous special effects and animation, their inside but open-to-the-public gags about Fairbanks as a personality, and their winking titles. Fleming's point of attack differs drastically from the scattershot topicality of animation like *Shrek 2*, with its "Farbucks" coffeehouse, or *Shark Tale*, with its transposition of Mob stereotypes onto undersea cartoons. He builds on the audience's authentic affection for broad comics like Lahr, dancing clowns like Bolger, and dapper entertainers like Haley, whose casting as the creaking Tin Man was one giant in-joke—and also the foundation for a touchingly frustrated character.

As Dorothy's friends attempt, with the aid of an intrepid Toto, to rescue her from the Wicked Witch's castle, the film reaches giddy heights of humorous self-reference even in dire conditions. There are few funnier sights in movies than the Tin Man holding on to the Lion's tail as they climb up a slippery mountain path, the Tin Man's tug bringing out the block-like outline of the tail's anchor in the lion costume.

That anchor was, according to Ambrose Schindler, "a thick hunk of shoe leather." And he should know. He was Haley's double in that scene, holding on to the tail of Lahr's stunt double. Schindler was a junior at the University of California and, when he wasn't quarterbacking the USC Trojans, earned the odd dollar doing stunts and background work at MGM. "I was the only guy at MGM who still knew how to drive a Model T," he recalls. "I had one all through high school, knew how to work the three pedals."

Just before he did the Tin Man stunt, Schindler had been a ballroom dancer in a Joan Crawford picture, *The Bride Wore Red.* "They came over and took me off that," and the following day Schindler found himself being fitted in a heavy costume made of tinny, metallic cloth, leather, and buckram, identical to the one Haley wore. Schindler practiced stepping on a trick two-by-two-foot boulder, scrambling for his life on the cliff when it gave way, and hanging on to the tail of the Cowardly Lion.

The Cowardly Lion splutters, "I—I—I hope my strength holds out."

The Tin Man replies, "I hope your tail holds out!"

But for Schindler, it didn't. "I was 185 pounds and I pulled the tail right off" and "fell like a hunk of lumber," Schindler says. "No way could I do this. So they had to take time out." He got a couple of extra paydays while the costume team made a lighter-weight outfit out of "some soft plastic material" and rejoined the Cowardly Lion's tail to the rest of Lahr's costume "with some kind of heavy leather belt. It was a real thick hunk of shoe leather down around the guy's waist and around the guy's tail." (Schindler says he recognized himself in the scene by his straight, long, prominent English nose; his football-team nickname was "banana nose.")

The characters are so full of fear, anguish, and self-mockery that the comedy and action—as well as the heartache—are intertwined. Someone is always breaking into tears or on the verge of them, and the effect on the audience is amusing, sad, and stirring. Haley said when he was working on *Oz:*

> I disparaged the work because I thought our roles were really just a quartet of people who were quaking all the time—a bunch of two-dimensional scaredy-cats. It wasn't until years later when I realized that children connected immediately with the fear in the *Oz* story, that overcoming this fear was the greatest bravery and heroism a child could imagine. It is what a child must live through each time he wakes in the night and sees a horrific shadow on the wall. Victor knew all this as he directed us.

("My dad had great regard for him," Jack Haley Jr. confirmed.)

The director kept the actors primed in the midst of their chagrin or befuddlement. John Lahr wrote that his father "was flattered when Fleming would take him aside and ask his opinion for improving a scene." Haley thought there was an ulterior motive to this questioning:

> Fleming had a wonderful understanding of people. He knew that the makeup was wearing on us. After a couple of hours, it was depressing to have it on. In order for us not to lose interest in the picture, to try and keep our animation, he would call all three of us together and say, "Fellahs, you've got to help me out on this scene." Well, I knew this guy was a big director, and he didn't need actors to help him. He'd say, "You guys are Broadway stars, what do you think we should do here?" . . . But I always thought he was just trying to keep our interest.

These sessions most famously bore fruit when Dorothy and her friends fall into a stupor in the poppy field only to be awakened by a snowfall. Lahr came up with the tension-breaking laugh line, "Unusual weather we're having." He told his son, "Fleming couldn't see it. I said, 'Vic, I'm sure it's a laugh.' He trusted me. In that situation, I was right. It was a big laugh." When our heroes are caught in the Wicked Witch's castle, the Lion exclaims, "Trapped, trapped like mice!" Then, as if realizing he's grown in stature since his cowardly days, he says, "Er, rats." It crackles like an improv.

As the Wicked Witch, Hamilton turned her voice into a cackle and her cackle into a nails-on-chalkboard screech. She let makeup artists expand her nose and chin, and gave her expressions a fierce jut that made her profile as menacing as the taloned clutch of her hands. She had already worked with Fleming in *The Farmer Takes a Wife*, and she praised him as "a very good director, one of the best in his day. He did a great job and was delightful and very easy to work for."

But she also noted that he could lose his temper when somebody was "wasting time, or making the studio lose time; or just being unprofessional . . . He could be very sarcastic. And his sarcasm could hit a little below the belt. He'd say something like, 'Tell me, is your memory as soft as it seems to be?' And this would be because you had stopped for a second or two to remember a line, or the sequence. And of course, at the time, I was much younger (thirty-six) and had no memory problems." Fleming once told Morgan, a heavy drinker who'd lose his bearings when he went too long without alcohol, "Get back on your champagne kick so we can live together." Yet Hamilton also said, "Fleming would sometimes tell you how good your performance was. And in my experience, many directors never tell you how you're doing, or whether or not they like what you're doing . . . But whenever I was unsure about my performance, Fleming would encourage and advise me."

Considering that his swift, demanding pace nearly immolated her, Hamilton was more than fair. The calamity occurred in December, after Fleming shot the Witch threatening Dorothy in Munchkinland with "I'll get you, my pretty—and your little dog, too!" In order to vanish in a scarlet puff of fire and smoke, Hamilton had to walk backward to an elevator platform without tripping on her billowing black skirt. Knowing a cut would wreck the illusion of her disappearance, Fleming wanted to capture the action in one shot. After several rehearsals, the first take was perfect. But he demanded another for insurance. The timing of the flames and smoke effects began to go awry. Fleming bellowed, "I want the shot done, and done right now!"

Hamilton backed away from Garland and landed on the platform—but the incendiary effects kicked up before she could get down:

> At first, I didn't realize I was on fire. But suddenly, my face felt very warm. Fortunately, when I was going down, I instinctively put my hands up to cover my face. When I got down I said, "Gee, they got it right that time!" The two men waiting for me thought I was getting hysterical. And they were very busy fussing over me. My skirt, my witch's hat and broom were on fire. So one of them quickly knocked the hat off my head. The other grabbed the broom out of my hand. I said, "What's the matter?" But they were too busy putting out the fire on my skirt to answer.

Her right hand, nose, and chin were burned, and her eyebrows singed; her green copper-based makeup seeped into her skin. She was out for six weeks, while Fleming shot around her. When she returned, she was wearing a glove on her right hand "because the nerves were still exposed." Fleming asked to see the hand, so she took off the glove and he "grabbed" it. "Well, the pain was so unbearable that I almost passed out. 'It looks fine,' he said. But I begged him to please leave my hand alone. Fleming apologized and said, 'Well, we have that scene and the shot was great!' "

Hamilton's stunt double, Betty Danko, wasn't so forgiving. During Hamilton's first day back, a second unit prepared to film the Witch's skywriting sequence over the Emerald City. Hamilton refused to do the whole sequence, reasoning that if the stunt were safe, as everyone was telling her, the studio would not have supplied her with a fireproof costume. She was willing to sit in a special steel saddle on a broomstick raised fifteen feet high on wires as a wind machine blew at her, but she wouldn't allow the filmmakers to connect the smoke-spewing pipe to the broom while she was on it. So after a few close-ups, Hamilton gave the seat to Danko.

The special-effects team had planned to pin down the Witch's cape so it covered both the saddle and the pipe, but when Fleming saw them and Danko making the shot, he decided, after two perfect takes, that the image would have more zing if the cape were flying freely. So the pipe was moved directly under the saddle, and the next time Danko pressed the button to release the smoke, the pipe exploded, blowing her off the seat.

No one could figure out why that happened. "But Fleming was the killer," Danko told Harmetz, blaming his ruthless pursuit of the clinching shot for the ordeal that left her grabbing the broomstick with both hands and one leg for dear life. The accident bruised her left leg from the knee up and broke the skin two inches deep almost all the way around the limb. The shot was never retaken Fleming's way. An embittered Danko recalled working a stunt for Greer Garson on Fleming's *Adventure* in 1945. "I felt a draft on my leg and I looked down and it was Fleming. He was trying to get a look under my skirt to see my scars."

With his lead performer, though, Fleming was sensitive and considerate—and Garland developed a deep, lifelong affection for both him and the picture. When Guilaroff was doing Garland's hair on *Oz*, he thought she already showed the nervousness and shrillness of amphetamine addiction and blamed MGM for assigning her an assistant makeup artist and dresser who doubled as a drug supplier. But everyone else on the set considered Judy a joy, maybe because Fleming calmed her down. He lovingly called her "Judalein" (which years later led Judy's sister Jimmie to name her daughter Judalein). At the end of filming, he gave her a motorbike, and she gave him a black cocker spaniel bitch for Victoria and Sally. The Flemings named the dog Judy.

"Judy was very, very fond of Victor Fleming," said Sid Luft, who in the early 1950s became both her husband and her business partner, producing her cult favorite *A Star Is Born* (1954).

> She only had the nicest things to say about him. He was a genius, as far as she was concerned. And she really enjoyed making that movie. It was the most fun she ever had working at MGM. The spirit of it all; she was sixteen, seventeen, with no problems, and she was a very, very sharp teenager who knew who she was and had a lot of experience by that time. She was close to being a full-grown woman, but she could look and act like a child. And you have to trust her judgment about Fleming. Being in this business as long as I have, and knowing it like I do, I have to think he was probably the undiscovered genius of our business.

As always, Fleming maintained a rough-and-ready humor on the set. Garland told a reporter, "Once I lay down for a nap in my dressing room and someone—never mind who—had put smudge pots under my bed. They slipped in and lit them, then ran out and yelled, 'Fire!' When I stumbled out through the smoke, they threw water in my face." Although she also told a version of this stunt that was set during the making of *Girl Crazy* and blamed Mickey Rooney, it has all the fingerprints of one of Fleming's practical jokes.

When Garland couldn't stop breaking into giggles at the pseudo-menacing advances of Lahr's Cowardly Lion, Fleming escorted her off the Yellow Brick Road, said, "Now, darling, this is serious," slapped her on the cheek, then ordered, "Now go in there and work." It must have been one carefully calculated slap from a man with impressive upper-body strength who was also a master of the "corkscrew punch."

Sally Fleming hoots at the notion that anyone could find such a slap cruel. "That wasn't abuse! People in those days weren't afraid of slapping a child in public for misbehavior. But he could be a little crude sometimes. When I was little, either three or four, I threw a tantrum. I just got hysterical. You know, the way small children do? And I got under the dining room table, and I was screaming. I was a very high-strung child. And Daddy apparently didn't quite know what to do with me. So he kicked me. Not hard, just enough to get my attention. And it worked."

It did with Garland, too. After Fleming got the shot, he asked Mahin to bop him on the nose "because of what I did to her." Mahin was there when Garland overheard that and retorted, "I won't do that, but I'll kiss your nose."

Apart from that smack, he stuck to his approach of treating young actors like adults—and the results could be startling. Pickford's biographer Eileen Whitfield says one of her "favorite moments in all movies" is when the four friends enter the Wizard's throne room. The disembodied Wizard's head shouts, "Silence!"—"and Garland, scrambling away to the safety of her group, says 'Jiminy Crickets!' with the same shock and fear that adults would use saying 'Holy shit!' " Reporters and fan magazines made much of this emerging star's dates and occasional crushes. When Garland told Sheilah Graham of Fleming, "I love him like a father," Graham quipped, "I can see what she means. But from my standpoint, I'd omit the father angle."

Donna Stewart-Hardway, one of the child performers who blended in with the little people playing the Munchkins, called Garland's reaction "a case of puppy love . . . She'd get very close to him, look up at him, and, literally, bat her eyes. It's something that a kid would do." To Stewart-Hardway and the others, Fleming "just was brisk. And brusque. He was always moving people and changing things and changing marks."

In her autobiography, *With a Feather on My Nose* (1949), Billie Burke, a renowned beauty and the widow of the theatrical impresario Florenz Ziegfeld (who died in 1932), called Glinda, the Good Witch of the North, "my favorite role." In 1939, she told an interviewer, "Vic was like a schoolboy, so excited about the film's possibilities." The Munchkin Gus Wayne said he saw Fleming yelling at Burke for a flubbed line or bit of business, but that would have been a rare occurrence. And Wayne might have mistaken Fleming for a tall assistant director who gave Burke a dressing-down after she failed to show up on time one day. "You're—you're—browbeating me," Hamilton recalled Burke saying, and as the man's jaw dropped and he went silent, Hamilton noted to herself, "My goodness, what a wonderful actress she really is."

The movie that would become the ultimate holiday attraction demanded that Fleming set a relentless pace through November and December. The Christmas layoff was just two days, including Christmas Day, which fell on a Sunday that year. Before the end of 1938, Fleming filmed the four friends meeting on the Yellow Brick Road, Dorothy and the Scarecrow goading the irascible apple trees, the quartet falling asleep in the poppy field, the scenes in the Witch's castle, and all the Munchkinland scenes.

The special-effects master A. Arnold Gillespie devised a dolly running on tubing instead of wheels for shooting the poppy field, and the Emerald City provided the most elaborate interiors. But no sequence was more of a challenge—in logistics, creativity, and tone—than Munchkinland. It was "probably the most difficult set to photograph," said Rosson, "a two-acre set of tiny villages." The gauntlet he and Fleming faced consisted of "dozens of shades of primary colors. We found it best to try no novel colors but to get variety in shades." Using a constantly moving camera on a boom was one way to seduce the viewer's eye into an active appreciation of the spectacle, keeping the Munchkins from blending into one big "mass of nothing when they all mob together."

Katharine M. Rogers, a biographer of L. Frank Baum, blames the movie for making the term "Munchkins" refer to "ridiculous little people," explaining, "In Baum's book, all the inhabitants of Oz were the size of Dorothy, a child of about six; the effect was to give her a comfortably child-proportioned world. In the film, all the characters, including Dorothy, tower over the Munchkins." But if the film's Munchkins were "ridiculous," they would not be so beloved.

MGM enlisted the impresario Leo Singer to deliver little people who were identical, except for height, to average-sized men and women. Singer had only eighteen little people under personal contract at the time (among them Charles Becker, who became the Munchkin Mayor), and some others, like the veteran circus performer Major Doyle, cut their own deal with MGM. But Singer bartered with other managers and used agents across the country to come up with 116 little people; eight children were added to fill in backgrounds. Cloaked in outrageous mock-European garb, seen in a mock-gemütlich land of cottages and gardens filled with lacquered flowers, the Munchkins are like a precision operetta corps: Ruritanian village life writ small.

Edward Hartman visited that set during a rehearsal. "Uncle Vic was trying to organize them, and they weren't doing what he wanted them to do, so he stormed off and someone else ended up doing it. When he was directing the Munchkins or anyone else, he'd get right up in their face. He didn't scream at anybody." Several Munchkins depict Fleming as a godlike figure on the camera boom, delivering instructions from on high via assistant directors. That didn't bother Margaret Pellegrini, who still thinks of him fondly: "Oh, boy, a great fellow, and a handsome man on top of that—easygoing, and nice and as friendly as he can be."

Jerry Maren, the middle member of the trio of toughs who "represent da Lollipop Guild," recalls Fleming saying, "Tell those three to move their mouths to the right and to the left, so they look more like three tough guys." Nearly seventy years later, Maren muses, in a comical blasé manner, "He thought it was more realistic—whatever, what the hell." Then he quickly adds, "It was hard to believe he could be so quiet and cool. It was probably a relief for him to do simple stuff like fairy tales."

An entire apocrypha has sprung up about the randy, hell-raising offscreen behavior that the diminutive performers, many of them veterans of the gritty road life of circuses and carnivals, supposedly displayed as soon as they hit Culver City. Most of that can be traced to Garland's 1967 appearance on a TV special called *A Funny Thing Happened on the Way to Hollywood—with Jack Paar.* In an appearance on

Paar's regular prime-time program a few years earlier, Garland told the affectionate story of Fleming keeping "three dirty hams" from elbowing her off the Yellow Brick Road. But in 1967, two years before her death, the fawning Paar and a receptive studio audience egged on a brittle and visibly ailing Garland into entertaining snarkiness.

"No one can tell show business stories like Judy Garland," Paar cooed as he introduced her, and Garland immediately set out to prove him right. Even before she took on the little people, she told Paar that Deanna Durbin had "one thick eyebrow that just wouldn't quit. Like a caterpillar!"

Then Paar brought up "Moonchkins." After correcting his pronunciation, she said, "They were very tiny, you know." When Paar asked, "They were kids?" she retorted, "They were *drunks*!"—and the explosion of audience laughter set off ever more theatrical exaggerations. "What'd they do?" Paar asked three times, excitedly, and when Garland repeated the question, he clarified, "What did the dwarfs do?" In 1967, it was still titillating to hear Garland tell of a "two-inch" forty-year-old asking her out to dinner. "I couldn't say I don't want to go out with you, I can't, because you're a midget; I just said, 'You know, my mother wouldn't like it' "—and he, according to Garland, responded, "Bring her along, too."

When Paar asked, "What could you do with him?" and then, "What could *he* do?" she got another blast of laughter by saying, "They evidently did a *lot* . . . [there were] hundreds of thousands! And they'd put them all in one hotel—not in one room, one hotel in Culver City, and they got smashed every night, and they'd pick them up in butterfly nets!" Garland had complained that she received no residuals from her MGM films. Her closing quip was "The poor things—I imagine *they* get residuals!"

The surviving Munchkins insist that such memories are exaggerated or just false. One of them, Clarence Swensen, a soldier ("Fourth row back, camera side") says that Garland was "a sweet sixteen" who at the time seemed as happy to see them on her breaks as they were to see her. In 1974, though, LeRoy tapped the same vein of comic hyperbole as Garland in his as-told-to autobiography, *Take One:* "I guess it's like any group who go to a convention in a distant city; somehow their inhibitions are left behind. Or maybe the little people, as they prefer to be called, have little inhibitions to go with their little stature. Whatever the reason, they were wild. Every night there were fights and orgies and all kinds of carryings-on. Almost every night, the Culver City police had to rush over to the hotel to keep them from killing each other." (An unpublished memoir by the Culver City motorcycle cop Ed Meese partially supports that version. Meese wrote, "They all went into the local bars . . . They were the cockiest little people I have ever seen in my life, and I had more trouble with them than anyone in town.") But not all of the little people stayed at the Culver Hotel; perhaps the tiniest of the women, Olga Nardone, stayed at an apartment house, and so did Billy Curtis and some others.

Langley called the Munchkins "hell-raisers." One was fired after threatening his estranged wife with a knife and dragging her from a restaurant, caveman style, by the hair. Two others and their adult manager were dropped after a disputed knifing incident. Still, these were isolated events. And even if some of the little people were carousers, what's so wrong about acting out in a surreal situation? When Maren looked out his hotel window the morning after his arrival in November, he saw a parade and thought it might be for the Munchkins; he didn't realize at first that it was Armistice Day. The future Culver City cop Charlie Lugo, then a radio store owner, would see them climb up bar stools, get drunk quickly, and often fall off. "Some of them just had way too much fun," he'd tell his family.

Many Munchkin tales—perhaps all versions of a single event—revolve around restroom mishaps. MGM provided the women with attendants from the outset, but not the men. Megan Rosenfeld of the *Washington Post* uncovered the story behind "twins Mike and Ike Matina . . . problem drinkers who liked to seduce into overindulgence less hardened colleagues, one of whom had to be rescued from a toilet into which he had fallen." (Billy Curtis told Harmetz the man wasn't found for forty-five minutes: "They had to clean him off like he was a baby.") Langley would tell a story about "the King of the Munchkins" landing in a studio commode; if he meant the Mayor, that would have been Charles Becker. But the bit player Shep Houghton provides the resolution. Houghton, who found the Munchkins "arrogant," says "all hell broke loose" when one man splashed into a toilet, and the studio's response was to have two propmen rig up a child's potty seat to prevent further incidents. However practical and safety minded that may have been, the Munchkins who confronted the device reacted as if it were a put-down and smashed it to pieces. (That's when the men got their attendants, too.) But the Munchkin soldier Swensen says, "Aw, that's a lot of hooey! Yeah!"

Lahr told a story about all hands searching for the fellow who played the Witch's chief Winged Monkey (Pat Walshe) and finding him "plastered" and facedown in one of those long horse-trough urinals. For the monkeys, the casting office had put out a call for "small, thin men," and some of the Munchkin actors filled in as well. Danny Windsor was small, thin, and not yet fourteen at the time he appeared as the flying mate of the Winged Monkey who soars off (on wires) with Toto in his furry arms. As Windsor says, the other monkey did the work and got the full-figure shot: "All you see is my rear end flying away." But it gave him "the most famous ass in show business."

His grandmother, who hoped he'd become a juvenile lead, had brought him to central casting on a dance call; he wound up with four days in a monkey suit. During two rehearsal calls and a day and a half of actual shooting (including a half day of pickup shots), Windsor witnessed Fleming on the boom and LeRoy on the floor, but took his orders from assistants. After serving in World War II (including time on Guam and Iwo Jima), he forged a career in nightclubs, casinos, and early TV, winning acclaim from the *San Francisco Chronicle* columnist Herb Caen for his work in a waterfront club as part of a comedy team called Doodles and Spider. He mastered a killer Ethel Merman impersonation. In 1938, though, his grandmother thought his fellow monkeys were far too outré to be casual company for her budding child star. "I don't know if they were from the circus or what, but strange-looking guys played the winged monkeys—heavy, heavy drinkers and smokers," Windsor says. "My grandma wouldn't let me near them too much."

These tales of ribald little people and hard-guy monkeys may be a legacy of carnival-sideshow fantasy and humor. But they also reflect the real-life tragicomic slapstick that little people or unconventional performers confronted in pre-OSHA times. At any rate, whether they were falling into bed after work or into a latrine before the day started, on the set the Munchkins seized any chance they had for the spotlight.

Meinhardt Raabe, who played the Coroner of Munchkinland, still speaks in the formal tones and locutions he feels won him the role. "Victor Fleming had a reputation of being a rather hard-driving director, but with the Munchkins he was, shall we say, an extremely sensitive, compassionate individual. I never heard him say, 'Get over here! Do it like this, do it now!' He'd always say, 'Let's try it this way; let's try it that way.' He never raised his voice with the Munchkins at all. All Munchkins had a very high regard for him. He was very, shall I say, concerned for the little people."

The choreographer Bobby Connolly's assistants, Dona Massin and Arthur Appel, had more contact with the Munchkins in rehearsals than Fleming and his directing team, and even that was limited. Olga Nardone, at three feet four the tiniest Lullaby League dancer and the first Sleepy Head to emerge, had been part of her own vaudeville act in Boston as "Little Olga," with a six-foot partner who was the brother of her dancing teacher, Mildred Sacco, one of Bolger's many terpsichorean friends. She says there were so many Munchkins, "We didn't get any individual attention. You had to learn by yourself," and Sacco helped prepare her and the others as much as the choreography team. As for being a Sleepy Head, she shrugs and says, "We [Karl Kosiczky, Pellegrini] were the only ones who could fit in that little nest they built."

Joan Kenmore, another of the child performers, says even when she was seven (and the youngest actor in Munchkinland), she wondered why the choreographers picked a signature step that was particularly difficult for little people: "They had to kick their legs up to execute that step." But Ruth Duccini speaks for most of her peers when she says that being among dozens of other little performers made it "exciting and fun."

Raabe says that they knew it was Fleming's voice that rang out at shooting time and when "something didn't look right, he'd say, 'Cut!' We had so many big arc lamps that as soon as he'd say, 'Cut!' an electrician would say, 'Save your arcs.' We'd say, 'Save your arches,' and squat wherever we would be, so we wouldn't lose our positions." A graduate of the University of Wisconsin, Raabe had worked for the Oscar Mayer company both as an accountant in the Chicago office and as "Little Oscar," their tiny trademark, "the world's smallest chef." Says Raabe, "I had done a lot of public speaking, and was used to enunciating clearly. So when it came time to cast the Munchkin Coroner, I knew how to speak, shall we say, appropriately. I did it once, and the casting director said, 'Okay, you're the Coroner.' "

Karl Kosiczky (he took the last name of Slover in 1943), who played one of the three Munchkin trumpeters, declares Fleming "a sincere gentleman, well liked by the Munchkins" because he was direct and approachable. When the lead trumpeter, Kayo Erickson, missed three cues, "I, Karl, suggested to put me in first. Mr. Fleming said, 'Change.' " Kosiczky, at just over three feet tall, was a movie veteran whose credits already included *They Gave Him a Gun* and Hawks's

Bringing Up Baby. Not only did he play multiple roles (including a townswoman), but Fleming also asked him to sing "We're Off to See the Wizard" for set visitors. He remembers Raabe making too much of a song out of the Coroner's report. "Mr. Fleming said, 'Don't sing,' this is serious." The verdict was, of course, "As Coroner, I must aver, I thoroughly examined her, and she's not only merely dead, she's really most sincerely dead."

When Fleming was advising them on line readings, though, it was really to bolster their physical performances. Before he shot Munchkinland, the MGM sound chief, Douglas Shearer, and the musical arranger Ken Darby devised a system of recording the dialogue and songs at a slow speed, with performers seasoned in radio and/or cartoons, including members of the singing groups the King's Men Octet and the Debutantes. When played back at normal speed, the voices had the soprano electricity of the high-pitched Munchkin sound. The speaking voices of only two little people ended up on the final sound track.

Raabe is certain that Fleming signed off on individual casting choices for featured roles such as his Coroner. But it's unclear how much the director had to do with the intricacies of the recording or, for that matter, the specifics of the choreography. And more legendry abounds: The whimsical and hyperbolic Munchkin Mickey Carroll once boasted, "Vic Fleming would stand there and say, 'Mickey, the marching soldiers don't look right. Go in there and make it right.' So I'd go in and make it right." However, Swensen says that Fleming gave the soldiers their marching orders directly for "Ding Dong! The Witch Is Dead" and guided their steps throughout while maintaining an air of "kindness."

MGM's top-tier stars visited Munchkinland; in 1938, there was no more elaborate Yuletide fantasy park. Norma Shearer, Myrna Loy, Spencer Tracy, and Mickey Rooney toured the sights; Greta Garbo peeked in, too. Joan Crawford brought her niece, and Wallace Beery his daughter.

The kids' visits often ended in disillusioned pratfalls. Warner LeRoy skipped down the Yellow Brick Road only to crash into a painted backdrop after about twenty feet. "That is when I learned the difference between fantasy and reality," he used to say. Victoria Fleming took one look at the talking apple trees and grew so scared she had to be taken out. Edward Hartman declared Garland "the ugliest thing

I'd ever seen. Her head seemed to be too large for the rest of her body." These visitors might have stoked Fleming's good-humored yet unblinking view of childish perceptions and behavior.

His conquest of *Oz* was so complete that it may have helped take him off the film: when Selznick fired Cukor from *Gone With the Wind*, Fleming was now more than ever, in the eyes of the producer and his MGM partners and distributors, the number-one choice to replace him. And when he did go to Tara, he never left *Oz* completely. He hiked over to the fantasy's cutting rooms from the sets of the Civil War epic. With the editor Blanche Sewell, he kept looking for ways to both tighten the movie and temper the Wicked Witch's villainy without defusing it; for example, he took the skywriting message—"Surrender Dorothy or Die WWW"—down to "Surrender Dorothy." He chopped off a montage designed to accompany Dorothy's return to Kansas. (Luckily, even before filming, the image of "a Negro baby in a bathtub" was cut from the list of joke sightings in the twister.) After three to five sneak previews, Fleming and Sewell had winnowed the rough cut from 121 minutes to a release print of 101. (Almost all movies then were 90 minutes or under.)

Before Fleming left, he oversaw the special-effects squad's creation of a Kansas cyclone from a muslin stocking. Fleming didn't get to guide Garland through the farm version of "Over the Rainbow." Once Selznick and Mayer whisked him off to Tara, Twelve Oaks, and Atlanta, King Vidor came aboard to direct all the Kansas scenes. "Victor was a good friend, and he took me around to all the sets that had been built and went through the thing," Vidor told Richard Schickel. But he told Harmetz, "Instead of telling me what I wanted to know, he'd say, 'Oh, you know what to do.' I'm not even sure that he took me down to see the sets." Vidor didn't take credit for any of his *Oz* work while Fleming was alive, but after his death he even took credit for "We're Off to See the Wizard," which he didn't shoot.

Vidor often said he was particularly proud of the way he handled Garland singing in the barnyard. "Previous to this," he told Harmetz, "when people sang, they stood still. I used 'Over the Rainbow' to get some rhythmical flow into a ballad." He did film the number with supreme limpidity. He fixes his camera on Garland as she ambles around the yard, reclines on a hay bale, tugs at a wheel, and comes to rest on some farm equipment with Toto sitting just above and behind her and touchingly holding out his paw. Nonetheless, Vidor's depiction of his staging as a movie-musical breakthrough for the mobile camera is mistaken. Even in Fleming's train wreck *Reckless*, the title number starts with the camera following Jean Harlow down a bar. And through all the musical numbers set in Oz, Fleming and Rosson keep the camera roaming.

In this era of CDs and DVDs, *Oz* fans have become familiar with its deleted musical snippets, which include a Busby Berkeley–choreographed extension of the Scarecrow's "If I Only Had a Brain" number with Bolger bouncing off fence posts as if they were billiard bumpers. Also, Dorothy reprised "Over the Rainbow" as she cowered in the Witch's tower, and the Emerald City staged a triumphal procession to "Ding Dong! The Witch Is Dead." One jazz-infused song was excised in its entirety: "The Jitterbug," about "a goofy critter" who "injects a jitter" that "starts you dancing on a thousand toes." The first number Arlen and Harburg wrote for the film (demonstrating their grasp of Freed's jazz concept) was performed in part of the Haunted Forest populated with "Jitter Trees" that grabbed at Dorothy and her friends.

At a Santa Barbara preview, Harburg said the scene had audience members dancing in the aisles. But this was not a plus for MGM's conservative executives. According to both Harburg and Hamilton, they feared that number tied in too closely with the jitterbug dance craze and would date the film. (When told Metro anticipated a decade-long life for *Oz*, Hamilton snorted, "You're out of your mind.") All that survives of the number is Arlen's home-movie footage, which is too haphazard to provide much evidence of how it might have worked, since the jitterbug itself was animated. Fleming wanted the number kept; he was even providing the jitterbug's owlish hoots on the dialogue track the way Walt Disney (back then) was lending his voice to Mickey Mouse. But Freed thought it pointless and distracting, and he won.

On the other hand, Harburg put Fleming on the side of the devils during the controversy that arose from "Over the Rainbow" being cut at the preview stage. In Harburg's version, "Mr. Fleming walked into the office and he said, 'I'm sorry to say that that whole first part of that show is awful slow because of that number . . . We gotta take it out.' Now, when a man like that comes in, who doesn't talk but makes pronunciamentos, you've got to listen." LeRoy, according to Harburg, "became little Mervyn Levine again," and "Harold ran to shul." For the moment the song was out of the picture.

Even Harmetz, hardly the president of the Victor Fleming fan club, doubts that story. Whoever gave the order to kill the number, Harburg and Arlen agreed that Freed earned an even bigger piece of the *Oz* legend by demanding its restoration. At the time, Arlen liked to tell newspapers that the unexpected controversy taught him that when doing a stage show, "it's your show and everyone else's," but when working on a movie, "it's never your picture. You're just getting paid."

The movie's price tag meant that its impressive $3.017 million gross in its first release would register—because of opening costs—a three-quarter-of-a-million-dollar loss. *Oz* didn't do better for a couple of good reasons: many of the movie's admissions were at cut-rate children's prices, and the flood of quality films in that benchmark year of 1939 prevented holdover runs. MGM publicity concentrated its efforts on a preopening push far different from the sustained, years-long build Selznick had already been giving to *Gone With the Wind*. What MGM gave *Oz* was more like a contemporary media blitz, and it may not have suited a movie that was meant for the long haul.

But with broad popular acceptance (even political cartoons adopted the imagery) and mostly ecstatic reviews nationwide—Russell Maloney of the *New Yorker* was a notable exception, labeling it "a stinkaroo"—MGM executives must have known that the investment would eventually pay off. And when it aired on CBS, on November 3, 1956, it became a pop-culture phenomenon, attracting well over half of that night's TV viewing audience. The film's network showings became hugely popular annual events beginning on December 13, 1959, when the network began airing it in a 6:00–8:00 p.m. time slot, often with CBS stars and their children as hosts, such as Red Skelton and his daughter, Valentina, and Richard Boone and his son Peter. Garland was set to introduce the film with one of her daughters in 1956, while she was performing at the Palace, but it didn't happen. Either CBS didn't want to lug its lights and cameras backstage at the Palace or the fragile Garland thought twice about juggling an introduction and her act. Bert Lahr and Liza Minnelli did the honors, with the help of an *Oz* expert. Color sets were so rare that CBS didn't even broadcast *The Wizard of Oz* in color in 1961 and 1962. It proved Fleming's contention that if he did his job right, children would accept the reality of Oz until the movie's end; Oz carried just as much authentic emotional weight as Kansas, even with both in black and white.

The movie would garner its largest number of viewers—sixty-four million—on March 15, 1970, for its first broadcast after Garland's death in 1969. Under Mervyn LeRoy's direction, Gregory Peck introduced the film that year for NBC, calling it an "unquestioned classic" that "through theater engagements and telecasts may well have been enjoyed by more people than any other entertainment production in the history of the world."

For her one-word capsule in the *New Yorker*, many years after Maloney's sneer, Pauline Kael simply exhaled, "Heaven." The production *was* a stairway to paradise—for the audience, and for Garland, Lahr, Bolger, Haley, Hamilton, and Morgan. And Fleming ushered them all in. Key contributions came from Freed, the design and special-effects teams, a slew of screenwriters—notably Langley—and, crucially, Arlen and Harburg. But the movie's schedule was stop-and-go, its sets hazardous, and its collaborative history tortuous. Without Fleming's exuberance, instinct, and strict hand—and his gifts for upheaval and excitement—the movie would have collapsed into campy chaos.

When a director goes full tilt, his or her greatest contributions are often spiritual, intangible. So in some ways it's reasonable that Fleming, who worked in many different forms, would be slighted as a prime creator of a picture that ranks near the top not only of all movie musicals but of all movies. In other ways, it's befuddling. In an enterprise like *The Wizard of Oz*, where the components are outlandish and the creative risks great, why wouldn't the director get more, rather than less, credit for holding it all together?

Harmetz reserves high praise for Arlen and especially Harburg. The lyricist pushed Lahr for the role of the Cowardly Lion, edited the pre-Mahin scripts into a lucid entity, and contributed dialogue as well as lyrics, notably in the scene of the Wizard handing the Scarecrow, Tin Man, and Lion their rewards. Understandably, Harburg's biographers take Harmetz's argument to its logical conclusion: that the movie "owes its coherence and unity—not to mention its lyrics—to Yip." Yet Freed was the one who brought up the entwined songs and narrative and the emotional hook of *Snow White and the Seven Dwarfs* in an exhaustive and influential memo. And it's Fleming's genius at setting and maintaining a robust tone that made it possible for the satiric and comedic turns and one heart-stopping ballad to score with equal zing.

The influence game has been a complicated one to play with every aspect of the movie or Baum's book. One academic reading presents Baum's story as a testament to the lure of urban life and the machine age. Another interprets it as an intricate allegory of nineteenth-century populism, with the magic slippers (silver in the book, made ruby in the movie so they'd show up better in Technicolor) representing the Populist cause of silver coinage. The historian David Parker put it best when he said these conflicting interpretations stem from Baum's success at writing a "modernized, American" fantasy. Baum produced "not only the first real American fairy tale, but one that showed American society and culture in all its wonderful diversity and contradictions, a story so rich, it can be, like the book's title character, anything we want it to be—including, if we wish, a parable on Populism."

With a cultural stew as eclectic as *The Wizard of Oz*, the wisest path may be the one J. R. R. Tolkien took with fairy stories: "We must be satisfied with the soup that is set before us, and not desire to see the bones of the ox out of which it has been boiled." Tolkien, translating the view of the Icelandicist George Webbe Dasent, proscribed: "By 'the soup' I mean the story as it is served up by its author or teller, and by 'the bones' its sources or material—even when (by rare luck) those can be with certainty discovered. But I do not, of course, forbid criticism of the soup as soup."

As soup, *The Wizard of Oz* is not beyond criticism, but its flaws scarcely mar the flavor. You can see why MGM executives got antsy during the Kansas episodes. Vidor's pacing is erratic, especially in the scene with Professor Marvel, though Morgan is so wonderful you wouldn't want to part with any of it. (Morgan also is brilliantly bogus as the Wizard, though not so much as a gatekeeper, a guard, and a coachman in the Emerald City.) Munchkinland is arguably more eye-popping than the interior of the Emerald City, but who cares when you're gazing at the Horse of a Different Color?

Despite his prominence in the credits, and his tireless work on the film, the chef of this inimitable soup hardly figured in its national publicity. A May 1 letter from the MGM publicist Teet Carle to the writer Grover Jones, who had done the story adaptation for *The Virginian*, pushes Fleming as a possible subject for a national magazine piece. He "is certainly one of the early-day screen directors who has still retained the color that directors used to have a long time ago . . . It occurred to me that since you were one of those also in the birth of motion pictures that Fleming might be used by you as an example of a director who has grown up in the business as compared with the influx in recent years of stage directors." Of course, there was a caveat: "I don't know how interested a magazine would be in a yarn on a director."

Or maybe just this director: after all, Frank Capra had been on the cover of *Time* in 1938. But Capra was both an endless self-promoter and a creator of his own easily recognizable blend of whimsy, uplift, and melodrama. Fleming was, as Steven Spielberg says, "one of the great chameleons . . . We honor his movies and don't know him, because he did his job so well." And rarely had he done it at a higher pitch of inspiration than in *The Wizard of Oz.*

22

Saving Tara and *Gone With the Wind*

The bond between a reformed rake and a headstrong woman is the imperfect union at the core of *Gone With the Wind.* If *The Wizard of Oz* crystallized Fleming's feelings for the resilience of children, *Gone With the Wind* drew out his understanding of the traumas of matrimony. The Civil War and the destruction of antebellum Georgia provide the film with its breadth—at its widest reach the movie is about how people react when social upheaval rends a settled way of life. The wedding of the dashing, piratical Rhett Butler (Clark Gable) to the Southern belle Scarlett O'Hara (Vivien Leigh) gives it the snap and heartbreak of a romantic tragicomedy.

Lu Fleming was no Scarlett. She was an affable housewife, not a grasping minx who thought she was in love with someone else. Unlike some of her contemporaries, she didn't seek social advantage as the wife of a powerful director. As a traditional spouse, she was happy to be "Mrs. Victor Fleming." Yet the marriage contained enough wrenches and twists to give Vic and Lu advanced degrees in emotional mechanics. She may have been the pursuer in their love match; Fleming had never before been intimately involved with a married woman, much less the wife of a friend. When it turned sour, he would charge that she tricked him into wedlock by claiming she was pregnant. Fleming's grip on the heated sentiment and harshness that romance can funnel into domestic life gives *Gone With the Wind* a shrewdness verging on wisdom.

By the time he directed the picture, Fleming was no longer automatically linked to his leading ladies, not even knockouts like Mary Astor, Harlow, or Loy. He had been faithful to Lu; it would take Ingrid Bergman's allure and more than a dozen years of household strains to break his resolve. The marriage was built on teasing as well as tender emotion; their mutual goading was part of their relationship. Vic and

Lu knew what they were getting into when they tied the knot. They seemed to know what they wanted.

With his daughters, his playfulness was caring and serene. Sally once saw him retrieve a hummingbird's nest and try to hatch the eggs with the warmth of a lightbulb. He doted on Victoria as Rhett does on his daughter, Bonnie Blue, and, just as Rhett took Bonnie with him to London, Fleming took Victoria with him on fishing trips on their good ship *Missy Poo.* (Many years later, she became a crack skeet shooter like her father.) His discipline was often silent, swift, and surgical. Victoria recalls that when she was five and Sally three (just after *Gone With the Wind*), "We were going down to Balboa in the car. And I was in the front with Daddy, and Sally was in the back with Mother. But we got into some sort of fight, anyway. And Daddy didn't say anything. He just turned the car around and drove us back home."

Fleming wasn't keen on directing *Gone With the Wind*, but he hadn't been in the mood to make *The Wizard of Oz*, either. He missed flying, and he'd had no time for one of his usual long vacations. In an interview with Sheilah Graham a week before he left *Oz* for Tara, and *before* he'd been asked to take over *GWTW*, she found him "nervous as a thoroughbred horse." He told her, "I've been working too hard." When she pointed out that his last picture, *Test Pilot*, had been months ago, he corrected her: "*Test Pilot* was my last credit, you mean," then listed *The Crowd Roars*, *Too Hot to Handle*, *The Great Waltz*, and *The Wizard of Oz*. "After this, I'm going away where no one can find me—not even me."

Still, find him they did. The how and why of it remain matters of conjecture. But Gable's preference for Fleming to direct *GWTW* instead of George Cukor was not only well-known; it was also reported before principal photography began. And ever since he joined the production, Gable had been out of sorts. He shot his first scenes in January 1939, two weeks after Leigh and Olivia de Havilland. Doubtless he felt uncertain in a new studio, acting with women who already had a close rapport with Cukor.

After Selznick fired Cukor, John Lee Mahin recalled, Gable made a late-night visit to Fleming's house to beg him to come onto *GWTW.* Mahin was probably thinking of the events of the early-morning hours of Sunday, February 12: a coup de théâtre straight out of screwball comedy and at odds with Selznick's denial that he consulted with Gable about the directorial change.

In this version, Selznick, Gable, and Eddie Mannix, after viewing *GWTW* rushes at Selznick's house, paid a 3:00 a.m. visit not to Louis B. Mayer but to Mervyn LeRoy at his Santa Monica beach house. The ruckus stirred LeRoy from slumber. He looked down from his bedroom window and demanded: "I'm in bed—what do you mean by busting in at this hour of the night?" Selznick shouted in return: "We want your director—we've got to have Victor Fleming!" It took a series of phone calls—including at least one to Mayer—but a few hours later LeRoy had released Fleming from *The Wizard of Oz.* Selznick announced Fleming's hiring two days later.

"My God, imagine picking up a project like that at this stage," Fleming was heard to muse that week on the *Oz* set. "Still, if Clark's going to sulk, I guess I'd better do it." As soon as Selznick made the switch, Norman Webb of *National Box Office Digest* wrote the producer that he was glad Fleming was taking over, because, unlike Cukor, "Victor Fleming has one of the very best box-office records in the industry."

So what did happen to Cukor, and why did Selznick summon Fleming? Contemporary columnists as well as latter-day analysts, trying to make sense of Selznick's decision, have often placed the onus on Gable. But several eyewitnesses contradict the notion that Gable catalyzed the crisis, no matter how central he was to its outcome. Susan Myrick, the film's Georgia dialect coach and technical adviser, provided an intimate account in a letter to the book's author, Margaret Mitchell. She wrote that Cukor told her he had "looked at the rushes and felt he was failing. He knew he was a good director and knew the actors were good ones; yet the thing did not click as it should." He demanded that they return to the original script by Sidney Howard. Selznick balked and offered his own ultimatum: "OK, get out." In 1954, Ed Sullivan wrote that Cukor reached the point of no return when he clashed with Selznick on how to film a scene of Ashley Wilkes (Leslie Howard) walking down the stairs to meet Scarlett: "I think Ashley, at that moment, would be scared to meet her," Selznick said. "I disagree wholeheartedly," Cukor replied.

Cukor was never specific in his own recollections. "David talked generally," he said in 1968, recalling the day he was summoned to Selznick's office. "He said something like, 'It's not coming along the way I want it to, I've taken complete responsibility and it has to be my way.' "

The way Selznick saw things—and remembered them, consistently, year after year—the issues were practical and artistic: Cukor's slow going on the initial scenes, the languid tempo and listless quality of his footage, and a clash over who had final authority over rewrites and on-set scene making. In 1947, Selznick told *The New York Times*, "We couldn't see eye to eye on anything. I felt that while Cukor was simply unbeatable on directing intimate scenes of the Scarlett O'Hara story, he lacked the big feel, the scope, the breadth of the production." Yakima Canutt, the stuntman hired to double Gable and to act a renegade in a bit part, backs Selznick up, writing that Cukor "didn't seem to understand the action part of films."

Selznick denied to Gable's biographer Charles Samuels that any one incident precipitated Cukor's ouster: "He was in disagreement with me on my concept of how *Gone With the Wind* should be done." And when Bosley Crowther interviewed Selznick in the late 1950s for his MGM history *The Lion's Share*, Selznick refuted the story that the firing was to please Gable. The producer said he "simply could not agree on points with [Cukor]."

Cukor was not an easy man when it came to brokering disagreements. Sid Luft's experiences with him on the 1954 remake of *A Star Is Born* resemble Selznick's. Tempo was a major problem—even the nonmusical scenes ran a third longer than their exact equivalents in the 1937 original directed by William Wellman, a director far closer in his emotional and artistic makeup to Fleming than to Cukor. (The overlength—not entirely Cukor's fault, since he had nothing to do with proposing the fifteen-minute "Born in a Trunk" showpiece with Judy Garland—led Warner Bros. to cut a half hour from the film after its big-city engagements.) Luft and Garland's production company produced the picture. They were intent on providing Cukor with everything the director wanted, including George Hoyningen-Huene—in Luft's words, "the photographic guru of his time"—as a special color design adviser. Still, the pugnacious Luft and the stubborn Cukor found themselves at loggerheads over Hoyningen-Huene's attempt to frame Garland in a red dress against red walls (Luft had them painted gray) or the way Luft cut a long dialogue scene in a nightclub. "Cukor was tough, but good-natured underneath," Luft said a half century later. "I think he had mellowed since *Gone With the Wind.*"

Getting Gable *had* been crucial for Selznick to put the picture together. He needed this star to satisfy the throngs who thought the King was destined to play Rhett Butler. In exchange for loaning out

Gable, Selznick's father-in-law, Louis B. Mayer, agreed that MGM would distribute *GWTW*, put up half its production money (up to $1.25 million), and receive half the film's profits for the first seven years. A critical goal for Selznick was keeping Gable confident and effective, if not happy.

The idea that Selznick thought Cukor was a "woman's director" who threw the movie to Scarlett insults the producer as well as Cukor. Fleming later told Mahin, "George would have done just as good a job as I. He'd probably have done a lot better on the intimate scenes. I did pretty well on some of the bigger stuff. George came from the stage and taught us what directing a dialogue scene was about. He knew. And nobody could direct a dialogue scene like George Cukor. It's bullshit that he's just a woman's director. He's not. He can direct anybody." Similarly, in a 1972 letter to Kevin Brownlow, Louise Brooks argued (albeit at Cukor's expense) against Fleming as a "man's director": "The best performance Clara Bow ever gave was in Fleming's *Mantrap*. And in *The Wizard of Oz* Fleming made Judy Garland the most adorable creature we will ever see in films. Yet Garbo allowed Cukor to destroy her in *Two-Faced Woman*. It is no more reasonable to think that pansies love women than to think that cats like birds."

The most up-to-date, politically correct theory about why Selznick let go his good friend and frequent collaborator Cukor has to do with sexual politics. Although Cukor's circle spread this explanation of his firing for years, it came to light only after his death and entered film history when Patrick McGilligan included it in his provocative 1991 biography of Cukor, based on what McGilligan calls a "precise contemporary account of it" from the papers of the screenwriter Donald Ogden Stewart. The theory hinges on the story that Gable, in the 1920s, had a brief erotic encounter with the openly gay star William Haines—a friend of Cukor's and a sometime visitor to the set of *Gone With the Wind*.

Supposedly, during the early weeks of shooting, Gable heard reports that a member of Cukor's circle, the actor Anderson Lawler, had said during a party, "George is directing one of Billy's old tricks"—infuriating the star. But Haines's own biographer, William J. Mann, can't conclude anything about the original Gable-Haines incident other than "it's clear *something* happened between the two men." (He doesn't entertain the possibility that *nothing* happened.) And Mann qualifies his interpretation of the *Gone With the Wind* snafu: "It would be too naïve to assume that gossip about Billy and Gable had nothing to do with the antagonism of the director—just as it would perhaps be too simplistic to say it caused Cukor's ultimate dismissal. Lawler's wagging tongue, however, might just have been the proverbial straw that broke the back of an already strained, angry, and frustrated star."

Leigh and de Havilland had bonded with Cukor; they didn't share Gable's elation. "I was not aware, when the change came, that Victor Fleming was a particular friend of Gable's and, in fact, knew nothing about him at all," de Havilland says. "My fear was that with a change of directors, I would lose my grasp of Melanie [Hamilton]'s character."

When they learned the news on February 13, each was costumed in black to grieve for the death of Melanie's brother and Scarlett's first husband, Charles Hamilton. De Havilland wrote of confronting Selznick immediately: "In our garb of deep mourning, Vivien and I stormed his office. For three solid hours, we beseeched him not to let George go. As tears rained on David, he retreated to the haven of his window seat, and when we unfurled the forlorn banners of our black-bordered handkerchiefs, he nearly fled out the window." According to Selznick, the two actresses were so "sore" they also went to his brother (and Leigh's American agent), Myron, and asked "if Fleming [was] a good man." He couldn't stave off sarcasm. "No," he shot back, "David's going all over town looking for a bad director." (Myron later threatened Leigh: he said were she to quit the picture, he'd see that she never worked in Hollywood again.) De Havilland took some comfort from her then-beau, Howard Hughes, who, "to my surprise, said something both perceptive and reassuring: 'Don't worry, everything is going to be all right—with George and Victor, it's the same talent, only Victor's is strained through a coarser sieve.' "

To her actor friend Anthony Bushell, Leigh protested Cukor's replacement with a man she called "a mere workaday hack." She expressed her anxiety more politely in a letter to her mother:

> Everyone is hysterical about this film, with the consequence that everything is disorganized—after two years they are still writing the script which means I don't know where I am. They have changed the director, which has upset me a lot, as I loved George Cukor (who was here before). I like this man alright, but the poor wretch is exhausted as he hasn't stopped working for ages, & he did not really want to do this film, as he was

> so tired, & has not even had time to read the book! Then the photography is appalling, they all say. So *how* can I have any confidence.

Figuring out who had read the novel became a parlor game for columnists throughout filming. One reported, with authority, that neither Leslie Howard nor de Havilland had done so. When Fleming took the job, he had not, but he eventually did, as his well-thumbed copy indicates. He and Mahin worked nights "for about a week" on script revisions, Mahin recalled. "Every night, Vic would say, 'Now look on page so-and-so.' He knew the novel by heart."

At the time of Fleming's hiring, the cast was working from revisions by Oliver H. P. Garrett, who was rewriting the playwright Sidney Howard's screenplay. Fleming quickly got down to business with Mahin after bluntly telling the producer, "Your fucking script is no fucking good." Selznick ended that arrangement. He was determined to be as independent from Mayer as possible—but Mahin had been spotted meeting with Mayer to discuss his new assignment, and Selznick suspected the writer was behind a *Hollywood Reporter* scoop crediting the MGM talent pool with rescuing his chaotic production. Next at bat was Ben Hecht—one of the most fecund minds in Hollywood and a fan of the director he called "aloof and poetical." (Hecht may have met him in 1934 when writing *The Prisoner of Zenda* for Selznick, who wanted Fleming for that picture; it was filmed in 1937 with John Cromwell directing John L. Balderston's script.)

Hecht's rollicking account in his memoir, *A Child of the Century*, told how he rewrote the first half of the *GWTW* script in a week for $15,000. (Sometimes he said he worked on the script for two weeks for $10,000; whatever the price, he did stay on to edit the second half of the script in week two.) Hecht's tale, however rife with hyperbole and inaccuracies, captures the dynamic idiosyncrasies of Fleming and Selznick as well as the excitement of boy-on-a-burning-deck filming performed on a grand scale. Hecht insisted that all he was given to eat was peanuts.

Initially, as Selznick laid out the story to an uncomprehending Hecht (who had *not* read the novel), "Fleming, who was reputed to be part Indian, sat brooding at his own council fires." Then, after Hecht gave his blessing to Howard's distillation of the narrative into "treatment" (really, screenplay) form,

> Selznick and Fleming discussed each of Howard's scenes and informed me of the habits and general psychology of the characters. They also acted out the scenes, David specializing in the parts of Scarlett and her drunken father, and Vic playing Rhett Butler and a curious fellow I could never understand called Ashley . . . After each scene had been discussed and performed, I sat down to the typewriter and wrote it out. Selznick and Fleming, eager to continue with their acting, kept hurrying me. We worked in this fashion for seven days, putting in eighteen to twenty hours a day . . . On the fourth day, a blood vessel in Fleming's right eye broke, giving him more of an Indian look than ever. On the fifth day, Selznick toppled into a torpor while chewing on a banana. The wear and tear on me was less, for I had been able to lie on the couch and half doze while the two darted about acting.

Hecht also said, many years later, "Fleming was a much better director than Cukor ever could be."

GWTW devotees have long wondered which chunky, bespectacled, wavy-haired man was the better Scarlett: Selznick or Cukor, who had acted the role when de Havilland read for Melanie. The casting doubtless was better when F. Scott Fitzgerald worked on the script and played Rhett and Ashley to Sheilah Graham's Scarlett and Melanie; Fitzgerald, not surprisingly, both understood Ashley and did his best screenwriting for this project on that character. (He edited the sequence of Ashley's Christmas leave.) Hecht thought he forestalled any future demands by snaring Selznick into his script process and gaining the producer's tacit assent, but more likely Selznick realized the wisdom of what Mahin had told him even before Hecht said anything: "For God's sake, let's get back to Margaret Mitchell's book and Sidney Howard's wonderful script." And Selznick *did* get Hecht back to write seven title cards in September.

Most accounts of *Gone With the Wind* focus on everything Selznick did before Fleming arrived: the search for Scarlett that ultimately landed Leigh; the previsualization of the movie in the elaborate storyboards of the production designer William Cameron Menzies; the many early reworkings of Howard's script; and even the burning of Atlanta (filmed in December 1938). But rewrites continued during filming, and as Fitzgerald wrote of Fleming for a 1939 lecture tour by

Graham, "[He was a] fine adaptable mechanism—which in the morning could direct the action of two thousand extras, and in the afternoon decided on the colors of the buttons on Clark Gable's coat and the shadows on Vivien Leigh's neck . . . Like all pictures, it has been a community enterprise . . . but the tensile strength of this great effort has been furnished by the director."

Fleming took up the gauntlet partly because Gable was a close friend and frequent colleague. Gable as Rhett presents a mature incarnation of the good-bad take-charge guy he and Fleming had been developing since *Red Dust.* That alone should derail the long-accepted narrative that Selznick was the sole artist and Fleming the hack following orders. Years after his judicious Selznick biography, *Showman: The Life of David O. Selznick* (1992), David Thomson concluded that Selznick "identified very much with the character of Scarlett O'Hara . . . He believed in her, he so much wanted her success, her survival, for himself." Selznick's director, though, identified with Rhett.

The producer had prized Fleming's abilities at Paramount in the 1920s, and in 1933, during Selznick's brief tenure at MGM, he argued to Mayer that Fleming should be made a staff director (with a long-term contract) precisely because "we would be better off with fewer supervisors and more producing directors." (Fleming's only long-term contract with MGM, negotiated before *GWTW,* guaranteed him the right to deny credit on his films to any producer.) They had enjoyed a close and respectful collaboration on *Reckless,* and Selznick hoped Fleming would direct the Carole Lombard–James Stewart marital soap opera, *Made for Each Other* (which John Cromwell directed while Fleming was in Oz).

Although they were never to be friends, Selznick gave a remarkably fair evaluation of Fleming to Gable's biographer Samuels in 1961. Samuels asked whether Fleming was "tough, sadistic," and Selznick responded, "I don't think he was sadistic. He was another of that extremely masculine breed. The most attractive man, in my opinion, who ever came to Hollywood. Physically and in personality. He had a kind of Indian quality. American Indian, that is. Women were crazy about him, and understandably so." Admitting that he never knew Fleming socially, he added, "I enjoyed working with him. A really expert craftsman. He had been a cameraman and he knew his cinematics thoroughly." Naturally, he didn't drop his refrain that other directors worked on the film, but he summarized Fleming's contribution by saying, "Fleming did beautiful work on it." (In an earlier interview with Bosley Crowther, Selznick said Fleming directed 60 percent of the picture, a higher percentage than anyone else gave him.)

Another disaster to be contained was "the terrible mess we have made of Gable's clothes," Selznick wrote in one of his fabled memos. Gable was told he couldn't use his favorite tailoring firm, Eddie Schmidt's in Beverly Hills. This fiat, Selznick concluded, "was an insane order to begin with. And it had the further effect of making Gable take a what-the-hell attitude."

Schmidt recalled a tempestuous Saturday conference on the second floor of his Rodeo Drive store, with David and Myron Selznick, Fleming, Gable, Gable's agent, Phil Berg, and the costume designer Walter Plunkett. It was not specifically about wardrobe: "It was an easy place for them all to meet with nobody else getting involved. And that's when they started talking about it, and well, of course, they talked about the wardrobe, too, you know." In Schmidt's recollection, Fleming told Selznick, "I've seen what's been shot, and if I'm going to do this picture, I'm going to start from the beginning." Selznick replied, "My God, it'll cost a fortune." Fleming moved to leave and said, "You know, I have two other commitments," and Gable chimed in, "If Flem walks down those stairs, I'm going to follow him, and you can replace me." It was up to Myron to say, "For God's sake, either let them make the picture or forget the subject."

Fleming didn't get to shoot the picture in continuity, as he'd wished, but Schmidt's firm stitched all of Gable's costumes. "We had about six people working on the weekend to make that red suit with the white stripe. I'll never forget that one as long as I live." Like Garland's in *Oz*, Gable's body needed restraint, but in a different area. Schmidt's crew shaped Gable's suits around a light corset he wore to maintain his heroic profile. "It was very short and tight," Schmidt says. "He had a good-size fanny on him, know what I mean? He was a big guy, you know, and he did that purposely, just for that picture." Schmidt's tailors cut Gable's trousers to fit snugly and his jackets to hang loosely as they fashioned nearly two dozen costumes. "We doubled up on the white outfit, because he'd get them soiled very quickly, and that one where he carried her up the stairs, we made a couple of those."

Selznick completed his reorganization of the project when he replaced the cinematographer Lee Garmes with Ernest Haller; it would be Haller's first color film, and he chose to light it as if it were black and white. The result is an overall look that's delicately shaded except at its expressionist extremes. (Technicolor had developed a film twice as fast as the stock used on *The Wizard of Oz* and required only half as many lights.) Fleming and Haller worked well together. One reporter found the director impersonating an Atlanta streetlight so the cinematographer could line up a shot, causing a propman to circle Fleming's feet in chalk and then advise the grips, "Here's where she goes, boys—and try to make it look like Mr. Fleming." (Fleming's frequent cinematographer Hal Rosson shot retakes without credit that autumn.)

Fleming knew the film would require generalship—maybe that's why he came on so strongly to the assistant directors Ridgeway Callow and Eric Stacey. He sent them a barbed double message when he greeted them: "They tell me that you're supposed to be the best team in the picture business. But I'm going to put both of you in the hospital before this picture is over."

It was up to Fleming to make sure that Menzies's intricate storyboards worked in propulsive movie terms—and that his sophisticated visual strategies didn't overwhelm the performers. Fleming succeeded. When asked why Menzies spent more time with the fill-in director Sam Wood than with Fleming, the assistant director Callow said, "I think he felt that Sam Wood simply needed him more than Fleming." The old 1.33:1 ratio of width to height (compared with today's typical 1.85:1) was often called the "golden ratio." In *Gone With the Wind*, you see why. There's a satisfying balance between the actors and their surroundings, which makes the moments when history floods the screen and engulfs the characters more potent.

Fleming came in like a lion on the first day of March and started directing the picture's first scene—the opening, with Scarlett making "war" sound like "woah" as she drawls to the Tarleton boys (Fred Crane and George Reeves), "War, war, war: this war talk's spoiling all the fun at every party this spring." (After taking a couple more stabs at it in June, Fleming got it right in mid-October.) Rewrites from Selznick arrived daily, on sheets of pink for the first and blue for the second. Fleming made an initial effort to shield the actors from the backstage anarchy: on March 8, the script supervisor Barbara Keon wrote Selznick, "I am not sending out pink pages, because they are simple changes and Mr. Fleming mentioned today that pink pages scare the actors."

Throughout the process, Selznick and Fleming massaged ambivalence and irony into the storytelling. Like Margaret Mitchell, they intuited that if you respect the traditions of florid romance, you can question the principles behind them more powerfully. If you glorify the courtliness of the Old South, you can also savage its dreaminess in the person of the gentleman farmer Ashley Wilkes. (Leslie Howard, who in his mid-forties was too old for the part, plays him in an often stiff, embarrassed manner as if he knows the man's a prig.) Rhett, the realist, who gets rich running Union blockades for the Confederacy, is in effect a mustachioed Cassandra, predicting the fall of the South. The whole movie is built on matched opposites like Rhett and Ashley: workmanlike or corrupt Northerners and gallant or trashy Southerners, spoiled whites and enduring blacks (Hattie McDaniel, as Mammy, plays omniscience with an uncanny, gutsy splendor; Butterfly McQueen, as Prissy, plays naïveté comically and superbly). Best of all, there's the contrast between aggressive, headstrong Scarlett and that domestic saint, Melanie (de Havilland, in a performance of admirable conviction), who becomes Ashley's wife. When Fleming announced that he was going to make a melodrama, he didn't specify a simple one.

Fleming featured the actor Rand Brooks in one of his first setups, on March 11: the dining room at Twelve Oaks where a gaggle of Southern men discuss the necessity for war. As Charles Hamilton, Brooks betrays his inexperience twice: first by insulting Rhett Butler when he gives his downbeat view of the South's chances, and then by tumbling for Scarlett when she decides to marry him to spite Ashley. "Vic was one of my favorite people," Brooks said. "He was really an unusually fine man's man, a good director, very sensitive, yet very rough. He didn't believe in phonies. I tried to be a little macho in the part, but he said, 'No, no, you're so in love with this girl, you're sick about it' . . . I was very disappointed [in the part] because I was such an ass."

Phillip Trent appeared in that scene, too:

> I remember thinking how well he had done his director's homework, and how smoothly things were going given the fact that the scene had over three dozen dress extras and principal players, and the set we were working in was quite small. Fleming took a lot of time with each of us. I was lucky enough to have a line in the scene. He coached us in our action and cho-

reographed how we should move so that we could give Gable access to the camera while he had his lines. As I recall, we shot the entire scene in one day, with several setups from different angles.

Fleming did a favor to the entire industry with the successful filming of that scene. Natalie Kalmus, the ex-wife of the inventor of Technicolor, Herbert T. Kalmus, and the color supervisor on every Technicolor film made in Hollywood up to then, insisted that the men would fade into the beige-and-wood walls of Twelve Oaks. After Selznick screened the footage for Dr. Kalmus, Technicolor exiled Natalie to England. Though her name continued to appear on American film productions, her dictates against experimentation were henceforth largely ignored.

Fleming also earned the trust of Susan Myrick, who had considered herself a die-hard Cukor loyalist. Writing for the *Macon Telegraph*, she described him as "a handsome, blondish man with keen eyes and a tendency to fire questions at you so fast that you can't even answer them." Myrick sensed that his "familiarity with details of Miss Mitchell's novel . . . bodes good for the production of the movie." She initially thought him a "sour puss," and he certainly was when filming the Southern gentry's response to the declaration of war. The swells swarmed out of Twelve Oaks to mount their steeds and ride off to battle, but the wranglers in charge of the horses, as a gag, didn't cinch the saddles, so the men flew off the horses at first gallop. It was a time-honored practical joke among movie cowboys; Fleming might have pulled it himself back in his Flying A days. But Shep Houghton, another of the Twelve Oaks gents, said the director was livid and promptly fired one of the equipment managers. "Get *him* out of here," he growled, "and then get *me* out of here."

Still, Fleming retained a brusque charm through much of the filming, and Myrick cottoned to his smile. "He grinned back of his ears the other day when he asked me if we ever had anything like this Twelve Oaks in the South. I shook my head, grinning wryly, and he said, 'Maybe the po' white trash would like it because they could say it was just like Grandpa's that Sherman burned down.' " They came to share a running gag: Fleming would whistle "Marching Through Georgia" whenever Myrick appeared on the set. (He diplomatically failed to mention his grandfather's service under Sherman in the Battle of

Atlanta.) To Mitchell, Myrick confided, "Vic Fleming laughs at the script situation and told me the other day to write him some ad lib lines, that God knows they'd had fifteen writers [and] I'd just as well try my hand on it and probably couldn't be worse than the others!"

His close friendship and working relationship with Gable have been used to delimit the director's contribution. But as James Harvey wrote in *Romantic Comedy* (he puts *GWTW* in the category of "tough comedy"), Gable's "apotheosis as Rhett Butler" is critical to the film's success. "Most of the scenes," he writes, "are focused on [Scarlett] but they are focused by him—by his bemusement, his disbelief, his final enchantment."

Fleming first relaxed, then vitalized Gable. "They talked each other's language and they yelled and hollered on the set with each other," said Adela Rogers St. Johns. "[Clark] knew what he was and what he had and I think he regarded Victor as his equal." Gable could be clumsy or wooden when directed by Jack Conway, but as Rhett Butler he's free as a performer. Fleming liberated him in part by treating him like Douglas Fairbanks. During the "marital rape" scene of Rhett carrying Scarlett up the tall stairs in their Atlanta mansion, technical snafus spoiled five takes. After take six, Fleming called to Gable, "Sorry, Clark! Just one more!" Gable wearily began lifting Leigh again until he heard "Cut!" followed by crew laughter. Fleming explained, "I don't really need another shot. I just had a bet you couldn't make it." Other cast members joined in. De Havilland, a slip of a thing at 105 pounds, presented no obstacle to Gable's strength when Rhett had to lift Melanie and carry her from her birthing bed to the carriage waiting to speed them out of Atlanta. But before the final rehearsal, she asked an assistant director to move a cement block under her bed and secretly tie her to it to give Gable a back-wrenching surprise. His face went red with struggle before the joke dawned on him. "He was really startled, but he was a very good sport."

Gable suffuses the movie's first half with his cockiness. He's at the apex of masculine self-confidence his smile and scowl were rarely more appealing and seductive. When he's still no more than a distant grin at the bottom of the staircase at Twelve Oaks, Scarlett asks who the man is "looking at us and smiling—the nasty dog," and her friend Cathleen Calvert (kittenish Marcella Martin) responds, "That's Rhett Butler! He's from Charleston and he has the most terrible reputation." Fleming slides the camera down the stairs to show Gable beaming brightly, his mint julep resting on the banister, as he swings his shoulders around to enjoy a cool, discerning look at Scarlett. He's anything but nasty—though, as Scarlett notes, "He looks as if—as if he knows what I look like without my shimmy!"

It's similar to that other great male introduction of 1939: the tracking shot that ratchets into a close-up of John Wayne as the Ringo Kid in John Ford's *Stagecoach.* But Ford was introducing Wayne as a star coming of age. Fleming's direction seems to state, "Here is Gable in his prime, in the role he was born to play." (To this day, audiences applaud Gable's close-up.)

Fleming's competence would stabilize the crew, renew Gable's sense of security, and inspire most of the male actors. "I don't think he 'directed' too much," Brooks recalled. "I think he knew the angles and he had the emotion inside, and he just talked to people about what he felt a scene should be . . . He was so strong and so well liked. It's funny to be that way; it wasn't the kind of strength you felt afraid of—you felt strengthened from him; not like John Ford, who was abusive. Fleming rehearsed quite a bit, but when a take came, he got it on the first or second take; he knew when it was ready to shoot, and that was it."

The female cast required more empathetic handling. Ann Rutherford, who played Scarlett's sister Carreen, "just sort of snapped to attention" whenever she saw Fleming. "He had marvelous command. He was head of the table wherever he was. He was the father image. He brooked no nonsense. We respected him deeply and liked him and tried to be very obedient to anything he wished us to do."

His relationships with de Havilland and Leigh had to be more complicated. The trickiness of their roles and the grain of their temperaments challenged his artistry—and his probable awareness that they continued to "moonlight" with Cukor challenged his ego. De Havilland explains:

> [Cukor] not only gave us wonderful direction but also confidence in what we were doing. To be severed from him and our relationship with him was a colossal blow, and the prospect of working with anyone else too unnerving to contemplate. I continued to need the assurance and insights which George provided and . . . went to him several times on days off to consult with him about an upcoming scene. These were secret sessions about which I felt guilty toward Vivien. Long after the film was

completed, I learned that Vivien had been doing the same thing—even more often than I.

No one is certain whether Fleming knew of this directorial intervention. But he was too smart and canny not to get a sense of it. He did connect more readily to de Havilland than to his leading lady. Both she and Leigh were born abroad to comfortable British families (de Havilland in Tokyo, Leigh in India); both were convent educated. But de Havilland's parents had divorced when she was three. She grew up in California, mostly in the San Francisco Bay area, and had been working at that no-nonsense dream factory, Warner Bros. She practiced a steady, can-do craft that Fleming understood. When Leigh wouldn't make retching sounds for Scarlett coughing up a radish before announcing she'd "never be hungry again," the dubbing supervisor asked de Havilland to fill in: "I said 'yes,' and proceeded to retch."

No matter how much she had learned and continued to derive from Cukor, de Havilland gained immediate confidence in her new director's insights during their maiden rehearsal. It was the scene when Melanie greets Scarlett at Twelve Oaks: Melanie tells Scarlett she admires her abundance of "life," and Scarlett replies that Melanie "mustn't flatter" her and say things she "doesn't mean"—leading Ashley to say, "Nobody could accuse Melanie of being insincere." Fleming thought somebody *could* accuse Melanie of flattery, at least as de Havilland first delivered her lines. "I responded to Scarlett's greetings in a friendly 'social' way. Victor then drew me aside and said just this: 'Whatever Melanie says, she means.' Thus he gave me not only the key to the playing of the scene but also the key to Melanie's whole character." She repaid Fleming with a performance that has a preternatural calm, a quiet alertness, and an unexpected emotional flexibility that binds her to Scarlett.

It's undisputed that Leigh, who had a cosseted British background, was often at odds with Fleming, who preferred actresses with a bit of rough-and-tumble in them. The authorized biography of Leigh and Olivier, published in 1953 with their input, has her "at first discouraged by his seemingly gloomy disposition."

How often they fought, and over what, vary with the source. But a single incident—a huge breach of professional etiquette—encapsulates the conflict and suggests that it came closer to the surface as everyone grew more fatigued. Six months into the production, Fleming was preparing the scene of Scarlett almost seducing Ashley in a paddock when Leigh suggested (or demanded) on the set that Fleming screen a Cukor-directed test of it. In Leigh's account, she was "shocked to find herself behaving ungraciously" after she told Fleming, "For goodness sake, let's go and see that test scene I did . . . when George was directing!" and was sorry afterward. (Fleming's reaction was not recorded, and reports differ on whether he ever watched it; he shot the scene on June 24.) Years later, Cukor gloated at the story. "Yes, that was much better in the test, and Vivien knew it," he said in 1970, recalling a Sunday (Leigh's only day off) when an exhausted Leigh visited him and dozed for hours, then, upon awakening, "giggled, and told me, 'I was an awful bitch on the set yesterday.' They'd been trying that very scene with Ashley, and she felt it wasn't right, so she made poor Victor Fleming trot over and screen the test. That was so typically straight-shooting of her, as an actress and a human being."

Some critics favorably compare that test to the more restrained version Fleming filmed. But the Cukor-Leigh Scarlett is too close for comfort—or credibility—to her Blanche DuBois in *A Streetcar Named Desire* (1951). Solid Douglass Montgomery, who played Ashley in the test, soaked up her histrionics (as he did for Katharine Hepburn as Laurie in Cukor's *Little Women*), but in this operatic mode she would have made Howard's mild, willowy Ashley look ridiculous. Blanche is what Scarlett might have become if her formidable survival mechanism had malfunctioned. Cukor did help Leigh shape her characterization—"Leigh hated Fleming [and] followed Cukor's direction to the end," Selznick told Crowther. But he shot fewer scenes in the picture than legend has it (notably Scarlett's first long sequence with Mammy). And if some of Cukor's work with her had a finer edge, going toe-to-toe with Fleming had its stiffening virtues.

For his part, Leslie Howard, sometimes effective as a premature elder statesman in his group scenes, was not happy as a romantic ideal. "Yesterday I put on my Confederate uniform for the first time and looked like a fairy doorman at the Beverly Wiltshire [*sic*]—a fine thing at my age," he wrote to his daughter. Although he was popular with the cast and assistant directors, his attitude never improved. Howard kept fumbling his lines, and Leigh once took the actor to task for not knowing his script.

Leigh's confidant Anthony Bushell later confirmed to the critic Michael Dempsey that she blamed Gable's complaints about Cukor for Fleming's hiring, and added that Fleming's "ONLY words to Viv in a directorial sense during the whole run of the picture were, 'Ham it up!' "—or as Sheilah Graham recorded, "Ham it, baby, just ham it!" delivered with a big smile.

Leigh wasn't the only one to hear that command. "Ham it up!" became one of Fleming's favorite proclamations to everyone from Leigh to Yakima Canutt. Butterfly McQueen recalled that the only time he berated her "was when I was sitting in the back of the wagon and we had to pretend that we were going through the fire—which we never saw—and he said to me, 'Ham it up, Prissy! Ham it up! You're not hammy enough!' " Using "ham it up!" as a direction ran against Fleming's temperament. On *The Farmer Takes a Wife* and *Oz*, "ham" was a dirty word: a synonym for mugging. But on *Oz*, his goal was to provide "a basis of reality" in outrageous fantasy. In *Gone With the Wind*, he had to breathe dramatic verve into a mammoth historical romance that had taken on a cultural reality of its own even before Selznick had invested it with state of the artisanship circa 1939. ("After the headache of pure imagination from *The Wizard of Oz*," Fleming wrote in a syndicated story, he now had to drill "down to the bed rock of reality, with millions of voices shouting, 'Hew to the line, mister.' ") "Ham it up," in this case, appears to be Fleming's way of urging the actors to scale their emotions to the size of the production. Thanks to Selznick and Cukor's canny casting choices as well as Fleming's guidance, most of the actors did just that.

Although Fleming altered his style from film to film and was known for his mastery of scale, he was rarely (at least up to then) a self-conscious or ostentatious storyteller. Part of the charm of *The Wizard of Oz* is its matter-of-factness. (When reviewing *Close Encounters of the Third Kind*, Pauline Kael noted, "Very few movies have hit upon this combination of fantasy and amusement—*The Wizard of Oz*, perhaps, in a plainer, down home way.") But Fleming had dabbled in pomp and circumstance on *The Great Waltz*—indeed, most of Hollywood gave him credit for that entire spectacle—and the elaborate Strauss biopic became one of Selznick's models for *GWTW.* In an early-March memo, the producer ordered his whole unit to screen the picture, calling it "Hollywood's best technical achievement in many ways in several years." Almost simultaneously he advised the production manager Ray Klune that Fleming would go after photographic effects and camera angles he'd achieved on *The Great Waltz* when shooting the Twelve Oaks barbecue and reshooting the Atlanta bazaar later that month.

Selznick wanted *Gone With the Wind* to be the sort of spectacle that announces every summit it means to scale. You want the Old South? You get it, with columns and flowing staircases and flaming sunsets. You want to see Atlanta burn? You see it, with Gable and Leigh moving in front of it, to boot. Luckily, Fleming understood that the naturalistic, conversational scenes had to hold their own in intensity with the splashy set pieces—and that those set pieces had to carry their emotional weight.

Few movies have made more vivid use of the Technicolor system's prodigious colors in scenes of spectacular destruction as well as expressionist strokes like Rhett and Scarlett clinching in front of a tangerine sky, or Scarlett raising her fist as dawn breaks over the plantation grounds of Tara. Martin Scorsese has extolled the capacity of this movie's imagery to unlock the audience's imagination. That's partly because Menzies worked out the central drama in vibrant hues. It's also because Fleming set a matching level of intensity in the performances. Color doesn't decorate the characters—it helps bring them to completion. When Scarlett outrages onlookers at the bazaar by dancing with Rhett despite her black mourning dress, or later faces down scandal by showing up at a party for Ashley in a garish crimson gown, the red and the black convey the volcanic essence of one of the screen's great divas.

Fleming also varied the performances so Gable and Leigh could perform unpredictable duets of ardor and manipulation. Rhett is both smitten with Scarlett and, until their mostly disastrous marriage, able to step back and appraise her. In one of several antiromantic pas de deux, he says, "You need kissing badly. That's what's wrong with you. You should be kissed, and often—and by someone who knows how." When she taunts him with "And I suppose you think you're the proper person," he wisely (at that point) keeps his distance, responding, "I might be . . . if the right moment ever came." He forces their first kiss on the road back to Tara from burned Atlanta, when Rhett, suddenly seized by the pull of Dixie's lost cause, asks her, sardonically, to think of herself as "a woman sending a soldier to his death with a beautiful memory." A witness captured Fleming bristling as he filmed that scene, with Leigh clinging to a fence to resist Gable's advances. "Resist, but don't resist too much, it takes up too much time," Fleming told her. After she softened for a second and Gable came on like gangbusters, she hauled off and smacked him. Fleming was "jiggling up and down with excitement. 'That's swell,' he said."

It took the gut feelings of a director like Fleming to keep alive the audience's hope that Scarlett will realize that swashbuckling Rhett is her man rather than overrefined Ashley. Leigh's give-and-take with Fleming—like Scarlett's with Rhett, but without love—resulted in the polar magnetism that powers the movie. Scarlett is simultaneously calculating and unconscious, and Leigh conveys her psychological shifts with lightning physical and verbal contortions. She's a virtuoso at knitting her forehead, and she makes unusual choices with her dialogue. As admiring men encircle her chair at the Twelve Oaks barbecue, she chatters to the brink of unintelligibility: "Now, isn't this better than speaking at an old table? A girl has only two sides to her at a table." She's being as coquettish with the audience as the heroine is with her adoring beaux.

Leigh and Fleming developed their own tense rapport. To Hedda Hopper, he lauded Leigh with, for him, the highest praise: "At first, I didn't give Vivien Leigh credit enough for the emotional depth she has. She's an amazing person and can stand more punishment than any woman I've ever met." Gladys Hall, who observed the filming for *Screen Romances*, thought it amusing that the director called his star "Miss Fiddle-de-dee" and that she called him "Mr. Boom-Boom" because of his predilection for boom shots. Ed Sullivan, witnessing Scarlett sport her famous green-curtain dress during her "horse jail" visit to Rhett, extracted a terse "She's terrific" from the director. Harrison Carroll visited the Twelve Oaks set during the library scene and watched Leigh repeatedly hurl a vase. In one rehearsal, Leigh's throw only got as far as the sofa, leading Fleming to crack, "There's one thing certain, my dear. You're no baseball player."

Afterward, Selznick wrote, "Vivien made no secret of her opinion of certain scenes as she went along; during the 122 days she was on the set . . . she groused plenty . . . and then, at a word from Victor Fleming, who was not merely a very fine director but a man who had the ability to conceal the iron hand in the velvet glove, she would walk into the scene and do such a magnificent job that everybody on the set would be cheering." In Leigh's account, she enjoyed Fleming's joking with the cast and crew: "Take it easy, we've only got three more days' work to do tonight!" And she understood that he had to put up with everything she endured, like the brick dust that simulated Georgia's red clay and made the actors' sweating faces cry crimson rivers.

"The separation from Larry [Laurence Olivier, whom Leigh married that coming September] was very, very upsetting for her," wrote

Sunny Alexander, who worked for Myron Selznick and lived with Leigh as her secretary/companion. "She was motivated by how fast she could get this movie over and get back to Larry. It was a horse race. She had a cute little way of going up to Vic Fleming and saying, 'Darling, could we do just two more shots?' "

Fleming brought out Leigh's fighting spirit, but Selznick's assistant Marcella Rabwin thought she was steely enough, and ready for action, from the tests—she loathed Fleming partly for the way he "targeted" his female star with his fury and sent her running to her "black-market director," Cukor. Fleming did coerce Leigh into belting down several slugs of real brandy for her drunk scene. (Maybe he was stealing the ploy from Emil Jannings.) He brooked no dissent from his insistence that she play Scarlett's bitchiness all out. But there was method to Fleming's intransigence and anger. Leigh had never taken on such a demanding movie role. Scarlett had to be a one-woman compendium of contrasts: selfish and self-destructive, rock-hard and changeable, decisive and procrastinating. A whiz at putting food on the table or launching a business, she's a loser when it comes to resolving her deepest feeling—the alternately inexplicable and heartbreaking longing she retains for Ashley, her childhood ideal. Most of all, though, she has drive. By the time Sherman marches through Georgia and Scarlett returns to the ravaged Tara, audiences are geared to applaud when she raises her fist against the sky and vows never to be hungry again. Fleming built that push into the beat he laid down from the moment he took charge of the movie.

Leigh, who had weak lungs, seldom complained publicly about her physical problems. (Early on, she took one afternoon off because her corset, which gave her a seventeen-inch waist, was making her ill.) She lost weight and body tone under the duress of twelve-hour (sometimes longer) shooting days. Other than Sundays, she had only three days off from March 2 to June 27. Her diminished appearance led Selznick to order Fleming to improve her "breastwork situation"—he wanted her looking "at least as good" in that department as Fox's singing star Alice Faye. (Selznick said Fleming "feels even more keenly about it than I do.") The director had Leigh's breasts taped up to improve her décolletage.

That task might have been on Fleming's mind a few years later when he teased MGM's up-and-coming musical star Kathryn Grayson in the studio commissary. In the early 1940s her prettiness was in full (and buxom) bloom, and her spats with Mayer over her desire to sing opera were the talk of the studio. "Oh, Katie," Fleming called out, to her momentary confusion, "you're the real Katie Scarlett. I wish you were here when we made that. We'd have had to tamp you down, but we had to build Vivien up."

Sidney Howard returned to California in April for additional script work. He soon discovered that Fleming, despite the constrictions of a producer's pet project, was commander of the set, committed to making every scene emotionally authentic. On April 5, Howard wrote his wife, "Footage wasted on spectacular shots of Scarlett's marriage to Charles. No room for Rhett to give back Melanie's wedding ring. Vic Fleming says: the screen is no place for trivial character. OK by me. Vic Fleming is the director."

Within two weeks Howard comprehended the grueling pace and pressure of Selznick's attempt to create a Hollywood sound epic comparable to *The Birth of a Nation.* "I can now, for the first time in my life, say with confidence that I know what the word 'tired' means. My own private weariness, apart from nausea whenever I look at a page of the script, is less my trouble than the miasma of fatigue which surrounds me." Selznick popped Benzedrine and chain-smoked. Fleming wore himself out with his own intensity, and chain-smoked, too. But Howard described the director getting what appeared to be vitamin shots as well: "Fleming takes four shots of something a day to keep him going and another shot or so to fix him after the day's stimulants. Selznick is bent double with permanent, and I should think, chronic indigestion. Half the staff look, talk and behave as though they were on the verge of breakdowns."

Even then, Fleming was in his element. He might have been speaking of himself as he yelled out directions to the extras for the hospital scene: "Remember, this is a hot summer day. This hospital is a filthy place. You are tormented by wounds, mosquitoes, flies, bedbugs, lice. Now everybody sound off in misery . . . I want a perfect litany of pain!" Adding to his own litany was an April 12 memo from Selznick, who hadn't shaken his *Great Waltz* fixation. Selznick advised Fleming, "If and when you get a moment and when you are not a wreck and haven't got nine million other things to do," he should discuss with Menzies how to get images of a waltz "at least as good as what they have had in other pictures in the way of waltz shots."

Published rumors of Fleming's possible departure began the first week in April. "Whatever I do, they're fighting me all the way," he confided to his brother-in-law Dick Kobe, who feared that a breakdown was imminent. On April 14—a Friday—Selznick sent out a memo stating that Fleming "is so near the breaking point both physically and mentally from sheer exhaustion that it would be a miracle, in my opinion, if he is able to shoot for another seven or eight weeks." Myrick wrote in her diary the same day, "Vic told me . . . he was tired to death and he thought he was getting the jitters and would just have to quit."

Yet Fleming maintained his family dinnertime schedule before returning to Culver City for night shoots or to edit *The Wizard of Oz*. That Sunday, he also summoned sufficient energy to fulfill an obligation to direct a live radio program—an episode of the *Gulf Screen Guild Theater* for the benefit of the Motion Picture Relief Fund. Although directing a tightly written half-hour program was nowhere near as strenuous as taking the helm of a movie, Fleming still had to be at the CBS studio for both the rehearsal and the broadcast. Oddly enough, the episode, "The Hand of Providence," written by Charles Tazewell (*The Littlest Angel*), involved a return to Kansas—this one starring James Cagney and Andy Devine as two escaped cons who go straight under the influence of a farm girl played by Priscilla Lane.

De Havilland explains that she was one of the few cast members to see the strain behind Fleming's bold facade in late April:

> I found that during the lunch hour, it did me good to repair for a while to a quiet spot on the back lot before returning to the set. One day, as I was eating in the fresh air and sunshine, Fleming—no doubt searching for similar solitude and relief from the oxygen-deprived confines of the soundstage—wandered into the same area and discovered me there. It was, I think, during our walk back to the set that he gravely told me that on the previous Saturday night he had driven to the top of a cliff and had contemplated leaping from its edge. As we presently can see, he was suffering from a depression which, now that I think about it, must surely have predated the filming of *Gone With the Wind* and not only required his absence but must also have continued in some measure after the film was finished. But on the film, despite his melancholy, he was unfailingly professional, capable, courteous, and considerate, I would never have guessed that he was a deeply suffering man—

serious, grave, aware of his enormous responsibility, yes, but not despondent to a profound degree. Fleming, finding me so unexpectedly in that quiet sunlit spot, may have sensed a kinship of some sort, and perhaps this impelled him to make his anguished admission.

Shortly after that, Fleming filmed Melanie's death scene, which included Mickey Kuhn, a seven-year-old actor, already a veteran of a half-dozen movies, playing four-year-old Beau Wilkes. No other fictional scenario would have cut closer to Fleming than a four-year-old boy losing a parent, but he knew how to control his emotions around children. Before filming, Fleming approached Kuhn's mother and said, "I want to talk to Mickey." In Kuhn's recollection:

> He just talked to me. He just knew how to get to people. He said, "You know, it's a very sad day. Your mother is dying." And he said, "How would you feel if your mother was dying? She's dying, and she's very, very sick." I cried easily in those days. He patted me on the back and handed me to Leslie Howard, and on the count of five, as I remember, we went out and did the scene. One take. What you see is what it was. Afterward, he picked me up and held me and took me back to my mother. Because I was crying, you know, pretty hard. I don't think what I did in that scene could be done just by acting ability. It needed someone like Victor Fleming to plant the seed, you know what I mean?

Kuhn, in turn, helped bring out Fleming's emotions, as Leigh's companion Sunny Alexander recorded. She wrote that Melanie's death "was so real and everybody so emotional and so tired from working so hard that when [Fleming] said 'Cut,' everyone on that set was crying—the crew, the electricians, the third and fourth assistant—everybody was weeping as if we'd been to a memorial service or something. That's how real it all seemed. Vic knew he had a good shot when he saw tears in everybody's eyes—including his own."

Gable didn't agree. It took two days of rehearsal and shooting for Fleming to wring just the right anguish from Gable for Rhett's mourning of Melanie. The director envisioned some exhausting takes on the horizon; he knew he would want Gable to shed tears when Rhett reacts to Scarlett's miscarriage. Yet he had to move on without pause to prepare his back-lot Atlanta for a night scene with Scarlett, Melanie, and Rhett's mistress, the notorious madam Belle Watling (Ona Munson). Once again, Leigh fought Fleming's determination to convey Scarlett's most unlikable qualities, such as her cynicism and snobbery toward Belle—but this time Fleming responded, "Miss Leigh, you can stick this script up your royal British ass!" Then he stomped off the set and didn't come back.

It was April 27. "Confusion redoubled today when doctors ordered Victor Fleming to quit work," Sidney Howard wrote his wife. Fleming said his doctor ordered him to bed after eighteen months of nonstop labor. He typically crashed from exhaustion at the start of his prolonged vacations. But no one in Hollywood had worked on such a relentless procession of complicated, big-budget projects (including *The Great Waltz*), and the pressure finally got to him, as it would two years later when his production of *The Yearling* collapsed in Florida. Victoria remembers exactly what happened during these episodes: her father was confined to his bedroom for two weeks, and the only person allowed to enter, other than his doctor, was his butler, Slocum.

Selznick announced the same day that Sam Wood, a competent and sometimes better-than-competent director (*Goodbye, Mr. Chips*), would spell Fleming. Wood was not in the same league as his predecessors, but, wrote Scott Fitzgerald, he "takes things a little less hard" than Cukor or Fleming. All the news reports indicated that Fleming would return in a week to ten days, but his absence did stretch into two weeks. During his recuperation, Selznick, Gable, and Leigh visited the director at his Balboa beach house. Selznick even offered Fleming a piece of the profits as part of his salary. But this risk-averse son of a citrus rancher responded with "What do you take me for, a chump?" On May 2, Charles Cotton, hoping to lift Vic's spirits, paid him a visit, and for that he did dress up and perk up, as caught in the Fleming family's home movies.

Gavin Lambert's perceptive yet frustrating *GWTW: The Making of "Gone With the Wind"* (1973) recounts a Selznick-oriented version of Fleming's departure in which the producer discovers from Fleming's doctor that the breakdown was "feigned"—"a protest against what he considered David's domination of the picture." In this skewed rendering, the collapse is a tactic conceived "under the false impression that Selznick would promise to reduce the pressure if he came back," and the hiring of Wood a ploy on the producer's part to rouse Fleming to his senses. Some members of Selznick's team, such as Rabwin, suspected Fleming of faking his illness—but Selznick's own intuition in the April 14 memo and the testimony of Myrick and Fleming's daughters back up its reality.

Wood shot the troublesome Belle Watling scene until early morning, then returned a few hours later to shoot Mammy helping Scarlett make her famous green-velvet-curtain dress. Working with the first unit and later with an alternate first unit (known simply in Selznick's memos as "the Wood unit"), he filmed many scenes with Leigh, including Scarlett's marriage to Frank Kennedy. (He directed for sixteen days when Fleming was out and eight more with his "Wood unit.") But Gable didn't warm to Wood. Although a May 3 Selznick memo says, "Mr. Gable has just told me he has withdrawn his opinion about Sam Wood and is very happy with him," after Fleming resumed shooting May 15, Selznick steered Wood toward scenes centered on Scarlett and Ashley. The producer's memos increasingly reflected his high evaluation of Fleming: Wood was being "very slow and obstinate," and Fleming was keen at catching miscues such as Union artillery speeding over a bridge too quickly while Scarlett is hiding underneath. (Fleming, like Selznick, was obviously reviewing all the footage, not just scenes he'd shot himself; Menzies had taken the first swipe at the bridge scene.) Selznick also grew to appreciate Fleming's feel for physicalizing drama: he liked Fleming's "addition of Scarlett throwing the dirt in Wilkerson's face," though he thought it needed some improvements.

Selznick eventually concluded that Fleming should "direct everything, however seemingly unimportant. Vic is more relaxed now and also is very hopped up about the picture, and I think we should have the extra quality that he can give even to these seemingly unimportant bits." Fleming also made an effort to show his approval of Leigh's performance, congratulating her instead of shouting "Cut!" after she enacted Scarlett's sobbing at Rhett's exit.

Not everyone found Fleming more relaxed. When Canutt, who had done stunts on *The Farmer Takes a Wife*, showed up to complete his scenes as the lowlife who attacks Scarlett on a bridge, he "was amazed at the difference in [Fleming's] appearance and behavior. He was cranky as all get out and seemed to have aged years. The first take on my scene with Scarlett was cut before I had hardly opened my mouth.

Fleming stalked over to me and sneered, 'All right, ham it up!' He then went back to the camera, leaving me bewildered. Whatever his disposition, it certainly did not affect his talent for making great pictures." Yet the bit player William Bakewell, an old friend of Fleming's (possibly from Pickfair days) who portrayed the Confederate cavalry officer advising Scarlett that she "had better refuge South," said he "got a warm greeting" for "one of the briefest parts I've ever had."

Fleming's first scene on his return was of Scarlett, ravaged by hunger and desperation, digging up a radish and declaring, "I'll never be hungry again!" It was an all-nighter; the crew, Leigh, and Fleming arrived in Lasky Mesa, near Agoura, after midnight so they'd be set up to catch the first rays of the morning sun. The scene in the film as Scarlett beats the earth with her fists is the fifth take, Leigh's exhaustion and anger real. A Leigh biographer wrote, "All the way back to town in the director's car she sulked with rage," but she apologized to Fleming the next day.

When Rhett finally proposes marriage to Scarlett, it's with the questions, "Did you ever think of marrying just for fun? You've been married to a boy and to an old man; why not try a husband of the right age, with a way with women?" But the courtship is far from triumphant. Scarlett says she'll marry him, but at least "partly" for money, and she won't say she's madly in love with him. A change comes over Rhett; he can no longer be his authentic self until he goes as far as he can with his love for Scarlett, even into faithful matrimony. His air of gaiety at her untamed liveliness, including her covetousness and greed, can't quite camouflage his longing for her to love him absolutely.

Rhett's hidden nobility comes to the fore in his devotion to Melanie and Mammy—each, in different ways, a pillar of rectitude. The romantic and domestic ideals beneath Rhett's amorous deal making emerge as the anchors of the movie. That's why it was so crucial for Fleming to get Gable to cry when Rhett feels that he has brought on Scarlett's miscarriage. The movie needs this cathartic revelation of Rhett's frustration at being unable to make his marriage work and his guilt over masking his marital pain with sarcasm and bravado. Afraid of the emotional exposure, Gable balked.

Rand Brooks, who wasn't present for that scene, summed up what the other actors believed: Fleming "got Gable drunk to get that crying scene. He would call him every name in the book, say you can't act worth shit, every name under the sun, go in and do it right or I'll go off and leave you. Gable was a consummate technician, but didn't have much range. But after that he did some very emotional things. You are what your directors tell you, and Fleming could say what he wanted to Gable, there was so much affection and respect there."

De Havilland, who was there, recalls no drunkenness or verbal abuse:

> Clark did rebel against crying in the scene . . . In the culture of that time, men were not permitted to cry. To weep was regarded as an act of ultimate unmanliness, a sign of unacceptable weakness. No wonder Clark rebelled. This reigning view (plus, perhaps, a fear that he might not be able to summon the tears—technically a difficult thing to do) explains Gable's resistance. The idea of crying not only embarrassed him as a man but was unsuitable, so he thought, to his career. He did not want to disappoint or alienate his vast and admiring audience. Victor insisted, of course, that it was essential to the scene and to the film that Gable weep. When Gable reluctantly agreed to film a weeping Rhett, not only Victor but also I tried to reassure and encourage him. Then, just before the scene began, we sensed that Gable had at last committed himself, and when the cameras rolled, the tears were there and Clark was wonderful.

Fleming actually shot the scene twice—once with tears, once without—so Gable would feel more at ease knowing he had a fallback. The journalist Gladys Hall observed that afterward, "Clark crept to his bungalow via the back porch of the sound stage, slithering across the yard as though afraid that someone would see him, would speak to him. He wasn't himself for the rest of the day."

Selznick's story editor Val Lewton, later known as RKO's master of low-budget horror filmmaking, conceived the most elaborate and expensive crane shot ever made: the camera pulling back and up to show Scarlett picking her away among hundreds of wounded Confederate soldiers in the Atlanta railroad yards. "I clearly remember my father talking about it," says Val Lewton Jr. "He said he wrote the scene as a joke, knowing it would be impossible to shoot." (Lewton had tried to dissuade Selznick from buying Mitchell's novel.) But if Lewton thought it up and Menzies designed it, on May 20, Fleming was the one who called "Action!" on this staggering vignette of the wages of war, ending on the tattered battle flag of the Confederacy. Mitchell had described Scarlett seeing the wounded remnants of the Confederate army "lining the tracks, the sidewalks, stretched out in endless rows under the car shed. Some lay stiff and still, but many writhed under the hot sun, moaning." What makes it breathtaking in the movie is that you never lose sight of Leigh as the stunned, groping Scarlett maneuvers among the wounded and the dead—consisting of extras, dummies, and, for a jolting dose of realism, amputees from Sawtelle Veterans Hospital.

"Get off those dummies!" Fleming snarled at the extras through a loudspeaker at anyone stepping on the mannequins as the eighty-five-foot construction crane began its ascent, with the camera operator Art Arling, the cinematographer Ernest Haller, and, of course, Fleming on the camera platform. To Leigh, he rasped, "Slower, dear—slower!" as she was "threading her uncertain path among them—past the stretcher-bearers, the nurses and the huge soup kettles." Wrote another observer, "The camera swings up and back, up and up until the lens embraces the whole scene with the small figure of Scarlett moving from upper right to lower left through the mass of men. Finally, the camera, high in the air, shoots past a Confederate flag. 'Cut!' yells director Victor Fleming. And that's that."

The same day Fleming doubly earned Leigh's nickname for him, "Mr. Boom-Boom." As for his nickname for Leigh: Arthur Tovey, a Civil War extra who also doubled for Leslie Howard, enjoyed saying that when the shot was finished, one of the amputees asked, "Is her name really Fiddle-de-dee?" He especially enjoyed telling that to Leigh.

It was Selznick who declared to Sidney Howard, "I, for one, have no desire to produce any anti-Negro film," and labored with the writers "to be awfully careful that the Negroes come out decidedly on the right side of the ledger." When two bottom-feeders try to drag Scarlett from her wagon as she passes through a shantytown, it's the "big ragged white man" (Canutt) who poses the urgent physical threat, not, as in the novel, a black man with "shoulders and chest like a gorilla" who "fumbles between her breasts" inspiring "terror and revulsion" as she'd never known. And when Scarlett's second husband, Frank Kennedy, Ashley, and others ride out to avenge her, they're not cloaked in the robes of the Ku Klux Klan, as in the book. Selznick noted, "A group of men can go out to 'get' the perpetrators of an attempted rape without having long white sheets over them and without having their membership in a society as a motive." Fleming kept a rugged feel to the sequence in which the men return home from their raid feigning drunkenness. When Gable, Howard, and Harry Davenport (as Dr. Meade) began rehearsing "Massa's in de Cole, Cole Ground," he berated them for not sounding properly stewed: "That's entirely too good! Why, you sound like a college glee club! It won't do! Mess it up, get off key!"

This film's Old South is full of happy slaves contented with their lot. We're introduced to the New South with a disdainful shot of a jolly, rotund black carpetbagger singing "Marching Through Georgia" next to the evil Jonas Wilkerson, who attempts to grab Tara when Scarlett has difficulty paying her tax bill. But the actors imbue their characters with individuality and consciousness—especially McDaniel. Thomas Cripps observes in *Slow Fade to Black* (1977) that the result of these compromises and contradictions is a "confused ideological view that made it conservative and somewhat avant-garde at the same time."

Cukor, Wood, and Menzies all did sublime work with the Kansas-born McDaniel (like the white actresses, she had to learn to drawl), but it was Fleming who shot the pivotal scene when Rhett and Mammy share a drink over the birth of Bonnie Blue Butler. It's a testament to the film's marvelous sense of characterization—and a tribute to Selznick, Howard, and the other screenwriters, as well as Fleming—that the scene celebrates the growing respect of Mammy for Rhett as much as it does the birth. "Who wants a boy?" Rhett asks drolly. "Boys aren't any use to anybody. Don't you think I'm proof of that?" A riptide of affection and approval surges through Mammy's laugh. Maybe some of her joy springs from an offscreen practical joke sprung by Gable, who substituted real Scotch for her fake bourbon. "Had anybody else perpetrated such a stunt as Gable had managed," Myrick later recalled, Fleming "would have hit the ceiling. As it was, he and the cast and crew had a ten-minute laugh and shooting was begun again."

The much-maligned Butterfly McQueen, a Broadway actress who later said, "I hate listening to that silly, stupid handkerchief head when I see the movie," also conceded that Prissy's signature line, "I don't know nothin' 'bout birthin' babies," gave her a sort of immortality. Even Prissy has her moments of revolt: as the Union soldiers approach

Atlanta, she turns a spiritual into a covert expression of rebellion, singing to herself, "Jes' a few more days fer to tote de weary load." McQueen fought against stereotypes and demeaning on-set behavior. "I didn't want to eat the watermelon"—she didn't—and "I didn't want [Vivien Leigh] to actually slap me." (In the slap, filmed by Cukor, no direct contact is shown, but there is a mighty thud on the sound track.) She later recalled that during filming, "Everyone was wonderful. Olivia made us laugh . . . and Clark Gable was such a considerate gentleman." McDaniel said, "When I'm working, I mind my own business and do what I'm told to do." Was that a statement of compromise or artistic discipline, or both? McDaniel told McQueen, "It was better to earn $1,250 a week playing the part of a maid than $12.50 being a maid," and urged her to be more cooperative.

Blacks might have chafed privately at taking stereotype dialect direction from Myrick. But whatever the underlying prejudices of cast and crew, the making of the film appears to be an instance of melting-pot cooperation. The Atlanta native Evelyn Keyes wrote that when playing Suellen, "I never thought one way or the other about black actors sitting among us, that Hattie McDaniel even had a chair of her own, that they were earning more than I (easy to do)." In the most unaffected description of the whole production, Canutt acknowledged some friction with Everett Brown as Big Sam, in the scene where Sam saves Scarlett from the rapist Canutt played. But Canutt chalked up their trouble to the predictable tensions of a hard-nosed specialist teaching the ropes to a touchy performer. "I told him to quit behaving like a temperamental actor. Stunt work and staging fights was my business. If he'd just listen, we'd get the scene shot in such a way that we could both be proud of. Brown calmed down and, after a few more rehearsals the fight was filmed in one take with two cameras."

The black extras didn't automatically get that same respect. Early on, a group of them threatened a walkout unless the production removed signs marked "White" and "Colored" that had been posted over some portable toilets on an outdoor set. The pianist and singer Lennie Bluett, an extra marching with the Negro troops through Atlanta, says he and a friend kick-started the protest. He never knew whether someone put up the signs as some kind of sick joke.

"I got with the older guys about it, and they didn't want to rock the boat, afraid we'd be kicked off the picture if we raised the stink. So I was the instigator—and a friend of mine, about eighteen or nineteen then—and we said, listen, we got to stick together." They worked up the nerve to knock on Gable's dressing-room door and asked the actor to inspect the offensive signs. "He followed me out and stepped across phone lines and cables, and we walked about twenty, thirty feet to where the toilets were." As Bluett remembers it, Gable said, "I'll be goddamned." He got on the phone to Fleming, who called the prop master and told him, "If you don't get those signs down, you won't get your Rhett Butler." The signs came off immediately.

Fleming was superbly caring in his direction of children—even babies. Phillip Trent's second scene, nearly three months after he appeared in the Twelve Oaks "war room," featured Melanie and Ric Holt as her now-eleven-month-old son, Beau. In the original setup, Trent, as a returning Confederate soldier, was eating on Tara's steps with a fork and a wooden spoon. But Fleming, Trent recalled, gave the spoon to the baby to play with instead:

> We rehearsed several times without the baby and it was okay, but when the cameras were rolling . . . he started crying when he was not supposed to cry. Four times Victor tried to shoot the scene, and each time the baby cried. Victor said, "He seems to think he gets a cue to cry from the camera." He sat down on the steps next to us, he cooed and chuckled for the baby and even had orange juice brought to him because he thought the baby might be thirsty. Never once did I see Fleming lose his temper. I saw script changes brought to him all the time. I never once saw him act unprofessional.

"First they give me a forty-year-old Ashley Wilkes, then a British Scarlett O'Hara, and now, by God, a brown-eyed Bonnie Blue Butler!" So Fleming exclaimed in a memory related to Cammie King Conlon, who played Bonnie Blue, by her mother. "Supposedly, Selznick said if we light her properly and dress her in blue, no one will notice," says Conlon. She had already performed in a Blondie movie. Most of her recollections come from her mother, who could curl her "stick-straight hair" and teach the young actress her lines. (Eleanor Conlon, a journalist, married the Technicolor founder, Herbert Kalmus, in 1949.)

Fleming was usually direct and honest with child actors, but he felt compelled to pull some strings with Cammie. When she turned "bratty" one day, as her mother said, and kept muffing her lines, he knelt down to eye level and adopted a concerned parental tone: "I have a little girl your age. That's why I come to the studio and work, so I can take care of my little girl. And you see all these men on the set? They have little girls and little boys, too. Well, when you don't know your lines, we can't do our work, and we won't be able to take care of our little boys and girls." She never blew her dialogue again.

As early as March 14, memos flew between Selznick and MGM regarding the director's credit. Matters heated up in October when MGM insisted that Fleming's name had to be placed on the last title card, following the cast of characters and immediately preceding the picture, according to the latest pact between the producers and the Directors Guild. Selznick ignored that rule, because his deal with Fleming predated the guild contract.

Throughout the autumn, Fleming assisted in the editing, and in October and November, he filmed numerous insert shots, additions, and retakes. Greg Giese, seen in close-ups of both Beau and Bonnie Blue as infants, learned from his mother that after the first preview on September 9 in Riverside, California, Selznick decided "the babies they'd used just didn't look newborn." Fleming shared that perfectionism—and instinct for emotional reality—and oversaw fresh baby shots featuring Giese.

During this period, Selznick made the disastrous suggestion to Fleming that the credits should thank the directors who received no official titles on the film. He got no further than Cukor and Wood before Fleming interrupted and told him he didn't think it was necessary. Then he huffed off to remake the night scene of Scarlett, Prissy, and Melanie and her baby hiding from Yankee soldiers in a swampy creek under a bridge during a thunderstorm.

Real rain began to fall. Fleming believed that the scene would be impossible to light. Klune disagreed, and Fleming (in Klune's recollection) snapped, "You do whatever these Jews want you to do, don't you?" This outburst has fostered Fleming's reputation as an anti-Semite. But there's an air of roughhouse workplace comedy to the gibe, more along the lines of anti-bossism than anti-Semitism. Only under Selznick's obsessive hammering is Fleming known to have uttered an ethnic remark on a set. The Paramount executive Sam Jaffe contended that Fleming was anti-Semitic when he knew him in the 1920s but, as evidence, cited one instance of Fleming imitating his Jewish Harlem accent before falling back on hearing the director call Selznick "that goddamned Jew" during the making of *Gone With the Wind.*

America's ethnic badinage before World War II was coarse and unabashed, but Fleming appears to have kept it out of his workplace almost all the time. George Sidney, who shot screen tests at MGM before becoming a successful director himself (*Annie Get Your Gun*, *Scaramouche*), knew Fleming well, and recalled, "I'm half-Catholic, half-Jewish—Irish-Hungarian—and I never got an anti-Semitic feeling from him. You have to be small to have that kind of feeling, and he was bigger than that kind of thing."

While Selznick was juggling credits and vanity (including his own), he was also battling censors to retain the most famous exit line in the history of motion pictures: Rhett brushing off a now-repentant Scarlett with "Frankly, my dear, I don't give a damn!" (Minus the "frankly," he has the same line in the novel.) Fleming had shot that scene twice—first, as a backup, with the weak "I don't care." The prospect of that substitution could not have pleased him any more than Selznick.

It wasn't the only "damn" spoken in the picture, but it was the only one heard. Under Fleming's direction (and, for a retake, Wood's), Frank Coghlan Jr. played the young soldier who collapses in Rhett's face during the retreat from Atlanta. Coghlan wrote that when the scene continues and another soldier tries to pick him up, he responds, "Put me down, damn ya, I can walk"—and that the cussing was audible when he first saw the film that winter in Los Angeles. Coghlan thinks that Selznick expunged the line, believing his "damn" undercut Rhett's. If you watch for Coghlan's bit in the current prints of the movie, his mouth does move visibly but without a sound, and the camera cuts away.

Selznick won the censorship war based on Rhett's "damn," not Coghlan's. He compelled the Motion Picture Association board to amend the Production Code. "Damn" and "hell" could now be used when they were "essential and required for portrayal, in proper historical context, of any scene or dialogue based on historical fact or folklore, or for the presentation in proper literary context of a Biblical, or other religious quotation, or a quotation from a literary work provided that no such use should be permitted which is intrinsically objectionable or offends good taste."

In 1940, Leigh toted up Scarlett's flaws and virtues with conciseness and lucidity. On the negative side: humorlessness, pettiness, and "selfish egotism." On the positive side: "Her courage. She had more than I'll ever have." Leigh saw through Scarlett *and* identified with her:

"While Scarlett wasn't the most easygoing type, neither am I." Just weeks before Leigh's death, the actress declared, "I never liked Scarlett"; maybe that's why she doesn't sentimentalize her. Seconds after Rhett walks out on Scarlett, this indomitable dame returns to form and lets the thought of Tara cheer her up: "I'll go home, and I'll think of some way to get him back. After all, tomorrow is another day!" Writing in *Esquire* in 1961, the skeptical Dwight Macdonald praised the movie's pace and tough-mindedness. Preferring it to a couple of Tennessee Williams misfires, Macdonald observed, "At least there is some doubt as to whether the heroine is a bitch—or as to whether the heroine is only a bitch. That makes it more interesting, more grown-up. Adult entertainment, that's what I like about *Gone With the Wind.*"

The invitation to the wrap party listed Selznick as Jonas Wilkerson and Fleming as Big Sam. If you summon the proper context for the joke, with Selznick at the height of his prestige and *Gone With the Wind* as his make-or-break project, the gag takes on a starry glow. (At the party, Leigh presented Fleming with a pair of budgies for his daughters. He thanked her with a kiss that showed he was someone who knew how.)

Unfortunately, the fault lines soon cracked into a full-fledged rift. Fleming suggested giving Wood and Cukor a special thanks in the official program, only to see this sentence in the finished playbill: "There were five directors on *Gone With the Wind*, all personally supervised by David O. Selznick." Fleming wrongly blamed Selznick for this insult instead of the writer, MGM publicity maestro Howard Dietz. Words flew between MGM and Selznick over the affront, with Selznick proclaiming his respect and affection for Fleming, who did receive sole directing credit on the screen.

Even so, the press allotting Selznick major praise for the success of the first sound-era blockbuster spurred discussion in the ranks of the Directors Guild. In a lengthy missive to Guild president Frank Capra (who, Selznick said, had badly wanted to direct *Gone With the Wind* himself), Selznick wrote that he didn't "mean in any way to detract from the brilliant job that Victor did." Yet he then went on to itemize the contributions of Menzies, Cukor, and Wood. And in a highly unlikely notion of events, he protested that after the program dustup, he and Fleming "threw our arms around each other and decided not to let any outsiders spoil a long and warm friendship; and I thought that was the end of it, until some others took the matter up and decided to make it their issue, even when it was obviously of no interest to Victor."

Selznick quotes Fleming telling MGM colleagues that Selznick didn't merely produce the picture, "He wrote it, and he half directed it," while assuring him, "This is your picture, David. I am doing exactly what you tell me to do, and I hope it turns out all right." Selznick's overall purpose was to persuade Capra that the more Directors Guild members "talk about it, the more they are going to reveal just how much this was a producer-made picture."

That was a contentious tone to strike—especially in a letter Selznick encouraged Capra either to destroy or to use "in whole or in part" as a presentation to his board, or (in an odd wording) "for the excrescence of the Guild." (It's anyone's guess whether he chose "excrescence" to mean that the letter would enlarge the guild's understanding or inflame it.) Capra admired Fleming; six years later, he invited him to be part of his Liberty Pictures company, along with George Stevens and William Wyler. Selznick must have known that his words would get back to Fleming. Maybe he really felt, as he indicates to Capra, that Fleming would agree with him. Fleming did stay with the movie, attending the Riverside sneak and the L.A. press screening.

Although Lu told both daughters that Vic refused to go to either Atlanta or the Oscars because of the way Selznick had treated him, Fleming made plans to participate in the premiere in Atlanta on Friday, December 15; he would have flown in on the same plane as Gable and Lombard. That undoubtedly was a topic of discussion on the preceding Sunday, when he spent the day visiting Douglas Fairbanks in Santa Monica. Fairbanks was planning to remake his great hit *The Mark of Zorro* as *The Californian*, although this time he would take a supporting role. Fleming probably thought his old friend and mentor needed a pep talk; Fairbanks, for most of the 1930s, had not been able to launch a number of announced projects, but this one was about to take wing, and despite having heart problems, he'd passed a recent physical.

The following morning, Fairbanks suffered a mild heart attack and was put on immediate bed rest. Thirteen hours later, he had a second heart attack, this one fatal, in his bedroom overlooking the Pacific. A nurse came into the room when she heard his mastiff, Marco Polo, growling. "Doug has taken his last leap," someone in the Fairbanks organization told the newspapers.

The funeral was set for Thursday. Fleming chose to stay in California. He issued a dignified public statement: "Douglas Fairbanks was outstandingly the man who put motion into motion pictures. He lived and breathed action. He set an example that will remain part of the history of the films forever. He was a stanch [*sic*] friend and a fine influence." To Ed Sullivan, Fleming said, "The stars of today are lazy people," adding that Fairbanks was "the last of the great stars who really enjoyed working."

In Atlanta, Selznick's publicity machine had merged with local boosters to create a premiere that made attendees feel that the South had risen again. Between industry favors and local freebies, he created a tidal wave of publicity on the cheap. No black actors were invited, not even McDaniel, who would win a deserved Oscar as best supporting actress for Mammy. America was in the thick of that post-Reconstruction, pre–civil rights era when sympathizing with the fallen South bordered on nostalgia for separatism.

As president of Eastern Airlines, World War I ace Eddie Rickenbacker provided the plane that flew in Selznick, de Havilland, Leigh, and Olivier. After Gable, Lombard, and Howard Strickling arrived on the MGM plane, they traveled in a motorcade down Peachtree Street to their hotel; Gable was scheduled to raise the Stars and Bars there, but an elderly Confederate veteran received the dubious honor. Then they joined the rest of the Hollywood contingent at a charity costume ball put on by the Junior League at City Auditorium. Atlantans dusted off Confederate uniforms and antebellum costumes they either found in attics or rummage sales or made themselves to compete for costume prizes. Ten-year-old Martin Luther King Jr., son of the pastor of Ebenezer Baptist Church, sang spirituals as part of a choir clothed in slave garb. Introducing them, Clark Howell Jr., publisher of the *Atlanta Constitution*, intoned, "Can you smell the wisteria? Can't you hear the darkies singing? They're coming to the Big House!"

North Carolina's comical musical celebrity Kay Kyser, in town to promote his movie debut, *That's Right, You're Wrong*, led his orchestra in "Dixie" to an approving roar, with several rebel yells. The novelty swing-band leader beckoned, "C'mon chillun—let's dance!" and soon had high-style Atlantans swaying to songs like "I'm Fit to Be Tied" sung by Ginny Simms. NBC carried his performance live, and before leaving the stage, Kyser thanked Selznick "as a Southerner." After witnessing two days of the celebration, a prominent local fertilizer dealer, Augustus D. Adair, recorded in his diary on December 16, "The *Gone With the Wind* festivities ended last night. I hope Atlanta will settle down once more. She's been frantic all week."

While Kyser's band played on, Fleming was hatching a meaningful memorial for Fairbanks during a long, drunken wake that ended up at Lucey's, an Italian restaurant near Paramount Studios. Doug's demise had leveled him as no death had done since his father's. Fleming's plan expressed his desire to relive the prank-filled days when he and Doug would cavort on trains, planes, and automobiles around the globe. Some friends of Doug's, including Fleming and Ted Reed, didn't like the brief, formal, invitation-only funeral held at the Wee Kirk o' the Heather in Forest Lawn Memorial Park. Fairbanks was laid out in morning clothes. The church held only about a hundred mourners; others had to sit outside and listen on loudspeakers; and many of Fairbanks's employees, left out of all that, held their own memorial service at his studio. His permanent grave was built later; that day, his coffin was placed in a temporary crypt, next to that of Will Rogers.

As Reed handed down the story to his son Robert:

> They felt [the formal funeral] did not honestly reflect Fairbanks's real personality. After a lengthy discussion, this group of five or six decided that the right thing to do was to exhume the freshly buried Fairbanks, sit him up at graveside, and have a final conversation with their friend. The conversation went on, punctuated with a lot of drinks, and the plan was eventually abandoned because no one was sober enough to carry it out. I remember my father recalling it with both remorse and relief.

The plan would come to life four decades later, in a movie: Blake Edwards's bleak 1981 Hollywood satire, *S.O.B.* Edwards knew Fleming from afar; he started out as an actor, and one of his first roles was in Fleming's *A Guy Named Joe.* He also had an uncle, the writer-director-actor Owen Crump, who was married to Fairbanks's niece Lucile, and Edwards heard the funeral story from him. The climax of *S.O.B.* is a case of one savvy, irreverent director paying homage to another. The friends of a late, crazed producer (Richard Mulligan)—his director (William Holden), PR man (Robert Webber), and doctor (Robert Preston)—decide to save him from a soundstage funeral full of the folks who drove him nuts. They steal his corpse from the mortuary, take him to his beach home so they can toast him, then *really* toast him when they shove him into a flaming rowboat for a makeshift Viking funeral.

The scene is similar to the tale Errol Flynn told about John Barrymore's pals stealing the Great Profile's body from a funeral home in

1942, then propping it up in Flynn's home as a lark. In *S.O.B.*, Preston says, "Good night, sweet prince," over Mulligan's body, in a direct reference to Barrymore. But Edwards confided to Fay McKenzie, who had a small role in *S.O.B.*, that he based the sequence on Fleming's scenario. "Blake did love to tell that story," she says.

Against all odds, *Gone With the Wind* was an immediate sensation. It turned the search for blockbuster combinations of art and extravaganza into the American movie dream.

Although he didn't usually attend premieres of his MGM films, Fleming went to the Los Angeles premiere at the Carthay Circle theater. He and Lu shared a limousine with Gable, Lombard, and Gable's father and new stepmother, William and Edna. They were the last to arrive, and when fans caught a glimpse of Gable, and Lombard in gold lamé, "pandemonium broke loose," the papers reported, and the Flemings took charge of William and Edna as Gable greeted his fans and posed for photos.

Fleming, nominated for best director, missed the Academy Awards ceremony at the Cocoanut Grove on February 29, 1940. The stated reason was influenza. Just as likely, however happy he was to play Selznick's "Big Sam" at the wrap party, he didn't want to do it on the industry's night of nights. In Hollywood's annus mirabilis of 1939, also nominated for best director were William Wyler for *Wuthering Heights*, John Ford for *Stagecoach*, Frank Capra for *Mr. Smith Goes to Washington*, and Sam Wood for *Goodbye, Mr. Chips*. *Gone With the Wind* went on to win a total of eight Oscars and two additional special awards. The film of Fleming accepting his Oscar from Mervyn LeRoy was taken on March 8 for a Warner Bros. short subject and was directed by Capra; columnists gleefully reported that Fleming and LeRoy kept blowing their scripted lines. In his brief remarks, Fleming never breaks his deadpan as he thanks the people he says really deserve the award—the crew, not the filmmakers who were hogging praise in print.

Although Fleming and Selznick didn't work together again, they did swap information and insight about projects and performers. Selznick's papers contain a plaintive note to his publicist, Whitney Bolton, several years later: "I wish you'd call Victor Fleming and tell him about the opening and ask him whether he'd like any tickets for himself and party with my compliments. Let me know what he says." There's no record of Fleming's response.

Right up to Fleming's death in 1949, Selznick exerted influence on the director's career and personal life. At the time he was mounting *Gone With the Wind*, Selznick had been concluding negotiations to sign a young Swedish beauty who had the potential impact of another Greta Garbo. Rand Brooks remembered sitting next to Leslie Howard under hair dryers. As they looked in the mirror, there she was—Howard's future co-star in *Intermezzo* and Fleming's last great love—Ingrid Bergman.

23

Dr. Jekyll and Mr. Hyde

Before Fleming did his epic salvaging of *The Wizard of Oz* and *Gone With the Wind*, he and Spencer Tracy, still flush with the success of their partnership on *Captains Courageous* and *Test Pilot*, planned on teaming up for an adaptation of Marjorie Kinnan Rawlings's superb novel *The Yearling*. After *Gone With the Wind* was finished, Fleming and Tracy approached John Steinbeck in December 1939 about filming *The Red Pony*, based on four linked stories set on a Salinas Valley, California, ranch early in the century. Its tale of a boy facing the death of a beloved animal and growing into a man made it close kin to *The Yearling*—with the added benefit of not requiring filming in Florida's Everglades. But Steinbeck stunned Fleming and Tracy when he treated them as big-picture men to be exploited for his own ends rather than as fellow artists or craftsmen.

No author fared better at the hands of Hollywood than Steinbeck with the back-to-back productions of *Of Mice and Men* (1939) and *The Grapes of Wrath* (1940), yet he proposed that the actor and director raise money by subscription and not offer anyone a salary—then he would give the story gratis as well as write the screenplay. He wanted the film distributed only where local governments could ensure that box-office revenue went to provide children's hospital beds. Although Fleming told Steinbeck he thought the movie could pull in $2 million, he and Tracy didn't respond to this offer, and Steinbeck took it off the table in January 1940. Instead, Steinbeck began discussing *The Red Pony* with his *Of Mice and Men* director, Lewis Milestone (who made it in 1949).

The repercussions of Steinbeck's non-negotiation with Fleming rattled through MGM for several months. Mayer wouldn't permit Tracy to voice the narration for *The Forgotten Village*, the Steinbeck-written documentary about modernization encroaching on a rural Mexican hamlet. When Fleming and Tracy returned to the idea of making *The Yearling*, Steinbeck spoke of taking court action if *The Yearling* movie used Rawlings's name for her boy hero, Jody, because the boy hero of *The Red Pony* was called Jody, too. (When Milestone filmed *The Red Pony*, the boy's name became Tom; Steinbeck's son, Thom, was born on August 2, 1944.)

After years of wrangling, Fleming signed his first long-term contract with MGM, to start on January 1, 1940, and last until December 31, 1944. To get his signature, the studio had to guarantee that he could terminate his contract if Eddie Mannix, Mayer, or Loew's president, Nicholas Schenck, left the company, pledge not to loan him out to other studios, and remove morality and insurance clauses that Fleming found insulting (he thought these clauses were "directed against troublesome actors and actresses, and he feels that he does not fall in this category as a troublemaker or drunkard, etc.," an MGM functionary reported). And, as summarized in a studio memo, "On pictures directed by Fleming, we agree there shall be *no producer credit* (this in lieu of his request that he be permitted to produce and direct every second picture if he so desires)."

Fleming kept operating much as he had before. He did prep work for *The Yearling*, including sussing out locations in Florida. He shot retakes of Tracy and Gable in Conway's *Boom Town* and laid plans for a Gable vehicle based on the nineteenth-century Western con man and outlaw Soapy Smith. (Jack Conway made it as *Honky Tonk*, with Gable playing a fictionalized version of Smith named Candy Johnson.)

That June, Fleming helped Gable buy a five-hundred-acre cattle ranch in Arizona. Hedda Hopper reported that they spent a week "putting up in tourist camps, and nobody recognized them." Fleming and Tracy looked at test shots for a potential Jody for *The Yearling*, then took their daughters (Tracy's son, John, stayed home with his mother) on a sailing vacation in British Columbia, where they visited Fred Lewis. Mannix wired a request for Fleming to okay the characters' wardrobes for scenic shots. "We should prepare immediately to get the best of all scenic beauty to be shot before the first September," wrote Mannix, but preproduction on *The Yearling* would stumble on for months.

Something about this career plateau made Fleming meditative with the press, and he gave a frank interview to Sheilah Graham. Her lover, F. Scott Fitzgerald, had written the 1939 speech for her that coined the comparison between Fleming as a "man's director" and Cukor as a "woman's director." But when she asked Fleming about that label (apparently she was the only person ever to ask him directly), he quickly tore it off, saying, "I like directing women, too." He discounted reports of his fights with Vivien Leigh. He painted himself, proudly, as one of the silent-film directors who "were thrown out on their ears and told they were through," naming others such as John Ford, King Vidor, Frank Borzage, and Henry King, then drily noted that only two of the stage directors brought in for sound had stayed on top, Cukor and John Cromwell. The way Graham quoted Fleming, he portrayed the end of his tenure at Paramount melodramatically: "After six months of idleness they decided to give me another chance. I made *The Virginian* (one of the most successful pictures of all time) and then walked out on them!" He also said he considered *Reckless* his worst picture. He acknowledged his new contract, and said, "But I was paid just as much fifteen years ago. The only difference was, you could save most of it then; now you give it to the government."

Back home, Lu's daughter with Arthur Rosson, Helene, divorced from Jaime del Valle and with a six-year-old daughter, began dating a young MGM contract player, Lee Bowman. Fleming emphatically did not approve—yet Helene's view of Fleming as an elegant man-about-town might have bled into her passion for Bowman. Helene revered her mom's husband. "I was practically in love with [Vic]," she told David Stenn. "Women just fell all over themselves to get at him, he was so attractive: tall, dressed beautifully." Helene regarded the debonair six-foot Bowman as a similar catch, but Fleming took an instant dislike to him. Bowman cut against Fleming's goal to keep his household out of the Hollywood limelight and untouched by phoniness and glamour.

When Helene and Bowman became a match, she'd been divorced for five years, and he'd just appeared in his finest picture by far, Leo McCarey's *Love Affair*, the apex of the "you'll laugh, you'll cry" kind of movie. (It's Charles Boyer and Irene Dunne's film.) Helene and Lee first met at the West Side Tennis Club in August 1939. Lee's younger brother Hunter says, "Helene was a good tennis player and she was not stupid, by the wildest stretch of the imagination. She set her sights on Lee, and got him." His meticulously publicized romances had included Joan Bennett, Lucille Ball, and Joan Crawford, but Hunter discounts that second Joan. "We were a pretty snobbish family," he says. "He might have laid her a few times, but no way would Lee have married someone like that." Snobbery—and the ambition that went with it—provoked Fleming's immediate disdain. "Daddy thought [Helene and Lee] were social climbers and kind of phony, you know, although [I thought] Lee was a wonderful man," Victoria says.

The director of *Bataan*, Tay Garnett, a hardy filmmaker like Fleming who'd been a Navy aviator and a silent-comedy gag man (and also, like Mahin, had been married to Patsy Ruth Miller), said Bowman "looked as if he were a young ambassador to the Court of St. James." Bowman's cultivated aura wasn't put on—he wasn't that good an actor. His thrice-married mother, Elizabeth "Bessie" Pringle Brunson Fauntleroy Bowman Clyde, grew up as Southern aristocracy on Kingstree, the Brunson family plantation outside Charleston, South Carolina. (They also had timber and hunting properties as well as farmland in Georgia and Florida.) But there was a hex on Bessie's private life. Both her mother and her grandmother would fatally burn—in accidents with a fireplace and an overheated stove, respectively. And her first husband, a dentist and mineral-water entrepreneur from Staunton, Virginia, contracted a debilitating illness.

Bessie bore her second husband, Luther Lee Bowman, three sons: Lee, Pringle, and Hunter. Luther, also from a wealthy Staunton family, was a handsome go-getter who tried to establish a brewery in Cincinnati with his brother; when it failed, he became an income tax collector. After that marriage fell apart, Bessie married a wealthy distant cousin, William Clyde, who supported Lee's pursuits of singing and dancing at the Cincinnati Conservatory of Music as well as varsity athletics (gymnastics and track) in public school.

Lee befriended the Cincinnati native Tyrone Power, and in state track meets challenged the future fastest man in the world, Cleveland's Jesse Owens. When Bowman entered Columbia University in 1932, he was bent on lawyering. Fred Astaire movies changed his life. "He saw the improvement Astaire had made [from film to film], and said, hell, if he can do it, I can do it," says Hunter. He enrolled at the American Academy of Dramatic Arts; a talent scout noticed him in his graduation play. At age nineteen he had a Paramount contract. Bowman drove to Hollywood in a Chrysler convertible with red leather seats. Even before he landed his first movie, in 1937, *Internes Can't Take Money* (the first film adaptation of a Max Brand Dr. Kildare story), he was popping up in Louella Parsons's column. But the Bowman hex continued. In

January 1937, Pringle, the middle Bowman brother, died of peritonitis after a Puerto Rican gang attacked him and his roommate, William Chatfield, an art student and old friend from Cincinnati, in Harlem. Neither had been robbed; both had been drinking.

Bowman's mottled family history might have rubbed Fleming the wrong way, and his behavior spurred the director's distaste and distrust. When the actor tapped a cigarette against the back of his hand to pack its tobacco—in front of King Vidor, no less—Fleming erupted, "Don't do that. I hate anybody who does that. That's really cheap and effete and that's awful to do that in front of somebody." (He, of course, was a roll-your-own kind of guy.) Winnie Weshler, a childhood friend of Victoria and Sally's, says Fleming used to call Bowman "that half-assed talent." Victoria says, "My father had certain ways of thinking about life, certain standards, certain ways to operate, as we all do. The Bowmans had another. And their way of operating was never approved of by my father, because he would consider that sort of phony. They were movie stars and getting into the movie magazines, and, you know, all that bullshit. Daddy did his best to keep us away from the movie scene." The Bowmans inflamed Fleming's frustration because they showed him that he *couldn't* keep his household at Moraga Drive distant from the movie scene. How could he? He'd become the biggest director at MGM. In February 1941, Helene eloped with Bowman to Tijuana. The idea of Bowman—who had just climbed from a Paramount contract to one at MGM—as part of his extended family sent Fleming into emotional orbit.

Luckily, another MGM purchase from Paramount put Fleming back into the director's chair. In March 1940, MGM announced that it had bought Robert Louis Stevenson's *Dr. Jekyll and Mr. Hyde* from the rival studio, including rights to a stage adaptation that had grafted two contrasting female characters onto Stevenson's sexless story. The studio saw it as a showcase for Robert Donat, the critical and popular favorite who beat Gable's Rhett Butler for the 1939 best actor Oscar with his moving performance in *Goodbye, Mr. Chips.* Donat doubted the story's dramatic possibilities. He also worried about Americans messing with its Englishness and asked an MGM executive whether the studio could hire a British director or "fly a first-line American director" over there. Mannix planned a London production in May, but by then German submarines were blocking commercial Atlantic crossings. The Battle of Britain began in July.

Victor Saville, head of MGM production in Britain, had commanded back-to-back successes with Sam Wood's *Chips* and King Vidor's *Citadel* (1938). Saville was vacationing in Hollywood when Mayer closed down his British office. The mogul persuaded him to stay on in America and handed him several prestige assignments, including *A Woman's Face*, a remake of a Swedish Ingrid Bergman vehicle, starring Joan Crawford as a woman whose facial disfigurement and its surgical cure mold and alter her behavior. So it was eerily natural for Saville to segue to *Dr. Jekyll and Mr. Hyde.*

When executives started looking for a Hollywood actor's actor to take Donat's place in the double role, the obvious choice was Tracy—and Tracy's favorite director was Fleming. As with many of Fleming's singular achievements, *Dr. Jekyll and Mr. Hyde* was an assignment that became personal. (It helped that Mahin had been writing the script for Donat.)

Fleming told the movie's publicists that he set out to make a version more realistic than the 1932 Rouben Mamoulian production that won an Oscar for Fredric March or the 1920 silent (directed by John S. Robertson, shot by Fleming's mentor Roy Overbaugh) that garnered raves for John Barrymore. Fleming meant he wanted his version to be *emotionally* more realistic—and he succeeded, thanks to his gut understanding of conflicting drives and his nose for the contemporaneity of classic tales. Yet the film would be more realistic physically, too. Tracy wished to play Hyde without any makeup or prosthetics. The filmmakers settled on a compromise: Hyde's makeup merely exaggerated Tracy's features. It was light-years removed from the ape-man look of March's Hyde or the bullet-headed bogeyman of Barrymore's. This *Dr. Jekyll and Mr. Hyde* makes you believe that Hyde *could* bring a pretty girl under his sadistic sway.

In an underrated performance, at once trenchant and sensually alive, Tracy combines his gifts for tortured nobility and raffish urbanity. As Jekyll, he conveys the frustration of being a "good" man in Victorian times. In polite company he can't be affectionate with Beatrix, his betrothed; even in the demimonde he's not supposed to receive and return a kiss from Ivy, the good-hearted barmaid. His frustrations become concrete in flamboyant hallucination sequences more effective than any of the suppressed-memory dream sequences in Hitchcock's *Spellbound.* Best of all, *Dr. Jekyll and Mr. Hyde* has Ingrid Bergman as Ivy, in full bloom. Bergman was under personal contract to Selznick, who ran footage of her for Fleming while they were working on *Gone*

With the Wind. Selznick knew that for his protégée, this director's interest would reap professional dividends.

George Sidney joked that in his early days at MGM he had "a secret service" arrangement with Fleming to prepare sets and conduct screen tests. The most memorable audition was for Ivy. He was shooting a redheaded starlet named Edythe Marriner when Fleming crossed the soundstage, crooked his finger at Sidney to come over, and asked to talk to Marriner for a moment. In a terrific illustration of what Hecht meant by "aloof and poetical," Fleming tried to make her understand the scene by telling her a parable. She should think of herself as a lady whose man "comes back from traveling around the world. Everybody else has brought their women big presents of satin and silk and jade and beautiful jewels. And all this boy has brought you is a precious vessel containing sacred waters from Africa and the Orient." As Sidney remembered, "Victor asks the woman if she understands, and she says, 'Oh yes, oh yes.' Then I tell the cameraman to get ready. I see Edythe's finger prodding me, come here." He goes over and she pleads: "Tell me, what the fuck did I say I understood?" Ingrid Bergman, as Sidney said, got the part instead, but right after that Edythe "broke loose"—under her screen name, Susan Hayward.

Both Saville and Bergman claimed that Ingrid was cast as Jekyll's virginal Beatrix, not Ivy; they said Lana Turner was cast as Ivy and that Bergman lobbied for the two to switch roles. Actually, Saville and Fleming handed Ivy to Bergman long before they cast Turner as Beatrix. (Bergman turns up on a January 28, 1941, cast list for *Dr. Jekyll and Mr. Hyde* as Ivy; no one is listed playing Beatrix, and it further notes that both Maureen O'Hara and Ruth Hussey were testing for the role. A studio memo dated five days earlier complains, "No sketches can be made or wardrobe started for Beatrix until she is cast.") Miriam Hopkins had scored a sensation playing "Champagne Ivy" against March's Jekyll and Hyde in the 1932 version, and Bergman, as she wrote in her memoir, "loved this girl, this barmaid Ivy," the opposite of "a Hollywood peaches-and-cream girl." In Bergman's account, she proposed playing Ivy to Fleming, who said, "That's impossible. How can you with your looks? It's not to be believed." According to Bergman, she made a test "without telling" Selznick, and it won Fleming over. When Selznick said, "But she just can't play that kind of role," Fleming sent him the test, and "David pulled a face and said, 'Well . . . okay.' "

Bergman may have been, as Selznick put it, "the Palmolive Garbo," but even in screen terms she was no virgin. She had broken through internationally in the Swedish and Hollywood versions of *Intermezzo* (1936, 1939), playing a young pianist who has an affair with her married musical mentor (Leslie Howard in the Selznick-produced American film). In the recently completed *Adam Had Four Sons*, none other than Hayward had stolen the picture from her as a bad girl. Bergman wasn't going to allow any similar kind of theft on *Dr. Jekyll and Mr. Hyde.* (Of course, Bergman would reach her peak five years later as the heroic ex-slut of Hitchcock's *Notorious.*)

Married since 1937 to Dr. Petter Lindström and with a three-year-old daughter, the twenty-five-year-old actress wrote that she fell in love with Fleming during filming (stories of her involvement with Spencer Tracy are apocryphal at best). Bergman, whose father died when she was twelve and whose first romance, at eighteen, was with the forty-one-year-old stage director Edvin Adolphson in Sweden, would, like Clara Bow, discover both a romantic focus and an inspirational father figure in Fleming. "Although I'd known many fine directors in Sweden, this man added another dimension to what I'd known before. As soon as he came close to me I could tell by his eyes what he wanted me to do, and this has happened with very few directors in my career; I could tell if he was satisfied, in doubt, or delighted."

Turner, for her part, was the Sweater Girl, undeniably sexy but not yet, in the public mind, the platinum blonde adulteress of her iconic role in Garnett's 1946 *The Postman Always Rings Twice* or even the doomed good-bad chorine of *Ziegfeld Girl*, which didn't come out till April 1941. (In fact, MGM's publicists put out feature stories saying *Dr. Jekyll and Mr. Hyde* would be the picture to help her shed that Sweater Girl image, even in the part of Beatrix.) In Turner's memoir, *she's* the one who wanted to exchange parts. She says she was cast as Ivy and implored Mayer to let her out of it, because "that role is so deep, I don't know if I could trust a director enough to let me try to reach those emotions." According to Turner, it was Mayer who said, "What about Beatrix? A nice, well-bred Victorian girl."

The truth: before Turner entered the picture, MGM announced Laraine Day as Beatrix. Whether because retakes were needed on Day's active project, *The Bad Man*, a Wallace Beery vehicle, or because the outré dream sequences scared off the proper Mormon actress, Day bowed out. Turner didn't join the cast until February 3, the day before shooting began. The idea that Bergman and Turner swapped parts just made for a better yarn. But the yarn is plenty strong without that knot.

Detail obsessed as always, Selznick urged Fleming and the cinematographer Joseph Ruttenberg to study how the cinematographer Gregg Toland had photographed Bergman on *Intermezzo:* "Toland did such wonderful things with her that you might as well all get the benefit of seeing the picture." But Fleming understood without anyone's help that Bergman could be the image of carnal purity. He and Ruttenberg did so well with Hyde's monstrosity and her imperiled animal innocence that Cukor and Ruttenberg duplicated the gaslit effects of *Dr. Jekyll and Mr. Hyde* for Bergman and Charles Boyer in the cat-and-mouse games of *Gaslight* (1944). "He got things out of me that were different from anything I had done before," she said of Fleming to a reporter for the *Times* of London. "What more can an actor want?"

Mahin's script sets a bold context for the story. It begins in church, with a minister (C. Aubrey Smith) praising Queen Victoria for her righteous example. The pews include Beatrix and Jekyll and his prospective father-in-law, Sir Charles Emery (Donald Crisp)—and also a heckler (Barton MacLane) who scoffs at Victoria for taking all the fun out of life. When other parishioners hustle the heckler out, Jekyll follows and learns that he'd been a model citizen and devoted husband before an explosion rocked his mind. Jekyll decides he's the perfect test case for separating good and evil in the soul of man. Unfortunately, the poor bloke dies before the doctor can put him to the test; Jekyll has been too busy juggling the demands of scientific research, free clinical work, an upscale practice, and a high-society catch like Beatrix. He reckons the only way to advance his research is to become his own guinea pig.

All the major *Dr. Jekyll and Mr. Hyde* films—Barrymore's, the March-Mamoulian production, and Fleming's—illustrate the Achilles' id of Jekyll's psyche in exactly the same way: the doctor encounters a demimondaine who makes him feel temptation without acting on it. In both Fleming's and Mamoulian's versions, Jekyll and his friend Dr. Lanyon rescue this lower-depths flower, Ivy, from an assault, then take her to her modest flat, where Jekyll briefly checks her aches and pains. Ivy doesn't know that Jekyll is a doctor and takes his examination as a proposition. In Mamoulian's version, the scene becomes a striptease, staged to the director's written specifications. Hopkins's Ivy, a saucy wench, makes a frontal assault on Jekyll. As soon as he checks out her bruised thigh, she grabs his hand and presses it down on her flesh. She asks Jekyll to turn his back as she gets ready for bed, then slithers off her stockings and undoes her dress and the rest of her underthings. When Jekyll turns his head, he sees what we do—her naked profile between the sheets. She pulls him to her for a kiss, her bare back to the camera, just as Lanyon enters and interrupts the scene. She keeps flashing her comely leg, rocking it back and forth on the side of the bed, as she asks Jekyll with a croon to come back "so-o-o-n." After he exits, the words seem to whistle through his head.

Ten years later, the Production Code put any similar streak of nudity out of the question. Fleming gives Ivy's come-on to Jekyll the even hotter glow of love at first sight. As we find out later, this Ivy isn't an entertainer like Hopkins's "Champagne Ivy," just a barmaid at the cabaret known as the "Palace of Frivolities" who amuses the customers when she sings along with the stage show. After Jekyll and Lanyon (Ian Hunter) chase off her attacker, Bergman's Ivy lifts her head to see Dr. Jekyll standing there appraising her, with a half smile. She beams at the sight of this calm gent. She's an embattled innocent with a sexual readiness and an instinctive, premoral integrity that make her difficult to resist. Every instant in the sequence becomes erotic from the moment Jekyll lifts Ivy to keep her off her twisted ankle. He carries her to her upstairs room and drops her on the bed and turns up the gaslight. He asks, "You want me to have a look at you, don't you?" Ivy reacts, "I don't know. Yer looking, ain't you?"

In Mamoulian's version, March reacts lightly and gaily to Hopkins's unrestrained lust. In Fleming's, Bergman's ardor deeply affects Tracy. Who wouldn't succumb to Bergman's Ivy? Everything about her is erotic and touching, from her voluptuous form to her Scandinavian-cum-Cockney vocalizing. Saville said he coached Bergman "most mornings to perfect her accent—we decided on the very posh upper-Tooting style—'Ouw, yereversonice, aren't yer.' " Bergman's Ivy is delighted that Jekyll asks to look at her side. "Yer aren't half the fast one, aren't you?" she asks, taking down her blouse. At that point, Jekyll could be another literary doctor, Tomas, in *The Unbearable Lightness of Being* (1988), telling his lovers, "Take off your clothes." He makes clear to Ivy that he and Lanyon are physicians. When she can't pronounce or comprehend the word "physicians" and is startled to learn he's a doctor, Tracy becomes more distant and comical in his demeanor. But she continues to come on to him. He's the one who's over his head when Bergman bares her ankle and leg for his inspection.

In a bit of business that Fleming and Mahin pick up from the earlier version but imbue with more sensuousness and gravity, Jekyll warns Ivy that her garter is too tight; it could impair the circulation. She offers it as partial payment for his care, then kisses him. She's mortified that he might think of her as a whore and not as a woman in love. "You're a girl with a heart just where it ought to be," he reassures her, "maybe a little too generous, that's all." He tells her that if she knew him, she'd know he didn't want to be there; they were just being "foolish." Ivy retaliates for the insult: she declares *she* knows that their kiss "wasn't all in fun"—and Tracy's sudden sober expression suggests Jekyll's agreement. Under Fleming's direction, these two robust performers manage liquid emotional shifts.

The composer Franz Waxman, in his potent, subtle score, uses the period song "See Me Dance the Polka" even before we hear it in Ivy's saloon. This merry strain grows ambiguous as it follows Jekyll and Ivy through their bedroom scene and then comes up again unexpectedly as Lanyon scolds Jekyll for loose behavior. ("Polka" had been a giant hit for the songwriter George Grossmith, co-author of *The Diary of a Nobody* and a sometime Savoyard; Martin Savage played him in Mike Leigh's *Topsy-Turvy*.)

The backdrop to the last temptation of Dr. Jekyll is the refusal of Sir Charles Emery to let his daughter Beatrix wed him soon. In Mahin's script, Sir Charles doubts Jekyll as much for his public displays of affection as for his misplaced professional priorities and his heretical view that he can isolate man's good and evil sides. As he locks horns with Sir Charles, Tracy's solid, confident Jekyll represents adult independence from meaningless proprieties, not youthful ardor like March's Jekyll, who urges his fiancée to push up their wedding date in their very first scene, and not innocence like John Barrymore's. (In the Barrymore silent, Jekyll's prospective father-in-law, a habitué of Victorian London's sexual underworld, thinks Jekyll isn't experienced *enough*.) Tracy's Jekyll moves from accompanying Beatrix at church to mock-nibbling her knuckles in the carriage outside. Rather than a matinee idol jumping out of his skin, he's a well-rounded grown man with a forward-looking sense of what it means to be well-adjusted. It makes more sense that when *his* cork pops—in one hallucination, literally—the effects are catastrophic.

Although Bergman said Tracy reassured her at the start of filming ("You know, I'm scared of my part, too, but then aren't we all? I guess it's the name of the game"), she thought he "wasn't really very happy" during the picture. She surmised, "He didn't like doing these two characterizations; the sane doctor and the monster Hyde. He wanted to play himself, his own personality, which of course was the warm and marvelous personality that made him a great movie star."

But there were practical reasons for his grouchiness. An illness kept him out of the studio for most of January, delaying the tailor Eddie Schmidt from properly adjusting the costumes, designed to contrast the grotesque dandy Hyde with the understated gentleman and shirt-sleeved researcher Jekyll. And Tracy wanted to undergo the transformation not just without tricks or makeup but even without a mysterious potion. He wished to portray Jekyll as a good doctor and Mr. Hyde as a result of drugs and alcohol, carrying on depraved acts of hedonism and/or cruelty in a disreputable neighborhood or town.

In Tracy's vision, Beatrix would still have been the virginal fiancée, but Ivy would have been Hyde's dream prostitute, aching for debauchery. Hepburn said he wanted her to play both parts. According to Mannix, "Mr. Mayer thought that if Spence flipped out when he drank booze and took dope, it would be too close to home for a lot of people, and besides, it would make a 'message picture,' which L.B. hated."

But Tracy's determination to steer Hyde away from out-and-out monstrosity persisted, to the ultimate good of the picture. "I even suggested that Hyde never be pictured, except maybe the back of his ear or something like that, but it never worked out," he said. The relatively spare makeup adjustments that Fleming approved flare Tracy's nostrils and sharpen his nose, give him devilish laugh-lines around unblinking eyes, and make his mouth more simian and his mane and eyebrows more ominously hirsute.

In the March-Mamoulian picture, the photographer, Karl Struss, revived a trick from the leper scenes in the silent *Ben-Hur* to depict what Vladimir Nabokov called Jekyll's "hydizations": Struss rendered jolting facial transformations in real time by shooting colored makeup with rotating colored filters. But MGM couldn't duplicate the results and didn't want to order special filters from the Corning Glass Company. And Fleming and his editor, Harold Kress, hoped to avoid imitating the previous picture, anyway. Kress observed that when Mamoulian and Struss shot the star's entire face and body, "Fredric March dropped his hands down, they cut to the hand, hair started growing, cutaway, cutaway, all cutaways." (In the pivotal scene, Mamoulian does, indeed, swing Struss's camera down from Jekyll's face, then jump-cut and move to one hand, then go back up and down and jump-cut again before descending to the other hand.)

Kress dismissed the notion that cartoonists should animate the change from Jekyll to Hyde over shots of Tracy's face, "the way they did the old flip cards." (Kress and Saville mentioned seeking advice from Walt Disney, but a studio memo specifies tests made by "Mr. Sprunk of the cartoon department.") Ultimately, Kress sought to direct the metamorphoses himself. He told Tracy, "I've got an idea. The motion picture [camera] will be locked off, steel riveted to the stage floor so nobody can move it. Next to you we'll have one of those old-fashioned cameras with the big plate behind it and an artist who will sketch you. I'm only going to shoot your face, it will be so effective if we can see your face changing. There will be a long makeup table, all the pieces for your changes will be laid out and you'll be in a barber chair with wheels." Fleming gave his blessing. But Saville, Kress recalled, said, "Young man, you're just the film editor on this picture, this is none of your goddamn business and I'm going to have you fired!" The assistant director, Tom Andre, called Kress at home and said, "We hear you're not on the lot, stick by the phone."

Saville soon learned that Fleming was fiercely protective of his crew. (And before the film reached the theaters, Saville would learn how adamant Fleming was about the details of his own contract.) The director canceled the day's shooting, though all three leads were on the set. Then he and Tracy marched into Mayer's office and backed up Kress. The editor remembered Mayer ordering Saville's return to England, but the producer did stay on the picture; Mayer simply barred him from the editing room and the stage where Kress and Tracy plied their magic.

Kress found Tracy "a dream to work with." An artist sketched his position to keep him in proper alignment, Kress operated a camera by remote control, and the star went through forty-six makeup changes. Kress talked Tracy through it like a silent director: "Okay Spence, get ready, we're rolling now, just a little grimace, a little more, you fight it, fight it, cut." In the end, Kress was able "to make a continuous series of dissolves," always staying on Tracy's face. (Mamoulian had used quicker, clumsier dissolves to show March's Hyde reverting to Jekyll.)

Franz Waxman's score made a signal contribution, too. Like Bernard Herrmann or John Williams at their best, Waxman imbued tension music with operatic sweep. (Christopher Palmer later crafted a symphonic suite out of his score; Waxman was working on full-scale opera version for the New York City Opera at the time of his death.) During one of Jekyll's hydizations, Waxman utilizes a string of half notes that Williams duplicated, consciously or not, as the shark's theme in *Jaws*. In the climactic scene, when Jekyll involuntarily changes back into Hyde and Lanyon shoots him dead, Tracy wanted to speak desperately through his dying action. Kress said, "We'll do it just like a music number with playback. We'll make the sound track first." Tracy mouthed the words to a playback disc. For his skill and ingenuity, Kress earned an Oscar nomination; so did Ruttenberg and Waxman.

Despite his beef with Fleming over Kress and a more intense one over final credit, Saville memorialized the director with fond respect. "Victor was not only well informed, he was, above all, never hurried into making a decision that required deep thought. Although of a completely different temperament—I've made a few slapdash decisions in my time—I enjoyed working with him because I learned much from his profound knowledge." As an example of Fleming's willingness to spend "long hours to make up his mind as to how many angels can stand on the head of a pin," Saville recalled a conference with the production designer Cedric Gibbons about the opening, set in a "fashionable West End church." Fleming sat silently as Saville and Gibbons discussed the scope of the scene, until Saville asked, "What's worrying you, Victor?" "You know," Fleming replied, "there is nothing so deadly as a hundred extras seated in pews listening to a sermon." After another period of silence, the director asked, "Couldn't we photograph architecture? A lot better than people." Saville remembered, with satisfaction, "the congregation represented by four heads framed at the bottom of the picture of a beautiful Gothic window."

There *are* dozens of extras, but the architecture does dominate the scene expressively—befitting the high-toned aspirations of the preacher. Fleming taught Saville that "impressions so often make a scene more believable than spelling everything out in detail." All they needed for "a perfectly convincing chase," for example, was "Tracy, with a cape flying" across a wet-down studio floor along with "a set of Palladian-type stairs, an arched bridge, a few set pieces of masonry, and a string of electric light bulbs shining through the misty night." (The athletic Hyde was the stuntman Gil Perkins.) Even negative reviewers singled out this sequence.

The most flamboyant sequences are the montages depicting

impulses darting through Jekyll's mind as he morphs into Hyde. Saville *did* take credit for these audacious surges of symbolism. "Robert Louis Stevenson, in his short story, talked about Plato's 'Twin Horses of the Soul.' I had read and reread Stevenson looking for something I could clue into the film. So, I materialized Plato's thought of the Twin Horses. We made a montage of fantasy with Tracy as a charioteer with lash, driving in harness Bergman and Turner, with windswept manes. It was a good piece of symbolism—*Life* magazine reproduced, in its two center pages, each frame of the montage." The scholar Christopher Falzon has noted the sole parallel in Stevenson's text: Hyde emerges from a horse-drawn cab as "these two base passions [fear and hatred] raged within him like a tempest." Falzon rightly sees that Saville and Fleming transform the "Platonic image of reason in control of the other parts of the soul" into a "metaphor for the unleashing of Jekyll's desires for sexual possession and domination."

Of course, the Production Code forced the filmmakers to "delete all scenes where Tracy is shown lashing the two girls"—Jekyll couldn't be shown with a whip in his hands. But the suggestion of the whip remains. Not so another montage, referred to in *Life*, depicting the myth of Leda and the swan (Zeus, as a swan, raping Sparta's queen Leda, presumably Turner) and apparently containing suggestive images of a stallion and a girl (presumably Bergman). Joseph Breen requested that Fleming excise two shots of Bergman's "unduly exposed breasts" as well as her closing line to Jekyll, "Next time you look at a girl, make up your mind." For the Palace of Frivolities, Breen ordered Fleming, "Delete the crotch shot of the dancing girls."

The hallucination of the stallion would have echoed Freud's comparison of the ego and the id to a rider and his steed. But what's wonderful about the movie is that it contrasts animal urges and rational conduct without any clinical categorizing. The expansive performances and surreal episodes explode formula. Fleming's depiction of Jekyll's second hallucination pictures Bergman and Turner in champagne bottles against volcanic backdrops; the uncorking of her bottle seems to decapitate Bergman, but she appears healthy and sexy in the very next shot.

In the March version, there's something too post-Freudian about the way Hyde proclaims himself "free," just as there's something too earthbound about his declaration to his absent, moralizing enemies, "If you could see me now, what would you think, eh?" He goes through a gavotte of confusion over his new state before giving in to giddiness. Fleming's emphasis is on Jekyll's immediate gaiety at his transformation. Tracy doesn't make himself jump when he shows up as Hyde, the way March does; his Hyde is delighted—ready to spend a night on the town.

And that interpretation fits Stevenson's perfectly: "There was something strange in my sensations, something indescribably new and, from its very novelty, incredibly sweet. I felt younger, lighter, happier in body; within I was conscious of a heady recklessness, a current of disordered sensual images running like a mill race in my fancy, a solution of the bonds of obligation, an unknown but not an innocent freedom of the soul." Jekyll was astonished to be "conscious of no repugnance, rather of a leap of welcome. This too was myself. It seemed natural and human." In Fleming's movie, Tracy asks, after his first hydization, "Can this be evil?"—then, in relief or disbelief, laughs.

Tracy's Jekyll is juicy enough to cast spells on underclass and upper-crust women alike, and Hyde, as his outgrowth, is charismatic enough to hold Ivy in his sway even after she comes to fear and loathe him. In Fleming's film, Jekyll's desires grow convincingly into Hyde's monstrous perversions.

Tracy demanded a closed set because of the film's athletic and emotional demands (which engendered more than the average amount of griping), but George Cukor requested that a celebrated friend, the author and playwright Somerset Maugham, observe the filming anyway. While Tracy threw himself into Hyde's sadistic excesses, Maugham, with his stutter, asked Cukor, "Wh-which one is he doing now?" Expecting applause at the end of the take, Tracy heard laughter—and this tale has often been told as a reason for Tracy's disillusionment with the role. But contemporaries viewed Maugham's quip as nothing more than a slick witticism. Tracy even spread it around in the movie's publicity handbook. He said Maugham kept him cued into the closeness of good and evil in the dual character. (As Vladimir Nabokov put it, the doctor's potion left "a halo" of Jekyll resting over Hyde.) Tracy contended that he'd wanted to play Jekyll and Hyde for years, and there's no reason to doubt the desire of a tortured character like Tracy to play the ultimate divided personality.

If Tracy (unlike Bergman) didn't look back with fondness on the filming, it's probably because even without the demands of the makeup, the role was physically exhausting. Bergman said that Tracy balked at having "to race up the stairs carrying me off to the bedroom for his immoral purposes." (Actually, the only time he carries her up to her bedroom is as Jekyll, out of care for her twisted ankle.)

Once again, Fleming tried to assuage the fears of a male star by demonstrating a stunt. "Big and strong, he picked me up and ran up the stairs as if I weighed nothing. Spencer wailed, 'What about my hernia?' So they rigged up a sling which supported me so they could hoist me upward while Spencer hung on and raced up behind me looking as if he were carrying me." At first, Tracy couldn't keep up with the rig. It took nearly a score of attempts to get the timing right and, "on the twentieth attempt, the rope broke. I dropped down into Spencer's arms. He couldn't hold me, and we went rolling head over heels to the bottom of the stairs. How either of us was not injured, I'll never know. It was just a miracle. But there we were at the bottom helpless with laughter, roaring with laughter, while Victor came racing up, all sympathy and concern, but really so relieved that both his stars were not hurt and could continue to work."

No wonder Fleming called in a frequent collaborator, the stuntman Gil Perkins. "To double Tracy as Mr. Hyde," Perkins recalled, "I had to get into the MGM makeup department at 5:30 in the morning, and it would take a couple of hours to put the rubber mask all over my head. Then they would make up the mask, and put a wig on top of it, and fill in down around the neck." For Perkins, it was business as usual: "Tracy did everything very professionally—he always was the ultimate professional. And Victor Fleming was one of the best directors in the business." Despite spurious reports that the star and the director had their disagreements during the production, Perkins said, "Spence had a great respect for Vic, and they got along very well." According to Fleming, when he and "Spence" had "differences of opinion" and the star was "mad as the devil about something," Tracy would sit on the divan in Fleming's office "and we'd tremble at each other without saying a word! Then, he'd get up and walk out and we'd both feel better."

Beatrix daunted Turner. She recalled that during the scene of Jekyll calling off their marriage (because Hyde has become an indelible part of him), "I was in a happy mood that day and I just couldn't force tears into my eyes." Fleming summoned camphor crystals; Turner begged, "Please don't blow anything into my eyes." Fleming expressed frustration; Tracy accused him of being too harsh and stormed to his dressing room. After she thought "of every sad thing I could," including a car running over her new puppy, Turner's eyes stayed dry. Finally, Fleming "rushed over to me, grabbed my arm, and twisted it behind my back, where he held it for so long I feared he would break it." She screamed for him to stop, that he was hurting her. "Out of either pain or sheer fury, I not only started crying but went on crying so hard and so long that my nose was red and my eyes were swollen. Makeup didn't do any good. They could only shoot Spencer for the rest of the day, while I gave him my lines off-camera. I heard later that Spencer had wanted to take a poke at Fleming for being so rough with me." Turner never wrote how Fleming shot the scene; maybe she used the sense memory of that twisted arm.

Bergman told a similar story about Fleming overcoming her inability to become sufficiently tearful with Hyde. "I just couldn't do it. So eventually he took me by the shoulder with one hand, spun me around and struck me backwards and forwards across the face—hard—it hurt. I could feel the tears of what?—surprise, shame—running down my cheeks. I was shattered by his action. I stood there weeping, while he strode back to the camera and shouted 'Action!' Even the camera crew were struck dumb, as I wept my way through the scene. But he'd got the performance he wanted." It's doubtful whether he could have smacked her that hard and still filmed the scene without revealing any welts. In an earlier account of the filming, Bergman noted, simply, "Fleming was very mean to me. He screamed at me, hit me and shook me. Deep down I realized he was doing this to help me, but I was very hurt and embarrassed. I kept saying 'I'm doing my best.' Finally I burst into tears."

It didn't affect Bergman's enthusiasm for the movie—or her growing passion for Fleming. Bergman confided to her diary:

> Shall I ever be happier in my work? Will I ever get a better part than the little girl Ivy Petersen, a better director than Victor Fleming, a more wonderful leading man than Spencer Tracy, and a better cameraman than Joe Ruttenberg? I have never been happier. For the first time I have broken out from the cage which encloses me, and opened a shutter to the outside world. I have touched things which I hoped were there but I have never dared to show. I am so happy for this picture. It is as if I were flying. I feel no chains. I can fly higher and higher because the bars of my cage are broken.

On March 6, Selznick wrote Fleming that he found the scenes he'd seen from the movie "enormously exciting" and "as for Ingrid, she's everything that both of us hoped she would be under your direction. I am delighted and very happy about it." Bergman wrote, "By the time the film was over I was deeply in love with Victor Fleming. But, he wasn't in love with me." Bergman concluded, "I was just part of another picture he'd directed."

So was Saville. In June, as the producer began the final dubbing and prepared to give orders for the main title, he sent a night letter to Fleming at the Meadowlark Ranch and copied it with a message to him at Moraga Drive. Saville begged that Fleming grant permission for MGM to give him a producer's credit—as only the director could do, based on his new contract. "I am certainly only human enough to wish for a recognized credit on *Jekyll and Hyde* on which I so willingly labored as producer. Believe me, working with you was both great pleasure and profit. I should not like my memories to be disturbed on such a pleasant association with regrets of the lack of recognition of my work."

Fleming didn't bend. Saville later said, "To tell the truth, I did not give a damn; I knew my contributions to the picture, and anyhow, my name stands on the Academy records as producer." But he added, "Both Fleming and Sam Wood died at a very early age from heart attacks; having listened to both for hours on end on their tirades against the Establishment about the amount of income tax they had to pay, I am convinced they died of Franklin Roosevelt!"

24

The Yearling That Wasn't

While Fleming was wrestling with *Dr. Jekyll and Mr. Hyde*, preparations for *The Yearling* were stumbling ahead. Fleming had juggled projects before, with *Red Dust* and *The White Sister.* But *The Yearling* would ultimately stymie him. *The Yearling* would eventually be made not by Fleming but by Clarence Brown, starring not Tracy but Gregory Peck. Fleming's reputation as a ruthlessly efficient fixer of faltering productions had taken on mythic proportions; that's why everyone was stunned when he aborted his production of *The Yearling.*

The director's link to the project dates back to MGM's acquisition of radio, TV, and motion picture rights for the book for $30,000 in May 1938. "I got them to buy it because I loved it so," John Lee Mahin said. "I was taken off because I 'didn't realize the sensitivity of it.'" It was always slated for Fleming, and it was a natural to follow *Captains Courageous.* Marjorie Kinnan Rawlings's novel, like Faulkner's classic "The Bear" and Steinbeck's *Red Pony*, chronicles a youth conquering the natural world and growing into manhood. The hero, Jody Baxter, and his father, Penny Baxter, share a long-standing vendetta against a bear, Old Slewfoot. The focus of *The Yearling*, though, is on Jody's love for an orphaned fawn he adopts and names Flag. Jody's struggle to keep Flag after the pet wreaks havoc on the Baxters' modest spread in the Florida Everglades exposes the strictures of a hardscrabble life and the schisms of a family.

The problems started at the script stage. Because Fleming was working nonstop in 1938 and 1939, Mahin had to consult instead with the producer Sidney Franklin, who decreed, "Oh, of course, we can't kill the deer"—to which Mahin responded, "What? You can't kill the deer? That's the *story*! This is the story of a boy growing up. He grows up because he's got to kill the deer!" Franklin replied, "We buy lots of things that we change"; Mahin retorted, "You're a fucking idiot and you're going to fuck up this picture." So Franklin decided whatever he was doing with the picture, he'd do it without Mahin. When Fleming's back-to-back rescue jobs on *Oz* and *Gone With the Wind* conflicted with *The Yearling*, Norman Taurog got the assignment to make it with Fleming's initial cast—Tracy as Penny and Gene Reynolds as Jody—but Taurog, too, moved on (he made four pictures in 1938, including *Boys Town*), and the project languished. But Fleming put it back in motion after saving Tara. Marc Connelly, having worked so well with him on *Captains Courageous*, took one run at the script. The playwright Paul Osborn, who'd recently penned his first screenplay, *The Young in Heart*, for Selznick, did the final version and got sole credit. He *did* retain the scene of the boy delivering the coup de grâce to the deer after his mother wounds it. That didn't satisfy Mahin, who told Franklin years later, "But you had him dreaming of the deer at the end instead of dreaming of digging the well, of killing the bear, of being a man."

After doing reconnaissance on Florida locations and meeting Rawlings, Fleming wrote to the author, on February 9, 1940, "By the time *The Yearling* has been made into a picture you will probably wish that you had never sold the rights to a moving picture company. Besides having us in your hair . . . you are bound to be delighted by every boy's mother and father who feel he would be a perfect Jody, everyone who has a pet deer and thousands of others who feel that they could in some way break into the movies." Fleming added, "As to personal interviews, why don't you inform your 'Black Adreena' to shoo them away with a studio address in their hand as they go out the front gate." ("Black Adreena" more likely reflects how Rawlings, a southern lady of the old school, referred to her maid Adrina in private conversation, rather than Fleming's own racial terminology.) He closed with a compliment to one of her lesser-known books: "By the way, I loved 'Golden Apples,' and you might as well know I've fallen in love with you."

In December 1939, Rawlings inscribed a copy of *The Yearling* for Tracy: "Nothing finer could happen to Penny Baxter than to be brought to life by your great gift for the portrayal of man's courage and man's kindness." Tracy remained on board as Penny, but Gene Reynolds had outgrown the juvenile lead. Howard Strickling sniffed a possibility for spectacular publicity: a talent hunt for Jody in its own way as elaborate as Selznick's for Scarlett O'Hara. Strickling issued the announcement the following February: "Most extensive nationwide talent search ever conducted for motion picture role begins this week . . . Qualifications are that youth be between ages of ten and twelve of slight build standing approximately four and one half to five feet tall. All attempts to locate such boy in Hollywood have failed." It's hilarious to think "all attempts to locate" a youth of that age range and height in Hollywood "have failed," but Strickling was aiming to bring unprecedented ballyhoo to a family adventure.

The ace MGM talent scout Billy Grady made stops in five southern cities, including, in April, Atlanta. In the *Atlanta Constitution* (as he did in the big papers at each stop), he placed an artist's rendering of a sensitive, almost girlish-looking Jody cradling the head of Flag. Police had to control the mob that showed up to try out. "It seems every other kid had a harmonica and none of them knew anything but 'Old Black Joe,' " Grady remembered. "There were kids who could double for Wallace Beery, and imitations of Jimmy Cagney and George Raft were common. Anything to get my attention."

But twelve-year-old Gene Eckman—by his own account "skinny and weak-looking. A towheaded blond. And very sensitive"—really did fit the likeness. His mother took him to the open casting call at the Henry Grady Hotel—Eckman recalls, "It was like, you know, 'you stay, you leave, you stay, you leave' "—and he became one of five finalists. His father, a Western Union electrician, stayed in Atlanta when Gene and his mom went to Hollywood, all expenses paid. Gene auditioned with Tracy on the *Boom Town* set. "You're supposed to look at him like he's your father," the test director told him.

In late summer, after Fleming and Tracy spent three days looking at footage of potential Jodys, they took their daughters on a sailing getaway to British Columbia. On September 9, Eckman got the part. He went back to Georgia before returning to California for what turned out to be a two-year stay. "And my mother came out," Eckman remembers, "and my brother Harold, who was four years younger than me, but we looked very much alike, and he was my stand-in. They gave him special shoes to make him look as tall as me." His training included spending time with fawns at the studio zoo.

Memos flew between MGM and the advance crew in Ocala, Florida. The unit manager Jay Marchant sought the advice of "forestry men" to help his inexperienced troupe round up fawns. He shipped sample nipples to MGM so studio workers could learn to feed the fawns as they were herded into a studio pen. He gathered eighteen fawns, two does, and one buck from Florida and from Pennsylvania's state game commissioner in Harrisburg and set out with them for the West Coast. From New Mexico, Marchant advised MGM that "2 sick fawn in crate should be moved separate from rest if they live today," though "hot animals traveling okay so far." A few days later, from L.A., he wired the Pennsylvania game commissioner, "All fawn arrived in fair shape with exception of 2 from your farm which died making a total of four delivered from you."

MGM underestimated the complexity of the production from the outset. Although Mannix had wanted a second unit to shoot all "atmospheric" shots by September 1940, the preproduction second-unit team headed by Richard Rosson didn't make it to Ocala until mid-January 1941. Once Rosson and his crew got there, what Mannix called Fleming's "exacting" nature sabotaged their productivity. Fleming had grown to love Selznick's use of Menzies's storyboards and production sketches on *Gone With the Wind.* Based on his and Marchant's location hunts, Fleming hired an artist to illustrate scenes in pastel colors. And he wanted Rosson to match this concept art precisely.

Fleming, like others at MGM planning the film, didn't realize the roughness and unpredictability of the environment. "Central Florida had become a huge cattle ranch," wrote the crewman Wallace Worsley. "In cold weather [the cattle] would sleep on the highway at night because the pavement was warm. There were lots of smashed cattle, cars and people, and one learned to drive carefully at night." Chain gangs moved beside them down the road or zipped along in their prison vans on the highway. Ocala itself was an impoverished small town, with one nighttime hangout, the Chicken Shack, where Rawlings would occasionally show up, "sit alone at a table, talking across to us, and tossing off shots of local whiskey." Once she went deep into the Big Scrub to fetch the grown man who as a child had been the model for Jody. He kept the 250-watt ceiling lamp in his motel room on all night, because, he said, "I thought that's the way it was supposed to be," never having slept in a room with electricity.

Because Fleming was so specific about his requirements for atmospheric images, the crew had to wait, and wait, for each scenic shot. Sunrises required 4:30 a.m. wake-up calls; if the sun didn't hit the earth perfectly, the company spent the rest of the day shooting snakes and alligators. It took two weeks to capture what Fleming had designated a must-have image of "two egrets in the foreground of a wide river with beautiful clouds." Sidney Franklin sent his brother Chester to Ocala in March to serve as a second-unit action director. Franklin wrote that Chester "had had great experience with animals, and had made the beautiful picture, *Sequoia*, about a deer and a mountain lion." He wanted Chester to take charge of "a great many animal scenes," including "a bear fight with dogs, and a very important sequence, almost a ballet, in which Jody and Flag, the fawn, run through the woods while a herd of deer dance behind them." But Chester, too, chafed under Fleming's demand that his shots follow production sketches; he thought Fleming had diverted power from the directing staff. "After all, Sid," wrote Chester, "when an art director comes in and tells the director to put the camera here or there, it's all wet."

The advance unit's most ambitious effort was to film the confrontation between Old Slewfoot, the bear, and Jody and his father, Penny (with doubles for Eckman and Tracy). The bear playing Old Slewfoot, though, was "not interested in pictures from any angle," Chester wrote Sidney, after the animal knocked his crew around. For the close-ups of Old Slewfoot, the filmmakers planned to use an actor who played plug-uglies, Harry Wilson, in a bear suit. By the time Wilson's big scene arrived, spring had become oppressively hot. The handlers released the hounds, Wilson stepped toward them, "waving his forelegs menacingly" (wrote Worsley), and promptly collapsed from the heat. To discover how to build a better bear suit and bear head, Fleming wrote to a hunter friend, James L. Clark, who was knowledgeable about techniques used for mounting and preserving animals in museums. "He wanted more finesse in the actual shaping of the head," wrote Clark, "and particularly the mouth and lips so that he could photograph a closeup of the head showing a wicked snarl."

Back in Hollywood, Grady still needed to fill the role of Jody's friend, the frail, magical Fodderwing, with a boy who could match Eckman's accent. Fleming and Franklin hadn't yet agreed on how to cast strict, grief-hardened Ma Baxter and the raucous Forrester men, partly because Fleming was intent on using fresh faces. Sidney joked, nervously, that Tracy "has been playing Mr. Hyde to such an extent that we're afraid to out him with the boy for fear he would tear him to pieces. It seems to be affecting his disposition, so we have to leave the poor guy alone until he gets out of character." Fleming settled on Anne

Revere to play Ma Baxter. Educated at Wellesley College and acclaimed on the Broadway stage, she seemed an odd choice for a matriarch to Franklin. But she'd go on to give a full-bodied, Academy Award–winning performance as a heroic rural mother in *National Velvet* (1944) and a piercing, haunting performance as a warping mother in *A Place in the Sun* (1951). Franklin commented, "On account of Vic liking her so much better than anyone else we had, we all seemingly agreed it wouldn't be a catastrophe."

On April 18, as Fleming boarded an eastbound train, Franklin wired him "a great deal of good luck and success on your new venture" and pledged support for anything the director "may need or desire." Fleming, Hal Rosson, and the cast arrived within days of one another at the end of April and the beginning of May. Thanks to Rawlings, the group enjoyed some instant, if fleeting, bonhomie. On first sight of Eckman, Rawlings hugged the boy and exclaimed, "You *are* Jody!" For the local press, Tracy reported himself content, but Worsley said the company's base, the former Ocala Country Club, "at best was a third-rate hotel, and with no air conditioning." Miles deep into the Big Scrub, MGM carved out service roads for passenger cars, trucks, and buses. Tracy soaked his legs in insecticide between shots. Fleming ordered air-conditioning.

A Hollywood production on primitive territory inevitably won wide attention. Dora Byron, on location for *The New York Times*, said the worst obstacle was the sand flying in the works of "many a smart Hollywood station wagon." Byron watched Fleming shoot Tracy and Eckman approaching the Forrester family manse. Getting the pigs scurrying and the chickens squawking and Tracy asking, "Is it all right for a feller to git down here?" with the right rhythms and cadences ate up most of the day. "Tobacco-chewing Spencer Tracy, dressed in a slouchy brown and gray outfit topped by a wide-brimmed hat, bears little resemblance to a glamorous Hollywood star," Byron told her readers. "Finally the scene is finished and Tracy sinks into his canvas chair with relief. A pig roots comfortably at his feet . . . In addition to pigs, chickens and 'houns' are twenty-four deer, six bears, a bobcat, eight coons, two foxes, twenty squirrels, quail, owls, doves, and 'buzzards.' "

Fleming directed Eckman twice. In the movie's very first scene, Jody, lolling on a creek bank after building a palm-frond mill wheel (or "flutter-mill," as Jody calls it), nervously scans the sky to guess the time of day and begins running home. Fleming wanted Jody to look worried as he ran up the road. Eckman fondly recollects, "He had me running about five times, and I thought the camera was not working. [Then] he got in my face and said, 'I'm not going to put up with this anymore!' He wasn't mean or anything, but I wanted to believe him, because he was that type of person. He got the scene." In a vignette dramatizing the boy's desire to have a pet, Jody spots a bird whistling outside his cabin window and tries to communicate with it. "He wanted me to try to whistle back at the bird, you know, copy the bird, and, of course, I had no idea how to do it. And because I didn't know how to do it, it turned out very well." (In Clarence Brown's film, Claude Jarman Jr. doesn't whistle; he just fixes his eyes on the tweeter.) As far as Eckman was concerned, Fleming "got what he wanted. He was a genius to do it, I think."

When the press wasn't looking, Eckman noticed that Tracy was getting antsy. A bunch of dogs "kind of screwed around on the scene, and Spencer didn't like it." Eckman also heard "through the grapevine" that Tracy "didn't like his accommodations." John Marquand later said Tracy declared that "he was goddamned if he would act with any little boy with an accent like that, it was too hot anyway, and the whole thing was corny and would ruin his reputation." *The New York Times*, too, would report that Eckman's "southern accent" and "the idiom of the dialogue" made his delivery hard to comprehend and "the contrast between his speech and Tracy's was so great that it was ridiculous."

Franklin wrote, "When on location, the director knows the cost per day is terrific, and this puts him under tremendous pressure. Hence he is over sensitive to interruption and delay." But Franklin's rain of wires didn't help dispel tension for Fleming, who once wired back: "JUST SAT DOWN AND READ SCRIPT AND YOUR TELEGRAM TO DEER + FEEL HE WILL DO BETTER HEREAFTER." Having an ambitious young man named Jerry Bresler on his production staff was no help to Fleming. Even after Bresler became a successful producer, he retained what Sam Peckinpah's biographer David Weddle characterized as a "nervous, hen-pecking manner" guaranteed to rile any tough, independent director. Rawlings reported that Bresler "made a lot of trouble, keeping everybody stirred up against everybody else."

On May 19, Fleming shut the production down and returned to Hollywood. On May 22, the publicist Eddie Lawrence wrote Rawlings not to believe what she'd be reading in the newspapers. He chalked up any bad PR to normal grousing: "When the boys get home, they relish telling what a hard time they had. I have a helluva time trying to keep them in line. This is a stupid town that delights in picking out the worst in anything, with trimmings . . . Too, Tracy and Fleming are worriers. They work best that way, seeing the dark side. If they are ever happy with a picture in the making, it is sure to be a bust. The more they worry, the harder they work and the better the final result."

But within days, Fleming stepped down, and MGM named King Vidor to replace him. Soon Eddie Mannix was telling Louella Parsons, "We didn't agree on the story and the production, and since Victor has the right to do things his way, he asked for his release. He felt that things had not been arranged properly for the company in Florida, and perhaps he had his grievance, too." *The New York Times* reported that "Fleming doesn't like producers, anyway," and that Franklin's supervision had given him a *Gone With the Wind* flashback.

Rawlings probably came up with the closest rendering of the truth in a letter to her friend Bee McNeil:

> I was only on the set twice and I could tell Fleming wasn't satisfied with Anne Revere or the boy. He was very nervous, taking sleeping tablets, etc., and felt he could handle things much better on the Hollywood sets. The wind registered on the soundtrack, not sounding like wind at all, etc. The boy Gene Eckman, in looks and personality, seemed quite all right, but the sound man had me listen in, and it was true, as he complained, that the boy was not enunciating and his lines were not registering. Tracy was bored and morose. Anne Revere is not Ma Baxter as I visualize her but had a fine pioneer look and I thought she was all right, but she didn't seem to "put out" emotionally in the one scene I saw her do.

Nonetheless, Franklin put the blame solidly on Fleming for being unable to handle the challenges of the location and the pressure of his own lofty standards. Franklin wrote to the screenwriter Paul Osborn, "Things became so bad and mounted so terrifically in Vic's mind, his sense of responsibility to the terrific overhead and the small number of scenes being shot every day deepened, and his discouragement continued to grow." Franklin contended that Fleming "hadn't gotten anything down there that was usable," but the Brown picture would use some of the atmospheric shots, and Brown adopted the Osborn script that Franklin and Fleming had prepared. Franklin said, "No one really knew what had happened to Vic, as we all knew him to be a very powerful, courageous and strong character, but on discussing it when he was back he made the declaration that he wanted to be taken off the picture."

Fleming passed his own view of the disaster down to Elia Kazan via Bud Lighton. According to Lighton, Fleming told Franklin and the MGM execs, "How can I make a picture whose essence is that people love each other, when no one in the cast loves anyone or loves being down there or loves making the picture? They only love themselves. The kid wants to be a goddamn star and thinks of nothing except his vanity. Tracy is only thinking how he can get away for a few days to go up to New York and see Hepburn. And the mother part is always between a shit and a sweat about something, but never about the goddamn picture." To Kazan, Fleming "had more experience and more guts" on *The Yearling* than Kazan had on *his* Tracy-Hepburn fiasco, *The Sea of Grass* (1947). So Fleming did on *The Yearling* what Kazan wanted to do on *The Sea of Grass* (but couldn't) and quit the picture.

Margaret Mitchell wrote Rawlings, "What ails the works of us Southern lassies? Why is it so hard to translate us into another medium? I have been wondering seriously if there is something about the Southern scene which is difficult to capture in the movies if it is to be captured honestly." Admitting "I do not pretend to understand the workings of the Hollywood mind any more than I understand the motives of Igorot headhunters," she voiced the "sincere hope that the movie mixup straightens out." Later she confessed, "*The Yearling* is such a beautiful book that I selfishly would rather have it never come to the screen than have it done wrong—or have half of it done by one director and half by another. Doubtless when it does come to the screen the Forrester boys will be dashingly portrayed by the Marx brothers." Actually, Jeff Corey did a screen test for Fleming as one of the Forresters. "He wanted me to play one of the wild brothers," Corey recalled. "What Anne Revere later told me was that things were so uncomfortable in the bayous in Florida that Spence began to drink heavily, which annoyed Fleming, and they just couldn't go on with it."

Clarence Brown, who turned *The Yearling* into a family-film masterpiece five years later, offered this explanation for the debacle: "Victor Fleming, one of the greatest directors, started the picture, but he had just come off the greatest picture ever made, *Gone With the Wind*, and he just wasn't at home with three people. He went on location in Florida and tried, but it was lousy. They shelved it for a year, and then I took it up. Fleming's problem was the kid. He was lousy."

The problem may have been the kid *and* everything else. Echoing what Lighton told Kazan, the MGM in-house magazine *Lion's Roar* reported several years later that Fleming overheard his principal actors on a film talk about their dinner plans at 2:00 p.m. on a shooting day. "Our minds are not on this picture," he said. "Let's all go home and come back when we really have our minds cleared of other things." And he did shut production down for the rest of the day. "But," he told his interviewer, "I was so sorry. It was terrible of me to act that way."

25

Bonhomie in Bel-Air and *Tortilla Flat*

Any MGM executive thinking *The Yearling* had extinguished Fleming's fire would soon change his mind. For three days in August, Fleming consulted with Eddie Mannix on the studio's attempt to keep the project going, then took off for a two-month vacation. While he was away, reports filled the entertainment wires of him and Hawks co-directing an adaptation of Ernest Hemingway's "The Short Happy Life of Francis Macomber," to star Gary Cooper, for Goldwyn. An assistant treasurer at Loew's shot a letter to Goldwyn, Hawks, Cooper, *and* Hemingway, demanding they respect MGM's exclusive-services contract with Fleming. Zoltan Korda made the film as *The Macomber Affair* five years later; Gregory Peck would be at his pinnacle both as the Great White Hunter in the Hemingway story and as Penny Baxter under Brown's direction in *The Yearling*. Fleming took notice. When he began preparing the biblical epic *The Robe* in 1948, he and his producer tapped Peck to be their star.

Rawlings heard from John Marquand that "Fleming had a nervous breakdown," and the report contained some truth. Edward Hartman visited Moraga Drive near the end of May 1941, shortly after Fleming's return from Florida. Slocum met him at the door and cautioned him, "There's been a bit of a disturbance here . . . Mr. Bowman and his wife are not to be allowed on this property, ever again." What set off the explosion was the Bowmans' decision to send seven-year-old "little Helene," big Helene's daughter from her first marriage, to Ojai for boarding school. Little Helene's daughter, Kate Harper, says Fleming "felt my mother was getting short shrift from her mother and stepfather. He already thought she spent more time with nannies than with them, so they could attend to their social whirl." (Sally Fleming never saw Lee and Helene Bowman at the house again "until after Daddy died," though little Helene and Lee Bowman Jr., born in 1943, did come for visits.)

Aside from the uproar over the Bowmans, Fleming's home became his haven, especially after Hawks bought a 105-acre spread at the tip of Moraga Drive and moved in with his ultrachic second wife, Nancy "Slim" Gross, who became a fast friend of Lu's. The Flemings welcomed Hawks and Athole Shearer's children into their home: Barbara, then five, and David, then eleven. David remembers, "Vic was more of a Victor McLaglen rugged sort, not Errol Flynn dashing. I thought he was the ultimate man's man: truthful, upright, not afraid to speak his mind," and interested in "knowing *your* mind." Says Barbara Hawks McCampbell: "He was Uncle Vic to me and she was Auntie Lu. I had no idea until I was much older that we lived next to someone so famous."

Shortly after Hawks became his neighbor, Vic expanded *his* Moraga spread by ten acres. "When he got that property," says Sally, "he became a country boy again." Soon a whiff of old San Dimas blew into this Bel-Air estate. Fleming planted nearly five acres of oranges and, on the canyon wall above the house, lemons, then plums, cherries, apples, walnuts, avocados, and cherimoya. Beehives pollinated the trees. He erected a chicken house and filled it with Rhode Island Reds. Any chicken-home invaders, mostly coyotes, ended up trapped or shot.

"There were occasionally feral cats on the property, and he'd shoot them, too," Victoria says. Once a stray mounted Victoria's female calico, K.C., by the pool. "He took his pellet gun and shot it . . . A single shot. He knew he wouldn't miss." Fleming dealt with animal nature the way he did with human nature, directly and instinctively. The family dog, Judy, killed a bird once, so he tied the avian corpse around the dog's neck. The dog hated to have that bird rotting around her neck, and so grew to hate catching birds. It was animal aversion therapy.

"We'd have big barbecues," Sally says. "And Fourth of July parties which were huge. I remember Hoagy Carmichael singing to me on the piano." Cookouts at the Flemings' were memorable for the Hawks kids, too. "Jimmy Durante was there a lot," says Barbara. "You'd go home to sleep and go back over for breakfast. Uncle Vic had dinner for breakfast; chops and steaks and things like that." Jules Furthman, now Hawks's (not Fleming's) steady writer, was still a social standby. And Tracy visited occasionally with his son, John. "He neither spoke nor signed, but we would try to play with him," says the girls' pal Winnie Weshler. "And Clark Gable came once in a while, and like every other movie-struck teenager we were hiding around corners trying to get a good look." Other regulars included Mahin, Lighton, "Uncle Hal" Rosson, and Douglas Shearer. Ward Bond "practically lived there," says Sally. "There was no ostentation. Daddy protected his family . . . from the sleazy people. We didn't even know what he did until we got older."

Barbara Hawks never went to Fleming's movie sets with his daughters as she did to the sets of her father's other friends. "Family was separate from business with them," she says emphatically, "one of the best ways to keep a family life." The Fleming girls rarely even went out to the movies or restaurants. When the servants were off, the Flemings ate dinner at the Bel-Air Country Club. Victor intended to give his daughters security and normalcy.

"He wanted us to be regular kids, and we were," says Victoria. To make sure of it, "he got involved in every detail of our wardrobes, down to our socks." Sally says, "We were always wearing shorts and T-shirts, and [we were always] in the garden, so that we were cloistered, and we were protected maybe a little too much . . . and our life was very plain. We were always within the bounds of the house, or the grounds, or we were in a car going to school. We were never, you know, out and about." Although not a churchgoer himself, Fleming sent the girls to Sunday school at a Methodist church and later enrolled them at Marymount, a Catholic school. "He wanted us to get some spiritual background and stay away from show business," says Victoria.

When he came home, he would sit in a swing on the lawn "and give the children some time that was just time," says their friend Weshler. "I remember making daisy chains and putting them around his neck." If problems dogged him at the studio, he dined with Lu and the girls at 6:30 on the dot, then returned to MGM that night. Lu, an accomplished cook, grew her own bean sprouts for Chinese meals. Weshler says dinners were "disciplined": "If we were eating Chinese food, we had to get it with the chopsticks; they would not let you eat with anything else." Fleming's daughters knew how to read him. Sally says, "He'd just fix you with a glare, and you knew. Whatever it was you were doing that you weren't supposed to be doing, you stopped. That was all he ever had to do."

Fleming stayed in constant touch with his mother and sisters, made occasional visits, and always arranged for them to have tickets to previews of his films if they wanted them. But he never sought their approval of Lu, and she never made much of an effort to be close to his family or make them feel welcome at Moraga Drive. Lu's mother, who had remarried, and her two sisters, Georgiana Kohler, a seamstress, and Evelyn Wenchell, a bill collector, all lived in Los Angeles by the 1930s but were kept at a similar chilly distance. "I never saw my aunt Georgie at the house, never saw any of my mother's relatives, never saw any of my father's relatives," says Sally. One Easter, Eva sent Fleming's niece Yvonne over with a gift of two baby chicks. Slocum took them at the door but didn't invite Yvonne inside. Whenever Edward Hartman was helping his father with repair work or performing some small jobs himself, "Lu was never around. I'd talk to Slocum, and if Clark Gable was visiting, I'd talk to him, but I never saw Lu. She was always out somewhere."

Fleming seldom took Lu and his daughters on his annual Christmas visit to his mother's house, but the always practical Eva demonstrated her own brand of hospitality. The Flemings wrapped their gifts to her in wide satin ribbons. Eva took the accumulated ribbons, shaped and sewed them, and gave them back to her son as a quilt. For the holiday, she would always make her son what she called a "sunshine cake" because of its multicolored sugar dots.

Sally says she and Victoria learned "constancy," also "friendliness, outdoor living. We all had little boats to go in, and we all learned to fish. We had bicycles and motor scooters." So did their father. In the years when gas rationing prevented Hollywood's sailors and pilots from exercising their wanderlust in yachts or planes, he and Hawks anchored a loosely organized Bel-Air motorcycle gang, the Moraga Spit and Polish Club. The bikers would gather at Fleming's place on Sundays for jaunts on local hills and canyons and across the San Fernando Valley, or for road trips as far away as Malibu or Las Vegas. Members included a third great director, William Wellman; Zeppo Marx; Gable, Robert Taylor, and an up-and-coming heartthrob, Van Johnson; the stalwart character actors Keenan Wynn and Andy Devine (who'd appeared in *The Farmer Takes a Wife*); the stunt driver Carey Loftin, who later worked on such milestones as *The Wild One* (1953) and *Bullitt* (1968); Bill Lear, who went on to create the Learjet; Vance Breeze, the pilot who tested the P-51 Mustang; and the aircraft manufacturer Al Menasco, also a close friend of Gable's.

Fleming never saw motorcycling as a men's-only activity. He took Judy Garland up and down the Bel-Air canyons in 1939; unfortunately, she nearly upended the actress Jean Parker and her husband, who were riding on horseback. And despite the Moraga Spit and Polish Club's macho aura, several wives rode with the bulls: Dorothy "Dottie" Wellman, Dorothy "Doagie" Devine, and Zeppo Marx's wife, Marion. Barbara Stanwyck occasionally came along, too, on the back of Taylor's bike. The Devines and the Wellmans made a fabled drive to Vegas, sending club clothes ahead; white-jacketed waiters served them a catered lunch behind a billboard in the Mojave Desert. Slim Hawks designed Moraga Spit and Polish Club sweatshirts and jackets. She was the one who named the group to mock the men as motorcycle dandies. "They spent more time fussing with [the bikes] than they did riding them, really," said Dottie.

The Harley-Davidson riders bought their bikes in Pomona from Ben Campanale, a Daytona 200 champion. "It was not what you think of today, in Harleys and black," Hawks's son, David, recalls. "They were mostly into English and foreign bikes." Fleming owned a turquoise Harley, but his favorite motorcycle was British, black with pinstripes, called the Ariel Square Four because of its unique engine design. "It had a cigarette lighter custom-mounted on the handlebars," David notes. The general wisdom of the club, says Devine's son Tad, was that it was engineered like a Swiss watch and hummed like a sewing machine.

It was "just a group of guys who like to go out and ride motorcycles on Sunday," said David. "Not ne'er-do-wells looking for people to bash—or a bunch of thugs, quoting the rumors." He compares it to "the camaraderie and clubbiness" of drivers in the early days of sports cars. Motorcycling hadn't won the notoriety that it would after *The Wild One.* Cyclists who passed each other would give each other a friendly wave or a thumbs-up. "We'd do it to motorcycle cops, too," said Dottie, "'cause they'd wave back to us unless they were in a mean mood, you know—and then they'd see there was a girl on a motorcycle!" Dottie had a Harley of her own. During one Sunday barbecue and tune-up session, Dottie told Fleming and Gable that her bike sounded "kind of funny." They "started pulling things out and testing and fussing." When Dottie asked, "Hey, do you guys know what you're doing?" they simultaneously said, "No!" They kept on fooling with the Harley until they put it back together, saying, "Now try it." "Scary," she thought. But it worked: "Oh, yeah, they knew what they were doing."

A score of bikers might take off from the Flemings' house, then stop at the Devines' five-acre "ranchette" in Van Nuys. Because the Flemings and the Devines farmed their land, they earned extra gas-ration coupons during the war and maintained their own gas pumps. (Fleming was always generous with his friends: "Howard [Hawks] borrowed large sums of money from Victor Fleming at various times," said the screenwriter Wells Root.) Taylor sported a leather jacket, which protected him when he fell after his bike hit gravel rounding a curve. But David Hawks says most of the guys showed up as if dressed for a tailgate party, wearing "Levi's or nice shirts or sweaters or jackets—sporting clothes, like you'd [wear] to go to a football game." At the Devines', they congregated under a walnut tree that spread between the house and the garage; carved on top of a large bench in the middle was "Liar's Bench, Moraga Spit and Polish Club." Tad Devine remembers that it would "take sometimes the better part of an hour for the group to assemble. Actors, directors, stuntmen, cameramen, grips, and electricians. It wasn't just an elite group."

Even though Mahin and Patsy Ruth Miller didn't like motorcycles, the group would sometimes stop at the Mahins' place in Encino, dubbed "the Farm." ("It wasn't exactly a farm," Miller wrote, "but we did have a cow, some chickens, a large, mean rooster and some horses in addition to a few fruit trees. Sometimes, with any luck, we had a few ears of corn and a cucumber or two.") Fleming would "exchange some studio gossip" with Mahin, Miller wrote, and tease her about her haircut, her woefully undisciplined dogs, or her "very conservative" politics—a session that might have shed some light on his own conservative but elusive politics. He was godfather to Mahin and Miller's son, Timothy, who most vividly recalls being deposited on Fleming's Kodiak bear rug: "I was put on a bear rug with a genuine bear head attached, fangs bared, and I was scared!"

The stars and directors generally left daredevil exploits to the stunt driver Loftin, the test pilot Breeze, or the roughrider Wynn, who later wrote, "I think [Vic] rode for the same reason I did—to hold onto the feeling of being still on the leeward side of forty." Van Johnson, Wynn said, would just go "plugging along, enjoying himself, and leaving the hell-for-leather stuff to hotter heads than his." David Hawks has "fond memories of nice calm cruises, and hill climbs up Topanga Canyon" when it was undeveloped. He says his dad and Fleming would "drive out and watch guys do the big hills; we'd do small hills."

Gable wasn't the biker that Fleming was. As Wynn wrote in his autobiography, *Ed Wynn's Son*, "He was converted into a steady rider, content to jockey along in the middle of whatever pack he was out with, just taking it easy." But Gable was adept at improvising in a crisis. Wynn recalled a Fleming spill in 1946 that occurred when he was "twenty or thirty miles from his house, scrabbling up a deep rutted track." Gable reworked his scarf into "a rough sling," then offered to get "a Jeep or something" to bring him and the motorcycle home. Fleming would have none of it. "Forget it," he said. "I rode this bike up here, and I'm going to ride it down." The gang helped him on and got the motorcycle going as he "pushed off, making one hand work for two," then endured "two hours of pounding" on what turned out to be a broken collarbone.

This bunch didn't actively court danger, says David Hawks: "They just enjoyed going on local trips and had a good time and socialized." Still, he wasn't around when Fleming, Gable, and Loftin played motor tag at ninety miles an hour on fifteen miles of open road outside Los Angeles. Fleming was on his Ariel, Gable on his Knucklehead Twin Harley, and Loftin on a Rudge Ulster. "We opened them up, full throttle," said Loftin. "Gable and Fleming didn't think I'd be able to keep up with them on that Ulster. But they were wrong. I sat straight up like a farmer and moved to the head of the pack. As it turned out, my bike could easily go to 120, while Clark's Harley could barely break 100."

Slim didn't ride motorcycles. Otherwise she was the perfect spouse to complete this picture. By the time Hawks married her, after a three-year wait for his divorce from Athole Shearer, she was competitive at manly sports. William Powell had called her "the Slim Princess," and even though only the "Slim" stuck, she comported herself like royalty. Slim became the muse for Hawks pictures from *Only Angels Have Wings* to *The Big Sleep* that immortalized "the Hawks woman"—a gal who could talk as smart and tough as any man and dish out and take as much emotional punishment. Slim brought Lauren Bacall to Hawks's attention after seeing her photo in *Harper's Bazaar*—and Bacall perfectly embodied the Hawks woman when the director paired her with Humphrey Bogart in her first movie, 1944's *To Have and Have Not*, then followed it up with *The Big Sleep*. Hawks even gave Bacall's character the same nickname in *To Have and Have Not:* she's billed as Marie "Slim" Browning.

With a homegrown sense of understated American high style, the real-life Slim decorated Hawks's Moraga ranch herself. It would eventually include stables, barns, and a riding ring. "She was clearly very, very bright, very original in looks and thought, and very straightforward," Bacall wrote of Slim. "And with humor." Bacall found Lu at least "friendly." Sally Fleming liked Slim's occasional flamboyance. "She painted the toenails on Oliver, her poodle. She was very much that way, you know. Very clever."

Before they made *To Have and Have Not*, Bacall was shocked when Hawks, over lunch, casually asked her, "Do you notice how noisy it is in here suddenly? That's because Leo Forbstein just walked in—Jews always make more noise." Slim told Bacall that her husband "didn't want any Jews in his house" except for his agent, Charles K. Feldman—as if Slim and Howard didn't know that Bacall was Jewish, too. Hawks's anti-Semitism wouldn't have upset Slim. Her father, Edward Gross, a prosperous German-born businessman, was an anti-Semite, also anti-Catholic and generally intolerant. Slim branded Lu with a tasteless nickname that reflected Slim's own upbringing. "Mother was not a beauty," says Victoria. "Her nose was not small and cute. And Slim decided this made her look Jewish. You know what she used to call her? Lu the Jew. All in love, you know."

Lu didn't have Jewish parents. Her father's family was Protestant, and on her mother's side some ancestors were German Catholics who had emigrated from Russia. But as with stories about Fleming's Cherokee ancestry, the nickname stuck. Slim "gave Mother a gold bangle, something you'd wear on a bracelet," says Sally. "On one side was engraved 'L the J,' and on the other side, 'I love you, Miss Schmaltz.' " Lu, whose real opinion of the nickname is not known, was outwardly accepting of it and attached the bangle to a gold bracelet that Clark Gable had given her.

Like many a rhyming nickname, it spread quickly. Fleming's relatives, who barely knew Lu and disliked her, anyway, found in it an explanation of her disdain of them. "You mean True Blue Lu, the Little Jew?" asked Yvonne Blocksom. "I always called her Truie. I never really liked her very much, and she didn't like me. She put me down as much as she could." Rodger Swearingen recalls being told that Lu really was Jewish.

Edward Hartman offers a gentler explanation for the family antagonism. "Lu literally blew Vic out of our lives when he married her. He just dropped Yvonne and Newell [Morris] after supporting them all their lives. It was a real blow to them."

Of course, in that era, even sophisticated adults found it difficult to sort out prejudice from banter. Some ethnic and racial goading derived from xenophobia and snobbery, some from the spirited give-and-take of a melting pot that was still bubbling. Leonora Hornblow, Arthur Hornblow's wife, thought Slim was purely affectionate, not anti-Semitic at all, when Slim told her, "I'm having lunch with Lu the Jew." Fleming's daughters said that whenever they heard him and his friends complain about "the goddamn Jews," it was about studio politics. Hornblow agrees. "David O. Selznick just ate up directors. Darryl Zanuck *wasn't* Jewish, and he could be appalling, and Harry Cohn *was* Jewish, and *was* appalling. Ben Hecht was a passionate Jew and he really liked Victor. It wasn't the place to be an anti-Semite."

More than her ethnic humor, Slim's chic would have rubbed Fleming the wrong way. Jane Greer did remember him playing croquet at the Hawks house. But Hedda Hopper reported that when Slim made a list of best-dressed women in 1945, he called Hawks to "razz him about the money it was going to cost him for her to live up to that reputation." Dottie Wellman recalled, "I know the first party we went to there, Slim said, 'Oh, we're going to barbecue.' I said, 'Fine, so it's casual.' And I go over there to barbecue, [and] the gals all have on—like a uniform—black pants, gorgeous satin blouses, with lots of jewelry. And this is barbecue dress?"

Not surprisingly, the ambitious Bowmans became Slim's fast friends. Slim was godmother to Lee junior. Bacall recalled a 1943 bash at Hawks's place where the luminaries included Bob Hope and Bing Crosby, Johnny Mercer and Hoagy Carmichael. She spent the evening dancing with Lee Bowman "and flirting, of course . . . I wanted something of my own, and, failing that, was willing to flirt outrageously with a man like Lee Bowman. I went a bit far that night and Helene Bowman was less than thrilled with me, for which I could not blame her one bit. Lee took me home—somewhere along the way it was daylight, and I remember sitting on a diving board in my evening dress and then dancing with him. Harmless, and I enjoyed it completely."

Nothing, however, not even Slim's friendship with the Bowmans, soured Fleming on Howard Hawks. "They were the very closest of friends," recalled Hornblow. "Howard was an ice cube, cold; Victor was not cold. Howard was a wonderful director, but they were different, and their work was different." Their boyish bond endured despite slashing contrasts in psychology and temperament. For reasons known only to themselves, they persisted in calling each other Dan or Ed.

"They used to make each other presents," Sally says. "He made Daddy these silver things that go around a casing for matches. He engraved it 'Ed and Lu.' "

They'd goad each other deliberately and playfully. Edward Hartman recalls, "Hawks had dogs over there that barked at night. They woke Vic up and it really pissed him off. So he had me collect tin cans, and he hung them up on a string on the fence between their properties. And he had a wire that ran into his bedroom, so the next time the dogs started to bark and howl, he'd yank the wire, rattle those cans, and make even more noise. That situation lasted about two weeks, and finally they found a way to shut their dogs up." Fleming may have found Hawks's notorious yarn spinning funny. Vidor said he and Jules Furthman "just told stories about Hawks" the way other Hollywoodians would tell stories about Sam Goldwyn.

Slim Hawks's family lived in Steinbeck country, but were hardly Steinbeck characters. She came from Pacific Grove, a fashionable spot at the top of the Monterey peninsula. Her father didn't work on Cannery Row—he *owned* most of Cannery Row. They were the hoity-toity opposites of the hoi polloi in Steinbeck's first best seller, *Tortilla Flat.*

Fleming directed an adaptation of that episodic novel during the winter of 1941–42. Other projects had come his way; MGM had started to develop Jules Verne's *20,000 Leagues Under the Sea* for Fleming while he was in the midst of *The Wizard of Oz.* But after the storms and strains of *Oz*, *Gone With the Wind*, *Dr. Jekyll and Mr. Hyde*, and his aborted *Yearling*, *Tortilla Flat* promised to be (and was) idyllic. It fit this easygoing moment of his life. For Steinbeck, writing the novel was a lark, and it reads like one: a relaxed comedy of bad manners set among the *paisanos* of Monterey, California. Steinbeck presents this mixed-Hispanic people as the salt of the earth—make that the tortillas and beans, since their children astonish authorities by achieving health with that staple diet. The novel teeters on the brink of condescension toward *paisanos* but never becomes a Monterey version of Erskine Caldwell's pandering *Tobacco Road.* (Jack Kirkland had adapted both books for the Broadway stage; *Tortilla Flat* proved as big a flop as *Tobacco Road* had been a hit.)

Building on anecdotes provided by Monterey friends as well as Monterey cops and others who lived and worked with *paisanos*, Steinbeck makes them figures of fable as well as earthy fun. A rascal named Danny sets the novel in motion when he inherits two houses in Monterey from his grandfather. What underlies the sprawling content is the idea that owning property entails life-altering risks. Steinbeck's madcap variation on Marxism pales before the secondary idea that when Danny, Pilon, and the rest of their friends adopt one house as their base (the other goes down in flames), they grow akin to Arthur and the Knights of the Round Table. But their code, as well as their camaraderie, rests on slackerdom, not chivalry.

It's sad and funny to read in literary studies that the movie softens the book or muddles its intentions. There's nothing softer or more muddled in either book or film than the novel's ending, which strains to turn Danny's house into a ruined Camelot by having him go mad. Aside from Steinbeck's sometimes ironic but always real attachment to its characters, what unifies the book is the *paisanos*' ability to believe in their own lies or illusions.

At best, Steinbeck's *Tortilla Flat* is a merry chaos. Fleming's movie is one, too. Fleming may have considered an all-Hispanic ensemble; he tested Desi Arnaz and Ricardo Montalban for Danny and tried to borrow Rita Hayworth from Columbia. But with Tracy as Pilon, Fleming needed a commensurate star, like John Garfield, for Danny, and Hedy Lamarr became a natural choice for Sweets: she and Tracy had scored a giant hit in *Boom Town* (1940). The picture's ultimate urban-ethnic cast, with its maelstrom of accents, would have suited a grown-up version of a Dead End Kids comedy. The whole movie is full of jolly incongruities. The collection of hangdog character actors mirrors the collection of reformed mutts and strays that follow around the most likable character, the Pirate, a dog lover and cutter of kindling. When the Pirate and his dogs witness a miracle, the scene itself is a miracle—the kind of far-fetched fantasy that Fleming pulled off repeatedly throughout his career.

The movie's genesis was haphazard. A former story editor at Paramount, Benjamin Glazer, persuaded the studio to buy screen rights for the novel in 1935, the year of publication, for a mere $4,000. Despite its best-seller status, *Tortilla Flat* acquired Hollywood heat years later, from the prestige of two other Steinbeck properties, *Of Mice and Men* (1939) and *The Grapes of Wrath* (1940), both best picture Oscar nominees and the latter a great popular success. By then, Glazer had left Paramount and bought the rights back from the studio, then sold them to MGM for (reportedly) $65,000. Steinbeck had no love for that studio. During his most recent attempt to launch a film of *The Red Pony*,

MGM had refused to grant the author total script control as well as a ton of money and the right to work at home.

When an MGM story editor attempted to interest Steinbeck in helping adapt *Tortilla Flat*, Steinbeck proposed extortionate terms. The movie's producer, Sam Zimbalist, set a meeting with Steinbeck at a Monterey bar. Mahin, who had already prepared a script from Glazer's draft—in eleven days, he told one interviewer—came with Zimbalist. They put across the message that they needed assistance; Steinbeck remained noncommittal. Then Tracy joined in. He and Zimbalist said they'd try to persuade MGM to hire Milestone, who'd done a superb job on *Of Mice and Men*, to direct the picture. But it wasn't to be; Milestone had long been in Mayer's doghouse. Steinbeck read the working draft, pronounced it a screwup, and wrote to his stage and screen agent, "I've planted all the seeds of uncertainty I could and then got out. They must hate Milestone because they offered me John Ford and they hate him too." In the MGM publicity account, Zimbalist and Mahin gave him the script one night in Monterey, "and when he returned it, to their amazement, he said it was all right." According to Mahin, Steinbeck thanked him for taking "all the drama and message out of it," expressing the wish that Kirkland had done the same in his flop play. And the final choice of directors suited him: Steinbeck felt friendly enough toward Fleming to socialize with him later in New York.

Maybe the friendliness of the finished movie got to Steinbeck; its affable air is its most seductive quality. At 105 minutes, it goes on fifteen minutes too long, with one redemption too many. And Fleming by now had begun to overvalue his own studio wizardry. The re-creation of shantytown Monterey in Culver City generated reams of publicity: "Its single dirt street meanders down to the bay flanked by shacks and outhouses in exquisite disrepair. Here a rusted iron bedstead serves as a gate; there a porcelain washbowl, once planted with flowers, sprouts weeds; geraniums in tin cans and clusters of abalone shells cling forlornly to fences or sag to the ground with them." But even with an infiltration of chickens, goats, and dogs, as well as pigeons that reportedly clocked themselves flying into a cyclorama, it never stops looking like what it is: a set. It's sorry indeed compared with the seamless blend of studio and location work in *Captains Courageous*.

Yet from the moment Pilon (Tracy) and Pablo (Akim Tamiroff) convince the jailer Tito Ralph (Sheldon Leonard) to parole Danny (John Garfield), it shows off what Fleming could do without breaking a sweat. He frames groups of men so naturally that you can tell their emotional closeness by the slump of their postures and the tilt of their heads. He conjures a sense of real-life leisure through a mixture of shambling inaction and vivid action. The men perk up an already virile, bubbly atmosphere when they take off into song, regularly. Fleming draws a stripped-wire performance out of a normally impassive actress, Hedy Lamarr. And he fully realizes an outrageous episode that would give other directors agita: Saint Francis visiting Pirate and his dogs.

Garfield's Danny enters marital bliss and Tracy's Pilon cheers him on his way—a far cry from Danny's descent into alcoholic depression and death in the book. But the film's ending is not as crippling as the book's, since Fleming and Mahin adopt a more emotional stance toward their characters. They embrace the slacker romanticism behind the Arthurian allegory. The Sweets Ramirez of the book, a Portuguese woman of highly variable charms, reacts with materialistic glee to Danny's gift of a vacuum cleaner. In the movie she becomes an equally virtuous and voluptuous Lamarr (at her most high-Fahrenheit), and she does end up marrying Danny. *The New York Times* paraphrased the producer, Zimbalist, saying that Danny's "fate in the picture is worse than death," and that after he becomes a husband and "a solid citizen," he "is as lost to his friends as if he had died." But there's no evidence of that in the movie: the wedding is unreservedly joyous. If Danny and Sweets drive toward a separate fate than Pilon and friends, the feeling is not sorrowful—just bittersweet.

Tortilla Flat prefigures Italian movies like Federico Fellini's *I Vitelloni* and Gabriele Muccino's *Last Kiss* and Barry Levinson's American classic *Diner* as tales of arrested adolescence. It's a natural outgrowth of Fleming's studies of male bonding from *The Virginian* through *Test Pilot*—not a summation, but in some ways a goodbye to all that. Fleming told the *Los Angeles Times* that it was something new for movies, a study more than a narrative, and that he even "tried to slow down his filmic tempo, proportionately." He wasn't blowing smoke. When Major T. C. Lee, a Chinese airman, toured the set, thc "tall and patrician" Fleming vented his worries that the film "would fail critically and financially."

For a studio picture of that time, or even *this* time, *Tortilla Flat* is refreshingly loose and anecdotal. Fleming and Mahin treat the *paisanos* as a mass character, as Steinbeck did. The moviemakers also build up two catalysts for change: Sweets, of course, and the Pirate—that devout, aging man who cuts kindling for two bits a shot and saves his money for a gold candlestick to dedicate to Saint Francis. Sweets and the Pirate expose the limits of a male commune built on cheerful irresponsibility. The filmmakers saturate the material with emotion, but don't soften it—certainly not the cockle-warming story of the Pirate. He had promised Saint Francis that he would buy a gold candlestick if the saint saved one of his dogs from illness; then, the Pirate admits, a truck struck and killed the canine anyway. But the Pirate retains his gratitude while piling up quarters, and in his passion the film touches the sublime.

Frank Morgan brings the Pirate to life in all his humility, hopefulness, and awe, and the canine flock that surrounds him never gets overly cute—these dogs are as wild and woolly and expressive as Toto. They're just like the ones in the book, from houndish Enrique and brown curly Pajarito to Rudolph, "of whom passersby said, 'He was an American dog.' Fluff was a Pug and Señor Alec Thompson seemed to be a kind of an Airedale. They walked in a squad behind the Pirate, very respectful toward him, and very solicitous for his happiness. When he sat down to rest from wheeling his barrow, they all tried to sit on his lap and have their ears scratched." Garfield was half-right when he said, "I tried to steal scenes from Hedy, Hedy tried to steal them from Spencer Tracy, Tracy tried to steal from Frank Morgan, Morgan tried to steal from me, and the dogs stole the show."

Garfield was selling himself short: he and Lamarr were also a bright and engaging spectacle. For Garfield, the loan-out from Warner Bros. to MGM was a working vacation, and the cast and crew of *Tortilla Flat* were good company. Major Lee thought Garfield "relaxed and clever" on the set. Fleming made him so, with his usual combination of rough hazing and humor. The director stopped Garfield in the middle of his first scene and declared, "For Christ's sake, Garfield, you have to do better than that. I fought like hell to get you in this picture, so don't make me look like a fool." Tracy laughed—he knew what would come next as Garfield asked Fleming for more guidance. Fleming responded, with a roar, "You want me to tell you how to act, Garfield? Hell, I don't know how to act, and I'd be making more money if I did. You're the actor, you have the reputation; now I just want you to be better." Yet when Garfield *did* get better, Fleming took him aside and said, "Take it easy, Garfield; don't get *too* good. A lot of your scenes are with Hedy Lamarr. She's not what you call un-outclassable, and we can't let that happen. Let's take it again. Be better than you were the first time, but worse than the second." As Garfield biographer Larry Swindell puts it, Fleming "liked to keep a picture moving. He thus would create an atmosphere in which actors could respond to his own style of pressure."

Tracy, as Pilon, with an accent as variable as Manuel's, works hard at being lower-depths casual—and, paradoxically, the audience rewards him for his effort. But Garfield really *is* at ease here. Although the film doesn't draw on his ability to express shades of feeling, it's a relief to see him so *agreeably* intense, and he's at his contentious sexual best with Lamarr, who is sensational. "It was an honest part and I was glad to get away from glamour," Lamarr told Hedda Hopper in 1951. She portrays so energetically a woman at war with herself that her conflicts make her more captivating. She and Garfield get at the underlying attraction that's needed to inflame the surface antagonism of an Apache dance. "John Garfield was wonderful to work with," she said in 1971, nearly twenty years after his death. Watching the film, you believe her.

Fleming's theory that a love scene is a fight scene gets one of its most seductive workouts during the courtship of Danny and Dolores. When Danny comes on too strong to her, she swings a knife at him, yet that doesn't keep Danny from going straight to Sweets for goats' milk when he and his friends take on the cause of a traveling widower with an ailing infant. Dismayed at Sweets and Danny's closeness, Pilon engineers a romantic spat that propels Danny into the hospital. As penance, Pilon promises to buy Saint Francis another candlestick if Danny recovers, then signs up to cut squid for a Chinese man, Chin Kee (played by Willie Fung, the houseboy from *Red Dust*). Luckily, a kindly priest says that buying a boat for Danny would be a better act of redemption. Henry O'Neill plays the cleric, who becomes a paternalistic Anglo-Saxon in the movie; the choice is especially jarring since the source character in the book is named Father Ramon. This Classic Comics priest contrasts with Fleming's startlingly effective and unexpected use of Jack LaRue as the priest in *Captains Courageous.* Here, the joy-riding director occasionally takes his hand off the wheel.

MGM did reckon correctly that *Tortilla Flat* would be an all-around success, and Zimbalist wanted credit for producing it. On February 20, 1942, Benny Thau advised Floyd Hendrickson of MGM's contracts department that Fleming had concurred. A back-and-forth culminated in the following pointed exchange:

For my records, I am dropping you this note to confirm the fact that you were kind enough to agree that Sam Zimbalist may be given credit as the producer of "TORTILLA FLAT," but this, of course, does not apply to any other picture.

With kindest regards, I am
Sincerely,

F. L. Hendrickson

A week later, Fleming replied.

On February 25, 1942 you sent me a note regarding my kindness in permitting Mr. Sam Zimbalist to put his name on "TORTILLA FLAT" as the producer of the picture.

So as to keep the records straight, you should know that it was no particular kindness on my part, but rather, the other half of a deal I made with Mr. Thau, that in exchange for the permission I am permitted to take an additional three months per year vacation together with the three months per year called for in my contract, making a total six months per year off without any extension of my contracted time.

Despite this insistence on protocol and status, and the incursion of sanctimony near the end of the film itself, *Tortilla Flat* siphoned something deeply congenial out of Fleming's nature. His work would never be so lighthearted again.

26

World War II with Tears: *A Guy Named Joe*

Before his death in 1936, Billy Mitchell, one of America's aviation heroes, had been predicting a Japanese air assault on the American fleet. The aftermath of the attack on Pearl Harbor on December 7, 1941, brought Fleming some embarrassment along with the same fear of an impending assault on Southern California shared by everyone else. Sid Deacon, who had suffered a stroke the previous year, wrote President Roosevelt to offer his services at discovering Japanese submarines off the California coast. "I think he had a special tip on his witching rod for that," Edward Hartman recalls. The White House didn't take him up on his proposal. The year before, Deacon had asked the Los Angeles Board of Supervisors for permission to dig on the grounds of the Hollywood Bowl for the treasure known as the Patriot Cache, supposedly buried by Mexican families in the 1860s for use against the French-appointed Austrian emperor Maximilian. But the supervisors turned him down, too. "That was a shame," Hartman says. "If they'd have let him dig, he may have found something. He was old, but he wasn't crazy."

The military swiftly adopted more conventional means for defending the waters outside California, including the appropriation of large yachts. Fred Lewis's *Stranger* had become a minesweeper earlier in 1941, and Frank Morgan's *Dolphin* likewise was painted gray and pressed into service. Fleming did not throw himself directly into the war effort, but it is possible that, like many other watercraft owners, he proposed some help to the Office of Naval Intelligence. Any services he might have rendered remain secret. John Ford did do some amateur spying on Japanese trawlers before he joined the Navy, but at fifty-two Fleming was six years older than Ford and had more than a decade on the other top-rank directors who went overseas to shoot documentaries.

As America's studios joined the information war, MGM enlisted its most consistent moneymaker in the cause. Fleming was preparing and shooting *Tortilla Flat* when the Japanese attacked Pearl Harbor, then advanced to Wake Island the next day for a battle that raged until the twenty-third, forcing an American surrender. On February 25, 1942, even before they settled on the credits for *Tortilla Flat*, Fleming and Zimbalist began developing a project called *Wake Island*, using the battle as the background for "a Gable-Tracy" story. They assigned MacKinlay Kantor to write it. James Agee noted that Kantor was "beloved by some" for "boiled-and-buttered native corn, fresh from the can." Indeed, MGM had found a berth for Kantor when he supplied the source novel for a successful dog picture, *The Voice of Bugle Ann*. (He would later garner acclaim as the author of *Glory for Me*, the verse novel that became William Wyler's Oscar-winner *The Best Years of Our Lives*, and *Andersonville*, the Pulitzer Prize–winning historical novel about the notorious Confederate POW camp.)

The *Wake Island* script went nowhere. But on March 5, Kantor and Fleming, in Kantor's words, "drifted away from an unproductive story line" and "started talking about Buffalo Bill, since both of us remembered having seen him and his circus in our respective boyhoods." Zimbalist ("who had a city-vaudeville-stage background") blurted out, "Jesus Christ, why are we talking about this other silly picture when there is such a thing as Buffalo Bill?"—and Fleming "immediately stood up, roaring with enthusiasm." Kantor, "digging deep into all Buffalo Bill sources available" and promising Fleming "a director's field day if you ever had one," delivered a treatment that had him "all ready to call up Central Casting." For the lead role there was no question: they intended to use Gable.

Zimbalist said, "By God, I'll see Eddie Mannix tonight, kidnap him and take him to dinner if necessary." But when Zimbalist called him back to the office a week later, he reported the sad news that MGM executives felt there was "no money to be made out of Buffalo Bill . . . They say that Buffalo Bill tried to make a picture about his own life, and it was a flop." Kantor responded, "Good lord, everybody knows that; the old idiot even tried to get some of the same Indians against whom he had fought, and have them in the picture. The poor old guys were limping around, and people were shooting off cap pistols, and it was a general mess. What's that got to do with our picture?"

Kantor later recalled, "About that time there was a dreadful rumble from the deep couch behind me, and I turned to see Victor arising from where he had been stretched out. He said, 'For blank blank blank blank's sake, let me tell you about the whole picture business as it's run at Metro. Don't you know that there are a whole bunch of blank blank blank blanks up on the third floor who would rather sit around and blank blank each other's blank blanks than make good pictures?" (Kantor provided the "blanks.")

In 1943, Kantor left MGM to work for the *Saturday Evening Post* as a war correspondent, and William Wellman began preparing *Buffalo Bill* to star Joel McCrea at Fox. MGM knew the Fox film was already in the works, and Warner Bros. was flirting with the subject, too. Wellman later admitted that he'd started a *Buffalo Bill* script in 1940, debunking the scout, hunter, and Wild West show impresario as "the fakiest guy that ever lived," until his initial writer, Gene Fowler, had second thoughts about defacing a hero's image and burned the screenplay. Wellman wound up filming a rah-rah version of Buffalo Bill's life, depicting him as a frontiersman at odds with civilization. "When that poor little crippled kid at the end stands up and says, 'God bless you, too, Buffalo Bill,' I turned around and damn near vomited," Wellman confessed. "And then Zanuck turned around and told me it was the second biggest moneymaker we've ever made." (The Pasadena-born McCrea, grandson of a stagecoach driver and son of a utility executive, would have been a good fit for Fleming. In 1946, he nearly redeemed a flaccid Technicolor version of *The Virginian.*)

The actor John Frederick called the Fleming of those years "intimidating yet compassionate—reminiscent of John Ford and his bluster." Fleming was even logging some hunting time with Ford's protégé John Wayne; when Wayne wasn't shooting his first MGM film, *Reunion in France*, for Jules Dassin, he was sometimes roaming the San Dimas area for small game with Fleming and others. Wayne had first gone on those jaunts a few years earlier, with Ward Bond along.

Like Ford at Fox, Fleming at MGM had become the director the studio could trust with everything from kids' adventures to gritty Americana. Right after Fleming's Steinbeck adaptation, another California writer, William Saroyan, who had visited the *Tortilla Flat* set with Garfield, called on Fleming for advice. Saroyan, a bold, eccentric humanist, had written a screenplay called *The Human Comedy* and, with no prior film experience, hoped to direct it himself. (He also turned it into a novel that hit bookstores before the movie reached theaters.)

The studio choice to direct *The Human Comedy* was King Vidor. Saroyan, to prove that *he* could make it, put together a short called *The Good Job*, from his story "A Number of the Poor," about the filching of a melon from a market, then showed it to Fleming and Zimbalist. Fleming told him it was "wonderful," but Mayer and his inner circle did not agree. Saroyan left the studio, and Clarence Brown became *The Human Comedy*'s director. Saroyan had asked for Fleming or Wyler.

With Gable in mind, Fleming and Zimbalist had also been revamping *Shadow of the Wing*, a five-year-old script about the Royal Air Force that they turned into the story of an adventurer joining the Army Air Forces. But Gable had already decided to join the Army Air Forces in real life—and his plans accelerated when Carole Lombard, Gable's third wife and the love of his life, died on the return trip of a bond-selling tour.

Lombard's plane crashed in Nevada on January 16, 1942. President Roosevelt awarded her a medal and declared her "the first woman to be killed in action in the defense of her country in its war against the Axis powers." Gable continued to work throughout his crisis, and MGM announced in March that he would follow his role as a war correspondent in *Somewhere I'll Find You* with *Shadow of the Wing*. But the military began courting him the day after Lombard's January 21 funeral: General Henry "Hap" Arnold wired the forty-year-old Gable with the offer of a "specific and highly important assignment." In August, Gable went to Officer Candidate School in Miami. In October, he received his commission and official task: to film the combat experience of aerial gunners.

To produce *Combat America*, Gable pulled in Mahin, who'd been teaching combat intelligence at a base in New Mexico. Gable and his crew flew with heavy-bomber groups from the Eighth Air Force, based in England's Midlands. After shooting nearly fifty thousand feet of film, he received the Air Medal "for exceptionally meritorious achievement while participating in five separate bomber combat missions," as well as the Distinguished Flying Cross. Gable edited *Combat America* at MGM (though assigned to the First Motion Picture Unit at the Hal Roach Studios), had enough left over for a quartet of additional instructional shorts (including an officer-recruitment film, *Wings Up*, featuring himself), and put together the compilation film *Show Business at War*. As for *Shadow of the Wing*—it never happened. MGM announced McCrea as a replacement for Gable after he went into the service, but by then McCrea was onto other things, including *Buffalo Bill.*

Meanwhile, Saroyan went back to Broadway, where he predicted the rise of the wartime weepie, a genre that would soon sweep up his friend Fleming. Saroyan's *Get Away, Old Man* parodied a Mayer-like studio mogul intent on mounting a sob story called *Ave Maria.* (Since Mayer's love of Catholicism was so well-known, onstage Ed Begley played Saroyan's Mayer figure as an Irishman.) "When the world is full of death—when men are killing one another—what do people think of?" asks the mogul. "They think of Mother." Or, sometimes, Father. Twentieth Century–Fox was already producing *Happy Land,* based on a Kantor novel about a Gold Star father who, from the ghost of his Civil War grandfather, gains perspective on the death of his son.

The real Mayer did get his blockbuster weepie when he assigned the producer Everett Riskin and Fleming to *A Guy Named Joe* and they got Dalton Trumbo to write the script. It's about a guy named Pete (Spencer Tracy) and another guy named Ted (Van Johnson). Pete is a flier's flier who dies bombing a German aircraft carrier. (The real German navy didn't have aircraft carriers, but the moviemakers wanted to portray both theaters of war, so in this film the Germans had them.) He enters an air veterans' version of the afterlife, becoming an unseen instructor to a novice pilot, Ted, and ultimately, at least in the finished film, the benign force that pushes his bereaved lover, Dorinda (Irene Dunne), to move ahead. He can throw his thoughts to these characters, but they never know he's there. The plotline alone conveys one reason why *A Guy Named Joe* became a smash as well as a consolation to many grieving families. The movie appeals to what Joan Didion has popularized as "magical thinking"—"thinking as small children think, as if my thoughts or wishes had the power to reverse the narrative, change the outcome." In the case of *A Guy Named Joe,* the magical thinking occurs on earth and in the heavens above. It fuels hope in a connection between at-risk or deceased loved ones and the folks they leave behind.

The family of a flier in the movie said they experienced such a connection shortly after they saw *Joe.* Army Staff Sergeant Arthur J. "Bud" Swartz Jr., a dive-bombing instructor, doubled for Tracy during second-unit shooting at Drew Field (now Tampa International Airport) in Florida, then became a tail gunner in the South Pacific. On his last furlough, Swartz had urged his mother to "look up at the North Star every night at eleven," saying he'd do the same; that way they'd know they were thinking about each other. On March 5, 1944, she woke the family with her screams. Her son's star had fallen out of the sky. It was the day his B-25 Mitchell bomber crashed in New Guinea, the climactic setting of *A Guy Named Joe*.

Premiering on Christmas Eve 1943 in New York and widening out to the rest of the country in early March (without a Los Angeles opening, it wasn't eligible for Oscars until 1944), *A Guy Named Joe* ended up grossing $5.254 million. In the more than two years since Pearl Harbor, 62,312 Americans had died in combat, and the number would triple by the end of 1944. The country was smack in the middle of the war, with costly battles raging in the Pacific and D day (June 6, 1944) still half a year away. But the reason this heartwarming hokum won the hearts and minds of audiences goes beyond timing. Fleming brought it his full commitment. Adela Rogers St. Johns, in a letter to Lu, recalled Vic visiting her house in 1944 right after she had received the personal effects of her son Bill, who had died flying for the RAF. St. Johns wrote:

> They sent me everything—pajamas that hadn't been washed, half a tube of toothpaste, his bathrobe which I'd had made because he was 6 foot 6 and couldn't wear the regular ones, his uniforms and great coat and flying reports. It was pretty rugged, as you know. And when Vic got there I was still choked up and shaking. I will never forget what he said to me as long as I live. He said, "You've got to bite on the bullet. USE everything. Use up the toothpaste, give the bathrobe to his kid brother, send the uniforms back to the RAF—they need 'em. Have the pajamas washed or wash them yourself and give them to somebody. That's life. That's the continuation of life. That's what your boy would want you to do. This country was created by that spirit. They couldn't afford to throw things away, they had to make use of everything, and they kept the usefulness of the one who was gone still part of their everyday life. You know your boy's all right. He was a man, doing a man's job, and he's still doing it."

The producer Riskin had already mounted one afterlife hit, 1941's *Here Comes Mr. Jordan*, about a prematurely dispatched boxer who finds a new body to house his soul. (It earned Oscars for best original story and best screenplay, and decades later evolved into the Warren

Beatty hit *Heaven Can Wait* and the Chris Rock flop *Down to Earth.*) But Riskin had failed to come up with an acceptable script for "Fliers Never Die," the original story of *A Guy Named Joe.* His son Ralph recalls a version called *Three Fliers,* in which a couple of brothers tutored their youngest brother from the great beyond.

Then Riskin convinced Metro to let him hire a prolific screenwriter named Dalton Trumbo, who would earn a measure of immortality as a witty radical. As a screenwriter he'd already shown an affinity with the afterlife—his novel and screenplay *The Remarkable Andrew* featured the ghost of Andrew Jackson. He'd endured an unproductive stint at MGM in the 1930s, then worked at nearly every major studio, notably Warner Bros. and RKO, and published an enduring antiwar novel, *Johnny Got His Gun,* before returning to MGM, where his friends included Sam Zimbalist. By the time Riskin signed him, in the middle of 1942, Trumbo already had a reputation as a radical. He wrote the liberal journalist Murray Kempton in 1957, "The proprietors of MGM were never deceived about my political affiliations . . . I informed each producer about those affiliations before I accepted an assignment from him. There were no objections."

Ralph Riskin remembers his father telling him that he had to order Trumbo to knock off writing pamphlets for Communist Party front groups and finish the script; Trumbo demanded two secretaries and did the whole second half in an afternoon and an all-nighter. "And they never changed a word. It was brilliant." There was good reason for Trumbo's accelerated political activity. Word had gotten out that some big names at MGM were forming a Red-hunting organization called the Motion Picture Alliance for the Preservation of American Ideals. Trumbo, "convinced there was going to be trouble," decided to join the Communist Party. "I didn't want to have the advantage of those years of friendship (with other writers) and then to escape the penalties. Now that may sound odd. I don't think it's odd at all . . . If they hadn't been my friends, I wouldn't have joined." Of course, Trumbo became one of the Hollywood Ten and served a prison term for contempt of Congress.

Fleming became a member of the MPA's executive committee, his name emblazoned on its letterhead. But he embraced Trumbo as a creative partner. Trumbo's playwright son, Christopher, thinks that what bonded them was their unashamed emotionality. Whatever the political differences, he says, "I know that they liked each other as men."

Fleming visited the writer on Trumbo's "pleasantly remote" 320-acre ranch, ninety miles north of Los Angeles. Fleming would come to have drinks and gaze across a valley where nobody else lived. In a monologue out of a Robert Towne script—the kind that's funny because it doesn't really go anywhere—Fleming would say, "You know, Trumbo, if you want to get rich, I can tell you how to get rich. See that field over there? Go out there and have somebody dig a pit about ten feet deep; then you have him put a lid over it; then you hide that lid so only you know where it is. Then every day around this time you go out there. The first day you go out, drop a dollar bill in it. The next day you drop two dollars. And you just keep doubling it." Christopher says his dad told the story, more than once, "because it continued to amuse him—I think it was a case of you think of the man when you think of the story."

As Fleming and Riskin revised the film, Pete began to look less (as one early version had it) "like Clark Gable," more like a regular guy. The propaganda got toned down, too. Pete and his best pal, Al Yackey (Ward Bond), no longer strafed German staff cars while fantasizing that one was carrying Hitler. Pete's best ghost buddy, Dick Rumney (Barry Nelson), portrayed at first as British, ended up solidly American like Pete. Originally, the great beyond also contained pilots from the Red Army and China, as well as a dissident German. When Pete asked the whereabouts of Nazis and Japanese, the commanding general, "with grim satisfaction," said, "There's a place for them." Now the heavenly fliers were all Yanks.

Even political enemies recognized Mahin as a formidable talent, but Trumbo's reputation as a screenwriter has oscillated according to political and aesthetic fashion. That's partly because Hollywood script credits, always mysterious, were never murkier than during the anti-communist blacklist of the early Cold War. Without credit or with the credit taken by "fronts" who lent their names to his work, Trumbo wrote the original scripts to such films as the harrowing 1951 noir *He Ran All the Way* (John Garfield's last picture) and the delightful 1953 romantic comedy *Roman Holiday* (which made a Hollywood princess out of Audrey Hepburn). His prominence in the Hollywood Ten colored perspectives on him even after he broke the blacklist with back-to-back credits on Otto Preminger's *Exodus* and Stanley Kubrick's *Spartacus* (both 1960). Though critics blamed Trumbo for the virtuous-rebel speeches in *Spartacus*, the film's producer-star, Kirk Douglas, gave Trumbo enormous credit for the movie's ultimate wit and pace and thump. Richard Corliss, the first to write critical history from the point of view of the screenwriter, found Trumbo's scripts fascinating "because of the disparity between a natural warmth and an imposed message"—especially in *A Guy Named Joe.*

The script for *A Guy Named Joe* is really *written,* with tones and moods suggested on the fly as Trumbo advances the melodrama. But it incorporated suggestions from all over. When Tracy asked Major T. C. Lee for some tips about playing a pilot, Lee replied, "Flying isn't tough. Crashing is tough." In the screenplay, that's how Pete feels, too.

In a scene Fleming pushed to include in the finished movie (it didn't appear until the shooting script), Pete passes five juvenile English aviation fans. Edward Hardwicke, the son of Sir Cedric Hardwicke, played a little boy in a striped shirt. He had just one line: "Pete . . . What would happen if you went way, way up high and you forgot to turn your oxygen tank on?" Pete gently explains how swiftly and thoroughly a pilot would get disoriented without oxygen. Then, prodded by his admirers, he looks around quickly to make sure no adult is watching and delivers a heartfelt description of the *good* kind of disorientation a real flier in his own ship can experience alone, feeling he's "halfway to heaven . . . The earth's so far below ya that it just doesn't matter anymore. The sky is the thing that's important." Pete tells them that up there, a flier says to himself, "Boy, oh boy, this is the only time a man is really ever alive—it's the only time he's really free!" Hardwicke, a sturdy and virile Mr. Brownlow in Roman Polanski's 2005 *Oliver Twist,* remembers Tracy as "a hugely avuncular figure; his relationship with the children in the movie is very much what it was like with him before the camera rolled."

Just getting the camera rolling was the first challenge—and keeping it rolling would remain a challenge. Although it was an inspirational fantasy, both the War Department and the Production Code Administration questioned the way the fantasy had been worked out. Politics weren't the issue. Trumbo, who thought "all wars are bad and can be prevented by intelligent and compassionate leadership," also "felt that World War II was a moral war from our point of view, and should be won." But the film's emotional salve was supposed to come from Pete and his lover, Dorinda Durston (another flier), uniting in the afterlife—and that climax triggered debate among military readers and censors.

Dorinda (pronounced "Drinda"), who flies for the Air Transport

Command, grows conflicted about her engagement to Ted and usurps his assignment to annihilate a Japanese ammunition dump. In Trumbo's treatment, she drops her plane on it "straight as a plummet" despite Pete's scolding her, "So you're going to be a heroine, eh? You love this jerk, so you're gonna commit suicide to save him?" In heaven, she tells Pete, "it was you all the time." When she says, "I almost died from loneliness," he replies, "You *did.* And if you weren't my girl, I'd paddle you."

Only one version of the ending made it to the theaters, but it required considerable tinkering at the script stage and a reshoot after filming was completed. And even without consideration of the romantic-suicide climax, the War Department readers' reactions zigzagged all over the map. Major Ralph Jester, in civilian life a costume designer at Paramount, applauded the script's "redeeming *Topper* twist" and Pete's "appealingly blithe spirit," and suggested it be called "The Ghost Knows Best." But Falkner Heard, a by-the-book San Antonio infantry colonel, thought it gave an impression of military aviation and discipline so misguided and wrong "that no degree of supervision could make this picture a contribution to the war effort." Colonel Edward Munson, with some justification, noted the "slightly schizophrenic character of the scenario." Part of his concern, though, came from the few moments the script treats the terrible swiftness of combat death. ("One minute," Ted says, in an early draft of the script, "a man is warm—alive—and then—so fast it's like the intake of breath—he's nothing." In the film, that became "It doesn't seem possible, when you stop to think about it, that they're not here anymore and they're not gonna be.") Colonel William Wright, chief of the Pictorial Branch in the War Department's Bureau of Public Relations, summarized: "Because the script offers nothing constructive to the Army Air Forces, and is based upon the *Mr. Jordan* theme of the living dead, it is doubtful if Army cooperation would be forthcoming."

But the filmmakers wouldn't give up. Trumbo, Riskin, and Fleming *had* built some flattery of the Army Air Forces into the scenario. Lionel Barrymore would play the heavenly general—and when Pete first sees him, he blurts out, in a Fleming suggestion for the final script, "One of the greatest guys that ever flew a ship!" (In the film, Tracy reads that as "What a flier he was!") Contemporary audiences knew that the general was patterned after Billy Mitchell. The general has a model plane on his desk—the Martin MB-2, the bomber Mitchell used to sink two captured German battleships in 1921 and prove the military potential of airpower. MGM continued to lobby for War Department support, and the film eventually passed a new review board. The final script, according to Lieutenant John T. Parker Jr. of the Review Branch, "presents a morale-building motif for the benefit of air cadets, as well as an interpretation of air combat casualties that can be helpful and perhaps comforting to the civilian point of view." Fleming moved to deploy his second and third units to military air bases to enlist military technical advisers.

Nonetheless, for the Production Code chief, Joseph Breen, the tag scene was unacceptable because in effect "Dorinda commits suicide." (It wasn't until early 1944 that Japanese fliers began their kamikaze suicide missions.) What Breen saw as the self-destructive amorality of Dorinda's decision made him suggest an alteration: Dorinda would "take on a dangerous job that might result in disaster for Ted, then loses her life in the attempt." After a subsequent reading, Breen extended his proposal to the specific detail of Japanese anti-aircraft fire shooting her down. "The point," he wrote, "is to get away from the definite suggestion that she deliberately goes out in a heroic way to commit suicide." It wasn't a big problem: the ack-ack fire was already in the script. But this ending ultimately took a ninety-degree turn that pleased audiences—if not critics or the film's creators.

In the early 1940s, Irene Dunne was at the midpoint—and apex—of her triplicate career as a musical star, a comedienne, and the dramatic center of many a prestige studio picture. She rarely gave a better serious performance than she did as Dorinda. Underneath the studio makeup, she's just a workingwoman having hard times in love and war; when Pete wins her over after a spat by presenting her with a glamourous dress, her exclamation, "Girl clothes!" takes her from moodiness to delight in seconds. Her character gets torn up in the action, and Dunne doesn't shy away from the ecstasy or ravages of true love. Even more than Tracy's peerless tough-tender turn, Dunne's rippling presence grounds the film in reality. Her evocation of a lover who loses her moorings in mourning had its roots in the volatility of the set.

"I suppose the film that I thought was most difficult was *A Guy Named Joe*," Dunne recalled thirty-five years later. In February 1943, she hated the midwinter dreariness that periodically settles on Los Angeles. She'd drive herself to work in early-morning darkness and pouring rain. There she'd come up against the challenges of a shifting crew (there *were* two top cameramen, George Folsey and Karl Freund, and, Dunne remembered, multiple makeup people) as well as a director surprisingly prone to ailments and a star intent on "calling the shots."

Dunne, who had hero-worshipped Tracy before she went to work with him, thought her co-star "got the idea that I thought he wasn't a hero anymore. Which was not true. But he had this big mental thing, and there was even talk of taking me off the film."

"This big mental thing" had a history she never knew about. While at Columbia, Everett Riskin, in 1938, had produced the exquisite *Holiday* for Cukor and Katharine Hepburn. He later tried to cast Hepburn in another picture, and she'd turned him down "rather nastily" (says his son Ralph). So Riskin wasn't about to cave in when Tracy demanded Hepburn be cast as Dorinda. According to Ralph Riskin, "Dad said, 'Screw you, Spence,' so Tracy was pissed off from the beginning, and Mr. Mayer was pretty tough to go through with it. There was always trouble on the set. It was pretty tough when they had to play a love scene in front of a fireplace."

Ralph says Fleming would call his father whenever Tracy acted up. "He's doing it again," Vic would say. "You've got to come down to the set." On the jungle site with the field headquarters and the P-38 parked in the background, Fleming announced they'd "take ten," and Riskin put his arm around Tracy and walked him behind the backdrop. "As soon as they were out of sight, my father grabbed him by the lapels and backed him against the soft, padded wall of the soundstage. Then he said, 'Make her cry one more time and I'll beat the shit out of you.' My father and his brother [the screenwriter Robert Riskin, co-inventor of the wised-up whimsicality that became known as the Frank Capra touch] were tough guys from the Lower East Side. They knew how to take care of themselves."

Convinced that whenever she and Tracy worked closely together things were going to get uncomfortable (one story accuses him of crude sexual come-ons), Dunne made the ultimate threat: she'd break the story to Louella Parsons. She also decided she would be performing at her peak: when Mayer reviewed the rushes, he'd see her at "my *best*—my best, my best, my *very* best." She made the right decision. When Mayer viewed an assemblage in early March, about five weeks into shooting, he came out saying, "If we're going to replace anybody, let's replace Tracy." It sealed Dunne's respect for Mayer. "And," said Dunne, "we ironed everything out, Tracy and I."

It was a gutsy move for Mayer, a smart one for both stars. Despite the unfair vilification of his Jekyll and Hyde, Tracy was *the* male actor on the MGM lot. He certainly was for Barry Nelson. "I used to go to the studio even when I wasn't needed just to see what he would do with certain lines," said Nelson. Tracy taught Nelson the importance of what Tracy called "the versatility of thought"—assuming a character's internal life and using it to convey feeling and attitude, rather than relying on "makeup or a special look."

Fleming knew what an artist he had in Tracy. "Spencer never acts," he told a reporter while making *Test Pilot*. "He's smart; he understands what he's supposed to be and while playing a scene he is that person." Fleming illustrated what he meant with a *Test Pilot* scene "in which he was supposed to falter. We made it—and it was so real that I thought he had forgotten his lines. It couldn't have been more natural—and it was a real performance for that very reason."

At quitting time one night, Fleming approached the young actor Don DeFore, who played one of ghostly Pete's unknowing students of flying. "I looked at the schedule and you're not going to work until tomorrow afternoon," Fleming said, "but I want you here at nine o'clock. I want you to watch something that you'll remember." The event was Tracy filming a demanding monologue that Pete recites while Dorinda, weeping, holds his picture and ponders her feelings about her new fiancé, Ted, and the dead flier whose memory she can't shake. Tracy had to recite a soliloquy that both sums up the selflessness of an unsung hero's life and—in Fleming's cut, anyway—compels Dorinda to reunite with her great love. The result was a lesson in naturalistic acting and wise, appreciative directing.

Fleming hadn't lost the taste for spontaneous invention he'd carried with him from the silent days, even after he fell in love with studio work and storyboarding. Trumbo had written, in a page and a half, a masterly compendium of bittersweet romantic kitsch: "I wish I told you how cute your nose is—the way it goes up all of a sudden at the end . . . how good the smell of your hair is . . . the way your eyes shine when you laugh . . . and I never thought for a minute to tell you how your voice sounds—like music, kind of . . . and how you fit into my arms . . . just as if you were made to fit in there." Tracy put over its melancholy essence and made it soar by mussing up the diction and collapsing some of the sentences and losing the bit about music, which would have jarred with Pete's personality. He sped it up *and* savored it ("just as if you were made to fit in there" became the quicker, more natural "just as though you belong there"). His physical performance, caught mostly in a tight two-shot, with Pete standing in profile as

Dorinda sits at her desk, simmered with pent-up passion. When Pete talks about the smell of Dorinda's hair, Tracy emphasized the point with the slightest downward movement of his head. He did all this in one take.

For DeFore, it was an inspiration. "And I thank Vic Fleming for that," he said, "because it was a great, great study in what to do in front of the camera, and what to do personally about yourself, and to know what you're going to do. Tracy was the epitome of knowing the technique of motion pictures." The scene gains immeasurably from Dunne's own understated and movingly tremulous performance, which, given her history with Tracy, was a triumph of commitment over chemistry. Indeed, Tracy remained a truculent presence on the picture. Trumbo recalled, during rushes of a Pete-Dorinda love scene, "a voice rumbled back from the darkness of the front row: 'Look at that pair of overage destroyers!' It was, of course, the incomparable Tracy in a moment of discontent."

That soliloquy ends with Pete saying, "Goodbye, Dorinda. We'd have made a great pair." Then Van Johnson's Ted walks in. He and Pete know something Dorinda doesn't: Ted is prepared to go on that suicide mission to bomb a Japanese ammo dump. So it's not insensitive, merely tragically ironic, that she picks this moment to tell Ted how she really feels: that Pete will always be her one and only. What she had with Pete was "*real* love—like food and drink and air and water!"—and she'd only be able to give Ted "a cheap imitation."

As Ted, Johnson glances at his watch and says, "I wish I could stay and talk with you" and walks out to a certain death. As himself, Johnson left the set in February and would not finish that scene until November. By then, he'd acquired scars, and a steel plate in his head, from a near-fatal motorcycle crash.

Johnson had been a real find for the studio. Billy Grady plucked him from the chorus of Broadway's *Pal Joey* when the major stars were off at war. June Caldwell, a secretary for the director W. S. Van Dyke and a producer actually named Orville Dull, remembered the first time she saw him on the lot. "He was a big guy sitting with his boots stuck out, waiting for a drama lesson. I had to step over him to deliver mail. And he was *beautiful*! I'd never seen a guy like him. He was big and he was nice-looking and friendly, with sandy-blond hair, and just anybody would turn around to take a look at him." His best showing before *A Guy Named Joe* was a brief role in *The Human Comedy; Joe* was going to be Johnson's breakthrough.

But on March 30, en route to a screening of the Tracy-Hepburn drama *Keeper of the Flame*, Johnson had a serious accident. Everett Riskin always told Ralph it was a motorcycle, not a car, accident, and that Johnson's biker friend Keenan Wynn and his wife Evie covered it up because he'd promised not to ride bikes during shooting. Irene Dunne said it was a motorcycle crash, too. Johnson suffered a fractured skull. Glass cut across his face and neck. The back of his head was skinned. Bone fragments bit into his brain. Miraculously, he stayed conscious.

"Van was lucky," says his daughter, Schuyler, because the spill "just crushed the top of his head and left his face relatively unscathed." When the Los Angeles ambulance came, Johnson discovered that Culver City, where the accident occurred, was just outside its jurisdiction. Johnson remembered, "I had to crawl across the road before they'd take me to the hospital." "Van would probably have served overseas if not for that accident," says Schuyler, who adds, "Evie [Schuyler's mother] said he was different afterward, a personality change."

Doctors ordered him off the road, for years he suffered incapacitating headaches, and he became a more remote character; Schuyler says what his "cold-fish" father started, "the accident finished." But Evie grew closer to Van after the accident. She divorced Wynn and married Johnson in 1947 at the behest of Mayer, who wanted to quash rumors of Johnson's homosexuality. Schuyler says Evie never wanted to see *Keeper of the Flame* for the rest of her life.

From the start, Johnson thought he hadn't impressed Fleming. He told *Photoplay*, "They had already tested so many guys so much more important than I and when Vic Fleming, the director, introduced me to Irene I knew just how interested he was when he said, 'Miss Dunne, this is Mr. Van Warren.' " But Fleming became Johnson's hero in the aftermath of the accident. In Hedda Hopper's adoring account, Fleming held an oxygen mask over Van's face at the request of a nurse, then waited to the end of an emergency operation. Victor Fleming "has more heart than most folks give him credit for," she wrote. A 1947 bobby-soxer-level biography of Johnson put Fleming "at the door of the doctors' dressing room," telling Van's surgeon that he's staying because "when a man goes through a door like that one, I think he'd like to know there's someone standing on the other side, waiting for him." (When the surgeon explains that Johnson is unconscious, Fleming says, "I understand that, but maybe he knows, all the same.") Beyond the hospital doors, Tracy and/or Dunne became Johnson's champion, refusing to continue the picture if Mayer thought of replacing him.

The day after the accident, MGM asked the AAF to extend Major Edward Hillary's term as the film's technical adviser. On April 4, the studio was able to announce that the completion of the movie would be postponed "as long as possible" for the young star's recuperation. Jimmie Fidler told his readers on April 9 that three weeks would be added to the shooting schedule; Louella Parsons declared on April 23 that Johnson would definitely return. In May, Johnson told reporters he'd be back sometime in June.

Ralph Riskin says it wasn't easy for his father and Fleming to rejigger the shooting schedule to fit Johnson's recovery, but a lot of variables worked in Johnson's favor. Second units went to work on April 7 to capture the aerial action shots. One unit spent six months hopscotching with heavy cameras from Columbia Army Air Base in South Carolina to Kelly Field in San Antonio and Drew and MacDill fields in Tampa, Florida. Another unit shot doubles for Tracy and Nelson at Luke Field in Arizona. Even with full military cooperation, it was difficult to rely on aircraft being available during wartime. The weather intervened, too, including a score of rainy days in Tampa in July. And then there was what Mannix called Fleming's "exacting" nature. Rather than rely on canned sound effects from the War Department, Fleming wanted MGM sound teams to record planes "right from fields wherever such planes are based, or might be moving in and out." (Fleming got his original sound effects, thanks to his old friend the pilot Paul Mantz.)

Johnson returned to *Joe* in late June—but not before MGM diplomatically judged his camera readiness by handing him a walk-on in *Madame Curie*. "They wanted to see how the scar would photograph," Johnson said. He passed the test with the help of makeup and diffused lighting. And he ended up appearing with Dunne in two movies simultaneously, *Joe* in the afternoon and Clarence Brown's *Mrs. Miniver*–esque *The White Cliffs of Dover* in the morning. "Which one am I in now?" Dunne would ask Johnson before each take. On September 19 the *New York Times* reported that *Joe* had been prolonged a total of thirteen weeks, attributing the delays to Johnson's accident, the difficulty of finding and shooting planes, *and* Dunne's assignment to *The White Cliffs of Dover*—which actually might have been shrewd double scheduling on MGM's part.

Everett Riskin's brother Robert spent the war in the overseas branch of America's propaganda arm, the Office of War Information. A small part of the OWI, the Bureau of Motion Pictures, reviewed Hollywood movies from every studio except (for the most part) Paramount between 1942 and 1945. The BMP's primary mission was to advise filmmakers on how to report and maintain the war effort. It also counseled them on how to present an image of America consistent with the Four Freedoms at the center of FDR's New Deal—freedom of speech and freedom of religion, freedom from want and freedom from fear. The BMP *never* liked the ending of *A Guy Named Joe.* The chief of its review and analysis section, Dorothy B. Jones, complained about it even before the Production Code did. Apparently it was all right to promulgate racist stereotypes in a Warner Bros. cartoon like *Bugs Bunny Nips the Nips,* but having Dunne commit suicide by ammo dump would sully America's wartime goals.

It may sound astonishing today that a government agency, determining that an Irene Dunne movie would damage civilian morale, brought its full force to bear on changing the film's ending. Yet that is exactly what occurred. Here's the scene as Fleming originally filmed it that September:

The script shows Dorinda thrusting the bomber's control stick as Pete shouts, "Look, Drinda, hear me. You always wanted us to fly together—remember? Well, we're flying together now, Drinda! I'm right here—I'm with you—and you've got to let me through—you've got to hear me!" Dorinda puts the bomber into a dive over the ammunition dump.

INTERIOR PLANE—CLOSE SHOT—PETE AND DORINDA

PETE: Pull out, Dorinda! You'll never make it! Pull out and let the Army do this job!

Dorinda seems to hesitate, but quickly overcomes the impulse and continues on her course.

PETE (*shouting*): Dorinda! Pull out!

FULL SHOT—SKY AND SEA AND CLOUDS AND ISLAND

From the island come puffs of anti-aircraft shells, aimed at the rapidly diving plane.

INTERIOR PLANE—CLOSE SHOT—DORINDA AND PETE

Through the front window, we can see the sickening approach of the cove. The ship shudders and bounces from AA shells exploding around it, illuminating the cabin weirdly.

PETE (*despairingly*): Back up on the stick, Dorinda. Nose up, girl. Up—nose up—up—up—UP.

CAMERA moves through smoke to:

EXTERIOR ISLAND—NIGHT—FULL SHOT

As the plane plummets into a mass of buildings, going sideways just enough to slip under an enormous craggy ledge which protects the dump from ordinary bombing. The SCREEN is completely enveloped in smoke.

PETE'S VOICE (*over scene*): Up, Dorinda—up.

CLOSE SHOT—FIGURE

Standing as if on a little eminence. The smoke is so thick that the figure can't be made out. The scene lights up gradually to reveal Pete. He is looking down, calling.

PETE: Up, Dorinda . . . up . . .

The scene becomes suffused with light. The smoke changes into sunlit mist. Up the brow of the incline we see Dorinda walking—first her head, then shoulders, then waist—with Pete beckoning her up.

PETE (*infinitely tender*): Up, girl . . .

Dorinda comes up to him, proud, erect, smiling. They do not embrace. Instead, they clasp each other's hands, stand silently for a moment looking into each other's faces.

DORINDA (*with a kind of delicious sigh*): Pete!

PETE (*almost with reverence, quietly*): Dorinda!
DORINDA: So it was you . . . all along.
PETE (*very gently, smiling*): Of course, darling.
DORINDA (*with a kind of reminiscent yearning, almost a whisper*): Oh, Pete—I've been so lonely. You'd no idea how lonely I've been!
PETE (*shaking his head slowly, smiling*): But not any more . . .

CLOSE SHOT—DORINDA

As she looks around at her new surroundings. Her expression is not one of bewilderment or confusion, but rather one of pleasant discovery and joyfulness.

CLOSE SHOT—PETE

Watching her.

MEDIUM SHOT—THE TWO

As Dorinda heaves a delicious sigh, snuggles her arm into his.

DORINDA: Oh, Pete . . . it's wonderful.

Pete nods. Both of them have on their faces an expression which indicates great joy, as if life were just beginning for them. As Pete nods in reply to her last line they start out of the scene.

ANOTHER ANGLE—FULL SHOT

Arm in arm they move away from the camera, walking with heads up, steps brisk. The mist grows lighter, the light brighter, as they recede from our view.

FADE OUT.

THE END

Perhaps anticipating that audience sniffles, if not outright bawling, might drown out the dialogue, Trumbo also wrote an alternate of that ending with no dialogue, with Dunne and Tracy conveying all the emotion on their faces.

While this ending placated Breen and the War Department, the BMP—shrewdly, it turns out—held its fire. As *Joe* slogged through its extended production period, the BMP acquired more Hollywood clout. When Congress cut the domestic budget of the OWI in July 1943, Ulric Bell assumed command of the Hollywood review office. He'd been the Washington bureau chief for the *Louisville Courier-Journal* and had chaired the interventionist group Fight for Freedom. He quickly pushed the BMP beyond its original advisory role. The wartime Office of Censorship now banned topics such as class conflict and rationing from American movies and imposed public morality more severely on film plots: lawlessness, for example, could never go unpunished.

When Bell's office denied overseas sales to B pictures like *Hillbilly Blitzkrieg, Sleepy Lagoon,* and *Secret Service in Darkest Africa,* the impact on the studios was slight. *A Guy Named Joe,* however, was the quintessential "major motion picture." When Bell's review staff watched a cut of it in November, they were delighted *and* appalled. They admired the movie's emphasis on combining individual expertise and teamwork and its demonstration that "every human being can contribute his measure to the building of the free world." What they didn't admire, in the words of Lillian R. Bergquist, was the movie's failure "to tell the important story of the women throughout the world who are losing men in this war and who are making the difficult adjustment and going on—instead of hysterically sacrificing themselves as Dorinda did." She closed the group's report by saying that with the film still being scored and edited, "It might be possible to persuade the studio to re-shoot the ending, with the heroine deciding to accept her responsibility as a human being, to live and marry the young flier when he successfully completes his dangerous mission."

Bell wrote directly to Eddie Mannix's assistant. "All I am entitled to say on behalf of the overseas OWI is that were the ending different, nothing we have seen—not one picture that we can readily recall—could make as great a contribution to the war job as *A Guy Named Joe.*" Bell cabled Robert Riskin in New York that the film "would be perfect but for Hollywood ending." No direct threats, but the message was clear. "The entire ending . . . was reshot as a result of OWI's criticism," said the BMP's analysis chief, Jones, years later, acknowledging it was unusual for any studio "to go to such lengths (and expense) to comply with OWI suggestions." In fact, it was unique.

How the orders went down is lost to history, but the incredibly swift Trumbo wrote a new ending in days, completing it on November 6. MGM called Dunne back from a Mexico City vacation for retakes that were shot and sent to the Production Code by November 9. At least it wasn't as square as the BMP suggestion. Dorinda, not Ted, explodes the Japanese ammo dump—only this time she lives. Bosley Crowther of *The New York Times* spoke for many critics and possibly the filmmakers themselves when he wrote, "The ending negates the whole thesis and the romantic ending is sour."

For Fleming, Riskin, and Tracy, the original ending had been one of the production's bragging points; they thought it gave them a satisfying resolution to a lopsided triangle. All through the film, the genuine romance centers on Pete and Dorinda—Ted is the pale reflection of a ghost, a point the filmmakers bring home when he adopts one of Pete's nervous tics and starts plucking at his eyebrows. The War Department reader was right: it *was* a clever twist to have Dorinda end up in Pete's arms like an Everyman and Everywoman version of Cary Grant and Constance Bennett in *Topper.* "And even if it does fizzle," Tracy told a reporter early in production, "you've got to admit it is a good try."

The filmmakers struggled to approximate that romantic feeling while letting Dorinda live in the government-approved ending. They kept Pete in the cockpit and had her sense his rightness when he says (in Tracy's realistic mussing up of Trumbo's text), "You're afraid of living—you're afraid of life—and that's double-crossing a lot of guys who are out there fighting for it." With Pete directing the mission like a macho angel and a backseat driver, Dorinda pulls the mission off and gets back safely.

En route back to the base, Pete tells her, "You're going to have a wonderful life"—a prefigurement of Trumbo's next assignment, an unproduced Cary Grant version of *The Greatest Gift*, the story that eventually became, yes, Frank Capra's *It's a Wonderful Life.* Fleming's movie, unlike Capra's, clicked with audiences—and later, with Steven Spielberg, who cried over it when he was twelve. Spielberg produced a 1989 remake, *Always*, miscasting Holly Hunter and Richard Dreyfuss in the Dunne and Tracy roles and, in Van Johnson's, *Brad* Johnson. (Was this nonactor cast for karma, because of his last name?)

Spielberg transposed Fleming's movie to a wilderness firefighting force; amazingly, the blockbuster auteur stuck to the revised flight plan that ends with the heroine alive. "Now that Spielberg is no longer twelve," asked Pauline Kael, "hasn't he noticed that there's a voyeuristic queasiness in the idea of playing Cupid to the girl you loved and lost, and fixing her up with the next guy?"

That's exactly what those old pros Trumbo and Fleming wanted to avoid in *A Guy Named Joe.* It remains an audience favorite, but Ralph Riskin confirms that the forced ending irked his father, Fleming, and Trumbo. "My dad and Mr. Trumbo and Mr. Fleming all wanted the original ending, which was a romantic and satisfying ending for the audience—that she get back to her beloved." Trumbo told an interviewer, "It had three endings, until we decided what to do with it." (According to his copy of the script, Trumbo cranked out *six* endings.)

In a proposal James Agee wrote for *Life,* he said "a good director like Victor Fleming" could serve as his model for a story about a "reliable journeyman." That didn't stop Agee from critically savaging *A Guy Named Joe:* "The picture will serve as well as two hours spent over the *Women's Home Companion.*" Agee returned to the subject, and *Happy Land,* too, several months later, recognizing that these movies had touched a war-wounded populace. Agee invoked Joyce's "The Dead" when describing the jealousy of a living character for a dead one over the love of a woman. "The emotions a ghost might feel who watched a living man woo and cajole his former mistress seem just as promising to me," he elaborated, and "the paralysis and slow healing of a bereaved woman is not a bad subject, of itself. But to make such a film—above all, at a time like this—would require extraordinary taste, honesty and courage." Agee bluntly decreed that "the makers of *A Guy Named Joe*" had only the courage of "a moral idiot."

Sergei Eisenstein was the movie's biggest highbrow fan. He loved the film's "American inventiveness and skill at extracting from situations a range of possibilities—from lyricism to farce, from low comedy to tragedy." Eisenstein felt that "the idea that the hands of each trainee would be guided by the thousands that perished before him attains the height of pathos." The Soviet artist and the patriotic agents of the BMP loved the movie for the same reason: because of Lionel Barrymore's spectral flying legions, "the chain of experience passed down is uninterrupted. And each flight is the creative action of all, collectively."

As the war ground on, the constrictions it placed on home-front life strained Fleming's appetites and patience, though the MGM commissary provided some goodies, like butter, sugar, bacon, and coffee. "I remember the bubble gum," says Sally. "It was one of the things you couldn't get during the war because of sugar rationing. He never said where it came from, but we always figured it came from the studio."

Fleming's wanderlust took the biggest hit. He couldn't sail his boat, and the Moraga Spit and Polish Club wasn't enough to satisfy his yen

PHOTOFEST

Hal Rosson and Fleming focus on Jean Harlow as Mary Astor and Gable watch during the making of *Red Dust* (1932).

JOHN KOBAL FOUNDATION/HULTON ARCHIVE/GETTY IMAGES

(above) Helen Hayes prays for divine guidance in *The White Sister* (1933). *(below)* Fleming clowns for the chorus line of *Reckless* (1935).

PHOTOFEST

PHOTOFEST

(above) Fleming; his new male star, Henry Fonda; and Janet Gaynor relax on the Fox set of *The Farmer Takes a Wife* (1935). *(below)* A member of the camera team checks the lighting as Fleming hovers over Vivien Leigh and Gable cools his heels in the background while they prepare to bring Scarlett and Rhett's marriage to life in *Gone With the Wind* (1939).

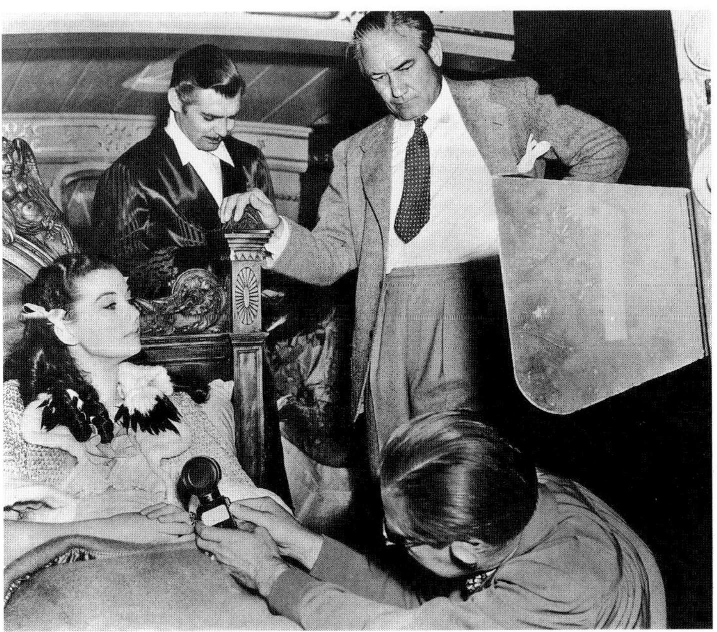

GREER GARSON COLLECTION, SMU

(left) "Gable's back and Garson's got him" went the tagline for *Adventure* (1946). Here Fleming's got Garson in his lap while he gives direction to Gable. *(below)* Ingrid Bergman pays rapt attention to Fleming as Spencer Tracy, dressed as Dr. Jekyll, looks on during the first day of shooting *Dr. Jekyll and Mr. Hyde* (1941).

MIKA RAATIKAINEN COLLECTION

WILLARD CARROLL COLLECTION

Mervyn LeRoy, Judy Garland, and Fleming tower over the Munchkins in *The Wizard of Oz* (1939). Fleming, holding Toto, is looking directly at tiny Olga Nardone and Lollipop Guild member Jerry Maren. Mickey Carroll is the Munchkin next to Maren.

KEVIN BROWNLOW COLLECTION

(above) Gary Cooper makes courtly love to Mary Brian in *The Virginian* (1929). *(below)* Emil Jannings won half of his best actor Oscar for his role as the devoted family man who falls from bourgeois grace in *The Way of All Flesh* (1927).

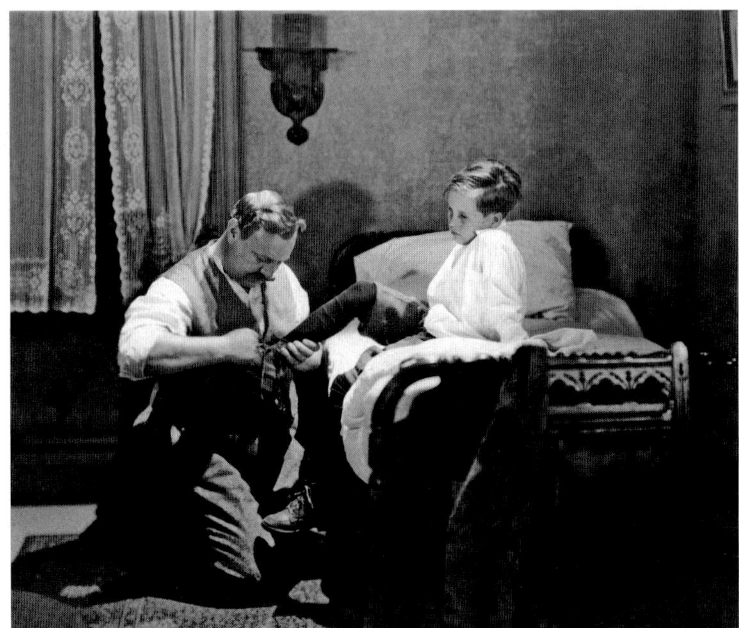

KEVIN BROWNLOW COLLECTION

JOHN KOBAL FOUNDATION/HULTON ARCHIVE/GETTY IMAGES

(above) Harlow at her comic peak, giving her dogs the run of the house in *Bombshell* (1933). *(below)* Vilma Banky snatches a door key from a fire in *The Awakening* (1928).

KEVIN BROWNLOW COLLECTION

PHOTOFEST

(above) Lupe Velez worked with two of her off-screen lovers, Fleming and Gary Cooper, on *Wolf Song* (1928). *(below)* City slicker Percy Marmont falls for a frustrated Minneapolis manicurist turned rural wife, Clara Bow, in *Mantrap* (1926).

KEVIN BROWNLOW COLLECTION

Norma Shearer learns about survival (and love) from Jack Holt in *Empty Hands* (1924). She actually fell for her director.

Percy Marmont forges a doomed bond with Shirley Mason in Fleming's adaptation of Conrad's *Lord Jim* (1925).

Gable interrupts Harlow's barrel bath in *Red Dust* (1932)—a scene Fleming later parodied in *Bombshell*.

Douglass Dumbrille as "Ugly" Israel Hands bows to Jackie Cooper's Jim Hawkins as Long John Silver (Wallace Beery) looks on in *Treasure Island* (1934).

Ray Bolger, Judy Garland, Jack Haley, and, of course, Toto in *The Wizard of Oz* (1939).

Rhett Butler inspects the hands of Scarlett O'Hara, who is wearing one of the most famous of all movie costumes in history: the green curtain dress in *Gone With the Wind*.

MGM star power at its peak: Tracy, Myrna Loy, and Gable in *Test Pilot* (1938).

Tracy stands up for Freddie Bartholomew (*left*) against John Carradine in *Captains Courageous* (1937).

A really eternal triangle: ghost Tracy witnesses the wooing of his former lover Irene Dunne by Van Johnson in *A Guy Named Joe* (1943).

Ingrid Bergman, flanked by Shepperd Strudwick *(left)* and Bill Kennedy, is led to the stake in the fiery climax of *Joan of Arc* (1948).

for travel. He yearned for the freedom of hopping in his car and going wherever his spirit would take him. In 1943, before he filmed *A Guy Named Joe*, Vic, Lu, Hawks, and Jim Jordan (radio's Fibber McGee) got called into federal court to testify in a black-market tire case. Fleming said he thought four tires he'd bought from Hawks were used, before the Office of Price Administration seized them. He told the judge, "What I don't know about this tire business is plenty." (The case was thrown out because the prosecution's case was flawed.)

"A very dour, sort of dry, charming fellow, but kind of a sour act," is how King Vidor once summarized his buddy Vic. "Sort of gruff with everything and everybody. Like a big dog can be gruff or something." One day in 1944, Fleming jumped into Vidor's office and asked his old friend to go with him on a road trip to Arizona. Fleming said they had to meet at Ash Fork. Vidor could get there only by train. When he asked Fleming how *he'd* get there, Fleming replied, "Don't start asking questions." When Fleming met Vidor at the station, he was with his pal Sterling Hebbard, who sold ranches and was swimming in extra gas coupons. With Fleming and Hebbard in the front seat and Vidor in the back, they started east. Whenever Vidor asked where they were heading, Fleming would growl, "What are you, a woman or a wife? You want to know where you're going? Why do you have to know where you're going?"

Vidor thought these interchanges reflected how Fleming had come to relate to his wife. "He was very sort of tough with his wife, [Lu] Rosson, always." Vidor was speaking after the fact, and reviewing his comments years later, Olivia de Havilland figures Fleming "may have been in a very tense state of mind" or enduring "a hangover." Beyond that she notes, "Actually the words were droll—it was the way they were said that upset King. And obviously, Vic had not yet decided where they were going—the whole adventure having been conceived as directionless."

Gradually, Vidor realized that Fleming and Hebbard "didn't know where they were going either," in a jaunt that stretched into a two-thousand-mile round-trip. They were "just going to look at ranches." When they came to a town like Albuquerque, Fleming "always went in first and asked did they have a good Mexican restaurant in this town, that's the first thing . . . I liked Mexican food about once a week or once every two weeks, but he liked it every night, every night and probably lunch if he could find it."

After Albuquerque they headed southeast to check out a ranch in minuscule Muleshoe, Texas. As they drove north, through New Mexico, they flirted with the idea of stopping at the ritzy Broadmoor Hotel in Colorado Springs, and Vidor got excited. He'd been to the town as a boy and wanted to see it again. But a hundred miles away Fleming decreed, "The Broadmoor Hotel—a lot of pimps and prostitutes lying around in short bathing suits around the pool. Who wants to see that? Let's turn around and go to Taos." They did Taos, then Santa Fe, where everyone seemed to have a good time. So when Fleming came to Vidor's room the morning after their night out in Santa Fe and said, "Come on, get up, we're going back to Phoenix," Vidor stood firm: he was staying put. "But that was typical," Vidor said. "Sort of gruff, ordering and bossy . . . But if you were a friend, that meant he could treat you this way."

27

A Confounding Political Life

George Sidney, who knew Fleming only in studio settings, said, "I can't tell you if he was Democratic or Republican!" Others assumed that he was conservative because he befriended men like the strident right-winger Ward Bond. He maintained a blunt and often confounding irreverence to the political turmoil of his day: Joseph L. Mankiewicz recalled him laying down bets in 1940 that Great Britain would tumble before the Germans in six weeks.

Although Fleming was well-read, and had acquired broad first-hand knowledge of the world as well as an idiosyncratic and elegant personal style, he retained some of the naïveté of a self-taught San Dimas boy. He couldn't gauge when a gambler's bravado could be taken for bias or malice, and he made some inane private political moves that he thought would have real repercussions. From age thirty-five until his death, Fleming registered as a Democrat for every election except two. But Lu told their daughters that he signed up to vote in the primaries for the weakest Democratic candidates and thus help the Republicans. His bogus party affiliation didn't stop him from continually grousing about President Roosevelt's tax policies or, in the mid-1940s, enlisting in a Hollywood crusade against communist infiltration. And it doesn't reveal his connection to any ideology or political platform.

Fleming was proud of his independence, disdainful of bosses and bureaucracies. He was likely drawn to particular leaders and issues. Politics didn't preoccupy him, but it wasn't alien to him, either: His mother's cousin H. H. Kinney had been the secretary to the corruption-prone Los Angeles mayor George E. Cryer. Kinney was the conduit for city jobs for the husbands of Fleming's sisters Arletta and Carolyn, and in 1927 briefly embroiled the family in scandal when Arletta's husband,

Ralph Morris, attained a research engineer position even though he had failed the civil service examination.

Elia Kazan was eulogizing Fleming's friend and partner Bud Lighton when he wrote, "He was against the New Deal of Roosevelt, believed that a real man would not accept relief, that it amounted to pity. He despised the East Coast, its ideology and the civilization there. He was for the frontiersman, who lived on a large tract of semiwilderness and asked no favors of his neighbor or of nature, the man who lived where he couldn't hear his neighbor's dog bark. Lighton despised communism but despised 'liberals' even more."

Fleming's own politics must have been similar—but just how similar, and how intensely they mattered to him, remain enigmatic. Unlike Lighton, Fleming enjoyed New York and sophisticated company and even the friendship of a known communist, Dalton Trumbo. Like Lighton, he believed in America as the country of the self-made man. "I have no use for a poor man, because he hasn't got the guts or intelligence to make something of himself," Fleming said in 1947 within earshot of Joseph Steele, Ingrid Bergman's manager/publicist in the 1940s (who also wrote that the director "laughed uproariously" after saying so).

Apart from griping about the tax bite the New Deal put on his income (he was in the confiscatory top bracket), Fleming kept close counsel on politics with friends like Mahin, Gable, and Hawks. Even his daughters are hazy on the subject. "I used to hear Daddy complaining about the communists," says Victoria. "He complained that Dore Schary was soft on them. Otherwise, I don't remember him speaking in terms of individuals. It was always just the communists in general." (Schary, production chief at RKO when that studio distributed *Joan of Arc*, was one of the few voices at the 1947 hearings of the House Un-American Activities Committee, or HUAC, to assert that communism was "not as great a danger as it is represented to be." He opposed the firing of the Hollywood Ten before they were jailed for contempt of Congress.)

During his days with Fairbanks, that other Roosevelt, Theodore, was Fleming's idea of a great man—and Theodore Roosevelt, of course, was a trust-busting, ecology-minded Republican, and later a Progressive. Fleming was equally hard to categorize. In the late 1930s, as a favor to Melvyn Douglas, he signed on as a sponsor of a benefit recital for war refugee relief given by Douglas's wife, the actress-singer

Helen Gahagan. She didn't enter Congress as a liberal Democrat until 1945, but Fleming's sponsorship is exactly the kind of well-intentioned activity that could have gotten him blacklisted or at least pegged as a fellow traveler of communists during McCarthyism's height in the early 1950s. (In their 1950 contest for a California U.S. Senate seat, Richard Nixon dubbed Douglas "pink right down to her underwear." The charge was scurrilous, but Nixon won. Douglas, in return, pinned Nixon with the sobriquet "Tricky Dick," which followed him to his grave.)

The sole sight of Fleming in direct political action comes from the deft liberal screenwriter Philip Dunne. With a Harvard degree and no future on Wall Street after the 1929 stock-market crash, Dunne, a son of the renowned newspaper humorist Finley Peter Dunne, used a letter of introduction from the movie critic of the *New York World* (where his brother was the drama editor) to get a job with the Fox studio boss, Winfield Sheehan. Dunne wrote skillful adaptations such as *The Count of Monte Cristo*, *How Green Was My Valley*, and the version of *The Last of the Mohicans* that was Michael Mann's inspiration for his politically aware 1992 remake. Dunne was present at the creation of the Screen Writers Guild (the forerunner of today's Writers Guild of America). "It was officially non-political," he wrote in his 1980 memoir, *Take Two*, "but inevitably it had a liberal bias, even though one of our most respected presidents, Charles Brackett, was a Republican. For one thing, the very right of labor to organize was in itself a major political issue in the 1930s; for another, the minority of ultraconservative writers had split off to form the rival Screen Playwrights, leaving us with a center and a left, but no right wing."

In 1937, the SWG sent Dunne to a Directors Guild board meeting to test union solidarity. There he observed a telling scene starring Fleming. It gives Fleming the charisma and professional stature John Ford had when he berated the right wing of the Directors Guild, particularly Cecil B. DeMille, for trying to depose Joseph L. Mankiewicz as its president. But Dunne's description puts Fleming in a comic, not heroic, light. "When we arrived before the meeting was called to order," Dunne wrote, "the directors were discussing the Detroit sit-down strikes." The CIO automobile workers had pioneered the strategy of going to their assembly lines and simply sitting down on the job—not doing the work. Fleming, "generally an engaging fellow," had an extreme "reply to this new gambit of militant organized labor. 'If I were running Ford or GM or Chrysler,' he growled, 'I'd get a lot of guys with machine-guns, poke them in through the windows, and mow the bastards down.' He pantomimed firing a machine-gun and repeated, 'Mow 'em down! That's what I'd do!' " Dunne went to the meeting with his fellow SWG member Albert Hackett, co-writer of *The Thin Man* and later *It's a Wonderful Life* and that tepid 1946 *Virginian* remake. They noted that discussion grew heated only when it turned to the studios' refusal to do business with the Directors Guild. "Vic Fleming jumped up and restored a semblance of order," Dunne wrote.

"Wait a minute, wait a minute, fellows," Vic said. "Let's not get excited. Let's not go off half-cocked. No strikes or demonstrations or any of that Communist shit." Fleming pointed to his fellow top-of-the-line directors, including Wyler, Capra, Ford, Milestone, and Mamoulian. "All you guys are working," he said. "I'm working. Here's what we do. Tomorrow morning we walk on the set as usual, sit down beside the camera—and that's it. We don't rehearse, we don't roll the camera, we don't do one goddamn thing. We just sit on our ass all day. Then we'll see what those bastards of producers will do about it."

After what Dunne called "reverent silence" from Fleming's directing peers, the screenwriter Hackett, looking all "wide-eyed innocence" but with "a lethal wit," responded, "That's a great idea, Vic, but what do you do when Louis B. Mayer pokes a machine-gun through the window and starts mowing you down?"

Fleming delivered his only other recorded and explicit political statement a half-dozen years later when he became a founding member of the Motion Picture Alliance for the Preservation of American Ideals—an organization for self-styled superpatriots and anticommunist zealots that grew out of the Screen Playwrights. The group officially lasted just sixteen years, sputtering into obscurity under the belligerent Bond. At its peak in the early 1950s, when John Wayne and the labor leader Roy Brewer were its presidents, it served as a clearinghouse of sorts for those wishing to get themselves removed from the Hollywood blacklist of real and suspected communists.

When it began, in a display of high-powered presumption and naïveté, farcical in its details and tragic in its consequences, a small core of vitriolic right-wingers—all from MGM—attempted to enlist a federal agency in their effort to clean house and scour away any taint of political subversion or radicalism. On November 30, 1943, the MGM security chief, Whitey Hendry, and the screenwriter George Bruce invited Bruce Baumeister, from the FBI's Los Angeles office, to a meeting at the studio. George Bruce mentioned (according to Baumeister's report) that "persons in the various studios were grouping together to combat influences degrading the motion picture industry generally with particular emphasis being placed on fighting the communistic elements." The following February the Motion Picture Alliance went public with its inaugural meeting at the Beverly Wilshire Hotel. Fleming was there; Mahin joined the group after he returned from service.

In the years just before America's entry into World War II, HUAC had tried to gin up outrage about supposed communist infiltration of the Hollywood workforce—and had gotten nowhere. (In one notable misstep from 1938, the committee's star witness implied that ten-year-old Shirley Temple was a communist dupe.) But despite a comical mixture of hubris and ineptitude more suitable for a Marx Brothers movie than an anti-Marxist movement—indeed, one MPA member, Morrie Ryskind, co-wrote *A Night at the Opera*, and another, James Kevin McGuinness, contributed to the story—the MPA created an environment of suspicion and fear in which political spite and paranoia flourished. It catalyzed the 1947 HUAC hearings, which brought on the blacklist of the 1950s.

Along with Gary Cooper and Donald Crisp (the only actors in attendance), Fleming was one of 75 directors, producers, executives, and writers (all Screen Playwrights) who gathered at that first session. MGM dominated the MPA leadership, with 13 out of 24 positions; in another month, when membership had grown to 225, the FBI estimated that 200 came from the studio. When Fleming participated in the MPA on its executive committee, in 1944, virtually all the organization's activities originated at MGM. James Kevin McGuinness, an MGM story editor as well as writer, had earlier founded the Screen Playwrights with Mahin, Howard Emmett Rogers (*Tarzan and His Mate*), and Patterson McNutt (*Curly Top*). McGuinness organized private meetings for the MPA in late 1943 and 1944 and was the first chairman of the MPA's executive committee. Sam Wood was the MPA's first president. The three vice presidents were Walt Disney (who contended that communists tried to wreck his studio), the director Norman Taurog, and the MGM designer Cedric Gibbons; the secretary was Louis Lighton (then at Fox); the treasurer, Clarence Brown; and George Bruce was executive secretary. Fleming was named to a ways and means committee with Gibbons and Brown.

In the MPA, ideology mixed with bile and professional envy. Wood's daughter Jean thought her dad's right-wing furor derived from his bitterness over losing the best director Oscar for *Goodbye, Mr. Chips*—though he lost to his MPA colleague Fleming!—as well as his hatred of Roosevelt and the New Deal. Wood became possessed by anti-Marxism, listing suspected communists in a black notebook. "He was such a charming man—gentle, generous, dear . . . until 'It' came up. 'It' invariably transformed Dad into a snarling, unreasoning brute; we used to leave the dinner table with our guts tangled and churning from the experience."

In FBI memos, Fleming's name appears solely on the roster of MPA officers. But he cast a giant shadow on men like Vidor, who also was a founding member of the MPA and part of its executive committee. In 1971, Vidor said it "did me harm for a while," but that he had joined "simply because [Fleming] came in [and said] 'You're going with me tonight' and we went to some sort of meeting and our name got in the paper. Not that I wouldn't have done it, probably, but I wasn't prepared to know what was going on and maybe I would have decided not. [We] got banned for being anti-Semitic and anti-everything and they got banned right and left from the radicals . . . They hopped on everybody."

William Ludwig, the screenwriter of Vidor's *An American Romance*, was an SWG steward at MGM in 1944 when, in one frantic day, he was invited to join the Communist Party in the morning and recruited by Vidor for the MPA that afternoon:

> I said, "What are they for, King?" and he said, "We're against this and against this, and against this, and especially against the Communists." I said, "I know what the Alliance is against, but what are they for?" And he said, "What do you mean?" I said, "King, I have made up my mind that I'm not going to join things just because they are against something. I want to find, if there is such a thing, something that's for what I'm for. What is your organization for, King?" There was a long pause, and King said, "I'll have to talk to Sam Wood about that," and he got up and left the office.

No wonder the *New Republic* wrote, "Possibly nowhere but in Hollywood could a group of eminent and representative creative workers form a quasi-political organization and [say] 'as Americans we have no new plan to offer. We want no new plan.' "

The MPA's ringleader, George Bruce, was a legendary, prolific creator of pulp novels in the 1930s, specializing in aerial adventures. He'd also published a couple of adventure-story magazines and briefly had his own radio series. In 1938, he boasted that by his own estimate, he had written more than twenty million words since 1920, "more words than any other author, living or dead, who wrote in English." But in that first meeting with Baumeister, Bruce didn't have anything to tell the FBI. Instead, he and other MPA founders fantasized that they could use the FBI as their own investigative force to vet potential members. Bruce knew that the agency had stepped up its surveillance of subversive groups after the outbreak of the war and, Hollywood being a gossipy place, also knew that the FBI had a list of Communist Party members. Los Angeles agents had first submitted that list, along with membership lists of other groups deemed subversive, to the FBI chief, J. Edgar Hoover, in August 1942.

The FBI's men hadn't learned that the few directors who had the power to make socially conscious films were often right-wingers like Vidor. "I did *Our Daily Bread* for King," the blacklisted actress Karen Morley told me a few years before her death, "and that made me popular in Russia; King was amused by that." Why? I asked. "He was conser-va-tive." But in a 1942 agency report, the Los Angeles bureau chief, Richard Hood, described Vidor as "beginning to show left-wing tendencies" because he had praised Russian films for not being dependent on the box office.

Still, the agency "was very, very effective in those days," Baumeister recalled. "Hoover was just fantastic. The boss was just loved by practically all the agents, because he stuck up for us, and defended us."

Officially, the FBI kept its distance from the MPA, suspecting that its leadership would zealously exploit any tie to the agency. But Hoover had a close connection to Ginger Rogers's mother, Lela Rogers (a story editor at RKO), and to Hedda Hopper. In May 1944, a typical Hopper passage ran, "If trying to be a good American citizen is harmful, then I'm gonna hang onto that. Sure, the MPA attacks petty parlor pinks and all fellow travelers. When it accused some picture writers of being commies, it didn't mince words."

While Hopper was extolling the MPA, however, Hoover was ordering his agents, "You should avoid becoming involved in any sort of controversy and at no time should the Bureau be permitted to be put in the position of taking any sides in this matter."

Baumeister, who joined the FBI in 1942 straight out of law school, received several visits from MPA organizers, who either registered complaints about attacks on them by Hollywood communists or provided minutes of MPA meetings. Six decades later, the affable Baumeister says, "I can't remember the details of any of the reports I made. I made most of mine to Hoover personally." But, he cautions, "a lot of things did not go into the record. That was done deliberately."

What did go into the FBI's L.A. office and its records from late 1943 throughout 1944 was nearly as much foot traffic as went through the Hollywood Canteen—the Bette Davis–founded entertainment center for visiting GIs that the FBI, in its initial overenthusiasm, branded "a possible Communist front" because it employed labor unions. (Walter Wanger would drop by to complain to agents about the MPA's attacks on him.)

With the FBI not budging on revealing its list of Hollywood communists to the MPA, the group leadership tried a reckless gambit that could have landed Fleming and others in prison for receiving classified information. For the previous two years, the group's secretary at its Beverly Hills office, Maribess Stokes, had worked for the Office of Naval Intelligence, then the nation's premier spy agency. (George Bruce evidently took pride in telling this to the FBI, unaware of the warning flag he raised.) The FBI had shared the communist list with the ONI and other agencies to ensure that communists weren't getting sensitive defense jobs.

A Navy officer, Lieutenant Dan Goodykoontz, in civilian life a special agent for the Treasury Department and in war an expert in counterespionage, gave Stokes access to the names. She took shorthand notes and planned to send mimeographed copies of them to all twenty-four MPA officers, including Fleming. Whether he actually received a copy of the FBI's communist list is a matter of conjecture. But the FBI quickly learned of the security breach, and Hoover made it a priority "to recover all copies of Stokes's transcribed notes, based on a list of outstanding copies assigned by one of the MPA officials." What happened to Stokes is not reflected in FBI memos, but Goodykoontz was transferred to the naval base in Keflavík, Iceland. Before he released the list to HUAC in 1947, Hoover knew some names had escaped, because in 1945 Wood boasted to a newspaper, "We even know their [party] card numbers."

The MPA was a launching pad for Lee Bowman. He later became TV's first Ellery Queen, but he couldn't maneuver himself into any decent big-screen parts after *Smash-Up* (1947); in 1948, he failed to parlay an appearance on the pilot episode of Lucille Ball's radio-comedy series, *My Favorite Husband*, into a regular role. (Jack Paar, then acting with Ball in *Easy Living*, recommended Richard Denning to replace him.) Gregg Oppenheimer, the son of the series writer Jess Oppenheimer, says he'd heard "Bowman was not a guy born to comedy; there was not a humorous bone in his body."

Politics was another matter. In the fall of 1946, George Murphy, the song-and-dance man who became a Republican senator from California, invited Bowman to make a speech in Whittier for "some young guy named Dixon or Nixon" running for Congress from a district that included San Dimas. "Murphy suggested he take my mother along and make a day out of it," Lee Bowman Jr. recalls. "My mother replied, 'Go to Whittier for a speech? You've got to be out of your mind! Call up *your* mother, she'll go anywhere to listen to you!' So he and my grandmother went, Richard M. Nixon defeated Jerry Voorhis, and the rest is history." Bowman's freshman congressman of choice became an influential member of HUAC. The lifelong friendship that ensued between the actor and the politician culminated in Bowman taking emcee jobs at the 1968 and 1972 Republican national conventions and subsequent inaugural balls, and a 1969 media consulting post with the National Republican Congressional Committee that gave him use of a Capitol Hill office. "He was acknowledged as a real pioneer in what is today a complete media-training industry," says his son, a media-training consultant in London. "He used his work with politicians to develop a corporate clientele. He advised all the Republicans in the House and Senate on how to deal with appearances in front of TV cameras and in radio interviews . . . with the objectives of having their key messages come through loud and clear as well as having their real personal attributes."

By contrast, the MPA did no good for Fleming and did lasting damage to his reputation because it opened him to charges of anti-Semitism. Both the communists and the anticommunist David O. Selznick used the known anti-Semitism of many MPA members to inveigh against the entire group. The MPA leaders attempted to defuse the issue, offering up Morrie Ryskind and other Jews as evidence of the organization's innocence. But the issue wouldn't go away, not with the likes of McGuinness and Mahin on the team. According to the FBI, "The attacks against the MPA have been successful to the point that the top figures in the motion picture industry such as Louis B. Mayer . . . and Jack Warner are both interested and worried." In February 1944, an informant reported that John Howard Lawson had labeled King Vidor and Fleming "notorious" anti-Semites. In March, an informant reported a conversation between Lawson and Yip Harburg, who was active in the Hollywood Democratic Committee. Harburg, according to the informant, said, "I have got a bunch of cowering, cringing big producers in this business who are worried that the opposition is going to say, 'You see, the Jews don't let the Christians organize.' Now that's what they were worried about."

Selznick leveled his accusations directly, after meeting Wood at a *Life* magazine party on February 25 and going on to a meeting of the MPA. (If Fleming was present, it was not noted.) George Bruce, the apparent informant, wrote the FBI: "Selznick spent the evening making unsubstantiated charges against [McGuinness] of the Executive Committee, charging him with being the biggest anti-Semitic person in Hollywood. He also charged that [name redacted] of the Lakeside Golf Club (which is closed to Jewish membership) harbors a nebulous anti-Semitic organization known as 'the Hundred Haters' within the confines of [the club] and intimated that this club used the lockers, rooms and facilities of Lakeside to foster anti-Semitism." (The Lakeside Country Club membership included Bing Crosby and the director Leo McCarey, and in 1944 provided the setting for the golf scenes in Crosby and McCarey's *Going My Way*.) In the early 1930s, Fleming had joined the Bel-Air Country Club—which was, like most others, restricted. But if he was anything more than "a country-club anti-Semite," it escaped the notice of Jewish colleagues and friends such as Ben Hecht and Zeppo Marx.

By 1947, Fleming was no longer on the MPA's executive committee, and his name was off its letterhead. Whether because of disillusionment or lack of interest, his MPA involvement dwindled beyond paying dues. His reputation would always transcend his amorphous politics. The MPA veteran Robert Vogel, MGM's director of international publicity under Mayer, recalled at age ninety-two, "Victor Fleming was a pretty intelligent, broad-minded man, and so was King Vidor."

Even a blacklisted director like Jules Dassin, who did his apprenticeship at MGM, never lost his admiration for Fleming and "the virility in all he did. And his self-assurance. He certainly was a master of his trade. This is the guy who had the muscle to handle Selznick. Not easy." For Dassin, one phrase would always fit Vic perfectly: He was "a hell of a director."

28

One Last *Adventure* at MGM

With Gable, the MPA catalyzed an embarrassing episode, one that betrayed him as a great star in need of great filmmakers. Upon his return from duty overseas, he became the featured speaker at an MPA gathering. McGuinness (who bore a broad resemblance to Gable) wrote a dunderheaded speech for him, which Gable dutifully read. "It has been said that there are no atheists in foxholes. There were no communists either in the foxholes where I was," said Gable. "The boys sit around and talk about home and what they want to find when they get back—and it's not communism." Since Gable was still on active duty, his commanding officer had to face objections that the actor-soldier had, in the words of a protesting letter writer, "cast aspersions on the Allies." At a meeting of motion-picture industry union officials in May 1944, Mary McCall, then head of the Screen Writers Guild, was reported to crack, "Put them wise to Gable, the foxhole flier."

Gable left the service in June seeking a career tune-up. In July 1944, MGM announced a Gable-Fleming film called *This Strange Adventure.* The source material was way off base for his persona. Clyde Brion Davis's *Anointed* was a wry, plainspoken novel about a walking tabula rasa named Harry Patterson who sets out to sea at age fourteen and makes it his quest to cross the Black Ocean and find "the reason for everything." *The Anointed,* like other weird, wispy, and distinctive properties, might have turned into a magical big-studio fluke (à la the Lighton-Hathaway-Cooper *Peter Ibbetson*). The resulting film, *Adventure, was* mighty odd, but not affecting *or* true to the book. Aside from some character names and a quest to find the meaning of life, the script derives only a handful of scenes, subplots, and lines from the novel. There are bar brawls and a glamourized version of the book's San Francisco librarian (Greer Garson) and a parade of romantic/marital spats between her and Gable's long-in-the-tooth but also childish Harry Patterson. There's a shipwreck; plenty of chatter about God, the final judgment, and the immortal soul; and a few scraps of Davis's imagery (a lot is made of water, smoke, and vine curling clockwise in the Northern Hemisphere, counterclockwise in the Southern). An understandably befuddled Gable went to Frances Marion for advice. She marched to her old friend Vic and berated him for casting Clark and Greer Garson in "a studio plot to kill off two stars." She advised Fleming that *Adventure* was "a great title" with "a false promise." Marion's tale seems exaggerated when you learn that Garson fought for her role and that, during filming, the movie was called *Strange Adventure* or *This Strange Adventure* or *The Big Shore Leave.* But Marion was spot-on about the "mish-mash" quality of Gable's role and indeed the entire production.

MGM first considered mounting a movie version of *The Anointed* in 1938, to star the age-appropriate Freddie Bartholomew, but the studio announced the film in 1941 as a vehicle for Spencer Tracy. Three years later a battery of writers, including John Huston's then-favorite co-writer, Anthony Veiller, conspired with Fleming and the producer Sam Zimbalist to turn Harry Patterson from a wandering teenage naïf into a take-charge merchant marine boatswain fit for Gable. The adaptation was difficult, and the process made Vic think, seriously this time, of retirement. Fleming's contract ran out on December 31, 1944, and MGM couldn't get him to renew it. The production executives were so eager to retain one of their most expert and consistent moneymakers that they extended the contract to March 15, 1945, and then continued to pay him at his highest contract rate while he worked on *Adventure.* Word may not have trickled down to each guard on the MGM lot. Early in April, an MGM gate cop stopped him from entering the studio and asked for his pass. Fleming, insulted, turned around and went home. Vidor sympathized with *this* kind of gruffness. When you worked as hard as Vic did at MGM, Vidor said, "You felt like you built the buildings." When asked for his name or a pass, Vidor "would continue on and try to get where I was going, but [Vic] would just go home."

On April 5, Vic packed up and moved out everything in his office. He stayed home for at least a week and a half. Then he went to Balboa for two days of boating with Spencer Tracy. He returned to MGM on April 20 and met with a financial executive in Zimbalist's office four days later to discuss the retirement plan but "gave no indication as to whether or not he was going to continue to render services." Actually, Fleming, an expert at tweaking studio bigwigs, worked with Zimbalist on the movie as soon as he returned. The capper to his bitter joking was asking Clyde Hartman to make a sign marked "Personal Parking for Victor Fleming" that he could plant across the street from MGM's executive offices.

As usual with Fleming, once he settled on making the picture, he went all out. If even a Mahin polishing job couldn't fix this script, the production itself would retain Fleming's new brand of energy and swank. At this point in his career, what this director wanted he got. No one experienced his insistence more directly than the rising actress Audrey Totter. "He was very stubborn," she says. "I had just come to Metro and made a few little motion pictures. He decided he wanted me to play this bit. I didn't want to be associated with such a small part and was mad at him because he was insisting." Gable advised her, "This is what you do: when the camera comes to you, turn your back to it." No one could spot her in the finished picture. *Adventure* opened to big business and shriveling reviews: it became one of those profitable movies perceived to be a bomb because so many people hated it. Totter was having lunch in the commissary when Vic stopped at the table and said, "I guess, Miss Totter, you knew something we didn't know."

Bosley Crowther would muse, in his withering review, "If you ask us, we'd guess that Metro simply said, 'Oh, boy—a Garson-Gable film! It can't miss!' " Yet *Adventure* has all the earmarks of a personal project. Fleming had such a major influence on the script that he was credited in the studio files as a co-writer, and its preoccupations reflect the changes in his life. Gable's version of Harry Patterson goes Vic or Doug Fairbanks one better: Harry doesn't just say "Action is the word," he says that action is everything. But he falls hard for Garson's San Francisco librarian, Emily Sears, who represents emotional commitment as well as book learning. After battling for a reel, they clinch under a tree in back of her dead parents' farm house. They get married, but Harry ships off again, and before he goes, Emily demands a divorce—she knows he isn't ready to leave the peripatetic life of a boatswain any more than Vic would have left the peripatetic life of a movie director in the footloose 1910s and 1920s. "It has everything except Little Eva floating up to heaven," wrote the *Chicago Tribune*'s Albert Goldberg. Actually, it almost has that, too. Only the final-curtain near death of his just-delivered infant son—Harry wills him back to life, commanding him to breathe—matures Harry as a man.

The best sequence, the bristling introduction that unfolds in Chile but was filmed in studio sets and on the back-lot shipping docks, establishes Harry Patterson as a man who believes solely in movement and energy. He enters the film in a carriage with the lovely Lina Romay as Maria, his steady girl in port. (He's left her three times; he cracks, "That makes me a one-woman man.") He kicks in a bar door marked "Cerrado" and swings through it with Maria on his arm. Harry's roistering ways delight everyone, even the abused bar owner—and that's okay with the audience as long as the film remains a roughhouse comedy. There's a Huston-Peckinpah kind of what-the-hell nihilism to Harry's bravado and to its contrast with the sentiment-filled Latin music that underlines his minutes with Maria. Romay had been part of the vocal ensemble for Xavier Cugat's orchestra and had little acting experience before *Adventure*, but she brings some nectarous vibrancy to the film. If Harry's eyes drift away from her to the bar band when she sings for him—if he can't muster any commitment even to this sweet gal—then it may not be in his nature. They amble arm in arm to the boat, where a Chilean man (Philip Merivale) introduces the great-grandson named after him, Ramon Estado (Tito Renaldo), to the boatswain; there's something funny and a little stirring, too, about the old Ramon entrusting the young Ramon to Harry. But Harry has no time for it. He and Maria embrace, and when Harry says he'll be back soon, Maria says, "I'll wait, Harry. I'll be like a statue facing the sea—I won't even move!"

Romay remembers that Fleming "wanted a young girl and someone with some kind of Latin background, which I had . . . I think he really wanted all that sweetness and innocence against all the others." He expanded her role with that bar scene and gave the character a backstory that suited her: Romay would play Maria as the daughter of a diplomat; Romay was herself the daughter of the Mexican vice-consul, first in Detroit, then in New York. She says she "absolutely loved [Fleming], because he was marvelous to me!" So was Gable. During the shooting of her second sequence with Gable, where they kiss, he had his makeup man at the ready with a cup of mouthwash. "When he spit out the mouthwash," she says, "his front bridge went with it" into the studio tank. "We had to hire a diver. And he went down, and sure enough, he found it." That really set her at her ease. "It could have been a tragedy, but it turned into a comedy. He was wonderful about it." During their clinch, Gable "was very gentle." Off the set, he was kind. "He would follow me home every night we shot late, and he would follow me until we got to Sunset Boulevard and he turned left. He lived in the Valley, and I lived in Brentwood, and he'd blink his lights before he turned. He was really very nice to me." If Fleming was stressed out, he didn't show it. "He'd just say what he wanted you to do, but he was warm and affectionate about it. He'd sit and hold my hand."

Fleming films Harry's departure from Chile with dramatic angles that capture the dash and hustle of men shoving off to sea and the mingled pride and sadness of the people waving goodbye to them. These were images he'd carried inside him since his months in the Signal Corps and as Woodrow Wilson's cameraman. A few oddball tropes in the onboard dialogue suggest Vic's personal imprint, too—Harry explaining to one of his crew that iron is a "machine" made up of atomic particles recalls Fleming telling Loos that fireflies are a scientific phenomenon because they produce light without heat.

Sadly, the movie's story revolves around what happens after the Japanese torpedo Harry's boat. Only a handful of crewmen survive, including Harry's best friend, Mudgin (Thomas Mitchell), and, briefly, Ramon Estado, who slips into unconsciousness and dies. Mudgin, panicking, vows to give all his money to the Church and swears off hard liquor, easy women, and using a knife in a fight (even with a bigger man). Instantly, a rescue plane appears. So when Harry and his men debark in San Francisco, Mudgin immediately tries to make good on his four promises. But Harry persuades them all to "drink down" the old ship. Before long Mudgin succumbs to a B-girl, and when a fight breaks out, he tosses his knife away, only to see it stab a man's arm. It's the last good scene: you can feel life closing in on Mudgin like a trap. When his friends find him sitting alone in a bar looking spooked the next morning, he says he watched helplessly as his "weepin' immortal soul" flew straight out of his chest, like, yes, a "firefly." Harry tries to help his buddy find a solution for his new feeling of emptiness and steers him into the library. While Mudgin dreams of heaven, the film goes to hell.

Was there ever worse romantic casting than Gable and Garson? Gable could be terrific with classy ladies like Astor in *Red Dust* and Loy in *Test Pilot*, and he and de Havilland made Rhett Butler's bond with Melanie as persuasive as his twisted passion with Scarlett. But throughout *Adventure* he affects a desperate, alienating bravado. Part of the problem is that he's playing a concept instead of a character. He seeks what he calls "It," and he defines "It" pretty much as everything that makes life viscerally exciting. He's a man of action turned into a post–World War II archetype of bottled-up vitality and restlessness. Only when, as Mudgin says, Harry "grows the thorny rose she planted in his heart" does he realize that there would be deeper thrills in marriage to Emily.

Clark "was jittery the first week until we got him settled down," Fleming told a reporter. Taking Dexedrine for weight loss was one possible cause of Gable's shakiness. During the second week, Gable said, "I stalled as long as I could, I just couldn't get up what it takes to come before these cameras. In uniform a guy fast develops an unbeatable sense of confidence; but when you come back you have nothing but an overwhelming sense of uncertainty." Later, Gable told Louella Parsons, "The trouble was, I had war jitters. Like every other guy back from the service, I was nervous and restless. I was pressing too hard. We were all pressing too hard."

Including Garson. This role model for home-front females earned five best actress Oscar nominations in a row from 1941 through 1945 (matched only by Bette Davis), and won in 1942 for embodying Britain's stiff-upper-lip perseverance in *Mrs. Miniver.* She'd been charming in *Goodbye, Mr. Chips* and *Pride and Prejudice* (1940), but by the end of that 1941–45 run even Garson was chafing at her own nobility. Unfortunately, in *Adventure*, she's tone-deaf and impenetrable. Her meet-cute with Harry in the library is more like a meet-ugly; think of the bookstore scene in Hawks's *Big Sleep* without the sexiness, or "Madame Librarian" in *The Music Man* without the charm. Harry walks in snickering at everything about the library, as well as the librarian. We're supposed to think they're elemental opposites who deep, deep down can't resist each other. But despite these big names signaling their characters' intentions all over the place, all we see are two glossily photographed stars. She glares as he growls and slits his eyes.

"A good hot fight. That's what real sex is," Fleming told the UPI reporter Virginia McPherson. "None of this moonlight and hearts and flowers smoosh where the guy gets goofy-eyed and says 'I love you' and the woman lisps, 'I love you tooooo.' No, sir!" He was getting ready to stage the scene that takes place right after the dramatic debacle in the library. Harry tags along to dinner with Emily and her good-time gal roommate, Helen (Joan Blondell), who immediately sparks to Harry. Emily, to prove that she's brash and entertaining, like Helen and Harry, dances away with Harry's crew and instigates a brawl. (She also crashes a plate over his head, though Harry doesn't notice Emily is the one who hits him.) "I've got a lulu of a fight in this," Fleming said. "That kind of stuff's Gable's meat, but Miss Garson is right in there pitchin', too." That theory worked in *Gone With the Wind*, when Scarlett's and Rhett's survival instincts meshed with their libidos. In *Adventure*, Harry and Emily simply try to out-spite each other.

Garson, too, plays a concept: the woman who must be knocked off her pedestal, then placed back on it. The script demanded the impossible—that Garson be convincing as a woman who falls in love with her man after she teams up with him to steal some chickens. It isn't exactly Hepburn telling Bogart that she never experienced anything as thrilling as shooting the rapids on the *African Queen*. Garson may have had the right instinct to try a movie like this one, but she didn't have the pluck to execute it. "Every time she had to work with [Gable], she wanted these black or navy blue velvet curtains all around the scene, with the directors and the actors," Romay says. Garson found it impossible to conjure intimacy with a co-star if the crew and the sets beyond her soundstage were in her sight lines. Being shut off with an insecure leading man didn't help her, either. "They did not get along personally at all. She was not easy to get along with." The MGM publicist Emily Torchia got a $250 bonus for coming up with the famous ad line "Gable's back and Garson's got him!" Garson didn't prefer the only alternative—"Gable puts the arson in Garson"—and counter-proposed, "Garson puts the able in Gable." But everyone could see that wasn't true. "He'd look at her as if she weren't even there," said Torchia. "It was the same with Jeanette MacDonald in *San Francisco*. With warm, earthy girls like Jean Harlow and Lana Turner, he was his usual charming self. With others he could be cold as ice."

"*Adventure* is definitely the worst picture I ever saw in my life," Davis, the author of *The Anointed*, wrote his son. "*Sign of the Cross* and *Sons of the Legion* were fine productions by comparison. Gable is the worst ham in the business. I feel very sick to the stomach and low. Wish I hadn't seen it. If I had seen the thing in preview I would have demanded that they take my name off it. It'll do me irreparable harm. And I had nothing to do with it."

Adventure marked Fleming's clean break from MGM. Aside from the parking-lot incident, the studio couldn't have been more respectful. The executives asked his permission to give Sam Zimbalist a producer's contract; he told them they were under no legal obligations to him and he'd accept Zimbalist's name on the film anyway. (It was still, of course, "A Victor Fleming Production.") They even composed a letter for his signature requesting a three-month leave, not wanting him to lose his place in the Pension Fund if he did come to terms during that time.

Fleming never came back. It may be that his friend Lew Wasserman, the innovative agent who would become famous for negotiating groundbreaking gross-package deals for his clients (notably Jimmy Stewart), encouraged him to bide his time and consider a new option: independence. Fleming flirted with his pal Vidor's plan to form a director's co-op along with Hawks and Tay Garnett. "That would have been a nice group," Vidor said, but nothing happened: Hawks thought he could do more movies on his own, and Garnett's story choices flummoxed Vidor. When the already-established independent directors' company Liberty Films, made up of Capra, Wyler, George Stevens, and the producer Sam Briskin, threatened to go aground after the release of its first movie, *It's a Wonderful Life*, Capra approached Fleming to join their partnership. Then Capra and Briskin went another way, persuading Wyler and a reluctant Stevens to accept the sale of Liberty to Paramount.

There were other reasons for Fleming to leave MGM. The MPA tainted the atmosphere at the group's home studio. Odd weeds now grew along political fault lines. In 1944, the former producer Maurice Revnes, a Mannix assistant and the liaison between MGM and the Office of Naval Intelligence (and the Bureau of Motion Pictures), had developed a hatred for the MPA and began sending out poison-pen letters to besmirch anyone he thought affiliated with it. In a letter to Arthur Freed's wife, Renée, he disclosed Freed's affair with the actress Lucille Bremer, who was playing the oldest sister, Rose, in Freed's *Meet Me in St. Louis.* Freed discovered Bremer when she was a featured dancer in nightclub acts, and his affair with her would have been a scoop at the time; *Meet Me in St. Louis* had begun filming the previous November. According to George Bruce and MGM's top in-house cop, Whitey Hendry (who'd hired a handwriting and typing expert to check the documents), Revnes was also behind a letter sent to Mildred Rogers, the wife of the MPA executive committee member Howard

Emmett Rogers; it contended that her husband was having an affair with Sue Ream, one of Louis B. Mayer's secretaries, who was engaged to the MPA vice president, Norman Taurog (and did marry Taurog that year). Hendry thought Revnes's attacks "were motivated by personal jealousy" and said "he is not acting as an instrument of the communists." Never a well-liked figure (in past studio jobs he'd alienated Preston Sturges when Sturges was on the way up), Revnes soon left his Thalberg Building office to work as a talent agent. But J. Edgar Hoover was a glutton for sexual gossip, so his agents found justification for passing along the story; not even a month after D day, they made sure Hoover could savor some Hollywood dish among reports of potential espionage. Freed's daughter, Barbara Saltzman, was surprised to learn that her father turned up in an FBI memo about communists and anti-communists: "My father was probably the most apolitical person around. He believed, 'My president, right or wrong,' you know. But probably he was involved in Republican politics sometimes, because Mayer, you know, was Republican."

The screenwriter George Oppenheimer said that after World War II "everybody was out for himself. [The producer Joe] Pasternak was delighted when Freed had a flop. Freed was delighted when Pasternak had a flop. The heart had gone out of it. [In the cafeteria] the center table, with McGuinness, Mahin and Rogers, referred to the writers' table as the Moscow Club." And the MGM executive committee was as oppressive as the MPA executive committee; it now contained almost a score of what Fleming had called those "blank blank blank blanks up on the third floor."

In retreat from the MPA and MGM, Fleming threw himself into family life. Responding to a 1946 polio outbreak, which catalyzed what health officials called "a moderate epidemic" in Los Angeles, he bought an island near Vancouver, British Columbia, and made it a family retreat. His old friend and fellow voyager Fred Lewis helped him buy horseshoe-shaped Knapp Island, which had been a Hudson Bay trading post and could offer anchorage and protection for large ships. (Lewis was already living on nearby Coal Island.) Fleming also purchased Frank Morgan's eighty-one-foot diesel cruiser, the *Dolphin*, docked at Newport Beach, and the four-man crew sailed it up the coast while the family flew to Knapp Island. (The Flemings sailed only on the calmer return trips down the coast.)

Knapp Island was an ideal place for Fleming to hobnob with Lewis and educate and amuse Victoria and Sally. He taught them how to paddle rowboats and fish for salmon. Victoria remembers that he conducted treasure hunts with candy: "Daddy used to hide rock candy on the beach. He'd hide it in the pebbles and we would have to find out which was the candy. That and the island are the best part of my memories." He had created an oasis of enchantment for his daughters. It lasted only for a moment.

29

Ingrid Bergman and *Joan of Arc*

The making of Fleming's last picture, *Joan of Arc*, became one of those behind-the-scene sagas far more fascinating than the finished film, like the productions of *Cleopatra* or *Apocalypse Now* or *Heaven's Gate*. It would span a decade and a half of creative flirtations, turbulent love affairs, and discordant ambitions. In the end it would humble a renowned playwright, Maxwell Anderson; a towering director, Fleming; and an adventurous producer, Walter Wanger. Even its presentation of Ingrid Bergman as an apple-cheeked warrior-saint—the ultimate tomboy heroine—backfired shortly after the film's release, when the American public condemned her for deserting her husband, Dr. Petter Lindström, and their daughter, Pia, for the Italian director Roberto Rossellini.

Released in December 1948, *Joan of Arc* would bear the credit "A Victor Fleming Production." But Anderson and Bergman were the catalysts for retelling the story of the peasant girl who was born in 1412 in the village of Domrémy, near the line dividing the provinces of Lorraine and Champagne. They were the ones committed, in contradictory ways, to celebrating her heroism (and martyrdom) when she responded to the voices of three angel-saints, rallied an army against the English, and crowned a king of France in the thick of the Hundred Years' War. The fight to transform Anderson's modernist 1946 play, *Joan of Lorraine*, into the church-pageant-like *Joan of Arc* became a battle royal.

In 1934, Anderson was at the crest of his fame as a dramatist who could turn contemporary and historical subjects into blank verse and Broadway hits. So when the producer Pandro S. Berman wanted to commission a prestige writer to do a Joan of Arc screenplay for the director-star team of George Cukor and Katharine Hepburn, the

RKO-based filmmaker commanded representatives in New York to go after the playwright. But Anderson was busy, so they signed Thornton Wilder instead, for a work that never got past the treatment stage.

In 1940, David O. Selznick took Wilder's treatment out of mothballs only because he knew Joan was one of Ingrid Bergman's dream roles. A shower of news items promised a Bergman *Joan of Arc* as Selznick's epic follow-up to *Gone With the Wind.* His New York story editor, Kay Brown, proposed hiring Winifred Lenihan, a veteran of George Bernard Shaw's *Saint Joan,* to assist Selznick's Swedish star with her characterization of the French saint as well as her command of English (her third language, after Swedish and German). But Selznick had aesthetic qualms about trying to push through a Joan of Arc movie, even with his prize protégée and the expatriate Jean Renoir attached to direct. (Renoir was appreciated here—his *Grand Illusion* had been nominated for an American best picture Oscar, running against *Test Pilot.*) In his usual blizzard of memos, Selznick doubted the vitality of Joan as a film subject and feared adulterating "Ingrid's natural talent" with stage technique. And he may have experienced the same qualms Victor Saville sensed at MGM when he was supposed to go back to England to direct Garbo in a Joan of Arc movie: "We never got around to it because the Allies invaded Normandy and I suppose they thought it was hardly the picture to make."

Whether Joan of Arc stuck in Anderson's mind for a decade or changing times suddenly made her story more relevant, eleven years later he wrote the stage piece *A Girl from Lorraine,* which eventually became *Joan of Lorraine.* Although the play hasn't worn well, it proved a commercial and critical comeback for Anderson. (He hadn't had a hit since *Key Largo* in 1939.)

Forsaking his usual blank verse for prose, he employed a play-within-a-play format to dramatize the conflict between idealism and compromise, which stirred returning veterans as well as home-front idealists. Should Joan stick to her vision of uniting France under its Dauphin, even if the Dauphin she aims to make king is a self-loathing coward surrounded by opportunists? Can she reconcile her divine dream of expelling the English with the subterfuge and decadence of the French court? How can any higher faith endure an environment that prizes power and money? Reading *Joan of Lorraine* (it's much easier to read than to perform), you can tell it came from the same period as *The Best Years of Our Lives.*

Because of Bergman, whom even a skeptical Anderson called "incandescent," it broke records on Broadway for a limited run. Casting Bergman was the idea of Anderson's common-law wife, Mab, and it clicked: Bergman told Anderson, as she had Selznick, that Joan was her ideal role. From the beginning, an eventual movie version was part of Anderson's prospectus. "I naturally want you to play Joan in the picture also," Anderson wrote Bergman, pledging that if she promised to star as Joan on-screen, he would "hold the rights in the hope that you and I together may be able to work out a project for producing the picture ourselves." To spur on Bergman, Anderson mentioned Hepburn as a possible competitor. But she didn't need much persuading. She signed the contract on a California beach on V-E Day (May 8, 1945). "I'm not making any of this up," Anderson wrote, recounting the tale in *The New York Times.* During the previous twelve months, Bergman had made *Spellbound*, *Saratoga Trunk*, the immensely popular *The Bells of St. Mary's*, and that nonpareil romantic thriller, *Notorious.* She was a huge film star at her peak—she and her *Bells* co-star, Bing Crosby, were voted the top box-office attractions of 1946—and a budding theatrical idealist.

In retrospect, *Joan of Lorraine* seems eerily observant and prophetic of the trials of Fleming's *Joan of Arc.* It's about backstage quarrels in a contemporary theater as well as Joan's verbal battles with the inquisitors who try her for heresy. Joan squares off against her foes in a play within the play; the framing story and the dramatic spine are a marathon rehearsal clash between a fictional director, Jimmy Masters, and his lead actress, Mary Grey. By the final revisions, Mary Grey and Ingrid Bergman bled into each other. "I have always wanted to play Joan," Mary says in the rehearsal scenes of *Joan of Lorraine.* "I have studied her and read about her all my life. She has a meaning for me. She means that the great things in this world are all brought about by faith—that all the leaders who count are dreamers and people who see visions." Mary objects to the way Masters allows the play to be revised. She wants the theme to be "if you die in a great cause," then "your sacrifice is not lost—and the world can be better and different because of your dying." Instead, the play within the play demonstrates that even a saint can strike deals with sinners (though, Mary discovers, only up to a point).

Almost two-thirds of the way through *Joan of Lorraine*, Mary says, ominously, "An actress is held responsible for the plays she chooses, remember." But she does come to see the wisdom of the director and the playwright. They characterize Joan as an idealist who can make earthly concessions—until they directly threaten her spiritual life. Several scenes would survive in some form all the way into the film version. Joan's ally, Dunois, the Bastard of Orléans, advises her to stay in King Charles VII's court and serve as a balance to her monarch's decadence and corruption rather than leave in disgust. Near the end, Joan tells her one clerical ally, Massieu, "To surrender what you are, and live without belief—that's more terrible than dying—more terrible than dying young." (She also says, "To live your life without faith is more terrible than the fire.")

Bergman told reporters she approved of Anderson's Joan. "She was the kind of young woman I think she was in life, a simple peasant girl who loved a home and children," neither "a tomboy" nor "the dangerous fanatic" of Shaw's *Saint Joan.* Echoing Mary Grey again (or was it vice versa?), Bergman continued, "She was driven on by an unswerving faith—a faith so strong she could not renounce it even to save her own life. It is faith of this kind that moves mountains and makes one succeed in any undertaking." On a USO tour through postwar Germany with Jack Benny and the harmonica virtuoso Larry Adler (who wrote that he was her lover), she performed monologues from the play, even though (in Adler's recollection) bored GIs were blowing up condoms like balloons and waving them at her.

"Ingrid was a dear, very sweet soul," recalls Maxwell's son Alan Anderson. "It was a scary, tough job for an actress who had not only the normal work of a devoted professional, but language was on her mind always." She had mastered English sufficiently to pull off a fragmented film schedule with ease. Conquering an entire stage play in her new language was still daunting—especially one that depended on her in every scene (unlike *Liliom,* in which Burgess Meredith co-starred).

Bergman began to show her clout during the Washington, D.C., tryout. She protested the racial segregation at George Washington University's Lisner Auditorium. And Anderson fired the original director, Margo Jones, because he felt she wasn't up to the challenge of making nuances heard and felt in a large, echoing auditorium. The producers wouldn't have made that move without their star's advice and consent (though Bergman in her 1980 book, *My Story,* says the firing shocked her). Bergman's co-star, Sam Wanamaker, who played Mary Grey's director, Masters, became Bergman's actual director, with uncredited assistance from Alan Anderson, who was already working as his father's stage manager. "I have a feeling everyone agreed, including Bergman," Anderson says. "Margo Jones really had no experience. Never should have been there."

When Masters falls into an old crush he had on Mary, he tells her, "You'll forgive an old admirer for sort of relapsing a bit and—admiring you?" By the time preproduction on Fleming's *Joan of Arc* began, with Anderson working on a new script, the backstage plot of *Joan of Lorraine* would come to life in two ways. Bergman and Fleming were having an affair—and some felt that Bergman had come to believe (in the words of Anderson's daughter, Hesper) "that she was the reincarnation of Joan."

On opening night, November 18, 1946, at the Alvin Theater in New York, she triumphed. "Six years ago," Brooks Atkinson wrote in *The New York Times*, "Miss Bergman paused briefly in New York to play in a revival of 'Liliom' en route to Hollywood. Her beauty was extraordinary then, and her gifts as an actress seemed to be considerable. Since then her gifts have multiplied and prospered, and Miss Bergman has brought into the theatre a rare purity of spirit." At the end of 199 sold-out performances *Variety* reported, "She is regarded as the most successful repatriate from the coast, in marked contrast to Spencer Tracy in *The Rugged Path*."

Terese Hayden, who joined the cast in January 1947 as the Dauphin's mistress, thought there was no question what made the play so popular. Bergman "was a magnificent physical presence," and audiences "were thrilled to just walk into the theater and [be] where she was. They don't make them like that anymore. This was Ingrid at the top of her powers." Those powers, Hayden cautions, were mesmeric, not thespian. "I don't think Ingrid was a first-class actress," she says. "I thought she was a marvelous girl. I don't think she was particularly fine in the play." Kevin McCarthy, who played the Bastard of Orléans, also admired her personally. "She was such an unusual person," he says. "She had a perfect kind of freshness." Critics sounded similar notes: Louis Kronenberger (in the leftist daily *PM*) and Atkinson called her "radiant." George Jean Nathan begged to differ: in the *New York Journal American* he called the production "a Readers' Theatre performance of Percy MacKaye's Joan of Arc, directed by a second cousin of Pirandello and interrupted from time to time by some old patent medicine doctor with faith and hope messages from Mr. Anderson and with a popular screen actress as ballyhoo."

"Everybody you ever heard of in Hollywood came to see the play," Hayden recalls. "The most beautiful, in my memory, was Gary Cooper." Bergman complained to Hayden that Greta Garbo never showed up. "I was in Stockholm last year, sent flowers, and made it very clear I would love to see her," Bergman said, "but she didn't even respond." Well, why wouldn't Bergman feel a little petulant about it? Every night a large group of fans who dubbed themselves "the Alvin [Theater] Gang" waited to greet her by the stage door. "Steinbeck and Hemingway saw the show," she reported to her English coach and lifelong friend Ruth Roberts, and "Hemingway said I was the greatest actress in the world."

Roberts was a good pal to have, for her loyalty *and* her industry savvy as the sister of George Seaton, who scored a critical and popular hit with his script for *The Song of Bernadette* (1943) and had just directed *Miracle on 34th Street* (1947). Roberts may have fostered Bergman's tendency to push Joan toward schoolgirl notions of uncomplicated sainthood. Bergman chose to perform half-hour radio condensations of *The Bells of St. Mary's* with Crosby on August 26, 1946—before rehearsals began for *Joan of Lorraine*—and on October 5, 1947, just after the start of Fleming's *Joan of Arc*. It was as if she thought playing the feisty yet wholesome Sister Mary Benedict, the feminine counterpart to Crosby's resourceful, unflappable Father O'Malley, was the best way of getting into character.

Dr. Petter Lindström was Bergman's strong, handsome husband—no pushover in matters of money or the heart. Hollywood types who found him a hard bargainer on his wife's behalf always referred to him as a dentist, but as Pia Lindström, his and Ingrid's daughter, testifies, "Petter never was a dentist. He got his Ph.D. and taught dentistry as part of his plan to pay for medical school." In the United States, he studied medicine at the University of Rochester in the early 1940s and then became a neurosurgeon in Los Angeles, holding teaching and clinical appointments at UCLA and USC and becoming chief of neurosurgery at Los Angeles County Harbor Hospital by 1949. During later stints at veterans hospitals in Pittsburgh and Salt Lake City, and the University of Pittsburgh and the University of Utah, he developed the use of ultrasound to perform bloodless brain surgery.

"He was very good-looking as a younger man. He was a professional-class ballroom dancer, a wonderful dancer," says Pia.

> We won contests together, and we had such fun. He also was a great skier—he took me skiing as a child. The myth is of "the interfering dentist." The fact is, he was educated, [Ingrid] was not, though she was a gifted actress. And she was also [eight years] younger, and he was of the old-fashioned European stock who would try to protect her. But he was a Swede with an accent and not in that world or that business, so calling him "the interfering dentist" was a way of diminishing him.

When Bergman's contract came up with Selznick early in 1946, the producer thought Lindström's demands were so exorbitant that both parties let the contract lapse; soon Bergman was bound for Broadway, anyway. Yet the critical and popular success of *The Song of Bernadette*, starring Selznick's new protégée and future wife, Jennifer Jones, as well as the flurry of interest around *Joan of Lorraine*, made the Joan of Arc story a sought-after property. Selznick copyrighted the title *Joan of Arc*, assigned Ben Hecht to the script, and floated it as a possible production for Jones, who insisted (Selznick said) that he offer it to Bergman first. In England, the producer Gabriel Pascal tried to launch a screen version of Shaw's *Saint Joan* with Deborah Kerr.

Just when Selznick and Bergman dissolved their relationship, Fleming's post–World War I acquaintance Wanger began to reorganize Walter Wanger Productions into a group of smaller companies, including the Diana Corporation (the director Fritz Lang, the writer Dudley Nichols, and the star Joan Bennett). With Wanger, Bergman formed the En Corporation (from the Swedish for "one"). Wanger hoped to snag Bergman for the lead in an adaptation of the British writer Rosamond Lehmann's international best seller *The Ballad and the Source*. Lehmann's novel spanned the Victorian and Edwardian eras, in Britain and in France; it told of a free-spirited woman's determination to be true to her lovers as well as her children. Wanger touted the heroine's "constant search for happiness and truth in a world shackled by the chains of a bigoted culture" and wooed Noël Coward for the screenplay. Wanger would later write that Bergman told him, "Walter, I could never play the part of a woman deserting her child and leaving her husband for someone else, because I could never do a thing like that."

In 1949, of course, Bergman *would* do that, for Roberto Rossellini. Pia says the humiliation her father endured from that public scandal and her mother's other infidelities left lasting scars:

> I was a young woman, seventeen or eighteen, when my father told me how he felt about it. Years after, it affected him. It was so disturbing and painful to him that he couldn't drive home after performing neurosurgery without stopping the car and getting sick by the side of the road. He felt shamed that it happened, and he wasn't of the generation that thinks everything is easy, you go to therapy or counseling, you work it through, you get over it. That kind of grief was damaging to his self-esteem. And for it to happen again and again: he was not from that world in which everyone was having affairs, so he felt humiliated, publicly humiliated, even when he went to the hospital. Life took its toll on him.

In January 1947, Anderson and Lindström had quarreled, and Bergman and Anderson had stopped talking to each other. The energetic Lindström negotiated for Bergman with Liberty Films, but turned Liberty down. "The good doctor is a hard man to do business with," Liberty's partner and producer Samuel Briskin told Bergman's publicist, Joe Steele. "If he had his way there would be nothing left for us." Bergman was getting tense with Lindström, too. "Business, business, it's always business. How I feel doesn't matter," she vented to Steele. But Wanger secretly sympathized with her husband. He later told an interviewer that Ingrid "was always going off half-cocked, making crazy financial commitments, and he was the one who had to extricate her. She had bum judgments, phony enthusiasms." After her triumph in *Joan of Lorraine*, Wanger said, she wrote him "that she was the happiest woman in the world and that, from now on, the theater was for her. But three months later, she was bored. She couldn't wait to rush back to Hollywood."

During the run of *Joan of Lorraine*, Hollywood's top filmmakers came to pay their respects at the Alvin Theater. The Liberty director George Stevens flew in to see the play and talk movie projects, but said his script was "not good enough for you and I won't even tell you what it is." (Instead of that comedy, Joseph Fields's *One Big Happy Family*, Stevens filmed the hit Norwegian-immigrant play *I Remember Mama* with Irene Dunne.) When Bergman let it be known that she'd do a Joan film without using Anderson's play, another Liberty director, William Wyler, began courting her and Lindström. Anderson thought his partnership with Bergman was through. He met with Jerry Wald of Warner Bros. to discuss a movie of *Key Largo* (John Huston eventually made it, with Bogart and Bacall), and Wald pitched *Joan of Lorraine* as a possible star-making vehicle for Viveca Lindfors (who never became a star) or a comeback vehicle for Garbo.

Wanger didn't give up easily on *his* dream movie, *The Ballad and the Source.* He asked Fleming to see Bergman in January, not to consider *Joan of Lorraine* as a movie, but to pitch that novel again. Fleming was feeling unusually unmoored. Many of his friends—Hawks, Mahin, Gable—were in marital limbo or upheaval, and though his own daughters had anchored his life on Knapp Island and Moraga Drive, he'd begun to get bored or frustrated with Lu. "He used to pick on her terribly at the dinner table, and she'd go crying up to her bedroom," says Victoria. "Mother told me that if Daddy had had two bourbons, she knew to watch it. I remember crawling under the bed one time because I was scared," says Sally. He started monitoring Lu's comings and goings, touching the hood of her car when he got home to see if it was warm.

Professionally, Fleming had been unattached for the first time since 1932. Although the deals with Vidor and Liberty didn't pan out, his new adviser, Lew Wasserman, continued to nudge him away from the studios. (Wasserman soon pioneered the epochal arrangement that netted half the profits of *Winchester '73* for James Stewart.) Wanger, a literate independent with studio-sized dreams and a cosmopolitan background, who knew Fleming from his days as President Wilson's cameraman, was a good fit for the director. Wanger enlisted him to bring a copy of Lehmann's book to New York in hopes of hooking Bergman for the lead. Theaters usually go dark on Monday, but *Joan of Lorraine* took its day off on Sunday, instead, out of deference to a devout audience. At the Monday, January 27, performance, the actress who thought herself just part of another movie Fleming made five years earlier became the center of his career and his emotional life.

Accounts conflict on just what happened next. In a publicity piece written for his byline, Fleming said he invited Bergman to lunch the next day and proclaimed, "Ingrid, you were magnificent! You ought to play Joan for the rest of your life."

But according to the publicist Steele,

> The white-maned lion stormed backstage and clamored to see her now, instantly. "Victor, Victor!" Ingrid cried out as they kissed and embraced with fervor.

> Words gushed from him in a violent torrent. "God damn it, Angel, why do you want to make a picture? You should play Joan for two years, ten years, all your life!" He grabbed her shoulders, held her off and gazed into her eyes. Tears streamed down the bronzed, part-Cherokee countenance.
>
> "I came here to talk to you about *The Ballad and the Source*—to hell with it, it's a lot of junk! I don't want to direct you or make pictures with you. God damn it, you belong here, out there on that stage!"
>
> "Oh, Victor! Victor!" she said, and they cried together.

Only in Bergman's version of events does Fleming sweep in, toss Lehmann's novel in the corner of the dressing room, grab, embrace, and praise her, and *then* say, "You must play Joan on the screen." For Bergman, "So there it was. The words I'd been waiting for as long as I could remember, certainly for the last six years since David Selznick said we were going to do it. I was so happy. At last it was serious."

Fleming called Wanger almost immediately to push Bergman as Joan, and his enthusiasm made Wanger move quickly. The next day Wanger phoned Anderson's office to open discussions on optioning his stage work and hiring Anderson himself to do the film script that became *Joan of Arc.* Fleming was on the train to California, heading back to Moraga Drive to attend Victoria's birthday. By the end of the week, Wanger and Fleming called Anderson to tell him they had a deal. Bergman was, as Anderson put it, "now 100 per cent on my side," and even Petter put his weight behind the film. Anderson wrote in his diary, "Wonders will never cease."

Fleming wrote a letter to Bergman from California:

> This was in my pocket when I arrived. Several more I destroyed. The *Lord* only knows what is written here, and no doubt His mind is a little hazy because he had not a very firm grip upon me at the time I was writing—we were slightly on the "outs." I was putting more trust in alcohol than in the Lord. And now I am putting all my trust in you when, without opening this, I send it, for you may think me very foolish.
>
> Then he folded another note inside the letter:

> Just a note to tell you dear—to tell you what? That it's evening? That we miss you? That we drank to you? No—to tell you boldly like a lover that I love you—cry across the miles and hours of darkness that I love you—that you flood across my mind like waves across the sand. If you care—or if you don't, these things to you with love I say. I am devotedly—your foolish—ME.

With Bergman fever heating up both coasts, the star herself "wore a simple gray suit and the usual Bergman glow" at a February 2 bash thrown in her honor by the artist Bernard Lamotte at his Manhattan atelier, Dorothy Kilgallen reported. Fleming hustled back to New York on February 6. The next day Wanger announced that he'd hired the designer Richard Day for a screen version of *Joan of Lorraine* to star Bergman under Fleming's direction. This public declaration had the desired effect of stomping out Pascal's *Saint Joan* and nullifying Wyler. (Lindström turned him down formally on February 9; "William Wyler's disappointed," wrote Hedda Hopper on the nineteenth.) A note from Bergman to Anderson read simply, "Max—come to me!" She and the playwright "made up formally, with embraces," he recorded. Anderson referred to Lindström as "the stupid ass" for wanting Walter Winchell to break the news of the film on his radio show. Louella Parsons was the columnist who did the honors. And Bergman announced that she would start the film as soon as the play's run ended in May.

The movie would be neither an En Corporation film nor a Walter Wanger picture but the product of a new entity, Sierra Pictures, whose principal corporate directors were Wanger, Fleming, and Bergman. Wanger was the biggest investor; he spent $50,000 of his own money for five thousand shares, purchased another forty thousand shares through Wanger Productions, and borrowed $200,000 to underwrite Bergman's twenty thousand shares. Fleming was in for $150,000. All deferred the major portion of their production salaries. (Wanger had to finance the costs of script writing and preproduction.) In a letter to J. Arthur Rank two years later, Wanger commented, "As poor Victor Fleming used to say, 'Everybody in Hollywood is worrying about making deals instead of making pictures.' Never a truer word was said." *Joan of Arc* was a gamble for all concerned. But they were each, in his or her way, fanatically devoted to the movie.

Fleming plunged into independent filmmaking—but he may have had more power with his ironclad contract at MGM. He was about to experience the dangers a director faced outside the studio system when partners had their own strong ideas and the star system was ascendant. Wanger, an Anglophile, was so enamored of Laurence Olivier's *Henry V* that he attempted to hire Olivier's costume and set designer even before Sierra was legally established. When the craftsmen themselves weren't available, Wanger tried to lease *Henry V*'s sets and costumes.

Still, Fleming *should* have been wary of Bergman. He was confident that he could direct her to a career-high performance. He didn't recognize the destructive potential of her intense identification with the role. Wanger and Fleming ended up hiring Barbara Karinska as the costume designer and Dorothy Jeakins, then a sketch artist, as her associate. Bergman told Karinska her Joan should wear red, since a red skirt was common to Joan's class and tradition held that she wore one when she made the rounds of French royalty. "What peasant wears red chiffon?" Karinska snapped. She had total faith in Fleming, not Bergman, even when Bergman was correct. (She did, in fact, wear red in the opening scenes.)

This historical epic would be filmed without the years of planning that went into *Gone With the Wind* or even *The Good Earth*. Fleming had to hurry. He initially made his base at the Waldorf-Astoria; within days he relocated to a thirty-third-floor suite at the Hampshire House, eight floors above Bergman. Steele said he suggested the transfer "to better facilitate conferences with Ingrid." (The $75-a-week rate put off the ever-practical Fleming; he managed to get a monthly deal.) As always a demon for physical authenticity (he shared that with Wanger), Fleming hired the costume artist Noel Howard, who sketched armor and period wear at the Metropolitan Museum of Art (a museum armorer would also work on the film). Then he commenced script prep with Anderson.

The playwright didn't realize—or was too sophisticated to record—that his director and star were having an affair. On February 8, when Fleming was still at the Waldorf, Anderson, who lived thirty-six miles north of Manhattan in New City, waited for the director to call him, then rung him up after midnight only to be told that Fleming was out. He concluded, "Probably Petter is kicking up some kind of hell-dust" on the phone from California and Fleming was sweeping away the fallout.

"I didn't like it," Anderson wrote after Fleming trooped him and Bergman off to see Carl Dreyer's *Passion de Jeanne d'Arc* at the Museum of Modern Art on Valentine's Day. This compressed black-and-white reenactment of Joan's five cross-examinations, a masterpiece of the silent era, features a performance by Maria Falconetti as Joan that makes starkly physical the heroine's tormented and exalted states of consciousness. It had little influence on Fleming, except in one regard. Dreyer shot most of the film in enormous close-ups. Fleming's *Joan of Arc* would contain more sustained close-ups of Bergman than *Hula* or *Mantrap* did of Bow, *The Wizard of Oz* of Garland, *Gone With the Wind* of Leigh, or all of them combined. Unfortunately, this was infatuation, not direction.

Fleming found himself at the center of the action on a high cultural level. He shot craps in his suite with Charles Boyer while John Steinbeck and Erich Maria Remarque discussed European politics. About ten days after the excursion to MoMA and following a week's delay created by a heavy snowfall, Anderson had lunch with Bergman and Fleming at the Hampshire House. Bergman told him she wanted to sing for him, and picked his hit from *Knickerbocker Holiday*, "September Song." But when Fleming listened to the lyrics about the "long, long while from May to December" (and the days growing short "when you reach September"), he knew she was singing the song for her lover and director. He had just turned fifty-eight; Bergman was thirty-one.

Fleming was in thrall to Bergman. Yousuf Karsh had printed up a portrait of Bergman for Steele, who hung it on his wall. When Fleming saw it, he took it. "Marvelous, just marvelous!" he exclaimed. "I've got to have it—it's mine!" Steele tried explaining it was unique and made for him. "You can't have it, Joe," Fleming insisted. "It belongs to me now." And he sped away with it.

John Lee Mahin's now estranged wife, Patsy Ruth Miller, got what was going on when she lunched with Vic at the Hampshire House:

> I had assumed that we'd meet in the lobby and lunch in the restaurant, but when I called to tell him I was there, he told me to come up to his room. It was a suite, actually; a living room and two bedrooms. And guess who was there when I entered—Ingrid Bergman, looking very poised and beautiful. It was our first meeting and I was thrilled because I was a great admirer of hers. Victor said we would have luncheon served there as

> Ingrid didn't want to appear in public; we could have a nice cozy chat without being interrupted by fans and autograph hunters. That certainly made sense. But it was hard to have a nice cozy chat under the circumstances.
>
> Of course, there's nothing wrong with a director having lunch with his star in his hotel suite, but when it's fairly evident that it was not only his, it was also hers . . . it's a bit awkward to talk about the old days back home. Victor knew that I was separated from my husband, John, and I knew that he was cheating on his wife. So we skirted around the subject of the old days in California and we made inane remarks about New York weather, about how the [USC] Trojans were doing, about God knows what. The most trivial of trivia. We parted with many assurances that we would get together again, but, of course, we never did.

Never appearing romantic in public, Vic and Ingrid were old-school discreet. But when Bergman's husband arrived without warning on February 28, Lindström's own discretion shredded theirs. Rather than meet her in her dressing room, Lindström went directly to the Hampshire House and waited in the lobby. After her performance that night, Fleming and Bergman had gone to 21. Bergman told Steele, "When we came to the hotel we went directly to the elevator. I said, 'Let me come up for a little while. I don't feel a bit sleepy!' " She didn't spot her husband sitting by himself in the lobby. And he didn't want to intrude on whatever he sensed was happening between Fleming and his wife.

Already, Petter and Ingrid's marriage had been turbulent. Petter had recently gotten wind of Bergman's affair with the celebrated war photographer (and womanizer) Robert Capa when the three were vacationing on the Sun Valley, Idaho, slopes. Capa's easy intimacy with Bergman and an impolitic remark he made about seeing her in New York suggested that their relationship transcended friendship—and Bergman didn't deny it. But, in Bergman's telling of the episode, when Lindström requested a divorce, she told him that she and Capa were through. And Bergman was sincere, writing Ruth Roberts that she and Capa had made "a clean operation so that both patients will live happily ever after."

Now, in Fleming, Lindström found a new and at least equally formidable rival staying with her in New York.

The morning after Lindström sighted Ingrid and Vic at the hotel, Joe Steele woke up to a phone call from Fleming in full bray:

> "Joe! Goddamn it, who are you that you shouldn't be disturbed in the morning?"
>
> Fleming's voice boomed against my ear like a trumpet blast.
>
> "What's the matter? Can't you sleep?"
>
> "Sleep, hell! You turned out to be a fine friend . . ."
>
> "Hey, wait a minute—What's eating you, Victor?"
>
> "Why didn't you let me or somebody know that Petter was coming?"
>
> "Petter? What are you talking about?"
>
> "Didn't you know that he was coming in last night?"
>
> "No, I didn't."
>
> "Well, damn it, he did. Ingrid didn't know he was coming, either. He went to her room and when he didn't find her there, he called me. It was damn near two o'clock. 'This is Petter,' he said. 'May I speak to Ingrid?' Damn embarrassing, that's what it was."
>
> "Then what?"
>
> "She got on the phone and told him she'd be right down. Pretty rough, my friend. Pretty rough."

When Steele and Bergman walked to the theater that night, he responded to her rare silence by saying, "Victor called me this morning and told me what happened last night. I want you to know I had no idea Petter was flying in." Bergman said, "I am just sorry for Victor. He was terribly embarrassed."

Anderson cryptically noted Lindström's appearance at a script meeting in Fleming's suite the next day: "No fireworks." For a man like Fleming, who treasured privacy and his own brand of honor, such an encounter would be deeply jarring. He managed to funnel any anger, remorse, or anxiety into revising the script. Fleming, Lindström, and Anderson gathered in early March, but the meeting broke up because of a snowstorm. In his own gentlemanly way, Fleming hectored Anderson about the writing; they and Bergman met to go over revisions. On

March 19, Anderson recorded that Fleming "compressed the siege of Orléans." Fleming returned to California on the twenty-third. Boarding the 20th Century Limited to Chicago, he called Bergman during his change of trains to the Santa Fe Super Chief. En route to California, he wrote a letter that he mailed upon arrival.

Dear and darling Angel.

How good to hear your voice. How tongue-tied and stupid I become. How sad for you. Then when you put the phone down, the click is like a bullet. Dead silence. Numbness and then thoughts. Thoughts that beat like drums upon my brain. My heart, my brain. I hate and loathe both. How they hurt and torment me—pain my flesh and bones. When they have had their fill of that, they quarrel and fight each other. My brain beats my heart into a great numbness. Then my brain pounds my heart to death. All this I can do nothing about.

In Arabian Nights it says: "Do what thy manhood bids thee do. From none but self expect applause. He best lives and noblest dies, who makes and keeps his self-made laws."

Time stopped when I got aboard that train. It became dark and in the darkness I was lost. Why I did not think to do some drinking I don't know. I went to bed for fourteen hours and I slept fourteen minutes, forgot to order breakfast on the Century, and had no food or coffee until 1 p.m. That much I remember. Someone met me at the train. I'm very much afraid she found me crying. A hundred years old and crying over a girl. I said, "There's no fool like an old fool."

The first Antoinette Perry Awards (or Tonys) were given on April 6—Easter Sunday. So it was either sacrilegious or fortuitous that Ingrid Bergman was one of two best-actress winners that year; the other was Helen Hayes, who presented the younger woman with the award.

Anderson enjoyed listening to Ingrid and Sam Wanamaker on the radio that night, but found writing the script a long haul. From the moment the movie became a real possibility, it was conceived as a straightforward historical drama, not a Pirandello-cum-Brecht hybrid like the play, and even though he'd worked on major movies years before, the scope of this epic was formidable. Attached to a package of revisions he sent Easter weekend, he wrote, "Just how long it's going to take to finish, I can't be sure. I'm trying to cover ground fast so that you'll have a script to work from. At the same time I'm trying to do a good job, and so I can't hurry too much." Anderson did relax for a few hours and paid a congratulatory call to Bergman and the cast at the Alvin on April 11. Three days later Wanger fired off a telegram asking Anderson to move to California forthwith. Wanger might have made the call, but Fleming's dissatisfaction fueled it. To Ingrid, Vic wrote:

> *Angel:*
>
> *About the script. It is not good. Much too long. Max has not done what he said, has not stayed on the story line, keeps on* Joan of Lorraine. *What's wrong? Walter Wanger and I have talked to several writers—we are going to put someone on at once. Yesterday I spent with Walter trying to bring him up to date on the story and the business. Today I came to the Roach studio. Our gang are all hard workers, like beavers, and all seem happy. Monday we have—or rather you have our new corporation business manager to see. He comes very well recommended having had charge of Columbia Studios. Walter and I hope he will keep the Corp on their toes and get the picture started on time.*
>
> *Angel—Angel—why didn't I get a chain three thousand miles long with a good winding device on the end. Better quit now before I start telling you I love you—telling you Angel I love you—yes—yes—yes—it's ME.*

Bergman saved her frank reactions for notes back west to her friend Roberts:

> *I get so angry when I read Fleming's letters. He seems to have to spend day after day with business people; everyone trying to find out where and how to get the last dollar out of the picture. I know Victor has talked business much more than story, but it is important I guess to get these things organized after all. He said, last time we spoke on the phone, that now he is only concentrating on story . . . I'll be the bridge for everyone who wants to come to Victor with ideas. Don't think for a moment I believe I can turn Victor round my little finger, but I'll try to talk like an angel, be strong like a god, and dangerous like a devil. Forward my friends. Now starts the battle for Joan!*

Though Bergman quotes Fleming's letters in *My Story*, they are not in her collected papers at Wesleyan University; her letters to him, which he tied up in ribbons, didn't survive his death. Sally recalls her mother telling her father that she'd found the letters. He snapped, "I am aware of your awareness." Lu mentioned the contents of just one of them. She told Sally, "Ingrid wrote that she adored [him] so much she'd gladly sleep in some hay—or whatever you call those things you keep hay in—at the foot of his bed."

On Anderson's first day back in Los Angeles, when he still had the energy to fulminate over an improperly worded press release, Fleming took the playwright to dinner at Wanger's house and introduced him to the screenwriter Andrew Solt. Since the war ended, Solt was on a hot streak that included a hit comedy, *Without Reservations* (1946), starring John Wayne and Claudette Colbert, for the director Mervyn LeRoy. In the course of that movie, Colbert's character, the author of a visionary and best-selling novel, was dubbed a contemporary Joan of Arc, and the search for an actor to play her hero was compared to Selznick's hunt for Scarlett O'Hara.

Whether any of that caught Fleming's attention, Solt was the man he hired to help Anderson learn (or relearn) the ropes of movie writing. (In the early sound era, Anderson had written *All Quiet on the Western Front* and *Rain.*) Solt earned his equal credit, and the two writers, and Fleming, had an amiable partnership, despite some obvious miscues between Anderson and his director. Anderson thought Fleming "agreed to the opening." That would have meant using actual voices for the saints, as Anderson had done on the stage. If Fleming entertained the notion of keeping the voices, it was because of *The Song of Bernadette*, which both pictured Bernadette's vision of the Virgin Mary (an uncredited Linda Darnell) and gave the Virgin a voice.

Indeed, on April 25, Fleming arranged for Anderson to screen *The Song of Bernadette* to see how a tale of tested faith, hinging on several rigorous cross-examinations, could have some narrative urgency to it. But *Bernadette* was about a very different country girl, halting and sickly, whose holiness became the foundation of a controversial healing shrine in France; the movie's modest, respectful approximation of her visions gave her sanctity much-needed dramatic credibility. *Joan of Arc* was about a heroine who spoke forthrightly and sometimes merrily of Saint Michael, Saint Catherine, and Saint Margaret and who succeeded in inspiring followers as long as she projected certainty. No wonder that in *Joan of Lorraine*, Masters, the director, complains about how difficult it is to get the voices right. As part of the straight-arrow big-screen narrative of *Joan of Arc*, it's hard to see how a director as tough, precise, and down-to-earth as Fleming could have gotten them right without shading into fantasy, horror, or bizarre comedy.

In his first pass at the script, Anderson simply lifted lines from the play as if they would work devoid of their old context. If he'd had his way, Saint Catherine would still have hectored Joan that it's been "four years since you heard our Voices first in your garden. And you have not yet begun what you must do." Well, what was it they wanted a girl to do? In Anderson's initial version, Saint Margaret provided the answer: "You must go to Sir Robert de Baudricourt and he will give you escort to the Dauphin. You will rescue France from the English and crown the Dauphin at Rheims [*sic*]." Happily, as filmed, this mission statement plays out across Bergman's face while a narrator summarizes her vision. And the Roger Wagner Chorale and the singing of eighteen-year-old Marni Nixon augment Bergman's wonder-struck reactions with their holy warbling. Nixon would go on to sing for Deborah Kerr in *The King and I* and for Audrey Hepburn in *My Fair Lady;* a fourteen-year-old Marilyn Horne stood next to Nixon, and later dubbed the movie "a disaster."

Fleming engaged yet another writer, Laurence Stallings, on April 26; Stallings had co-authored the 1924 play *What Price Glory* with Anderson, and Fleming thought he could pitch in on the battle scenes. Sadly, whatever rapport Anderson and Stallings shared in the 1920s had vanished. Anderson referred to him as "a headache" and chalked up Stallings's knowledge of medieval warfare to reading Arthur Conan Doyle's *White Company*.

Fleming relieved his own stress with civilian sport flying, which had become legal again in early November. He applied for a student license, bought a tiny Navion two-seater, and, the following April, passed his licensing flight test in Burbank. Charles Cotton's son—Charles Cotton Jr.—remembers flying to the Mojave Desert with his wife, Audrey, as well as with his dad and Fleming. They landed near a dive that the older men deemed unsuitable for the younger Cotton's spouse. It was the barnstorming female pilot Pancho Barnes's rowdy Happy Bottom Riding Club—the watering hole made famous in the book and film of *The Right Stuff*. (Barnes's biographer states that this colorful aerialist deserved partial credit for the script of *Test Pilot;*

there's no evidence for that claim, and it fits the pattern of friends horning in on Fleming's successes.)

On May 11, the day after *Joan of Lorraine* closed in New York, Bergman returned to California. Consultations with Anderson began immediately, and the playwright swiftly grew exasperated, even depressed. He couldn't lick the opening scene, which Bergman disliked; he couldn't deliver the pastoral scene Fleming wanted and simply "gave it up." On May 13, according to his diary, "Vic wanted Voices out"—and when Anderson talked to the star about it, he was chagrined to find "she wants Voices out," too. The next day, at her first preproduction meeting, Anderson found Bergman "very simple and gracious."

Stallings, however, in 1950, depicted everything negatively. From that initial meeting, Stallings wrote, "it was plain that Miss Bergman was not going to do Anderson's play. She was going to do Ingrid Bergman's play, not yet written, about Joan of Arc. This was not only a whacking surprise, but a very great pity. Do not think that Miss Bergman was the ordinary run-of-the-mill piece of temperament who wanted to have her own way. On the contrary, she approached the work with the deepest humility, the utmost desire to do the right thing. Soon, there came as many days of debate as there were in Joan's own days." (Of course, he was writing for an audience that had already condemned Bergman for her adultery and out-of-wedlock pregnancy with Rossellini.)

"It was like being back in the Middle Ages," wrote Stallings. Actually, it was like a vision of Hollywood yet to come, when superstars wielded unprecedented power as the most dependable draws in the business and the bosses of their own production companies. Fleming had been thought of as a wily pro able to get the best out of a variety of stars. But having Bergman as his business and love partner as well as his marquee player must have rattled him.

It didn't help that Anderson, the man with the most stubborn artistic conscience on this project, was uncomfortable with the screenwriting form and producing prosaic results. Fleming complained that Anderson kept getting stuck on his old work in *Joan of Lorraine.* The playwright set the nettlesome voices in a sheepcote where Joan was tending to a sick little "ramkin"; Anderson was analogizing her to King David, the shepherd summoned by God's own voice to rule Israel. But Bergman's objection to the voices, and Vic's, grew into a dislike for everything about the scene.

In *My Story*, Bergman depicted the success of *Joan of Lorraine* as a result of her cajoling Anderson into revising his modern/medieval structure to incorporate more of her favorite lines and episodes from the life of the saint. *Joan of Arc* would be even more her movie than *Joan of Lorraine* was her play, and her view of Anderson's intransigence or film incompetence led her to draft some scenes herself, further alienating the playwright. (It may not have helped Anderson in Bergman's eyes that Ruth Roberts's brother, George Seaton, had written the script to an unsuccessful film based on Anderson's *Eve of St. Mark*.)

On June 5, Anderson wrote in his diary, "I told Ingrid if the sheepcote went out, I'd quit." His partnership with Solt became a creative refuge. Solt liked the new trial and execution scenes, Anderson noted, and "says I've learned to write for pictures—or am learning." But the issues of the voices and the sheepcote scene rankled Anderson, and on June 11 he told Wanger that "if it turned out we were doing a child's Joan out of Ingrid's little book [Willard Trask's 1936 *Joan of Arc: Self Portrait*], I wouldn't be likely to write it. Said I wouldn't rock the boat at the moment."

He was sincere about the "moment" part. On June 15, the *Los Angeles Times* published an interview in which Anderson said "he had no choice" in the final shaping of the script but hoped "the idea that faith can meet the challenge of corruption will stand out strongly." Four days later, Anderson elaborated his regrets to *The New York Times*, stating that Hollywood producers "feel compelled to take into account in whatever they do" the entertainment demands of the broadest possible mass audience. "We've had no quarrel with Max about these things," Fleming said, for the public. "He knew when he came out here that he would have to make a lot of changes. In fact, he started making them before he came here."

But in private, two days earlier, Wanger, at breakfast at the Polo Lounge, tried to persuade Anderson "to soft-soap Ingrid," and at lunch Fleming said, even more ominously, "The reins have been snatched from my hands." That afternoon Bergman presented her version of the script from Joan receiving that wake-up call from her voices right up to the Battle of Orléans. "I pointed out that she had taken out the little girl feeling from the script altogether," wrote Anderson. On June 23, he turned in the introductory sequence of Joan at Domrémy in Lorraine, and Bergman read Fleming and Anderson her version of the Battle of Orléans. "I disagreed violently on two points," Anderson wrote, "and she gave in on both." But Bergman held her ground on the elimination of the voices and the sheepcote. The next day she came to see the writers in Solt's office and "kissed us both for the 'wonderful opening'—told us she knew now nobody could write like us."

After so many pitched battles, Anderson had grown fatigued. The script had gotten away from him, and so had Bergman's interpretation of Joan. Whatever faith he had in the production rested on Vic and an isolated casting coup or two. One was Fleming's casting of José Ferrer as the Dauphin; Ferrer had acted in the original production of *Key Largo* and won a Tony for his *Cyrano de Bergerac* when Bergman won for *Joan of Lorraine*. Ferrer did prove to be one bright spot in the finished movie, creating a medieval weasel without resorting to camp mannerisms. Ferrer's Dauphin is a small man in every sense of the word; what makes him piquant is that he knows it. Fleming said, "I chose him . . . not only because he approximates a physical resemblance to the character, but because I knew he would attack the part with more enthusiasm than some actor who wished to return home to the swimming pool." As a matter of fact, he was taking a rare public swipe at Lee Bowman, who'd appeared in Wanger's Susan Hayward hit *Smash-Up* and had tested for the Dauphin. For his part, Ferrer told the technical adviser Father Paul Doncoeur that he took the role "to earn some money" and would "not come back" to Hollywood. But *Joan of Arc* ended up launching Ferrer on a significant film career as an actor and an actor-director.

For a rising star like Ferrer, *Joan of Arc* held the excitement of a baptism by fire. But Anderson, a Broadway luminary for two decades, was in the unusually demeaning position of being dependent on a star's approval, of feeling succored (or was it suckered?) when Bergman declared that she liked the new scene in which Joan converts the army to Christianity. Prolonged conferences over battle scenes and the coronation and trial sequences became ever more exhausting, and the Los Angeles heat exacerbated Anderson's discomfort. On July 31, he told Fleming he wanted to return home, but it wasn't soon enough to elude one last set-to with Bergman. Two days later, she presented her version of the trial. It pushed Anderson past his breaking point: in his diary he wrote that he "told her she was an amateur." Bergman apologized by note, but Anderson, responding in an abrasive letter of his own, would not be placated. When he finally headed back east on August 7, he made a leisurely, digressive road trip with his daughter, Hesper, including a visit to his boyhood home in North Dakota.

Hesper's account doesn't jibe with her dad's diary, but probably reflects his feelings. She wrote that he'd quit and left no forwarding numbers. But he did stay in contact with Solt, Wanger, and Fleming along the way; he even called Fleming to apologize for his scathing letter to Bergman. Hesper remembered their homecoming this way: when they arrived in New City, "My father got out of the car and walked straight to the ringing phone. He picked it up, listened for a second, and then shouted, 'You big, dumb goddamn Swede!' The explosion had happened, and, standing outside the window, I looked at South Mountain to see if it was shaking."

"It is a question of erasing all that remains of Anderson," Father Paul Doncoeur would write just two weeks later. There was some truth in this exaggeration. The movie retains scraps of Anderson's dialogue, set pieces, and themes. At times it even hits the same note of postwar disillusionment, such as when Joan's captor, John, the Count of Luxembourg (J. Carrol Naish), declares that he's on neither the English nor the French side: "I'm on the ME side."

But as the film sped closer to production, drama retreated before hagiography. The National Legion of Decency and the Production Code fretted from the beginning over *Joan of Arc* because no movie could turn clergy into villains, even though the historical record showed that Bishop Cauchon, who governed Joan's trials, operated a kangaroo court. When Selznick projected doing a *Joan of Arc* film with Jennifer Jones, the legion's Martin Quigley advised, "While no right-minded person can ask for historical distortion, the fact remains that the Catholic people are not to be pleased with the presentation of a Catholic bishop in a despicable light. The part played by the Jewish priestcraft in the crucifixion of Christ is a clear historical fact, but it is entirely understandable that Jews, the world over, today are not made happy by the focusing of attention on that historical incident." (Quigley, the publisher of *Motion Picture Herald*, was reflecting Catholic doctrine of the time.) The legion's advocate to the studios was Monsignor John Devlin of St. Victor's Catholic Church in West Hollywood. Puffed up by *The Song of Bernadette*, the legion and Devlin had grown so influential that they successfully demanded that Cardinal Richelieu in George Sidney's 1948 *The Three Musketeers* become *Prime Minister* Richelieu.

To make sure *Joan of Arc* would land on the side of these dubious angels, Wanger and Fleming hired Father Doncoeur, a sixty-six-year-old French Jesuit scholar and the editor of a Jesuit weekly, *Étude*, as their reigning arbiter on all things Joan. But he wouldn't besmirch his international reputation as a published authority on the subject just to please Devlin and Quigley. Doncoeur thought that Pierre Cauchon, the bishop who controlled Joan's trial, "was an ambitious and venal tool of the English." The finished film reflects his view. But by the time Doncoeur, the researcher Michel Bernheim, Bergman, and Roberts had finished influencing the script, it would have been suicidal for any prominent Catholic to complain about *Joan of Arc*, because Joan had become an unblemished and uncomplicated paragon. The movie makes Joan's quest for moral clarity easy. She is the true Catholic: her antagonist is both listed in the credits and cited in the dialogue as a political figure, "Count-Bishop" Cauchon.

Joan forswears her saintly voices merely because she becomes temporarily confused by her desire to be placed in a church prison (as opposed to a secular jail) and given women guards. Furthermore, the movie frames the trial with explanatory scenes between Cauchon and the Earl of Warwick (Alan Napier), ensuring that audiences see the proceedings as political rather than religious. Cauchon contends that executing Joan would martyr her in the eyes of the French and that the key to destroying her power would be compelling her to abjure her voices and her mission. Warwick says that Cauchon's future depends on his ability to see that she burns.

Led by Father Massieu (Shepperd Strudwick), her bailiff, several good clerics counsel Joan to petition that the pope review her case. In the movie, that request becomes pivotal, its denial crucial to the audience's perception that Joan's persecutors are a political hanging court in churchly glad rags, not an authentic religious body. Of course, historically, there was little chance that the papacy would save her and risk the wrath of the English. And even simplified for the movie in order to conjure rooting interest for Massieu, these proceedings are too clunky for poetic tragedy and too tortuous for satisfying melodrama. All the backstage machinations behind Joan's trial take the focus away from Anderson's modern attempt to redefine faith and reconcile spiritual purity and compromise.

Doncoeur dismissed Devlin as "a man very sure of himself, and unpleasant in his self-importance," but considered Fleming "very refined, distinguished, mild, direct." Fleming told an interviewer that he had read more than a hundred books himself, "including Mark Twain's version, which he considers the finest of all modern accounts" (making the self-educated Fleming the sole fan of Twain's 1896 *Personal Recollections of Joan of Arc*, with its idolatrous portrait of the one "entirely unselfish person" in "profane history").

The final rewrites leaned heavily on historical accounts. Fleming had procured a translation of the detailed rendering of Joan's trial that the French scholar Jules Quicherat put together between 1841 and 1845. These volumes had inspired the movement to canonize Joan, and Fleming's ability to quote from them directly led Doncoeur to observe that the director "doesn't miss a thing" and to say that in his "very ambitious" production "one senses a very serious desire for the truth." As captivated with Fleming as many a collaborator before him, Doncoeur wrote that the director "has the charming manners of a very great nobleman." When the Jesuit recommended wooing the French cardinals to surmount the legion's opposition to the trial scene, the director "took my hand and kissed it."

At Fleming's behest and with Bergman's urging, Doncoeur replaced language from Anderson and Solt's working draft with chunks from the 1431 trial "transcript" (a consensus account of the proceedings, created afterward). Doncoeur wrote in longhand, in French; Michel Bernheim translated; and Bergman and Roberts concocted their own versions of scenes, drawing heavily on Trask's *Joan of Arc: Self Portrait*, a verbal album of Joan's greatest hits. (In Trask's version, Joan exhorts her troops at Orléans, "In God's name! Let us go on bravely! Courage! Do not fall back. In, in, the place is yours!" The movie gets that down to "Frenchmen, there is no turning back! We will have victory, God wills it!") Roberts, a Protestant, told Doncoeur "that through prayer, we will find what is missing: the spirit and the heart."

As production approached and the drafting of the trial grew even more critical, Bergman often consulted separately with Fleming. Any new material, from full sequences to mere lines, still went through Solt's typewriter under Fleming's eye. But this hydra-headed monster of collaboration squeezed out Anderson's attempt to bring some twentieth-century complexities to his Joan. The process itself became a theatrical spectacle to at least one of its participants. "The whole thing amazes me," wrote Doncoeur.

In a way, Bergman seduced Doncoeur, too, impressing him with her daily Bible reading and hinting that she might convert from the Lutheran Church to Catholicism. "A very simple woman," he thought. "She wants to live the life of Joan as deeply as possible." He interrogated her with an intimacy and intensity beyond the usual domain of a production or script adviser, then concluded "she is not familiar" with Catholicism "at all."

She had just played Sister Mary Benedict, but in that role her chief actions were secular, such as teaching a bullied schoolboy how to throw a punch. Doncoeur felt compelled to ask whether she was "bothered by Joan's Catholic behavior." He noted she'd had no

> in-depth engagement with the religion . . . What attracts her about Joan is her love for France, for her people, for whom she sacrifices herself, her simplicity, and her honesty. She herself [is] very straightforward without any kind of affectation, not in dress (I am a country girl, she said, and people chide me for dressing as such), nor in thoughts, and without complication. She has a very simple nature, and I believe that she finds herself in Joan without having to become a character.

She and Bernheim attended a Mass for Saint Joan, and when she invited Doncoeur in October to watch her and Crosby record the radio version of *The Bells of St. Mary's*, to be broadcast the following night, he dubbed it "in good taste, except for the Camel advertisement."

Fleming managed to stave off Devlin and the legion with an incomplete script late in August ("the whole picture, as visualized by you, will not in any way give offense to any member of the Catholic Church," wrote Devlin), and as September rolled around, Doncoeur thought his work was done. But when he asked the movie's star, "Do you really need me, because they need me in Paris?" Bergman pleaded, "Help me to be correct, I pray you." Doncoeur determined, "I believe I must not abandon her now, but rather play with her the great part that eclipses personalities, interests, pettiness, and see only Joan." He had already proven his willingness to side with Bergman against Fleming. The priest thought her August makeup tests made her look like "a courtier," but Fleming knew what he was doing. He was trying to accent his star's youthfulness, which he also emphasized by surrounding her with older female performers. Even so, the novelist Mary Gordon would rightly lump Bergman together with other big-screen Joans as "too old and too feminine to get the important element of Joan's boyish youthfulness."

The pressure on Fleming was tremendous when filming started on September 16. The trial portion of the script was, Doncoeur reported, still in "complete upheaval"; Fleming eventually dispatched Solt to Anderson in New City, hoping this team could create sequences playable for the actors and acceptable to the National Legion of Decency. (The filmmakers didn't submit final pages for the group's approval until October.) Fleming's feelings for Bergman and hers for him hadn't dissipated, even if no one at the Hal Roach Studios suspected an affair. Yet here he was, living with his wife and daughters and commanding a project that would rise or fall entirely on Bergman's star power. For the first time in fifteen years, he wouldn't have the safety net of MGM's marketing and distribution prowess. (In addition to demands that Wanger reduce his budget, MGM had wanted 50 percent of first revenues to distribute the film; Wanger went to RKO, which agreed to 35.)

Among the usual displays of theatrical temperament, the chief costume cutter, disgruntled over her pay, threw her scissors in Wanger's face and walked off the film with most of her staff. *L'affaire Bergman*, though, was paramount for Vic. Doncoeur, convinced that Fleming was a devout husband (he'd met Lu at a Wanger dinner party), considered the director's behavior toward Bergman the height of chivalry. "Before beginning, on the set, it was beautiful to see Victor Fleming caressing her, paternally, kissing her hand, then embracing her."

Reading Doncoeur's descriptions of Fleming's generalship, you wonder whether the director's love for Bergman was spurring him on or unhinging him. Watching Fleming shoot Joan's arrival at the army camp, with "extras, horses, dogs, etc.," "45 meters of track" to move the camera, and "100 electricians and two wind machines," all at the cost of $80,000 a day, Doncoeur declared, "But what waste! When everyone was in place, Victor Fleming decided that Joan's helmet was not to his taste. (Three months ago they tested it and approved it, and again the day before yesterday, seen, reseen, etc.) He stopped the take for 30 or 40 seconds to arrange the gorgerin [the chain-mail necking]. Cost, thousands of dollars for nothing." Well, maybe not for nothing: Fleming made sure that Bergman looked even more captivating in armor than she had in a nun's habit.

On Halloween, Bergman raided her makeup room for a raven

fright wig and green cosmetics; she crafted warts and a hooked nose from putty and fit crooked teeth over her real ones. Chauffeured by Steele, she swooped into the Flemings' house as a witch astride a broom, dispensing candy to Sally and Victoria as she cackled her way through the living room. Even weirder for Fleming and everyone else were the occasions when, as Sally remembered, Ingrid "came sometimes with her husband. He was terrific, a very nice guy. He played games with us. One time she came over and gave us some presents—scarves and some kind of gold bracelets. I remember her in our sunroom."

Fleming had quoted a motto from the *Arabian Nights* to Bergman once—"He best lives and noblest dies, who makes and keeps his self-made laws"—but the lesson hadn't stuck in his own mind. Suddenly all sorts of boundaries Fleming had established for himself and his family went by the wayside. Fleming had always kept his movie life and home life separate; the signed copies of *The Wizard of Oz* were the rare mementos allowed inside Moraga Drive. Now he was giving his daughters bows and rubber-tipped arrows used by *Joan of Arc*'s soldiers. "Victoria and I used to shoot them from the driveway to the pool," Winnie Weshler said. "One metal-tipped one got in there and landed near the pool man when he was working. He was very unhappy and left," she recalled, giggling. Even more oddly, Fleming presented Victoria with the shears used to crop Joan's hair into a pageboy cut. She then used them to bob her own hair. "I did it because I thought [Ingrid] was so beautiful, and I wanted to look like her," Victoria says. The act "killed my mother." And her dad "hated it, of course."

Bergman's behavior kept jolting the long-suffering Lindström during the autumn of 1947. One night, when she said she would be staying at Ruth Roberts's apartment, Lindström arrived there unannounced. "At first, Ruth mentioned that Ingrid had locked herself up in a room to work there," Lindström recalled. "I searched the apartment. There was no Ingrid there, and Ruth had to admit that Ingrid had gone out for the night with a boyfriend. A few days later, [Lu] came to me and said, 'You must help me! My husband has got to stop this relationship!' " (It was the reverse of the scene between Lionel Atwill and Luise Rainer in *The Great Waltz*.) Lu huddled with Lindström, but he understood that the only solution to *his* problem was divorce. "I was never perfect and the marriage was anything but ideal," Lindström told Bergman's biographer Donald Spoto. "One of my many mistakes was that I did not proceed with the divorce I firmly proposed. She pleaded with me and assured me that she was changing her life." She counter-proposed that they have another child following her next picture for Hitchcock (*Under Capricorn*). Lindström said he agreed, and made plans to expand their house.

The affair did cool, though Fleming tried to put a happy face on his and Bergman's movie partnership. "She's not superhuman," he said. "She can be stubborn, but her stubbornness is based on an instinct for what makes the best picture."

"Except for *Joan of Arc*," said Alfred Hitchcock, the man Selznick once groomed as his next Victor Fleming, Bergman "could never conceive of anything that was grand enough." (She chalked that comment up to the pressures of making *Under Capricorn*.) Sympathetic and skeptical observers alike thought Bergman was torn three ways: she had overidentified with Joan, she had personal ambitions to (in Hitchcock's words) "appear in masterpieces," and she was also a partner in Sierra Pictures. Fleming was screening David Lean's *Great Expectations* when Stallings noted "a magnificent crane shot" following the boy Pip through Miss Havisham's mansion. "I spoke of Fleming's great take on the carpet of Rhett Butler's stairway which won Hattie McDaniel an Academy Award. 'But the cost,' Ingrid said. 'Think of the cost!' " (The screening may have led to the apt casting of Lean's Mr. Jaggers, Francis L. Sullivan, as Joan's show-trial antagonist, Cauchon.)

Fleming had made movies with lovers before, but never with one who knew her own force as a producer-star. It was not a dilemma a man like him could readily "talk out." On the surface she seemed gracious and appreciative. Bergman later said,

> Vic Fleming wore himself out on the picture. He was here and there and everywhere. I loved just to watch him; he moved beautifully, he was so graceful, and he had this great warmth toward everyone, always pleasant and helpful . . . Union practices very often got on his nerves. He could never wait for the man who was to come and do it to arrive; if a plug had to be put in, he put it in himself; if something needed carrying, he carried it. They were all union jobs, but he did them himself, and got away with them, so obviously they all liked him. But it was a very tight budget we were working on, and it was difficult because there wasn't much belief in Hollywood that the picture

> was going to be any good . . . Nobody thought there was any box office in a young girl saving her country, especially with no love story.

The budget tight? Only because the ambitions were spectacular. At $4.65 million, few pictures would rival it, most notably *Duel in the Sun* (the final cost of that Selznick epic was $5.25 million), and this was no "Lust in the Dust." Not much belief in Hollywood that the picture was going to be good or successful? Hedda Hopper was Fleming's biggest fan; the life of a saint was Louella Parsons's type of picture; and at one time or another it seemed as if every major independent producer or director in Hollywood wanted his own Joan picture, preferably with Bergman, the most popular female star. "I think the pressures got to Victor Fleming," Bergman said. "He was so anxious to make this a great success because he knew I was in love with Joan and her story." She left the ultimate pressure unsaid: Fleming's love for her.

The schedule *was* tight: a costume worker and machine operator strike hit Hollywood in August—one reason, along with the script problems, that the film was moved to mid-September. And the work space *was* cramped; the Hal Roach Studios were nothing like the quarters Fleming used to inhabit at MGM. The flu took Fleming out of commission for a week. Doncoeur observed:

> He came, wrapped in blankets, to direct the set with a fever. I admire the courage of someone who, six days a week, does not allow himself an hour of rest. Most often, he doesn't even come to the commissary. I have seen him at noon eating a sandwich brought to him in paper, staying all alone on the soundstage . . . In her bungalow, Bergman eats a wedge of cheese from Holland with pumpernickel bread. That's all, with a cup of coffee. She just had a cook, a Christian Scientist who as soon as she entered the house said, "I did not come here to cook, but to accomplish my mission." It was as worrying to their stomachs as it was to their spirits.

No matter how great his fortitude (and hers), it was proving impossible for Fleming to manage his last romantic fling with a business and artistic partner. Never before had he been heard to say "the reins have been snatched from my hands." Pride and fiscal responsibility wouldn't permit him to walk away as he had on *The Yearling*. And Wanger had laid another weighty mantle on the director's shoulders. Wanger always conceived of this film as his and Fleming's counterpart to Olivier's *Henry V.* Given the success of Anderson's play, Wanger might have reasoned that its messages of idealism and compromise would hit home with postwar audiences the way Olivier's puissant patriotism did in wartime. But Anderson, Solt, and Stallings were not churning out Shakespeare, and *Henry V,* though a box-office phenomenon for an import, grossed only $1 million as it traveled from town to town, first as a road-show presentation and later in general distribution. Wanger wanted the same rollout for *Joan of Arc.*

Fleming genuinely adored Bergman as an actress. To Stallings he said, "Brother, she is bulletproof. There never has been another figure like her before a camera; you can shoot her at any angle, any position. It doesn't make any difference . . . you don't have to protect her. You can bother about the other actors on the set. But Ingrid's like a Notre Dame quarterback. An onlooker can't take his eyes off her!"

Jimmy Lydon, the popular juvenile who played Pierre d'Arc, Joan's younger brother, says the director wasn't interested in any of the other actors. He offers a snapshot of Fleming at his weakest or most distracted. "He would approach a scene like this," says Lydon.

> "Okay, we're in the French farmhouse (or whatever), scene 27 (or whatever). You guys know this scene? Kick it around while I go talk to Joe [Valentine, the cinematographer]." He would go off for forty-five minutes or an hour with Joe while the cast would rehearse and stage the scene. Then he'd say two or three things—"It stinks," or "Kick it around again," or "That's fine." And he'd say, "Joe, put the camera there," and that was it. Actors need guidance or encouragement; you've got to suggest, cajole, or pat them on the head to get them up to doing what they want to do . . . Mr. Fleming didn't know anything about that. He depended on the marvelous people he hired. Maybe 90 percent of the time he was not far wrong. But in my experience, he never told an actor anything. We were working in cold soundstages in winter, for five or six weeks—very difficult conditions. We were all taken with Mr. Fleming's background, but I was terribly surprised at this man who seemed to have only camera setups and visuals to attend to, and there's a lot more to making a motion picture than that.

Lydon's one scene *was* a travesty of exposition, establishing the viciousness of pro-English Burgundians and introducing Joan's uncle, Durand Laxart (Roman Bohnen), as her means of reaching de Baudricourt, the governor of Vaucouleurs (George Coulouris). Fleming remembered Rand Brooks from *Gone With the Wind* and cast him as Joan's older brother, Jean. As Brooks said, "You couldn't even see me." Still, he loved Fleming:

> I'll never forget this; we walked off the set the day we finished shooting, and he says, "I've given you all these goddamned little parts, next time we'll give you a real good one." Of course for Vic, there would be no next time. I always thought actors loved him. I think he knew the angles and he had the emotion inside, and he just talked to people about what he felt a scene should be. A lot of actor-directors get into the part and have actors mimic them; that wasn't Vic's way.

But on *Joan of Arc,* only the most heroic scenes, or the intimate ones with Ingrid, got Fleming's blood running. Even the admiring Doncoeur complained about the coronation of Charles VII: "Very cold, and without spirit, above all, without prayers."

Fleming's on-set behavior never suggested an affair with Bergman. "We were all in love with Ingrid as a professional and as a sweet and wonderful lady," Lydon says. "But I don't think he treated her differently than anyone else. The quality of this woman! Working at the Hal Roach Studios under difficult conditions, getting in and out of this ugly fake armor; one day she came in later, at nine, and apologized to Fleming and the cast and crew, saying, 'I have no excuse. I'm terribly sorry. The alarm went off and I went back and I am terribly sorry for holding up the company.' And Fleming just said, 'Let's go to work.' "

Off the set, though, Fleming was effusive: "She's no bovine girl with cow eyes," he told the *Saturday Evening Post.* "She's got more warmth than anyone I know. She has temperament, but she controls her temperament. She's never really happy when she's not working. All her other pleasures are secondary to that. I've never known anyone so buoyant over a good scene or a good bit. Nor have I ever seen any human being suffer more over a bad picture. When she is in a bad picture, her fits of depression amount to actual physical nausea."

The character actor and acting teacher Jeff Corey, who played Joan's guard during her imprisonment and inquisition, thought that

Fleming didn't *need* discussions with actors and that he handled his star lovingly and gracefully. The historical adviser Bernheim emphasized to Bergman the sewer-like foulness of Joan's cell, and she passed the knowledge along to Corey. "Fleming was happy with what I did," Corey said. "I played the guard as a man who was hurt, who was trying to say to her, 'I care about you,'—who had a crush on her, in spite of her smelling so badly." There *is* a sensitive shot of Corey and Bergman through the cell grate, the guard staring dreamily at Joan before he moves on her and she responds aghast.

That's what Corey remembered when he said,

> It was quite wonderful in one particular scene the way [Fleming] talked to Ingrid, when she acquiesced to the inquisition and had to realize the saints were turned against her. In the scene, she's looking through the bars of her cell . . . Victor came close to her and said, "Ingrid, you've turned your back [on the saints], and they're not listening to you, and you break down," and he gently broke an ammonia capsule and swept it under her nose, and the medicinal tears merged with the real tears, and he very quietly turned to the crew and said, "Action."

Corey would soon become a victim of the blacklist, and the repercussions of the Motion Picture Alliance reverberated throughout the set. Several other left-leaning actors performed in *Joan of Arc*, including the Group Theatre mainstay Roman Bohnen, Selena Royle (who, off the set, made a speech attacking HUAC while the film was being shot), and Kate Drain Lawson, the wife of the communist screenwriter and MPA opponent John Howard Lawson. Doncoeur noted that Wanger was part of a group of twenty-five producers and stars (including Charles Boyer) who purchased radio time to protest the witch hunt, invoking the First Amendment and demanding that the government and patriotic groups accuse specific people openly and halt their mass indictment of the industry as a whole.

Despite those dark clouds, Corey made *Joan of Arc* sound like an actor's holiday: "Half my Hollywood friends—Aubrey Mather, Alan Napier, Herb Rudley, Shepperd Strudwick—all wonderful friends and very good actors I'd worked with onstage and in films, all of us enjoyed being in this all-star cast." None of them, according to Corey, knew of Fleming and Bergman's romantic entanglement.

Unfortunately, little of their joy infused the action; Ferrer's proudly shallow Dauphin was the most amusing sideshow. (George Coulouris Jr. said that George senior, who played the governor of Vaucouleurs, "had a higher opinion of Ferrer" than of Bergman.) In the movie's 146 minutes, there was room for only one character with any breadth—Joan—and her leading man was God. "If Ingrid hadn't insisted on taking out all human touches and making Joan a plaster saint, the thing might have had some quality," Maxwell Anderson complained to John Mason Brown after Brown panned the film in the *Saturday Review.* ("England's Harry was more fortunate in his ghostwriter," Brown noted.) "She wrecked that one," Anderson insisted, disavowing the film's pedestrian demotic language. "She had the power to wreck it and she did. Moreover, she's completely unscrupulous. She doesn't keep her word and she has no respect for a writer's work."

Each time Fleming stages some juicy bit of traditional Joan legendry, the movie comes momentarily to life: when Joan arrives at the Dauphin's court in Chinon, his poet-jester (Vincent Donahue) puts an impostor on the Dauphin's throne in order to addle and expose her and amuse the court. It's one of the few scenes in which Bergman seems genuine—betrayed and confused—and Fleming's camera follows her with tensile grace as she picks her way through the mingled noblemen to the true Dauphin. But, Ferrer aside, the supporting performances are too arch, especially Donahue and Gene Lockhart as the mercenary counselor Georges de la Trémouille. Also, John Emery as Joan's supporter Jean, Duke d'Alençon, the Dauphin's cousin, is woefully miscast: a distinguished gentleman of a certain age rather than a dashing young warrior.

Fleming seized on one detail from the trial to provide some fleeting humorous counterpoint. Historically, Cauchon asked Joan whether her saints had hair, a question that Anderson put in the mouth of another august questioner and framed to mock the pseudo-dignity of Cauchon's court. (Although for fifteenth-century Catholics, it was a reasonable query: they wanted to know just what emanations of faith *would* look like in the flesh.) Fleming, however, had the question posed by yet another cleric, Jean de la Fontaine, played by Corey's friend Aubrey Mather (the police inspector in *Dr. Jekyll and Mr. Hyde*). Mather was a British character actor with a slick bald pate. When *he* asks the question about hair, it contains a comic element of yearning.

Though Fleming could choreograph a rousing vignette of Frenchmen rising to Joan's cause, the scenes of her with her closest military supporters are leaden when they should be steely. Kevin McCarthy had played Dunois, the Bastard of Orléans, onstage; to this day he hasn't seen the film. When I told him Leif Erickson got his part, he laughed and said, "That's not bad." But Erickson lacks personality in the role, and you have to concentrate even to notice Hurd Hatfield as Joan's chaplain. John Ireland offers little more than a few sardonic or regretful glances as Jean de la Boussac, and Ward Bond does his standard bumptious military-man turn as the profane La Hire.

It would have taken considerable conviction and a less love-struck director to elicit performances that could have survived the soldiers' discus-shaped hairpieces and their historically correct, pictorially clumsy helmets, whose uplifted visors look deadlier than any riposte Anderson and Solt give to the men. These actors resort to masculine heartiness the way most of the trial's ecclesiastics succumb to bitchery. "That fell apart before it even started," sneered Ireland. "I was paid $15,000 a day and would have done it for $1,000. I think all I did was raise my mask and say something once."

Although the rap on the film is that Fleming filled it with pageantry and battle scenes, there's only one war sequence, depicting Joan's victory at the Battle of Orléans. Fleming had assigned Stallings to work on it with the montage master and second-unit director Slavko Vorkapich, who, after Fleming's death, took full credit, except for the intercut scenes of Joan being wounded and then rallying her troops. "Fleming wanted to direct those, too," said Vorkapich, "so I was there to suggest how it would fit into the rest of my battle." He criticized Fleming as well as Bergman for the film's conventionality and reverence. "Fleming wanted to make her sweet and all that. She was very tough; I read that in some French history. Preparing the battles, I read about her. She knew about military things and so on. She even swore." Vorkapich blamed Fleming for making "a virginal Holy Mary out of her. He was not up to the thing."

The man who shot Vorkapich's segments disagreed: Winton C. Hoch, one of Hollywood's great cinematographers, then at the start of his career. Hoch got his first big break on *Joan of Arc* and ended up sharing a best cinematography Oscar for it with the top-billed Joseph Valentine and the Technicolor expert William V. Skall.

> I started on second-unit work on *Joan of Arc*, and then they had all this battle stuff on the stage and Slavko Vorkapich was directing that. When I met him, he had sketches. He was a pretty good artist himself. He had some sketches of what he

> wanted to get on the camera. He was going to show Victor Fleming the sketches, and I gulped when I saw them. I said, "Vorky, you're not going to get these in the camera. You've cheated on perspective. Before you show them to Fleming, let's get a still camera and go out on the set and demonstrate exactly what we can get." Which we did, and then he revised his sketches, so we didn't promise Fleming something we couldn't deliver, which I thought was quite important.

Fleming called Hoch back to work on the first unit and gave the cinematographer his usual practical-joke hazing. Fleming demanded Hoch pull off "a dolly shot that went through the rafters of the church to a close-up of Joan" without "winging the (boom) tracks," that is, "when the camera has gotten into a certain position you smooth the tracks back into position so you can keep going." When Hoch protested, Vic walked away as if he didn't hear him. Of course, Hoch told the head grip, "Wing it back." (It would become the film's elegant opening shot.) Hoch grew to appreciate Fleming's showmanship.

> Fleming tested me there. But after that he was very pleasant to work with . . . He would drop me a cue once in a while. For instance, we had one scene when Joan was praying, and as she lifted up her face, of course, a key light here is deadly. But when your face is down, you have to have a key light. So he said when he gave me the setup, he said, "If I were you I'd hang a light over her head and bring it on as she lifts her face up." In those days that was a no-no. You never put a light on a dimmer. But those no-no's all have to be taken with a grain of salt. I put both key lights on a dimmer, so as she raised her head one light faded out and the other light came in. Now there was a color temperature change, no doubt about it. But in the movement and the spirit of the scene you didn't mind or notice, you accepted it. It's a dramatic scene; it's not a technical thing. It's a dramatic moment. There's drama and entertainment you're putting onto this technology. This is what so many people tend to forget.

Joan of Arc led directly to Hoch's celebrated partnership with Ford on *3 Godfathers* and *She Wore a Yellow Ribbon* (which won him a second Oscar).

Fleming's direction of Bergman, though, was more pictorial than dramatic. It would be bad enough if she were merely playing to an unseen God all the time; she's also playing to theatrical posterity. Bergman interprets Joan with such an actorish notion of single-minded purity that her idealism seems like narcissism. The battle sequence clicks not just because of Vorkapich's dynamic diagonals and skewed angles but also because it tests Joan's certainty in the most direct way. Again, fleetingly, the strength of the material saves the filmmakers. The script follows the legend of Joan ordering Sir William Glasdale (Dennis Hoey) to abandon his bastille and return to England, because if he does not, she says, she will "make such a hahay among you that it will be eternally remembered." She demands surrender for *their* sake. Glasdale calls her a harlot. The conquest begins with an impressive display of spears and arrows and siege machines but reaches its emotional apex when Joan takes an arrow in her shoulder and then rallies her troops. She comes face-to-face with Glasdale, who refuses to surrender and meets a fiery end on a collapsing drawbridge.

Otherwise, the audience yearns for any emotional intensity or spontaneity. Young Pia Lindström provides a glimpse of it—she's a beautiful blond child waving and smiling at Joan and urging her to save herself when she momentarily abjures her visions in hopes of entering a church prison and getting female guards and chapel privileges. "I was paid a hundred dollars and was paid in pennies, which I thought was funny," says Lindström. "Of course I would see [Fleming]. I would sit on the camera boom with him, play with the other children on the set. He was a very handsome man, a very elegant and rather imposing figure. Of course, a director has a great psychic connection with his actress. I guess I was vulnerable to my director, too!" Despite her identification with her betrayed father, she laughs at the memory. "Gentle, I would call him. I don't remember meeting Maxwell Anderson. He probably wasn't as good-looking as Victor Fleming!"

Columnists fanned advance publicity with their accounts of the celluloid Joan's conflagration, which Fleming started filming shortly after sunrise on a chilly mid-December day in 1947, on the RKO medieval set that famously hosted the 1939 version of *The Hunchback of Notre Dame*. Fleming took a microphone and intoned, "This is May 30, 1431, and Joan of Arc is going to be burned. You are excited." Among the 350 extras calling for Joan to burn was a future president of Disneyland, Jack Lindquist. The twenty-one-year-old son of an RKO purchasing agent had played bit parts for the past five years. "I was just part of the rabble coming out for the burning," he says. "I remember being reminded that [we didn't have] the luxury to put that event in perspective. We were just a bunch of peasants watching a woman burn at the stake . . . Like any other film, it was an all-day thing, but in spurts and bits." All morning he and the rest of the extras jeered at Joan as a cart carried her in chains to her fate, and punctuated the reading of her death sentence with howls and wails. A double replaced Bergman as Joan's executioners lit the tinder, then a dummy replaced her double on the stake as the kerosene-fed flames licked the sky.

A week later the home front heated up. A Cartier gold necklace with gold dragons that Fleming had ordered for Bergman came to Moraga Drive by mistake. "Daddy had never bought my mother much of anything jewelry-wise," Sally remembers. "Mother came across it in a closet we used to keep gift boxes in," Victoria recalls. "Mother tore up the whole house after that, looking for whatever." It may well have been a lover's gift, or merely a token of friendly reconciliation. For this was also the time when the columnist Jimmie Fidler was asking, "Wotzis about a red-hot feud between Ingrid Bergman and Victor Fleming?" The necklace never reached Ingrid's neck; it was disposed of in the trash at the Bowmans' house in Santa Monica.

When principal photography ended on December 18, the movie entered the phase when expectations remain out of this world and the various participants divide their concentration between postproduction and launching their next project. Even the title was haggled over. Despite Anderson's objections that it would make the film seem like a schoolbook assignment (exactly what it turned out to be), Sierra officially bought the title *Joan of Arc* from Selznick for $25,000 (to be paid after the negative cost was recouped). In doing so, RKO and Sierra followed their own poll and ignored an independent poll that showed the title would be less immediately popular for a Bergman vehicle than *Joan* or *Joan of Lorraine*.

More important, there were test screenings. Wanger couched the results in compliments. A memo from early April 1948 coos that *Joan of Arc* is "a picture that is way off the beaten track . . . Not a formula picture of the Hollywood type . . . It cannot be cut down or speeded up like 'Northside 777' or a snappy DeMille spectacle." He says that in two screenings for "regular film audiences," in Santa Barbara and Phoenix, "both audiences were completely enchanted and mesmerized and sat from beginning to end." He hailed "the great artistic quality of the picture from the standpoint of color and composition." But he did feel compelled "to repeat that I think there are certain parts of the picture that could be vastly improved." In the family breakfast scene, "the arrival of the Uncle is one of coming for a week-end," and the discussion of France resembled an American clan's "afternoon discussion of a Kaltenborn broadcast." (The producer is dead right.) He complained about intrusive Americanisms, in the scenes both at Vaucouleurs and in the military camp, and reactions so broad in the battle scenes that they bordered on inadvertent comedy. Wanger, though, did appear to be sincere when he said these were all problems that could be fixed. "Can you imagine if *Henry V* had been previewed at Santa Barbara and Phoenix, and then turned over to the professionals in Hollywood, what they would have done to Mr. Shakespeare's script and picture!"

Delaying personal business, as he always had, until the end of filming, Fleming addressed the emotional aftermath of the Bergman affair only after he completed all retakes in April 1948. The following month he had his lawyer draft a separation agreement. Although it indicated, in the standard legal language, that Fleming and Lu had been living apart, according to both daughters neither one of them had moved out. Fleming settled on paying $1,000 a month in alimony and an additional 20 percent of all gross income he might receive apart from investments. He agreed to buy a house for Lu and the children if it didn't cost more than $50,000, and (probably in expectation of spectacular profits from *Joan of Arc*) to create a $100,000 trust fund for Lu, so long as she remained unmarried. Fleming was to keep more than $205,000 in cash, his commercial properties in Los Angeles and Beverly Hills, $20,000 in bonds, Knapp Island, what remained of his Meadowlark Ranch property, and all his stock in Sierra Pictures.

The agreement was never signed and divorce papers never filed. That might have been the couple's last moment of panic in the Bergman era. By summer, both Victoria and Sally agree, they had reconciled. Working with Bergman this time—and viewing the results of their joint creative effort—may have disillusioned Fleming.

He certainly homed in on the finishing touches to *Joan of Arc* as if his career were at stake. In June, he was making sure his top editor, Frank Sullivan, would also supervise the dubbing. He rode herd on John Fulton's special effects and enlisted William Cameron Menzies to create some of the opening art shots and the credit backgrounds clearly patterned after those of *Gone With the Wind.* Fleming compressed the introduction Solt and Anderson wrote and then sent it back for two rewrites at different lengths, forty-five seconds and a minute. Very much the director in command, he ordered Wanger to ditch the narrator, who "sounds like a radio newscaster," and strive to find "a fine stage voice such as that of Mr. Joseph Cotten." They settled on additional work for Shepperd Strudwick.

Wanger was declaring to the press that *Joan of Arc* would take in $20 million and had RKO convinced of its assured success, too. Fleming appeared to be riding high in the epic mode. So the producer Frank Ross considered it a coup to attach Fleming to his adaptation of Lloyd C. Douglas's *The Robe.* Ross had prepared a script by Ernest Vajda and Albert Maltz; Fleming brought in his own team—none other than Anderson and Solt. Fleming cast Gregory Peck as Marcellus Gallio, the Roman tribune who supervises the Crucifixion. He wins Christ's robe as a gambling prize and gives it up to his Greek slave, Demetrius, only to accept Jesus as his savior and the robe as a divine relic with healing powers. In June, Ross announced filming would start late in 1948 or early in 1949, possibly in Italy.

Anderson rented a beach house in Santa Monica, but did most of his writing at Fleming's remodeled guest house, commuting with a car the director lent him. Even more than Mahin's testimony, Anderson's diary provides the best evidence for Fleming as a director who cared about script and went back to literary sources. Anderson and Solt started work on June 7, and on June 8 they and Ross and Fleming decided to break down the picture into five sequences. Just three days later, the entire picture was laid out. On June 12, Fleming came by with a Bible and a copy of George Bernard Shaw's *Androcles and the Lion.* They spent the afternoon reading the New Testament accounts of the Crucifixion and the preface to Shaw's play.

At the same time he was screenwriting *The Robe*, Anderson was preparing for rehearsals of his new play, *Anne of the Thousand Days,* for a New York opening that fall. Anderson gave Fleming a copy of *Anne* and recorded that the director was "very enthusiastic," adding, "for him." He hoped Fleming would direct the film version right after *The Robe.* Neither happened. The RKO chief, Howard Hughes, ended up dumping *The Robe* and concentrating on Fleming's old Paramount colleague Josef von Sternberg's *Jet Pilot*, featuring supersonic fore-and-aft cleavage from aerodynamic jets and a voluptuous, jump-suited Janet

Leigh as a Soviet pilot. *Anne of the Thousand Days* wasn't made until 1969 with Richard Burton, Geneviève Bujold, and a revamped script. But Fleming got something out of Anderson's work on *The Robe.* While the writer was in town, he persuaded him to contrive a new opening speech for *Joan of Arc.* And if he had lived to see the producer Ross turn *The Robe* around and land it at 20th Century Fox, the director might have mastered one more movie milestone. *The Robe* became the first movie in CinemaScope, the widescreen process designed to draw 1950s audiences into theaters and away from their TV screens—and for a while the sole competitor for *Gone With the Wind*'s box-office crown.

When Hesper Anderson turned fourteen on August 2, Fleming presented her with two bottles of wine "for her hope chest." The gift touched her deeply. Maxwell Anderson noted, "On the way home she said, 'That was about the most moving thing anybody ever did for me. He must have learned a lot about girls. I felt like just sitting there and crying.' " But her and her father's feelings for Vic didn't cushion their reactions to *Joan of Arc* when they saw it the following week, along with Mab, Marion Hargrove, and Andrew Solt. Anderson kept his feelings private, not even recording them in his diary. In her memoir, *South Mountain Road*, Hesper recalled it as a terrible, depressing afternoon, the silence in the screening room broken only by Hargrove's crack, "It just goes to show, a woman's place is over a hot stove."

Fleming sounded off to Mahin: "I don't know what's wrong . . . Everything is so beautiful. Ingrid is just so marvelous. I don't know what's wrong." Graham Lee Mahin said his dad responded, "Well, Victor, it's the first picture *she* ever directed."

Men of Fleming's generation would sneer at a phrase like "midlife crisis." But the deep humiliation of *Joan of Arc* aged Fleming beyond the virile grand-old-man status he'd enjoyed for more than a decade. Bergman's high-toned ardor and sense of her own power disarmed him and damaged the movie. And their affair had thrown a wrench into the family life that he'd managed for a decade to keep out of scandal or Hollywood foolery. Alain Bernheim, the brother of Michel, thought Fleming a proper family man who seemed "very Catholic" to him. When Bernheim found out about Fleming's romantic involvement with Ingrid, he thought it "didn't mesh" with the rest of what he knew about him.

Bergman wasn't the tragicomic figure that Bow was—someone Vic could look back on with unself-conscious fondness. He was passionate about both of them, but with Bergman he had what Ward Bond in *A Guy Named Joe* called "that slow poison kind of love." When it passed through his system, could it have strengthened him as a man and an artist? Fleming had been developing a reflective strand to his moviemaking, similar at his best to William Wyler's. Just as his friend Hawks had turned Hemingway's then-worst novel, *To Have and Have Not*, into a first-rate escapist romance, Fleming might have turned Hemingway's new-worst novel, *Across the River and into the Trees*, into a stinging summing-up.

As Wanger set out to orchestrate the publicity campaign for *Joan of Arc*, Fleming returned to his mechanic roots, restoring a 1932 Ford Model A as a hot rod. "It looked stock on the outside, but it screamed. It was a really fast thing," said Graham Mahin. Fleming's partner in the restoration was Ormond "Red" Ruthven, a sometimes screenwriter and full-time troubleshooter for MGM. "Apparently, when Victor wanted to get away or something without going on vacation, he'd go and work on the car with Red."

Meanwhile, Bergman, the star in the driver's seat of his latest screen vehicle, was falling out of favor with the press. The columnist Edith Gwynn blamed Joe Steele's departure. "Ingrid has always been difficult with the 'press' and others, taking herself too seriously perhaps. And what a job the diplomatic and hardworking Joe did, to keep most of the world from finding it out!" When fall arrived and the advance reviews began spilling out, there were indications that even the critical community was falling out of love with her. "Miss Bergman presents a splendid figure as Joan," wrote *Variety*. "But her part demands long speeches amounting almost to soliloquies, and force of these is lost as spectator watches endless scenes of the trial." The *Hollywood Reporter* was unqualified in its praise, especially for Fleming as "a director whose sensitivity can merge subtle characterizations and human emotions into the pageantry."

By the time *Joan of Arc* opened to the public at the Victoria Theatre on Times Square in New York on November 11, the luster was gone from the fleur-de-lis. November 10, the night of its charity premiere, was rainy, and there were few stars visible on the ground. Bergman arrived from Sweden and stood stiffly next to Fleming for photographers; Barbara Bel Geddes and Guy Kibbee were the biggest showbiz names among a phalanx of Catholic clergy. Wanger had made sure to win the approval of New York's Cardinal Spellman and the National Legion of Decency with a special screening the month before. The RKO publicist John Springer knew movie fans were still in love with the Bergman of *The Bells of St. Mary's*, and she seemed to live up to that image: she took him to St. Patrick's Cathedral every day when they were promoting *Joan of Arc.* Wanger and company gave the film's opening the old college try. Putting together Bergman and the movie's second- and third-most-popular selling points—the spectacle of medieval battle and the spectacle of conflagration—RKO erected a huge electric sign of Bergman resplendent in Joan's armor, surrounded by orange flames.

In his last interview, Fleming reiterated the themes of *Action Is the Word*, saying, "I'm getting my history this way, to make up for quitting school in the seventh grade. It's like a fairy land to me." The reviews were no fairy tale. *The New York Times*'s Bosley Crowther wrote similar pans for Fleming and his star, saying just as "the spiritual ordeal of the maiden is confused in the pageant of the trial," the "agony of the execution is likewise lost in the surge of the big show," and Bergman, "while handsome to look on, has no great spiritual quality. Her strength seems to lie in her physique rather than her burning faith."

Adela Rogers St. Johns said, "The one time [Vic] failed, poor man, I felt so sorry for him, when he made *Joan of Arc* with Bergman . . . I went to see it with him one night, and he sat and cried all the way through it. That was his heartbreak." In December, Fleming appeared at the Fox Beverly in Beverly Hills for the movie's West Coast premiere. He greeted the crowd, then slipped quietly inside the theater. This time Bergman stood by Alfred Hitchcock. Robert Mitchum came, and, with Shelley Winters as his date, Farley Granger was there, too, having recently appeared in Hitchcock's *Rope.* A slew of older female stars paid tribute to Bergman, including Joan Crawford, Ann Miller, Esther Williams, Susan Hayward, and, reminding Fleming of his Fairbanks days, Mary Pickford.

The next day the hometown reviews appeared. They were shriveling. " 'Joan of Arc' sprawls awkwardly, in episodic lumps," wrote the reviewer for the *Los Angeles Daily News.* He also shrewdly noted, "All hands concerned would have been better off had they stuck to Maxwell

Anderson's original 'Joan of Lorraine,' which at least stuck to the one basic theme of faith-as-a-compromise—and from a modern standpoint at that." As for Fleming's direction, it was "almost insensate."

Two days later it was Christmas, and Fleming was at his mother's house passing $20 gold pieces to a collection of young relatives and softly admitting to Rodger Swearingen, "It's a disaster, that picture."

30

Death in the Desert

Fleming had declared that he wanted to be a director of epics ever since the late 1920s. But *Joan of Arc*, his one independent foray into epic territory, was a creative debacle. *Time*'s movie column, generally sympathetic to him, said the heroine "becomes a lifeless symbol in a pageant." RKO found no better way of promoting the film than *as* a pageant. The critical reception scotched the idea of sending it out as the American-produced equal to Olivier's *Henry V:* Crowther put the two heroic-medieval portraits head-to-head and declared *Joan of Arc* competitive only in its pictorial "perfection," because Fleming, unlike Olivier, allowed "this whole drama to be played in the wide frame of a pageant, with consequent lack of real insight and intimacy." (It's "score one for Henry," he quipped.) The studio hedged its bets from the start, showcasing it as a reserved-seat, road-show presentation in some theaters and a continuously run film in others.

The initial returns *were* solid, and Wanger's hopes of awards, despite the bad reviews, still high. But he and Fleming had misjudged their audience. Shepperd Strudwick, Joan's idealistic bailiff, shortly afterward appeared as an idealistic doctor in 1949's *All the King's Men*, a torn-from-the-headlines melodrama based on Robert Penn Warren's Pulitzer Prize–winning novel. *All the King's Men* ultimately became a box-office success and won Academy Awards for best picture and best actor, Broderick Crawford (a Fleming family friend), and best supporting actress, Mercedes McCambridge. That movie, with its democratic hero turning into a demagogue, boasted the kind of direct, dynamic ambivalence and street credibility postwar critics wanted.

Under Bergman's spell, Fleming had succumbed to holiday-season poster art and siphoned any bit of ambivalence out of *Joan of Arc*. Even its cost became a joke. Wanger accepted a *Look* magazine achievement award for the film in February. When the presenter, Bob Hope, asked in his usual teasing-wheedling fashion why there'd been no role for Hope in *Joan of Arc*, Wanger said, in a scripted quip, "If a man has a $200 pipe, would he smoke Dr. Scholl's foot pads in it?" It was nominated for seven Academy Awards, but won only for cinematography and costume design; Wanger shamelessly campaigned for, and received, a special award for "distinguished service to the industry in adding to its moral stature in the world community by his production of *Joan of Arc*." Bergman and Ferrer, though nominated, were never considered contenders. When Wanger accepted his award, he said, "Notwithstanding this citation, I cannot accept this award except in the name of my partners, Ingrid Bergman and Victor Fleming, who made this great picture possible."

By then Sierra Pictures was mired in debt, and Bergman had run off with Roberto Rossellini, leaving her daughter, Pia, behind with Petter Lindström.

And Victor Fleming was dead.

"We had the same dentist, or my husband did at least, and the dentist, I was convinced, killed Vic—gave him too much Novocain or took out too many teeth and weakened him," said Leonora Hornblow. But *Joan of Arc* took more out of him than any dentist could. The mature, seductively melancholy Fleming was no longer the Beau Brummell who could laugh off broken dreams with Clara Bow. Bergman said she delighted in observing him run a set. Fleming, however, must have been in agony watching her there and in the editing room, where he could see her slipping away from his personal and professional grasp. Bergman forced Fleming to face the contradictions of his life and to consider whether sustaining his marriage for the previous dozen years had simply been a matter of marital will and parental devotion. His antidote to gloom, as usual, was action. He had dental surgery the day after Christmas, and a mere two days after that drove Lu and his daughters to the Beaver Creek guest ranch, twenty miles east of Cottonwood, Arizona.

In many ways, it was a journey into his past, to the country where he'd played escalating pranks with Douglas Fairbanks and navigated perilous location scouts on horseback with Lois Wilson. He stopped to visit Lighton at his Wine Glass Ranch in Prescott. Watson Webb, who hosted the Flemings and Lightons for dinner whenever Hope and Bud came back to Los Angeles, always found Fleming to be "very gracious and down-to-earth" with his wife in that smaller group. Hope would display a cigarette box adorned with custom-made jewelry charms patterned after Lighton's favorite productions, including a little boat for *Captains Courageous* and a parachute for the next Lighton-Fleming production, *Test Pilot.* And "Lu was very warm, very nice, very easygoing." Webb had no sympathy for Fleming's affair with Bergman: "The two most promiscuous women in Hollywood were Grace Kelly and Ingrid Bergman. We used to call a dame a porcupine: a million pricks stick into her. Ingrid was a real porcupine."

Watching them at Wine Glass Ranch and Beaver Creek, Victoria thought her father and mother had come closer together. "Daddy had rediscovered Mother after the Ingrid Bergman affair was over," Victoria says. And to Sally's eyes, too, they *were* more friendly. Hornblow, who knew the couple well in the 1940s, thought there *was* something for Vic to "rediscover" in Lu: "She wasn't the beauty of the world, but she was an awfully nice woman. I think he cared for her in a way; she made his life comfortable. If he would have left her for anyone, it would have been for Ingrid Bergman. There may have been a lot of little in-between with the starlets, but nothing to affect his home life until Ingrid: she was a glorious creature and so was he." Hornblow said until the Ingrid episode, Lu might even have basked in his off-set reputation: "Women like womanizers. It's very simple: you know there's honey in the honeycomb. That was part of Vic's warmth, charm, and vitality."

On the dude ranch Fleming reestablished family norms. When Sally, eleven and still prone to childhood ailments, complained of nausea, Fleming found something she could hold down—frozen strawberries. When Victoria went out riding on Thursday, January 6, 1949, she saw that her father "had an arm around Mother. I had never seen that before in my life." Later that morning, Victoria says, "I got this flash—'something's wrong'—and we went back and I galloped back to the house." Fleming had gone hunting coyotes, then lost his strength, complaining of chest pains. The ranch hands took him back to the cabin. Sally recalls her mother saying that she poured some brandy into him before they put him in the backseat of a car. Lu cradled her big man as best she could.

Vic never made it to the Marcus Lawrence Hospital in Cottonwood. He died in her arms en route, Lu said. An ex officio county coroner ruled it death from heart failure, but there was no autopsy. Family members agreed with Hornblow that he might have died because of the dental operation, possibly from a pulmonary embolism, especially given the complications of the earlier kidney surgery.

Sally had wandered into the main lodge, where a man told her that her father had taken sick. "And I said, 'Well, he'll be all right, won't he?' The guy said, 'How old is he?' That's all I needed to hear; that was it. And he said, 'Oh, sure, he's gonna be fine.' So when I saw Mother coming through the doorway, you know, she was completely dissolved. That's when I knew."

The hospital transported Fleming's body to the Scott and McMillan Mortuary, in Jerome. The press reported that Lee and Helene Bowman and Hal Rosson went to Arizona on Friday to arrange for the body's return to Hollywood, but Victoria saw them only at the airport. Graham Lee Mahin said the undertaker John McMillan called Graham's father to handle the funeral. "So [John Lee Mahin] went out there, and they had picked out this bronze casket. It was going to be [thousands of dollars] for the whole funeral thing." Mahin looked McMillan in the eye and asked, "What do you bury the indigents in?" McMillan replied, "It's a $7 pine box." Mahin declared, "That'll be fine for Victor." McMillan had a fit of pique, saying, "But I picked out all the stuff." Mahin tried to explain, "You don't understand Victor. He was a very simple man. He wouldn't have wanted to waste the money." They finally agreed on an unpretentious walnut coffin. The total for embalming and the coffin was $175. Then Howard Hughes sent a plane to fetch Fleming's body from the Prescott airport.

Wanger and Joan Bennett immediately wired Lu:

> Words are inadequate to express our shock and grief at yours, Sally's and Victoria's great loss; and believe me, our own and the industry's loss cannot be measured in words. Please accept our deepest sympathy in your tragedy and our deepest love, and do not hesitate to call upon us for anything at all at this time. Love, Joan and Walter

Spencer and Louise Tracy and their children, Susie and John, were dining at Romanoff's in Beverly Hills. Susie remembers, "It was Mike Romanoff who told my dad—who told him Vic died. My father just sat for a couple of minutes and looked down, and said, 'I'm going to have to go,' and left. He was very moved and sad, and he left the three of us there. He just couldn't say what there was to say. They were very good friends. To have Mike Romanoff come over and tell him something like that—I was a teenager, but I understood even then that it was important, and unusual."

Fleming's other great star Clark Gable was making *Any Number Can Play* for Mervyn LeRoy, who shut down the set for a day. "The pall of gloom . . . was so great that Gable couldn't talk," wrote Hedda Hopper.

There had been a cold wave in Southern California since the beginning of the year. On January 10, the day of the funeral, snow fell in Los Angeles, accumulating to a foot in outlying areas and covering the ground in Westwood, the location of St. Alban's Episcopal Church. The Reverend John A. Bryant, the church rector, read the Episcopal funeral liturgy and Psalm 23 before delivering Mahin's terse eulogy, "Man of Iron":

> Victor Fleming was an inviolate man.
>
> He was inviolate in his love for his country, standing as he always strove to help it stand, for the dignity and freedom of people before God.
>
> He was inviolate in his passion for work, and the absolute purity of fine workmanship. He held his home and his family inviolate—as the only earthly source of human goodness.
>
> For those unrelenting principles, his friends and the world that knew Victor Fleming loved and respected him beyond measure.
>
> To many of his fellows, he was, affectionately, "The Iron Man." In Victor, we discovered and learned the simple axiom: "Iron has the gentlest touch—when springing from the heart of Man as he was meant to be."

Mahin, Gable, Harold Rosson, Charles Cotton, Al Menasco, Sterling Hebbard, and Victor Ford Collins, Fleming's attorney, served as his pallbearers. Among the honorary pallbearers were Wanger, Ward Bond, Spencer Tracy, Eddie Mannix, Leland Hayward, Sam Zimbalist, Jack Conway, Jules Furthman, Robert Peyton, Laurence Stallings, Douglas Shearer, Ormond Ruthven, Richard Rosson, Louis Lighton, Henry Hathaway, King Vidor, Howard Hawks, Fred Lewis, Cedric Gibbons, and Lew Wasserman.

Approached to comment on his friendship with Fleming a half

century later, Wasserman predictably answered, "I do not give interviews." Then he added, "You have my best wishes for the success of the biography you are doing on Victor Fleming. He was a great man."

The other mourners included John Wayne, Louis B. Mayer, Andy Devine, Sam Goldwyn, James Stewart, Hoagy Carmichael, Van Johnson, and Brian Aherne. A year later Stallings remembered seeing Bergman at the funeral, too. But Stallings focused on what he would no longer see: "The great Fleming's lithe figure (his fierce eyes beneath the high forehead and the crest of silver hair) standing behind a camera to control the destiny of a movie set." Stallings wrote that *Joan of Arc* was "a killer-film": Joe Valentine and the set decorator Casey Roberts also died in 1949. So did Roman Bohnen, who played Joan's uncle and succumbed to a heart attack on February 24, while under the gun from government investigators to testify before HUAC.

Fleming's secretary, Nan Hinds, and his relatives guessed that the cross of Lorraine made of lilies of the valley and topping his rose-covered coffin came from Bergman, and they resented what they saw as a brazen gesture. "I think that Nan was quite sure about it. It was so obvious to me, for heaven's sake, that she had sent it," said Yvonne Blocksom.

And just as brazenly, at least from their point of view, Bergman was sitting in a front pew. Of course, she had no control over the seating arrangements. Whoever had made them simply observed Hollywood protocol by seating the big movie stars, including Gable, in the front and wasn't aware of what was then still a closely held secret.

Bergman's sorrow at Fleming's death, as she occasionally would tacitly acknowledge in interviews years later, was genuine. And as for the cross of Lorraine, she, probably more than anyone else, knew that Fleming had died on the long-accepted birthday of Joan of Arc.

As the mourners filed out of the church, "I remember that Gable was crying," Swearingen recalls. Sally and Victoria did not attend. "The Bowmans decided that Sally and I shouldn't go to the funeral, because it was too sad," says Victoria. Instead, they sent the girls to a movie. Fleming's mother chose the grave plate for his burial in a mausoleum at Hollywood Memorial Park. Above his name and the years of his birth and death, it reads, "He Leadeth Me."

"I was in London making *Night and the City* when I read about his death," said Jules Dassin, who was already on the run from the blacklist. "That we had different political opinions did not stop me from reading this with sadness." A year later Fleming's friend from Paramount days the director Herbert Brenon compared his own "peaceful, happy life" in retirement to the pressures of directing. "I am positive that those splendid men, like Victor Fleming and others, cracked under the strain."

One encomium after another poured into Wanger's office. They came from collaborators on *Joan of Arc*, including Father Doncoeur and the costume designer Karinska, and from the nation's film exhibitors. Wanger passed the most personal ones to Lu. Lee Bowman thanked Wanger: "Of all the old friends of Victor's, you certainly came to the fore in your offers to help in any way she needed you." Putting the best face on his and Fleming's past, he added, "We have lost a great friend and an even greater man."

Adela Rogers St. Johns wrote Lu to describe Vic helping her get through her son Bill's death in the war. He had urged St. Johns to act as if Bill were still looking on. St. Johns urged Lu to do the same:

> We have completely dropped into the conviction of our Bill just being "away." And I am 100% sure that Vic's wonderful advice helped more than anything. So may I give it back to you, so that it makes a true circle, and please know that I feel so sure the friendship Vic and I began . . . hasn't been broken . . . When my Bill went on, I know it did help me to find how many people loved him, how many were praying for him, how surrounded I was by love and sympathy. Nothing can change the sorrow but it did help to endure it, and so I wanted to add my little bit to the flood of affection, admiration, and love and prayers that must be going out to you and Vic. There was a *man!*

Nothing could comfort Lu. "She was very grim when he died," says Winnie Weshler. "Vic was the one thing that kept her straight, and he was gone."

"I think she was so knocked away by what happened," Sally reflects. "I thought she felt my father was sort of a god. I think she really did."

"I remember it being very quiet and not the same at all at his house," says Barbara Hawks McCampbell. "He just made a big impression in the house . . . He was just a very special person, and I felt about him like I did about my dad; they threw away the molds of a lot of these people. I only saw a wonderful side of him."

The public was soon to see another side. "Widow, Cut Off If She Reweds, Accepts Will," ran the headline in the *Los Angeles Times* on February 2. The estate, when probated, amounted to a little over $453,500, with nearly half of that in cash. (His fifteen thousand shares of stock in Sierra Pictures had "no value.") Lu, Sally, and Victoria received one-third shares of the estate in trust. But Lu's income would be managed by the trust for the rest of her life (with what was left, at her death, to be divided between daughters), while the girls controlled theirs outright after they turned thirty-five. Were she to remarry, Lu got nothing.

Harsh terms indeed—yet to Fleming's extended family, they reflected badly on Lu, not Vic. Yvonne Blocksom said, "There was an earlier version of that will, which we all saw for some reason or other. He left, I think it was, $5,000 to each member of the family. Well, [Lu] blew a cork, and he changed it, and he didn't leave any of that money to anybody. She really had him by the hooks, which was typical."

The real meaning of the will was that Fleming—at least on December 11, 1939, when he signed the document, and was already in a foul mood over Selznick—didn't trust Lu's side of the family or her judgment in the potential choice of a third husband. Not only did the will ensure that there would be no stepfather in his daughters' lives: it cut off any money to Victoria, Sally, and their guardians "during any time they may live with the relatives of [Fleming's widow] Lucile Fleming." In this case, Fleming was referring not to Helene and Lee Bowman but to Lu's sisters, Evelyn and Georgiana, who were heavy drinkers. Lu's sisters were to stay out of her daughters' lives.

Lu's first order of business was to sell the Moraga Drive estate for the fire-sale price of $113,000; she then moved to a smaller house on Rockingham Drive in Brentwood. Fleming's mother and sisters made a bittersweet trek to Knapp Island before Lu sold that, too. "Each of them brought a souvenir home, something that had belonged to him," Blocksom said.

Lu and the daughters drifted further apart from the Deacons and the Hartmans. The last time Lu and her mother-in-law, Eva, met was at attorney Collins's office so that Eva could sign over a half-million dollars' worth of oil stocks that Fleming had put in his mother's name as a tax dodge. Afterward, Lu told Eva, "Mother Deacon, if you're ever in need of anything, let me know." Collins quietly set her straight: "Mrs. Fleming, this isn't a patch on Mrs. Deacon's wealth."

The will hemmed Lu in, defining her, until her death in 1966, as Victor Fleming's widow. But it didn't serve Fleming's intended purpose of preserving his household values. "As soon as [Victor] died, people that we'd never seen started coming to the house," Weshler says. "Helene and Lee Bowman and their crowd then came in profusion." The Bowmans removed the girls from Marymount and enrolled them in the fashionable Marlborough School. Sally says her half sister, Helene, "swooped in to rule" and "took over our lives, and I think my mother pretty much just abdicated. Don't know why—must've been her personality." Lu did feebly try to find new ways to while away the hours, such as playing bridge with other single women. Among Vic's gang, only Ward Bond stayed close to her. "Clark Gable took her out for dinner once. Broderick Crawford took her out to dinner once, and that was about it. Joan Fontaine kept up her friendship, and so did Joseph Cotten," says Victoria.

In August 1954, when MGM first rolled out *Gone With the Wind* in wide-screen and stereophonic sound, Selznick held a bash at Ciro's, Louella Parsons reported. Gable didn't come, nor did Vivien Leigh, who was still recovering from a bout of bipolar disorder. Selznick's guests included Charles and Shirley Temple Black, Merle Oberon and Dr. Rex Ross, "and sitting sadly out of the range of the photographers' flashing bulbs was Mrs. Victor Fleming."

"She never recovered from [the death]," Victoria says. "She stayed in the house. She took to her bed and began drinking, which she had never done, and smoking, which she had never done. She just went to pot." As the family downsized, all but three of Fleming's movie scrapbooks were lost. Lu gradually dispensed with Vic's collection of hunting rifles and a menagerie of safari trophies: one leopard skin, zebra skins, a mounted cheetah, and a boar skull.

While Lu was getting rid of those mementos, Fleming's pals and coworkers were bringing back their buddy's hunting days in two different movies that came out in 1953. John Wayne conjured one of his most invigorating star turns as the title character in *Hondo*. While the star was scouting Utah locations for the gritty Western, Fleming had been on his mind. Wayne told an Ogden reporter, "For a girl to get into the movies, I'll use Vic Fleming's size-up: 'To take in the movies, a girl must have a challenge in her face.' I think he was about right." (That certainly applied to his *Hondo* co-star, Geraldine Page.) A U.S. cavalry scout in Indian country, Hondo dreams of nothing more than to return to a scruffy ranch outside San Dimas. The reference to San Dimas appears only in James Edward Grant's screenplay; it is not in Louis L'Amour's original short story or his later novel based on the screenplay. For that matter, San Dimas didn't even exist in the 1870s, the setting of the story. But the mention of it does hark back to the Duke shooting small game with Fleming in the San Dimas Wash. And Hondo as a man has Flemingesque charisma, with an instinct for emotional truth that makes him irresistible to the widowed rancher-woman played by Page, even though Hondo is the man who widowed her. Wayne essayed a Westerner making his rules up as he goes along and sticking to a code of strength and honesty and teaching Page's son a thing or two with tough love—all lessons out of the Fleming playbook.

At the same time, Zimbalist and Mahin were cooking up *Mogambo*, a remake of Fleming's first smash for MGM, *Red Dust*, for Wayne's favorite Western director, John Ford. Astonishingly, it once again starred Gable as the supercompetent hero torn between a good-time gal and a lady. Gable had actually planned to go big-game hunting with Vic in Africa in 1939, before *Gone With the Wind* dragged on. Mahin may have known about that aborted trip: Gable had boasted that he'd purchased a .50-caliber elephant gun. So this time, instead of a rubber-plantation manager as he was in *Red Dust*, Gable played a Great White Hunter, but one devoted to trapping animals and sending them off to zoos, not slaughtering them. (Fleming would sometimes say, later in life, that he regretted the killing he did just for sport.)

Mahin rewrote Gable's character for a star then in his early fifties, not the smoldering thirty-one-year-old of *Red Dust.* Mahin acknowledged the older Gable's mellower if still undeniable appeal, but gave him some of Fleming's youthful traits and oddities, from smacking around incompetents to turning a boa constrictor into a pet. Gable's co-stars would be Ava Gardner as an international playgirl (a considerable social upgrade from Jean Harlow's prostitute) and Grace Kelly as the wife of an anthropologist who's gone to Africa to study gorillas (the Mary Astor role). In this movie they each embodied, in different ways, the cosmopolitanism that would increasingly take hold of postwar high-end escapism. Both were nominated for Oscars. Gardner delivered and possibly provoked the best line in the movie—after a bull elephant lifts its trunk, she says, "That reminds me of someone."

"He's a very attractive burglar," Gardner later says of Gable's thief of hearts. In this picture, Gable represents something timeless: a man whose years of adventure have poeticized as well as hardened him. He falls into a clinch with each woman only after she succumbs to the heady sights of his environment. He doesn't make romantic conquests—he gives in to them. The Gardner character appreciates his experience: he's been around the way she has. The Kelly character appreciates his freshness: to her eyes he's a natural phenomenon, like the African sunsets and waterfalls. In the end, he realizes that the playgirl understands him better—and the wife is better off with her husband. He only pretends not to feel the pain.

The exotic setting puts into stark relief the mixture of firsthand knowledge, shrewdness, resilience, and hard-knocks lyricism that audiences around the world, thanks to Fleming movies like *The Virginian* and *Red Dust* and *Captains Courageous* and *Test Pilot*, recognized as quintessentially American. In *Mogambo*, Mahin and Zimbalist called this character Vic.

AFTERWORD

A Great American Movie Director

"Someday someone's going to bring up what Fleming meant to this business," Arthur Freed said in 1974. More than twenty years later, Todd McCarthy conjectured in *Variety* that a biography of Victor Fleming would be "highly unlikely" because he left no extensive letters or memoirs and had not "given lengthy interviews or been prone to undue self-promotion." As McCarthy observed, "The modern reputations of some filmmakers from Hollywood's golden age are directly related to how long they managed to live, and whether or not they lasted long enough to be enshrined through career interviews, biographies and honorary awards."

Luckily, Fleming left his mark on everyone in his personal and career orbit, including a succession of columnists and reporters who chronicled his every professional move. And many of the world's top moviemakers, from Philip Kaufman and Steven Spielberg to David Lynch and Guillermo del Toro, have never ceased to look to him for inspiration. Spielberg, himself a prodigy of reinvention, calls Fleming "one of the great chameleons. He reinvented himself every time he took on a new project. He was what I call a general-education director—meaning that rather than specialize in and master a single subject, or exercising simply one muscle, he threw himself into all these different categories."

Fleming found creative satisfaction wrestling with material that was fresh to him. He worked in every style, from the plainspoken lyricism of *The Virginian* to the outlandish musical fantasy of *The Wizard of Oz* and the rousing spectacle of *Gone With the Wind.* No wonder America's leading proponent of the auteur theory, the critic Andrew Sarris, put Fleming in his "Miscellany" category in his seminal *The American Cinema* (1968). Unlike Alfred Hitchcock or John Ford, Fleming didn't place his signature on a favorite genre. And unlike Hawks, he didn't concoct variations on the same brand of group chemistry whether in a comedy or a Western or an aerial adventure.

Fleming didn't distance himself from his more single-minded colleagues, nor did they from him. They all labored to put out first-class entertainment. The novelist and screenwriter Daniel Fuchs memorialized men like "William Wellman, Howard Hawks, Sam Wood, Clarence Brown, Victor Fleming" as "a gaudy company, rambunctious and engrossed. What they produced, roistering along in those sun-filled, sparkling days, was a phenomenon, teeming with vitality and order, as indigenous as our cars or skyscrapers or highways, and as irrefutable. Generations to come, looking back over the years, are bound to find that the best, most solid creative effort of our decades was spent in the movies, and it's time someone came clean and said so."

In failure or success, Fleming's movies were not predictable. Most popular artists contend with commerce and accommodation—or, as Fleming memorably put it, the "blank blank blank blanks" on the third floor of the Thalberg Building—as they build a body of work. Until Fleming's misguided love letter to Ingrid Bergman in *Joan of Arc*, his films, however uneven or compromised, were rarely boring. Sarris conceded, "This mysterious figure probably expressed more of Hollywood's contradictions than did most of his colleagues. Yet, aside from Cukor, he was the only Metro director who could occasionally make the lion roar."

"Mysterious" became the word for Fleming after his death because so little effort was made to preserve his legacy. He left behind a shattered widow and two young daughters, no journals, few letters. Before film preservation became an artistic cause, many of his silent pictures turned to dust or celluloid soup, including the Oscar-winning *The Way of All Flesh* and the epic *The Rough Riders*. Before the rise of classic movie channels on cable TV, it was difficult to see his landmark films like *The Virginian*, *Red Dust*, and *Bombshell*.

Fleming's supporters, such as Kevin Brownlow, wondered about the wild trajectory of a career that oscillated between spirited masterpieces like *Mantrap* and leaden studio properties like *Abie's Irish Rose*. Critics enamored of Hawks and Vidor couldn't see that these genuine old masters were still working out old rivalries or bitterness when they spoke of their friend Fleming. And other writers may have found it hard to believe that a self-tutored boy from San Dimas could have been part of so much general history (the use of film for military training, intelligence, and propaganda) *and* film history (the changes from independent two-reelers to studio features, from silence to sound, from black and white to color). All the while, Fleming contributed key images to the American photo album, from Woodrow Wilson in his top hat to Gary Cooper on a horse—and Judy Garland tentatively stepping into Munchkinland and realizing that she's not in Kansas anymore.

Most film chroniclers chalked up Fleming's two most famous credits to the efforts of producers. Critics viewed *The Wizard of Oz* as a paradigm of big-studio artistry rather than a feat for its director. Aljean Harmetz's essential production history *The Making of "The Wizard of Oz"* was taken as the final word on its subject, because the smart, skillful Harmetz was the last person to grill almost all the major participants. Yet Fleming, although long dead, rubbed Harmetz the wrong way. She vastly preferred the lyricist Yip Harburg, the production executive Arthur Freed, and King Vidor, who directed *Oz* according to Fleming's game plan for only three and a half weeks as opposed to Fleming's three and a half months. When Mahin—described by Harmetz as Fleming's "drinking and motorcycle buddy"—told her that the director "had the fingers of an artist," Harmetz commented, "Nothing else in his outward appearance or personality suggested an artist in the least." Most of Fleming's contemporaries, including seasoned, sophisticated observers such as Ben Hecht, never thought of him any other way.

Thomas Schatz, author of *The Genius of the System* (1988), blithely noted, "Fleming received director's credit on both [*The Wizard of Oz* and *Gone With the Wind*], but each was ultimately a producer's picture." Fleming, though, was the only creative force on *Oz* who had been raised on a farm by a benevolent uncle and aunt, and the only major figure on *Gone With the Wind* with a family tree that boasted Civil War veterans on both sides of the conflict. Selznick's prestige and tsunami of memos inevitably diminished Fleming's contribution to *Gone With the Wind.* (And with Selznick elevated to sole auteur of that film, it became easier, in retrospect, to credit all of MGM, or sometimes just Mervyn LeRoy, with *The Wizard of Oz.*) Part of the reason is that *GWTW* influenced Hollywood in matters that ultimately may mean more to producers and film-industry historians than to directors.

The Wizard of Oz, with its delayed-reaction TV success, heralded the phenomenon of movies from *It's a Wonderful Life* to *Austin Powers: International Man of Mystery* achieving their greatest popularity in a home-video afterlife. *Gone With the Wind* instantly changed the moviemaking practices and habits of a nation. In the 1930s, Hollywood movies were at their zenith as a popular art, one that filmgoers could plan on attending as casually as going to the corner diner. In that era, only the studios' biggest, most prestigious efforts—like MGM's *Mutiny on the Bounty*—clocked in at much more than two hours (*Bounty* and Capra's Columbia production of *Lost Horizon* were 132 minutes, *Oz* only 101). No producer besides Selznick dared to test audiences with an almost four-hour running time. Selznick wanted MGM to "road-show" *Gone With the Wind* with limited showtimes, inflated prices, and an intermission, in the manner of silent epics like *The Birth of a Nation* and *Ben-Hur* (1925). He had to settle for (in Rudy Behlmer's words) "a modified road-show policy," with optional reserved seats, higher pricing for "preferred" seats, and an intermission whose length was up to the discretion of exhibitors and the local distributor's agent. Starting with "event" films like *Around the World in Eighty Days* (1956), Selznick saw his strategy carry Hollywood into a new road-show era with movies like the remake of *Ben-Hur* (1959) and *Lawrence of Arabia* (1962).

The studios no longer present films road-show style, but every time a sprawling, colorful costume picture, whether *Amadeus* or *The Lord of the Rings*, wins a fistful of Oscars and a gigantic chunk of the box office, you're witnessing part of the influence of *Gone With the Wind*. After *GWTW*, producers began pulling for a giant brass ring, and audiences began lining up for movies they'd been hearing about for years in advance. Some moviemakers feel that it broadened Hollywood's appetite for manufacturing blockbusters of any kind, regardless of cultural clout. As Spielberg says, "I think studios were spoiled the first day *Gone With the Wind* made more money than any movie ever. I think from that moment on, decision makers wanted movies that would be hugely successful."

Selznick wisely exploited a three-year plan of escalating publicity. Headlines screamed about everything from the burning of Atlanta to the casting of Gable and Leigh to the premiere in the real Atlanta. But the hoopla would have evaporated without a film that delivered the goods. Overall, its failings hardly matter—largely because it boasts Scarlett O'Hara and Rhett Butler at its core. They remain startlingly contemporary and compelling as antiheroine and antihero. James Cameron says that when he made *Titanic*, "*Gone With the Wind* was the film to beat—it showed the path you could take to do the epic story and capture people's hearts beyond the normal movie experience."

Scarlett and Rhett as well as the impact of their twisted love and marriage also are the main (but not the only) reasons Fleming, the credited director, should receive the same honor today as when the movie first went out with his name on it. Over the course of his career, he, as much as anyone, showed Hollywood how to create tarnished protagonists who still glittered. In *Bombshell*, Harlow's Lola Burns resembles a burlesque version of Scarlett, supporting a sponging family and resisting the go-getting cynic who's perfect for her, because she prefers classier gents. Directing Gable in *Red Dust*, Fleming brought a new sexual dimension and knowing humor to the figure of the can-do guy and anticipated the attractiveness of a wised-up fellow on a grander scale, like Rhett.

Unlike Selznick, whose biographers portray his forays into womanizing as pathetic or laughable, Fleming, like Rhett, was a ladies' man *and* a man's man who became a devoted family man. He'd learned about the esprit and weariness of military service in the Signal Corps and observed the aftermath of war in Europe. He'd even assisted on *Intolerance*, D. W. Griffith's follow-up to *The Birth of a Nation*, *Gone With the Wind*'s obvious predecessor. So he was a natural to connect with this material. *Gone With the Wind* would never have become the resplendent thing it is without Selznick, but it never would have found its voice—its bark *and* its bite—without Fleming. Nothing Selznick threw at him was too big a stretch. Fleming's temperament, background, and aptitude made him more than a journeyman enjoying a stroke of luck. He was the ideal director to save and vitalize the movie.

Years later, Dalton Trumbo, Fleming's collaborator on *A Guy Named Joe*, became part of another phoenixlike production when the cocky young Stanley Kubrick took over the reins from Anthony Mann on Kirk Douglas's production of *Spartacus*. Chafing at Kubrick's high-handed alterations of his work on the set and in the editing room, Trumbo put his own track record on the line, writing to the director in a lengthy and blistering memo, "In the past I have worked with, or my screenplays have been directed by, such competent, successful, and even brilliant artists as Sam Wood, Mervyn LeRoy, Preston Sturges,

Garson Kanin, René Clair, and Victor Fleming, whom I consider the king of them all."

From the point of view of a producer who thought directors were overrated anyway, Saul David asked in *The Industry*, "Who directed *The Wizard of Oz*? Mervyn LeRoy? Nope. And who directed *Gone With the Wind*? Selznick? Uh-uh. Both were directed by Victor Fleming—a man who never makes the auteur lists and whose work is therefore a reproach to serious cineastes. Maybe his obscurity is a bitter injustice to Fleming." Without question.

Acknowledgments

Individuals whom I interviewed or corresponded with: Evangela Anderson, Dorothy Barrett, Rex Bell Jr., Alain Bernheim, Lennie Bluett, Rand Brooks, Kevin Brownlow, June Caldwell, James Cameron, Keith Carradine, Cammie King Conlon, Jeff Corey, Charles Cotton, Thomas Cripps, Jules Dassin, Cecilia DeMille, André de Toth, Ruth Duccini, Sally Fleming, Victoria Fleming, Julie Garfield, Vera Gebbert, Norman Geiger, Kathryn Grayson, Jane Greer, Andy Griffith, Jack Haley Jr., Stan W. Haley, Edward Hardwicke, David Hawks, Leonora Hornblow, Shep Houghton, Joan Kenmore, Gavin Lambert, Frank Leonetti, Val Lewton Jr., Pia Lindström, Norman Lloyd, Julian Ludwig, Sid Luft, James Lydon, Graham Lee Mahin, Tim Mahin, Tom Mankiewicz, Jerry Maren, Patricia Marmont, Barbara Hawks McCampbell, Kevin McCarthy, Karen Morley, Joan Marsh Morrill, Joseph Newman, Marni Nixon, Robert Nott, Gregg Oppenheimer, Margaret Pellegrini, Meinhardt Raabe, Luise Rainer, Maurice Rapf, Gene Reynolds, Ralph Riskin, Mickey Rooney, Ambrose Schindler, Budd Schulberg, Martin Scorsese, John D. Seelye, Vincent Sherman, George Sidney, Andrew Solt, Steven Spielberg, John Springer, Robert Stack, David Stenn, Rodger Swearingen, Larry Swindell, Bob Thomas, Audrey Totter, Susie Tracy, Phillip Trent, Christopher Trumbo, William Tuttle, Lew Wasserman, Watson Webb, Dottie Wellman, William Wellman Jr., Winnie Weshler, Danny Windsor, Ralph Winters, Jane Withers.

Individuals whom my research associate, Kurt Jensen, interviewed or corresponded with: Bette Jean Ahrens, Alan H. Anderson, Lawrence Bachmann, Pamela Morris Baker, Elizabeth Bartholomew, H. Bruce Baumeister, Yvonne Blocksom, Hunter Bowman, Lee Bowman Jr., Julie Lugo Cerra, George Coulouris Jr., Patrick Curtis, David Brion Davis, Tad Devine, James Drury, Gene Eckman, Sally Fleming, Victoria Fleming, Richard Foelsch, John Frederick, Greg Giese, William Goodykoontz, Kate Harper, Edward C. Hartman, Olivia de Havilland, Terese Hayden, Marsha Hunt, Schuyler Johnson, Thomas Jones, Christy Kelso, Mickey Kuhn, Helen Reed Lehman, Betty Lighton, Jack Lindquist, Ian Mackersey, John McCabe, Fay McKenzie, Olga Nardone, Micky O'Donoughue, Robert Rampton, Robert Reed, Lina Romay, Arthur H. Rosson Jr., Barbara Saltzman, Eddie Schmidt Jr., Sheila Shay, John Sheffield, Karl Slover, Tim Soules, Martin Spellman, Donna Stewart-Hardway, Rodger Swearingen, Clarence Swensen, Robert Terry, Melissa Wells, Harriet Wheeler, Richard V. Wyman.

Interview collection, Columbia University: Mary Astor (1971), Pandro S. Berman (1971), Marc Connelly (1959), Jackie Cooper (1959), Janet Gaynor (1958), Ben Hecht (1957), James Wong Howe (1971), Mervyn LeRoy (1971), Myrna Loy (1959), Adela Rogers St. Johns (1971), Edward Sutherland (1959).

Interview collection, Southern Methodist University: Don DeFore (1986), Irene Dunne (1986), Mervyn LeRoy (1978), Gil Perkins (1986), Gene Raymond (1986), Emily Torchia (1984), Slavko Vorkapich (1975).

J. D. Marshall interviews, Recorded Sound Reference Center, Library of Congress: Howard Estabrook (1978), John Lee Mahin (1978), and Dalton Trumbo (1973).

Robert Gottlieb, who hired me at the *New Yorker* and often edited me there, championed Fleming as a subject, prodded the book to completion, and applied his pencil cunningly to the manuscript. In person and in writing, he has an uncanny knack for course correction—which he can accomplish with a word of encouragement or a penetrating critique. No one has been more patient or sanguine about this book's long gestation—except, perhaps, for Sarah Lazin, an agent who is also an ally and close reader, and Glenda Hobbs, my wife, who applied her diamond cutter's eye to the text.

The biography would not have been possible without my research associate, Kurt Jensen, the best pure reporter I know as well as a first-rate editor and fact-checker. He came aboard to crack the family history and, by his dexterity with databases and tenacity with human sources, cleared up many a clannish mystery. He soon became organically connected to the process of establishing a life story for a man who left a sparse written record. Kurt sifted through prodigious amounts of data to nail down individual details and was crucial to the coverage of such varied topics as the Atlanta celebration for *Gone With the Wind*, the birth of the anticommunist Motion Picture Alliance, and the vagaries of Joan of Arc scholarship, which, he was delighted to find, encompassed Bob Hope, Bing Crosby, Jack Benny, and Fred Allen. He has a keen nose for the truth, and I can't think of a nonfiction book that couldn't be taken to its highest possible level with Kurt's participation.

Sally Fleming kindly shared all the family material she had and helped persuade Turner Entertainment in Atlanta to open her father's MGM legal files to me. Victoria Fleming offered her prodigious memory and insights, including this sly, deceptively simple advice: "If there's ever a question of whether Daddy and some woman did or they didn't, assume they did!"

Christy Kelso not only shared her extensive files documenting the background and the westward trek of the Hartman family; she also lent her formidable skills as a genealogist to turn up a substantial trove of correspondence and legal documents. Edward C. Hartman divulged his detailed memories of San Dimas and "Uncle Vic" with a generosity matched only by his sanity and natural good humor: he said that when Fleming was at his peak, making *The Wizard of Oz*, "You have to remember that I was fourteen years old, and if it had nothing to do with sports, I couldn't care less."

Kate Harper, whose childhood memories include personalities as diverse as Cecil B. DeMille and Jimmy Durante, aided the vast effort to locate interviewees.

The man who's done more than anyone since James Agee to revive the popularity of the silent film, Kevin Brownlow, gave the first big boost to this biography. At the 1998 Telluride Film Festival, he expressed his enthusiasm for Fleming as a director and a personality, then opened up, and *kept* open, voluminous data and research on early Hollywood, including correspondence with Louise Brooks from the 1960s and early 1970s, an unpublished memoir by Sidney Franklin, and interviews with Howard Hawks (1970), Bessie Love (1971), and Dorothy Jordan Cooper (1972). Throughout this book's own long history, Brownlow overflowed with information, photographs, and insights, and he never said no.

Elizabeth Anthony, editor of the Web site ReelClassics.com, made marvelous contributions on several fronts. In addition to assiduous library work, she translated Sergei Eisenstein and Father Paul Doncoeur from the French; she deciphered Bosley Crowther's handwriting; and she made the kinds of suggestions for further research that could come only from a three-strip Technicolor dyed-in-the-celluloid movie lover.

The biographer of Jean Harlow and Clara Bow, David Stenn, scoured the David Stenn collection for quotations from acquaintances and co-workers of Fleming's and kept finding untapped sources of testimony to the director's drive and creativity. Selden West provided anecdotes from her research on Spencer Tracy. William Wellman's biographer, Frank Thompson, put me in touch with John Gallagher, author of the first important monograph on Fleming. And Gallagher was invaluable: he delivered tapes of rare films, dozens of contemporary reviews and publicity stories, several of his own original interviews, and even a program for the road-show presentation of *The Rough Riders.*

Scott Eyman, while researching, writing, and promoting his book about Louis B. Mayer, shared his knowledge of and sources on MGM in the 1930s and 1940s and even came up with a budget sheet for *Around the World in Eighty Minutes.* Joseph McBride, while completing his life of John Ford, gave me a score of leads on filmmakers (or family members of filmmakers) from Fleming's generation.

Todd McCarthy, Howard Hawks's biographer, put me in touch with Hawks's family and sent me his notes on Fleming from Norma Shearer's unpublished autobiography. He also cheered the project on, although he knew it wouldn't always view *his* subject favorably. So did David Thomson, who lent me the Fleming-related research he did for his life of David O. Selznick, *Showman.* Matthew Bernstein, Walter Wanger's biographer, provided pointers on the Wanger Collection at the University of Wisconsin; the indefatigable and prolific Milwaukee-based biographer Patrick McGilligan (a colleague since Boston alternative-weekly days in the 1970s) navigated it for me. McGilligan also sank back into his fifteen-year-old notebooks on George Cukor to locate the source of a now-crucial piece of *GWTW* lore.

John Fricke, who keeps proving the last word can't be written or spoken on *The Wizard of Oz,* was always open to questions, as was Willard Carroll, who was profligate in his generosity with *Oz* photographs, memorabilia, and lore. Anthony Slide provided key early assistance on silent-film resources, and Lee Tsiantis of Turner Classic Movies offered practical and aesthetic support from beginning to end.

My longtime friend and ace professional movie researcher, Joan

Cohen, gave the project a shot of energy with her in-person research in London as well as her forays into many Los Angeles archives and libraries. Amy Glover and Jennifer Clark operated like brainy sharpshooters, homing in on every request with immediate perception and clarity and invariably coming up with more than I asked for. Meg Singley discovered eloquent testimony to Fleming's standing at MGM in Bosley Crowther's unused notes for his book on the studio.

Don Rogier's effort to trace Clara Strouse and her family even involved a hike through an Ohio cemetery.

"Several friends and colleagues" of Dave Smith, director of the Walt Disney Archives, spent a weekend, on their own time, casting their experienced eyes on several vintage Mickey Mouse cartoons to determine whether any footage was recycled into *Around the World in Eighty Minutes.*

Neal Graffy generously offered his own research, aided by his friendship with Lulu Phelan, to add detail to Fleming's professional launch—and his romance with Charlotte Burton—at the Flying A studio in Santa Barbara.

Most of the research originated at the facilities of the Library of Congress. Zoran Sinobad and the rest of the staff of the Motion Picture Reading Room lent their wide-ranging expertise at every turn. But a biography with widely scattered source material can only come about with the skilled assistance of archivists and reference librarians nationwide. Foremost on this list are Barbara Hall at the Margaret Herrick Library, Ned Comstock at USC's Cinema and Television Library, and Charles Silver at the Museum of Modern Art. And Fleming's story could not have been fleshed out without the knowledgeable help of volunteers at local historical organizations from Columbia County, Pennsylvania, to San Dimas and Santa Barbara, California.

Everyone involved in this enterprise felt the adventure of Fleming's life and the thrill of retracing its bold trajectory from the orange orchards of Pasadena to the top of the entertainment world. Everything of quality in this book owes a huge debt to the people mentioned or listed here, and many others. Responsibility for inaccuracies and shortcomings lies with me alone.

Additional thanks go to: Dennis Aig, Paula Allen, Kathryn Ashe, Pat Atkinson, Lutz Bacher, Sarah Baker, Frank D. Balzer, Joseph Bendersky, Stella Bendoris, Betty Birk, Alice Birney, Gregory D. Black,

Olivier Bouzy, Connie Breedlove, Roy M. Brewer Jr., James Breyley, Richard Brody, Faith Brook, John Burrud, James E. Butler, Ben Campanale, Larry Ceplair, John Christensen, Ian Christie, Gerry Chudleigh, Judy Colgrove, Ralph Cooper, Greg Cumming, James Curtis, Ron Cuskelly, James D'Arc, Ron DeFore, William Drew, Dana Driskel, K. O. Eckland, Jan Edwards, Karren Elsbernd, Ann Evans, Christopher Falzon, Harry Forbes, Alexa Foreman, Leatrice Gilbert Fountain, Jeannine Wagner Gallardo, Lynn Gamma, Cara Gilgenbach, Leo Gorcey Jr., Luther Greene, Rick J. Gunter, Rosemary Hanes, Stacey Hann-Ruff, Barbara Hartley, Dorinda Hartmann, Karen L. Hathaway, Bob Heald, Daniel Hobbins, Abraham Hoffman, Richard Hutson, Maria Cooper Janis, Latane Jones, Chris Kaltenbach, Chiaki Kawajiri, David Kessler, Dickran Kouymjian, John Lahr, Margarita Landazuri, Ludwig Lauerhass Jr., Lee Lawrence, Richard LeComte, Laura Leff, Judy Lewis, John Lindner, Anne Lockhart, Patrick Loughney, Lloyd MacFadyen, Tim Mahin, Madeline Matz, Stan McClain, Hamilton Meserve, Dwight Miller, Ted Mills, Langdon Morrill, Robert Morris, Kirk Myers, Victor Navasky, Harold Osmer, Erin Overbey, Sam Ratcliffe, Maria Reachi, Michael Redmon, Eric Rentschler, Bill Robie, Elizabeth Robnett, Carole Sampeck, Rodney Sauer, Hans-Joachim Schlegel, Sandy Slater, David Smit, Victoria Sturtevant, Lawrence Suid, Glenn Taranto, Russ Taylor, Ned Thanhouser, Sandra M. Thomas, Pat Tone, Dan Van Neste, John Waxman, and Eileen Whitfield.

Archival and research resources: Air Force Historical Research Agency; American Museum of Natural History; Arizona State Archives; Brigham Young University (Bosley Crowther Papers); British Film Institute; Catholic University of America (National Catholic Welfare Conference Papers; Archbishop John Timothy McNicholas correspondence); Centre Jeanne d'Arc, Orléans, France; Columbia University (Oral History Research Office and University Archives); the Walt Disney Archives; Federal Aviation Administration; Federal Bureau of Investigation; Filson Historical Society, Louisville, Kentucky (Cleves Kinkead Papers); Georgetown University (Martin J. Quigley Papers, Lawrence Suid Papers); Harry Ransom Center for the Humanities, University of Texas, Austin (Maxwell Anderson Papers, David O. Selznick Archive); the Henry Ford Museum and Research Center; Herbert Hoover Presidential Library (Westbrook Pegler Papers); Kent State University (Lois Wilson Collection); Library of

Congress Manuscript Division (Maxwell Anderson Papers, H. H. "Hap" Arnold Papers, Ray Stannard Baker Papers, Ruth Gordon and Garson Kanin Papers, Cary Grayson Papers, MacKinlay Kantor Papers, Rouben Mamoulian Collection, Groucho Marx Papers, Harold Sintzenich diaries, Woodrow Wilson Papers, Owen Wister Papers); Library of Congress Motion Picture Reading Room (preservation copies of many of Victor Fleming's silent films, including fragments of *The Rough Riders*); Library of Congress Prints and Photographs Reading Room (*Look* photo collection, *New York Journal American* photo collection); Library of Congress Performing Arts Reading Room (Irving Berlin Papers); Library of Congress Recorded Sound Reference Center (Bob Hope scripts); Los Angeles County Registrar-Recorder's Office; Margaret Herrick Library, Academy of Motion Picture Arts and Sciences (Anthony Slide Collection, Herrick Library Oral History Collection, Paramount Script Collection, Production Code file, SMU Oral History Collection (Greer Garson Collection), Turner/MGM Script Collection, Victor Fleming clipping file); Museum of Modern Art, New York (Sergei Eisenstein Collection, special screenings of *When the Clouds Roll By*, and fragments of *The Rough Riders*); National Archives and Records Administration, College Park, Maryland (Records of the U.S. Army Military Intelligence Division, Records of the Bureau of Motion Pictures, Records of the War Department Bureau of Public Relations, U.S. Army Signal Corps films); National Archives and Records Administration, Washington, D.C. (Civil War military records); Richard Nixon Presidential Library and Birthplace (Lee Bowman file); Newberry Library, Chicago (Ben Hecht Papers); San Diego Natural History Museum; San Diego Zoological Park; Stanford University (John Steinbeck Collection); Steinhart Aquarium; Supreme Court of California; University of Arkansas, Fayetteville (Lighton Family Papers); University of California, Berkeley (Sidney Howard Papers); University of California, Los Angeles (Betty Bronson Papers, Hedda Hopper Papers, Oral History Project, UCLA Film Archive for special screenings of *Common Clay* and *American Aristocracy*); University of Florida, Gainesville (Marjorie Kinnan Rawlings Papers); University of Indiana, Bloomington (Upton Sinclair Papers); University of North Dakota (Maxwell Anderson Papers); University of South Carolina (Jules Furthman scripts); University of Southern California (Constance McCormick Collection, Cinema and Television Library Archives); University of Virginia (Booton Herndon

Papers); Wisconsin Center for Film and Theater Research (Dalton Trumbo Papers, Walter Wanger Collection); U.S. Conference of Catholic Bishops; Film and Broadcasting Office (National Legion of Decency files); Columbia County (Pa.) Historical Society; Culver City Historical Society; Harold Bell Wright Society; Hoboken Historical Society; Institute of Texan Cultures, San Antonio; Jerome (Ariz.) Historical Society; Pasadena Historical Society and Museum; Pasadena Public Library; San Dimas Historical Society; Santa Barbara Historical Society; Sedona (Ariz.) Historical Society; Seneca County (Ohio) Historical and Genealogical Society; Texas County (Mo.) Historical Society; Wood County (Ohio) Historical Center and Museum.

For permissions to quote confidential or copyrighted material, thanks go to Roger L. Mayer of Turner Entertainment (MGM files); Daniel Selznick of Selznick Properties, Ltd. (Selznick Archive); Dixon Adair (the diary of A. D. Adair Jr.); Christy Kelso (Fleming letters); and Maria Cooper Janis ("Well, It Was This Way: Gary Cooper Tells His Story").

Notes

Direct quotations in the text that do not have a corresponding note identifying the source are drawn from interviews or correspondence with the author or his research associate. The names of such sources are provided in the acknowledgments.

Introduction

3 "A composite between": Paramount publicity, 1928; the screenwriter cited is Louise Long (*Rough House Rosie*, 1927; *Interference*, 1928), who never worked on any of Fleming's pictures.

3 "the Lincoln type of melancholia": *Lion's Roar*, Jan. 1944.

3 an appreciation of her father: *The New York Times*, Nov. 15, 1998.

4 "a man like Fleming": Carle to Grover Jones, May 1, 1939, Victor Fleming file, Margaret Herrick Library, Academy of Motion Picture Arts and Sciences.

5 When the author of: Schulberg, *Moving Pictures*.

5 "Clark Gable on the screen is Fleming": Henry Hathaway's description of Fleming as Gable is from his interview in the Ronald L. Davis Oral History Collection, DeGolyer Library, Southern Methodist University, Dallas, collection number A1980.0154; viewed at Margaret Herrick Library.

5 "Every man that ever worked": Interview in *Focus on Film*, No. 7, 1991.

6 "Nice legs, sister!": From a letter written by Eleanor Saville to her husband after the U.S. Olympic swimming team, escorted by Johnny Weissmuller, visited MGM that July, shortly before the Summer Olympics began in Los Angeles. The team met Fleming and other movie directors at a reception at the Ambassador Hotel. Letter held by Roger van Oosten.

6 he wired back, simply: The telegram is recalled by Louis Lighton's sister Betty.

6 "He is probably the only guy": *Lion's Roar*, Jan. 1944.

6 "Fleming was quite inarticulate": Kaplan to David Stenn.

7 "Every dame he ever worked with": Kobal, *People Will Talk*.

7 "Victor Fleming knew as much": Maltin, *Behind the Camera.*

7 "Fleming was the realist": Hathaway, SMU oral history.

8 "he had an inner power": Lewis, *The Creative Producer.*

8 "Eddie Sutherland, the gay sophisticate": Brooks to Kevin Brownlow, Jan. 6, 1971.

9 "he was part Indian": Interview with John Lee Mahin in McGilligan, *Backstory.*

9 "He was always the biggest star": Torchia made this comment to Selden West when the latter was researching the life of Spencer Tracy. Katharine Hepburn told West that when she first entered MGM to make *The Philadelphia Story*, she saw Gable and Tracy flanking an imposing figure and asked her group, "Who's the one in the middle?" It was Fleming.

10 When Hathaway, Tracy, Gable: For example, Hedda Hopper devotes her entire column of January 23, 1944, to the comparison of Rhett Butler to Fleming, and begins with Tracy calling him "the Clark Gable of directors."

1 Born in a Tent

11 February 20, 1888: The date is indicated in an autograph book signed by friends and neighbors of the Flemings the day before they left Missouri.

11 tornado: The date of that tornado is in the 1889 *History of Laclede, Camden, Dallas, Webster, Wright, Texas, Pulaski, Phelps & Dent Counties, Missouri, from Earliest Times to the Present.*

12 "publicity, settlement agents": McWilliams, *Southern California Country.*

12 "half an acre in lemons": Dumke, *Boom of the Eighties.*

12 claims of Cherokee blood: According to a Bledsoe County historian Elizabeth Robnett, the earliest traced Fleming ancestor is Samuel Fleming, born in 1795. In 1850, he, his wife, and nine children lived south of Pikeville, Tennessee. Since in that Census his place of birth is given as "Unknown," the family roots beyond him are open to speculation.

14 pig roasts and brass bands: Dumke, *Boom of the Eighties.* Irving Stone memorialized the period in *Men to Match My Mountains:*

> It was said that the boom did not burst, it gradually shriveled up. By April 1, 1888 a few harsh facts began to emerge: tourists simply had not settled in anything like the numbers expected.

The banks, nervous about the paper boom, had cut down on credit involved in real estate. Many who had made large profits buying and selling land realized that their gains amounted to soft signatures by people who had been speculating precisely as they had. Those who had property left to sell saw that they had to sell their land quickly and get out some cash, or they would be left empty-handed.

15 February 23, 1889: Since his death, for reasons unknown, Fleming's birth year has often been reported as 1883. It seldom was recorded or reported correctly during his lifetime, either. Among the accurate records: the 1900 census, the 1910 census, and Fleming's Army record. The volume for births registered for February 1889 is missing from the Los Angeles County Registrar Recorder's Office, as is the 1891 volume recording his sister Arletta's birth. However, his sister Ruth's birth in 1893 *is* recorded. Fleming sometimes fudged his age. His 1909 marriage license application records his birth year as 1887 because, at twenty, he was not legally an adult. Starting at age thirty-nine, he occasionally recorded his birth year as 1890. It's written that way on applications for his pilot license and on his 1933 marriage license application.

17 "There is little room in my life": Fleming, *Action.*

19 spacious three-bedroom bungalow: The house is still there, with the kitchen window Fleming's aunt Mamie had lowered. One of the oddities of Fleming's history—especially for someone who grew up in Southern California—is that nearly every dwelling in which he lived still exists.

19 Chinese peddler: San Dimas Historical Society.

19 "an old postcard": Robert Towne, preface and postscript to *Chinatown*, included in Ulin, *Writing Los Angeles.*

21 put their faith in dowsing: Wyman, *Witching for Water, Oil, Pipes, and Precious Minerals.*

2 Cars, Cameras, Action!

25 in 1903: Oldfield's first Los Angeles appearance was that November; he returned the following December.

25 Charles Soules and Joe Nikrent . . . Ted "Terrible Teddy" Tetzlaff: Soules, one of five racing brothers, was a journeyman racer with a brief career. Along with his brother George, Charles is believed to have won

the first twenty-four-hour race, in Columbus, Ohio, in 1905. Nikrent was, like Soules, part of a family of racing brothers, and finished first in the 1909 endurance race from Los Angeles to Phoenix known as the Cactus Derby. It is likely Fleming had more racing experiences with Tetzlaff, a prominent early racer with twenty-two races between 1909 and 1915. Five of those were in Santa Monica, including the first Santa Monica road race on July 10, 1909. Because Fleming, in 1911, raced on the Santa Monica road course used for the 1914 Vanderbilt Cup, this became distorted into the often-published claim that he had been a Vanderbilt Cup racer. It is possible Fleming was Soules's ride-along mechanic, or "mechanician," in a race at Santa Monica on August 9, 1913. Soules, driving a Cadillac, finished sixth. There are no newspaper mentions of Fleming as anyone's mechanician. Except for George Hill, who worked for both Tetzlaff and Oldfield, mechanicians seldom were mentioned in newspaper accounts of races. Mechanicians often had to do hand pumping to maintain gas and oil pressure, and made repairs during the course of the race. In the notes used to compose *Action Is the Word*, Fleming mentioned that he had begun racing at Agricultural Park in 1907.

26 Thomas Flyers: The same make, although not the same model, that won the 1908 race from New York to Paris.

27 "We'd wait until it rained": Howe's anecdote about Fleming and the cowcatcher is contained in the Reminiscences of James Wong Howe (1971) in the Oral History Collection of Columbia University, pp. 17 and 18.

27 Brian J. Leavitt: One of the more colorful figures in early Southern California racing, he sponsored racers and races—including a three-hundred-mile contest against a Stearns in August 1909, with winnings of more than $10,000—and occasionally got behind the wheel himself.

29 "That's where you get a job": Behlmer, *Henry Hathaway*.

30 Allan Dwan: He continued to direct into the early 1960s. He became a favorite of film historians for his detailed anecdotes of early filmmaking—although many failed to notice that sometimes he was cheerfully putting them on—and a favorite of film critics for finding the energy in low-cost projects like the *High Noon* rip-off *Silver Lode* (1954). He died in 1981, age ninety-six.

31 "A chauffeur in those days": Harmetz, *Making of "The Wizard of Oz."*

31 Charlotte Burton: She possibly was born earlier than 1893, the year she usually gave, or 1892, the year on her death certificate, since her daugh-

ter was born in 1906. Burton had been married to a man named Wooldridge when she returned to Santa Barbara, where she had family roots. In 1917, she married the cowboy actor William Russell when they both were acting in a serial, *The Diamond from the Sky.* She appeared in fifty-five films and serials until 1920. The marriage ended in divorce, and she is known to have married at least twice after that. As Charlotte Stuart, she died in 1942. Her daughter, Charlotte Burton Coombs, died in 1986, age eighty.

31 "superb figure": *Moving Picture World,* Nov. 16, 1912.

31 "We developed some sort of engine trouble": Interview in Bogdanovich, *Who the Devil Made It.* In a 1970 interview with Richard Schickel, Dwan said Fleming had his back to the vehicle and announced, "One of your tappet valves is missing," without looking up. Dwan, trained as an engineer, would undoubtedly have been impressed.

32 Roy Overbaugh: Fleming credited Overbaugh and his assistant, R. D. Armstrong, with helping get him a job in the developing lab at Flying A, something that may have happened when Armstrong tried his hand at acting in 1913. Fleming moved up to be Overbaugh's assistant cameraman after that.

33 "I used to drive a race car": Interview in Schickel, *Men Who Made the Movies.*

33 "True, false, or merely exaggerated": McCarthy, *Howard Hawks.*

33 "we used to load": Victor Fleming, "Directing—Then and Now," *Lion's Roar,* July 1944.

35 "There were quite a few incidents": "In the Days of the Flying A," *Noticias,* March 17, 1954, reprinted by the Santa Barbara Historical Society, Fall 1976.

35 "They didn't make any comment": Bogdanovich, *Who the Devil Made It.*

35 "In the 'middle ages' ": Fleming, "Directing—Then and Now."

36 "a tremendous figure": Slide, *Silent Players.*

36 "Quite a lady himself": Interview in *Bright Lights* (online), Sept. 1996.

36 raw kidding: Mentioned in Mann, *Behind the Screen.*

37 Neilan established a new site: *Moving Picture World,* Dec. 27, 1913.

37 "With both alcohol and fury": Brownlow, *The War, the West, and the Wilderness.*

37 "The legend": Koszarski, *Evening's Entertainment.*

38 "the Hollywood version": Spears, *Hollywood.*

38 "Mickey was a genius": Eyman, *Mary Pickford, America's Sweetheart.*

38 "You must remember": Ibid.

38 "Oh, shit!": Samuel Marx, *Mayer and Thalberg.*
39 "Irishmen like Mickey": Eyman, *Mary Pickford, America's Sweetheart.*
39 "beauty, personality, charm": Marshall Neilan, "Acting for the Screen: The Six Great Essentials," in *Opportunities in the Motion Picture Industry* (Los Angeles: Photoplay Research Society, 1922).
40 "used dozens of assistants": Brown, *Adventures with D. W. Griffith.*

3 The Importance of Shooting Doug

41 "he often enjoyed": Fairbanks to Schickel, March 27, 1972, evaluating Schickel's article on Douglas Fairbanks Sr. in the December 1971 *American Heritage.* Part of the Booton Herndon Papers, University of Virginia.
42 presumed *he* was half-Indian: Lu Fleming's daughter from her first marriage, Helene Rosson Bowman said, "I think he probably was," to David Stenn, but neither of Vic and Lu's daughters recalls ever being told that he was, or that people said he was. Neither had Fleming's niece Yvonne Blocksom, born in 1915. Those who did included Allan Dwan (who described Fleming as "half-Indian" to Fairbanks's biographer Booton Herndon), David O. Selznick (who mentioned Fleming's "American Indian" quality to Charles Samuels), and Ingrid Bergman's publicist, Joseph Steele (who wrote of Fleming as "part Cherokee").
42 "has definitely abandoned": *Variety,* Sept. 24, 1915.
42 "He went out West": Fairbanks to Schickel, March 27, 1972.
42 "The director is much overestimated": *New York Telegraph,* Nov. 24, 1918.
43 "Once even I found myself": Kael, *When the Lights Go Down.*
43 "shattered, messy childhoods": Ibid.
45 "this nocturnal scene": Bingham, *Great Lover.*
45 "My tits!": Carey, *Anita Loos.*
45 "bears the taint": *The New York Times,* June 11, 1916.
45 "Griffith was not pleased": The traditional quotation can be found most recently in Basinger, *Silent Stars;* the original text is in *Photoplay,* Sept. 1929.
46 "has already proven himself": *Variety,* Sept. 24, 1915.
46 "The fact of the matter is": Fairbanks to Schickel, March 27, 1972.
46 "You had to keep working": *Bright Lights* (online), Sept. 1996.
47 "We all did": Bogdanovich, *Who the Devil Made It.*

47 "very actorish, petulant": Richard Schickel, "Good Years, Bad Years," *Harper's*, Oct. 1970.

47 "If something went wrong": Undated notes, interview with Booton Herndon, Herndon Papers.

47 "Douglas Fairbanks was a man": Harriman, *Vicious Circle*.

47 "It was no secret": Slide, *Kindergarten of the Movies*.

48 "basically an actor": Interview with Booton Herndon, March 10, 1975, Herndon Papers.

49 "called for a degree": Jacobs, *Rise of the American Film*.

49 "was the abnormal norm": Cooke, *Douglas Fairbanks*.

50 "Gee whiz!": Jacobs, *Rise of the American Film*.

50 "whole damn crew": Herndon, *Mary Pickford and Douglas Fairbanks*.

50 Bessie Love: She never indicated when she and Fleming were a couple; most likely they became romantically involved during their time with Fairbanks. She is now best known for *The Broadway Melody* (1929). After marrying and divorcing William Hawks, she moved to London in the 1930s, where she occasionally appeared in plays. In 1972, she was Aunt Pittypat in a short-lived London musical production of *Gone With the Wind*. Her last film role was a cameo in *Ragtime* in 1981. She died in 1986, age eighty-seven.

50 avert the boredom: Fairbanks's and Fleming's daredevil offscreen jokes were celebrated on both sides of the Atlantic. David Lean referred to them in his final film, *A Passage to India* (1984): Dr. Aziz (Victor Banerjee) walks on the outside of a railroad car as it crosses a dizzying viaduct and proclaims, "I am Douglas Fairbanks!"

50 "to see which of them": Love, *From Hollywood with Love*.

50 they'd shout "Boo!": Dan Thomas column, May 10, 1927.

51 "Vic Fleming [was] taller": Dwan to Herndon, March 10, 1975. Herndon Papers.

51 "a suitcase of valuable bonds": Harmetz, *Making of "The Wizard of Oz."*

51 Fleming once asked Fairbanks: The version in Oscar Levant's *Memoirs of an Amnesiac* is what Milestone told him on his TV program, though in his book Levant credited Henry Hathaway. In 1948, the Hollywood columnist Erskine Pearson wrote another variation on that anecdote, calling it "a wonderful story" told by James Stewart. That version involved Fleming, a stuntman, and a flight of steps, and a slightly different punch line: "See," Fleming said, "that's exactly what I want. Now do it that way. And call an ambulance for me. I think I broke my leg."

51 *The Good Bad Man, The Half-Breed:* Cinematographer Glenn MacWilliams

told John C. Tibbetts in *American Classic Screen*, January–February 1979, "By 1917, Doug was nuts on cowboy stuff. His idea of life was to make western pictures. He wanted to go on location among the Indians. . . .

"In those days we had to shoot with available lights and diffusers. There would be many a day when we couldn't shoot and Doug would organize a footrace. One day he had a marathon, up Sunset, up Vermont to Hollywood Boulevard back to the studio. Doug would put up five dollars and get everybody in on it. . . . He was very energetic, very nervous, but it wasn't really nervous energy. It was just that he enjoyed everything and he loved making pictures. When he was making westerns, he was in his glory. He was like a little boy playing cowboy. A lot of people don't believe this, but the whole time I was with him, he never had a stunt man. He kept real cowboys around him all the time. And he never sat still. He was always rehearsing, building up stunts, practicing, working. He'd figure out a stunt and we'd build the whole picture around it."

51 an impossibly wide ravine: The effect is described in Herndon, *Mary Pickford and Douglas Fairbanks*.

51 Dwan remembered: Booton Herndon often was frustrated by the memories of old-time moviemakers who had no intention of telling any unembellished stories. On September 5, 1973, he wrote a friend, Jim Card:

> Allan Dwan told me at great length how he attached a steel rod to a sapling in this picture [*The Half-Breed*] so that Fairbanks could use it as a catapult to throw himself up a big redwood tree. Dick Talmadge said that even with the steel rod, it just wouldn't work. It was done by reversing the film. I went back to Dwan and he said yes, this stunt was frequently done by reversing the film, and also by using a piano wire, but on this occasion, they just wanted to do it the easy way and did so using the steel rod. Who am I supposed to believe?

Herndon just needed to run that scene backward. Herndon Papers.

52 "the names of actresses": *Motion Picture News*, undated copy.

52 Howard Hawks: His biographer, Todd McCarthy, describes his first job in motion pictures this way:

> The most Hawks ever said about his motivation for entering the film business was, "I just wanted a job during summer vaca-

tion. Somebody I knew at Paramount got me a job in the prop room." He further explained that an emergency had arisen on the Fairbanks picture—the film needed a modern set built in a hurry at a time when the studio's sole official art director was away. Hawks, with his limited architectural training, volunteered his services—or perhaps was recommended by Fleming. Fairbanks liked the work as well as the young man who did it, which led to further employment at the studio.

4 In Manhattan for the Great War

55 "with what appeared to be the rest of Hollywood": Fleming, *Action.*

56 Major Charles Wyman: Wyman, suffering from tuberculosis, moved to Southern California in 1920 to improve his health, and his family expected him to die soon. He died at age eighty-seven, in 1971. He was the technical adviser for *Ten Gentlemen from West Point* in 1942, directed by Henry Hathaway.

57 Starting in September 1917: Nye, *Carbine & Lance.*

57 only four motion picture cameramen: "Monthly Report to the Chief Signal Officer for March of 1918," Records of Allied Expeditionary Force, National Archives, College Park, Md.

57 Olin O. Ellis and Enoch Garey: In the spring of 1917, Ellis and Garey, then lieutenants at the federal military training camp at Plattsburgh, New York, co-authored *The Plattsburg Manual,* a handbook for civilians entering training camps for military reservists. Photographs in the manual illustrated everything from exercise positions to the correct way to march in formation. Published that April, the book was briefly a best seller. Ellis later headed the ROTC program at Johns Hopkins University in Baltimore; for a short time, Garey was superintendent of the Maryland State Police.

57 He and twelve others: The record of that remarkable group of filmmakers is included in Fleming's Military Intelligence Division file at the National Archives.

58 "should their work at Columbia": From Fleming's own file of correspondence from his military career.

58 "Vic Fleming, cameraman": Diaries of Harold A. C. Sintzenich, 1912–73, Library of Congress Manuscript Division.

59 "I taught them": Brownlow, *The War, the West, and the Wilderness.*

59 "news value, historical record": From the catalog of the U.S. School of Military Cinematography, Columbia University archives.
59 "Jewish tastes and standards": Charyn, *Gangsters & Gold-Diggers.*
60 Al Jolson in *Sinbad:* Sintzenich's diary records many group visits to Broadway and vaudeville shows. In keeping with anti-German sentiment, the producers of that version of *Maytime* changed the setting from Austria to old New York. Fleming's group attended *Sinbad* a month before Jolson first interpolated "Swanee."
61 "Akeley's talents": Brownlow, *The War, the West, and the Wilderness.*
61 Akeley improved searchlights: Bodrey-Summers, *Carl Akeley.*
62 Under the category noted: Fleming's Military Intelligence Division review is included in Military Intelligence Division files in the National Archives.
63 The shadow of DeMille: DeMille's nativism led to scorn and condemnation at a famous meeting of the Screen Directors Guild in October 1950, when, while attacking the guild president, Joseph Mankiewicz, for opposing a loyalty oath for guild members, he read a list of alleged communist front groups and deliberately mispronounced the names of directors such as William Wyler and Fred Zinnemann to emphasize that they weren't born in the United States. That performance resulted in a vote of confidence for the Mankiewicz faction of the guild and the end of the loyalty oath question.
63 In 1914, seventeen German ships: Hoboken Historical Society.
65 "Suggest you 'hold fast' ": Fleming's military correspondence file.
65 "My orders were to accompany him": Fleming, *Action.*

5 Filming the Conquering Hero

66 "No one in America": Clements, *Woodrow Wilson.*
67 "We replied": Shotwell, *At the Paris Peace Conference.*
68 "We have at our table": Whiteman, *Letters from the Paris Peace Conference.*
68 "So up we went": Benham's diary is included in Link et al., *Papers of Woodrow Wilson*, vol. 53.
69 "an enterprising young photographer": Starling and Sugrue, *Starling of the White House.*
69 "At the end": Fosdick's diary is included in Link et al., *Papers of Woodrow Wilson*, vol. 53.

69 "Nothing has pleased": *The New York Times*, Dec. 12, 1918.

70 "The town was a veritable mud-hole": Grayson's diary is included in Link et al., *Papers of Woodrow Wilson*, vol. 53.

71 "a very jolly boy": Shotwell, *At the Paris Peace Conference.*

71 "my cameraman": Brownlow files.

71 placed at the president's disposal: Wilson toured European capitals because, as Thomas Fleming writes in *The Illusion of Victory*, when the opening of the peace conference was postponed until January 12, 1919, the French, eager to see Germany punished in the peace settlement, urged Wilson to visit battlefields and view damaged cities in France and Belgium, which he resisted, not wanting to inflame passions. His way out—and also a way to build up his image as a global peacemaker—was to schedule ceremonial visits to Great Britain and Italy. But Vic's November 27 letter to his mother indicates that a European tour was always planned.

71 dozens of iconic images: President Wilson, incapacitated by a stroke in 1919, did not see any of them until November 1920 in the East Room of the White House, using a projector given to him by Douglas Fairbanks. Ray Stannard Baker, who wrote about that event in *American Chronicle*, recalled, "With the first brilliantly lighted episode we were in another world; a resplendent world, full of wonderful and glorious events," but Wilson "sat bowed forward, looking at all this, absolutely silent . . . Was there ever such marching regiments of men, such bowing dignitaries, so many lords and lord-mayors? And here he was, the President, riding behind magnificent horses with outriders flying pennants, and people shouting in the streets, coming down from Buckingham Palace with the King of England." But when the film was over, "the symbols of that glory had faded away with a click and a sputter. It was to us sitting there as though the thread of life had snapped; as though we had fallen from some vast height into the dim, cold, dreary reality of this lesser world." Wilson left the screening, Baker recorded, without speaking a word.

72 "a tremendous demonstration": *The New York Times*, Jan. 7, 1918.

6 The Importance of Directing Doug

75 " 'Look!' said Douglas": Chaplin, *My Autobiography.*

75 Jerry Lewis would use: Publicity for *The Ladies Man* in 1961 asserted that his four-story cutaway of a women's boardinghouse was the largest indoor set ever built at Paramount.

77 rolled-up script pages: On-set photos of Fleming from the 1920s to 1947 show him with script pages either put in the left back pocket of his trousers or, more characteristically, stuffed into his left jacket pocket.

79 "a room open": *Literary Digest*, July 3, 1920. Tibbetts and Welsh quote the article in their study *His Majesty the American* and also draw the comparison to *Royal Wedding* and *2001: A Space Odyssey*.

80 "the one about the old maid in the sleeping car": Jokes about old maids in sleeping cars had been around since the first Pullman sleeping car in 1857.

80 "We had even passed": Fleming, "Directing—Then and Now," *Lion's Roar*, July 1944.

81 "intensely unselfconscious": *Los Angeles Times*, July 3, 1921.

81 for Irene Castle to suspect: Castle, *Castles in the Air.* She sneered particularly at Clifford's outfit that day: a purple wool suit and a purse emblazoned with "KC" in what Castle described as diamonds. Castle, known as the embodiment of tasteful couture, was describing the typical flashy getup of vaudeville performers.

82 "Right now I want you": Letter auctioned on eBay in 2007.

82 "Just another day away": Letter held by Robert Birchard.

82 "Darling, my love": Letter auctioned by Sotheby's in 1993.

82 "perfectly good husband": Fleming and Clifford were not, in fact, ever married, and common-law marriages had been illegal in California since the 1890s. In 1926, she married the banker Mirimir Illitch, a union lasting until her death in 1962.

83 "extraordinary scenes": *The New York Times*, June 14, 1920.

84 knocked off early one day: Dan Thomas column, April 16, 1924.

85 "outdoes anything of the kind": *The New York Times*, June 14, 1920.

85 "Only the cinema": Greene, *Graham Greene Film Reader.*

7 Scaling Paramount Pictures

87 "John chose a newcomer": Loos, *Talmadge Girls.*

91 "two scenes where double exposure": *The New York Times*, Jan. 9, 1922.

91 "Thalberg says you know": McBride, *Hawks on Hawks.*

91 "a dandy little household": Sutherland's description of the Hawks brothers' house is in the Reminiscences of Edward Sutherland (1959) in the Oral History Collection of Columbia University, p. 93.

91 *Behind the Front:* A raucous service comedy co-starring Wallace Beery

and Raymond Hatton, and the film that launched Sutherland as a comedy director.

91 "a world-weary homosexual": Samuel Marx, *Mayer and Thalberg.*

92 "Howard had class, you see": McGilligan, *Backstory.*

93 "He'd say, 'Dan, what are you gonna do?' ": McBride, *Hawks on Hawks.*

93 "I think I got about an hour": Ibid.

93 "built a couple of airplanes": Bogdanovich, *Who the Devil Made It.*

94 "a collection of puppets": *The New York Times,* Nov. 19, 1922.

94 Betty Bronson: Her unpublished memoir tells of Fleming's help in landing the role of Peter Pan. She wrote that she found him

> a very adorable and encouraging person. I told him . . . of my real desire of securing a test for Peter Pan. This seemed to surprise him somewhat and he said he didn't quite know if they would take someone unknown but that he would see what could be done—since he really didn't have anything in his picture that would fit me. However, the following week or so, Herbert Brenon returned to Hollywood to begin work on his productions and I found that an appointment had been arranged for me to meet him. Of course, I was very nervous during the interview, and feared that I had not made a very good impression and was quite surprised when I received a call a few days later to make a test.

94 "far more," "It never seems real anywhere": *Photoplay,* Sept. 1923.

95 "In direction": *Variety,* June 21, 1923.

95 Virginia Valli: In 1921, she had married Demmy Lamson, a location manager and assistant director who later became a personal manager. When they divorced in 1926, court papers said he had deserted her in December 1924 and that they had not lived together since 1923. With her career fading, she married Charles Farrell in 1931, retired from the screen, and moved to Palm Springs. She died in 1968, age seventy.

95 "a pine tree": Drew, *Speaking of Silents.*

95 "gave me a half-broke horse": *Los Angeles Times,* April 1, 1928. The eight thousand thorns presumably were hyperbole.

95 "Vic Fleming wanted to go": Tuska, *Filming of the West.*

96 " 'that kills two birds' ": *Motion Picture News,* Dec. 22, 1923.

97 "a silhouette picture": Interview with Howe in *Filmmakers Newsletter,* Feb. 1973.

97 "We were riding along the trail": Howe's anecdote about Fleming killing the rattlesnake is contained in the Reminiscences of James Wong Howe (1971) in the Oral History Collection of Columbia University, p. 19.

97 "right through the finger!": Likely an exaggeration, since Stout retained all his fingers. Stout, an assistant to Howe in the 1920s, later worked for John Ford. In 1951, he was director of photography for Ida Lupino's production company, and for a *Collier's* article published May 12 he gave Lupino what he considered his highest praise: "Ida has more knowledge of camera angles and lenses than any director I've ever worked with, with the exception of Victor Fleming."

98 "just a very attractive bright boy": Drew, *Speaking of Silents.*

98 Seal Beach speed trap: *Victor Fleming v. Superior Court of the County of Orange, et al.*, L.A. No. 8360, decided by the Supreme Court of California, July 1, 1925. Upton Sinclair's novel *Oil!*, in its opening pages, articulates what rugged Westerners thought of "officers hiding in the bushes and spying on citizens: it was undignified, and taught motorists to regard officers of the law as enemies."

98 "a judicial knockout": *Los Angeles Times*, Sept. 11, 1924.

98 "The finished photoplay of today": From a Paramount publicity item.

8 Courage and Clara Bow

102 *Riders to the Sea:* A bleak one-act play written by John Millington Synge and first performed in 1904, set on an island in the west of Ireland.

102 "was mistaken for the leading man": Paramount publicity item, but it has the ring of truth to it.

102 "desert island stuff": *Variety*, Aug. 20, 1924.

103 "After a few days": According to Todd McCarthy, Shearer began writing her autobiography shortly after the death of Irving Thalberg in 1936, and left it uncompleted at her death in 1983, at age eighty. (Shearer's biographer Gavin Lambert wrote that she began it in 1955, while laid up from a ski accident, and abandoned it the next year, after the Random House executive Bennett Cerf deemed it "too bland and too sentimental.") Howard Strickling held on to it before passing it to one of his relatives, Barbara Blane, who allowed McCarthy to study the manuscript for his biography of Hawks. McCarthy furnished me with the sections describing Shearer's affair with Fleming.

103 Norma and Vic's fling: The circumstances of her breakup with Fleming

remain unknown; Lambert's *Norma Shearer* says Fleming initiated the split. They attended their last public event together in July 1926; he became "engaged" to Clara Bow that September. Shortly afterward, newspaper items hinted that Shearer was getting serious with Irving Thalberg, whom she married the following year. After Thalberg's death, she acted in a half-dozen more movies, including *The Women* (1939). She retired from acting in 1942, when she married Martin Arrougé, a ski instructor twenty years her junior.

103 "When Lasky saw the finished picture": McBride, *Hawks on Hawks.*

104 "a breezy, refreshed style": *Los Angeles Times,* Aug. 11, 1924.

104 "a group of people": *Lion's Roar,* July 1944.

104 "For the first time in my life": *Photoplay,* July 1926.

104 "nearly drowned": Undated, from 1925, syndicated newspaper article about swimming safety.

104 "a compact serial": *The New York Times,* April 28, 1925.

104 "one more of": *Variety,* Sept. 30, 1925.

104 "asked him, frankly": Love, *From Hollywood with Love.*

104 "I asked him why": Love to Kevin Brownlow.

106 until her death: Ruth Kobe died in 1977.

106 "I have just witnessed": *Moving Picture World,* Aug. 28, 1925.

106 "should be the translation": Greene, *Graham Greene Film Reader.* Considering film "more truly comparable with the novel" than with the stage, Greene saw it progressing the way the novel had from Defoe to Henry James and Conrad, "from action to thought."

107 "in all except bulk": *The New York Times,* Nov. 16, 1925.

110 "I hear the train coming now": Ralston quoted in Drew, *Speaking of Silents.* Ralston incorrectly recalled the train as the Super Chief, which was not in existence in 1926. Likely, as in the improvisational early days of silent film, Fleming put Ernest Torrence on a regularly scheduled Santa Fe train at the station in Fullerton, then waited for it to come by.

112 "a straight, out-and-out romance": A quotation that Lewis supplied to Paramount publicity in 1926, before he saw the movie.

112 "always amusing": James Harold Flye, *Letters of James Agee to Father Flye* (Boston: Houghton Mifflin, 1962).

112 "social climber": Noted by the language maven William Safire in *The New York Times,* Nov. 15, 1998.

112 He told an audience: Schorer, *Sinclair Lewis, an American Life.*

113 "He had me open up": Interview in Higham, *Hollywood Cameramen.*

113 "You go ahead and shoot": Interview in Eyman, *Five American Cinematographers.*

113 "She was what we called": Atkins, *Arthur Jacobson.*

114 "older a great deal": "The Love Life of Clara Bow," *Motion Picture*, Nov. 1928.

114 "I liked him at once": *Photoplay*, March 1928.

115 "She was bad in the book": *Los Angeles Times*, July 15, 1926.

115 "Just before the lights": *Toronto Star*, April 5, 1991.

9 A Lost Epic

118 "Clara did strange things": Atkins, *Arthur Jacobson.*

118 "But as for movie people being themselves": Astor, *Life on Film.*

119 enjoying an aerial bout of tag: *Washington Post*, June 7, 1928.

119 "a good 'big production' man": Astor, *Life on Film.*

120 "The town was lousy with movie people": Wellman's unreliable, albeit entertaining, *Rough Riders* stories are in Wellman, *Short Time for Insanity.*

121 "get the feel of the period": Astor, *Life on Film.*

121 "the Armageddon": Wellman, *Short Time for Insanity.*

121 "the high spot": Astor, *Life on Film.*

121 "We notified all our exchanges": Lasky's *Rough Riders* stories are in Lasky, *I Blow My Own Horn.*

122 "The heat bore down": The rest of Astor's *Rough Riders* stories in this chapter are in Astor, *My Story.*

123 "a crude version": Interview in Eyman, *Five American Cinematographers.*

123 "Well, I never saw": Howe's *Rough Riders* stories are in the Reminiscences of James Wong Howe (1971) in the Oral History Collection of Columbia University, pp. 16 and 18.

123 "Fleming was sitting": Hathaway's *Rough Riders* stories are in Behlmer, *Henry Hathaway.*

124 at 4:00 a.m.: *San Antonio Express*, Sept. 16, 1926.

124 Roland told a reporter: United Press, Sept. 16, 1926.

124 "We were quite sure": *Los Angeles Times*, Sept. 19, 1926.

124 "I did not consider myself engaged": Clara Bow, "If I Had My Life to Live Over," *New Movie Magazine*, May 1932.

125 Fleming had proposed in a letter: *San Antonio Light*, Sept. 20, 1926.

126 "a little flirtation": Stenn, *Clara Bow.*

126 "You couldn't deceive him": *Photoplay*, March 1928.

128 "considerable trouble": *Variety*, March 30, 1927.
128 the audience's delight: *The New York Times*, May 17, 1927.

10 From *The Way of All Flesh* to *Abie's Irish Rose*

130 "a large, beaming, childlike personage": *New Yorker*, Oct. 28, 1928.
131 "have had a slight disagreement": Associated Press and many other news outlets, Dec. 2, 1926.
131 "feeling for each other": *Photoplay*, March 1928.
131 "I couldn't live up to his subtlety": *Los Angeles Times*, June 8, 1930.
131 "He's hung like a horse": Arce, *Gary Cooper*.
131 Alice White: Her acting career took a downturn in the early sound era, and she made few films after that, ending with *Flamingo Road* in 1949. Following her divorce from Sidney Bartlett in the 1930s, she wore a gold "divorce ring" inscribed "liberty and freedom." She died in 1983, age seventy-nine.
131 "so stubby and fat": White told different versions of how she gained movie stardom. This version is from the United Press, April 21, 1938.
131 "a nice little-boy kiss": "Alice White's Diary," *Screen Secrets*, Feb. 1929.
131 "a girl can't help liking Victor": *Motion Picture*, Dec. 1928.
132 Meadowlark Ranch: The property is now part of an unincorporated area north of San Diego. A remnant of the former Leo Carrillo Ranch next door is now a park operated by the city of Carlsbad.
133 "Mr. Fleming and Mr. Schulberg": *Los Angeles Times*, July 10, 1927.
133 "discussed every scene": Jannings, *Theater, Film—Das Leben und ich*. He also wrote of Fleming, "Not misguided by formal education or training, he was straightforward and explicit and had absolutely no notion of the art of acting as we understood it in Berlin. But he knew all of my films and had a high opinion of me, which, however, did not keep him from speaking his mind. I owe it to Fleming that I overcame the mental ocean between Europe and America rather quickly." (Translation by Christiane Faris, professor emerita of German and humanities, Oklahoma City University.)
134 "the situation so thoroughly": A Paramount publicity item that closely matches Jannings's later account of the filming.
134 "about three or four slugs of whiskey": Behlmer, *Henry Hathaway*.
134 "would bathe him in gloom": Von Sternberg, *Fun in a Chinese Laundry*.
135 "For him, suffering is a prism": Buñuel, *Unspeakable Betrayal*.

135 "ballast of American hokum": Edmund Wilson, *The Twenties: From Notebooks and Diaries of the Period*, ed. Leon Edel (New York: Farrar, Straus and Giroux, 1975).

135 "Gary was big and strong": *Photoplay*, March 1928.

135 "that great shaggy head of his": Hedda Hopper column, Feb. 24, 1940. Hopper was the only columnist to mention both Fleming's San Dimas roots and his first marriage. She continued to write her column until nearly the end of her life and died in 1966 at age eighty.

136 "Beau Brummells of Hollywood": *Motion Picture*, March 1929.

136 "We worked down on": Behlmer, *Henry Hathaway*.

137 "For all the acting I did": *Photoplay*, March 1928.

137 B. P. Schulberg had a fallback plan: Stenn, *Clara Bow*.

137 "a poor man's Clara Bow": Ayres to David Stenn (via Pam Prince of the William Morris Agency), David Stenn collection.

138 "noted as graceful dancers": *Los Angeles Times*, July 27, 1927.

138 "He went out of town": Victor Fleming notes on *Bombshell*, June 6, 1933, MGM Collection, USC Cinema and Television Library.

138 "showy": Stenn, *Clara Bow*.

138 "she was never much of an actress": LeRoy, *Take One*.

138 "perfectly devoted": *Los Angeles Times*, Oct. 30, 1927.

139 "Practically every major studio": Lasky, *I Blow My Own Horn*.

140 "one great trouble in that picture": "Hoofing to Fame with Nancy Carroll," *Screen Secrets*, Jan.–Feb. 1931.

140 "Do it this way": Rogers to Stenn.

140 "two hours and ten minutes of title gags": *Variety*, April 25, 1928.

141 "The laborious sentimental play": Ibid.

141 "a glass of water": Skutch, Ira, and David Shepard, eds. *Joseph Youngerman: My Seventy Years at Paramount Studios and the Directors Guild of America*. Directors Guild of America oral history, 1995.

142 "One of the things that we had": Interview in Maltin, *Behind the Camera*.

142 Lili Damita: Married to Errol Flynn from 1935 to 1942, she died in 1994, age eighty-nine.

142 "When I first come": *Motion Picture*, Aug. 1929. It was the custom of that time, in both newspapers and magazines, to quote foreign speakers of English in dialect. African-Americans, particularly, were most often quoted—if they were quoted at all—in what was known as the "plantation dialect" of the minstrel stage.

143 Lupe Velez: Married to Johnny Weissmuller from 1933 to 1939 and the star of several "Mexican Spitfire" films, she committed suicide with an overdose of Seconal in 1944, age thirty-six.

143 "Victor Fleming": *Motion Picture*, Jan. 1929.

144 Disney did try to broker a deal: Elements of Marion's story, the Disney archivist Dave Smith says, "could have happened in January 1930," but if Disney screened any cartoons at MGM with Mayer present, he did not record it. In 1928, he visited New York trying to sell his series of Oswald the Lucky Rabbit cartoons. At that time, MGM was not interested and told him, as he wrote in a letter on February 28, 1928, that "their theatre dept. reported that cartoons were on the wane." The first Mickey Mouse cartoon, *Steamboat Willie*, was released on November 18, 1928. His Silly Symphony series began with *The Skeleton Dance* in August 1929, and those were distributed by Columbia. In January 1930, Disney was looking for a new distributor, and the MGM sales manager Felix Feist recommended a contract, but studio attorneys vetoed that, not wishing to enter into a protracted legal fight with Disney's current distributor.

11 Creating Gary Cooper

145 *Burlesque:* David O. Selznick wanted to remake it with Fleming, according to a Selznick interoffice communication dated May 31, 1938. John Cromwell, who made it in 1929 under the title *The Dance of Life*, was an able craftsman (the 1934 *Of Human Bondage*) and often a backup director for Selznick when he couldn't land Fleming for films such as the 1937 *Prisoner of Zenda*. Blacklisted in the early 1950s, Cromwell directed on Broadway before returning to the screen with *The Goddess* (1958). The father of the actor James Cromwell (*Babe*), he acted himself in two Robert Altman films, *Three Women* (1977) and *A Wedding* (1978).

145 "Come on": Eyman, *Speed of Sound.*

145 "Are you only going": Behlmer, *Henry Hathaway.*

146 "Too late": Stenn, *Clara Bow.*

146 "He's on everybody's love-list!": *Motion Picture*, Jan. 1929.

146 "Coop loved him": Interview in Kobal, *People Will Talk.*

146 "I know he adored Victor": Veronica Cooper Converse to Stenn.

147 "wanted Lupe to be so sexy": Head and Calistro, *Edith Head's Hollywood.*

147 "his Mexican spitfire" "Kees Tony for me, Tom": Herbert Coleman with Judy Lanini, *The Hollywood I Knew* (Lanham, Md.: Scarecrow Press, 2003).

146 *The Hired Hand:* It's a lyrical flight of a Western—ninety minutes of impassioned imagery about marital and fraternal loyalty, manhood, and (what's rarer for a Western) womanhood, too. It picks up a pair of

decent, affable drifters, Peter Fonda and Warren Oates, just when Fonda has sickened of the winding trail that was supposed to lead to California and has decided to go home to the wife and daughter he abandoned seven years before. (Verna Bloom is mortified and sexy as the wife.) The film opened to positive reviews and slow box-office returns in 1971, but has since acquired a considerable cult, especially among filmmakers.

148 "I didn't seem to myself": Fairbanks to Wister, May 31, 1924, Owen Wister Papers, Library of Congress.

149 "The film is about": Richard Hutson, "Early Film Versions of *The Virginian,*" in Graulich and Tatum, *Reading "The Virginian" in the New West.*

150 "Gary Cooper on a horse": Anthony Mann, director of such classic "adult Westerns" as *The Naked Spur* said this on the Universal lot, to Philip Kaufman, who was in the process of writing *The Great Northfield Minnesota Raid;* told to author by Kaufman.

151 writing his first lines: From a letter from Mankiewicz to Cooper, June 12, 1953: "The first writing I ever did for the screen, many years ago for both of us, was a love scene I wrote—at the request of Bud Lighton—for you and Mary Brian in *The Virginian.* It was a silly scene, as I remember, something about 'Why the hell didn't Romeo get a ladder, if he was so in love with the girl?' " In Lower and Palmer, *Joseph L. Mankiewicz.*

152 "What is needed now": Robert Warshow, "Movie Chronicle: The Westerner," *Partisan Review,* March–April 1954.

153 "I was extremely impressed": David Lewis, *Creative Producer.*

153 "was serious when he needed to be": Interview in Leonard Maltin's *Movie Crazy,* no. 2 (Autumn 2002).

153 "The air was chilly": Weld, *September Song.*

154 Arlen once said: Hedda Hopper column, Jan. 31, 1942.

155 "The most underrated": Hathaway interview, *Focus on Film,* No. 7, 1971.

157 "Cooper was so hesitant": Estabrook to J. D. Marshall, Recorded Sound Reference Center, Library of Congress.

158 "No, I think it's *The Virginian*": Hedda Hopper column, Feb. 10, 1961.

12 A Woman's Film and a Man's Adventure at Fox

159 "epics, not melodramas": Report for Mr. Schulberg from David O. Selznick, Nov. 22, 1929, Selznick Archive, Harry Ransom Center, University of Texas, Austin.

159 "impossible for talking pictures": Selznick, "High Lights in the Recent Management of B. B. [*sic*] Schulberg," undated and possibly unsent, Selznick Archive.
160 "the tragedy": *Variety*, Aug. 6, 1930.
161 In January 1930: Document labeled "Col. Joy's Resume," Jan. 24, 1930. MPAA Production Code Administration files, Margaret Herrick Library.
161 "He had been handed me": Ayres to John Gallagher. Undated, unpublished interview, courtesy Gallagher.
162 "Constance Bennett had that audience": Louella Parsons column, *Los Angeles Examiner*, Aug. 15, 1930.
163 "a happy film": Kotsilibas-Davis and Loy, *Myrna Loy*.
163 "I was supposed to operate": *Los Angeles Times*, Nov. 16, 1930.
164 at a preview in New York: Varconi, *It's Not Enough to Be Hungarian;* except Varconi misidentified the director and is corrected in Lennig, *Immortal Count*.
165 his supposed secret marriage: *Los Angeles Examiner* memo dated April 27, 1932, USC Cinema and Television Library.
165 "Of all the men I've known": Bow quoted by Teet Carle, to Stenn.
165 "I only met Clara Bow once": Miller, unpublished memoir, circa 1991, intended as a follow-up to *My Hollywood.* Like Louise Brooks, Miller was astonished that Fleming had "been ignored" by "the film historians, the old-movie buffs, the early-Hollywood biographers." And despite her discomfort over his affair with Bergman, "I admired Victor as a director—but I liked and admired him even more as a man—and a friend."
166 "Hey, Rex!": Harrison Carroll's column of June 30, 1930, has Fleming politely asking, "Well, Rex, how's our girl?" Another unbylined version has Fleming shouting, "Hey, Rex!" Bow and Bell married in December 1931. "I have no idea why mother and Victor broke up," Rex Bell Jr. told me in 2007. "I do know she was very fond of him and always spoke very highly of him." Although "she didn't say she was upset that they broke up," she said Fleming was "a great guy" and "a great director."
167 "a small Jewish neighborhood": Harpo Marx, *Harpo Speaks!*
168 "head mistress": Richard DeMille, *My Secret Mother, Lorna Moon.*
169 "to spend Saturday evening": Astor, *My Story*.
170 "I want you to make pictures for me": Macklin and Pici, *Voices from the Set.*
171 Chuck Lewis said: Hancock and Fairbanks, *Douglas Fairbanks.*
171 "Just give her your autograph": Ibid.

172 "When Doug went abroad": Love to Kevin Brownlow.

173 the rarest Mickey Mouse cartoon: Also, at eighty seconds, shortest.

173 "These cartoons get their tremendous appeal": Schickel, *His Picture in the Papers.*

174 "Shit, she had been with Clark Gable?": Quinn, *One Man Tango.*

175 crashed the plane on its first flight: *Los Angeles Times*, Aug. 3, 1930. Lockheed repossessed the plane after Hutchinson couldn't pay all the costs from the crash, including damage to the plane and a lawsuit filed by a woman who was struck by the plane during takeoff. A work order signed by Fleming and Carl Squier, president of Lockheed, in November 1931 called for dual controls (for Hutchinson, the craft had an additional fuel tank in the front in place of the forward cockpit), a new instrument panel, removal of two fuel tanks, and installation of a smaller oil tank, a new fin and runner, and repairs to the tail and fuselage, among other items. Fleming also had a 450-horsepower Pratt & Whitney engine installed.

13 Guiding Gable in *Red Dust*

176 *Variety* announced: *Variety*, Oct. 6, 1931.

176 "in the case of one man": From the Reminiscences of Pandro S. Berman (1971) in the Oral History Collection of Columbia University, p. 20.

176 "When I finish": Harris, *Upton Sinclair.*

176 "For God's sake": Ibid.

177 "came to work": Abrams to David Stenn.

177 "very sensitive": Dorothy Jordan Cooper to Kevin Brownlow.

177 "could not make a Prohibition picture": Mary Craig Sinclair, *Southern Belle.*

177 "They're grooming me for drama": *Photoplay*, June 1932.

177 "Moyna": Kotsilibas-Davis and Loy, *Myrna Loy.*

177 "because it didn't take a stand": Mahin interview with J. D. Marshall.

177 "I think it's the best thing": McGilligan, *Backstory.*

178 "a thin, reedy juvenile": Interview with J. D. Marshall.

178 "work with us": McGilligan, *Backstory.*

178 "one of the half dozen best": Fitzgerald to Tom F. Carey Jr., June 9, 1939, in Turnbull, *Letters of F. Scott Fitzgerald.*

178 "the way women do when close": Mahin in Lyn Tornabene collection of recorded interviews for her Gable biography, *Long Live the King*, Margaret Herrick Library.

179 "He had a lot of talent": Bogdanovich, *Who the Devil Made It.*
179 "A Bob Sherwood picture": Fitzgerald to Matthew Josephson, March 11, 1938, in Turnbull, *Letters of F. Scott Fitzgerald.*
179 "I never wrote 'close shot' ": Hoopes, *Cain.*
180 "made out a ship": Fleming, *Action.*
180 Kodiak bear cubs: Zoo records show that the bears were named Pinky and Jimmie.
181 "We were starting the picture": Mahin, Tornabene collection.
181 "There's this guy, my God": Ibid.
182 "I wish I could do something": Dillon to Mayer, Aug. 13, 1931, MGM legal files.
182 "a sweet, delicate Frenchman": Mahin, Tornabene collection.
182 "famous for his departures": *Los Angeles Times,* Aug. 3, 1932.
183 studio conference notes: MGM script collection, Margaret Herrick Library; the description of Barbara and Dennis's kiss is dated September 4, 1932.
184 "a marvel": Weales, *Canned Goods as Caviar.*
185 "He had a knack": Kaplan to Stenn.
185 "being tough": Astor, *Life on Film.*
185 "fix one of 'em": United Press, Dec. 30, 1938.
190 "Something for the boys": Stenn, *Bombshell.*
191 "Very hard-nosed": Sheldon to Stenn.
191 "I felt he": Tetrick to Stenn.
191 "one of the shabbiest acts": Stenn, *Bombshell.*
192 "This staying around home": *Los Angeles Times,* Sept. 13, 1932.
192 "The day she came back": Stenn, *Bombshell.*
192 "How are we going": Astor, *Life on Film.*
192 "I'm sure you don't": Stenn, *Bombshell.*
192 "I'm sorry, honey": Marx and Vanderveen, *Deadly Illusions.*
193 "there was never a family": Cecil B. DeMille, *Autobiography.*
193 "He went up to San Francisco": McBride, *Hawks on Hawks.*
194 "What man doesn't": Kael, *When the Lights Go Down.*
194 "male fascism": Kael, *Deeper into Movies.*
194 "I remember one lovely story": From the Reminiscences of Ben Hecht (1957) in the Oral History Collection of Columbia University, p. 50.
195 "worked around the clock": In a statement he wrote called "A Formula for Screen Success," in Hughes, *Truth About the Movies, by the Stars,* Fleming said, "Work would be my formula . . . You must know your stuff and be prepared to deliver it. And you must also give it without

stint—without thought of the hard, grinding effort and often-times long hours."

195 "sure-fire b.o.": *Variety*, Nov. 8, 1932.

14 Pioneering the Screwball Comedy

197 "were a daily delight": Stewart, *By a Stroke of Luck.*

197 "When Vic got a scene going": Abrams to David Stenn.

198 "In the carnival scenes": From an undated newspaper clipping John Gallagher found in the Theater Collection of the Philadelphia Free Library. It's a filler item of unusually grave character, consistent with the weightier pronouncements Fleming had been handing the press since the mid-1920s. Under the headline "Direction Very Important," Fleming, described as a successful cameraman turned director of films such as *The Wet Parade* and *Red Dust*, says, "The thing that every motion picture director must keep in mind is that motion pictures do move: to create a single beautiful composition isn't sufficient. Beauty must be combined with action or the whole structure is of little value."

198 Stewart, under the rear end: In *By a Stroke of Luck*, he wrote, "Every producer, incidentally, seemed to have some similar signature-tune for use in conferences with writers. Irving [Thalberg] would constantly toss and catch a coin. Others would have their nails manicured, their shoes shined, or their hair trimmed. It was very impressive. I added my own identifying symbol during the shooting of the carnival scene in *The White Sister* when Vic Fleming let me play the rear end of a trick horse."

198 Fleming wanted to close: *Variety*, Feb. 26, 1933.

199 "had achieved certain effects": Gish, *The Movies, Mr. Griffith, and Me.*

199 one of the best: Ed Sullivan column, Nov. 10, 1938.

199 "The Gable blow-torch style": Jordan, *Clark Gable.*

199 "Pre-eminently a woman's picture": *Variety*, March 21, 1933.

199 "continues to interest Hollywood": Louella Parsons column, March 30, 1933.

199 "That came in, again": McGilligan, *Backstory.*

200 "He has a crush on Lola": MGM studio conference notes on *Bombshell*, USC Cinema and Television Library.

201 satire, burlesque, and wallow in the mud: *Bombshell* is both one long in-joke and a collection of in-jokes, many of which were known only to the filmmakers. A partial list: Frank Morgan's "Pops" is based loosely

on Clara Bow's father; Una Merkel's embezzling secretary is based on Daisy DeVoe, Bow's secretary; Lola Burns must do retakes on *Red Dust* because of Hays Office complaints; Lola's sheepdogs are based on those of Jeanette MacDonald and Alice Brady; two extras in white nun habits are in the background in the studio—a reference to Fleming's *White Sister.* Hugo, the phony marquis, is a composite. At least three actresses—Mae Murray, Gloria Swanson, and Constance Bennett—had been married to, or involved with, questionable "royalty." Brogan calls the cameraman Hal (Rosson). Brogan calls Lola "Baby," Harlow's real-life nickname. Brogan doesn't want anyone loafing on his set. Fleming was famous for this. The mention of the Monarch casting director, "Ben Veranda," is a reference to the MGM casting director, Ben Piazza.

204 took credit for ad-libbing: "As a matter of fact, I created the 'barefoot' line myself. I was pitching woo to Harlow and it just popped into my head. Victor Fleming, the director, liked it so much he kept it in the picture." Interview in *Hartford Courant*, Aug. 1, 1966.

205 "disconcerted by": Eyman, *Lion of Hollywood.*

205 an epic Don Juan: Kundera, *Unbearable Lightness of Being.*

207 Royal Hawaiian Hotel: *Honolulu Advertiser*, Oct. 13, 1933.

207 spent the next two months: *Honolulu Advertiser*, Oct. 25, 1933. The specimens were confirmed by the Steinhart Aquarium.

207 "the shyest, most bashful guy": Howard Strickling, Tornabene collection.

208 "alienating the affections": *Paul A. Lockwood v. Victor Fleming and John Doe, Seduction, Alienation of Affection*, Los Angeles Superior Court No. 367168.

208 become "infatuated": *Los Angeles Times and Examiner*, July 7, 1934.

208 could not grant: *Los Angeles Times and Examiner*, July 11, 1934.

208 divorce went through: Marjorie DeHaven Lockwood is known to have married once more after her 1936 divorce from Paul Lockwood, in a union that lasted just under six months, ending in divorce in 1939. Her screen dancing credits included *Pigskin Parade*. She died in 1975, age sixty-two.

209 "I worked alone": Booth to Stenn.

209 "*Bombshell* was a SENSATION": Stenn, *Bombshell.*

209 night letter: Oct. 5, 1933, MGM legal files.

209 "Box office returns": Letter to Louis B. Mayer, Dec. 20, 1933, MGM files.

209 *Singin' in the Rain: Movieline*, April 1990.

15 *Treasure Island*

210 "the scum of the earth": Black, *Hollywood Censored.*

211 lobbied in vain: Cooper, *Please Don't Shoot My Dog.*

211 "If Fleming didn't do it": Jackie Cooper, Turner Classic Movies interview conducted by Margarita Landazuri on November 30, 1994; from a complete transcript, courtesy of Alexa Foreman.

211 "If you dove in the water": The Reminiscences of Jackie Cooper (June 1959) in the Oral History Collection of Columbia University, p. 852.

211 wear a wig: Cooper, TCM interview.

211 "the leisurely start": *Los Angeles Times*, Sept. 2, 1934.

212 "Character to the boy": Robert Louis Stevenson, "A Humble Remonstrance." The essay is Stevenson's reply to his friend Henry James's quibble in "The Art of Fiction" that he felt distant from *Treasure Island* because "I have been a child in fact, but I have been on a quest for buried treasure only in supposition." Stevenson responded, "If he has never been on a quest for buried treasure, it can be demonstrated that he has never been a child."

212 "a picture so good": Wilson, *Film Criticism of Otis Ferguson.*

213 "Lionel Barrymore was just marvelous": Mahin in Marshall, *Blueprint on Babylon.*

213 Oakland riding-academy manager: *Oakland Tribune*, April 5, 1934.

213 an "exact picturization": Dan Thomas column, May 13, 1934.

214 "and not at all pictorial": *Teacher's Key to "Treasure Island,"* MGM publicity department.

214 "One thing I hate," "a great kid": *Washington Post*, Jan. 6, 1935.

215 "all the pirates were good": Mahin in Marshall, *Blueprint on Babylon.*

216 "Beery was in terrible pain": Cooper, Columbia Oral History Collection.

216 "Fleming would tell me": Cooper, *Please Don't Shoot My Dog.*

216 "When I was a kid": Prelutsky, *Secret of Their Success.*

216 "the last shot": Mahin in Marshall, *Blueprint on Babylon.*

216 "a sort of a large rowboat": Cooper, Columbia Oral History Collection.

217 "Jackie's perch": *Teacher's Key.*

217 "the most difficult scene mechanically": Ibid.

217 "A small charge of dynamite": *Los Angeles Times*, April 29, 1934.

217 "But at this point": *Los Angeles Times*, Sept. 2, 1934.

217 Final cut: Cooper, *Please Don't Shoot My Dog.*

218 "We were all unhappy," "Fleming nearly had a stroke": Cooper, *Please Don't Shoot My Dog.*

218 "The story of *Treasure Island*": Greene, *Graham Greene Film Reader.*
219 "Fleming was very sort of tough": Vidor, sound recording (1971), UCLA Library Department of Special Collections.

16 Introducing Henry Fonda, Farewell to Jean Harlow

220 using the pseudonym: Haver, *David O. Selznick's Hollywood*, who also reports that Fleming helped Selznick/Jeffries with the story.
220 Ten writers: MGM legal files.
220 Libby Holman: Jon Bradshaw, *Dreams That Money Can Buy: The Tragic Life of Libby Holman* (New York: Morrow, 1985).
221 "nothing ever done": Night letter from Howard Strickling to Dietz, April 3, 1935, MGM legal files.

The only other letter in the studio's files about *Reckless* is this bizarre joke missive, complete with misspellings out of a B-movie ransom note:

MGM Pictures Corporation,
Hollywood California
From Hollywood, California
May 14, 1935

Dear Mr. President:

This is just to remind you that we are going to Anhiliate YOU if you don't come across with the profits on "Reckless" amounting to exactly to $100,000 and if you don't come across with the money that you owe us on account of that script we loaned you we will find other ways of doing it and this is just a reminder that there will be plenty more. So don't think that you will get out of playing us and DONT FORGET

VERY truly yours,
FRANK CaPrA,
Chief DirEcToR FoR CoLuMbia PiCtUrES CoRpOrAtIoN

221 "I thought she could do well by it": Behlmer, *Memo from David O. Selznick.*
223 "a real gentleman": John McCabe to Kurt Jensen, 2003. McCabe added, "This, coming from gentle, gentle Rosina, who hated the profanity she heard everywhere on the sets of her films, was genuine tribute." She was,

he said, "an observant person" and one "not given to idle prattle or politeness for its own sake."

223 "falling out all over the place": Machu to David Stenn.

223 "was working with Franchot Tone": Allan to Stenn.

223 "Harlow was fun, and nice": Light to Stenn.

223 "Pursuant to an understanding": F. L. Hendrickson, of the contracts department, Nov. 2, 1938. "There is no card or contract on Victor Fleming; he has been working pursuant to an understanding he had with Mr. Mannix." MGM legal files.

224 "very fortunate in my director": This quotation and Fonda's anecdote about mugging are in Shay, *Conversations.* Fonda rejiggered this tale several times. To Howard Teichmann in *Fonda: My Life,* the actor emphasized how green he was—he didn't know what a "dolly" referred to when he read the script—and how genial Fleming was, even allowing Fonda to use his adopted saloon cat, George, as the canal boat cat. In *Hollywood Speaks,* however, he told Mike Steen that Fleming and the film editors didn't recognize that a stage pause could produce a laugh on-screen; he then repeated the dolly and the mugging stories and gave Fleming credit for steering him toward "total naturalness."

224 "I was in love with him": "An Interview by Curtis Lee Hanson: 'Henry Fonda: Reflections on 40 Years of Make-Believe,' " *Cinema* (Calif.) Dec. 1966.

226 "putting some realism": United Press, June 13, 1935.

226 "a very big and rugged man": From the Reminiscences of Janet Gaynor (1958) in the Oral History Collection of Columbia University, p. 26.

227 "set up unlawful housekeeping": Brooks Atkinson review in *The New York Times,* Oct. 31, 1934.

227 John Ford *wanted* to include: Bogdanovich, *John Ford.* "For example," said Ford,

> I had a lovely scene in which Lincoln rode into town on a mule, passed by a theater and stopped to see what was playing, and it was the Booth Family doing *Hamlet;* we had a typical old-fashioned poster up. Here was this poor shabby country lawyer wishing he had enough money to see *Hamlet* when a very handsome young boy with dark hair—you knew he was a member of the Booth family—fresh, snobbish kid, all beautifully dressed—just walked out to the edge of the plank walk and looked at Lincoln. He looked at this funny, incongruous man in a tall hat

riding a mule, and you knew there was some connection there. They cut it out—too bad.

228 "The narrative starts slowly": *Variety*, Aug. 14, 1935.
228 "an affectionately amusing photoplay": *The New York Times*, Aug. 9, 1935.
229 "seems subject to a jinx": *The New York Times*, April 21, 1935.

17 Bagging Game on Safari, Losing *The Good Earth*

230 Cotton's safari diary: Provided by Charles Cotton Jr.
231 A *Hollywood Reporter* review: June 10, 1935.
232 "250 cases of film," Under the direction of General Ting-Hsui: *The New York Times*, June 3, 1934.
233 "It is a story": Associated Press, Nov. 16, 1935.
233 "Throw 'em all out": Thomas, *Thalberg*.
233 air race publicizing a casino: *Los Angeles Times*, Nov. 24, 1935.
233 "the most nonchalant": Associated Press, Dec. 2, 1935.
233 Lewin's reports: MGM Collection ("The Good Earth"), USC Cinema and Television Library, casting test memos from Albert Lewin.
234 "Here was a great picture": MGM publicity, Kevin Brownlow files.
234 "too Occidental": Franklin's account of *The Good Earth* is in his unpublished memoir, "We Laughed and We Cried."
234 "his usual lack of imagination": Kael, *5001 Nights at the Movies.*

18 Spencer Tracy and *Captains Courageous*

235 "Vic's parenthood": Undated note, Lighton Family Papers, University of Arkansas, Fayetteville.
236 "perhaps because he had no children": Kazan, *Life*.
236 "a happily married lady codfish": Kipling, *Something of Myself.*
236 "A good actor": Kazan, *Life*.
237 "cinema's no. 1": *Time*, April 25, 1938.
237 "Spencer always thought": Hepburn, *Me.*
237 unsatisfying five years at Fox: An excellent overview of those films is John C. Tibbetts, "Pre-MGM Spencer Tracy," *Films in Review*, Nov./Dec. 1995.
237 "arranging introductions": *Variety*, June 23, 2006.

237 "a great and bitchy gossip": Cukor to Ruth Gordon, Nov. 12, 1941, Ruth Gordon and Garson Kanin Papers, Manuscript Division, Library of Congress. Cukor was referring to Lawler's reaction to a screening of *Two-Faced Woman*, saying that "he condemned it lock, stock and barrel," but "it represents a point of view that many of his ilk will have—and with some justice."

238 he ordered the studio's security chief: Berdie Adams, interviewed by Eyman in *Lion of Hollywood.*

238 "I would get drunk": Granger, *Sparks Fly Upward.*

238 "I was lying there feeling like death": Ibid.

239 "Vic sat at one end": Sidney's story is confirmed by an item in Virginia Wright's column, Oct. 1, 1936: "Victor Fleming and Jules Furthman not too mad at each other to continue lunching, although for a time it looked as if fisticuffs might interfere."

239 "to capture a single": Kazan, *Life.*

239 "Spencer does it": Andersen, *Affair to Remember.* On June 9, 1940, Howard Barnes, critic of the *New York Herald Tribune*, wrote, "It is not easy to catalogue Mr. Tracy's acting gifts. For one thing, he is enormously direct, in a field where it is easy to get a showy effect by being oblique. For another he is aware of all those small clues to universal experience which gives the spectator the feeling of sharing in living rather than watching a reconstruction of it. Meanwhile he has the great talent of seeming at ease amid himself."

239 "That business of not being typecast": *Los Angeles Times*, Nov. 18, 1962.

240 "Fox had him playing villains": Mayer quoted in "What Makes a Star," *American Weekly*, June 8, 1958.

241 "pomp and respectability": Daniel Selznick, interviewed by Eyman in *Lion of Hollywood.* Rabbi Edgar F. Magnin of the Wilshire Boulevard Temple recalled Mayer's attitude toward Catholicism in a 1975 oral history for the University of California, Berkeley. He said when he asked Mayer why he didn't make pictures about Jews, his reply was, "Rabbis don't look dramatic. A priest has all these trimmings and all this stuff."

241 Cantwell . . . had summoned: This account is in the Archbishop John Timothy McNicholas Papers, Catholic University. "You will be glad to know," Cantwell wrote a week later to McNicholas, "I was assured that there have been no bad pictures made in the last three months." That June, Irving Thalberg visited Cantwell to complain about Father David Lord, who helped author the Production Code and headed the Sodality of Our Lady in St. Louis. Lord had written in his publication,

The Queen's Work, that Thalberg "made of his wife a harlot in her pictures."

241 "Most of the men and women": Breen to McNicholas, March 1934, McNicholas Papers.

241 "The priests are all such superior men": Kanin, *Tracy and Hepburn.*

242 "America's faults": Seelye's expansive essay on the book and film of *Captains Courageous* serves as the introduction to the 2005 Penguin Classics edition. Among the piece's many felicities, Seelye calls the character of Disko Troop "a Puritan Ulysses, for whom the voyage out is the voyage home, the whole irradiated with a triumphant sense of a job well done."

242 Luke 5:1–11: In verses 4–6 (King James Version): "Now when he had left speaking, he said unto Simon, Launch out into the deep, and let down your nets for a draught. And Simon answering said unto him, Master, we have toiled all the night, and have taken nothing: nevertheless at thy word I will let down the net. And when they had this done, they inclosed a great multitude of fishes: and their net brake."

243 "backbreaker about heaven": *New Republic*, June 16, 1937.

243 "the only one with which I was truly happy," "Instead of the usual concoction": From the Reminiscences of Marc Connelly (1959) in the Oral History Collection of Columbia University, pp. 11 and 12.

245 "Geez, this is a beautiful kid": McGilligan, *Backstory.*

246 "The film of a book": Powell, *Million Dollar Movie.*

246 "half Portuguese and half black": Mahin in Marshall, *Blueprint on Babylon.*

246 "in which white children": Seelye, introduction to *Captains Courageous.*

247 Rooney said he couldn't resist: Rooney, *Life Is Too Short.*

247 a contemporary profile states . . . a mere three days: *Los Angeles Times*, Nov. 16, 1937.

247 coaching from Fred Lewis: Witnessed by Thomas Jones, one of the Sea Scouts. Jones is the current owner of Fleming's Bel-Air estate.

248 "iron egg": MGM production notes detail the workings of this device and the "self-wiping windshield." They describe the iron egg as "a heavy egg-shaped mass of solid iron suspended from a framework, and to which the camera is attached, permitting it to swing like a pendulum. The result will be stability within five degrees, no matter how a boat may toss." And the "self-wiping windshield" is "a disc of plate glass, about eight inches in diameter, rotated before the camera lens at high speed, by a motor. Pressure plates about its circumference keep it wiped and polished at all times, so that spray, waves, or drops of sea water can never obstruct the lens."

248 "You'll never know": *Los Angeles Times*, May 16, 1937.

248 "*Courageous* is all done": Lighton's Christmas letter to his family, December 1936, Lighton Family Papers.

249 "will not move the camera": James Wong Howe interviewed by Alain Silver for UCLA Oral History Program (1969).

250 "Freddie always came in": Mahin in Marshall, *Blueprint on Babylon.*

250 "You never have to fake": Gladys Hall, "You Can't Put Spencer Tracy into Words," *Motion Picture*, Nov. 1937.

250 "one long outing": *The New York Times*, Jan. 24, 1992.

251 "When a man gets angry": Kazan, *Life.*

251 "I didn't want to play Manuel": Many articles about Tracy's discomfort with the role were published. This one is from Hall, "You Can't Put Spencer Tracy into Words." But Tracy later wrote in his daybook, "Best picture ever made. Best part ever, too. Once in a lifetime . . ." (These lines can be seen in the 1986 documentary *The Spencer Tracy Legacy*, directed by David Heeley.)

253 one of his own top three: Ed Sullivan column, Nov. 10, 1938.

253 "in iced water": Paul Harrison column, June 11, 1937.

253 "a corking yarn": *New Republic*, June 16, 1937.

254 "One must be insensitive": *Paris-Soir*, Oct. 29, 1937.

254 "have shown here a remarkable capacity": *Times* (London), May 6, 1937.

254 "they had made a good show of it": *National Board of Review Magazine*, June 1937.

254 "leave the lot": From unsigned memorandum in Fleming's MGM file; it quotes a note from Fleming dated Feb. 5, 1937. MGM legal files.

254 united behind Shearer: From Lambert, *Norma Shearer:* "He was directing *Captains Courageous* at the time, and in March, 1937, when attorneys for both sides had still failed to reach any kind of agreement, he called the General in New York. Almost everyone at the studio, he said, felt that Mayer and [Robert] Rubin had cast themselves as heavies opposite Norma's true-blue heroine, and the situation was bad for the company's image. Schenck agreed."

254 "It looks all right": Lighton to his family, Dec. 1936.

254 "To my dying day": From the audiotape of Bartholomew's interview for the 1992 documentary *When the Lion Roars,* produced for Turner Network Television.

254 "He was a fabulous character": Rooney, *Life Is Too Short.*

255 a father and son once again: The film cast an afterglow on all the families involved with it. For John Carradine's son Keith, "It's one of my favorite of all Dad's films, a beautiful picture." After making it, John Carradine bought a sixty-three-foot Gloucester-style schooner—and years later,

Keith bought a hurdy-gurdy like Manuel's. Similarly, Tracy handed down his scale model of the *We're Here* to his daughter, Susie. Sally Fleming has her father's leather-bound edition of *Captains Courageous.*

19 *Test Pilot*

256 "They're still trying names": Louella Parsons column, April 18, 1937.

257 Vic's fidelity to Lu: McCarthy, *Howard Hawks.*

258 Nine writers: MGM legal files. The studio later gave the estate of the test pilot Jimmy Collins, who died in a power dive, $5,000 to settle a plagiarism suit. He'd written a series called "Flying Stories" for New York's *Daily News,* and his editor compiled them into a book called *Test Pilot.* Fleming never cited Collins's articles. He does put over the sensations that they described: "Centrifugal force, like some huge, invisible monster, pushed my head down into my shoulders and squashed me into that seat so that my backbone bent, and I groaned with the force of it," becoming "blind as a bat," "dizzy as a coot." As the pilot takes a power dive, Collins wrote, the land shows up "like something looming out of a morning mist."

258 Fleming, Wellman, and Tay Garnett: McCarthy, *Howard Hawks.*

258 "Vic Fleming was the most exacting": Unused notes for *The Lion's Share,* Bosley Crowther Papers, Brigham Young University.

259 "It's incredible": Hedda Hopper column, Nov. 12, 1939.

259 "I wanted out": *Los Angeles Times,* May 15, 1955.

259 "a personal favorite": Kotsilibas-Davis and Loy, *Myrna Loy.*

259 "I just didn't have the heart": Susan Myrick, *White Columns in Hollywood.*

260 "exchanged glances and smiled": *Chicago Tribune,* Nov. 9, 1934; mention of Fleming's cracked oil tank appeared in the *Sportsman Pilot,* Dec. 15, 1934. The Lockheed Sirius "was notoriously difficult to fly and unforgiving of pilot error," says the New Zealand writer and historian Ian Mackersey, a biographer of Kingsford Smith. Mackersey has written that the aviator was afflicted with a morbid fear of flying over the sea.

260 "of what big-studio moviemaking could be": Kotsilibas-Davis and Loy, *Myrna Loy.*

260 "King and Queen of Hollywood": The competition for the crowns was set up as a one-day-only contest. On November 28, 1937, the fifty-five North American newspapers in the *New York Daily News–Chicago Tribune* syndicate asked readers to send in votes for their top three movie actors and actresses to their local papers. Sullivan presented Gable and Loy with the crowns (they sported the newspapers' mastheads) on

MGM's radio house organ, the Maxwell House *Good News* program. Initially delighted with the honor—"this will be the nicest souvenir the movies ever gave me"—Gable later felt compelled to mock it with disclaimers like "I'm just a slob from Ohio."

260 wooden manner in front of a camera: Sullivan hosted his eponymous variety program on CBS TV from 1948 to 1971.

261 "Stop being nervous": Ed Sullivan column, Dec. 16, 1937.

261 "Don't worry about it": Ed Sullivan column, Jan. 6, 1940.

263 "Spencer Tracy as a gay man": DiLeo, *100 Great Film Performances You Should Remember but Probably Don't.*

264 "very motherly": October production conference notes, MGM Collection, USC Cinema and Television Library.

264 one reviewer in 1938: *Hollywood Reporter,* April 15, 1938.

264 "amazing": Mahin in Tornabene collection, Margaret Herrick Library.

264 "had a lively exchange": Kotsilibas-Davis and Loy, *Myrna Loy.*

264 "I remember him working out": Geist, *Pictures Will Talk.*

264 "Tracy would give his right arm": Strickling, Tornabene collection.

265 "with a long shot": *Hollywood Reporter,* Jan. 24, 1938.

265 "got a little out of hand": Kotsilibas-Davis and Loy, *Myrna Loy.*

265 *Only Angels Have Wings:* Mahin in McGilligan's *Backstory* derided Hawks for doing "an aviation picture in South America that was stolen directly out of *Test Pilot.* He asked me to get the script for him for that. I wouldn't do it. I said, 'Howard, I can do just so much. It's Vic's script, ask Vic.' [The movie] had come out. I guess he wanted the script so he wouldn't have to go to the movie."

267 "absolutely true": Bogdanovich's *Who the Devil Made It* includes Hawks's most extreme statements about his supposed authorship of *Test Pilot.*

268 "the unsung heroes": From prepared remarks dated April 21, 1938 (and marked second revision), Henry H. "Hap" Arnold Papers, Manuscript Division of the Library of Congress.

268 "plane, spinning like a top": *Los Angeles Times,* May 8, 1938.

268 "One of the outstanding successes": *Hollywood Reporter,* April 15, 1938.

268 "A bang-up aviation drama": *The New York Times,* April 16, 1938.

268 "many critics were shocked": *Economic and Trade Notes,* June 9, 1939. Those fleeing the Third Reich at the time of the movie's release included the families of André Previn and Mike Nichols, who both came to New York from Berlin on the S.S. *Manhattan;* the first film they saw when they arrived was *Test Pilot.*

269 "Don't you like my papa?": *Los Angeles Times,* May 13, 1938. When I asked her about this item in 2003, Susie Tracy laughed and said, "Do you

think I'd deny saying something like that?" She also talks in the 1986 documentary *The Spencer Tracy Legacy* about the "devastating" experience, at age five, of seeing her father "die" in *Captains Courageous.* (Her mother reassured her it was only a movie, but to this day she finds it "too sad" to watch.)

269 "Why don't we": James Salter confirmed this anecdote in an e-mail on July 25, 2003.

20 Salvaging *The Great Waltz*

270 "almost cracked up": *Hollywood Reporter,* April 19, 1938.

270 "I am the only farmer": Fleming, *Action.*

271 "he demanded": Day, *This Was Hollywood.*

272 Clinton Hale's extended family: Although Fleming worked as a chauffeur only for the Hale family in Santa Barbara, Julian Ludwig could not recall the woman's name, and her identity has eluded inquiry.

273 "sensitivity—that quickness": Fleming, "Directing—Then and Now," *Lion's Roar,* July 1944.

273 "there wasn't a single American": Interview in *Focus on Film* (Winter 1975).

273 "Strauss having died": D. O. Decker, Aug. 19, 1938, MGM legal files.

274 "made magnificent pictures": *The New York Times,* April 16, 1939.

275 Hyman declared: The playwright S. N. Behrman's account of that remark and other indignities inflicted by producers was in *The New York Times,* July 17, 1966.

275 "They gave me two million dollars": Desrichard, *Julien Duvivier.*

275 "New policy at MGM": Ed Sullivan column, Nov. 7, 1938.

277 "her eyes suddenly filmed over": Jimmie Fidler column, June 30, 1938.

278 he called her "Angel": Paul Harrison column, Nov. 21, 1938.

278 direction from the producer Reinhardt: Sheilah Graham column, Sept. 27, 1938.

278 "the lowest ebb": Interview in Truffaut, *Hitchcock/Truffaut.*

280 Gravet said: Interview in *Focus on Film* (Winter 1975).

280 "When they learn to work": *Independent,* June 19, 1992.

281 "a dazzling contrast": Paperno, *Notes of a Moscow Pianist.*

281 "She never did fully believe me": Plisetskaya, *I, Maya Plisetskaya.*

281 "he would rise from his seat": Korjus died in 1980 at age seventy-one. Evidence of her continued popularity in the former communist-bloc nations still surfaces from time to time, says her daughter Melissa Wells,

U.S. ambassador to Estonia from 1998 to 2001. In 2002, when the Chinese president, Jiang Zemin, was on a state visit to Estonia, "toward the end of the dinner, when the toasts take place, he said, 'I'd like to sing a song.' And he sang 'One Day When We Were Young.' And the Estonians recognized it right away . . . And now she's gone, but the fact that even the Chinese president sings her song, my God!"

281 "and weep like a baby": Although that sounds like Cold War propaganda, it was told to Korjus, and a distinguished observer, the director Grigory Kozintsev, did think the dictator had trouble distinguishing the screen from reality. Kozintsev recalled Stalin's running commentary during a screening of his 1935 film, *The Youth of Maxim.* "He immediately gave vent to his irritation if the people on the screen didn't work well, say, or praised them when they acted correctly" (quoted in the *Independent,* June 19, 1992).

21 Putting Oz into *The Wizard of Oz*

282 "You may wonder": *MGM Studio News,* Aug. 14, 1939.

283 "Isn't Victor Fleming an inspired": Brooks to Brownlow, March 10, 1969.

284 "Here Vic": Harmetz, *Making of "The Wizard of Oz."*

284 "a picture that searched": LeRoy's comment comes from an audio recording on the main commentary track of Warner Home Video's 2005 three-disc reissue of *The Wizard of Oz;* it expands slightly on Mahin's comment to Harmetz in *Making of "The Wizard of Oz."*

285 "I'd wanted to make the picture": Interview with Vernon Scott, UPI, May 17, 1973.

286 "whose work is often rich in imaginative qualities": Oct. 26, 1938. MGM publicity item.

286 "Parting her hair": Guilaroff, *Crowning Glory.*

286 "that man was a poet": Kobal, *People Will Talk.*

286 "I wish I was as good": George Stevens Jr., ed., *Conversations with the Great Moviemakers of Hollywood's Golden Age* (New York: Alfred A. Knopf, 2006).

286 "We got along": Thompson, *Between Action and Cut.*

288 He commanded Harburg and Arlen: At least one MGM interoffice memo from Keith Weeks, dated Dec. 21, 1938, confirms this.

288 "The primer provided": Harmetz, *Making of "The Wizard of Oz."*

289 *A Matter of Life and Death:* Released in the United States as *Stairway to Heaven.*

289 in his memoirs: Powell, *Life in Movies* and *Million Dollar Movie.*

289 *his* jumping-off point: Harmetz, *Making of "The Wizard of Oz."* In a *Washington Post* interview published on Feb. 12, 1939, Langley chalked up the framing of *Oz* in a dream sequence as a "compromise" to "box office." But that compromise has haunted the vision of filmmakers as cutting-edge as Guillermo del Toro (*Pan's Labyrinth*).

290 Harburg, likewise: Meyerson and Harburg, *Who Put the Rainbow in "The Wizard of Oz"?*

291 "the place where we belong": Hearn, *Annotated Wizard of Oz.*

291 Jane Withers could pack: When I asked Shirley Temple Black in 2003 about a publicity still, circa 1938, that posed her with Fleming, she said she had no memory of him, "but I am certainly an admirer of his work." Jane Withers, on the other hand, asserts, "They tried many times to borrow me from Fox to play Dorothy, but MGM had Judy under contract, and I loved Judy Garland."

291 "an Orphan in Kansas": Fricke, Scarfone, and Stillman, *"The Wizard of Oz."*

292 "It is a song": Meyerson and Harburg; *Who Put the Rainbow in "The Wizard of Oz"?*

292 "If Miss B will sing my song": Berlin to Arlen, April 28, 1969, Irving Berlin Papers, Library of Congress. Arlen's parody lyrics evidently are lost. A letter from Berlin to Arlen indicates that he sent the parody to Streisand in early June.

293 "artistically curled mane": *The New York Times*, Aug. 18, 1939.

293 "I viewed the replacement": Worsley, *From Oz to E.T.*

294 "to light 550": McClelland, *Down the Yellow Brick Road.*

294 "I worked in a shiny suit": United Press, Jan. 6, 1939.

295 "I then told Vic": Haley, *Heart of the Tin Man.*

295 "I tried to get a sound": Harmetz, *Making of "The Wizard of Oz."*

295 "Smith's Premium Ham!": Lahr, *Notes on a Cowardly Lion.*

295 "Vic Fleming had never": Ibid.

296 "I'm a professional dancer": Burke, *With a Feather on My Nose.*

296 "Ah—the hot seat!": Paul Harrison column, Feb. 21, 1939.

296 Langley would regale: The *Norfolk Virginian-Pilot* entertainment writer Mal Vincent expanded on the details of his Nov. 12, 1998, article about Langley to me in 2002. According to Vincent, "Langley loved to put on a gruff persona . . . he didn't have anything good *or* bad to say about Fleming."

297 Schindler was a junior: Ambrose "Amblin' Amby" Schindler, a standout high-school athlete from San Diego, was the starting quarterback at USC in 1936, 1937, and 1939 and is best remembered as the MVP of the

1940 Rose Bowl, when USC defeated Tennessee 14–0. Even *Oz* experts have often misidentified Schindler as one of the Winkie Guards of the Wicked Witch of the West; he said he didn't even know what a Winkie was when first asked about his appearance in the film.

298 "I disparaged the work": Haley, *Heart of the Tin Man.*

299 "a very good director": Undated interview with Margaret Hamilton by Gregory J. M. Catsos. It was reprinted in slightly shorter form as "That Wonderful Witch: A Lost Interview with Margaret Hamilton" in *Filmfax,* Oct./Nov. 1993. My copy of the original interview, supplied by John Gallagher, does not contain publication information.

299 "Get back on your champagne kick": Harmetz, *Making of "The Wizard of Oz."*

299 "Fleming would sometimes tell you": Catsos interview.

299 "I want the shot done": Harmetz, *Making of "The Wizard of Oz."*

300 "At first, I didn't realize": Catsos interview.

300 Betty Danko: Harmetz, *Making of "The Wizard of Oz."*

300 During Hamilton's first day back: Catsos interview.

301 "Once I lay down": Interview in *Los Angeles Times,* Oct. 8, 1939.

302 "Now, darling, this is serious" to Fleming "because of what I did to her," and Garland, "I won't do that but I'll kiss your nose": Fricke, Scarfone, and Stillman, *"The Wizard of Oz."*

302 "favorite moments in all movies": Whitfield was studying the work of the deadpan genius Buster Keaton when she made this observation and was keen to the subject of entertainers who hit the comic bull's-eye with the most colloquial means.

303 "I love him like a father": Sheilah Graham column, Nov. 7, 1939. Fan magazines went along with the story line about Garland's crush on Fleming (as well as her well-publicized crush on the bandleader Artie Shaw). In an interview in *Screenland* in August 1939, Garland was quoted: "If you really want to know a perfectly wonderful man, you should meet Victor Fleming . . . He has the nicest low voice, and the kindest eyes. Besides, he realizes that a girl who is sixteen is practically grown up. He shows me all of the courtesies he would to Hedy Lamarr. That's very important to me. He rises when I enter the room and places a chair for me. He notices my clothes and the way I do my hair and remarks about them."

303 "Vic was like a schoolboy": Fricke, Scarfone, and Stillman, *"The Wizard of Oz."*

303 "You're—you're—browbeating me": Harmetz, *Making of "The Wizard of Oz."*

303 "probably the most difficult set": McClelland, *Down the Yellow Brick Road.* "I'd forgotten how great were the composition of those crowd shots of Munchkins and the great mob at the Emerald City and the excitement and sheer opulence of the chase through the witch's castle," wrote the *New York Herald Tribune* television critic John Crosby after the film's 1959 showing on CBS.

303 "In Baum's book": Rogers, *L. Frank Baum.*

305 "I guess it's like any group": LeRoy, *Take One.*

306 "They all went into the local bars": Unpublished memoir held by the Culver City Historical Society. (Ed Meese the motorcycle cop was not related to the future U.S. attorney general Ed Meese.)

306 "hell-raisers": Mal Vincent to author, 2002.

306 "twins Ike and Mike Matina": *Washington Post,* June 20, 2001.

306 "King of the Munchkins": Mal Vincent to author.

309 "Vic Fleming would stand there": *Palm Beach Post,* March 13, 2006. Some of the little people became grand tall-tale tellers, none more so than Carroll, who has also taken credit for advising Fleming that the troupe should skip down the Yellow Brick Road: "They can come out and have some motion."

309 "That is when I learned": *Washington Post,* July 18, 1986.

310 "Victor was a good friend": Interview in Schickel, *Men Who Made the Movies.*

310 "Instead of telling me": Harmetz, *Making of "The Wizard of Oz."*

311 At a Santa Barbara preview, "Mr. Fleming walked into the office": Meyerson and Harburg, *Who Put the Rainbow in "The Wizard of Oz"?*

312 "it's your show": *The New York Times,* July 4, 1943.

312 preopening push: Newspaper ads from 1939 demonstrate that the film was not regarded the same way it is today. One ad touted, "Broadway's great musical masterpiece," adding, "Alluring dancers!" When the film was rereleased in 1949, Garland had top billing, but some ads trumpeted the recent Broadway successes of Bolger, Haley, and Lahr.

312 "a stinkaroo": *New Yorker,* Aug. 19, 1939.

313 "owes its coherence": Meyerson and Harburg, *Who Put the Rainbow in "The Wizard of Oz"?*

314 "modernized, American": David B. Parker, *Journal of the Georgia Association of Historians,* vol. 15, 1994.

314 "We must be satisfied": Tolkien, "On Fairy Stories," in *Tolkien Reader.*

314 "one of the early-day screen directors": Carle to Jones, May 1, 1939, Victor Fleming file, Margaret Herrick Library.

22 Saving Tara and *Gone With the Wind*

317 "nervous as a thoroughbred": Sheilah Graham column, Feb. 10, 1939.

317 Mahin recalled: Flamini, *Scarlett, Rhett, and a Cast of Thousands.*

318 3:00 a.m. visit: International News Service, March 5, 1939. This entertaining version of events even has Selznick and Gable drinking "a quick toast to their benefactor" after LeRoy was able to extract Fleming from *The Wizard of Oz.*

318 "My God": Flamini, *Scarlett, Rhett, and a Cast of Thousands.*

318 "Victor Fleming has one of the very best": Selznick Archive.

318 "looked at the rushes": Harwell, *Margaret Mitchell's "Gone With the Wind" Letters, 1936–1949.*

318 "I think Ashley": Ed Sullivan column, June 5, 1954.

318 "David talked generally": Interview with Joyce Haber, *Los Angeles Times,* Feb. 11, 1968. Years later, Cukor was the evident source of the story in Jesse Lasky Jr.'s book *Love Scene* (New York: Crowell, 1978) that the firing wasn't done by Selznick himself but by Henry Ginsberg, Selznick's general manager.

319 "We couldn't see eye to eye": *The New York Times,* Oct. 26, 1947.

319 "didn't seem to understand": Canutt, *Stunt Man.*

319 "He was in disagreement": David O. Selznick, unpublished interview with Charles Samuels, March 25, 1961, Selznick Archive.

319 "simply could not agree": Unused Crowther notes, Bosley Crowther Papers, Brigham Young University.

320 "George would have done": McGilligan, *Backstory.* Fleming's evaluation of Cukor's talent at that point of his career is spot-on. The total of Cukor's footage in the finished film is slight. But it includes two memorable dialogue scenes (Mammy dressing Scarlett for the barbecue, Rhett presenting Scarlett with her Parisian hat) and two intense small-scale scenes (Scarlett and Prissy serving as Melanie's midwives, Scarlett gunning down the Union deserter at Tara).

320 "The best performance": Brooks to Brownlow, April 19, 1972.

320 Gable . . . had a brief erotic encounter: McGilligan, *George Cukor.*

320 "it's clear *something* happened": Mann, *Wisecracker.*

320 "It would be too naïve": Ibid.

324 "In our garb": Olivia de Havilland, *Look,* Dec. 12, 1967. It's possible that Leigh and de Havilland *were* in widow's weeds if preparing to reshoot the Atlanta bazaar, but Haver in *David O. Selznick's Hollywood* says the scenes being shot were Scarlett and Melanie's hurried preparation to

leave Atlanta. Cukor himself liked the story of his female stars in mourning clothes so much he repeated it to Lambert in *On Cukor.*

321 "looking for a bad director": Unused Crowther notes, Crowther Papers.

321 never worked in Hollywood again: Walker, *Vivien.*

321 "a mere workaday hack": Bushell to Michael Dempsey, March 12, 1993, David Stenn collection; in another letter to Dempsey, dated September 9, 1991, Bushell articulates Leigh's perspective: "It was [Gable's complaints], bred of years of unbroken star-success, that Cukor was making it a 'woman's picture,' that led Selznick, D. to the preposterous course of firing Cukor and replacing him with a run-of-the-mill MGM staff director."

321 "Everyone is hysterical": Leigh's letter is included in Vickers, *Vivien Leigh.*

322 "Every night, Vic would say": McGilligan, *Backstory.*

322 revisions by Oliver H. P. Garrett: Harwell, *GWTW.* Also reported by columnist Harrison Carroll, Feb. 16, 1939.

322 "Your fucking script": Lambert, *GWTW;* this was adopted by Flamini; Haver in *David O. Selznick's Hollywood* has "Your script is no fucking good"; Thomson in *Showman* uses "You haven't got a fucking script," from an interview with Marcella Rabwin.

322 MGM talent pool: "Selznick, Fleming, Mahin Fix 'Wind,' " *Hollywood Reporter,* Feb. 17, 1939.

322 "aloof and poetical": Hecht, *Child of the Century.* Hecht's account of his sessions with Fleming and Selznick is taken from this fiercely engaging memoir.

322 *The Prisoner of Zenda:* Selznick Archive.

323 "Fleming was a much better director": From the Reminiscences of Ben Hecht (1957) in the Oral History Collection of Columbia University, p. 50.

323 edited the sequence: Harwell, *GWTW.*

323 "For God's sake": McGilligan, *Backstory.*

323 everything Selznick did: As recounted in Thomson's *Showman,* his masterstroke may have been the first one: pursuing and landing the rights to the novel. His New York story editor, Kay Brown, plumped for it; his Los Angeles story editor, Val Lewton, called it "ponderous trash"—a self-revealing evaluation, since *GWTW* would become the splashiest of blockbusters and Lewton would become the poet-producer of low-budget horror movies at RKO. Brown was essential to the purchase. After a month and a half (May 20–July 7) of worrying over competing

offers and deliberating on his ability to cast the lead parts, Selznick made the bid. Brown had convinced the book's agent, Annie Laurie Williams, of Selznick's commitment—and would not let the agent leave her office without accepting Selznick's $50,000 offer, despite Williams's desire for $10,000 more (and a competitive bid from Harry Warner's daughter, Doris).

324 "fine adaptable mechanism": The entire speech, which is credited to F. Scott Fitzgerald, is in Graham, *College of One.*

324 "we would be better off": Selznick Archive.

324 *Made for Each Other:* Ibid.

324 "I don't think he was sadistic": Selznick interview with Samuels.

325 60 percent: Unused Crowther notes, Crowther Papers.

325 "the terrible mess": Selznick Archive.

325 "red suit with white stripe": tailored for a scene cut from the film.

326 an Atlanta streetlight: *Atlanta Constitution,* June 4, 1939.

326 Hal Rosson: Haver, *David O. Selznick's Hollywood;* also American Film Institute Oral History with Hal Rosson, interviewed by Bill Gleason, 1971, © AFI 1975.

326 "best team": American Film Institute Oral History with Ridgeway Callow, interviewed by Rudy Behlmer, 1976, © AFI 1976.

326 "Sam Wood simply needed him": Ibid.

327 "I am not sending out": That memo appears in Harmetz, *On the Road to Tara.*

327 he was going to make a melodrama: Lambert, *GWTW.*

328 Natalie Kalmus: Jones, *Glorious Technicolor.*

328 "a handsome, blondish man": Myrick, *White Columns in Hollywood.*

329 "apotheosis as Rhett Butler": Harvey, *Romantic Comedy.*

329 "They talked each other's language": The Reminiscences of Adela Rogers St. Johns (1971) in the Oral History Collection of Columbia University, p. 32.

329 Rhett carrying Scarlett: Barker, *Oliviers.* Several different versions of this story have appeared; the main difference among them is the number of times Fleming had Gable carry Leigh. Six seems reasonable, but two sources have a dozen. A Jimmie Fidler column from May 21, 1940, says Gable, on the set of *Boom Town,* was reminiscing about Fleming's cruelty in making him do it twenty-two times. According to Fidler, that's when Fleming let Gable know "the third take was okay—you carried her upstairs the other nineteen times for exercise!" Barker also wrote that Leigh discovered Fleming "possessed a somewhat unusual sense of humor."

329 "He was really startled": Associated Press, June 28, 1998.
330 "just sort of snapped to attention": Hinton, *Making of a Legend.*
330 "moonlight": Lambert, *On Cukor.*
331 "at first discouraged": Barker, *Oliviers.*
332 "shocked to find herself": Ibid.
332 "that was much better in the test": Lambert, *On Cukor.*
332 Some critics favorably compare: Hinton, *Making of a Legend;* Lambert, *On Cukor.*
332 "Leigh hated Fleming": Unused Crowther notes, Crowther Papers.
332 "Yesterday I put on": Howard's letter is in Leslie Ruth Howard, *A Quite Remarkable Father.*
332 "ONLY words to Viv": Bushell to Dempsey, Sept. 9, 1991, David Stern Collection.
333 "Ham it, baby": Sheilah Graham column, July 13, 1939.
333 "Ham it up!": Canutt, *Stunt Man;* Butterfly McQueen, *The New York Times,* Jan. 29, 1989.
333 "After the headache": Victor Fleming, syndicated story, Dec. 15, 1939 (*Atlanta Journal* reprint).
333 "Very few movies": Kael, *When the Lights Go Down.*
333 *The Great Waltz*: Behlmer, *Memo from David O. Selznick;* also Selznick Archive.
334 "jiggling up and down": International News Service, April 6, 1939.
335 "didn't give Vivien Leigh credit": Hedda Hopper column, Feb. 24, 1940.
335 "Miss Fiddle-de-dee": Gladys Hall, "On the Sets of *Gone With the Wind,*" typescript of article as submitted to *Screen Romances,* pencil dated October 15, 1939, Margaret Herrick Library.
335 "You're no baseball player": Harrison Carroll column, April 10, 1939.
335 "Vivien made no secret": Behlmer, *Memo from David O. Selznick,* from autobiographical remarks placed before each section of reprinted Selznick memos.
335 "Take it easy": Barker, *Oliviers.*
335 brick dust, "The separation from Larry": Vickers, *Vivien Leigh.*
336 "targeted," "black-market director": Rabwin, *Yes, Mr. Selznick.*
336 seventeen-inch waist, sickness: Hall, "On the Sets."
336 "breastwork situation": Behlmer, *Memo from David O. Selznick;* also Selznick Archive. Why Selznick thought that day of Alice Faye remains a mystery for the ages. As Faye herself once sang, "You'll never know."
337 "Footage wasted": Sidney Howard to his wife, April 5, 1939, Sidney Howard Papers, University of California, Berkeley.

337 "what the word 'tired' means": Letter to Mrs. Howard, April 18, 1939, Howard Papers.

337 "Remember, this is a hot summer day": Hall, "On the Sets."

337 "If and when you get": Selznick Archive.

338 "Whatever I do": Kobe to Edward Hartman.

338 "is so near the breaking point": Ibid.

338 "Vic told me": Myrick, *White Columns in Hollywood.*

339 "was so real": Alexander's letter is in Vickers, *Vivien Leigh.*

339 Rhett's mourning of Melanie: Haver, *David O. Selznick's Hollywood.* Haver puts equal emphasis on Gable's "intransigence" and Leigh's rebelliousness as direct motivations for Fleming's walkout. His rendering of the event derives partly from Mahin's eyewitness account collected in McGilligan's interview book *Backstory,* though Haver provides a more plausible description of the shooting day (Mahin has Gable balking at saying, "Frankly, my dear, I don't give a damn").

340 "Confusion redoubled": Letter to Mrs. Howard, April 27, 1939, Howard Papers.

340 "takes things a little less hard": Graham, *College of One.*

340 "What do you take me for, a chump?": Crowther's notes, Crowther Papers. In *The Lion's Share,* Crowther changed that to "What do you think I am, a chump?" In 1961, speaking to Charles Samuels, Selznick—ever the showman—either recovered some memory or enhanced what Fleming said: "Do you think I'm a damn fool, David? This picture is going to be the biggest white elephant of all time." Sometimes, that quotation is distorted to begin with "Don't be a damn fool, David."

340 "feigned": Lambert, *GWTW.*

341 suspected Fleming of faking his illness: Rabwin, *Yes, Mr. Selznick.*

341 "the Wood unit": Selznick Archive.

341 But Gable didn't warm to Wood: The most accurate estimate of Wood's contribution is Lambert's in *GWTW*—15 percent of the completed film—and Lambert's outline of Wood's participation suggests how crucial Fleming's presence was to Gable's performance. For example, Wood shot "Scarlett going to Atlanta in search of Rhett, excluding the scene with Rhett," and "the first half (up to Rhett's entrance) of the sequence in which Scarlett, Melanie and the others wait for Ashley and Kennedy to return from the raid on Shanty Town."

341 The producer's memos: Selznick Archive.

341 "direct everything": Ibid.

341 congratulating her: Hall, "On the Sets."

342 "was amazed at the difference": Canutt, *Stunt Man.*
342 "got a warm greeting": Bakewell, *Hollywood Be Thy Name.*
343 "All the way back to town": Robyns, *Light of a Star.*
344 "Clark crept to his bungalow": Hall, "On the Sets."
344 "lining the tracks": Mitchell, *Gone With the Wind.*
344 "Get off those dummies," "Slower, dear": *Los Angeles Times* (witnessed by Philip Scheuer), May 28, 1939.
344 "The camera swings": Harrison Carroll column, June 13, 1939.
344 "Is her name really Fiddle-de-dee?": *Los Angeles Times,* Jan. 19, 1986.
344 "no desire to produce": Behlmer, *Memo from David O. Selznick.*
345 "Massa's in de Cole, Cole Ground": Annie Kurtz, *Atlanta Constitution,* May 14, 1939. Kurtz, the wife of the technical adviser Wilbur Kurtz, was, like Hall and Myrick, an on-set diarist; her reporting emphasized the Southern connections of cast and crew, such as the Southern Negro cook at the Gable household.
345 "confused ideological view": Cripps, *Slow Fade to Black.*
345 "Had anybody else": Myrick, *White Columns in Hollywood.*
345 "I hate listening": *Toronto Star,* Oct. 23, 1988.
346 "I didn't want to eat the watermelon": *The New York Times,* Jan. 29, 1989.
346 "Everyone was wonderful": *Toronto Star,* Oct. 23, 1988.
346 "better to earn $1,250": Different versions of McDaniel's remarks have been written over the years; this one, with dollar figures attached, is what Butterfly McQueen told Greg Giese in 1979.
346 "I never thought": Keyes, *Scarlett O'Hara's Younger Sister.*
346 "quit behaving like a temperamental actor": Canutt, *Stunt Man.*
347 superbly caring in his direction of children: Patrick Curtis, who played the newborn Beau, was the baby of Daniel Curtis, the comptroller of Republic Pictures. His mother, Helen, was a friend of Cukor's—that's how she knew about the role. His father was a motorcyclist like Fleming—and that may be why he got the part and kept it, he says, jokingly. He's on-screen "for about as little time as anyone can be in the movies. I'm on there for those few seconds in which Olivia de Havilland is holding me, and she's saying, 'Ashley is coming home!' " But Sam Wood was the one who directed *his* scene.
348 memos flew: Selznick Archive.
348 "You do whatever these Jews want": Haver, *David O. Selznick's Hollywood.*
348 anti-Semitic: *An Oral History with Sam Jaffe.* Interviewed by Barbara Hall. Beverly Hills, Calif: Academy of Motion Picture Arts and Sciences 1992. Margaret Herrick Library.

349 his "damn": Coghlan, *They Still Call Me Junior.*

349 "essential and required": *Gone With the Wind* file, Production Code Administration Collection, Margaret Herrick Library.

350 "selfish egotism": *Motion Picture,* Feb. 1940, quoted in Walker, *Vivien.*

350 "I never liked Scarlett": *Los Angeles Times,* March 31, 1968.

350 "At least there is some doubt": Macdonald, *Dwight Macdonald on Movies.*

350 "to detract from the brilliant job": Behlmer, *Memo from David O. Selznick.*

351 "Doug has taken his last leap": *Los Angeles Times,* Dec. 13, 1939.

351 "Fairbanks was outstandingly": *Los Angeles Times,* Dec. 14, 1939.

352 "The stars of today are lazy": Ed Sullivan column, Dec. 14, 1939.

352 "Can you smell the wisteria?": Herb Bridges, *Gone With the Wind: The Three-Day Premiere in Atlanta,* Macon, Georgia: Mercer University Press, 1999.

352 "C'mon chillun—let's dance," "as a Southerner": From the recording of the NBC broadcast, Recorded Sound Division, Library of Congress.

352 "The *Gone With the Wind* festivities": Adair also recorded that his daughter Roline attended the costume ball with one Jimmie Newton, who "had on an old Confederate uniform he bought at a rummage sale on Decatur Street."

354 "pandemonium broke loose": *Los Angeles Evening Herald* (and other papers), Dec. 29, 1939.

354 the industry's night of nights: It also was the first time Bob Hope played master of ceremonies on Oscar night. "I think it's a fine thing, this benefit for David Selznick," he cracked as *Gone With the Wind* neared the end of its awards sweep. It also was the night Hope first trotted out a joke he would recycle in years ahead: "But I like it here in Hollywood. In fact, Hollywood is the only place you can let your hair down—and then put it back in the box."

354 "I wish you'd call Victor": Selznick Archive.

23 *Dr. Jekyll and Mr. Hyde*

356 yet he proposed: Simmonds, *John Steinbeck.*

357 spoke of taking court action: Benson, *Short Novels of John Steinbeck.*

357 first long-term contract: MGM's legal files demonstrate the studio's determination to sign him to an exclusive deal. Mannix proposed one for three years in October 1935 and another for seven years in October 1938 and got nowhere. The contracts department made roughly a dozen

requests for Fleming to sign an agreement. Fleming finally agreed to a five-year contract drafted November 13, 1939, to start Jan. 1, 1940, with an expiration date of December 31, 1944. The Nov. 13 contract dropped the morality and insurance clauses and enabled him to direct radio or theater not connected to MGM.

357 "putting up in tourist camps": Hedda Hopper column, July 11, 1940.

357 "We should prepare immediately": Mannix to Fleming, Aug. 8, 1940, MGM legal files.

358 "I like directing women, too": Sheilah Graham column, Jan. 18, 1940.

358 His meticulously publicized romances: Bowman was a busy man-about-town in the 1930s. In print, he also was linked to Joy Hodges (in 1938, she announced she was going to marry him), the Broadway actress Virginia Peine (*Lady in the Dark*), the ballerina Irina Baronova, the ice-skater Sonja Henie (who reportedly advised him to get fitted for a toupee), and Wendy Barrie, with whom Bowman had a lengthy affair.

359 "looked as if": Garnett, *Light Your Torches and Pull Up Your Tights.*

359 hex on Bessie's private life: The story of her grandmother's death was in the *Charleston Post and Courier*, Nov. 10, 1912. The fireplace accident is a family story. Her first husband, Dr. Thomas T. Fauntleroy of Staunton, Virginia, was a young dentist from one of the area's most prominent families. Her second husband, Luther Lee Bowman, also was from a Staunton family who owned a department store and hotel. Luther Bowman, who was active in harness racing, started a local department store himself in 1912 before moving Bessie and his sons to Cincinnati in 1914 to start the brewery. He died in the mid-1920s. Bessie Clyde died in 1967, age eighty-four.

359 when it failed: *Cincinnati Enquirer*, May 10, 1916.

359 the Bowman hex: It would continue with Lee. He died on Christmas Day 1979, just before his sixty-fifth birthday. While cleaning up his kitchen at his home in Brentwood, California, late on Christmas Eve, he fell backward into a glass door. A shard pierced an artery in his back, and he bled to death. His family, however, announced that he had died of a heart attack.

360 "Don't do that": King Vidor recorded interview, June 17, 1971, Department of Special Collections, UCLA Library.

360 "fly a first-line American director": *The New York Times*, March 11, 1940.

360 planned a London production: *The New York Times*, May 13, 1940.

362 "loved this girl": Bergman and Burgess, *My Story.*

363 "Although I'd known": Ibid.

363 "that role is so deep": Turner, *Lana*.

364 "Toland did such wonderful things": Selznick to Fleming and Ruttenberg, Jan. 22, 1941, Selznick Archive.

364 "He got things out of me": *Times* (London), Jan. 13, 1971.

364 In Mamoulian's version: Mamoulian's script has his penciled-in striptease for Miriam Hopkins. Rouben Mamoulian Collection, Manuscript Division, Library of Congress.

365 "most mornings to perfect her accent": Saville, *Evergreen*.

366 "You know, I'm scared of my part, too": Ingrid Bergman, "My Favorite Film," *National Enquirer*, Feb. 17, 1974.

367 "Mr. Mayer thought": Davidson, *Spencer Tracy*.

367 "I even suggested": *Chicago Tribune*, Feb. 22, 1941.

367 "hydizations": Vladimir Nabokov, *Lectures on Literature*, ed. Fredson Bowers (New York: Harcourt Brace Jovanovich, 1980). Nabokov told his students to "ignore the fact that ham actors under the direction of pork packers have acted in a parody of the book, which parody was then photographed on a film and showed in places called theatres; it seems to me that to call a moviehouse a theatre is the same as to call an undertaker a mortician." But even Nabokov recognized the weakness of the author's portrayal of Jekyll's whispered-about pleasures and Hyde's "monstrous exaggerations" of them—and that weakness is one reason all the major movie versions, heretical though it may sound, are dramatically far sturdier than the more poetic story.

368 "I've got an idea": Kress told this story a number of times. This version is in Lobrutto, *Selected Takes*.

369 "Victor was not only well informed": Saville, *Evergreen*.

370 "Robert Louis Stevenson": Ibid.

370 "these two base passions": Falzon, *Philosophy Goes to the Movies*.

370 "delete all scenes," "unduly exposed breasts": Breen to Mayer, June 3, 1941, Production Code Administration Files, Margaret Herrick Library.

370 "If you could see me now": Mamoulian added the first "Free" in this: "Free, free at last! Free to dare and to do! (Then, with a sudden change of mood) Mad, Twaddle, eh, Lanyon? Eh, Carew? Hypocrites! Deniers of life! (He mimics Carew) You must wait, my dear fellow. Wait! Slaves! Slaves! If you could see me now, what would you think, eh?" Mamoulian's note to himself for March's appearance after his transformation is written in Russian: "Shy and frightened on the floor," then Hyde "glancing back" at the "change of room." (Translation by Olga Golosinskaya, Library of Congress.)

371 "Wh-which one": Kanin, *Remembering Mr. Maugham*.

372 "to race up the stairs," "Big and strong": Bergman and Burgess, *My Story.*
372 "To double Tracy": Mank, *Hollywood Cauldron.*
372 "differences of opinion": *Lion's Roar,* Jan. 1944.
372 "I was in a happy mood": Turner, *Lana.*
373 "I just couldn't do it": Bergman and Burgess, *My Story.*
373 "Fleming was very mean to me": Bergman, "My Favorite Film."
373 "Shall I ever be happier": Bergman and Burgess, *My Story.*
374 "enormously exciting": Selznick to Fleming, March 6, 1941, Selznick Archive.
374 "By the time the film was over": Bergman and Burgess, *My Story.*
374 "I am certainly only human enough": Night letter, Saville to Fleming, sent to Meadowlark Ranch, also retyped and sent by messenger to 1050 Moraga Drive, June 26, 1941. MGM Collection, USC Cinema and Television Library.
374 "To tell the truth": Saville, *Evergreen.*

24 *The Yearling* That Wasn't

375 "I got them to buy it": McGilligan, *Backstory.* Mahin's story of locking horns with Sidney Franklin is one of the highlights of this interview, and, indeed, the whole anthology.
376 "By the time *The Yearling*": Fleming to Rawlings, Feb. 9, 1940, Marjorie Kinnan Rawlings Papers, University of Florida, Gainesville.
377 "It seems every other kid": Grady, *Irish Peacock.*
377 "skinny and weak-looking": Eckman eventually grew to a height of six feet and enjoys perfect health.
378 "2 sick fawns in crate": Marchant to Charles J. Chic, June 16, 1940. MGM legal files.
378 "All fawn arrived": Marchant to Richard Gerstell, June 19, 1940. MGM legal files.
378 "Central Florida had become": Worsley, *From Oz to E.T.*
379 Sidney Franklin sent his brother: Franklin's account of the filming is in his unpublished memoir, "We Laughed and We Cried."
379 "He wanted more finesse": Clark to George Lofgren, May 13, 1941. MGM legal files.
380 "many a smart Hollywood station wagon": *The New York Times,* May 25, 1941. MGM legal files.
381 "he was goddamned": Marquand's biographer Millicent Bell (*Marquand: An American Life*) wrote that he told a colorful version of *The Yearling*

debacle in a speech he gave that December, quoting Tracy excoriating Eckman, the heat and the corniness of it all. Anne Revere later told Selden West, "I would be the first to say I was not ready [to play Ma Baxter in the movie], but I was not the cause of this debacle."

381 "JUST SAT DOWN": Hay, *MGM.*

381 "nervous, hen-pecking manner": Weddle, *"If They Move . . . Kill 'Em!"*

381 "made a lot of trouble": Rawlings to Bee McNeil, June 24, 1941, Rawlings Papers.

382 "When the boys get home": Lawrence to Rawlings, May 22, 1941, Rawlings Papers.

382 "We didn't agree": Louella Parsons column, May 29, 1941.

382 "Fleming doesn't like producers": *The New York Times,* June 8, 1941.

382 "I was only on the set twice": Rawlings to Bee McNeil, June 24, 1941, Rawlings Papers.

383 "How can I make": Kazan, *Life.*

383 "What ails the works": Mitchell to Rawlings, June 27, 1941, Rawlings Papers.

383 "Victor Fleming, one of the greatest": Interview in *Focus on Film* (Winter 1975).

384 "Our minds are not": *Lion's Roar,* Jan. 1944.

25 Bonhomie in Bel-Air and *Tortilla Flat*

385 shot a letter: Aug. 27, 1941. Having finally persuaded Fleming to sign a long-term deal with the studio, MGM's contracts department wasn't going to tolerate any contrary publicity about the director's independence or availability: "We desire to notify you that Mr. Fleming is under contract to us under the provisions of which contract we are entitled to his exclusive services during the term thereof, which is not scheduled to expire prior to . . . several years from this date. This letter is written to advise you that we are insisting and will insist upon the full protection of our rights under said contract." MGM legal files.

385 "Fleming had a nervous breakdown": Rawlings to Bee McNeil, June 24, 1941, Rawlings Papers.

389 she nearly upended: *Los Angeles Times,* March 6, 1939.

390 "It wasn't exactly a farm": From Miller's unpublished memoir.

390 "for the same reason": Wynn, *Ed Wynn's Son.*

391 "We opened them up, full throttle": *Cycle World,* Aug. 1993.

392 "She was clearly": Bacall, *By Myself.*

392 "Do you notice": Ibid.

392 "Lu the Jew": Having a nickname herself may have prompted Slim to bestow them on others. According to Hoagy Carmichael (*Sometimes I Wonder*), she liked to refer to Howard Hawks as "Great White Father" because of his prematurely gray hair.

393 "razz him about the money": Hedda Hopper column, Jan. 31, 1945.

393 "and flirting, of course": Bacall, *By Myself.*

394 "just told stories about Hawks": Vidor, sound recording (1971), UCLA Library, Department of Special Collections.

395 acquired Hollywood heat: MGM announced its production of *Tortilla Flat* in 1940 in the wake of the success of *The Grapes of Wrath;* Ruth Hussey at one point was announced to play Sweets Ramirez.

396 MGM had refused to grant: Steinbeck to Annie Laurie Williams, June 24, 1941, John Steinbeck Collection, Stanford University.

396 set a meeting: Simmonds, *John Steinbeck.*

396 "I've planted all the seeds": Steinbeck to Annie Laurie Williams, Aug. 5, 1941, Steinbeck Collection.

396 "and when he returned it": *The New York Times,* Nov. 30, 1941.

396 According to Mahin: Marshall, *Blueprint on Babylon.*

396 "Its single dirt street": *Los Angeles Times,* Jan. 11, 1942.

397 "fate in the picture": *The New York Times,* Nov. 30, 1941.

397 "tried to slow down": *Los Angeles Times,* Jan. 11, 1942.

397 "tall and patrician": Lee, *Chasing Hepburn.*

398 He had promised Saint Francis: Joseph R. Millichap gets this whole episode wrong in his *Steinbeck and Film.* He writes, "In the novel [Pirate] mentions that the dog was later run over by a truck; in the movie the little dog is right up there, on the screen, wagging his tail in close-up." Actually, the movie is faithful to the original anecdote.

398 "I tried to steal scenes": *Life,* June 1, 1942.

398 "for Christ's sake, Garfield": Swindell, *Body and Soul.* Swindell told me his source for this dialogue was MGM talent scout Billy Grady.

399 "It was an honest part": Hedda Hopper column, August 4, 1951.

399 "John Garfield was wonderful to work with": Ibid.

399 pointed exchange: MGM legal files.

26 World War II with Tears

401 Deacon had asked: *Los Angeles Times,* Jan. 9, 1940. Deacon's mental decline continued after his stroke, but not his ability to place ads. In

1951, his ad read, "For $1 I will tell you what is killing the major portion of the trees." He died in a Pasadena nursing home in 1952, age ninety-two. In death, he would suffer the same exclusion from the family circle he had in life; Eva bought the crypt above Victor for herself but buried Deacon in a plot outside the mausoleum at Hollywood Memorial Park.

402 "boiled-and-buttered native corn": Agee, *Agee on Film.*

402 "drifted away": Kantor included this account of the aborted *Buffalo Bill* project in his papers, along with his treatment and memos to Fleming and Zimbalist; they reside in the Manuscript Division at the Library of Congress.

403 "the fakiest guy": Interview with William Wellman, in Schickel, *Men Who Made the Movies.*

404 Fleming told him: Dickran Kouymjian, "Saroyan Shoots a Film," in Hamalian, *William Saroyan.*

404 "the first woman": Warren G. Harris, *Clark Gable* (New York: Harmony Books, 2002).

404 "specific and highly important assignment": Gable's military career is outlined in detail in Steven Agoratus, "Clark Gable in the Eighth Air Force," *Air Power History* (Spring 1999).

405 "magical thinking": Didion, *Year of Magical Thinking.*

406 "They sent me everything": Letter from St. Johns to Lucile Fleming, sent just after Fleming's death. St. Johns didn't like to waste lachrymose anecdotes and recycled this one in her 1969 memoir, *The Honeycomb.* But in the new version, which ends the book, Fleming, whom she described as looking a lot like the *Gunsmoke* star James Arness, mixed compassion with a patriotic homily: "Never forget that cutting down Papa's pants for Junior was what made the United States great in the first place. The day we forget to use up everything, the Constitution and the Bill of Rights and the half-used cans of toothpaste, we won't be the USA any more."

407 "The proprietors of MGM": Trumbo to Kempton, 1957, published in the *Nation,* April 5, 1999.

407 "convinced there was going to be trouble," "I didn't want to have": Cook, *Dalton Trumbo.*

408 "like Clark Gable": Trumbo's treatment for *A Guy Named Joe,* called *Three Guys Named Joe,* is included in the War Department review file in the National Archives, College Park, Maryland. Also in that version, the characters of Pete Sandidge and Al Yackey open the film with some randy dialogue with a British farm girl about pullets.

409 "because of the disparity": Corliss, *Hollywood Screenwriters;* "Dalton Trumbo," appreciation by Corliss.

409 "Flying isn't tough": Lee, *Chasing Hepburn.*

409 "all wars are bad": *The New York Times,* June 28, 1970.

410 "redeeming *Topper* twist": Comments from Mayor Ralph Jester, Colonel Falkner Heard, Colonel Edward Munson, Colonel William Wright, and Lieutenant John T. Parker Jr. are in the War Department review file for *A Guy Named Joe,* National Archives.

411 "take on a dangerous job": Joseph Breen's suggestions for the ending are in the Production Code file for *A Guy Named Joe,* Margaret Herrick Library.

411 "I suppose the film," "got the idea that," and "my *best*—very best": Interview appendix to Harvey, *Romantic Comedy.*

412 "I used to go to the studio": Interview in *Films of the Golden Age* (Summer 2004).

413 "Spencer never acts": Associated Press, April 3, 1938.

413 "I looked at the schedule": DeFore's story about Spencer Tracy's scene is from his interview in the Ronald L. Davis Oral History Collection, DeGolyer Library, Southern Methodist University, Dallas, Texas, collection number A1980.0154; viewed at Margaret Herrick Library.

414 "a voice rumbled back": Letter from Trumbo in the *The New York Times,* Aug. 6, 1967.

415 motorcycle crash: Johnson verified to Spencer Tracy biographer Bill Davidson (*Spencer Tracy: Tragic Idol*) that it was a motorcycle accident.

415 "I had to crawl across": Interview with Johnson in the *Toronto Star,* Jan. 26, 1988.

415 "They had already tested": Van Johnson, "My Life," as told to Ruth Waterbury, *Photoplay,* March 1945.

415 "has more heart": Hedda Hopper column, May 7, 1944.

415 "at the door": Beecher, *Luckiest Guy in the World.*

416 MGM asked: War Department file.

416 "as long as possible": *Los Angeles Times,* April 5, 1943.

416 One unit spent: The War Department file details the work of the second units and includes suggestions on increasing cooperation between MGM and the military. The Army Air Forces embraced the second-unit footage and in January 1944 asked permission to use clips from *Joe* plus stills showing P-38 tactics. The AAF's then-classified General Information Bulletin published them—the first time a commercial motion picture was used for training purposes.

416 "right from fields": Letter from Carter Barron, MGM's Washington, D.C., liaison, in the War Department file.

416 "They wanted to see": Interview with Johnson in the *Toronto Star*, Jan. 26, 1988.

417 The BMP's primary mission: For a historical overview of the bureau, see Koppes and Black, *Hollywood Goes to War*. Mention of the "Four Freedoms" is in the Office of War Information publication "Government Information Manual for the Motion Picture Industry."

417 *Bugs Bunny Nips the Nips:* The 1944 cartoon has the indestructible Bugs on a Pacific island confronting bucktoothed Japanese soldiers. He refers to one of them as "monkey face." The BMP files also question the 1943 Jack Benny comedy, *The Meanest Man in the World*. The bureau argued that overseas audiences probably would not recognize that Benny and his valet, Eddie "Rochester" Anderson, were a comedy team, so might interpret their relationship as the true nature of race relations in the United States.

417 The script shows: Trumbo's script copy is in his papers at the Wisconsin Center for Film and Theater Research, Wisconsin Historical Society, Madison.

420 The wartime Office of Censorship: Koppes and Black, *Hollywood Goes to War*.

420 "every human being": The BMP script review, including comments by Lillian R. Bergquist and telegrams from Ulric Bell, is in the records of the Office of War Information at the National Archives.

420 "The entire ending": The only known interview with a member of the BMP staff was conducted by Harry A. Sauberli Jr. for "Hollywood and World War II: A Survey of Themes of Hollywood Films About the War, 1940–1945" (master's thesis, University of Southern California, June 1967).

421 "The ending negates": *The New York Times*, Jan. 9, 1944.

421 "And even if it does fizzle": United Press, March 15, 1943.

421 "Now that Spielberg": Pauline Kael, *Movie Love: Complete Reviews, 1988–1991* (New York: Dutton, 1991).

422 "It had three endings": Trumbo interview with J. D. Marshall, Dec. 1973, Phoenix House, Tempe, Arizona, Recorded Sound Reference Center, Library of Congress.

422 *six* endings: The original in the treatment, the two endings that were filmed, and Trumbo's wordless version, plus two additional ones. In the first of Trumbo's final unused endings, Dorinda radios the airfield for

landing instructions, adding, "And if Lt. Ted Randall is still there, tell him I'd like to talk to him about a new assignment." Smiling "gaily," she adds, "Something we might do together." In the second, a note of inappropriate humor goes to Pete, who watches Dorinda run to Ted after she lands the bomber, then says quietly to himself, "That's my boy . . . that's my girl . . . and four million bucks!" He follows that with "a little whistle to emphasize his awe."

422 In a proposal: Agee's memo to his *Life* editors appears in Wranovics's *Chaplin and Agee.* Agee had been intending to do a story on a representative Hollywood director. "[John] Huston could be the director story we discussed," he tells his editors. "But I suggest that he's worth a story to himself and that the director should be a medium-talented reliable journeyman, not so far above the average as Huston, Ford, Wyler, & such. Say, a good director like Victor Fleming." Agee's middling-positive estimation of Fleming may reflect the director's uneven output during Agee's years as a reviewer for *Time* and the *Nation*, 1942–48.

422 "The picture will serve": Agee, *Agee on Film.*

422 "The emotions a ghost": Ibid.

422 "American inventiveness": Eisenstein, *Beyond the Stars.*

422 "the chain of experience": The French edition of *Eisenstein's Memoirs* (*Mémoires* 2 [Paris: Union Génerale d'Éditions, 1980]) from the chapter "Judith." The critic and film historian Ian Christie, co-editor with Richard Taylor of *Eisenstein Rediscovered*, supplied these pages. (Translated by Elizabeth Anthony.)

423 "What I don't know": *Los Angeles Examiner*, Jan. 13, 1943.

423 "A very dour, sort of dry": Vidor interview, 1971, which contains the full story of the 1944 road trip, UCLA. Olivia de Havilland's comments are in a 2003 letter to Kurt Jensen.

27 A Confounding Political Life

425 laying down bets: Mankiewicz told this story to Selden West while she was researching the life of Spencer Tracy. Fleming was not, however, a member of the isolationist group America First.

425 registered as a Democrat: Lu Fleming always registered Republican, as did Fleming's mother.

426 "He was against": Kazan, *Life.*

426 "I have no use for a poor man": Steele, *Ingrid Bergman.*

427 "It was officially non-political": Dunne, *Take Two*.

429 "persons in the various studios": Richard B. Hood, Special Agent in Charge, Los Angeles FBI bureau, to FBI chief J. Edgar Hoover, Feb. 9, 1944, MPA file. Hood, an FBI agent from 1934 to 1953, died in 2005, age ninety-seven. Federal Bureau of Investigation: File on the Motion Picture Alliance for the Preservation of American Ideals.

429 one notable misstep: In August 1938, James B. Matthews, a former Communist Party member who was the committee's star witness, named Temple as a communist dupe because she, along with Clark Gable, Robert Taylor, and James Cagney, had sent congratulatory wires to the French communist newspaper *Ce Soir*. Matthews—who coined the term "fellow traveler"—went on to declare (in a statement reported by newspapers but expunged from the official HUAC transcript), "In fact, almost everyone in Hollywood has been signed up for some communist front organization except Mickey Mouse and Snow White." To that, Alabama representative Joe Starnes inquired, "What about Charlie McCarthy?"

429 the FBI estimated that 200: Hood to Hoover, March 22, 1944, FBI, MPA file.

429 James Kevin McGuinness: Born in Ireland, he was a close friend of John Ford's. In 1940, he married his second wife, the German baroness Lucie von Ledermann-Wartburg. He was ousted from MGM in 1949 in a restructuring blamed on the studio's declining box-office returns, although fervent anticommunists claimed it was retaliation for his MPA activities. He went on a three-month national speaking tour on the communist threat, wrote *Rio Grande* for Ford, then died of a heart attack in 1950, age fifty-six.

430 "He was such a charming man": Ceplair and Englund, *Inquisition in Hollywood*.

430 "did me harm": Vidor interview, 1971, UCLA.

430 "banned for being anti-Semitic": McGuinness, Mahin, and Howard Emmett Rogers had been tagged in print as anti-Semites in January 1941 when the *Daily Worker* observed them at the Brown Derby discussing "aliens" in Hollywood and attacking the forthcoming *Citizen Kane* with G. Allison Phelps, a virulently anti-Semitic broadcaster and pamphleteer. Phelps discussed that meeting on a subsequent broadcast on KMTR. But Vidor probably was thinking of a mass booklet mailing from the Council of Hollywood Guilds and Unions shortly after the MPA began. As noted in a memo from Hood to Hoover on September

13, 1944, the booklet accused the MPA "of having been sympathetic to the German-American Bund, implying connections with Father Coughlin's Christian Front, the Ku Klux Klan, Gerald L. K. Smith [a notoriously anti-Semitic minister and agitator for right-wing causes], Joe McWilliams [head of the anti-Semitic Christian Organizers], and those individuals now on trial in Washington, D.C., for sedition." *Communist Activity in the Entertainment Industry: FBI Surveillance Files on Hollywood, 1942–1958.*

430 "What are they for, King?": Schwartz, *Hollywood Writers' Wars.*

431 "Possibly nowhere but in Hollywood": *New Republic,* June 26, 1944.

431 "more words than any other author": *Los Angeles Times,* July 5, 1938.

431 "beginning to show left-wing tendencies": Hood to Hoover, Feb. 18, 1943, in *Communist Activity in the Entertainment Industry.*

431 "If trying to be": Hedda Hopper column, May 6, 1944.

432 "You should avoid": Hoover to Hood, May 1, 1944. FBI, MPA file.

432 straight out of law school: After leaving the FBI at the end of the war, Baumeister was general counsel for KTTV in Los Angeles.

432 "a possible Communist front": Hood to Hoover, Feb. 18, 1943. An informant added, "There is very little doubt that the inspiration for the creation of the Hollywood Canteen originated in communist circles," *Communist Activity in the Entertainment Industry.*

432 Maribess Stokes: Hood to Hoover, July 14, 1944. Ibid. Stokes was married to a Navy officer. She sometimes was named in FBI memos as Mary Bess Stokes. FBI memos do not indicate that she was prosecuted, but further information about her has eluded inquiry.

432 "to recover all copies": D. M. Ladd to Hoover, July 9, 1945. Ibid. On July 14, Ladd filled in the rest of the story in response to Hoover's request, explaining that Stokes "admitted" on October 18, 1944, that she had been securing FBI materials through Lieutenant Daniel Goodykoontz, and that the agent Hood had discussed the matter with commanders of the Los Angeles ONI office. This was done, Ladd reminded Hoover, "in accordance with your instructions that the situation be adjusted on a local level before it was taken up with Naval Intelligence at the seat of government." In other words, Hoover, who was renowned for his skill as a bureaucratic infighter, had asked that the matter be handled quietly, lest it become known not only that the FBI had shared documents but that a security breach had occurred. In addition to Wood, a memo from L. B. Nichols to Clyde Tolson on November 10, 1944, indicates that Lela Rogers said that she, too, had seen the FBI's list of Hollywood communists.

432 Goodykoontz was transferred: In the 1950s, Goodykoontz helped prosecute the gangster Mickey Cohen for tax evasion. Says Bill Goodykoontz, "My father always spoke positively about his time in Iceland, so the suggestion that he was banished there surprises both me and my mother."

433 "We even know their [party] card numbers": Ibid.

434 "The attacks against the MPA": Hood to Hoover, March 22, 1944. FBI, MPA file.

434 In February 1944: Ibid.

434 "I have got a bunch": Ibid.

434 "Selznick spent the evening": Ibid.

434 [name redacted]: An appeal to the FBI to uncover the names was turned down. The FBI still classifies the long-defunct Motion Picture Alliance under "domestic terrorism."

435 "pretty intelligent": An Oral History with Robert Vogel. Interviewed by Barbara Hall. Beverly Hills, CA: Academy of Motion Picture Arts and Sciences, 1991. Margaret Herrick Library.

28 One Last *Adventure* at MGM

436 "It has been said": Hood to Hoover, May 10, 1944. FBI, MPA file.

436 "Put them wise": Hood to Hoover, May 24, 1944. Ibid.

437 "a studio plot": Beauchamp, *Without Lying Down.*

437 vehicle for Spencer Tracy: *The New York Times*, Aug. 28, 1941.

437 Fleming's contract: MGM legal files.

437 "You felt like you built the buildings": Vidor interview, 1971, UCLA. Vidor was often of two minds when discussing his friend Fleming. Sometimes he told interviewers Fleming would mutter "Happy days" as a put-down of anyone he didn't see at work on the set; at other times, the phrase was a wistful expression of Fleming's longing for the relaxed atmosphere of shooting on location, away from the studio.

438 "gave no indication": MGM legal files.

438 "If you ask us": *The New York Times*, Feb. 8, 1946.

438 "It has everything except Little Eva": *Chicago Tribune*, March 9, 1946.

439 "When he spit out the mouthwash": Gable had finally learned the foul smell of his false teeth was turning off his on-screen love mates. On Sept. 9, 1991, Anthony Bushell wrote to Michael Dempsey of Leigh's experience with Gable on *Gone With the Wind:* "She regards her celebrated partner with only the ghostliest touch of the disapproval she

couldn't help feeling for him. It was the old question of BREATH and its unacceptability, and Vivien figured he had been in pictures long enough and played opposite enough outspoken colleagues to have done something about it." David Stenn collection.

441 "was jittery": *Los Angeles Times*, June 14, 1945.

441 "The trouble was": Louella O. Parsons, "Mister 'King,' " *Photoplay*, Nov. 1947.

442 "Gable's back": The anecdote of Torchia coming up with the slogan and winning $250 is from her interview in the Ronald L. Davis Oral History Collection, DeGolyer Library, Southern Methodist University, Dallas, Texas, collection number A1980.0154; viewed at Margaret Herrick Library.

442 Garson didn't prefer: Troyan, *Rose for Mrs. Miniver.*

442 "He'd look at her": Warren G. Harris, *Gable.*

442 "definitely the worst picture": Clyde Brion Davis to David Brion Davis, March 31, 1946, collection of David Brion Davis. Before he finally saw the picture at a theater in upstate New York, Davis joked to his son, "I hear it isn't so hot, but there'll be a newsreel."

443 producer's contract: MGM legal files.

443 "a nice group": Dowd and Shepherd, *King Vidor.*

444 "were motivated by personal jealousy": Hood to Hoover, July 14, 1944. FBI, MPA file.

444 Never a well-liked figure: Herman Mankiewicz said of Revnes, "His job, in the event he sees a glacier moving down Washington Boulevard, is to apprise Louis B. Mayer of the fact with all possible speed" (Hoopes, *Cain*).

444 "everybody was out for himself": Eyman, *Lion of Hollywood.*

29 Ingrid Bergman and *Joan of Arc*

446 the American public condemned her: Two weeks after giving birth to Roberto Ingmar Rossellini in March 1950, before getting a divorce from Lindström, Bergman was condemned on the floor of the U.S. Senate by Senator Edwin Johnson of Colorado as "a free-love cultist" and called one of "Hollywood's two current apostles of degradation." (The other was Rita Hayworth.) Earlier that year, citing "exhibitor resistance," the Motion Picture Association of America also ordered the excision of a *Joan of Arc* clip from an advertising short about history in films. After

separating from Roberto Rossellini in 1956, Bergman made a triumphant return to American movies with *Anastasia,* for which she won her second Academy Award. In 1972, Senator Charles Percy of Illinois apologized for Johnson's attack and called her "a true star in every sense of the word." Bergman won her third Oscar in 1975 in the supporting actress category for *Murder on the Orient Express.* She died on her sixty-seventh birthday in 1982.

447 "Ingrid's natural talent": Selznick to Kay Brown, Feb. 6, 1940, Selznick Archive.

447 "We never got around to it": Victor Saville, National Film Archive program, British Film Institute. He was planning to do Shaw's *Saint Joan* in a manner close to the stage version of *Joan of Lorraine:* "The style was a treatment of light and close-up leaving it to Shaw and the imagination to provide the scenery."

448 "I naturally want you": Anderson to Bergman, April 23, 1945, in Avery, *Dramatist in America.*

448 "I'm not making any of this up": *The New York Times,* Dec. 1, 1946.

448 top box-office attractions: As named by *Boxoffice.*

449 "She was the kind of young woman": *The New York Times Magazine,* Dec. 29, 1946.

449 bored GIs: Adler, *It Ain't Necessarily So.*

450 "that she was the reincarnation": Hesper Anderson, *South Mountain Road.*

450 "Six years ago": *The New York Times,* Nov. 19, 1946.

450 "She is regarded": *Variety,* May 9, 1947.

450 Louis Kronenberger: *PM,* Nov. 18, 1946.

450 "a Readers' Theatre performance": *New York Journal American,* Dec. 2, 1946. Percy MacKaye wrote a 1907 pageant-like play about Joan of Arc. Julia Marlowe, its star, was forty at the time.

452 "constant search for happiness": Bernstein, *Walter Wanger.*

452 wooed Noël Coward: *The New York Times,* May 27, 1946.

452 "Walter, I could never play": Wanger to Robert Haggiag, Aug. 18, 1955, Walter Wanger Collection, Wisconsin Center for Film and Theater Research, Wisconsin Historical Society, Madison.

453 "The good doctor": Steele, *Ingrid Bergman.*

453 "Business, business": Ibid.

453 "was always going off half-cocked": Davidson, *The Real and the Unreal.*

453 "not good enough for you": Steele, *Ingrid Bergman.*

454 "Ingrid, you were magnificent!": "Ingrid Bergman Had a Dream" is

included in *Hollywood Album*, a 1947 collection of publicity pieces compiled by Ivy Crane Wilson, Hollywood correspondent for the London *Star.*

454 "The white-maned lion": Steele, *Ingrid Bergman.*

455 "You must play Joan": Bergman and Burgess, *My Story.*

455 "Wonders will never cease": Anderson's account of the travails of *Joan of Lorraine*, Fleming's work in New York, and the writing of the script of *Joan of Arc* in California in this chapter are from his 1947 diary, with his papers at the Harry Ransom Center.

455 "This was in my pocket": Fleming's three letters to Bergman are all as published in *My Story*, but here, for the first time, put in their correct sequence. The letters are not now with Bergman's collected papers at Wesleyan University.

456 "wore a simple gray suit": Dorothy Kilgallen column, Feb. 8, 1947.

456 Wanger was the biggest investor: He also bought out Fleming's shares after his death. Stressed from his *Joan of Arc* debts, Wanger served a four-month term on a prison farm after shooting Jennings Lang, his wife Joan Bennett's agent at Music Corporation of America, in a jealous rage in 1951 because he believed they were having an affair. Newspapers decorously reported that Wanger shot Lang in "the groin." Shortly after that, the radio wit Fred Allen wrote Groucho Marx (in his customary lowercase) on December 27, "There is a rumor around here that because of missing members, mca is going to erect a statue of jennings lang to be called 'penis de milo.' this rumor, I might add, is not sweeping the city. there is no handle on it." (Groucho Marx Papers, Library of Congress.) Wanger lost his clout as a producer after the financial disaster of *Cleopatra* in 1963. He kept developing projects, though, until he died of a heart attack in 1968, age seventy-four.

456 "As poor Victor Fleming used to say": Wanger to Rank, Jan. 18, 1949, Wanger Collection.

457 "What peasant wears red chiffon?": Bentley, *Costumes by Karinska.*

457 "to better facilitate conferences": Steele, *Ingrid Bergman.*

458 He shot craps: Ibid.

458 "September Song": Evidently this serenade took place in the restaurant at the Hampshire House, since Anderson recorded that he also saw the producer Peter Cusick there.

458 "Marvelous, just marvelous!": Steele, *Ingrid Bergman.*

458 "I had assumed": Miller, unpublished memoir.

459 "When we came to the hotel": Steele, *Ingrid Bergman.*
459 "a clean operation": Spoto, *Notorious.*
460 "Joe! Goddamn it": Steele, *Ingrid Bergman.*
461 "Just how long": Undated, probably April 6, draft of a letter from Anderson to Fleming, Anderson Papers, Harry Ransom Center.
462 "I get so angry": Bergman and Burgess, *My Story.*
464 "four years since you heard": From Anderson's pen-script first draft of the *Joan of Arc* script included in his papers at the Manuscript Division of the Library of Congress.
464 "a disaster": Marilyn Horne, *My Life* (New York: Atheneum, 1983).
464 Barnes's biographer states: Kessler, *Happy Bottom Riding Club.*
465 "it was plain": Laurence Stallings, "The Real Ingrid Bergman Story," *Esquire,* Aug. 1950.
465 the nettlesome voices: Anderson's pen-script draft.
465 analogizing her to King David: From 2 Samuel 7:8 (King James Version): "Now therefore so shalt thou say unto my servant David, Thus saith the Lord of hosts, I took thee from the sheepcote, from following the sheep, to be ruler over my people, over Israel."
466 *Joan of Arc: Self Portrait:* "William R. Trask: A Universal Garland," *Literary Review* (Winter 1957). The article doesn't quote Trask, a famous translator of his time, but evidently he was the source of a quoted Bergman letter in which she called his book "her Bible, and kept it by her bed" as she prepared for the role of Joan. The National Legion of Decency recommended to Fleming a 1944 book by T. Lawrason Riggs, *Saving Angel: The Truth About Joan of Arc and the Church,* but he relied instead on the Quicherat transcripts.
466 "feel compelled," "We've had no quarrel": *The New York Times,* July 27, 1947.
467 "I chose him": *New York Herald Tribune,* Nov. 11, 1948.
468 "My father got out of the car": Hesper Anderson, *South Mountain Road.*
468 "It is a question": Father Paul Doncoeur's remarkable "Lettres de Hollywood" written to his Jesuit brothers in Paris from July 21 to the end of November 1947, as used in this chapter, were published in June 1979 in *Cahiers Paul Doncoeur.* Doncoeur came to Hollywood at the recommendations of the Production Code chief, Joseph Breen, and Tom Lewis, Loretta Young's producer husband, who was a regular at a Jesuit retreat near Los Angeles. He also was used to promote the film to Catholic audiences. Of Fleming, Doncoeur wrote in the Catholic weekly *America* on November 13, 1948: "How often have I seen him on the set, anxious,

his face drawn, running a fever perhaps, but striving to draw from a scene its maximum of dramatic truth." Doncoeur died in 1961, age eighty. (Translation by Elizabeth Anthony.)

468 "While no right-minded person": Quigley to Selznick, Oct. 8, 1946, from the National Legion of Decency file on *Joan of Arc.*

469 "was an ambitious and venal tool": *The New York Times,* Aug. 10, 1947. Doncoeur's comment, while historically accurate, raised concerns with Devlin. "Evidently the historian in Father Doncoeur refuses to be dominated," Devlin wrote on August 13 in a letter to his superior, Father Patrick J. Masterson, executive secretary of the National Legion of Decency. Masterson suggested in a letter on September 4 that Devlin look into the possibility of having the Los Angeles archbishop "put him under your paternal guidance and jurisdiction." But that was not done. Letter, National Legion of Decency file.

470 "Mark Twain's version": *New York Herald Tribune,* Nov. 11, 1948.

470 "The whole thing amazes me": Fleming also arranged a screening of *Gone With the Wind* for Doncoeur, since he had never seen it. Doncoeur found it "mammoth," but also "downright unendurable. Excess itself." He wrote that he promised Fleming he would tell him how he felt, but his letters don't record Fleming's reaction.

471 "the whole picture, as visualized by you": Devlin to Fleming, Aug. 22, 1947, National Legion of Decency file. Doncoeur wrote that Devlin "is very proud of the movie *Song of Bernadette,* which 100 million Americans and English loved. 'I care little what they thought of it in France,' he says." Doncoeur also wrote that Devlin told him, "What I want is not historical accuracy; it is the service of the Catholic Church."

472 "too old and too feminine": Gordon, *Joan of Arc.*

472 "Before beginning": Doncoeur described Fleming and Bergman on the set on the first day of shooting.

473 "At first, Ruth mentioned," "I was never perfect": Spoto, *Notorious.*

474 "She's not superhuman": Pete Martin, "Big, Beautiful Swede," *Saturday Evening Post,* Oct. 30, 1948.

474 "Except for *Joan of Arc*": Truffaut, *Hitchcock/Truffaut.*

474 She chalked that comment up: *Times,* Jan. 13, 1971.

474 "a magnificent crane shot": Stallings, "Real Ingrid Bergman Story."

474 "Vic Fleming wore himself out": Bergman and Burgess, *My Story.*

475 "I think the pressures": Ibid.

476 "Brother, she is bulletproof": Stallings, "Real Ingrid Bergman Story."

477 "She's no bovine girl": Martin, "Big, Beautiful Swede."

479 "If Ingrid hadn't insisted": Anderson to Brown, May 18, 1949, in Avery, *Dramatist in America.* (Alan Anderson adds: "He called her 'that Swedish bitch' to the end of his life." Anderson died in 1959, age seventy.)

479 "England's Harry": *Saturday Review*, Dec. 18, 1948.

479 whether her saints had hair: The French historian Régine Pernoud writes in *Joan of Arc and Her Witnesses* that because Cauchon himself was asking the questions that day—March 1, 1431—Joan's answer was sarcastic and hostile: "It is good to know that they do!" In Fleming's version, Bergman answers it defensively, not sarcastically. Anderson's diary entry of October 14, 1947, records that Solt mentioned "giving Joan a bit more comedy."

480 "That fell apart": *Globe and Mail* (Toronto), Oct. 25, 1980.

480 "I started on second unit work": Hoch to John Gallagher, courtesy of Gallagher.

482 "This is May 30, 1431": Associated Press, Dec. 15, 1947. The reporter Bob Thomas added, "It made a lovely blaze."

483 "Wotzis about a red-hot feud": Jimmie Fidler column, Dec. 28, 1947. On January 10, 1948, Erskine Johnson fired back: "Oops, sorry. Ingrid Bergman and director Vic Fleming definitely are not feuding—despite what the Hollywood grapevine may say."

483 Despite Anderson's objections: Anderson to Wanger, Jan. 7, 1948: "*Joan of Arc* is a stale, flat, worn handle—with no freshness, no promise of a new slant or any entertainment value. It's a chapter out of a history assignment which bored the children in the fifth grade." On January 3, Anderson wrote in his diary, "Seems I'll have to take my name off it." Anderson Papers, Harry Ransom Center.

485 Anderson's diary: His account of working on the script for *The Robe* is in his 1948 diary, with his papers at the University of North Dakota.

487 "Ingrid has always been difficult": Edith Gwynn column, Dec. 2, 1948. On November 23, Dorothy Kilgallen had sneered, "This sounds far-fetched, but a rumor sweeping the theatrical set has it that Ingrid Bergman fainted three times while reading the more lukewarm reviews on *Joan of Arc*, which she considers her greatest effort."

487 "Miss Bergman presents": *Variety*, Oct. 20, 1948.

487 "a director whose sensitivity": *Hollywood Reporter*, Oct. 20, 1948.

488 "I'm getting my history this way": *New York Herald Tribune*, Nov. 11, 1948.

488 "the spiritual ordeal": *The New York Times*, Nov. 12, 1948.

488 "The one time [Vic] failed": St. Johns's anecdote about watching *Joan* with Fleming is contained in the Reminiscences of Adela Rogers St.

Johns (1971) in the Oral History Collection of Columbia University, p. 31.

488 "sprawls awkwardly": *Los Angeles Daily News,* Dec. 23, 1948.

30 Death in the Desert

490 "becomes a lifeless symbol": *Time,* Nov. 19, 1948.

490 *Joan of Arc* competitive only: *The New York Times,* Nov. 21, 1948.

491 "If a man has a $200 pipe": *Bob Hope Swan Show,* Feb. 15, 1949, Recorded Sound Division, Library of Congress.

491 "I cannot accept this award": Associated Press, March 25, 1949.

493 The total for embalming: Records of the Scott and McMillan Mortuary at the Jerome (Ariz.) Historical Society.

493 "Words are inadequate": Walter Wanger Collection, Wisconsin Center for Film and Theater Research, Wisconsin Historical Society, Madison.

494 "The pall of gloom": Hedda Hopper column, Jan. 14, 1949.

494 "Man of Iron": Copies of John Lee Mahin's eulogy are held by several members of Fleming's family.

495 "The great Fleming's lithe figure": Laurence Stallings, "The Real Ingrid Bergman Story," *Esquire,* Aug. 1950.

495 front pew: Told by Helene Rosson Bowman to Sally Fleming.

495 birthday of Joan of Arc: January 6 has been her accepted birthday since her church rehabilitation proceedings in the 1450s—she was declared innocent in 1456—and is based on a reference in a letter written in 1429. Also sharing that birthday: the devout Catholic actress Loretta Young.

496 "I am positive": Goodman, *Fifty-Year Decline and Fall of Hollywood.*

496 "Of all the old friends": Wanger Collection.

498 "Mrs. Fleming, this isn't a patch": Recalled by Yvonne Blocksom, evidently because her mother, Ruth Kobe, was present. Eva Deacon died in Los Angeles in 1960, at age ninety-two. During the years following Sid Deacon's death, she gave away most of her fortune to her six grandchildren in annual installments.

498 wide-screen: Most of the movie was blown up to a 1.6:1 ratio; a matte was used to reshape the most spectacular scenes from square to broader rectangular compositions. Howard Dietz devised an ad line—"*GWTW*—Greater With the Wide-Screen and stereophonic—as an added tonic—sound"—that inspired part of Cole Porter's song "Stereophonic Sound" in *Silk Stockings.*

498 "and sitting sadly": Louella Parsons column, Aug. 13, 1954.

498 "For a girl": *Ogden Standard-Examiner*, Nov. 16, 1952.

499 *Mogambo:* If Ford knew that the picture was a Fleming tribute, he didn't talk about it later. "I never saw the original picture," he told Peter Bogdanovich (in *Who the Devil Made It*). "I liked the script and the story, I liked the setup and I'd never been to that part of Africa—so I just did it."

499 Gable had boasted: In 1938, several columnists mentioned both this and the planned African safari with Fleming.

Afterword

501 "Someday someone's going to bring up": Kobal, *People Will Talk*.

501 "highly unlikely": Todd McCarthy column, *Daily Variety*, Nov. 3, 1995.

502 "a gaudy company": From a 1962 essay reprinted in Fuchs, *Golden West*.

504 "a modified road-show policy": Behlmer, *Memo from David O. Selznick*.

505 "In the past": Trumbo's memo was reprinted in *Cineaste* 18 (1992).

Filmography

With the exceptions of Victor Saville's producing title on *Dr. Jekyll and Mr. Hyde* and the section on Fleming's own uncredited work, the following list adheres to official credits. I frequently cite additional collaborators elsewhere in the book: readers will notice that the screenwriter John Lee Mahin participated in nearly every important Fleming film from 1932 on, whether his name appeared on-screen or not. But in most cases it's impossible to tell (at this distance) whether the weight and nature of anonymous labor deserves the same standing as the credited work. To judge from Mahin's marked-up copy of his *Captains Courageous* script, which scrupulously apportions authorship to each writer on the project, the old studios did make an effort to evaluate who did what in their movies.

Most of Fleming's silent films have been lost. The approximate running times below are based on current copies or contemporary reviews; in cases where neither is available, the number of reels provides a clue (a reel usually ran about ten minutes). For Fleming's MGM films, I've provided additional detail wherever possible on the dates of his involvement. Although the body of the book contains similar information about his Paramount films, MGM was the only studio to open up its files for specific verification.

The artists and craftsmen are called by their most familiar names, so, for example, the "James Howe" of the silent-film credits appears below as "James Wong Howe."

DIRECTED BY VICTOR FLEMING

1919

When the Clouds Roll By (United Artists) Released December 29. Length: 77 minutes. Preservation status: 35 mm preserved. Cast: Douglas Fairbanks, Kathleen Clifford, Frank Campeau, Herbert Grimwood, Albert McQuarrie.

Production: Fairbanks, producer; Tom J. Geraghty, screenwriter; Harry Thorpe and William McGann, cinematographers; Ted Reed, assistant director.

1920

The Mollycoddle (United Artists) Released June 13. Length: 86 minutes. Preservation status: 35 mm preserved. Cast: Douglas Fairbanks, Ruth Renick, Wallace Beery, Paul Burns, Morris Hughes, George Stewart, Charles Stevens, Albert McQuarrie, Frank Campeau. Production: Fairbanks, producer; Tom J. Geraghty, screenwriter (from story by Harold McGrath); Harry Thorpe and William McGann, cinematographers; Ted Reed, assistant director.

1921

Mamma's Affair (Emerson-Loos Productions, released by First National) Released January 23. Length: 60 minutes. Preservation status: 35 mm preserved. Cast: Constance Talmadge, Effie Shannon, Katherine Kaelred, George Le Guere, Kenneth Harlan. Production: Joseph M. Schenck, producer; John Emerson and Anita Loos, screenwriters (from Rachel Barton Butler's play); Oliver T. Marsh, cinematographer.

Woman's Place (Emerson-Loos Productions, released by First National) Released October 17. Length: Six reels. Preservation status: Lost. Cast: Constance Talmadge, Kenneth Harlan. Production: Joseph M. Schenck, producer; John Emerson and Anita Loos, screenwriters; Oliver T. Marsh and J. Roy Hunt, cinematographers.

1922

The Lane That Had No Turning (Paramount) Released January 15. Length: Five reels. Preservation status: Lost. Cast: Agnes Ayres, Theodore Kosloff, Mahlon Hamilton, Frank Campeau. Production: Adolph Zukor, producer; Eugene Mullin, screenwriter (from Gilbert Parker's screen treatment of his own novel); Gilbert Warrenton, cinematographer.

Red Hot Romance (Emerson-Loos Productions, released by First National) Released February 13. Length: Six reels. Preservation status: Portions of the first two and final two reels are at the Library of Congress. Cast: Basil Sydney, May Collins, Edward Connelly, Tom Wilson, Snitz Edwards. Production: Emerson and Loos, producers; Emerson and Loos, screenwriters; Ernest G. Palmer and Oliver T. Marsh, cinematographers.

Anna Ascends (Paramount) Released November 19. Length: Six reels. Preservation status: Lost. Cast: Alice Brady, Robert Ellis, David Powell, Nita Naldi.

Production: Adolph Zukor, presenter; Margaret Turnbull, screenwriter (from Harry Chapman Ford's play); Gilbert Warrenton, cinematographer.

1923

Dark Secrets (Paramount) Released February 5. Length: Six reels. Preservation status: Lost. Cast: Dorothy Dalton, Robert Ellis, José Ruben, Pat Hartigan. Production: Adolph Zukor, presenter; Edmund Goulding, screenwriter; Harold Rosson, cinematographer.

The Law of the Lawless (Paramount) Released July 22. Length: 67 minutes. Preservation status: Lost. Cast: Dorothy Dalton, Theodore Kosloff, Charles De Roche, Fred Huntley. Production: Jesse L. Lasky, presenter; E. Lloyd Sheldon and Edfrid Bingham, screenwriters (from the story in *Ghitza, and Other Romances of Gypsy Blood* by Konrad Bercovici); George R. Meyer, cinematographer.

To the Last Man (Paramount) Released September 23. Length: 75 minutes. Preservation status: Lost. Cast: Richard Dix, Lois Wilson, Noah Beery, Robert Edeson, Fred Huntley, Leonard Clapham, Frank Campeau, Eugene Pallette. Production: Jesse L. Lasky, presenter; Doris Schroeder, screenwriter (from the novel by Zane Grey); James Wong Howe and Bert Baldridge, cinematographers; Henry Hathaway, assistant director. (Remade in 1933, directed by Hathaway.)

The Call of the Canyon (Paramount) Released December 16. Length: 75 minutes. Preservation status: Lost. Cast: Richard Dix, Lois Wilson, Noah Beery, Marjorie Daw, Ricardo Cortez, Fred Huntley, Leonard Clapham, Lillian Leighton, Mervyn LeRoy. Production: Jesse L. Lasky, presenter; Doris Schroeder and Edfrid Bingham, screenwriters (from the novel by Zane Grey); James Wong Howe, cinematographer; Henry Hathaway, assistant director.

1924

Code of the Sea (Paramount) Released June 2. Length: 61 minutes. Preservation status: 35 mm preserved. Cast: Rod La Rocque, Jacqueline Logan, George Fawcett, Maurice B. Flynn, Lillian Leighton. Production: Adolph Zukor and Jesse L. Lasky, presenters; Bertram Millhauser, screenwriter (from a story by Byron Morgan); Charles Edgar Schoenbaum, cinematographer.

Empty Hands (Paramount) Released October 13. Length: 80 minutes. Preservation status: Lost. Cast: Norma Shearer, Jack Holt. Production: Adolph Zukor and Jesse L. Lasky, presenters; Carey Wilson, screenwriter; Charles Edgar Schoenbaum, cinematographer.

1925

The Devil's Cargo (Paramount) Released February 2. Length: 75 minutes. Preservation status: Lost. Cast: Wallace Beery, Pauline Starke, William Collier Jr., Raymond Hatton. Production: Adolph Zukor and Jesse L. Lasky, presenters; A. P. Younger, screenwriter (from a story by Charles E. Whittaker); Charles Edgar Schoenbaum, cinematographer.

Adventure (Paramount) Released April 27. Length: 78 minutes. Preservation status: Lost. Cast: Pauline Starke, Tom Moore, Wallace Beery, Raymond Hatton, Duke Kahanamoku, Noble Johnson. Production: Adolph Zukor and Jesse L. Lasky, presenters; A. P. Younger and L. G. Rigby, screenwriters (from the novel by Jack London); Charles Edgar Schoenbaum, cinematographer.

A Son of His Father (Paramount) Released September 21. Length: 75 minutes. Preservation status: Lost. Cast: Bessie Love, Warner Baxter, Raymond Hatton, Walter McGrail. Production: Adolph Zukor and Jesse L. Lasky, presenters; Anthony Coldeway, screenwriter (from the novel by Harold Bell Wright); Charles Edgar Schoenbaum, cinematographer.

Lord Jim (Paramount) Released December 14. Length: 67 minutes. Preservation status: 35 mm preserved. Cast: Percy Marmont, Shirley Mason, Noah Beery, Raymond Hatton, Joseph Dowling, George Magrill, Nick De Ruiz, Duke Kahanamoku. Production: Adolph Zukor and Jesse L. Lasky, presenters; George C. Hull, screenwriter (from John Russell's screen treatment of Joseph Conrad's novel); Faxon Dean, cinematographer. (Remade in 1965, directed by Richard Brooks.)

1926

The Blind Goddess (Paramount) Released April 12. Length: 77 minutes. Preservation status: Lost. Cast: Jack Holt, Ernest Torrence, Esther Ralston, Louise Dresser. Production: Adolph Zukor and Jesse L. Lasky, presenters; Gertrude Orr, screenwriter (from Hope Loring and Louis D. Lighton's adaptation of Arthur Cheney Train's novel); Alfred Gilks, cinematographer.

Mantrap (Paramount) Released July 24. Length: 68 minutes. Preservation status: 35 mm preserved. Cast: Ernest Torrence, Clara Bow, Percy Marmont, Eugene Pallette, Patty DuPont. Production: Adolph Zukor and Jesse L. Lasky, presenters; B. P. Schulberg and Hector Turnbull, associate producers; Adelaide Heilbron and Ethel Doherty, screenwriters, and George Marion Jr., titles writer (from the novel by Sinclair Lewis); James Wong Howe, cinematographer; Henry Hathaway, assistant director. (Remade as *Untamed* in 1940, directed by George Archainbaud.)

1927

The Rough Riders (Paramount) Released March 15 in New York City, October 21 nationwide. Length: In premiere version, thirteen reels; cut to ten reels (app. 100 minutes) for nationwide release. Preservation status: Fragments at the Library of Congress and the Museum of Modern Art. Cast: Noah Beery, Charles Farrell, George Bancroft, Charles Emmett Mack, Mary Astor, Frank Hopper. Production: Adolph Zukor and Jesse L. Lasky, presenters; B. P. Schulberg, associate producer; Robert N. Lee and Keene Thompson, screenwriters, and George Marion Jr., titles writer (from an adaptation by John Fish Goodrich of an original story by the technical adviser Hermann Hagedorn); James Wong Howe, cinematographer; Henry Hathaway, assistant director. (The writer-director John Milius did his version of the story for television in 1997.)

Hula (Paramount) Released August 27. Length: 64 minutes. Preservation status: 35 mm preserved. Cast: Clara Bow, Clive Brook, Agostino Borgato, Arnold Kent, Albert Gran, Patty DuPont. Production: B. P. Schulberg, associate producer; Ethel Doherty, screenwriter, and George Marion Jr., titles writer (from Doris Anderson's adaptation of Armine von Tempski's novel); William Marshall, cinematographer; Henry Hathaway, assistant director.

The Way of All Flesh (Paramount) Released October 1. Length: 90 minutes. Preservation status: Lost. Cast: Emil Jannings, Belle Bennett, Phyllis Haver. Production: Adolph Zukor and Jesse L. Lasky, presenters; Jules Furthman, screenwriter, and Julian Johnson, titles writer (from Lajos Biro's adaptation of a story by Perley Poore Sheehan); Victor Milner, cinematographer; Henry Hathaway, assistant director. (Remade in 1940, directed by Louis King.)

Academy Award: Jannings, best actor, winner, for this film and *The Last Command.*

1928

The Awakening (Samuel Goldwyn, released through United Artists) Released November 17. Length: 90 minutes. Preservation status: Lost. Cast: Vilma Banky, Walter Byron, Louis Wolheim. Production: Samuel Goldwyn, producer; Carey Wilson, screenwriter, and Katherine Hilliker and H. H. Caldwell, title writers (from an original story by Frances Marion); George Barnes, cinematographer (assistant, Gregg Toland); William Cameron Menzies, art director.

Academy Award nomination: Menzies (submitted, not an official nomination).

1929

Abie's Irish Rose (Paramount) Released January 5. Silent with sound sequences. Length: 129 minutes. Preservation status: 35 mm preserved except for some musical sequences. Cast: Charles "Buddy" Rogers, Nancy Carroll, Jean Hersholt, J. Farrell MacDonald. Production: Adolph Zukor and Jesse L. Lasky, presenters; B. P. Schulberg, associate producer; Jules Furthman, screenwriter, and Herman J. Mankiewicz, Julian Johnson, and Anne Nichols, title writers (from Nichols's play); Harold Rosson, cinematographer. (Remade in 1946, directed by Edward Sutherland.)

Wolf Song (Paramount) Released March 30. Silent with sound sequences. Length: 75 minutes. Preservation status: 35 mm preserved except for some musical sequences. Cast: Gary Cooper, Lupe Velez, Louis Wolheim, Russell "Russ" Columbo. Production: Adolph Zukor and Jesse L. Lasky, presenters; Fleming, producer; John Farrow and Keene Thompson, screenwriters, and Julian Johnson, title writer (from Harvey Fergusson's novel); Allen Siegler, cinematographer.

The Virginian (Paramount) Released November 9. Length: 90 minutes. Cast: Gary Cooper, Walter Huston, Mary Brian, Richard Arlen, Eugene Pallette, Willie Fung. Production: Adolph Zukor and Jesse L. Lasky, presenters; Louis D. Lighton, producer; Howard Estabrook, screenwriter, and Edward E. Paramore, dialogue writer (from Grover Jones and Keene Thompson's adaptation of Owen Wister's novel and the theatrical adaptation by Wister and Kirk La Shelle); J. Roy Hunt and Edward Cronjager, cinematographers; Henry Hathaway, assistant director. (Previously made in 1914 with Dustin Farnum and in 1923 with Kenneth Harlan; remade in 1946 with Joel McCrea; later the basis of a 1960s TV series with James Drury and a 2000 TV movie directed by and starring Bill Pullman.)

1930

Common Clay (Fox) Released August 13. Length: 89 minutes. Cast: Constance Bennett, Lew Ayres, Tully Marshall, Matty Kemp, Beryl Mercer. Production: William Fox, presenter; Jules Furthman, screenwriter (from the play by Cleves Kinkead); Glen MacWilliams, cinematographer. (Previously made in 1919.)

Renegades (Fox) Released October 26. Length: 84 minutes. Cast: Warner Baxter, Myrna Loy, Noah Beery, Bela Lugosi, Victor Jory, Noah Beery Jr. Production: William Fox, presenter; Jules Furthman, screenwriter (from the novel *Le renégat* by André Armandy); L. William O'Connell, cinematographer.

1931

Around the World in Eighty Minutes (United Artists) Released December 12. Length: 80 minutes. Cast: Douglas Fairbanks, Fleming, Sessue Hayakawa, Duke Kahanamoku, Mickey Mouse. Production: Fairbanks, producer; Robert E. Sherwood, screenwriter; Harry Sharp and Chuck Lewis, cinematographers.

1932

The Wet Parade (MGM) Released March 26. Length: 122 minutes. Principal shooting took place January 18–February 23, but Fleming began developing the project on September 21, 1931, and did retakes from February 24 to March 8. Cast: Dorothy Jordan, Lewis Stone, Robert Young, Walter Huston, Jimmy Durante, Wallace Ford, Myrna Loy, Joan Marsh, Clarence Muse, Clara Blandick. Production: Hunt Stromberg, producer; John Lee Mahin, screenwriter (from the novel by Upton Sinclair); George Barnes, cinematographer.

Red Dust (MGM) Released October 22. Length: 84 minutes. Production dates: August 10–October 8; retakes on October 11. Cast: Clark Gable, Jean Harlow, Gene Raymond, Mary Astor, Donald Crisp, Tully Marshall, Willie Fung. Production: Hunt Stromberg, producer; John Lee Mahin, screenwriter (from the play by Wilson Collison); Harold Rosson, cinematographer. (Remade as *Congo Maisie* in 1940, directed by H. C. Potter, and as *Mogambo* in 1953, directed by John Ford, also with Clark Gable, also written by John Lee Mahin.)

1933

The White Sister (MGM) Released April 14. Length: 110 minutes. Fleming originally signed a contract for this picture on July 29, 1932, but it was waived so he could work on *Red Dust*. Production dates: December 1932–March 1, 1933, retakes on March 2. Cast: Helen Hayes, Clark Gable, Lewis Stone, May Robson, Edward Arnold. Production: Hunt Stromberg, producer; Donald Ogden Stewart, screenwriter (from the novel by F. Marion Crawford); William Daniels, cinematographer. (Previously made in 1915 with Viola Allen and in 1923 with Lillian Gish.)

Bombshell (MGM) Released October 13. Length: 96 minutes. Fleming went on contract May 6. Production dates: August 7–September 15, 1933, with retakes on September 20 and 21. Cast: Jean Harlow, Lee Tracy, Frank Morgan, Franchot Tone, Pat O'Brien, Ted Healy, Louise Beavers, Isabel Jewell, C. Aubrey Smith. Production: Fleming, producer; Hunt Stromberg, associate producer; John Lee Mahin and Jules Furthman, screenwriters (from a play by Caroline Francke and Mack Crane); Harold Rosson and Chester Lyons, cinematographers.

1934

Treasure Island (MGM) Released August 17. Length: 105 minutes. Fleming went on payroll on February 8. Production began March 20 and ended May 29, with retakes on June 8, 9, 25, and 27. Cast: Wallace Beery, Nigel Bruce, Jackie Cooper, Lionel Barrymore, Otto Kruger, Lewis Stone, Charles "Chic" Sale, Charles Bennett, Douglas Dumbrille. Production: Hunt Stromberg, producer; John Lee Mahin, screenwriter (from the novel by Robert Louis Stevenson); Ray June, Clyde DeVinna, and Harold Rosson, cinematographers. (*Treasure Island* has been filmed numerous times, most famously by Byron Haskin for Walt Disney in 1950, with Robert Newton and Bobby Driscoll; in 2002, Disney also produced and distributed the futuristic comic cartoon feature *Treasure Planet*, which in many ways pays homage to Fleming's version.)

1935

Reckless (MGM) Released April 19. Length: 99 minutes. Production dates: November 27, 1934–February 25, retakes on March 8, 9, and 11. Cast: Jean Harlow, William Powell, Franchot Tone, May Robson, Ted Healy, Nat Pendleton, Rosalind Russell, Mickey Rooney. Production: David O. Selznick, producer; P. J. Wolfson, screenwriter (from a story by Selznick under the pseudonym Oliver Jeffries); George Folsey, cinematographer.

The Farmer Takes a Wife (Fox) Released August 2. Length: 91 minutes. Fleming moved to the Fox lot on February 26 and returned to MGM for the reshoots on *Reckless*, before this film's principal photography took place from early April to mid-May. Cast: Janet Gaynor, Henry Fonda, Charles Bickford, Slim Summerville, Andy Devine, Jane Withers, Margaret Hamilton, Siegfried "Sig" Rumann, John Qualen. Production: Winfield Sheehan, producer; Edwin Burke, screenwriter (from Frank B. Elser and Marc Connelly's stage adaptation of Walter D. Edmonds's novel *Rome Haul*). (Remade as a Betty Grable musical in 1953, directed by Henry Levin.)

1937

Captains Courageous (MGM) Released June 25. Length: 116 minutes. Production dates: second-unit photography began in October 1935, principal photography began September 22, 1936, and Fleming didn't finish doing retakes until March 18, 1937. Cast: Freddie Bartholomew, Spencer Tracy, Lionel Barrymore, Melvyn Douglas, Mickey Rooney, John Carradine, Leo G. Carroll, Jack LaRue. Production: Louis D. Lighton, producer; John Lee Mahin, Marc Connelly, and Dale Van Every, screenwriters (from the novel by Rudyard Kipling); Harold Rosson, cinematographer. (Remade for TV both in 1977, with Karl Malden, Jonathan Kahn, and Ricardo Montalban, and in 1996, with Robert Urich, Kenny Vadas, and Colin Cunningham, in the roles originally played by Barrymore, Bartholomew, and Tracy, respectively.)

Academy Award nominations: Metro-Goldwyn-Mayer, outstanding production; Tracy, best actor (winner); Elmo Veron, film editing; Mahin, Connelly, Van Every, screenplay.

1938

Test Pilot (MGM) Released April 22. Length: 118 minutes. Production dates: December 1, 1937–February 18, 1938, with retakes March 30–early April. Cast: Clark Gable, Myrna Loy, Spencer Tracy, Lionel Barrymore, Louis Jean Heydt, Gloria Holden, Virginia Grey, Samuel S. Hinds, Martin Spellman. Production: Louis D. Lighton, producer; Vincent Lawrence and Waldemar Young, screenwriters (from an original story by Frank "Spig" Wead); Ray June, cinematographer.

Academy Award nominations: Metro-Goldwyn-Mayer, outstanding production; Tom Held, film editing; Wead, original story.

1939

The Wizard of Oz (MGM) Released August 25. Length: 101 minutes. Production dates: September 30, 1938 (recording); October 13, 1938 (filming, under Richard Thorpe, whose footage was scrapped)–March 16, 1939 (under King Vidor, who shot the Kansas scenes; Jack Conway and W. S. Van Dyke are often cited as contributors according to an erroneous column item). Fleming began shooting November 4, 1938, and continued until February 17, 1939. Cast: Judy Garland, Frank Morgan, Ray Bolger, Bert Lahr, Jack Haley, Billie Burke, Margaret Hamilton, Charley Grapewin, Clara Blandick. Production: Mervyn LeRoy, producer; Noel Langley, Florence Ryerson, and Edgar Allan Woolf, screenwriters (from the novel by L. Frank Baum); Harold Rosson, cinematographer.

Academy Award nominations: Metro-Goldwyn-Mayer, outstanding production; Cedric Gibbons, William Horning, art direction; Rosson (submitted, not an official nomination), color cinematography; Herbert Stothart, original score (winner); song, "Over the Rainbow," Harold Arlen, E. Y. Harburg (winners); special effects, A. Arnold Gillespie, Douglas Shearer. Special award to Judy Garland "for outstanding performance as a screen juvenile during the past year."

Gone With the Wind (Selznick International, released by MGM) Released December 15. Length: 222 minutes. Production dates: December 10, 1938–February 15, 1939. Fleming directed from March 2 to April 27, and from May 5 to July 1, with reshoots during the first two weeks of October. Cast: Clark Gable, Vivien Leigh, Olivia de Havilland, Leslie Howard, Thomas Mitchell, Hattie McDaniel, Butterfly McQueen, Victor Jory, Evelyn Keyes, Ann Rutherford, Laura Hope Crews, Harry Davenport, Rand Brooks, Cammie King, Mickey Kuhn, Ward Bond. Production: David O. Selznick, producer; Sidney Howard, screenwriter (from the novel by Margaret Mitchell); Ernest Haller, cinematographer.

Academy Award nominations: Selznick International, outstanding production (winner); Gable, actor; Leigh, actress (winner); de Havilland, supporting actress; McDaniel, supporting actress (winner); Lyle Wheeler, art direction (winner); Haller, Ray Rennahan, cinematography (color) (winners); Fleming, direction (winner); Hal C. Kern, James E. Newcom, film editing (winner); Max Steiner, original score; Samuel Goldwyn Studio, sound recording; John R. Cosgrove, Fred Albin, Arthur Johns, special effects; Howard, screenplay (winner). Special award to William Cameron Menzies for outstanding achievement in the use of color; scientific/technical award for several technical advances.

1941

Dr. Jekyll and Mr. Hyde (MGM) Released August 12. Length: 127 minutes. Production dates: February 4–April 18. Cast: Spencer Tracy, Ingrid Bergman, Lana Turner, Donald Crisp, Ian Hunter, Barton MacLane, and C. Aubrey Smith. Production: Victor Saville, producer; John Lee Mahin, screenwriter (from the novella by Robert Louis Stevenson); Joseph Ruttenberg, cinematographer. (This was a remake of the 1932 Paramount film directed by Rouben Mamoulian, with Fredric March.)

Academy Award nominations: Ruttenberg, black-and-white cinematography; Harold F. Kress, film editing; Franz Waxman, musical score of a dramatic picture.

1942

Tortilla Flat (MGM) Released May 21. Length: 105 minutes. Production dates: November 23, 1941–February 12, 1942; retakes February 23–24. Cast: Spencer Tracy, Hedy Lamarr, John Garfield, Frank Morgan, Akim Tamiroff, Sheldon Leonard, John Qualen, Donald Meek, Connie Gilchrist, Allen Jenkins, Henry O'Neill. Production: Sam Zimbalist, producer; John Lee Mahin and Benjamin Glazer, screenwriters (from the novel by John Steinbeck); Karl Freund, cinematographer.

Academy Award nomination: Frank Morgan, supporting actor.

1943

A Guy Named Joe (MGM) Released December 24. Length: 118 minutes. Production began February 15; the *The New York Times* reported on September 19 that Fleming completed principal shooting that week. He shot a new closing sequence for the film starting on November 10. Cast: Spencer Tracy, Irene Dunne, Van Johnson, Ward Bond, James Gleason, Lionel Barrymore, Barry Nelson. Production: Everett Riskin, producer; Dalton Trumbo, screenwriter (from Frederick Hazlitt Brennan's adaptation of Chandler Sprague and David Boehm's original story); George Folsey and Karl Freund, cinematographers.

Academy Award nomination: Sprague, Boehm, original story.

1946

Adventure (MGM) Released February 19. Length: 125 minutes. Production dates: Fleming began preparing the project in February 1945, started shooting in mid-May, and completed principal photography on September 21. He concluded postproduction on November 12 and left the studio for a three-month leave that turned out to be permanent. Cast: Clark Gable, Greer Garson, Joan Blondell, Thomas Mitchell, Tom Tully, Richard Haydn, Lina Romay, Harry Davenport, Tito Renaldo. Production: Sam Zimbalist, producer; Frederick Hazlitt Brennan and Vincent Lawrence, screenwriters (from Anthony Veiller's and William H. Wright's adaptations of Clyde Brion Davis's novel); Joseph Ruttenberg, cinematographer.

1948

Joan of Arc (Sierra Pictures, released by RKO) Released November 10. Length: Cut to 100 minutes in 1950, restored to 153 minutes in 1998. Production dates: September 16–December 18, 1947; retakes February 16–25, 1948. Cast: Ingrid Bergman, José Ferrer, Leif Erickson, John Ireland, George

Zucco, George Coulouris, John Emery, Gene Lockhart, J. Carrol Naish, Jeff Corey, Hurd Hatfield, Shepperd Strudwick. Production: Walter Wanger, producer; Maxwell Anderson and Andrew Solt, screenwriters (from Anderson's play *Joan of Lorraine*); Joseph Valentine, cinematographer.

Academy Award nominations: Ferrer, supporting actor; Bergman, actress; Richard Day, Edwin Casey Roberts, Joseph Kish, art direction (color); Joseph Valentine, William V. Skall, Winton Hoch, color cinematography (winners); Dorothy Jeakins, Barbara Karinska, costume design (color) (winners); Frank Sullivan, film editing; Hugo Friedhofer, music; Walter Wanger, special award "for distinguished service to the industry."

UNCREDITED WORK

1938

The Crowd Roars (MGM) Released August 5. Length: 92 minutes. Production dates: April 25–May 27. Richard Thorpe is credited director. Fleming did retakes in mid-July. Cast: Robert Taylor, Edward Arnold, Frank Morgan, Gene Reynolds, Maureen O'Sullivan, Lionel Stander, Jane Wyman, Nat Pendleton. Production: Sam Zimbalist, producer; Thorpe, director; Thomas Lennon, George Bruce, and George Oppenheimer, screenwriters (from a story by Bruce); John Seitz and Oliver Marsh, cinematographers. (Remade as *Killer McCoy*, directed by Roy Rowland.)

Too Hot to Handle (MGM) Released September 16. Length: 105 minutes. Jack Conway is credited director. Eleven reels. Production began on May 9 and ended in August. The *Hollywood Reporter* stated on July 30, "Jack Conway collapsed on the set . . . stricken with flu, taken home, Victor Fleming assigned to direct." Cast: Clark Gable, Myrna Loy, Walter Pidgeon, Walter Connolly, Leo Carrillo, Marjorie Main, Willie Fung. Production: Lawrence Weingarten, producer; Laurence Stallings and John Lee Mahin, screenwriters (from a story by Len Hammond); Harold Rosson, cinematographer.

The Great Waltz (MGM) Released November 4. Julien Duvivier is credited director. Length: 102 minutes. Production began in early May. The *Hollywood Reporter* announced on September 19, "After seven weeks work on *The Great Waltz*, Victor Fleming and John Lee Mahin leave for Rogue River fishing." After Fleming remade substantial portions of the film, Josef von Sternberg lent a hand on montages and the concluding scenes and finished up on September 21. Cast: Luise Rainer, Fernand Gravet, Miliza Korjus, Hugh Herbert, Lionel Atwill, Curt Bois, Leonid Kinskey, Herman Bing, Sig Rumann, Henry Hull. Production: Bernard H. Hyman, producer; Samuel Hoffenstein and Walter Reisch, screenwriters (from Gottfried Reinhardt's story); Joseph Ruttenberg, cinematographer.

Academy Award nominations: Korjus, supporting actress; Ruttenberg, cinematography (winner); Tom Held, film editing.

1940

Boom Town (MGM) Released August 30. Length: 118 minutes. Jack Conway is credited director. Production started in March; a Jimmie Fidler column dated May 21 reports on Fleming shooting retakes. Cast: Clark Gable, Spencer Tracy, Claudette Colbert, Hedy Lamarr, Frank Morgan, Lionel Atwill, Chill Wills. Production: Sam Zimbalist, producer; John Lee Mahin, screenwriter; Harold Rosson, cinematographer.

FILMS NOT MADE, OR DIRECTED BY OTHERS

1924

In February, Fleming announced as director of *The Mountebank*, from the novel by William J. Locke. Released in September as *The Side Show of Life*, directed by Herbert Brenon.

In April, Fleming announced as director of *The Honor of His House*, a remake of the 1918 film directed by William DeMille, with Sessue Hayakawa. Not made.

In June, Fleming announced as director of Zane Grey's *Border Legion*. Released in October, directed by William K. Howard. Also that month, Fleming announced as director of *Tongues of Flame*, from the novel by Peter MacFarlane, starring Thomas Meighan and Bessie Love. Released in December, directed by Joseph Henabery.

In October, Fleming's Paramount production of Bret Harte's *Outcasts of Poker Flat* (first filmed by John Ford at Universal in 1919) is canceled when the actress Patterson Dial breaks her jaw in an accident.

1925

Fleming announced as director of *White Heat*, from a *Saturday Evening Post* story by R. G. Kirk, screenplay by Percy Heath, starring Thomas Meighan. Made at First National in 1926 as *Men of Steel*, directed by George Archainbaud and starring Milton Sills, who also got a screenplay credit.

In December, Fleming takes himself off *Behind the Front* to replace James Cruze on *The Blind Goddess.* Edward Sutherland directs *Behind the Front,* released in 1926.

1928

In July, Fleming announced as director of *Burlesque*, the first all-talking picture for Paramount. Released as *The Dance of Life* in 1929, directed by John Cromwell and Edward Sutherland.

1930

In May, Fleming announced as director of *Painted Lady* at Fox, later made as Spencer Tracy film *The Painted Woman* in 1932, directed by John Blystone.

In September, Fleming signs with Columbia to direct *Arizona*, starring Jack Holt. The studio cancels the film and later reactivates it with George Seitz directing.

1934

In June, Fleming announced as director of *Indochina*, to star Joan Crawford. Not made.

1936

On January 10, Sidney Franklin takes over direction of *The Good Earth* following complications from Fleming's kidney stone surgery.

1937

In October, Fleming and Lighton announced as director and producer of *Kim*, based on the Rudyard Kipling novel. Finally made by MGM in 1950 and released in January 1951, directed by Victor Saville.

1938

In May, Fleming announced as director of Clark Gable/William Powell picture based on P. C. Wren's novel *The Spur of Pride.* Not made.

1939

In December, MGM backs out of a planned film of John Steinbeck's *Red Pony*, to star Spencer Tracy. Later made independently, directed by Lewis Milestone, and released in 1949.

1940

In May, Fleming announced as director of Clark Gable picture based on life of nineteenth-century outlaw Soapy Smith. Released October 1, 1941, as *Honky Tonk*, directed by Jack Conway, with the name of Gable's character changed to Candy Johnson.

1941

On May 19, Fleming ends production of *The Yearling* in Ocala, Florida, after seventeen days in production. The picture, using Fleming's second-unit footage and directed by Clarence Brown, is released in 1946.

On August 30, Fleming and Howard Hawks announce plans for a co-production of the Ernest Hemingway story "The Short Happy Life of Francis Macomber," to star Gary Cooper. Their version is not made. *The Macomber Affair*, directed by Zoltan Korda, is made in 1947, starring Gregory Peck.

1942

In early March, MacKinlay Kantor writes a treatment for *Buffalo Bill*, to star Clark Gable. The project is turned down by the MGM front office.

In mid-March, Fleming is announced as director of *Shadow of the Wing*, a production canceled when Clark Gable joins the Army Air Forces.

1948

In July, RKO pulls out of plans to film *The Robe*, with a script by Maxwell Anderson and Andrew Solt, to star Gregory Peck. It eventually is made at 20th Century–Fox in 1953, with a screenplay by Albert Maltz and Philip Dunne, starring Richard Burton.

WORK AS CINEMATOGRAPHER

Apart from *The Envoy Extraordinary*, which he shot for the short-lived Santa Barbara Motion Picture Company in 1914, Fleming's entire output as a director of photography was linked to the director Allan Dwan, the writing-directing team of John Emerson and Anita Loos, and the producer and star Douglas Fairbanks. Many silent-film credits have been lost even for films that have survived. But strong written and/or anecdotal evidence suggests that Fleming was behind the camera for the following films:

WITH DWAN

Betty of Greystone (Fine Arts–Triangle, 1916). Starring Dorothy Gish.

WITH DWAN AND FAIRBANKS

The Habit of Happiness (Fine Arts–Triangle, 1916). With Dorothy West.

The Good Bad Man (Fine Arts–Triangle, 1916). With Bessie Love.

The Half-Breed (Fine Arts–Triangle, 1916). With Alma Rubens and Jewel Carmen.

Manhattan Madness (Fine Arts–Triangle, 1916). With Jewel Carmen.

WITH EMERSON, LOOS, AND FAIRBANKS

His Picture in the Papers (Fine Arts–Triangle, 1916). With Loretta Blake.

The Americano (Fine Arts–Triangle, 1916). With Alma Rubens.

In Again, Out Again (Artcraft-Paramount, 1917). With Arline Pretty.

Wild and Woolly (Artcraft-Paramount, 1917). With Eileen Percy.

Down to Earth (Artcraft-Paramount, 1917). With Eileen Percy.

OTHER FAIRBANKS FILMS SHOT BY FLEMING

American Aristocracy (Fine Arts–Triangle, 1916). Directed by Lloyd Ingraham. With Jewel Carmen.

The Matrimaniac (Fine Arts–Triangle, 1916). Directed by Paul Powell. With Constance Talmadge and Winifred Westover.

The Man from Painted Post (Artcraft-Paramount, 1917). Directed by Joseph Henabery. With Eileen Percy.

His Majesty, the American (United Artists, 1919). Directed by Joseph Henabery. With Marjorie Daw and Lillian Langdon.

Bibliography

BOOKS

Adler, Larry. *It Ain't Necessarily So.* New York: Grove, 1987.

Agee, James. *Agee on Film (Volume 1), Reviews and Comments.* New York: McDowell, Obolensky, 1958.

Andersen, Christopher. *An Affair to Remember: The Remarkable Love Story of Katharine Hepburn and Spencer Tracy.* New York: William Morrow, 1997.

Anderson, Hesper. *South Mountain Road.* New York: Simon & Schuster, 2000.

Anderson, Maxwell. *Joan of Lorraine.* Washington, D.C.: Anderson House, 1946.

Arce, Hector. *Gary Cooper: An Intimate Biography.* New York: Morrow, 1979.

Armandy, André. *My Story.* Garden City, N.Y.: Doubleday, 1959.

———. *Renegade.* New York: Brentano's, 1930.

Astor, Mary. *A Life on Film.* New York: Delacorte, 1971.

Atkins, Irene Kahn, ed. *Arthur Jacobson.* Directors Guild of America Oral History Series. Metuchen, N.J.: Scarecrow, 1991.

Avery, Laurence G., ed. *Dramatist in America: Letters of Maxwell Anderson, 1912–1958.* Chapel Hill: University of North Carolina Press, 1977.

Bacall, Lauren. *By Myself.* New York: Alfred A. Knopf, 1978.

Baker, Ray Stannard. *American Chronicle.* New York: Scribner, 1945.

Bakewell, William. *Hollywood Be Thy Name.* Metuchen, N.J.: Scarecrow, 1991.

Barker, Felix. *The Oliviers: A Biography.* London: Hamish Hamilton, 1953.

Barrios, Richard. *A Song in the Dark: The Birth of the Musical Film.* New York: Oxford University Press, 1995.

Basinger, Jeanine. *Silent Stars.* New York: Alfred A. Knopf, 1999.

Baum, L. Frank. *The Wonderful Wizard of Oz.* Chicago: George M. Hill, 1900.

Beauchamp, Cari. *Without Lying Down: Frances Marion and the Powerful Women of Early Hollywood.* Berkeley: University of California Press, 1997.

Beecher, Elizabeth. *The Luckiest Guy in the World.* Racine, Wis.: Whitman Publishing, 1947.

Behlmer, Rudy, ed. *Henry Hathaway.* Directors Guild of America Oral History Series. Lanham, Md.: Scarecrow, 2001.

———. *Memo from David O. Selznick.* New York: Viking, 1972.

Bell, Millicent. *Marquand: An American Life.* Boston: Little, Brown, 1979.

Bennett, Joan, and Lois Kibbee. *The Bennett Playbill.* New York: Holt, Rinehart & Winston, 1970.

Benson, Jackson, ed. *The Short Novels of John Steinbeck.* Durham, N.C.: Duke University Press, 1990.

Bentley, Toni. *Costumes by Karinska.* New York: Abrams, 1995.

Bercovici, Konrad. *Ghitza, and Other Romances of Gypsy Blood.* New York: Boni and Liveright, 1921.

Bergman, Ingrid, and Alan Burgess. *My Story.* New York: Delacorte, 1980.

Bernstein, Matthew. *Walter Wanger: Hollywood Independent.* Berkeley: University of California Press, 1987.

Bessie, Alvah. *Inquisition in Eden.* Berlin: Seven Seas Publishers, 1967.

Bing, Rudolf. *5,000 Nights at the Opera.* Garden City, N.Y.: Doubleday, 1972.

Bingham, Madeleine. *The Great Lover: The Life and Art of Herbert Beerbohm Tree.* New York: Atheneum, 1979.

Black, Gregory. *Hollywood Censored: Morality Codes, Catholics, and the Movies.* New York: Cambridge University Press, 1994.

Bodrey-Summers, Penelope. *Carl Akeley: African Collector, Africa's Savior.* New York: Paragon House, 1991.

Bogdanovich, Peter. *Allan Dwan: The Last Pioneer.* London: Studio Vista, 1971.

———. *John Ford.* London: Studio Vista, 1967.

———. *Who the Devil Made It.* New York: Ballantine, 1997.

Breivold, Scott, ed. *Howard Hawks: Interviews.* Jackson: University Press of Mississippi, 2006.

Bronson, Betty. Unpublished autobiography, Betty Bronson Papers, University of California, Los Angeles.

Brown, Karl. *Adventures with D. W. Griffith.* New York: Farrar, Straus & Giroux, 1973.

Brownlow, Kevin. *The Parade's Gone By.* New York: Alfred A. Knopf, 1968.

———. *The War, the West, and the Wilderness.* New York: Alfred A. Knopf, 1978.

Buñuel, Luis. *An Unspeakable Betrayal: Selected Writings of Luis Buñuel.* Translated by Garrett White. Berkeley: University of California Press, 2000.

Burke, Billie. *With a Feather on My Nose.* New York: Appleton-Century-Crofts, 1949.

Butler, Rachel Barton. *Mamma's Affair.* New York: Samuel French, 1925.

Callow, Ridgeway. *An Assistant Director in Hollywood.* Edited by Rudy Behlmer. Glen Rock, N.J.: Microforming Corporation of America, 1977.

Canutt, Yakima. *Stunt Man.* With Oliver Drake. New York: Walker, 1979.

Carey, Gary. *Anita Loos: A Biography.* London: Bloomsbury, 1988.

Carmichael, Hoagy. *Sometimes I Wonder.* New York: Farrar, Straus & Giroux, 1965.

Castle, Irene. *Castles in the Air.* With Bob Duncan and Wanda Duncan. Garden City, N.Y.: Doubleday, 1958.

Ceplair, Larry, and Steven Englund. *The Inquisition in Hollywood: Politics in the Film Community.* Garden City, N.Y.: Anchor/Doubleday, 1980.

Chaplin, Charles. *My Autobiography.* New York: Simon & Schuster, 1964.

Charyn, Jerome. *Gangsters & Gold-Diggers: Old New York, the Jazz Age, and the Birth of Broadway.* New York: Four Walls Eight Windows, 2003.

Clements, Kendrick A. *Woodrow Wilson: World Statesman.* Boston: Twayne, 1987.

Coghlan, Frank, Jr. *They Still Call Me Junior: Autobiography of a Child Star.* Jefferson, N.C.: McFarland, 1993.

Connelly, Marc. *Voices Offstage.* New York: Holt, Rinehart & Winston, 1968.

Conrad, Joseph. *Lord Jim.* Edinburgh: Blackwood, 1900.

Cook, Bruce. *Dalton Trumbo.* New York: Scribner, 1977.

Cooke, Alistair. *Douglas Fairbanks: The Making of a Screen Character.* New York: Museum of Modern Art, 1940.

Cooper, Jackie. *Please Don't Shoot My Dog.* With Dick Kleiner. New York: William Morrow, 1981.

Corliss, Richard, ed. *The Hollywood Screenwriters.* New York: Avon, 1972.

Cox, Stephen. *The Munchkins of Oz.* Nashville: Cumberland House, 1996.

Crawford, F. Marion. *The White Sister.* New York: Macmillan, 1909.

Cripps, Thomas. *Slow Fade to Black: The Negro in American Film, 1900–1942.* New York: Oxford University Press, 1977.

Cronin, Paul, ed. *George Stevens: Interviews.* Jackson: University Press of Mississippi, 2004.

Crowther, Bosley. *Hollywood Rajah: The Life and Times of Louis B. Mayer.* New York: Holt, Rinehart & Winston, 1960.

———. *The Lion's Share: The Story of an Entertainment Empire.* New York: Dutton, 1957.

David, Saul. *The Industry.* New York: Times Books, 1981.

Davidson, Bill. *The Real and the Unreal.* New York: Harper & Brothers, 1961.

———. *Spencer Tracy: Tragic Idol.* London: Sidgwick & Jackson, 1987.

Davis, Clyde Brion. *The Anointed.* New York: Farrar & Rinehart, 1937.

Davis, Ronald L. *Just Making Movies.* Jackson: University Press of Mississippi, 2005.

Day, Beth. *This Was Hollywood.* London: Sidgwick & Jackson, 1960.

DeMille, Cecil B. *Autobiography.* Englewood Cliffs, N.J.: Prentice-Hall, 1959.

DeMille, Richard. *My Secret Mother, Lorna Moon.* New York: Farrar, Straus & Giroux, 1998.

Desrichard, Yves. *Julien Duvivier: Cinquante ans de noirs destins.* Paris: BiFi, 2001.

Didion, Joan. *The Year of Magical Thinking.* New York: Alfred A. Knopf, 2005.

DiLeo, John. *100 Great Film Performances You Should Remember but Probably Don't.* New York: Limelight Editions, 2002.

Doherty, Thomas. *Pre-code Hollywood: Sex, Immorality, and Insurrection in American Cinema, 1930–1934.* New York: Columbia University Press, 1999.

Dos Passos, John. *1919.* Boston: Houghton Mifflin, 1932.

Dowd, Nancy, and David Shepherd, eds. *King Vidor.* Directors Guild of America Oral History Series. Metuchen, N.J.: Scarecrow, 1988.

Drew, William M. *Speaking of Silents: First Ladies of the Screen.* Lanham, Md.: Vestal, 1989.

Dumke, Glenn S. *The Boom of the Eighties.* San Marino, Calif.: Huntington Library, 1944.

Dunne, Philip. *Take Two: A Life in Movies and Politics.* New York: McGraw-Hill, 1980.

Edmonds, Walter D. *Rome Haul.* Boston: Little, Brown, 1929.

Eisenstein, Sergei. *Beyond the Stars: The Memoirs of Sergei Eisenstein.* Edited by Richard Taylor. Calcutta: Seagull Books, 1995.

Erens, Patricia. *The Jew in American Cinema.* Bloomington: Indiana University Press, 1984.

Eyman, Scott. *Five American Cinematographers.* Metuchen, N.J.: Scarecrow, 1987.

———. *Lion of Hollywood: The Life and Legend of Louis B. Mayer.* New York: Simon & Schuster, 2005.

———. *Mary Pickford, America's Sweetheart.* New York: D. I. Fine, 1990.

———. *Print the Legend: The Life and Times of John Ford.* New York: Simon & Schuster, 1999.

———. *The Speed of Sound: Hollywood and the Coming of Talkies.* New York: Simon & Schuster, 1997.

Falzon, Christopher. *Philosophy Goes to the Movies.* London: Routledge, 2002.

Fergusson, Harvey. *Wolf Song.* New York: Alfred A. Knopf, 1927.

Flamini, Roland. *Scarlett, Rhett, and a Cast of Thousands.* New York: Macmillan, 1975.

———. *Thalberg.* New York: Crown, 1994.

Fleming, Thomas. *The Illusion of Victory: America in World War I.* New York: Basic Books, 2003.

Franklin, Sidney A. "We Laughed and We Cried." With Kevin Brownlow. Unpublished autobiography.

Fricke, John, Jay Scarfone, and William Stillman. *"The Wizard of Oz": The Official 50th Anniversary Pictorial History.* New York: Warner Books, 1989.

Fuchs, Daniel. *The Golden West: Hollywood Stories.* Boston: Black Sparrow Books, 2005.

Gabler, Neal. *An Empire of Their Own: How the Jews Invented Hollywood.* New York: Crown, 1988.

———. *Walt Disney: The Triumph of the American Imagination.* New York: Alfred A. Knopf, 2006.

Garceau, Jean. *"Dear Mr. G——": The Biography of Clark Gable.* With Inez Cocke. Boston: Little, Brown, 1961.

Garnett, Tay. *Light Your Torches and Pull Up Your Tights.* With Fredda Dudley Balling. New Rochelle, N.Y.: Arlington House, 1973.

Gehring, Wes. *Irene Dunne: First Lady of Hollywood.* Lanham, Md.: Scarecrow, 2003.

Geist, Kenneth L. *Pictures Will Talk: The Life and Films of Joseph L. Mankiewicz.* New York: Scribner, 1978.

Gish, Lillian. *The Movies, Mr. Griffith, and Me.* Englewood Cliffs, N.J.: Prentice-Hall, 1969.

Goldstein, Laurence, and Ira Konigsberg, eds. *The Movies: Texts, Receptions, Exposures.* Ann Arbor: University of Michigan Press, 1996.

Goodman, Ezra. *The Fifty-Year Decline and Fall of Hollywood.* New York: Simon & Schuster, 1961.

Gordon, Mary. *Joan of Arc.* New York: Viking, 2000.

Grady, Billy. *The Irish Peacock.* New Rochelle, N.Y.: Arlington House, 1972.

Graham, Sheilah. *College of One.* New York: Viking, 1967.

———. *Hollywood Revisited: A Fiftieth Anniversary Celebration.* New York: St. Martin's, 1985.

Granger, Stewart. *Sparks Fly Upward.* New York: Putnam, 1981.

Graulich, Melody, and Stephen Tatum, eds. *Reading "The Virginian" in the New West.* Lincoln: University of Nebraska Press, 2003.

Greene, Graham. *The Graham Greene Film Reader.* Edited by David Parkinson. London: Carcanet, 1994.

Grey, Zane. *The Call of the Canyon.* New York: Harper & Brothers, 1924.

———. *To the Last Man.* New York: McKinlay, Stone & Mackenzie, 1922.

Gruber, Frank. *The Pulp Jungle.* Los Angeles: Sherbourne, 1967.

Guilaroff, Sydney. *Crowning Glory.* With Cathy Griffin. Santa Monica, Calif.: General Publishing Group, 1996.

Haley, Jack. *Heart of the Tin Man: The Collected Writings of Jack Haley.* Edited by Mitchell Cohen. Beverly Hills, Calif.: Tinmanonline.com, 2000.

Hamalian, Leo, ed. *William Saroyan: The Man and the Writer Remembered.* Madison, N.J.: Fairleigh Dickinson University Press, 1987.

Hancock, Ralph, and Letitia Fairbanks. *Douglas Fairbanks: The Fourth Musketeer.* New York: Holt, 1953.

Harap, Louis. *Dramatic Encounters: The Jewish Presence in Twentieth-Century American Drama, Poetry, and Humor and the Black-Jewish Literary Relationship.* New York: Greenwood, 1987.

Harmetz, Aljean. *The Making of "The Wizard of Oz."* New York: Alfred A. Knopf, 1977.

———. *On the Road to Tara: The Making of "Gone With the Wind."* New York: Harry N. Abrams, 1996.

Harriman, Margaret Case. *The Vicious Circle.* New York: Rinehart, 1951.

Harris, Leon. *Upton Sinclair: American Rebel.* New York: Thomas Y. Crowell, 1975.

Harty, Kevin J., ed. *Cinema Arthuriana.* Jefferson, N.C.: McFarland, 2002.

Harvey, James. *Romantic Comedy in Hollywood, from Lubitsch to Sturges.* New York: Alfred A. Knopf, 1987.

Harwell, Richard, ed. *GWTW: The Screenplay by Sidney Howard.* London: Lorrimer, 1980.

———. *Margaret Mitchell's "Gone With the Wind" Letters, 1936–1949.* New York: Macmillan, 1976.

Haver, Ronald. *David O. Selznick's Hollywood.* New York: Alfred A. Knopf, 1980.

———. *"A Star Is Born": The Making of the 1954 Movie and Its 1983 Restoration.* New York: Alfred A. Knopf, 1988.

Hay, Peter. *MGM: When the Lion Roars.* With Woolsey Ackerman. Atlanta: Turner Publishing, 1991.

Head, Edith, and Paddy Calistro. *Edith Head's Hollywood.* New York: Dutton, 1983.

Hearn, Michael Patrick, ed. *The Annotated Wizard of Oz.* New York: C.N. Potter, 1973.

———. *The Wizard of Oz: The Screenplay*. New York: Delta, 1989.

Hecht, Ben. *A Child of the Century*. New York: Simon & Schuster, 1954.

Hemingway, Ernest. *Green Hills of Africa*. New York: Scribner, 1935.

Henabery, Joseph. *Before, In, and After Hollywood*. Edited by Anthony Slide. Lanham, Md.: Scarecrow, 1997.

Hepburn, Katharine. *Me: Stories of My Life*. New York: Alfred A. Knopf, 1991.

Herndon, Booton. *Mary Pickford and Douglas Fairbanks*. New York: Norton, 1977.

Higham, Charles. *Hollywood Cameramen: Sources of Light*. Bloomington: Indiana University Press, 1970.

History of Laclede, Camden, Dallas, Webster, Wright, Texas, Pulaski, Phelps & Dent Counties, Missouri, from Earliest Times to the Present. Chicago: Goodspeed, 1889; repr. Salem, Mass.: Higginson Book Co., 1997.

Hobbins, Daniel. *The Trial of Joan of Arc*. Cambridge, Mass.: Harvard University Press, 2005.

Hoopes, Roy. *Cain*. Carbondale: Southern Illinois University Press, 1982.

House, Boyce. *Oil Boom*. Caldwell, Idaho: Caxton Printers, 1941.

Howard, Leslie Ruth. *A Quite Remarkable Father*. New York: Harcourt, Brace, 1959.

Howard, Ronald. *In Search of My Father*. New York: St. Martin's, 1981.

Hughes, Laurence A., ed. *The Truth About the Movies, by the Stars*. Hollywood, Calif.: Hollywood Publishers, 1924.

Jablonski, Edward. *Harold Arlen, Happy with the Blues*. New York: Da Capo, 1985.

Jacobs, Lewis. *The Rise of the American Film*. New York: Teachers College Press, 1939.

Jannings, Emil. *Theater, Film—Das Leben und ich*. Berchtesgarten: Zimmer & Herzog, 1951.

Jordan, René. *Clark Gable*. New York: Pyramid, 1973.

Kael, Pauline. *Deeper into Movies*. Boston: Little, Brown, 1973.

———. *5001 Nights at the Movies*. New York: Holt, Rinehart & Winston, 1982.

———. *When the Lights Go Down*. New York: Holt, Rinehart & Winston, 1980.

Kanin, Garson. *Remembering Mr. Maugham*. New York: Atheneum, 1966.

———. *Tracy and Hepburn: An Intimate Memoir*. New York: Viking, 1971.

Kazan, Elia. *Elia Kazan: A Life*. New York: Alfred A. Knopf, 1988.

Keith, Slim. *Slim: Memories of a Rich and Imperfect Life*. With Annette Tapert. New York: Simon & Schuster, 1990.

Kellow, Brian. *The Bennetts: An Acting Family*. Lexington: University Press of Kentucky, 2004.

Kelly, Catriona, and David Shepherd, eds. *Russian Cultural Studies: An Introduction.* Oxford, U.K.: Oxford University Press, 1998.

Kessler, Lauren. *The Happy Bottom Riding Club: The Life and Times of Pancho Barnes.* New York: Random House, 2000.

Keyes, Evelyn. *Scarlett O'Hara's Younger Sister: My Lively Life in and out of Hollywood.* Secaucus, N.J.: Lyle Stuart, 1977.

Kinkead, Cleves. *Common Clay.* New York: Samuel French, 1917.

Kipling, Rudyard. *Captains Courageous: A Story of the Grand Banks.* New York: Century, 1897.

———. *Something of Myself: For My Friends Known and Unknown.* London: Macmillan, 1937.

Kobal, John. *People Will Talk.* New York: Alfred A. Knopf, 1985.

Koppes, Clayton R., and Gregory D. Black. *Hollywood Goes to War: How Politics, Profits, and Propaganda Shaped World War II Movies.* Berkeley: University of California Press, 1990.

Koszarski, Richard. *An Evening's Entertainment: The Age of the Silent Feature Picture, 1915–1928.* New York: Maxwell Macmillan International, 1990.

———. *The Man You Loved to Hate: Erich von Stroheim and Hollywood.* London: Oxford University Press, 1983.

Kotsilibas-Davis, James, and Myrna Loy. *Myrna Loy: Being and Becoming.* New York: Alfred A. Knopf, 1987.

Kundera, Milan. *The Unbearable Lightness of Being.* New York: Harper & Row, 1984.

Lahr, John. *Notes on a Cowardly Lion.* New York: Alfred A. Knopf, 1969.

Lambert, Gavin. *GWTW: The Making of "Gone With the Wind."* Boston: Little, Brown, 1973.

———. *Norma Shearer: A Life.* New York: Alfred A. Knopf, 1990.

———. *On Cukor.* New York: Putnam, 1972.

Lamparski, Richard. *Whatever Became Of . . . ? Fifth Series.* New York: Crown, 1975.

Lasky, Jesse. *I Blow My Own Horn.* With Don Weldon. Garden City, N.Y.: Doubleday, 1957.

Lawton, Stephen. *Santa Barbara's Flying A Studio.* Santa Barbara, Calif.: Fithian, 1997.

Leab, Daniel, ed. *Communist Activity in the Entertainment Industry: FBI Surveillance Files on Hollywood, 1942–1958.* Bethesda, Md.: University Publications of America, 1991. Microfilm.

Le Chanois, Jean-Paul. *Le temps des cerises.* Arles: Actes Sud, 1996.

Lee, Gus. *Chasing Hepburn: A Memoir of Shanghai, Hollywood, and a Chinese Family's Fight for Freedom.* New York: Harmony Books, 2002.

Leggett, John. *A Daring Young Man: A Biography of William Saroyan.* New York: Alfred A. Knopf, 2002.

Lennig, Arthur. *The Immortal Count: The Life and Films of Bela Lugosi.* Lexington: University Press of Kentucky, 2003.

LeRoy, Mervyn. *Mervyn LeRoy: Take One.* With Dick Kleiner. New York: Hawthorn, 1974.

Levant, Oscar. *The Memoirs of an Amnesiac.* New York: G. P. Putnam's Sons, 1965.

Levy, Emanuel. *George Cukor, Master of Elegance.* New York: Morrow, 1994.

Lewis, David. *The Creative Producer.* Edited by James Curtis. Metuchen, N.J.: Scarecrow, 1993.

Lewis, Sinclair. *Mantrap.* New York: Harcourt, Brace, 1926.

Link, Arthur S., et al., eds. *The Papers of Woodrow Wilson.* Princeton, N.J.: Princeton University Press, 1966–94.

Lobenthal, Joel. *Tallulah: The Life and Times of a Leading Lady.* New York: HarperCollins, 2004.

Lobrutto, Vincent. *Selected Takes: Film Editors on Editing.* New York: Praeger, 1991.

London, Jack. *Adventure.* New York: Macmillan, 1911.

Loos, Anita. *The Talmadge Girls.* New York: Viking, 1978.

Love, Bessie. *From Hollywood with Love.* London: Elm Tree Books, 1977.

Lower, Cheryl Bray, and R. Barton Palmer. *Joseph L. Mankiewicz.* Jefferson, N.C.: McFarland, 2001.

Lycett, Andrew. *Rudyard Kipling.* London: Weidenfeld & Nicolson, 1999.

Maas, Frederica Sagor. *The Shocking Miss Pilgrim: A Writer in Early Hollywood.* Lexington: University Press of Kentucky, 1999.

Macdonald, Dwight. *Dwight Macdonald on Movies.* Englewood Cliffs, N.J.: Prentice-Hall, 1969.

Macklin, F. Anthony, and Nick Pici, eds. *Voices from the Set: The Film Heritage Interviews.* Lanham, Md.: Scarecrow, 2000.

Maguire, James. *Impresario: The Life and Times of Ed Sullivan.* New York: Watson-Guptill, 2006.

Maltin, Leonard. *Behind the Camera: The Cinematographer's Art.* New York: New American Library, 1971.

Mank, Gregory W. *Hollywood Cauldron: Thirteen Horror Films from the Genre's Golden Age.* Jefferson, N.C.: McFarland, 1994.

Mann, William J. *Behind the Screen.* New York: Viking, 2001.

———. *Kate: The Woman Who Was Hepburn.* New York: Henry Holt, 2006.

———. *Wisecracker: The Life and Times of William Haines.* New York: Viking, 1998.

March, Joseph Moncure. *"The Wild Party" and "The Set-Up."* New York: Blue Ribbon Books, 1932.

Marion, Frances. *Off with Their Heads: A Serio-Comic Tale of Hollywood.* New York: Macmillan, 1972.

Marshall, J. D. *Blueprint on Babylon.* Tempe, Ariz.: Phoenix House, 1978.

Marx, Harpo. *Harpo Speaks!* With Rowland Barber. New York: B. Geis Associates, 1961.

Marx, Samuel. *Mayer and Thalberg: The Make-Believe Saints.* New York: Random House, 1975.

Marx, Samuel, and Joyce Vanderveen. *Deadly Illusions: Jean Harlow and the Murder of Paul Bern.* New York: Random House, 1990.

McBride, Joseph. *Frank Capra: The Catastrophe of Success.* New York: Simon & Schuster, 1992.

———. *Hawks on Hawks.* Berkeley: University of California Press, 1982.

———. *Searching for John Ford.* New York: St. Martin's, 1999.

McCarthy, Todd. *Howard Hawks: The Grey Fox of Hollywood.* New York: Grove, 1997.

McClelland, Doug. *Down the Yellow Brick Road.* New York: Bonanza, 1989.

———. *Forties Film Talk.* Jefferson, N.C.: McFarland, 1992.

McGilligan, Patrick. *George Cukor: A Double Life.* New York: St. Martin's, 1991.

———, ed. *Backstory: Interviews with Screenwriters of Hollywood's Golden Age.* Berkeley: University of California Press, 1986.

McWilliams, Carey. *Southern California Country: An Island on the Land.* New York: Duell, Sloan & Pearce, 1946.

Meyerson, Harold, and Ernie Harburg. *Who Put the Rainbow in "The Wizard of Oz"?* Ann Arbor: University of Michigan Press, 1993.

Miller, Patsy Ruth. *My Hollywood: When Both of Us Were Young.* Atlantic City: O'Raghailligh, 1998.

———. *That Flannigan Girl.* New York: William Morrow, 1939.

———. Unpublished sequel to *My Hollywood,* supplying more of "the memories of Patsy Ruth Miller."

Millichap, Joseph R. *Steinbeck and Film.* New York: Ungar, 1983.

Mitchell, Margaret. *Gone With the Wind.* New York: Macmillan, 1936.

Molt, Cynthia Marylee. *"Gone With the Wind" on Film.* Jefferson, N.C.: McFarland, 1990.

Moore, Gene M., ed. *Conrad on Film.* Cambridge, U.K.: Cambridge University Press, 1997.

Myers, James M. *The Bureau of Motion Pictures and Its Influence on Film Content During World War II.* Lewiston, N.Y.: Edwin Mellen, 1998.

Myrick, Susan. *White Columns in Hollywood.* Macon, Ga.: Mercer University Press, 1982.

Negri, Pola. *Memories of a Star.* Garden City, N.Y.: Doubleday, 1970.

Nichols, Anne. *Abie's Irish Rose.* New York: Harper & Brothers, 1927.

Noble, Peter. *Hollywood Scapegoat: The Biography of Erich von Stroheim.* New York: Arno, 1972.

Nye, Wilbur. *Carbine & Lance: The Story of Fort Sill.* Norman: University of Oklahoma Press, 1937.

Ogden, August. *The Dies Committee.* Washington, D.C.: Catholic University of America Press, 1945.

O'Reilly, Kenneth. *Hoover and the Un-Americans.* Philadelphia: Temple University Press, 1983.

Paperno, Dmitry. *Notes of a Moscow Pianist.* Portland, Ore.: Amadeus, 1998.

Parker, Gilbert. *The Lane That Had No Turning, and Other Tales Concerning the People of Pontiac.* New York: Doubleday, 1900.

Pernoud, Régine. *Joan of Arc: By Herself and Her Witnesses.* New York: Stein and Day, 1966.

Pernoud, Régine, and Marie-Véronique Clin. *Joan of Arc: Her Story.* New York: St. Martin's, 1999.

Plisetskaya, Maya. *I, Maya Plisetskaya.* New Haven, Conn.: Yale University Press, 2001.

Powell, Michael. *A Life in Movies.* London: William Heinemann, 1986.

———. *Million Dollar Movie.* New York: Random House, 1995.

Prelutsky, Burt. *The Secret of Their Success: Interviews with Legends and Luminaries.* Houston: Expanding Press, 2008.

Previn, André. *No Minor Chords: My Days in Hollywood.* New York, Doubleday, 1991.

Pyron, Darden Asbury, ed. *Recasting: "Gone With the Wind" in American Culture.* Miami: University Presses of Florida, 1983.

Quinn, Anthony. *One Man Tango.* With Daniel Paisner. New York: HarperCollins, 1995.

Raabe, Meinhardt. *Memories of a Munchkin.* With Daniel Kinske. New York: Watson-Guptill, 2005.

Rabwin, Marcella. *Yes, Mr. Selznick: Recollections of Hollywood's Golden Era.* Pittsburgh: Dorrance, 1999.

Rainsberger, Todd. *James Wong Howe, Cinematographer.* San Diego: A. S. Barnes, 1981.

Ralston, Esther. *Some Day We'll Laugh.* Metuchen, N.J.: Scarecrow, 1985.

Rapf, Maurice. *Back Lot: Growing Up with the Movies.* Lanham, Md.: Scarecrow, 1999.

Robyns, Gwen. *Light of a Star.* London: Frewin, 1968.

Rogers, Katharine M. *L. Frank Baum: Creator of Oz.* New York: St. Martin's, 2002.

Rooney, Mickey. *Life Is Too Short.* New York: Villard Books, 1991.

Roosevelt, Theodore. *The Rough Riders.* New York: Scribner, 1899.

Rose, Brian A. *Jekyll and Hyde Adapted: Dramatizations of Cultural Anxiety.* Westport, Conn.: Greenwood, 1996.

St. Johns, Adela Rogers. *The Honeycomb.* Garden City, N.Y.: Doubleday, 1969.

Samuels, Charles. *The King.* New York: Coward-McCann, 1962.

Saroyan, William. *Get Away, Old Man.* New York: Harcourt, Brace, 1944.

Sarris, Andrew. *The American Cinema.* New York: Dutton, 1968.

Saville, Victor. *Evergreen: Victor Saville in His Own Words.* Edited by Roy Moseley. Carbondale: Southern Illinois University Press, 2000.

Sayer, Michael, and Albert E. Kahn. *Sabotage! The Secret War Against America.* New York: Harper & Brothers, 1942.

Scarfone, Jay, and William Stillman. *The Wizardry of Oz.* New York: Gramercy, 1999.

Schatz, Thomas. *The Genius of the System.* New York: Pantheon, 1988.

Schickel, Richard. *D. W. Griffith.* New York: Simon & Schuster, 1984.

———. *His Picture in the Papers: A Speculation on Celebrity in America, Based on the Life of Douglas Fairbanks, Sr.* New York: Charterhouse, 1973.

———. *The Men Who Made the Movies.* New York: Atheneum, 1975.

Schorer, Mark. *Sinclair Lewis.* Minneapolis: University of Minnesota Press, 1963.

———. *Sinclair Lewis, an American Life.* New York: McGraw-Hill, 1961.

Schulberg, Budd. *Moving Pictures: Memories of a Hollywood Prince.* New York: Stein and Day, 1981.

Schwartz, Nancy Lynn. *The Hollywood Writers' Wars.* New York: Alfred A. Knopf, 1982.

Server, Lee. *Screenwriter: Words Become Pictures.* Pittstown, N.J.: Main Street, 1987.

Shay, Don. *Conversations.* Albuquerque, N.M.: Kaleidoscope, 1969.

Sherman, Vincent. *Studio Affairs.* Lexington: University Press of Kentucky, 1996.

Shotwell, James T. *At the Paris Peace Conference.* New York: Macmillan, 1937.

Simmonds, Roy. *John Steinbeck: The War Years, 1939–1945.* Lewisburg, Pa.: Bucknell University Press, 1996.

Sinclair, Mary Craig. *Southern Belle*. Jackson: University Press of Mississippi, 1999.

Sinclair, Upton. *My Lifetime in Letters*. Columbia: University of Missouri Press, 1960.

———. *Oil!* New York: Albert and Charles Boni, 1927.

———. *The Wet Parade*. New York: Farrar & Rinehart, 1931.

Sklar, Robert. *Movie-Made America: A Social History of American Movies*. New York: Random House, 1975.

Slide, Anthony. *The Kindergarten of the Movies: A History of the Fine Arts*. Metuchen, N.J.: Scarecrow, 1980.

———. *Silent Players: A Biographical and Autobiographical Study of 100 Silent Film Actors and Actresses*. Lexington: University Press of Kentucky, 2002.

Spears, Jack. *Hollywood: The Golden Era*. South Brunswick, N.J.: A. S. Barnes, 1971.

Spoto, Donald. *Notorious: The Life of Ingrid Bergman*. New York: Harper-Collins, 1997.

Starling, Edmund, and Thomas Sugrue. *Starling of the White House*. New York: Simon & Schuster, 1946.

Steele, Joseph Henry. *Ingrid Bergman: An Intimate Portrait*. New York: D. McKay, 1959.

Steen, Mike. *Hollywood Speaks: An Oral History*. New York: Putnam, 1974.

Steinbeck, John. *Tortilla Flat*. New York: Grosset & Dunlap, 1935.

Stenn, David. *Bombshell: The Life and Death of Jean Harlow*. New York: Doubleday, 1993.

———. *Clara Bow: Runnin' Wild*. New York: Doubleday, 1988.

Stevenson, Robert Louis. *The Strange Case of Dr. Jekyll and Mr. Hyde*. New York: Scribner, 1886.

———. *Treasure Island*. London: Cassell, 1883.

Stewart, Donald Ogden. *By a Stroke of Luck*. New York: Paddington, 1975.

Stone, Irving. *Men to Match My Mountains*. Garden City, N.Y.: Doubleday, 1956.

Stringer, Arthur. *Empty Hands*. Indianapolis: Bobbs-Merrill, 1924.

Studlar, Gaylyn. *This Mad Masquerade: Stardom and Masculinity in the Jazz Age*. New York: Columbia University Press, 1996.

Swindell, Larry. *Spencer Tracy*. New York: New American Library, 1969.

———. *Body and Soul*. New York: William Morrow, 1975.

Taylor, Patrick Gordon. *Pacific Flight: The Story of the* Lady Southern Cross. Sydney: Angus & Robertson, 1935.

Teichmann, Howard. *Fonda: My Life as Told to Howard Teichmann*. New York: New American Library, 1981.

Thomas, Bob. *Selznick.* Garden City, N.Y.: Doubleday, 1970.

———. *Thalberg: Life and Legend.* Garden City, N.Y.: Doubleday, 1969.

Thompson, Frank. *Lost Films: Important Movies That Disappeared.* New York: Citadel Press, 1996.

———, ed. *Between Action and Cut: Five American Directors.* Metuchen, N.J.: Scarecrow, 1985.

Thomson, David. *Showman: The Life of David O. Selznick.* New York: Alfred A. Knopf, 1992.

Tibbetts, John C., and James M. Welsh. *His Majesty the American: The Films of Douglas Fairbanks, Sr.* Cranbury, N.J.: A. S. Barnes, 1977.

Tolkien, J. R. R. *The Tolkien Reader.* New York: Ballantine, 1966.

Tornabene, Lyn. *Long Live the King.* New York: Putnam, 1976.

Train, Arthur Cheney. *The Blind Goddess.* New York: Scribner, 1926.

Trask, Willard R. *Joan of Arc: Self Portrait.* New York: Stackpole, 1936.

Troyan, Michael. *A Rose for Mrs. Miniver: The Life of Greer Garson.* Lexington: University Press of Kentucky, 1999.

Truffaut, François. *Hitchcock/Truffaut.* New York: Simon & Schuster, 1967.

Turnbull, Andrew, ed. *Letters of F. Scott Fitzgerald.* New York: Scribner, 1963.

Turner, Lana. *Lana: The Lady, the Legend, the Truth.* New York: Dutton, 1982.

Tuska, Jon. *The Filming of the West.* Garden City, N.Y.: Doubleday, 1976.

Ulin, David L., ed. *Writing Los Angeles: A Literary Anthology.* New York: Library of America, 2002.

U.S. Congress, Special Committee on Un-American Activities. *Investigation of Un-American Propaganda Activities in the United States.* Washington, D.C.: U.S. Government Printing Office, 1938–44.

Varconi, Victor. *It's Not Enough to Be Hungarian.* Denver: Graphic Impressions, 1976.

Vertrees, Alan David. *Selznick's Vision: "Gone With the Wind" and Hollywood Filmmaking.* Austin: University of Texas Press, 1997.

Vickers, Hugh. *Vivien Leigh.* London: Hamish Hamilton, 1988.

Vidor, King. *A Tree Is a Tree.* New York: Harcourt, Brace, 1953.

Von Sternberg, Josef. *Fun in a Chinese Laundry.* New York: Macmillan, 1965.

Von Tempski, Armine. *Hula: A Romance of Hawaii.* New York: Frederick A. Stokes, 1927.

Walker, Alexander. *Vivien: The Life of Vivien Leigh.* New York: Weidenfeld & Nicolson, 1987.

Ward, Larry Wayne. *The Motion Picture Goes to War: The U.S. Government Film Effort During World War I.* Ann Arbor: UMI Research, 1985.

Watts, Jill. *Hattie McDaniel: Black Ambitions, White Hollywood.* New York: Amistad, 2005.

Weales, Gerald. *Canned Goods as Caviar: American Film Comedies of the 1930s.* Chicago: University of Chicago Press, 1985.

Weddle, David. *"If They Move . . . Kill 'Em!": The Life and Times of Sam Peckinpah.* New York: Grove, 1994.

Weld, John. *September Song.* Lanham, Md.: Scarecrow, 1998.

Wellman, William. *A Short Time for Insanity.* New York: Hawthorn Books, 1974.

Whiteman, Harold B., Jr., ed. *Letters from the Paris Peace Conference.* New Haven, Conn.: Yale University Press, 1965.

Wilson, Robert, ed. *The Film Criticism of Otis Ferguson.* Philadelphia: Temple University Press, 1971.

Winters, Ralph. *Some Cutting Remarks.* Lanham, Md.: Scarecrow, 2001.

Wister, Owen. *The Virginian: A Horseman of the Plains.* New York: Macmillan, 1902.

Wister, Owen, and Kirk La Shelle. *The Virginian: A Play in Four Acts.* New York, 1904.

Worsley, Wallace. *From Oz to E.T.: Wally Worsley's Half-Century in Hollywood.* Edited by Charles Ziarko. Lanham, Md.: Scarecrow, 1997.

Wranovics, John. *Chaplin and Agee: The Untold Story of the Tramp, the Writer, and the Lost Screenplay.* New York: Palgrave Macmillan, 2005.

Wright, Harold Bell. *A Son of His Father.* New York: D. Appleton, 1925.

Wyman, Walker. *Witching for Water, Oil, Pipes, and Precious Minerals.* River Falls: University of Wisconsin Press, 1977.

Wynn, Keenan. *Ed Wynn's Son.* Garden City, N.Y.: Doubleday, 1959.

BROADCAST PROGRAMS

The Bells of St. Mary's. Screen Guild Theater. CBS Radio, Oct. 6, 1947.

Bob Hope Swan Show. NBC Radio, Feb. 15, 1949.

A Funny Thing Happened on the Way to Hollywood—with Jack Paar. NBC TV, May 14, 1967.

"The Hand of Providence." *Gulf Screen Guild Theater.* CBS Radio, April 16, 1939.

Kay Kyser and his orchestra at the Atlanta Junior League costume ball. Special broadcast. NBC Radio, Dec. 14, 1939.

DOCUMENTARIES

Driskel, Dana. *An American Film Company.* Mountain View Productions, 2003.

Heeley, David. *The Spencer Tracy Legacy: A Tribute by Katharine Hepburn.* WNET, 1986.

Hinton, David. *The Making of a Legend: "Gone With the Wind."* Selznick Properties, Ltd., and Turner Entertainment, 1998.

Jones, Peter, director. *Glorious Technicolor.* Peter Jones Productions and Turner Classic Movies, 1998.

Index